LANDSCAPE ARCHITECTURE

About the Authors

Barry W. Starke has been a leader in the profession of landscape architecture for more than 40 years. He graduated with a degree in landscape architecture from the College of Environmental Design at the University of California, Berkeley, in 1967. While at Berkeley, he was introduced to the first edition of *Landscape Architecture,* which became a major influence on his career. In 1974, Mr. Starke co-founded the award-winning, multidisciplinary landscape architecture and environmental design firm Earth Design Associates, Inc., and continues to serve as President. In 1988, he was elected to the faculty of the University of Virginia School of Architecture, where he taught Professional Practice. Mr. Starke served as the Centennial President of the American Society of Landscape Architects in 1999, leading ASLA's 100th-anniversary celebration. He is a Fellow of the ASLA, is a member of the American Institute of Certified Planners, and served as Chairman of the Renewable Natural Resources Foundation. In 2003, Mr. Starke received the inaugural M. Meade Palmer Medal for outstanding contributions to landscape architecture. He is the 2010 recipient of the VA ASLA Landmark Award and Honor Award in Communications for the fourth edition of *Landscape Architecture.*

John Ormsbee Simonds, who died in May 2005, was one of the twentieth century's most important figures in landscape architecture and environmental planning. He was recognized worldwide for his visionary thinking and innovative spirit. Mr. Simonds's work and career spanned more than 70 years, bridging an era during which the profession of landscape architecture expanded from a small number of individuals in the early 1900s to more than 30,000 land use and environmental planners in the United States today. His many contributions, including *Landscape Architecture,* helped lay the groundwork for today's focus on environmentally responsible planning and design. Mr. Simonds was President and a Fellow of the American Society of Landscape Architects, which awarded him its highest honor, the ASLA Medal, and its one-time Centennial President's Medal. He was a member of the President's Task Force on the Environment and Florida Governor's Task Force on Natural Resources, and was a Fellow of the Royal Academy of Design in Great Britain.

LANDSCAPE ARCHITECTURE

A Manual of Environmental Planning and Design

FIFTH EDITION

BARRY W. STARKE
JOHN ORMSBEE SIMONDS

New York Chicago San Francisco Lisbon London Madrid
Mexico City Milan New Delhi San Juan Seoul
Singapore Sydney Toronto

Cataloging-in-Publication Data is on file with the Library of Congress

Copyright © 2013, 2006, 1998, 1983, 1961 by McGraw-Hill Education, LLC. All rights reserved. Printed in the United States of America. Except as permitted under the United States Copyright Act of 1976, no part of this publication may be reproduced or distributed in any form or by any means, or stored in a data base or retrieval system, without the prior written permission of the publisher.

1 2 3 4 5 6 7 8 9 0   DOW/DOW   1 9 8 7 6 5 4 3

ISBN 9781265899868
MHID 1265899868

Sponsoring Editor
Michael McCabe

Copy Editor
Virginia E. Carroll,
North Market Street Graphics

Editing Supervisor
Stephen M. Smith

Proofreader
Stewart Smith,
North Market Street Graphics

Production Supervisor
Richard C. Ruzycka

Indexer
Virginia E. Carroll,
North Market Street Graphics

Acquisitions Coordinator
Molly T. Wyand

Art Director, Cover
Jeff Weeks

Project Manager
Virginia E. Carroll,
North Market Street Graphics

Composition
North Market Street Graphics

Printed and bound by RR Donnelley.

McGraw-Hill Education books are available at special quantity discounts to use as premiums and sales promotions, or for use in corporate training programs. To contact a representative, please e-mail us at bulksales@mcgraw-hill.com.

Information contained in this work has been obtained by McGraw-Hill Education, LLC from sources believed to be reliable. However, neither McGraw-Hill Education nor its authors guarantee the accuracy or completeness of any information published herein, and neither McGraw-Hill Education nor its authors shall be responsible for any errors, omissions, or damages arising out of use of this information. This work is published with the understanding that McGraw-Hill Education and its authors are supplying information but are not attempting to render engineering or other professional services. If such services are required, the assistance of an appropriate professional should be sought.

This book is dedicated

To Marj

Marjorie Todd Simonds, 1920–2012

Wife of John Ormsbee Simonds for 63 years, without whose "help and inspiration" the first and subsequent editions of this book would not have been written.

I also wish to acknowledge that this edition would not have been possible but for the generous contributions of my landscape architect colleagues, firms, and agencies around the world; the many outstanding photographers; the support of my wife, Laurie; the work of my staff; and, especially, the enthusiasm, dedication, and tireless devotion of my assistant, landscape architect Breanna Rau.

Barry W. Starke

Contents

Prologue ix
Foreword xiii
The Hunter and the Philosopher xvii

1. THE HUMAN HABITAT AND SUSTAINABILITY 1
The Human Animal 1
Nature 7
The Natural Sciences 10
The Ecological Basis 13
Earthscape 15
Sustainability 18

2. CLIMATE 23
Climate and Response 23
Social Imprint 24
Accommodation 25
Microclimatology 30
Climate Change/Global Warming 36

3. WATER 39
Water as a Resource 39
Natural Systems 43
Management 46
Water-Related Site Design 50

4. LAND 57
Human Impact 57
Land as a Resource 60
Land Grants 62
Land Rights 62
Surveying 63
Use 64
Reuse 66
Topography 67
Surveys 70
Supplementary Data 72

5. VEGETATION 75
Topsoil Mantle 75
Plants in Nature 76
Plant Identification 78
Plant Culture 79
Introduced Plantations 81
Invasive Species 82
Vanishing Green 83
Urban Agriculture 84
Urban Forestry 85

6. THE VISUAL LANDSCAPE 87
The View 87
The Vista 91
The Axis 94
The Symmetrical Plan 100
Asymmetry 104
Visual Resource Management 110
Landscape Character 112
Modification 114
The Built Environment 120

7. THE PLANNED ENVIRONMENT 131
A Conservation Credo 132
Environmental Issues 132

8. COMMUNITY PLANNING AND GROWTH MANAGEMENT 143
The Group Imperative 143
Problems 144
Possibilities 148
New Directions 158
Growth Management 164
Scatteration and Urban Sprawl 169
Restoration 171

9. THE REGIONAL LANDSCAPE 179
Interrelationships 179
Regional Form 188
Open-Space Frame 189
Greenways and Blueways 190
The Essentials 191
Regional Planning 191
Governance 192

10. URBAN DESIGN 195
Cityscape 195
The City Diagram 198
The Ubiquitous Automobile 207
People Places 208
Urban Green, Urban Blue 209
The New Urbanity 210

11. SITE PLANNING 213
Program Development 213
Site Selection 214
Site Analysis 216
Comprehensive Land Planning 220
The Conceptual Plan 226
Computer Application 231
Site Development 233
Site-Structure Plan Development 245
Site-Structure Unity 247
Site Systems 251

12. SITE SPACES 259
Spaces 259
The Base Plane 272
The Overhead Plane 275
The Verticals 277

13. CIRCULATION 289
Motion 289
Sequence 300
Pedestrian Movement 303
The Automobile 307
Complete Streets 314
Travel by Rail, Water, and Air 317
People Movers 323

14. STRUCTURES 327
Common Denominators 327
Composition 329
Structures in the Landscape 337
The Defined Open Space 339
Habitations 341
Dwelling-Nature Relationships 342
Human Needs and Habitat 344
Residential Components 346

15. LANDSCAPE PLANTING 353
Purpose 353
Process 354
Guidelines 355
Advances 361
Landscape Plantings in Low-Impact Design 363

PERSPECTIVE 367
Disavowal and Quest 367
Findings 369
Insights 370
Evolution and Revolution 372
The Planned Experience 373

Retrospective 379
Project Credits 389
Quotation Sources 391
Bibliography 393
Index 395

Prologue

In 1961, over 50 years ago, the first edition of *Landscape Architecture* was published and instantly filled the void that existed for a comprehensive presentation of the profession and how to plan for the human use of land harmoniously with the environment. These were the early days of what became known as the environmental movement, sparked by a series of wake-up calls, such as Rachel Carson's book *Silent Spring*, sending a signal throughout the country—and, indeed, the world—that people had to fundamentally change the way they viewed and interacted with their surroundings. No longer could we continue to think we had dominion over the Earth and ignore the fact that we are an inseparable part of nature and nature is part of us. No longer could we destroy our forests, abuse our soil, pollute our air and water, squander our natural resources, and overpopulate the Earth without dire future consequences.

The fledgling profession of landscape architecture, which had come into being less than a hundred years earlier, was in the right place at the right time, so to speak, with the right skills and knowledge to take on the leadership role among the design professions in this new movement. Educated and trained in architecture, civil engineering, botany, geology, horticulture, the natural sciences, and social issues, landscape architects were uniquely qualified to assume this role. At the time, however, the profession was relatively unknown and misunderstood, and its literature then was for the most part outdated and focused on a previous era. John Simonds would change that.

John had studied landscape architecture at Michigan State University, traveled the world, studied Eastern philosophy, lived among the native people of Borneo, worked in conservation, became a student of the environment, and embraced the principles of the emerging science of ecology. In 1939, John—a member of the infamous "class of rebels" that included Garrett Eckbo, Dan Kiley, and Charles Rose—graduated from Harvard with a master's degree in landscape architecture.

This placed him in a unique position that enabled him to become the profession's major advocate for the environmental movement and to tell the story of the role of landscape architecture in it. John wrote the first edition of *Landscape Architecture* "because," he said, "I felt compelled to get the word out about the comprehensive profession of landscape architecture." Over the next 30 years, two revised editions were published with John as the sole author. The story of my role as coauthor began some ten years later.

On the afternoon of December 12, 2004, my phone rang, the caller ID read "John Simonds," and a dreadful thought flashed through my mind. It had been several years since John and I had talked, following two years of intense communication preparing for the American Society of Landscape Architect's Centennial Celebration. John was not well at that time and I feared it was his family calling to say that he was gravely ill or had passed away. Following my hello, the sound of John's voice engendered a sigh of relief, and what he was about to say would shift my emotions from fear to total elation.

"Barry, would you consider working with me as the coauthor of the fourth edition of *Landscape Architecture*?" I couldn't believe what I was hearing. Then another flash—a flashback to November 22, 1963. Most people who were old enough at the time remember this as the day President John F. Kennedy was assassinated and, to a person, remember where they were and what they were doing at that time. On that day I was in the library at the University of California, Berkeley, completely absorbed in John Simonds's first edition of *Landscape Architecture*. Of course, the assassination of John F. Kennedy was an event that touched everyone, but for me personally the impact that event would have on my life and career was clearly secondary to the one that John Simonds's book would have on my future and future generations of landscape architects.

When John first published *Landscape Architecture* in 1961, it was before the digital revolution and modern methods facilitating the practice of the profession, including computer-aided design and Geographic Information Systems. However, what John presented in the first and subsequent editions of *Landscape Architecture* is as applicable today as it was when first published. John's genius in communicating the principles of landscape architectural planning and design, through his writing, sketches, and shared words of the wisdom of others, is indeed timeless and will no doubt help shape this century as it did the last.

During the following months, we exchanged ideas and worked on the fourth edition. John's role was to complete the revised manuscript, and mine was to review the manuscript and gather photographs—as John described, "Best in Show"—of works of landscape architecture and related subjects to illustrate the book. He considered the writing of *Landscape Architecture* his most significant professional accomplishment, and, of course, working with John as coauthor has been one of the great honors of my career.

Then, on May 26, I received the phone call that I had feared that December 12 call to be. After a fall and a brief stay in the hospital, John returned home, where he passed away near family and friends. When John died, he had already finished the manuscript for the fourth edition, leaving his wife, Marj, in charge of final editing. With renewed vigor and commitment to John's legacy—the legacy of one of the most influential landscape architects of the twentieth century—my work shifted into high gear, and, as Marj liked to say, "the rest is history." (Marj Simonds died in April 2012.)

The fourth edition of *Landscape Architecture* has been published in three languages—English, Chinese, and Japanese—and distributed worldwide. For the first time, it is also available in digital format. This fifth edition is the first to be published without John's direct input. However, much care has been taken to preserve the essential character and timelessness of what he first created in the early 1960s, while updating other material and providing refreshing new images and illustrations. It is my hope that further editions of this book will continue to be published into the indefinite future, thus extending the legacy of John Ormsbee Simonds and his contributions toward making the world a better place.

Barry W. Starke

Foreword

Landscape Architecture has been written in response to the need for a book outlining the land-planning process in clear, simple, and practical terms. In a larger sense it is a guide book on how to live more compatibly on planet Earth.

It introduces us to an understanding of nature as the background and base for all human activities; it describes the planning constraints imposed by the forms, forces, and features of nature and our built environment; it instills a feeling for climate and its design implications; it discusses site selection and analysis; it instructs in the planning of workable and well-related use areas; it considers the volumetric shaping of exterior spaces; it explores the possibilities of site-structure organization; it applies contemporary thinking in the planning of expressive human habitations and communities; and it provides guidance in the creation of more efficient and pleasant places and ways within the context of the city and the region.

This book is not intended to explain all forms of the practice of the profession or to explicate the latest technology. Nor is it proposed that the reader will become, per se, an expert land planner. As with training in other fields, proficiency comes with long years of study, travel, observation, and professional experience. The reader should, however, gain through this book a keener and more telling awareness of our physical surroundings. The reader should also gain much useful knowledge to be applied in the design of homes, schools, recreation areas, shopping malls, trafficways . . . or any other project to be fitted into, and planned in harmony with, the all-embracing landscape.

This, at least, has been the express intent.

The work of the landscape architect
(architect of the landscape)
is to help bring people,
their structures, activities, and communities
into harmonious relationship
with the living earth—
with the "want-to-be" of the land.

The Hunter and the Philosopher

Once there was a hunter who spent his days tracking the wide prairies of North Dakota with his gun and dog and sometimes with a small boy who would beg to trot along.

On this particular morning, hunter and boy, far out on the prairie, sat watching intently a rise of ground ahead of them. It was pocked with gopher holes. From time to time a small striped gopher would whisk nervously from the mouth of his den to the cover of matted prairie grass, soon to reappear with cheek food pouches bulging.

"Smart little outfits, the gophers," the hunter observed. "I mean the way they have things figured out. Whenever you come upon a gopher village, you can be sure it will be near a patch of grain where they can get their food and close by a creek or slough for water. They'll not build their towns near willow clumps, for there's where the owls or hawks will be roosting. And you'll not be finding them near stony ledges or a pile of rocks where their enemies the snakes will be hiding ready to snatch them. When these wise little critters build their towns, they search out the southeast slope of a knoll that will catch the full sweep of the sun each day to keep their dens warm and cozy. The winter blizzards that pound out of the north and west to leave the windward slopes of the rises frozen solid will only drift loose powder snow on top of their homes.

"When they dig their dens," continued the hunter, "do you know that they do? They slant the runway steeply down for 2 or 3 feet and then double back up near the surface again where they level off a nice dry shelf. That's where they lie—close under the sod roots, out of the wind, warmed by the sun, near to their food and water, as far as they can get from their enemies, and surrounded by all their gopher friends. Yes, sir, they sure have it all planned out!"

"Is our town built on a southeast slope?" the small boy asked thoughtfully.

"No," said the hunter, "our town slopes down to the north, in the teeth of the bitter winter winds and cold as a frosty gun barrel." He frowned. "Even in summer the breezes work against us. When we built the new flax mill, the only mill for 40 miles, where do you think we put it? We built it right smack on the only spot where every breeze in the summertime can catch the smoke from its stack and pour it across our houses and into our open windows!?"

"At least our town is near the river and water," said the boy defensively.

"Yes," replied the hunter. "But where near the river did we build our homes? On the low, flat land inside the river bend, that's where. And each spring when the snows melt on the prairie and the river swells, it floods out every cellar in our town."

"Gophers would plan things better than that," the small boy decided.

"Yes," said the hunter, "a gopher would be smarter."

"When gophers plan their homes and towns," the boy philosophized, "they seem to do it better than people do."

"Yes," mused the hunter, "and so do most of the animals I know. Sometimes I wonder why."

LANDSCAPE ARCHITECTURE

NASA

1
THE HUMAN HABITAT AND SUSTAINABILITY

People are animals, too. We still retain, and are largely motivated by, our natural animal instincts. If we are to plan intelligently, we must acknowledge and accommodate these instincts; the shortcomings of many a project can be traced to the failure of the planner to recognize this simple fact.

The Human Animal

Homo sapiens (the wise one) is an animal (a superior type, we commonly assume, although neither history nor close observation altogether support this assumption).

A human standing in the forest, with bare skin, weak teeth, thin arms, and knobby knees, would not look very impressive among the other creatures. As an animal, the bear with powerful jaws and raking claws would clearly seem superior. Even the turtle seems more cunningly contrived for both protection and attack, as do the dog, the skunk, and the lowly porcupine. All creatures of nature, upon reflection, seem superbly equipped for living their lives in their natural habitat and for meeting normal situations. All except the humans.

Lacking speed, strength, and other apparent natural attributes, we humans have long since learned that we can best attack a situation with our minds. Truth to tell, we have little other choice.

Intelligence, by one definition, must be the ability to respond adaptively to the environment—that is, the ability to plan a course of action based upon information gained through the senses.
John Todd Simonds

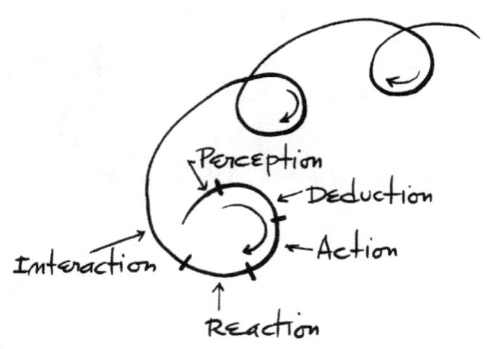

The thought processes of *perception-deduction* are in turn implemented by the physical processes of *action, reaction, and interaction*. These five dynamic drives form ever-repeating cycles and spin the intricate webbing of all human life.

And what is man? Amongst other things he is an organism endowed with a multiple organ, the brain, supported by the senses and the glands, in which the formative property of organic processes is applied to the memory records of experience. The brain orders its own records, and all mental processes express this basic activity. Art and science, philosophy and religion, engineering and medicine, indeed all cultural activities are based on the ordering of experience and the exploitation of the resulting design.
Lancelot Law Whyte

We alone of all the animals have the ability to weigh the factors of a problem and reason out a solution. We are able to learn not only from our own experiences but also from the disasters, the triumphs, and the lesser experiences of untold thousands of our fellows. We can borrow from and apply to the solution of any problem the accumulated wisdom of our species.

Our essential strength—the very reason for our survival and the key to all future achievement—is our unique power of perception and deduction. Perception (making oneself aware of all conditions and applicable factors) and deduction (deriving, through reason, an appropriate means of procedure) are the very essence of planning.

Down through the dim, chaotic ages, the force of the human mind has met and mastered situation after situation and has raised us (through this planning process) to a position of supremacy over all the other creatures of the earth.

We have, in fact, inherited the Earth. This vast globe on which we dwell is ours, ours to develop further, as an agreeable living environment. Surely, we, with our twinkling minds, should by now have created for ourselves a paradise upon this earth.

Have we? What have we done with our superlative natural heritage?

> We have plundered our forests.
> We have ripped at our hills and laid them open to erosion and ever-deepening gullies.
> We have befouled our rivers until even the fish and wildlife have often been killed or driven off by the stench and fumes.
> Our trafficways are lined with brash commercial hodgepodge and crisscrossed with senseless friction points.
> We have built our homes tight row on dreary row, with little thought for refreshing foliage, clean air, or sunlight.

Looking about us with a critical eye, we find much to disturb and shock us. Our cluttered highways, sprawling suburbs, and straining cities offend more often than they please.

We are the victims of our own building. We are trapped, body and soul, in the mechanistic surroundings we have constructed about ourselves. Somewhere in the complex process of evolving our living spaces, cities, and roadways, we have become so absorbed in the power of machines, so absorbed in the pursuit of new techniques of building, so absorbed with new materials that we have neglected our human needs. Our own deepest instincts are violated. Our basic human desires remain unsatisfied. Divorced from our natural habitat, we have almost forgotten the glow and exuberance of being healthy animals and feeling fully alive.

Many contemporary ailments—our hypertensions and neuroses—are no more than the physical evidence of rebellion against our physical surroundings and frustration at the widening gap between the environment we yearn for and the stifling, artificial one we planners have so far contrived.

Life itself is dictated by our moment-by-moment adjustment to our environment. Just as the bacterial culture in the petri dish must have its scientifically compounded medium for optimum development and the potted geranium cutting its proper and controlled conditions of growth to produce a thriving plant, so we—as complicated, hypersensitive human organisms—must have for our optimum development a highly specialized milieu. It is baffling that the nature of this ecological framework has been so little explored. Volumes have been written on the conditions under which rare types of orchids may best be grown; numerous manuals can be found on the proper raising and care of guinea pigs, white rats, goldfish, and parakeets, but little has been written about the nature of the physical environment best suited to human culture.

The naturalist tells us that if a fox or a rabbit is snared in a field and then kept in a cage, the animal's clear eyes will soon become dull, its coat will lose its luster, and its spirit will flag. So it is with humans too long or too far removed from nature. For we are, first of all, animals.

Everything we have to do to live, nature makes us do with lust and pleasure.
Seneca

Human reason is rooted to the earth.
Kenneth Clark

We have learned to unleash the awesome power contained within the atom. Now we must learn the means by which to control it.

The Human Habitat and Sustainability 3

We are creatures of the meadow, the forest, the sea, and the plain. We are born with a love of fresh air in our lungs, dry paths under our feet, and the penetrating heat of the sun on our skin. We are born with a love for the feel and smell of rich, warm earth, the taste and sparkle of clear water, the refreshing coolness of foliage overhead, and the spacious blue dome of the sky. Deep down inside we have for these things a longing, a desire sometimes compelling, sometimes quiescent—but always it is there.

It has been proposed by many sages that, other things being equal, the happiest person is one who lives in closest, fullest harmony with nature. It might then be reasoned: Why not restore humans to the woods? Let them have their water and earth and sky, and plenty of it. But is the primeval forest—preserved, untouched, or simulated—our ideal environment? Hardly. For the story of the human race is the story of an unending struggle to ameliorate the forces of nature. Gradually, laboriously, we have improved our shelters, secured a more sustained and varied supply of food, and extended control over the elements to improve our way of living.

*. . . and when he looked
At sky or sea, it was with
the testing eyes
Of the man who knows the
weather under his skin,
The man who smells the weather
in the changed breeze
And has tried himself against it
and lived by it.
It is a taut look but there is a
freedom in it.*
Stephen Vincent Benét

*These are the Four that are
never content, that have never
been filled since the Dews
began . . .
Jacola's* mouth, and the
glut of the Kite, and
the hands of the Ape, and the Eyes
of Man.*
Rudyard Kipling

*Jacola is the hyena.

Ecological design is simply the effective adaptation to and integration with nature's processes.
**Sim Van der Ryn
Stuart Cowan**

We are trapped in the roadside workings of our own machinery.

What alternatives, then, are left? Is it possible that we can devise a wholly artificial environment in which to better fulfill our potential and more happily work out our destiny? This prospect seems extremely doubtful. A perceptive analysis of our most successful ventures in planning would reveal that we have effected the greatest improvements not by striving to subjugate nature wholly, not by ignoring the natural condition or by the thoughtless replacement of the natural features, contours, and covers with our constructions, but rather by consciously seeking a harmonious *integration.* This can be achieved by modulating ground and structural forms with those of nature, by bringing hills, ravines, sunlight, water,

4   LANDSCAPE ARCHITECTURE

plants, and air into our areas of planning concentration, and by thoughtfully and sympathetically spacing our structures among the hills, along the rivers and valleys, and out into the landscape.

The visual clutter of strip roadside development.

There is that stupendous whole of a constructed environment, which, like fate, envelops civilized life. It must not be allowed to conflict seriously with . . . natural laws.

The ancient idea of a world wisely ordered to function affords an emotional gratification that has shown eminent and long tested survival value. It is the inspiration for all planning and designing.
Richard J. Neutra

The basic premise of science is that the physical world is governed by certain predictable rules.

Genius of place symbolizes the living ecological relationship between a particular location and the persons who have derived from it and added to it the various aspects of their humanness. No landscape, however grandiose or fertile, can express its full potential richness until it has been given its myth by the love, works, and arts of human beings.
René Dubos

We are perhaps unique among the animals in our yearning for order and beauty. It is doubtful whether any other animal enjoys a "view," contemplates the magnificence of a venerable oak, or delights in tracing the undulations of a shoreline. We instinctively seek harmony; we are repelled by disorder, friction, ugliness, and the illogical. Can we be content while our towns and cities are still oriented to crowded streets rather than to open parks? While highways slice through our communities? While freight trucks rumble past our churches and our homes? Can we be satisfied while our children on their way to school must cross and recross murderous trafficways? While traffic itself must jam in and out of the city, morning and evening, through clogged and noisy valley floors, although these valley routes should, by all rights, be green, free-flowing parkways leading into spacious settlements and the open countryside beyond.

We of contemporary times must face this disturbing fact: our urban, suburban, and rural diagrams are for the most part ill-conceived. Our community and highway patterns bear little logical relationship to one another and to our topographical, climatological, physiological, and ecological base. We have grown, and often continue to grow, piecemeal, haphazardly, without reason. We are dissatisfied and puzzled. We are frustrated. Somewhere in the planning process we have failed.

The Human Habitat and Sustainability 5

Sound planning, we can learn from observation, is not achieved problem by problem or site by site. Masterful planning examines each project in the light of an inspired and inspiring vision, solves each problem as a part of a total and compelling concept, which upon consideration should be self-evident. Stated simply, a central objective of all physical planning is to create a more salubrious living environment—a more secure, effective, pleasant, rewarding way of life. Clearly, if we are the products of environment as well as of heredity, the nature of this environment must be a vital concern. Ideally it will be one in which tensions and frictions have been in the main eliminated, where we can achieve our full potential, and where, as the planners of old Peking envisioned, man can live and grow and develop "in harmony with nature, God, and with his fellow man."[1]

Such an environment can never be created whole; once created, it could never be maintained in static form. By its very definition it must be dynamic and expanding, changing as our requirements change. It will never, in all probability, be achieved. But striving toward the creation of this ideal environment must be, in all land planning and design, at once the major problem, the science, and the goal.

All planning must, by reason, meet the measure of our humanity. It must meet the test of our senses: sight, taste, hearing, scent, and touch. It must also consider our habits, responses, and impulses. Yet it is not enough to satisfy the instincts of the physical animal alone. One must satisfy also the broader requirements of the complete being.

As planners, we deal not only with areas, spaces, and materials, not only with instincts and feeling, but also with ideas, the stuff of the mind. Our designs must appeal to the intellect. They must fulfill hopes and yearnings. By empathetic planning, one may be brought to one's knees in an attitude of prayer, or urged to march, or even elevated to a high plane of idealism. It is not enough to accommodate. Good design must delight and inspire.

Aristotle, in teaching the art and science of persuasion, held that to appeal to any person an orator must first understand and *know* that person. He described in detail the characteristics of men and women of various ages, stations, and circumstances and proposed that not only each person but also the characteristics of each person be considered and addressed. A planner must also know and understand. Planning in all ages has been an attempt to improve the human condition. It has not only mirrored but actively shaped our thinking and civilization.

---

[1]Translation from a manuscript in the possession of H. H. Li, descendant of architects of the imperial family.

Our planning professions have a common goal in their aim to determine, to create, and then keep current optimum relationships between people and their environments. . . .

Like the modern medical practitioner, we seek to bring about in humans a psychosomatic balance, an all-over health in the whole man. This involves psychological factors as well as physical and physiological ones. . . .

The success of a work of design may be soundly evaluated only by its over-all long-term effect on the healthy, happy survival of humans. Any other evaluation of architecture, landscape architecture, or city planning makes little if any sense.
Norman T. Newton

Our five senses together give us an organ of acquaintance, with which we perceive and experience the outer world.
Hans Vetter

Spiral nebula.

Nature

Nature reveals itself to each of us according to our interests. To the naturalist, nature unfolds a wonderland of spiderweb, egg mass, and fern frond. To the miner, nature is the tenacious yet prodigious source of minerals—coal, copper, tungsten, lead, silver. To the hydroelectric engineer, nature is an abundant reservoir of power. To the structural engineer, nature in every guise is an eloquent demonstration of the universal principles of form creation to be understood and applied.

With our prodigious store of knowledge we have it within our power to create on this earth a veritable garden paradise. But we are failing. And

Nature is more than a bank of resources to draw on: it is the best model we have for all the design problems we face.
**Sim Van der Ryn
Stuart Cowan**

Forms in nature.
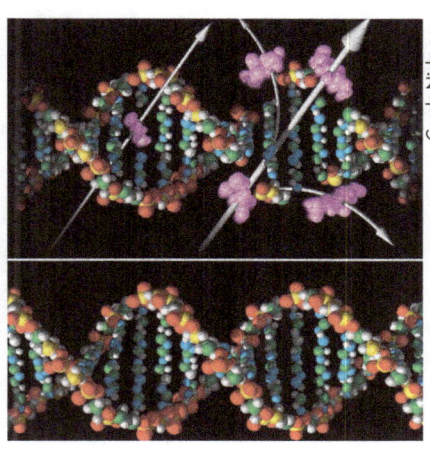

The Human Habitat and Sustainability

Dust bowl.

The Greeks and Romans had never bothered about the future but had tried to establish their paradise right here upon the earth....

Then came the other extreme of the Middle Ages when man built himself a paradise beyond the highest clouds and turned this world into a vale of tears for high and low....

The Renaissance was not a political or a religious movement. It was a state of mind. In the Renaissance men no longer concentrated all of their thoughts and their efforts upon the blessed existence that awaited them in Heaven. They tried to establish their paradise upon this planet, and truth to tell, they succeeded in a remarkable degree.
Hendrik Van Loon

The first chart of the Gulf Stream was prepared about 1769 under the direction of Benjamin Franklin while he was deputy postmaster general of the colonies. The board of customs in Boston had complained that the mail packets coming from England took two weeks longer to make the westward crossing than did the Rhode Island merchant ships. Franklin, perplexed, took the problem to a Nantucket sea captain, Timothy Folger, who told him this might very well be true because the Rhode Island captains were well acquainted with the Gulf Stream and avoided it on the westward crossing, whereas the English captains were not. Folger and other Nantucket whalers were personally familiar with the stream because, he explained, "In our pursuit of whales, which keep to the sides of it but are not met within it, we run along the side and frequently cross it to change our side, and in crossing it have sometimes met and spoke with those packets who were in the middle of it and stemming it. We have informed them that they were stemming a current that was against them to the value of three miles an hour and advised them to cross it, but they were too wise to be counseled by simple American fisherman.
Rachel Carson

we will fail as long as our plans are conceived in heavy-handed violation of nature and nature's principles. The most significant feature of our current society is not the scale of our developments but rather our utter disdain of nature and our seeming contempt for topography, topsoil, air currents, watersheds, and our forests and vegetal mantle. We think with our bulldozers, plan with our 30-yard carryalls. Thousands upon thousands of acres of well-watered, wooded, rolling ground are being blithely plowed under and leveled for roads, homesites, shopping centers, and factories. Small wonder that so many of our cities are (climatologically speaking) barren deserts of asphalt, masonry, glass, and steel.

For the moment, it seems, we have lost touch. Perhaps, before we can progress, we must look back. We must regain the old instincts, relearn the old truths. We must return to the fundamental wisdom of the gopher building a home and village and the beaver engineering a dam. We must apply the planning approach of the farmer working from day to day in the fields, fully aware of nature's forces, forms, and features, respecting and responding to them, adapting them to a purpose. We must develop a deeper understanding of our physical and spiritual ties to the earth. We must rediscover nature.

To the physical planner, nature reveals itself as the eternal, living, formidable, yet beneficent setting for every project and plan. It is essential to the success of our efforts that we come to know and understand nature.

Rape by the excavator.

8   LANDSCAPE ARCHITECTURE

Tao, the Way—the basic Chinese belief in an order and harmony in nature. This grand concept originated in remote times, from observation of the heavens and of nature— the rising and setting of the sun, moon, and stars, the cycle of day and night, and the rotation of the seasons—suggesting the existence of laws of nature, a sort of divine legislation that regulated the pattern in the heavens and on earth. It is worth noting that the original purpose of ritual was to order the life of the community in harmony with the forces of nature (tao) on which subsistence and well-being depended.

Mai-mai Sze

*Kyoto,
Mountain Green,
And water clean.*

Sanyō Rai

Improbable as it may sound, it is a fact that the contemporary architect or engineer faces few problems in structural design which nature has not already met and solved. By our own standards, her designs are structurally more efficient and esthetically more satisfactory than ours.

We should—to paraphrase that forthright pre-Civil War critic, Horatio Greenough— learn from nature like men and not copy her like apes. But the truth of the matter is that we have only recently perfected the means whereby her structures can really be understood.

Fred M. Severud

Just as a hunter is at home with nature—drinks of the springs, uses the cover, hunts into the prevailing winds, knows when the game will be feeding on the beechnuts and acorns of the ridges and when on the berries in the hollows; just as he senses the coming of a storm and instinctively seeks out shelter; and just as a sailor is at home on the sea, reads the shoal, senses the sandbar, interprets the sky, and observes the changing conformation of the ocean bottom—just so must planners be conversant with all facets of nature, until for any major tract of land, local building site, or landscape area we can instinctively recognize the natural characteristics, limitations, and fullest possibilities. Only by being thus aware can we develop a system of compatible relationships.

History shows us inspiring examples of humanized landscape planned in harmony with nature. One such example was the breathtakingly beautiful city of Kyoto as it existed at the turn of the twentieth century. Until only recently it could be said:

> Set amidst a national forest of pine and maple trees, Kyoto overlooks a broad river valley in which clear mountain water slides and splashes between great mossy boulders. Here in ordered arrangement are terraced the stone, timber, and paper buildings of the city, each structure planned to the total site and fitted with great artistry to the ground on which it stands. In this remarkable landscape, each owner considers his land a trust. Each tree, rock and spring is considered a special blessing from his gods, to be preserved and developed to the best of his ability, for the benefit of city, neighbors, and friends. Here, as one overlooks the wooded city or moves through its pleasant streets, one realizes the fullest meaning of the phrase "the stewardship of land."

Kyoto, as an illustrious example of oriental land planning, was laid out in accordance with the precepts of geomancy. These deal with the location and design of land use patterns and structural forms in response to, and in harmony with, the paths of energy flow through the earth and the atmosphere.

To the Western mind, this practice may seem dubious. In the more mature cultures, its efficacy is unquestioned. Unfortunately its principles have been veiled in religious mysticism and never clearly defined in technological terms. Let it be said only that historically architects, planners, and engineers have expressed in their constructions an intuitive feeling for those geological conditions and natural forces which have shaped and continue to govern the physical landscape and which have a powerful influence on all elements introduced. Such pervasive conditions include surface and subsurface rock formations, strata, cleavages, fissures, drainageways, aquifers, mineral seams and deposits, and lines and upwellings of electrical flow. They include also the air currents, tides, variations in temperature, solar radiation, and the earth's magnetic field.

The Human Habitat and Sustainability

The Natural Sciences

The landscape architect's unique strength and contribution to the comprehensive planning process is a general knowledge of the natural sciences. Especially applicable are geology, hydrology, biology, botany, and ecology. These are in addition to such sciences as chemistry, physics, electronics, the humanities, and graphic communication. All are essential to sound landscape design.

Geology

To understand the topographical base for any building project it is essential to know the structure and soil type of the earth's surface layers. The geologist learns early on that the tops of hills and ridges are generally underlaid with the denser subsoil or rock—which make for solid footing. They make excavation more difficult and expensive, however. This suggests the design of buildings without basements or lower levels. Such costly excavated space is replaced where feasible with on-grade building units around courts, which also serve to block hilltop winds and hold the warming winter sun.

Volcano.

Sloping topography suggests terraced structures, open to the outward view and with low retaining walls. Except in regions of drought, lower ground and especially valley bottoms below vegetated uplands can be expected to have deeper, moister, richer soils for crops and gardens. Here basements or deeper foundations may be required to reach bearing, but the digging is easy.

William Smith's *Strata of England & Wales,* one of the first geologic maps.

10   LANDSCAPE ARCHITECTURE

All organisms turn energy and food into living matter while producing waste materials of various kinds. This waste matter becomes food for legions of saprophytes, literally "decay eaters." These decomposers, which outnumber species of all other kinds, include beetles, fungi, nematodes, and bacteria. Through their complementary metabolic pathways, they return both essential nutrients and trace minerals to active circulation.

**Sim Van der Ryn
Stuart Cowan**

The level site, as on the plain, suggests an expanded building plan form, with wings to catch and check the breeze and courts to protect from the wind and drift. The study of geology also makes one extremely conscious of the deep-lying and shifting tectonic plates, the fault lines, volcanic cores, and the potential hazards of tornados and flooding. On a more modest scale it teaches of the various soil types and their qualities such as erosion resistance, fertility, and structural bearing. In land use planning, these are to be avoided for major transportation/transitways or settlements where lives are endangered. They are better reserved for welcome open space—left natural or with limited use, as for game lands or recreation. In storm-prone areas, early detection and monitoring techniques provide for early evacuation, saving thousands of lives and untold destruction.

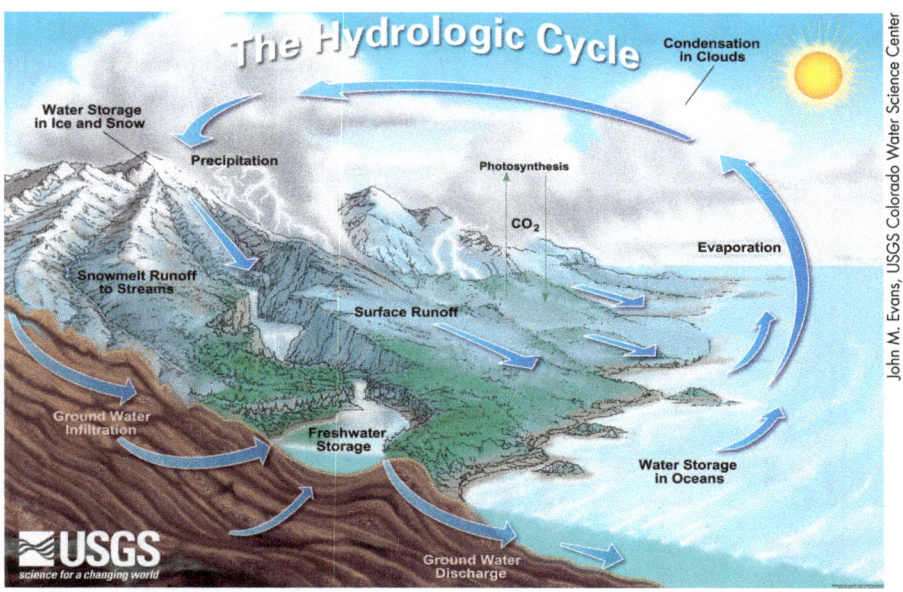

The water cycle.

Hydrology

Hydrology relates to land and resource planning in the form of water management. Those with an understanding of topography have learned to develop land use patterns in which extensive drainage inlets and deep sewer mains are not needed. Instead, surface drainage is conducted by swales to retention ponds or natural streams. Wastewater also flows by gravity in shallow laterals to outfall mains which follow the slope of the land. Water management has become increasingly important in regional planning since potable water shortage has become common. Irrigation and the transmission to urban centers have drained once-abundant rivers and watersheds. Population growth along both coasts has drawn down well fields to the point where saltwater intrusion is serious. This problem can no longer be overlooked. Nor can the large sweeps of lawn irrigated with freshwater be allowed. Irrigation of lawns and croplands will soon be treated by wastewater. With dual potable and treated wastewater systems, our freshwater reserves can be replenished.

Biology

With biology being the study of all forms of life and their interaction, one would believe it to be central in all planning considerations. It is not. Usually, more attention is paid to appearances than to people. It is the biology-conscious designer or team member who tests each proposal against the experience of the users—who brings the project to life.

Botany

A first-year botanist has learned the value of vegetation. In the immense cloud of carbon dioxide or exhaust fumes that surround planet Earth it is only by the transpiration of vegetation that the essential oxygen of the fresh air we breathe is produced. Moreover, it is the earth's vegetation that catches, transpires, and transmits to the aquifers the water on which all life depends. If that weren't enough, it is from the worldwide store of vegetation that we gather an astounding variety of foods, fibers, and timber. This knowledge should make conservationists of us all. It may in time. Meanwhile, in most unmindful construction a first thought is to clear the land.

In comprehensive land planning the botanist will be quick to point out the areas of natural cover that should be preserved. Costly clearing and

Botanical specimen.

ground cover replacement will thus be precluded. In the landscape planning process a botany doctorate is not needed, except in special cases. It is enough to know the local plants, their characteristics, and the conditions of growth under which they thrive. When existing plants are left undisturbed they need little care. Exotic ornamentals, needing more attention, are to be used sparingly.

Ecology

Ecology is the scientific study of the relationship of living things and their environment. As such it should be the primary science that informs humans about their environment and how to plan their activities and the use of land in a compatible, thus sustainable, way.

Other

A generalized knowledge of the natural sciences is the mark of a well-schooled landscape architect. No other profession is trained in this vital aspect of comprehensive land use planning.

The Ecological Basis

From the time of Earth's beginnings there has evolved an interacting, counterbalancing framework for all life.

Biosphere

In Spengler's most moving passage, where he identifies the "landscape" as the base of the "culture," he says that . . . man . . . is so held to it by myriad fibres, that without it life, soul, and thought are inconceivable.
Stanley White

This life matrix, or *biosphere*, born of earth, air, fire, and water, constitutes the whole of our living environment. It is as vast as the space between the basalt floor of the deepest ocean bed and the highest rarefied reaches of the outer ionosphere. It is as awesome as the towering thunderheads, the roaring hurricane, and the crashing surf. It is as tough as the granite hulk of a mountain. It is "as fragile as frost at dawn."[2] The biosphere, so fearfully and wonderfully contrived, is home to countless plant and animal communities that range in type and size from the invisible virus cluster to the roaming elephant herd or the pod of sounding whales. The biosphere is home as well to all members of the human race. As yet, we have no other.

The biosphere of the planet Earth is divided into several major habitats: the aquatic, the terrestrial, the subterranean, and the aerial.

Interdependence

Natural systems supply, transport, treat, and store water; modify the climate, oxygenate and purify the air; produce food; treat or assimilate waste; build land; maintain beaches; and provide protection from hurricanes. . . .
If essential components are destroyed, or if the system as a whole is overstressed, the process will break down and the system will fail.
Albert R. Veri et al.

We are just beginning to learn the extent to which all organisms are interrelated and interdependent and the sometimes critical effects of almost imperceptible changes in the temperature, chemistry, moisture content, soil structure, air movements, and water currents on our habitat. The slightest change in the delicate web of life may have repercussions throughout the whole of a natural system such as that of a marsh, pond, watershed, or receiving ocean basin.

As living, breathing human beings, inextricably related to all other organisms and creatures, we are utterly dependent upon the life-giving

[2]Ernest Braun and David E. Cavagnaro, *Living Water.*

There is a creature native to Kenya called the flattid bug, and I was introduced to it in Nairobi, some years ago, by the great Dr. L. S. B. Leakey. What Dr. Leakey introduced me to was a coral-coloured flower of a raceme sort, made up of many small blossoms like the aloe or hyacinth. Each blossom was of oblong shape, perhaps a centimetre long, which on close inspection turned out to be the wing of an insect. The colony clinging to a dead twig comprised the whole of a flower so real in its seeming that one could only expect from it the scent of spring. . . .

The coral flower that the flattid bug imitates does not exist in nature. The flattid bug has created the form . . . from each batch of eggs that the female lays there will always be at least one producing a creature with green wings, not coral, and several with wings of in-between shades.

I looked closely. At the tip of the insect flower was a single green bud. Behind it were a half dozen partially matured blossoms showing only strains of coral. Behind these on the twig crouched the full strength of flattid bug society, all with wings of purest coral to complete the colony's creation and deceive the eyes of the hungriest of birds.

Leakey shook the stick. The startled colony rose from its twig and filled the air with fluttering flattid bugs. They seemed no different in flight than any other swarm of moths that one encounters in the African bush. Then they returned to their twig. They alighted in no particular order and for an instant the twig was alive with the little creatures climbing over each other's shoulders in what seemed to be random movement. But the movement was not random. Shortly the twig was still and one beheld again the flower. The green leader had resumed his bud-like position with his varicoloured companions just behind. The fullblown rank-and-file had resumed its accustomed places. A lovely coral flower that does not exist in nature had been created before my eyes.

Robert Ardrey

All forms of life are interdependent with the environment.

productivity of the remaining un-built-upon landscape areas of the Earth. Should their life-support functions be diminished or disrupted to the point that they fail, we would then cease to exist. Only very recently, in the face of burgeoning population growth, rising indices of pollution, and the rapid depletion of our land and water reserves, has such a catastrophe seemed a remote possibility. Today, however, those scientists best able to assess trends and conditions have this very much on their minds.

What does all this mean to the planner, the designer of communities, the highway engineer, or the builder of home and garden? Simply that the integrity of the natural or cultivated landscape and the quality of the water within it and the air above it are to be in all ways protected. Land

Nature's ingenious process of pollination. As the honeybee lands and presses into the blossom after nectar, it triggers the flower stamen, forcing it down in an arc to make contact with and deposit on the bee's body. Bee, flower, mechanism—what have we humans made to compare?

14   LANDSCAPE ARCHITECTURE

Every process in nature has its necessary form. These processes always result in functional forms. They follow the law of the shortest distance between points: cooling only occurs on surfaces exposed to cooling, pressure only on points of pressure, tension on lines of tension; motion creates for itself forms of movement— for each energy there is a form of energy.

All technical forms can be deduced from forms in nature. The laws of least resistance and of economy of effort make it inevitable that similar activities shall always lead to similar forms. So man can muster the powers of nature in another and quite different way from what he has done hitherto.

If he but applied all the principles that the organism has adopted in its striving toward useful ends, he will find there enough employment for all his capital, strength and talent for centuries to come. Every bush, every tree can instruct him, advise him, and show him inventions, apparatuses, technical appliances without number.

Raoul France

The occupied landscape may be richer by far in all the subtle amenities of the original land if only the designs we apply are . . . becoming to the form as well as to the complexion of the meadows, woods and slopes we presume to compliment. . . . Landscape character should be intensified, not obliterated; and the ultimate harmony should emerge as a blend in which the native quality of the region and the spot still prevails. . . . These "humanized" landscapes are to us the most inviting and beloved, and we are pleased and inspired largely insofar as the whole structure and sentiment of the landscape can be preserved. . . .

There can be no deviation from the rule that the newly prepared landscape must be . . . a distillate or sublimation of the original myriad forms if it is to be a work of art in the sense of a high art form, timeless and historical.

Stanley White

Hermann Eisenbeiss, courtesy LIVING LEICA

areas can no longer be treated as little more than pictorial stage sets of forest, billowing grass, limpid water, or lavender hills amid which constructions can be blithely aligned or indiscriminately plunked. It is no longer acceptable that any land area be considered an isolated private domain, to be shaped at will to the heart's desire or carved up unfeelingly into cold geometric patterns. No smallest parcel can any longer be considered apart from all other contiguous land and water areas. For it is now well recognized that each draws upon the other and in turn affects them. Ecologically, all land and water areas are interconnected and interrelated.

Natural Systems

It is fundamental to intelligent land and resource planning that the natural systems which protect our health and well-being be understood and sustained. That those most sensitive and productive, together with nature's superlatives, may be preserved in their natural condition; that protective support and buffer areas be conserved and devoted to limited and compatible uses; that the less critical areas selected for development be so planned as to do no significant harm to their environs; and that all land use plans be so conceived as to bring people into the best possible relationships with each other and with the living landscape.

Earthscape

We have come to learn through the centuries that the spinning orb on which we live is a minor planet suspended in limitless space—an infinitesimal speck of matter in the universal scheme of things. Yet it is our world—vast, imponderable, and wonderful to us, a world of marvelous order and boundless energy. It is illumined and warmed in rhythmic cycles by the heat of our sun, bathed in a swirling atmosphere of air and moisture. Its white-hot core is a seething mass of molten rock; its thin, cool crust, pocked and creased with hollows and ridged with hills, mountain ranges, and towering peaks. The greater part of its area is immersed in saltwater seas, which ebb and flow with heaving tides and are swept to their depths by immense and intricate patterns of current.

From the ice-sheathed poles to the blazing equator, the earthscape varies endlessly. Wandering over it for something close to a million years, the human Earth dwellers have learned first to survive and later to thrive through a process of adaptation. This process, if wisely continued, should gain for us an ever-improving way of life. The study of the human-nature relationship is as old as humans themselves. In long-range perspective it is probably still a very young science, but, everything considered, it is the most basic science of all.

In our lifetime, we have for the first time scaled earth's highest peak, plumbed its deepest ocean trench, and penetrated outer space. We are tempted to believe that we have conquered nature. There are those who hold that in the years ahead we will finally subject nature to our control. Let us not delude ourselves. Nature is not soon to be conquered by puny man.

Conquer nature! How can we conquer nature? We are—blood, bone, fiber, and soul—a very part of nature. We are spawned of nature, rooted in nature, nourished by nature. Our every heartbeat, every neural impulse, and every thought wave, our every act and effort are governed by nature's all-pervading law. Conquer nature! We are but fleeting traces of life in nature's eternal process of evolving life and growth. Conquer nature! It is far better that we turn again to nature's way to search out and develop an order consonant with the universal systems, that our living may tap the vital nature forces, that our cultural development may have orientation, that our form building, form organizing, and form ordering may have meaning, that we may know again the rich, pulsing harmonies of life at one with nature.

Ignoring natural processes results in disaster.

For centuries European art has turned its back on the fundamental conception of nature in art, and Western man has imagined himself and nature as being in antithesis. In reality, his much-vaunted individuality is an illusion, and the truth which the Orient now reveals to him is that his identity is not separate from nature and his fellow-beings, but is at one with her and them.
Christopher Tunnard

The history of our progress on this earth is the history of an increasing understanding of nature's vitalities and powers. The wisdom of the wisest among us is no more than a comprehension of the simplest natural principles. The knowledge of our most perceptive scientists is gained through a faint insight into the wonder of natural phenomena.

Our labored development is the development of those sciences that reveal to us a way of life more closely attuned to nature's immutable way. Those of the forests, jungles, and sea are keenly sensitive to their natural surroundings and instinctively shape their living patterns to comply

Wildlife management area.

with nature's rhythms and cycles. They have learned that to do otherwise is to court inevitable disaster.

Years ago the urge to wander to strange new lands led the coauthor to live for some months in lonely, exotic British North Borneo (Sabah). There he came to be profoundly impressed by the tremendous joy of the people in simply being alive—exultantly healthy and happy sons and daughters of nature. On the islands, all live not only close to nature but by nature. Their whole life is guided day by day and hour by hour by the sun, the storms, the surf, the stars, the tides, the seasons. A full moon and an ebbing tide give promise of successful milkfish spearing on the shoal. The wheeling and screeching of the birds give warning of an approaching storm. In the quiet freshness of early morning, a hunter may draw his little daughter to his side and, crouching, point a long brown finger to the peak of Mount Kinabalu looming high above the palm fringe. "Tiba, little Tiba," he may caution. "Look now at the clouds on the mountaintop. Soon it will be blowing and raining there, and the streams will be rushing full. So stay away from the banks today and play at home with your mama." On the islands, clearly, the closer one's life is adapted to nature, the happier one's life will be. But not only on the islands. This observation is fully as true of our life on our farms and in our suburbs and cities. Sometimes we tend to forget this salient fact as we go about our living and planning for living. And often this forgetting is the root of much distress.

Interaction between man and environment in the West is abstract, an I-it relationship; in the East it is concrete, immediate, and based on an I-Thou relationship. Western man fights nature; Eastern man adapts himself to Nature and nature to himself. These are broad generalizations and, like all generalizations, should be taken with a grain of salt. But I believe that they may help to explain some of the essential differences out of which the different attitudes of East and West to life and environment develop and which are each in its own right destined to play its part in the transformation of the present and the future.
E. A. Gutkind

Sustainability

Webster defines *sustain* as "provide with nourishment; keep going; suffer; support or provide." The popular online encyclopedia Wikipedia offers a broader definition of the meaning of the word as used today: "The word sustainability is derived from the Latin *sustinere (tenere.* to hold; *sus.* up). Dictionaries provided more than ten meanings for *sustain,* the main ones being to 'maintain,' 'support,' or 'endure.' However, since the 1980s *sustainability* has been used more in the sense of human sustainability on planet Earth and this has resulted in the most widely quoted definition of sustainability and sustainable development, that of the Brundtland Commission of the United Nations on March 20, 1987: 'sustainable development is development that meets the needs of the present without compromising the ability of future generations to meet their own needs.'"

There is no doubt that *sustainable* has become the buzzword of the day and is used, perhaps too often, to address almost any issue, situation, or product. In landscape architecture and planning, the term has grown out of and is synonymous with environmental planning and design.

Although most, if not all, humans cannot comprehend really deep time, having a basic understanding of geologic time in the development of

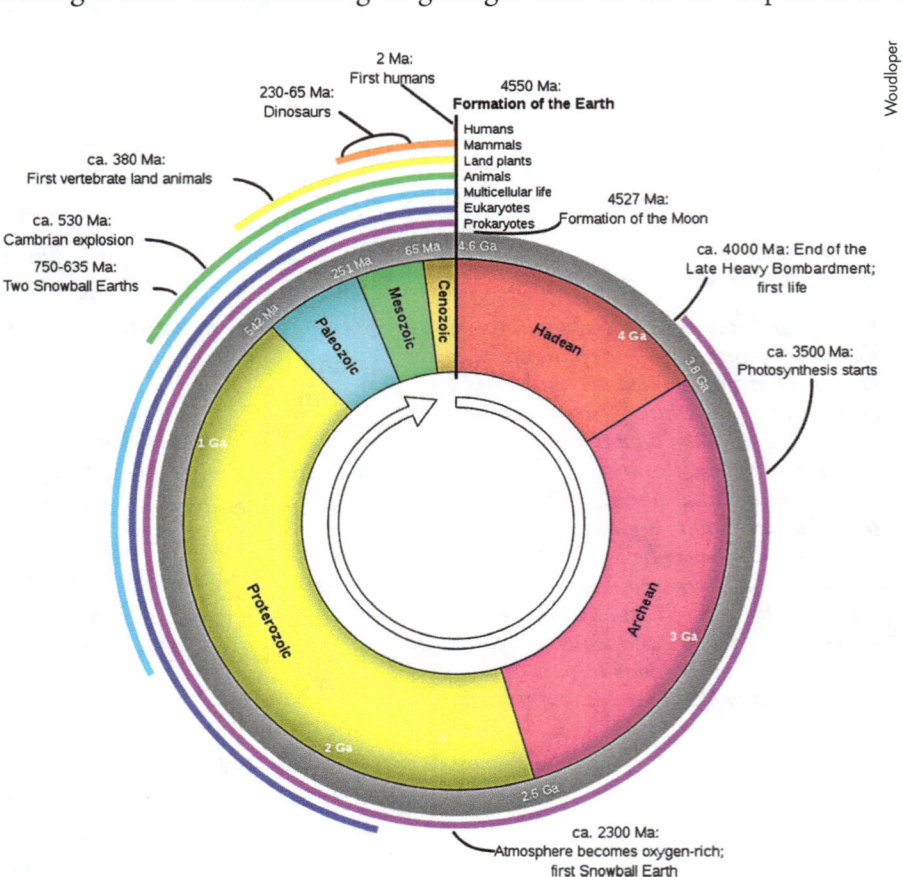

The way we treat land is largely symbolic and indicative of our lack of understanding of our place in the universe. . . . It is all tied with our comprehension of time. The human mind may not have evolved enough to understand deep time. It may only be able to measure it.
John McPhee

Geologic time.

18   LANDSCAPE ARCHITECTURE

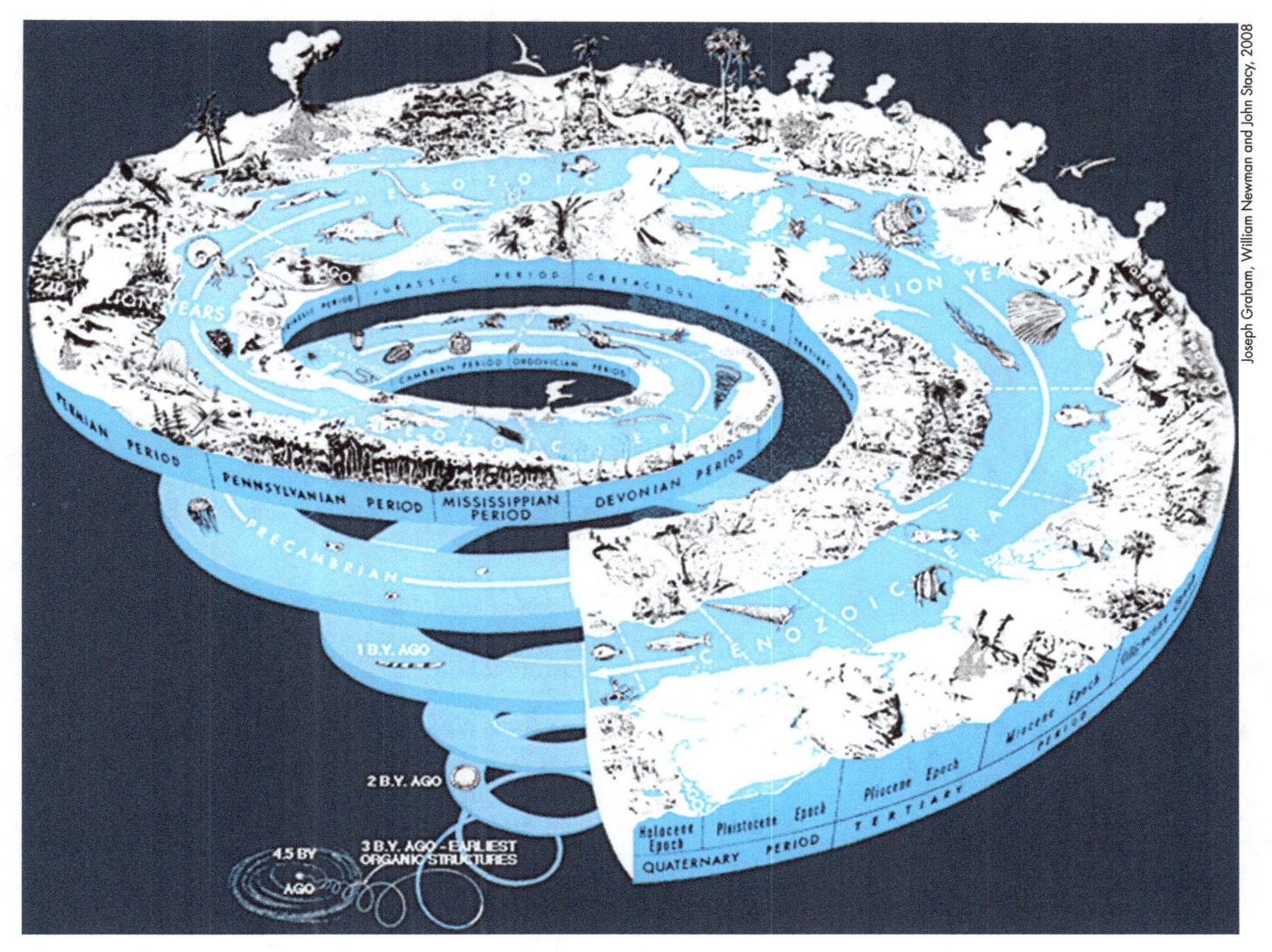

Earth's evolution.

planet Earth and human evolution is important in understanding sustainability in its larger context. Geologic time is time measured from the beginning of the formation of the planet. Expressed in numbers of "years ago," using today as the baseline, geologic time and human evolution are as follows:

	Years ago
• Earth is formed	4,500,000,000
• Beginning of life	3,000,000,000
• First humanoids (prehumans)	7,000,000
• First modern humans (*Homo erectus*)	2,000,000
• Modern man (*Homo sapiens*)	200,000
• Beginning of civilization	7,000
• Beginning of Industrial Revolution	200

The Human Habitat and Sustainability 19

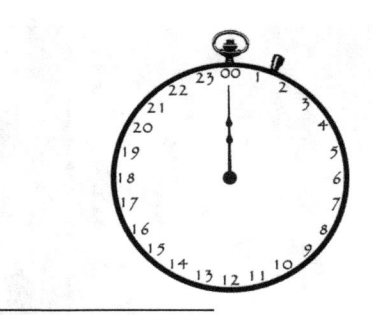

00:00 Prehumans appear.

16:08 p.m. *Homo erectus* appears.

23:19 p.m. *Homo sapiens* appears.

23:58:34 p.m. Civilization begins.

23:59:57 p.m. Industrial Revolution.

Understanding the scope of time of human evolution is aided by comparing it to a clock and a 24-hour day, with the first humanoids or prehumans appearing at the beginning of the day, or 00:00 (12:00 a.m.). *Homo erectus* appeared at 16:08 (4:08 p.m.), and *Homo sapiens* emerged at approximately 23:19 (11:19 p.m.). Civilization began about 23:58:34 (11:58:34 p.m.), and the Industrial Revolution began at 23:59:57 (2.47 seconds before midnight). The important point is that mankind has evolved as one of Earth's animals over a very long period of time and as part of the Earth itself.

During 97 percent of the time of human evolution, before the advent of agriculture, humans survived by hunting other animals and gathering plants for food directly from nature. Humans are part of the Earth, and the Earth is part of humans, who are inseparable from it. As such, humans are subject to the laws of nature, and their attempts to separate themselves from nature or to control it in the long term are doomed to failure.

During the first 7 million years of human evolution, as hunter-gatherers, the species, as with all other species, was biologically coded through DNA with a set of instructions regarding its relationship to its environment and how to survive as part of that environment. Simplified, modern biology tells us that humans have been programmed through DNA to do three basic things: stay alive as long as we can, reproduce and perpetuate the species, and accumulate things that facilitate staying alive and reproduction. This programming has served humans very well until recent times.

Modern humans, *Homo sapiens,* despite a relatively frail body as compared to other animals, have survived for over 200,000 years and have increased their life span from 20 years to the current world average of 67.2 years. In the 200,000 years since first appearing on Earth, they have reproduced, increasing their numbers from zero to 8 billion.

Although there are disparities among different human populations on Earth, by and large, humans have been able to accumulate more and more, to sustain longer lives, and increase their population. Ironically, the human species has been so successful at what it has been biologically programmed to do that longevity, population expansion, and the resulting increase in consumption have exceeded the planet's supply of renewable natural resources. The result is the destruction of the environment that sustains not only human life but the existence of countless other species.

In 1800, at the beginning of the Industrial Revolution, world population had reached 900 million people. Since then there has been explosive population growth, resulting in increased demands on the Earth's available resources, as outlined:

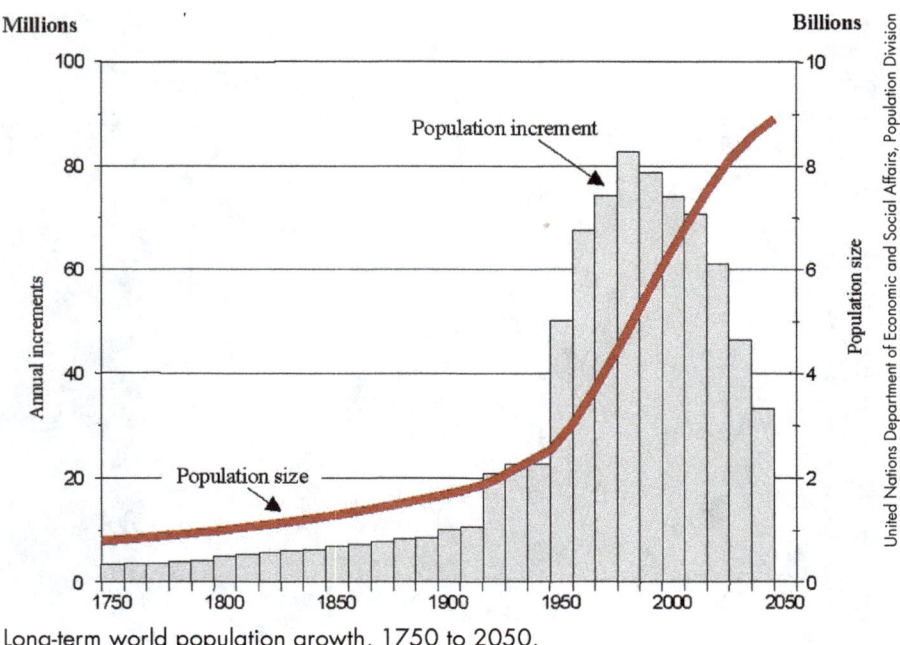

Long-term world population growth, 1750 to 2050.

- 1900—Earth's population increased to 1 billion people.
- 1961—There were 3 billion people, consuming 50 percent of the Earth's renewable natural resources.
- 1986—Population increased to 5 billion, consuming 100 percent of Earth's renewable natural resources.
- 2000—Earth's total population reached 6 billion, consuming 120 percent of renewable resources.

Since 1986, human population has continued to grow and consumption is eating away the renewable natural resource base, compounding the loss. Increased consumption has resulted in over-fishing, over-grazing, over-timbering, etc. The by-products of consumption are polluting land, air, and water and changing the biosphere, contributing to global warming.

If human sustainability is defined as meeting the needs of the present without compromising the ability of future generations to meet their own needs, it is clear that the combined effects of longer life spans, population growth, and ever-increasing consumption render human activity since the beginning of the Industrial Revolution unsustainable.

To become sustainable, humans must learn to control the basic activities that the species has been biologically programmed to do through controlling population growth and overconsumption.

The raging monster upon the land is population growth. In its presence, sustainability is but a fragile theoretical construct. To say as many do, that the difficulties of nations are not due to people but to poor ideology or land use management is sophistic.

Edward O. Wilson

The Human Habitat and Sustainability

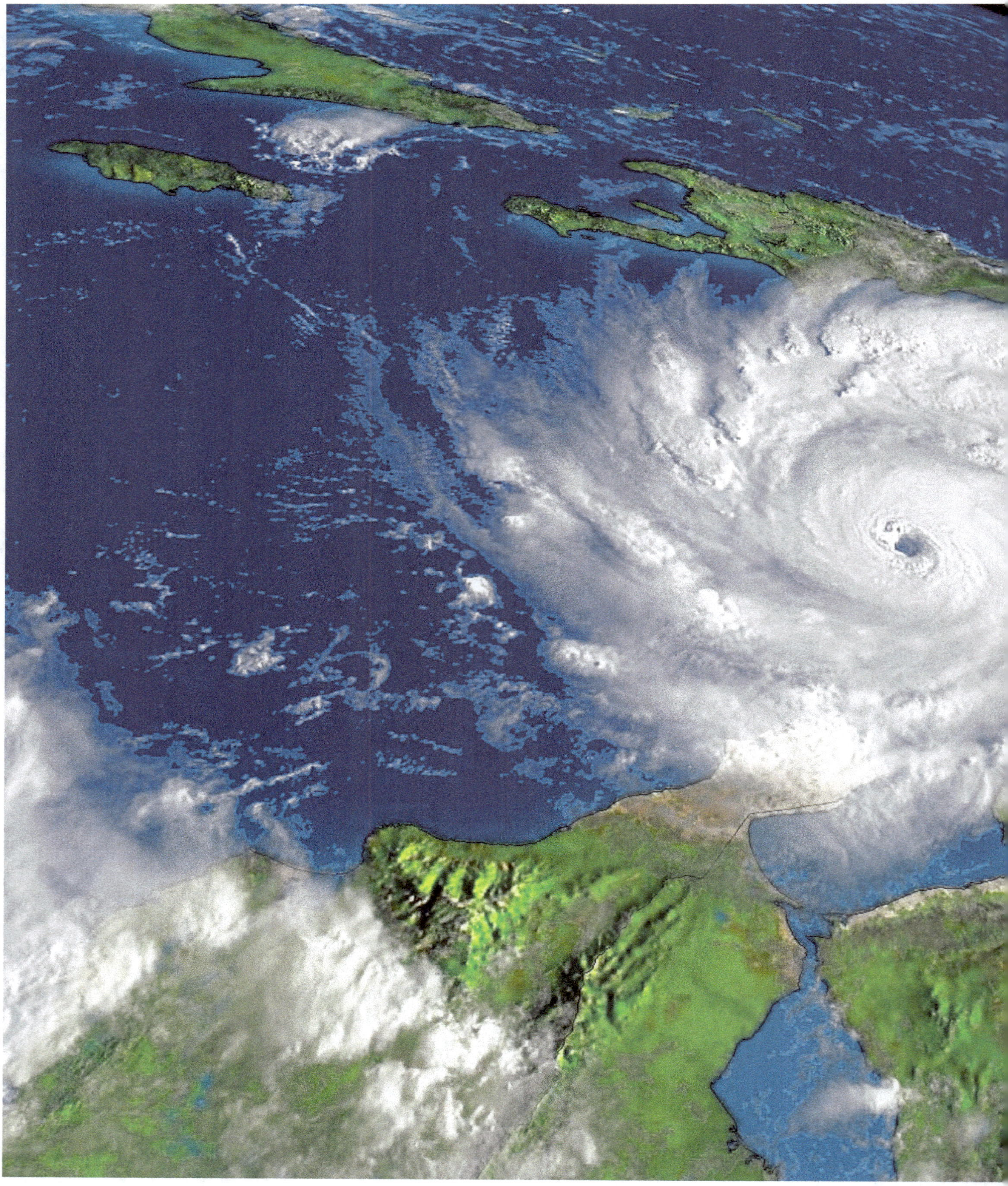

2 CLIMATE

Climate is the average weather condition at a place over time.

If a central purpose of planning is to create for any person or group of persons an environment suited to their needs, then climate must be a first consideration. It is fundamental, first, in the selection of an appropriate region for the proposed activities and then, within that region, in the selection of the most appropriate property. Once a site has been chosen, two new considerations suggest themselves. How do we best respond to the climatic givens in terms of site and structural design, and by what means can we modify the effects of climate to improve the situation?

Climate and Response

Perhaps the most obvious facts of climate are the annual, seasonal, and daily ranges of temperature. These will vary with changing conditions of latitude, longitude, altitude, exposure, vegetation, and proximity to such weather modifiers as the Gulf Stream, water bodies, ice masses, or desert. The amount of precipitation in the form of dew, rainfall, frost, or snow is to be recorded, as well as seasonal variations in humidity. The duration of sunlight in hours per day is of planning and design significance, as are the angles of incidence at prescribed times. The direction and velocity of the winds and the date and path of violent storms are to be charted. The availability, quantity, and quality of potable water are to be noted, together with the depths at which it occurs. The geologic structure is to be

NOAA

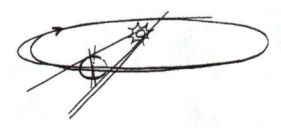

The planet Earth, with tilted axis, moves in its yearly loop around the sun. The incidence of the sun's radiation is a function both of our sphere's elliptical orbit and of its oscillating axial tilt. This variance in radiation accounts for climactic differentials and seasonal temperature change.

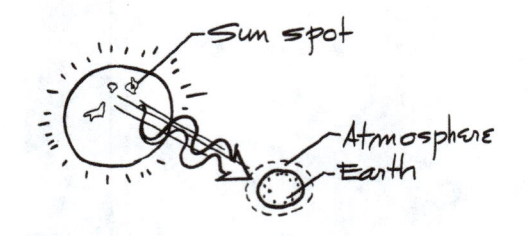

All terrestrial heat (energy) derives from the sun. The amount of energy received is related to the position of the earth in its elliptical orbit and in some yet inexplicable way to variations in the pattern of sunspots. In a lesser way energy reception is affected by conditions pertaining within the earth's intervening atmosphere.

The cyclic buildup and melt of polar ice are unpredictable. The periodic advance and retreat of the polar caps as they respond to solar forces in turn exert a massive influence on world weather conditions.

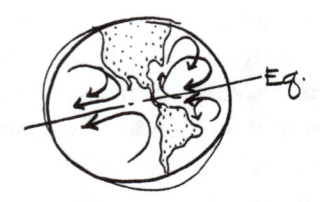

The ocean currents help to distribute the solar energy input to all areas of the globe. The thermal currents of the ocean, like the currents of the troposphere, are solar-generated. They sweep in counterrotary patterns and help to distribute the earth's store of sun-emitted heat.

described, together with soil types and depths and the existing vegetation and wildlife. Finally, the working together of all the physical elements as an ecological system is described to complete the story of regional climate.

Social Imprint

The physical well-being and attitudes of people are directly affected by climate, and these in turn prescribe the planning needs. It is well, therefore, in the study of climatic regions to note behavioral reactions and patterns of community organization that are unique and attributable to the climate or the weather. The special foods and dishes, the manner of dress, and the traditional customs are indicative. And so it is with the favored types of recreation, the level of education, and cultural pursuits. Economic factors such as agricultural yields and the production of goods are to be noted. The forms of government and political trends are analyzed, as are the general state of public health and the incidence of particular health and safety hazards and types of disease. A person's height, weight, circulation, respiration, perspiration, and dehydration have a direct relationship to climate, as do the factors of hardiness and acclimatization. It is no happenstance that the birdlike form of the maidens of the high Andes, with their thin ankles and capacious chests, differs from the squat and heavy build of Eskimo women. There are sound climatological reasons. In short, what one eats, drinks, believes, and is, is climate-induced and characteristic of the region. Literature, art, and music all give illuminating insights into the character of the various regions and their inhabitants. Travel and direct observation give even more vivid impressions, and if one is to work and plan for the people of any area, detailed on-site research is essential.

Regional dress responds to climate.

24   LANDSCAPE ARCHITECTURE

Color and plants characteristic of their region.

Accommodation

There is little to be done about the world climate except to adjust to it. The most direct form of adjustment is to move to that region which has a climate best suited to one's needs or desires. Such migrations or attempted migrations are the basis of much of human history. The alternative approach is to make the best of existing conditions wherever one may be. In broad terms, the climatic regions of the earth are four: the cold, the cool-temperate, the warm-humid, and the hot-dry. North America provides examples of all four. While the boundaries of these regions or zones cannot be defined precisely and while there are within them considerable variations, each has its distinctive characteristics and its strong influences upon any site development or structures to be planned. As in the two-dimensional plan layout of farm, home, and community, so it is with the three-dimensional design of sites and structures within a region. Just as the use area or trafficway is oriented "into the breeze," "away from the wind," or "across the sun" in some instances, so are site and architectural volumes shaped to afford exposure to the sun's warmth and light summer airs or protection from glare, oppressive heat, or fierce winter winds. All site and architectural spaces of excellence are weather-responsive; their form, materials of construction, and even colors are all climate-related. A postcard received from any part of the world depicting people, their dress, or their buildings will convey at a glance an informative story of region. It is proposed that within each region there is, for a given climatological condition, a logical planning-design response. The accompanying examples show for various conditions an appropriate accommodation in the shaping of community patterns, site plans, or building designs.

Climate

Condition

1. Extreme winter cold.
2. Deep snow.
3. Strong winds.
4. High windchill factor.
5. Deep frost.
6. Scrub forest cover.
7. Short winter days.
8. Long winters.
9. Alternating freeze and thaw.
10. Rapid spring melt.

The Cold Region

Community

1. Orientation to warming sun.
2. Provision for snowplowing and snow storage.
3. Utilization of all protective ground forms and covers as windscreens and soil stabilizers.
4. Crosswind alignment of trafficways and linear site use areas.
5. Reduction in size of plan areas to minimize costly excavation and frostproof construction.
6. Preservation of all possible vegetation, with the strong wind-resistant edges left intact.
7. Grouping of activity areas to reduce travel time.
8. Provision of community recreation and cultural centers within or near concentrations of dwellings.
9. Alignment of trafficways to fall within shadow bands to preclude ice buildup.
10. Avoidance of low ground, natural drainageways, and floodplains.

Site

1. Creation of enclosed courts and sun traps; use of textured construction materials and warm, "primitive" colors.
2. Use of short accessways, grouped entries, raised platforms, and covered walks.
3. Preservation or planting of windscreens; installation of snow fencing; use of low, strong vertical enclosure to brace for the gale.
4. Provision of intermediate points of shelter on a long traverse; placement of structures to block or sideslip the wind.
5. Use of post, beam, and platform construction to avoid the need for extensive excavation and foundations. Move with the ground surface by the use of stepped horizontal planes.
6. Clearing of small and clustered use areas, or "rooms," and meandering paths of interconnection within the scrub and tree growth. Developed areas should be limited in size to leave natural growth undisturbed insofar as possible.
7. Maximum utilization of daylight; orientation of buildings toward sunlit spaces with views to the sky and sunlit hills.
8. Utilization of the clustered-compound plan approach, which tends to engender pleasant community life and close social ties.
9. Use of decks, raised walkways, and flexible ground surfacings to preclude frost heave and keep people out of the slush and mud.
10. Provision of positive surface drainage to the natural lines of storm-water flow, with the soils, grasses, and other covers left undisturbed to prevent soil erosion.

Building

1. Design of massive, low-profile, well-insulated structures, with maximum exposure of walls and roof areas to the sun and minimum exposure to the wind; heat loss to be reduced in all ways possible, including limitation of the window area.
2. Protection of approaches from snow drift; the raising of entrance platforms above anticipated levels. The hazard of roof collapse may be reduced by steep-roof-and-storage-loft architecture.
3. Placement of windows away from prevailing winds; orientation of the long building axis into the wind and utilization of all possible topographic shielding and tree screens.
4. Location of entrances in the lee of the structure, with short protected passageways to limit the time of exposure.
5. Reduction of building perimeter and ground contact to reduce foundation problems and heat loss.
6. Forest cover preserved and buildings nestled against the protective slopes and tree masses.
7. Design of windows and living areas to exact the full contribution of the sun.
8. Attention lavished on comfort, architectural interest, and detail. In frigid climates particularly the "home is a castle."
9. With condensation and ice formation a problem, elimination of vulnerable joints and hazardous surfaces insofar as possible.
10. Use of steep roof pitches, deep overhangs, and exaggerated storm drainage gradients and capacities to facilitate rapid runoff.

Condition
1. Variable temperatures, ranging from warm to hot in the summer, cold in winter, and moderate in spring and fall.
2. Marked seasonal change.
3. Changing wind directions and velocities.
4. Violent storms occur infrequently.
5. Periods of drought, light to heavy rain and frost and snow may be expected.
6. Soils are generally well drained and fertile.
7. Many streams, rivers, and freshwater lakes.
8. An abundant supply of water.
9. Land cover varies from open to forests with rich vegetative variety.
10. Topographically scenic, including marine, plain, plateau, and mountainous areas.

The Cool–Temperate Region

Community
1. Definition of land use and trafficway patterns to reflect local temperature ranges and other climatic conditions. Extremes suggest compact plan arrangements; more moderate conditions permit dispersal.
2. Accommodation. Community plans must stand the test of function in all seasons.
3. Alignment of streets and open spaces to block cold winter winds and admit welcome summer breezes.
4. Design of streets, utility systems, and drainage channels to meet extreme conditions.
5. Consideration of high winds, flooding, and occasional snowstorms as important design factors.
6. Provision of extensive park and open-space systems as distinguishing attributes.
7. Incorporation of the natural waterways into the community plan for the use and enjoyment of the public.
8. Widespread installation of private and public gardens as regional features.
9. Preservation of indigenous vegetation within the open-space framework.
10. Planning of each community as a unique expression of its setting.

Site
1. Possibility of, and necessity for, wide variety in the type and size of outdoor activity areas.
2. Dramatization of the seasonal variations; consideration of spaces for winter, spring, summer, and fall activities.
3. Design recognition of the prevailing wind and breeze patterns.
4. Construction to withstand the worst of the storms.
5. Provision for all-weather durability and maintenance.
6. Protection of prime regional forest and agricultural lands.
7. Sensitive planning and zoning of all water-related lands to preserve their scenic and ecological values.
8. Use of pools and fountains to enhance community parks and gathering places.
9. Adaptation of community plan forms to provide the best possible integration with the natural-landscape features.
10. Full utilization of scenic possibilities.

Building
1. Elimination, by design, of extremes of demands for cooling, heating, and ventilating.
2. Consideration of the special design requirements and possibilities suggested by each season in turn.
3. Architectural plan organization and detailing in response to the cooling and chilling effects of local breezes and winds.
4. Structural design to meet the most severe storm conditions.
5. Consideration of shrinkage, swelling, condensation, freezing, and snow loadings.
6. Expansion and extension of plan forms when desirable, since excavation and foundation construction are not generally a problem.
7. Full utilization of the recreation values of each site.
8. Water catchment and storage is not a prime consideration.
9. Design of building areas and form in response to the topography.
10. Treatment of each building site to realize the full landscape potential.

Condition

1. Temperatures high and relatively constant.
2. High humidity.
3. Torrential rainfall.
4. Storm winds of typhoon and hurricane force.
5. Breeze often constant in the daylight hours.
6. Vegetative covers from sparse to luxuriant and sometimes junglelike.
7. The sun's heat is enervating.
8. Sky glare and sea glare can be distressing.
9. Climatic conditions breed insects in profusion.
10. Fungi are a persistent problem.

The Warm–Humid Region

Community

1. Spacing of habitations in the dispersed "hunter" tradition.
2. Adjustment of community patterns to channels or areas of air movement.
3. Avoidance of floodplains and drainageways. Disturbed areas are subject to heavy erosion.
4. Location of settlements in the lee of protective land masses and forest and above the level of storm-driven tides.
5. Alignment of streets and placement of gathering places to capture all possible air currents.
6. Avoidance of natural growth insofar as feasible. Disturbance of the ground-cover subjects soils to erosion.
7. Use of existing tree masses and promontories to provide a sunscreen to public ways and places. Supplementary planting of shade trees is often desirable.
8. Planned location of settlements with the arc of the sun to the rear, not seaward, of the building sites.
9. Location of settlements upwind of insect-breeding areas.
10. Admittance of sun and breeze to building areas to reduce fungi and mildew.

Site

1. Design of site spaces to provide shade, ventilation, and the cooling effects of foliage and water.
2. Provision for air circulation and evaporation.
3. Protection against driving rains and adequate runoff capacity.
4. Location of critical-use areas and routes in unexposed places, above the reach of tides and flooding.
5. Maximization, by exposure, channeling, and funneling, of the favorable effects of the breeze.
6. Use of lush foliage masses and specimen plants as backdrop and enframement and for the interest of form, foliage, or floral display.
7. Planning of outdoor activity areas for use in the cooler morning and evening hours. Heat-of-the-day gathering places should be roofed or tree-shaded.
8. Reduction or elimination of glare by plan location and well-placed tree plantings.
9. Elevation of use areas and walkways by deck and platform construction to open them to the breeze and reduce annoyance by insects.
10. Use of stone, concrete, metals, and treated wood only in contact with the ground.

Building

1. Induction of cooling by all feasible means, including the use of open building plans, high ceilings, broad overhangs, louvered openings, and air conditioning of local areas.
2. Provision of air circulation; periodic exposure to sunlight and artificial drying where required.
3. Architectural use of the colonnade, arcade, pavilion, covered passageway, and veranda; orientation of entranceways and windows away from the path of the storm track.
4. Design of wind-resistant structures or lighter temporary and expendable shelters.
5. Design of rooms, corridors, balconies, and patios as an interconnected system of breezeways.
6. Utilization, indoors and out, of indigenous plant materials for the cooling effect of their foliage.
7. Provision of shade, shade, shade.
8. Positioning of viewing points away from the glare and provision of well-designed screening.
9. Elevation of structures above the ground, facing into the breeze, and insectproofing of critical points and areas.
10. Provision of open, well-ventilated storage areas; use of fungus-resistant materials and drying devices as needed.

Condition

1. Intense heat in the daytime.
2. Often intense cold at night.
3. Expanses are vast.
4. Sunlight and glare are penetrating.
5. Drying winds are prevalent and often raise devastating dust storms.
6. Annual rainfall is minimal. Vegetation is sparse to nonexistent except along watercourses.
7. Spring rains come as a cloudburst, with rapid runoff and heavy erosion.
8. Water supply is extremely limited.
9. Limited agricultural productivity necessitates the importation of food and other goods.
10. Irrigation is a fact of life.

The Hot–Dry (Desertlike) Region

Community

1. Creation of cool and refreshing islands of use within the parched surroundings.
2. Provision of opportunities for group activity. Chill evenings in the desert, as on the tundra, suggest the need.
3. Adaptation of "outpost," "fort," and "ranch" plan patterns.
4. Within the dispersed compounds the planning of compact spaces with narrow passageways and colonnades to provide relief from the sun.
5. Location of homesteads and trade centers in areas of established ground covers; use of shelterbelt tree plantations.
6. Protection of all possible natural growth surrounding the development.
7. Avoidance of flood-prone areas. Those who have experienced desert freshets will keep well out of their way.
8. Minimization of irrigation requirements by compact planning and multiple use of planted and seeded spaces.
9. Location of settlements and community centers close to transportation and distribution nodes.
10. Coordination of land use and traffic patterns with existing and projected irrigation canal routes and reservoir locations.

Site

1. Amelioration of heat and glare by orientation away from the sun, by shading, by screening, and by the cast-shadow patterns of well-placed building components.
2. Adoption of the corral-compound (herder) arrangement of homesteads and neighborhood clusters.
3. Recognition of the automobile as the crucial means of daily transport and a dominant site-planning factor.
4. Screening of use areas and paths of movement from the direct blast of the sun.
5. Protection of outdoor activity spaces from exposure.
6. Preservation of native plant materials as self-sustaining and handsome components of the desert landscape.
7. Avoidance of arroyos and floodplains as development routes and sites.
8. Limitation in the size of parks, gardens, and seeded areas.
9. Use of tubbed and container-grown plants, drip irrigation, and hydroponic gardening.
10. Incorporation of irrigation canals, ponds, and structures as attractive site features.

Building

1. Architectural use of thick walls, high ceilings, wide roof overhangs, limited fenestration, light-reflective colors, and a precise design response to the angles and arcs of the sun.
2. Exclusion of the chill night air by insulation, reduction of heat loss, and use of localized radiant heat. The open fireplace is a desert tradition for good reason.
3. Low ranch-type spreads are a logical architectural expression of the hot–dry climate and desert topography.
4. Provision of cool, compact, and dim interior spaces in contrast to the stifling heat and brilliance of the great outdoors.
5. Sealing of all buildings against dust and wind. Airtight openings and skillful architectural detailing are required.
6. Grouping of rooms or structures around planted and irrigated courts and patios.
7. Provision of spring rainfall catchment and storage. Water from roofs, courts, and paved areas can be directed to cisterns.
8. Recycling of wastewater is prescribed. The type of use will determine the degree of treatment and purification required.
9. The provision of food and fodder storage is an important consideration in desert building design.
10. Adaptation of irrigation to interior courts and garden spaces. The evaporation of moisture from paved surfaces, fountains, spray heads, mulches, or foliage provides welcome relief from the heat.

Climate

Different responses to microclimate.

Microclimatology

Microclimatology is the study of climatic conditions within a limited area. It is sometimes referred to as the "science of small-scale weather." It may be inferred that the purpose of the scientific study is to discover facts and principles which may be applied to improve the human condition. This is precisely the case.

An Example

As a hypothetical example, let us consider a small walled courtyard in a hot-dry (desert) setting. It is proposed that by the application of well-known principles of microclimatic design, an ambient air temperature at a point 3 feet above the ground surface could be reduced by as much as 30 to 40°F. This could well improve the existing condition from an intolerable situation to one of comfort and delight—all in all, a worthy enterprise.

As a base condition, let us assume the worst. Let us assume that the enclosing walls are solid, admit no breeze, are high enough to provide an extensive sun-receiving, heat-radiating area, and are dark in color to maximize their heat absorption. Let us then compound the disaster by flooring the empty courtyard space with solid concrete, thick enough for massive heat buildup and radiation and colored in a dark-red hue. To complete our experimental volume, let us imagine the courtyard to be so oriented as to receive the full force of the burning midday sun. It can be seen that a subject seated on a metal chair in the center of this unfortunate cube would be properly grilled, and that shortly.

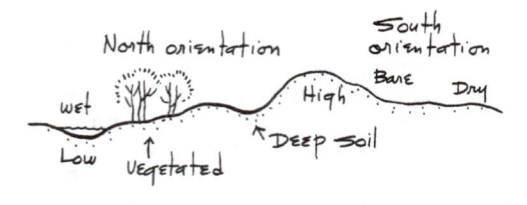

Every property has to some degree a variety of microclimates. These are dependent upon orientation, wind and breeze direction, land conformation, vegetation, soil depth and types, moisture content—and even colors. Such off-site conditioners as hills, forests, rivers, water bodies, and urbanization make a difference too.

30   LANDSCAPE ARCHITECTURE

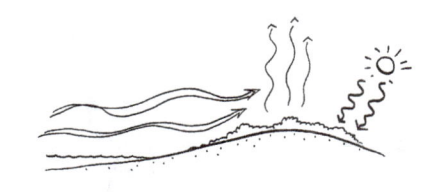

As the daytime sun heats the land surface and warm air rises, the cool moist air from adjacent water bodies moves landward to fill the void.

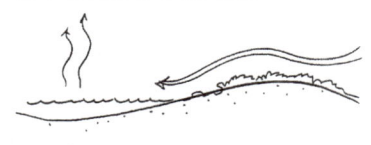

At night the cooler air from the vegetated land mass flows toward the water bodies.
THE DAILY LAND-WATER AIR EXCHANGE
Note: The temperature advantage gained by alert siting and landscape improvement may sometimes be measured in no more than a few degrees. But aside from the factor of increased comfort the savings of energy required in cooling and heating can be significant.

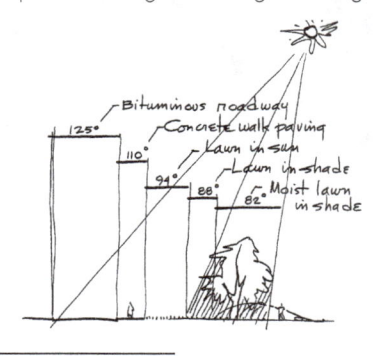

On a hot summer noontime the temperatures may vary widely on any given site.
RELATIVE SURFACE TEMPERATURES

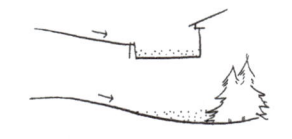

Since cool air flows downhill, local depressions or obstructions can form welcome "pools of cool"—or unwelcome frost pockets.

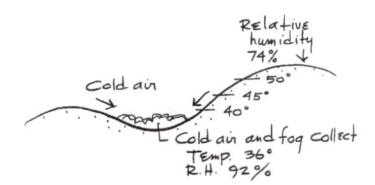

In colder climates the favored site is usually the upper slope below an exposed crest. Slopes facing south are warmer.

But exposure to cold winds at the crest may offset the temperature advantage.
TOPOGRAPHY AFFECTS THE MICROCLIMATE

In contrast, wishing to create a cool and refreshing courtyard in the same locality, let us "wing out" and open the side walls to catch the slightest breeze that might be channeled through the space. The walls themselves could be formed of light-gray textured concrete or stone rough enough to be heat-refractive and to receive several clumps of vines. A pool, a brimming basin, or a splashing fountain installed on the base plane would introduce water. Water would also be used as a spray to moisten low mounded beds of planting edged with gravel mulch for rapid evaporation. From the irrigated planting bed, a multistemmed shade tree might support a canopy of foliage and flowers, to cast patterns of shadow across the wall and paving. Additional shade could be provided on the overhead plane by light sails or panels of cool-colored nylon fabric. Tubbed and potted plants would add green relief and decorative interest. With webbed rattan furniture, iced drinks, and the sound of wafting music, the oasis would be complete.

The example is extreme, but it serves to illustrate the possibilities of small-scale climate improvement.

Design Guidelines

Whatever the climate or weather, when it comes to planning an agreeable living environment there are many microclimatic principles that can be applied to advantage. Among them are these:

- Eliminate the extremes of heat, cold, humidity, air movement, and exposure. This can be achieved by intelligent site selection, plan lay-

Outdoor space responds to solar orientation.

Climate

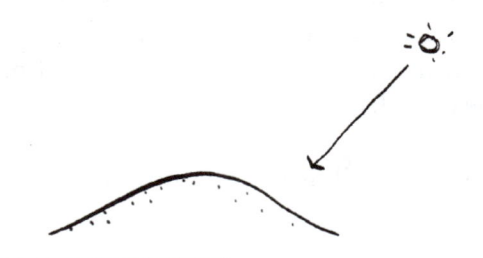

Slopes with southerly exposure receive the most hours and greatest intensity of solar heat each day. Spring can come weeks earlier on the sunny side of a hill.

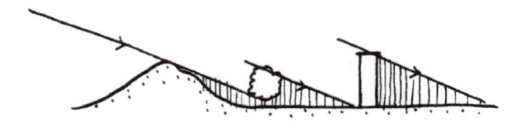

Topographical forms, tall buildings, trees, or other objects may reduce the total hours of daylight. Depending upon the climatic situation, full sun all day may or may not be desirable.

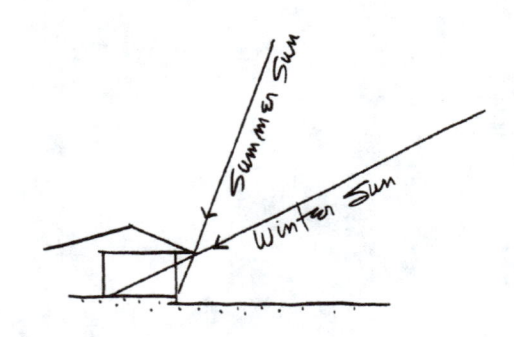

The sun's orbit and angle of incidence vary with the seasons. By orientation, screening, and overhang the amount of sunlight admitted to the interior can be precisely controlled.

Evaporative cooling.

out, building orientation, and the creation of climate-responsive spaces.
- Provide direct structural protection against the discomfort of solar radiation, precipitation, wind, storm, and cold.
- Respond to the seasons. Each presents its problems; each provides its opportunities for adaptation and enjoyment.
- Adjust community, site, and building plans to the movement of the sun. The design of living areas, indoors and out, should ensure that the favored type and amount of light are received at the favored time.
- Use the sun's radiation and solar panels to provide supplementary heat and energy for cooling energy.
- Utilize the evaporation of moisture as a primary method of cooling. Air moving across any moist surface, be it masonry, fabric, or foliage, is thereby made cooler.
- Maximize the beneficial effects of adjacent water bodies. These temper the atmosphere of the warmer or cooler adjacent lands. Introduce water. The presence of water in any form, from film to waterfall, has a cooling effect both physically and psychologically.
- Preserve the existing vegetative cover. It ameliorates climatic problems in many ways:

It shades the ground surface.
It retains the cooling moisture of precipitation.
It protects the soils and environs from the freezing winds.
It cools and refreshes heated air by evapotranspiration.

32   LANDSCAPE ARCHITECTURE

The glare from water, sand, or other reflective surfaces can increase heat loads.

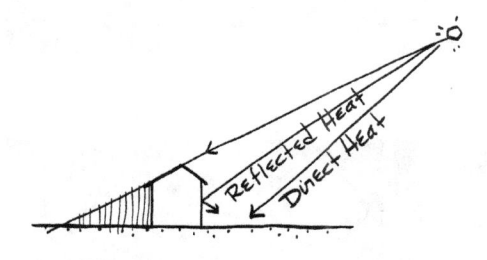

Buildings are temperature modifiers. By their positioning as well as by their form and character they suggest related uses.

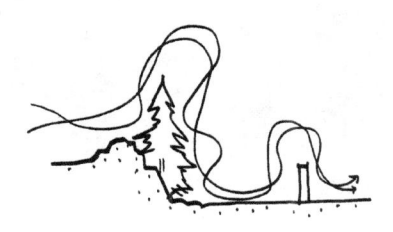

Abrupt forms cause unpleasant air turbulence.

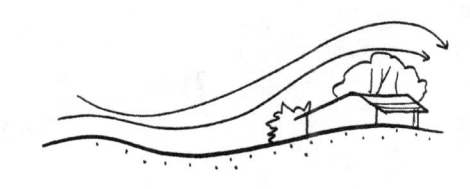

Smooth forms induce the smooth flow of air.

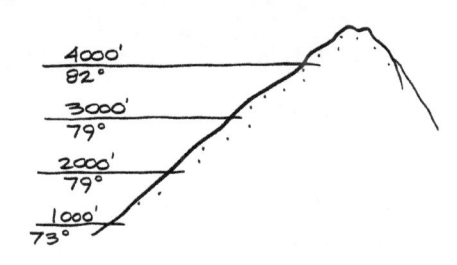

Temperatures vary with elevation—by about 3°F for each 1000 feet in the daytime. Nighttime differentials are greater.

It provides sunscreen, shade, and shadow.

It helps to prevent rapid runoff and recharges the water-bearing soil strata.

It checks the wind.

- Install new plantings where needed. They may be utilized for various types of climate control. Windscreens, shade trees, and heat-absorptive ground covers are examples.
- Consider the effects of altitude. The higher the altitude and latitude (in the northern hemisphere), the cooler or colder the climate.
- Reduce the humidity. Generally speaking, a decrease in the humidity effects an increase in bodily comfort. Dry cold is less chilling than wet cold. Dry heat is less enervating than wet heat. Humidity can be decreased by induced air circulation and the drying effects of the sun.
- Avoid winter winds, floods, and the paths of crippling storms. All can be charted.
- Explore and apply all natural forms of heating and cooling before turning to mechanical (energy-consuming) devices.

Reduction of Heat Loss

- Avoid exposure to prevailing winds and cold downdrafts from upper slopes.
- Avoid extremes in elevation.
- Avoid site areas with wet, impervious soils, dead-air basins, and frost pockets.
- Provide wind shielding by ground forms and existing tree cover (preferably evergreen).
- If exposure cannot be precluded, plan compactly and for a slip-stream effect, with narrow and solid building walls facing into the winter winds.
- Protect the dwelling entrances.
- Orient building facades to the east, southeast, and south and to the high arc of the sun.
- In cold climates, locate use areas and structures in the lee of windbreaks to utilize snow outfall for ground and building insulation.
- Provide open space around buildings for air circulation and the play of the winter sun.
- Deciduous tree cover provides summer shade and casts shadows while admitting winter sunlight.
- Dig in. Partially buried structures receive insulation from the earth and present a lower profile.
- Select construction materials, surface treatments, and colors that absorb and radiate solar heat.

Reduction of Cooling Requirements

- Face use areas and buildings into the natural airstreams.
- Provide an overhead tree canopy.
- Utilize structural sun shields. Colonnades, arbors, wide overhangs, and recessed openings are familiar in hot climates.

Climate 33

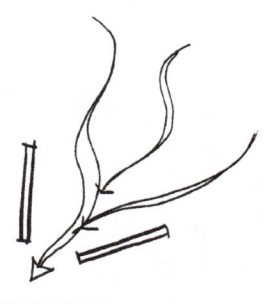

A mild summer breeze can be amplified by the venturi effect of well-placed buildings, walls, hedges, or mass plantings.

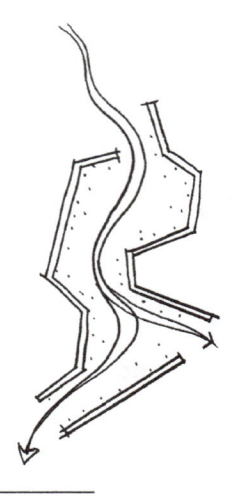

A breeze may be channeled and directed from space to space.

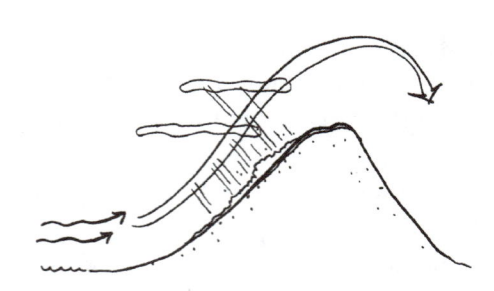

An air mass cools as it is driven up a mountain slope by prevailing winds, often to the point of precipitating its moisture content before reaching the crest. The windward slopes therefore tend to be humid and heavily vegetated, while the lee slopes, robbed of rainfall and subjected to the downdraft that warms as it falls, tend to be hot and arid. To a lesser extent any landform, such as a hill, island, or forest, can have the same effect.

Windbreak.

Solar orientation.

Shade.

Overhead screen.

Flowing water.

- Compose buildings, ground forms, walls, fencing, and planting to channelize summer breezes through exterior and interior spaces. A broad, dispersed plan arrangement is indicated.
- Excavate for foundations. Structures built into well-drained slopes are warmer in winter and cooler in the summertime.
- Reach for the breeze. Utilize open planning, flying decks, and balconies.

34   LANDSCAPE ARCHITECTURE

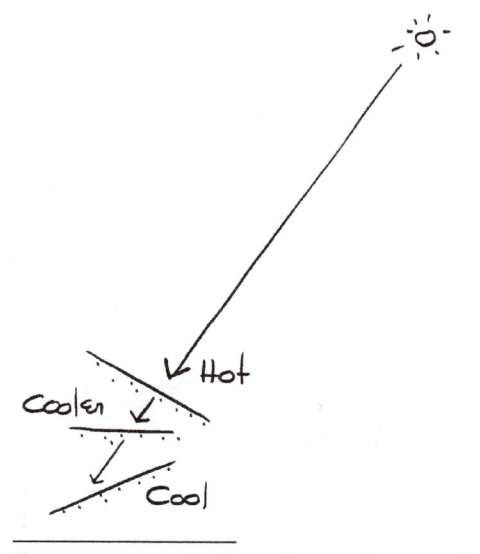

The more perpendicular a slope to the rays of the sun, the warmer the surface temperature.

- Promote ventilation by the use of breezeways, screened patios, louvered walls, and fans.
- Feature the use of water for its cooling effects. Utilize porous soils, mulches, ground covers, and irrigation to promote evapotranspiration.
- Use heat-reflective materials, rough textures, and cool colors.

Utilization of Natural Thermodynamics
- Consider energy generation by such sources as wind power, falling and flowing water, and solar panels.
- Maximize the warming effects of the sun and the cooling effects of shade, air currents, and moisture.

Useful Observations. Whatever the climate or weather—in siting land uses or structures, there are countless phenomena to be learned and applied. The temperature advantage gained by alert siting and landscape improvement may sometimes be measured by no more than a few degrees. But aside from the increased comfort and pleasure derived, the savings in energy in cooling and heating may be a telling factor.

Spring: Children playing in the fountain.

Fall: Evening performance.

Summer: Fourth of July celebration.

Winter: Ice skating.

Climate 35

Climate Change/Global Warming

For a decade or more the phenomenon of climate change and global warming has become a major focus of the scientific community. Throughout geologic time there have been shifts in world climate from extreme cold periods or ice ages and glaciations to periods of thaw during which glaciers retreated. The Earth is currently in a state of sustained rising temperatures, and, as evidence builds, most scientists agree that the rise in temperatures is due, at least in part, to human activity.

Air pollution contributes to global warming.

It should be noted that this is the first time in the history of the Earth that the effects of living organisms (humans) are changing world climate. With the coming of the Industrial Revolution and the beginning of the release of large amounts of carbon and other greenhouse gases into the atmosphere, an increase in Earth's atmospheric temperature is occurring which is widely believed to be changing world climate. The results will have profound effects on the environment of entire regions and planning for human habitation. The results of climate change brought about by global warming that most affect human habitation include more severe weather events (hurricanes, tornadoes, flooding, droughts, etc.), sea-level rise, and threats to and the migration of plant and animal species.

There is much debate regarding what to do about global warming and what can be done to abate or reverse the process causing it. Many believe it is already too late to reverse that process and the only thing for humans to do is adapt to it. Planners and designers can contribute to the efforts to slow down the process by employing the practices of conservation and sustainable, low-impact design, from the regional to the site-specific scale. However, they must also focus on adapting to change that is already taking place and that which is inevitable. This includes planning and designing for sea-level rise, which will have a large impact on coastal areas, ranging from the inundation of coastal wetlands to significant flooding of urban areas. In some cities and communities, the impact will be so significant that certain existing land uses in low-lying areas will have to be relocated and replaced with aquatic open spaces. Others may be redesigned to address the effects of more significant and frequent flooding.

The increased severity of individual weather events will also require different responses from the planning and design community. The location of communities out of harm's way from flooding, hurricane, and tornado impacts will require more consideration than has been given in the past. The potential short- and long-term impact of climate change on animal and plant communities will have to be taken into account in determining the future land use of an area or a specific site.

The reaction to the need to address climate change in planning and design has been mixed. Certain localities, such as Manhattan in New York City and several coastal European cities, have conducted extensive studies, created models, and prepared plans to address sea-level rise. Many equally vulnerable localities are ignoring the problem.

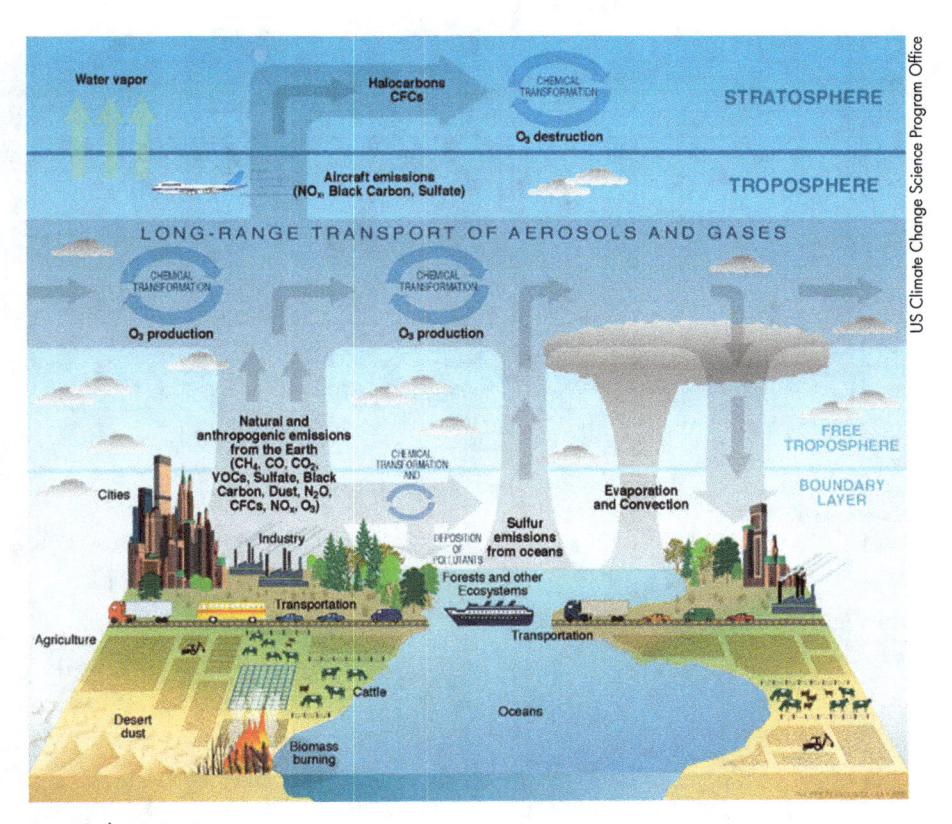

Atmospheric composition.

Climate 37

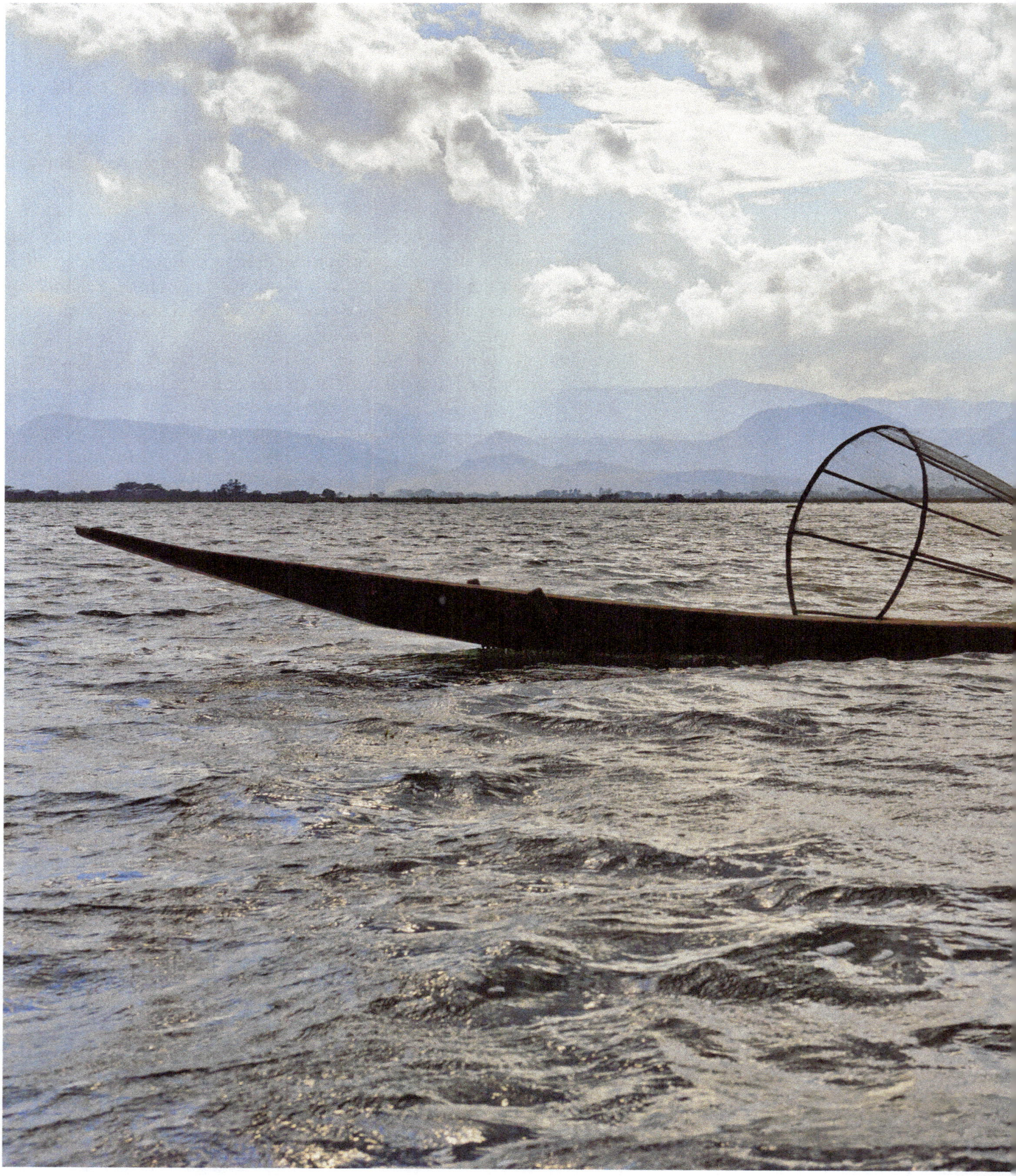

3 WATER

Tom Lamb, Lamb Studio

Free water is the shining splendor of the natural landscape. From the bubbling spring and upland pool to the splashing stream, rushing rapids, waterfall, freshwater lake, and brackish estuary and finally to the saltwater sea, water has held for all creatures an irresistible appeal. To some degree, we humans still seem to share with our earliest predecessors the urgent and instinctive sense that drew them to the water's edge.

Perhaps at first they were drawn only for drink, to lave hot and dust-streaked bodies, or to gather the bounty of mollusk and fish. Later, water for the cooking pots would be dipped and carried in gourds, skins, hollow sections of bamboo, and jars of shaped, fire-baked clay. Perhaps our affinity for water has increased with the discovery of its value in gardens and irrigation and with the knowledge that only with moisture present can plants flourish and animals thrive. It may be because in the deep, moist soils of the bottomlands the grasses are richer, the foliage more lush, and the berries larger and sweeter. Here, too, the refreshing breeze seems cooler and even the song of the birds more melodious.

Water as a Resource

Almost every human activity is dependent upon the use of fresh water, but of all the water found on planet Earth only 3 percent is fresh and, of that, most is frozen in glaciers and polar regions, making less than 1 percent of the Earth's fresh water potentially available for human use.

Distribution of Earth's Water

More than two-thirds of the earth's surface is submerged in saltwater. The balance of surface area is generally underlaid with fresh water that fluctuates slowly in elevation and flows imperceptibly through the porous aquifers toward the waiting sea.

In Florida at least 65 percent of all marine organisms, including shrimp, lobsters, oysters, and commercial and game fish, spend part of their life cycle in the brackish waters of tidal estuaries and coastal wetlands.

Within the past century, over half of the state's wetlands have been dredged, filled, or drained.

The only way to protect fish and wildlife is to protect their habitat.

In planning the use of land areas in relation to waterways and water bodies, a reasonable goal would be to take full advantage of the benefits of proximity. These benefits would seem to fall within the following categories.

Water Supply, Irrigation, and Drainage

When these are important considerations, the area of more intensive use will be located near the sources. Those site functions requiring the most moisture in the soil or air will be given location priority. Usually gravity flow will have much to do with the plan layout.

Irrigated fields will be established below points of inlet where possible and be so arranged that lines or planes of flow will slope gently across the contours to achieve maximum percolation and continuity.

Drainage will be maintained whenever possible along existing lines of flow, with the natural vegetation left undisturbed. It would be hard to devise a more efficient and economical system of storm drainage than that which nature provides. Runoff from fertilized fields or turf will be directed to on-site retention swales or ponds so that the water may be filtered and purified before reentering the source or percolating into the soil to recharge the water table.

Use in Processing

When drawn from surface streams or water bodies for use in cooling, washing, or other processes, water of equal quantity and quality is to be returned to the source. Makeup water may be supplied from wells or public water supply systems.

Transportation

When waterways, lakes, or abutting ocean are to be used for the transport of people or goods, the docking installations and vessels are to be so designed and operated that the functional and visual quality of the water is at all times ensured.

Microclimate Moderation

The extremes of temperature are tempered by the presence of moisture and by the resulting vegetation. This advantage may be augmented by the favorable placement of plan areas and structures in relation to open water, irrigated surfaces, or water-cooled breeze.

Wildlife Habitat

Lakeshores, stream edges, and wetlands together form a natural food source and habitat for birds and animals. When flora and fauna are to be protected, the indigenous vegetation is to be allowed to remain standing whenever feasible, and continuous swaths of cover are to be left intact to permit wildlife to move from place to place unmolested. The denser growth is usually concentrated along water edges and converging swales.

Recreational Use

Our streams and water bodies have long provided our most popular types of outdoor recreation such as boating, fishing, and swimming. Along their banks and shores is found the accretion of cottages, mobile home parks, and campsites that attest to our love of water. It is proposed that in long-range planning, with few exceptions, all water areas and edges to the limits of a 50-year flood would be acquired and made part of the public domain.

Scenic value.

Recreation value.

Scenic Values

For most people, the glimmer of sunlight on open water is sure to elicit an exclamation of discovery and delight. The feelings may be expressed as a shout of triumph or as a silent upsurge of the spirits. Not only the sight but as well the sounds of water evoke a sense of pleasure. It would seem that we are so acutely attuned to the language of water—the trickle and gurgle of ice melt, the splash of the stream, the lapping of water on lakeshore, the surf crash, even the cry of shorebirds—that we can almost see with our ears.

If there is magic on the planet, it is contained in water . . . its substance reaches everywhere; it touches the past and prepares the future; it moves under the poles and wanders thinly in the heights or air. It can assume forms of exquisite perfection in a snowflake, or strip the living to a single shining bone cast up by the sea.

Loren Eiseley

The subsurface reservoir of fresh water may be tapped and used freely as long as the local supply is not thereby depleted. Depletion is caused not only by overuse but also, and more often, by destruction of the natural ground covers and vegetation, which would otherwise retain precipitation for filtration to the aquifer.

A glimpse, a view, an unfolding panorama of the aquatic landscape is a scenic superlative. Streams and water bodies are the punctuation marks in reading the landscape. They translate for us the landforms and the story of their geologic formation. They set the mood; they articulate; they intensify. They give the essential meaning. What is a prairie without its sloughs? A meadow without its meandering brook? A mountainside without its cascade? A valley without its river?

Site Amenity

Fortunate is the landowner whose property includes or borders upon an attractive stretch of water or affords even a distant view. In landscape and architectural planning, a chief endeavor will be the devising of relationships that exact the full visual and use possibilities.

Submarine ecosystems.

Aquatic environment.

42   LANDSCAPE ARCHITECTURE

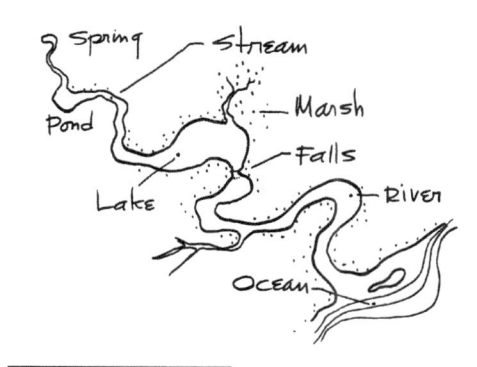

From upland spring to ocean outfall the river basin, river, and all its tributaries are part of a unified system.

Fresh water is a renewable resource, yet the world's supply of clean, fresh water is steadily decreasing. Water demand already exceeds supply in many parts of the world and as the world population continues to rise, so too does the water demand. Awareness of the global importance of preserving water for ecosystem services has only recently emerged as, during the 20th century, more than half the world's wetlands have been lost along with the valuable environmental services for Water Education. The framework for allocating water resources to water users (where such a framework exists) is known as water rights.
www.wikipedia.com

Attribute

Most attributes of nature—the hills, the trees, the starlit sky—are usually taken for granted, but the value of free water is not. Where it exists, as in the form of pond, stream, lake, or ocean, the adjacent landholdings are eagerly sought. They are prized as sites for parks and parkways, for homes, institutions, resort hotels, and other commercial ventures. It could almost be stated as a law of land economics that "the closer a site to open water, the higher its value as real estate."

Natural Systems

In the past, freshwater in all its forms has been used, and too often misused or wasted, as if these were God-given privileges. Except in irrigated lands, where water rights and supply are jealously guarded, there has been little concern for what is happening upstream or downstream unless the flow should be cut off or increased to the point of flooding.

Water flows, inevitably, from source to receiving ocean basin. This continuity of rivulets, streams, and rivers can be readily observed. Not so obvious are the sequential and interacting relationships of the ponds, lakes, and wetlands. These, too, are links in the chain of flow. They are affected not only by the things that happen at their sides but by all that transpires within the upper watersheds or the subsurface aquifers that feed and help sustain them. These same subsurface water-bearing, water-transporting, water-yielding strata provide, also, the groundwater essential to farmland, meadow, and forest and to maintaining the level of the well fields from which our water supplies are drawn.

Water and water areas well used can benefit all who live within their sphere of influence. If, however, they are unwisely used, contaminated, or wasted, dependent life is thereby threatened, sometimes with minor

Tidal wetlands.

Water 43

loss or inconvenience, sometimes with major disaster, as by devastating drought or overwhelming flood.

It is only recently that entire river basins have come to be studied as unified and interrelated systems. Such a rational approach increases rather than limits the possibilities of fuller use and enjoyment and sets a workable framework within which all subareas may then be better planned.

Any consideration of the flow of surface or subsurface water leads one to the obvious conclusion that only comprehensive watershed management makes any sense at all. A parcel-by-parcel approach to the use of river-basin lands can only fracture the contiguous water-related matrix and disrupt the natural systems.

Problems

The problems to be precluded are those of overuse, rapid runoff, erosion, siltation, flooding, induced drought, and contamination. Simply stated, any use that causes one or more of these abuses to any significant degree is improper and should not be condoned. It can be left to biologists and legal experts to define a significant impact. But it can no longer be left to individuals or groups to determine whether or not their activities may cause harm to their neighbors, no matter if the "neighbors" live next door or at the river mouth 1,000 miles downstream.

What happens in the wheat fields of North Dakota can have a telling effect on the working of the lower Missouri and Mississippi rivers. What happens or doesn't happen on the forest slopes of the upper James River may decimate the wildfowl yield of the distant salt marsh or contaminate the oyster beds of Chesapeake Bay. In Florida a cloud of spawning shrimp may die where the Apalachicola River debouches, because of an oil spill on a tributary two states away.

In most nonarid parts of our land it is assumed that the supply of freshwater is limitless. It is not. It has recently been common for reservoirs and wells to reach such low levels that whole regions are alerted and rationed. Along much of our coastline, the aquifers that flow underground to the oceans have been so lowered by drawdown that saltwater intrusion for many miles inland has been a vexing problem.

The normal solution to such shortages has been to extend aqueducts, no matter how far, to tap additional sources. Serious thought has even been given to the massive melting of the arctic icecap as a source of supply. This, even as we are beginning to realize the disastrous effects of global warming. Today the supply of freshwater is not equal to our use (or misuse) and demands. This has become a major land planning consideration.

Widespread irrigation and its exhaustion of the freshwater reserves is believed to have caused the demise of the ancient Mayan culture. In the United States in contemporary times it is not far from posing an impending threat to our style of life as we have known it.

Every activity which impacts a resource, such as the Chesapeake Bay, imposes a cost and that cost must be paid by someone. For years, we cheerfully operated under the assumption that where the environment and natural resources were concerned we could operate outside the laws of nature and economics. Cities disposed of their sewage for "free" by simply directing their outfalls to the nearest river. Factories poured wastes into the bay and its tributaries at little or no cost—to their owners. Unfortunately, even though the cost of such activities did not show up on any ledger book, they were being paid for, with heavy interest, by—the downstream municipality forced to find another water supply, the waterman facing condemned oyster grounds, the seafood packer forced to look further and further afield for products to market—all of them picked up the tab for this "free" activity.
W. Tayloe Murphy

44   LANDSCAPE ARCHITECTURE

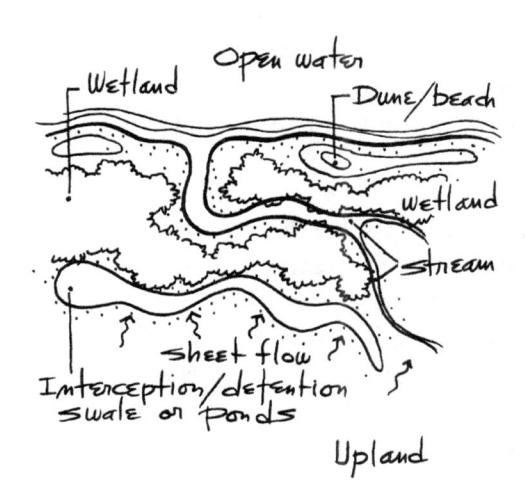

Ten Axioms of Water Resource Management
Within each rationally defined hydrographic region:
- Protect the watersheds, wetlands, and the banks and shores of all streams and water bodies.
- Minimize pollution in any and all forms and initiate a program of decontamination.
- Gear land use allocation and development capacities to the available water supply, rather than vice versa.
- Return to the underlying aquifer water of quantity and quality equal to that withdrawn.
- Limit use to such quantities as will sustain the local fresh-water reserves.
- Conduct surface runoff by natural drainageways insofar as feasible rather than by constructed storm sewer systems.
- Utilize ecologically designed wetlands for wastewater treatment, detoxification, and groundwater recharge.
- Promote dual systems of water supply and distribution, with differentiated rates for potable water and that used for irrigation or industrial purposes.
- Reclaim, restore, and regenerate abused land and water areas to their natural healthful condition.
- Work to advance the technology of water supply, use, processing, recycling, and recharge.

The irrigation of thousands upon thousands of acres of otherwise parched semidesert, converting it into lucrative farmland, was a good thing as long as the water was abundant. Overuse, however, has dried the beds of such rivers as the Colorado and lowered the levels of water tables nationwide. Recently, newly assembled macrofarms with rolling irrigation machines gush fountains of potable water skyward, while in nearby homes, faucet flows have been reduced to a trickle.

Beyond and exceeding the drain of agricultural irrigation, the sprinkling of untold thousands of lawn areas has caused a major depletion of our nation's water supply. It is said that the vast nationwide acreage of lawn under irrigation exceeds that of all cropland in New England. These are but examples of our prodigious waste. We think nothing of using 30 gallons in the taking of a shower, while in many countries the daily water consumption of an entire family is carried home from the stream or well each morning in a jar on the daughter's head. It is time for planners to adopt a new approach to water conservation, use, abuse, reuse, and replenishment.

Clearly, the amount of water drawn from streams, water bodies, and well fields must be reduced and brought into balance with sources of replacement. The area of irrigated agricultural land must be reduced—phased out instead of expanded as presently. It is to be permitted only where freshwater is abundant and can be used without depletion of local and regional reserves. This must be a factor also in the allocation of development sites of all types.

Priority attention is to be given to reducing the vast areas of mowed and irrigated residential lawns. The American homeowner's dream seems to be that of widely spaced single-family homes fronted or surrounded by as much closely shorn and well-watered green lawn as possible. With both land and water now at a premium, we must look to smaller lots, attached homes, and multifamily apartment living with lawn areas confined to walk borders, game courts, and other specialized areas.

With wise land use planning and water resource management, we can have in the United States an adequate supply of freshwater for centuries to come.

Possibilities

If there may be problems, there are possibilities also. These include the preservation of those areas of wilderness or wild river yet unspoiled. They include the conservation and compatible uses of those water-related areas which are rich in soils, cover, or scenic quality and which in their natural or existing state are important contributors to our ecological well-being. The possibilities include the restoration of depleted farmlands and dilapidated urban wastelands to productive use by regrading, soil stabilization, and replanting of eroded slopes and slashings. Well-planned agricultural districts, recreation lands, towns, and cities could

Ecologically managed wetlands are rapidly becoming an important alternative to conventional wastewater treatment systems.

Open lake and reservoir shoreline is becoming limited.

Avoid the water-edge ring of roads and buildings that seal off water bodies and limit their use.

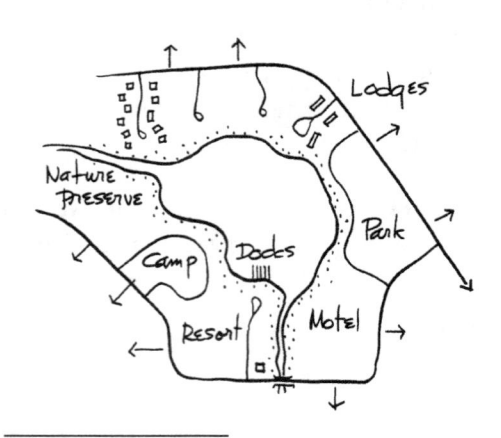

By expanding the traffic-free lake environs to include park, wildlife preserve, and public areas as well as private cottages and resorts, the use and enjoyment of the lake (and surrounding real estate values) are enhanced.

then be clustered within a green-blue surrounding of field, forest, and clean water, linked with parklike transportation ways. Far more than many may realize, we are already well on our way to such a concept, and ethic, of land and water management.

Proficient land and site planning will help solve the water-related problems and ensure that the possibilities are fully realized. The level of performance should be continually improved in the light of increasing public support and advancing technology. It is quite possible that within the span of our lifetimes wide reaches of our land and waterways may be restored to the fairer form that our naturalist friends Thoreau, Muir, and Aldo Leopold once found so exhilarating.

Management

In considering the site development of any landscape area, a first concern is the protection of the surface and subsurface waters both as to quality and as to quantity. *Quality* is maintained by precluding contamination in any form, as by the flow or seepage of pollutants, by groundwater runoff charged with chemicals or nutrients, by siltation, or by the introduction of solid wastes. The assurance of acceptable water *quantity* is largely a matter of retaining surface runoff in swales, ponds, or wetlands to prevent the flooding of streams or water bodies, to sustain the level of the underlying water table, and to replenish the deep-flowing aquifers.

Utilize

Since propinquity to water is so highly desirable, since there is only so much water area and frontage to go around, and since the protection of our water and edges has become so critical in our environmental planning, it would seem reasonable that all water-oriented land areas should be planned in such a way as to reap the maximum benefits of the water feature while protecting its integrity. This goal often resolves itself into the simple device of expanding the actual and visual limits of water-related land to the reasonable maximum. This is not as difficult as it might seem.

In practice, the rim of frontage is extended landward from the water edge in such a manner as to define an ample protective sheath. This variform vegetated band, at best following the lines of drainage flow and responding to the subtle persuasions of the topography, will provide frontage for compatible development and serve as access to the water. The possible variations are limitless, but the principle remains always the same. Each variable diagram must stand the test of these three underlying conditions:

1. All related uses are to be compatible with the water resource and landscape.
2. The intensity of the introduced uses must not exceed the carrying capacity or biologic tolerance of the land and water areas.

46 LANDSCAPE ARCHITECTURE

As a breakthrough in the treatment of wastewater and toxic effluents it has been discovered that ecologically engineered wetlands can be devised to extract and retain the contaminants while storing the clarified water and providing habitat.

3. The continuity of the natural and built systems is to be ensured. If these three principles are adhered to, it can be seen that all land-water areas, from homesite to region, can be planned and developed in such a way that both the scenic quality and the ecologic functions are maintained.

Open water is fast disappearing from the American scene. Expanding agricultural lands and development continue to follow the drainage ditches and tile fields across prairie wetlands and everglades. The urgent compulsion to dredge and fill, while slowed by recent conservation legislation, continues to reclaim the marsh, the cedar bog, and the mangrove strands. Rivers, lakes, and oceanfront are being hidden from public view and shielded from public access by a rising wall of apartments and office towers.

Is it not too late.

It is not too late!

Protect

Where water features exist, protect them. Work to preserve not only the open water but the supporting watershed covers, the natural holding ponds, the swampland, the floodplain, the feeding streams, and the green sheath along their banks. To be protected as well are the coastal wetlands, the landward dunes, and the outward reefs or sandbars.

In the planning of every water-related project site there is an opportunity to demonstrate sound management principles. Each well-designed example not only serves the interest of the client but also stands as a lesson to others.

Rediscover

Many water features of great potential landscape value have been bypassed in the process of building or roadway construction. They remain "out back" or "yonder," often in their natural state, more often as silted or polluted drainage sumps or dump sites. They are waiting to be reclaimed by the community as parkland or open space preserves. Preserved or modified, they may be rediscovered and featured in new public or private landscape development.

Restore

Again, a spring, a pond, or a section of stream may have been enclosed in a culvert or buried in fill. Or it may have been used as a dumping ground and covered with brush and trash. Sometimes, to add to the disgrace, such water features have been shamefully polluted with oils and chemicals and are coated with scum. In most urban and suburban

Xeriscape landscape construction, planting, and gardening is that requiring a minimum of irrigation.

Constructed wetlands.

Only in America with its abundance of buildable land and fresh water has it been the fashion to surround single-family homes and apartments with irrigated lawn. With land and water supplies in short supply it will no longer be affordable or acceptable.

Lawns cover over fifty thousand square miles of the surface of the United States—an area roughly equal to Pennsylvania, and larger than that occupied by any agricultural crop.
Wade Graham

precincts and often in the open countryside, there are to be found such unrecognized landscape treasures waiting to be reclaimed.

Conserve

The alarming drawdown and depletion of our freshwater reserves underscores the need for new attitudes toward water use and resource management. Even in times of moderate drought, many city reservoirs are emptied. While in most parts of the world water is considered a precious commodity and used sparingly, in the United States it is squandered as though the supply were unlimited. It is not.

To conserve our diminishing supply in the face of ever-increasing demands, several courses of action are proposed:

> Limit consumption.
> Regulate household use by sharply escalating the rates on a sliding scale for use above a basic norm.
> Preclude use of well water for irrigation.

Recycle wastewater. In urban areas this suggests a dual system of water supply—one for drinking, cooking, and bathing, the other for all other purposes. Treat and sanitize wastewater (at a much lower unit cost) to be used exclusively for irrigation, air-conditioning, street washing, and industrial processing.

Replenish

In undisturbed nature, the subsurface water reserves are sustained automatically—by the retention and soil filtration of precipitation. When trees,

48 LANDSCAPE ARCHITECTURE

grasses, and other vegetative covers are removed—and especially when replaced by paving or construction—the water tables are thereby lowered.

Three feasible remedies are suggested:

- Protect and replant the upland watersheds.
- Restore the natural drainageways (to the 50-year flood stage) to public ownership or restricted private use, and sheathe them in vegetation.
- Require of new development that the storm-water runoff be retained in catchment basins, swales, or ponds, for percolation and aquifer recharge.

Preplan

Sometimes in the necessary process of mining or in the excavation of open extraction pits, there exists the need to create new water areas. From the air in some regions these can be seen to dot the landscape, usually in the form of dull rectilinear dragline creations. Each may now be recognized as a lost opportunity. With advanced planning and sometimes little additional cost, these pits and the bordering property area could have been, and yet can be, shaped into new and attractive waterscapes, with free-form lakes, grassy slopes, and tree-covered mounds. This reasonable preplanning approach, as a condition of obtaining exca-

Use of native vegetation conserves water.

vation permits and combined with soil conservation and afforestation, provides the opportunity to preclude new scars on the countryside and, instead, to create new landscapes from the old. With enterprise, many existing extraction pits could be acquired, reshaped, and transformed into highly attractive and valuable real estate.

Water-Related Site Design

In the development of land-water holdings, special care is required in the delineation of use areas, in the location of paths of vehicular and pedestrian movement, and in site and building design.

Natural Streams and Water Bodies

Where these exist, they represent the resolution of many dynamic forces at work—precipitation, surface runoff, sedimentation, clarification, currents, wave action, and so forth. It can be seen that to alter a natural stream, pond, or lake will set in motion a whole chain of actions and interactions that must then be restored to equilibrium. It is soon learned, therefore, that a first consideration in the site planning of water-related areas is to leave the natural conditions undisturbed and build up to and around them.

In their existing state, the banks of streams and rivers are lined by a fringe of grasses, shrubs, and trees that stabilize soils and check the sheet inflow of surface storm water drainage. The bank faces are held in place by stones, logs, roots, and trailing plants that resist currents and erosion.

Lakeshores and beaches, armored with wave-resistant rock or protected by their sloped edges of sand or gravel, are ideally shaped to withstand the force and wash of wind-driven waves. Even the quiet pond or lagoon is edged with reeds or lily pads, which serve a similar purpose.

Where a water feature such as a spring, pond, lake, or tidal marsh occurs in nature, it is usually a distillate of the surrounding landscape and a rich contributor to its ecologic workings and the scene. Such superlatives are to be in all ways protected. This is not to preclude their use and enjoyment, for the purpose of sensitive planning is to ensure protection while facilitating the highest and best use of the landscape feature.

Canals and Impoundments

Parts of the American landscape are laced and interlaced with a network of canals. Some have been in operation since colonial times. Many have been long abandoned. When "rediscovered" and reactivated in rural or urban settings, these waterways, with hiking or biking trails alongside, become treasured community features. All are to be preserved and protected.

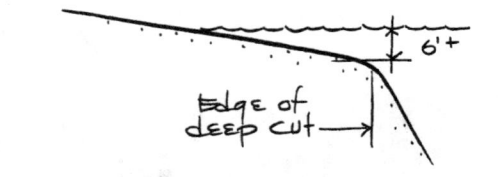

For safety, a beach should slope to a depth exceeding a swimmer's height (6 feet plus) before reaching a deep-cut line.

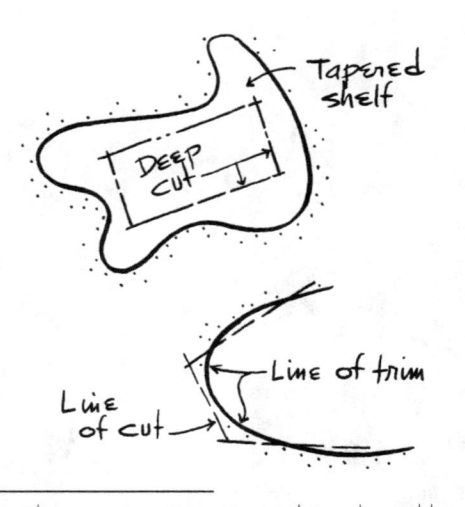

Rectilinear excavation pits can be reshaped by supplementary grading to create free-form lakes.

Ocean beaches are built and rebuilt by the forces of currents, storms, and tides. They are essentially temporary, since the forces that built them can also alter them beyond recognition—sometimes during a single great storm. Even the most costly stabilization projects have proven ineffective against. . . . beach evolution.

Albert R. Veri et al.

Often, and particularly in large parks and nature preserves, the migratory aspect of beaches and shores is acknowledged, and they are allowed full freedom to assume and constantly adjust their natural conformation. This eminently sound approach deserves far wider application.

The water in many city reservoirs is hidden from public view. In its storage and processing it could be used to refresh and beautify urban surroundings.

Ribbon path at river's edge.

At a miniscale, a trickling rivulet can be impeded by a few well-placed stones to increase its size and depth. By the construction of a proper dam, larger and deeper pools can be created for fishing, swimming, or boating or as landscape features.

At a greater scale, huge reservoirs or lakes may be impounded for water storage, flood control, or the provision of hydroelectric energy. Provided the drawdowns are not too severe or frequent, such large impoundments offer the opportunity for many forms of water-related recreation and often become the focal attraction for extensive regional development. To ensure their maximum contribution and benefits, all major reservoirs and the contiguous lands around them should be preplanned before construction permits are issued, with dedication provided for necessary rights-of-way and for appropriate public and private uses.

From the smallest dam to the largest, the location must be well selected to ensure its stability, for a failure and surging washout can bring serious problems downstream. Water levels are to be studied in relation to topographical forms so that the edges of the pond or lake may create a pleasing shape well suited to adjacent paths of movement, use areas, and structures.

Where the feeding streams are silt-laden or subject to periodic flooding, upstream settling basins with weirs and a gated bypass channel will be required.

Paths, Bridges, and Decks

People are attracted to water. It is a natural tendency to wish to walk or ride along the edge of a stream or lake, to rest beside it enjoying the sights and sounds, or, in the case of streams, to cross to the other side.

These desires are to be accommodated in site planning. Routes of movement will be aligned to provide a variety of views and will in effect combine to afford a visual exploration of the lake or waterway. It is fitting that water-edge paths or drives be undulating in their horizontal and vertical curvature and constructed of materials that blend into the natural scene. At points where water-oriented uses are intensified or where the meeting of land and water is to be given more architectural treatment, the shapes and materials of the pathways and use areas will become more structural, too.

Overlooks may be as unprepossessing as a bench in the widened bend of a path. Or they may be decked, terraced, or walled, to bring the user into the most favorable relationship to the water for the purpose intended, be it viewing, relaxing, fishing, diving, or entering a boat.

Bridges, too, are designed with regard for much more than basic function. At their best they provide an exhilarating experience of crossing.

Water 51

Seen from many directions and angles, they are to be given sculptural form. Every bridge is to be designed with utmost simplicity as a clear expression of its materials, structure, and use. Each will derive distinctive character from the locality and the nature of the site.

Water Edges

The meeting of land and water presents a line of special planning significance.

It has been noted that where the uses are mild and where the banks or shores are attractive, they are best left essentially undisturbed. As water-related uses are intensified and the need for space increased, the degree of edge treatment is correspondingly increased until in some instances it may become entirely architectural.

Water's edge in urban environment.

In the shaping of water bodies it is desirable that the outline be curvilinear, rather than angular, to reflect the undulating nature of water.

Often, to provide more efficient use of the bordering land, the pond or lake is first excavated along straight lines, which are often softened by curvature and by rounding intersections.

Since in most methods of excavation, as by dragline or pans, straight, deep cuts are more economical, the central body of a lake is often a rectangle or a polyhedron in shape, with a widened perimeter shelf sloped to the deeper excavation pit and trimmed to more natural form.

From no point along the shore should the expanse of the water surface be seen in its entirety. If possible, the shoreline should be made to dip out of sight at several points to add interest and to set free the observer's imagination. By this design device not only is the water body made more appealing, but its apparent size is increased.

In water-edge detailing these are some of the fundamentals to be kept in mind:

- *Minimize disruption.* Where the banks or shores are stable, the less treatment, the better.
- *Maintain smooth flows.* Avoid the use of elements that obstruct currents or block wave action.
- *Slope and armor the banks, if necessary, to absorb energy where flows are swift or wave impacts are destructive.*
- *Provide boat access to water of desired depth by the use of docks, piers, or floats with self-adjusting ramps.*
- *Avoid the indiscriminate use of jetties and groins or the diverting of strong currents.* The effects are often unpredictable and sometimes calamitous.

52 LANDSCAPE ARCHITECTURE

The qualities of water are infinite in their variety.
    In depth, water may range from deep to no more than a film of surface moisture.
    In motion, from rush to gush, plummet, spurt, spout, spill, spray, or seep.
    In sound, from tumultuous roar to murmur.
Each attribute suggests a particular use and application in landscape design.

- *Design to the worst conditions.* Consider recorded water levels and the height of wind-driven surf.
- *Preclude flooding.* Hold the floor level of habitable structures above the 50-year-flood stage as a minimum.
- *Promote safety by the use of handrails, nonslip pavement, buoys, markers, and lights.*
- *Use weather- and water-resistant materials, fastenings, and equipment.* Corrosion and deterioration are constant problems along the waterfront.
- *Prevent the flow of polluted surface runoff into receiving waters.* Such runoff should be intercepted and treated, or filtered by the use of detention swales.

Pools, Fountains, and Cascades

It is hard to imagine any planned landscape area—patio, garden, or public square—that would not benefit by the introduction of water in natural or architectural form. Its sound, motion, and cooling effects give it universal appeal.

Inside the cascade.

Water

Fountains add interest and refreshment.

54   LANDSCAPE ARCHITECTURE

Water has become symbolic. It connotes and promotes refreshment and stimulates verdant growth. Its presence can convert seeming desert into seeming oasis.

Where water is plentiful and its use is to be featured, as in urban courts, malls, or plazas, its treatment is often carried to an exhilarating scale and high degree of refinement. Many a city is remembered for the delight of its exuberant fountains and rushing cascades.

In even the smallest garden also, water has its essential place. Wherever plants are used, for example, irrigation is needed and is to be considered in the design. A trickling spout or well-placed spray can moisten and cool a patch of gravel mulch, a bed of ivy, or a square of sunlit paving. The simplest container of water placed out for the birds adds interest and refreshment, as does a quiet pool, a dripping ledge, or a splashing fountain. Such water features, easy to devise and construct, can yield long hours of watching and listening pleasure.

Water's symbolic journey from mountain to sea.

Water 55

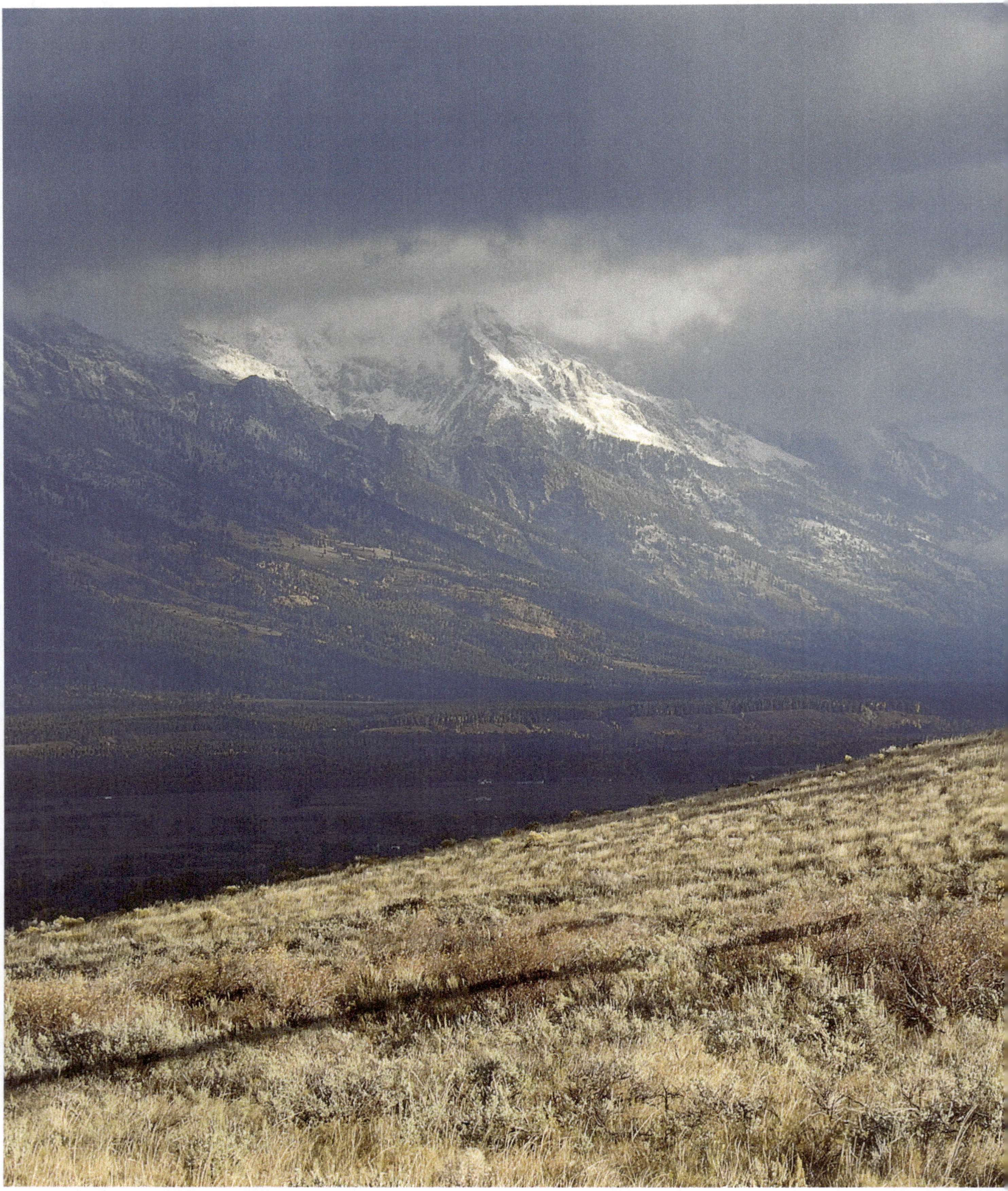

4 LAND

How often in their ceaseless wanderings over the face of the earth must men have paused as they topped the ridge or gained the pass to study the lay of the land?

Each topographic form had its message. Mountains were forbidding; craggy ravines were perilous; broad valleys, beckoning. Prairies, plains, and savannas stretched to the far horizons to be laboriously crossed on foot, on horseback, by travois, or by lumbering wagon trains.

Wherever their urgings or headings led them, our forebears avoided the unfavorable situation and sought those conditions within the landscape best suited to their needs. Sometimes these were as immediate as water, food, or forage, sometimes as permanent as fortification or homestead. With the same atavistic instinct, each of us by habit still constantly surveys the landscape about us to avoid areas of hazard or discomfort, to trace the most favorable path, and to attain the most suitable situation. This feel for the land is inborn; it is in our bones and blood.

Human Impact

For many thousands of years, our predecessors have gathered the bounty of the grasslands, waterways, and forests without causing significant damage. As they fished, set their snares, or hunted game, they left the land and waters as they found them. Their canoes glided silently through

Every day some 12 square miles of American farmland is usurped by development.

In the past decade we have lost farmlands equivalent to the combined areas of Vermont, New Hampshire, Massachusetts, Rhode Island, Connecticut, New Jersey and Delaware.
Peter J. Ognibene

the unspoiled wilderness, their horses were tethered, and their herds grazed without lasting disruption of the natural cover. Their early encampments left no lasting scars and were soon overgrown. Even the first settlements and clearings fitted to the slopes and water edges were of little ecologic consequence.

As populations increased, however, the effects of people's working have become more and more evident. Blazed trails have become roadways. Scattered farms have been consolidated to push back the marsh and woodland, sometimes to extinction. The early villages on the banks of a stream have swallowed the stream and usurped the banks of the nearby river. Village and town limits have been extended relentlessly outward to be interconnected with additional roads and with railways and, often canals. Within a few bustling centuries, our native American landscape has been transformed into an expanse of farmsteads, subdivisions, burgeoning cities, sprawling industrial complexes, and far-flung transportation systems. Often the only vestiges of wilderness left are those isolated fringes too difficult of access, too deep in the ooze, too dry, or too close to the rock for economic development.

Where the uses of land have been well suited to the sites, the resulting farms, roadways, and communities may be in all ways agreeable. We have flown over such settlements that seem nestled into the countryside.

Sonoran Preserve.

We have traveled inviting roads that weave pleasantly through the landscape, introducing us to woodland, meadow, streams, well-ordered fields, orchards, and abundant valleys. We have delighted in towns that seem to have blossomed spontaneously upon the crown of a hill or in cities terraced gracefully down to the river edge or harbor.

Well-suited developments intelligently planned can produce an integration of designed forms and modified landscape superior to the original. The best of the indigenous features can be preserved and incorporated. Or they may be conserved for limited uses and to maintain the native setting. The natural attractions may thus be enjoyed and appreciated daily to enrich the living experience. Such installations convey a sense of stability and fitness. They "sing" in the landscape, and they sing in harmony.

Adapt to the landforms:
    To diminish landscape disruption
    To reduce the costs of earthwork
    To prevent the wasting of topsoil
    To preclude the need for erosion control and replanting
    To make use of existing drainageways
    To blend into the natural scene

Existing topographical profile—suggesting a rich variety of structural forms conceived in harmony with the natural landscape

"Ideal" profile of the typical American builder

The code of the American subdivider and homebuilder (as it would seem to the casual observer)
    Axiom 1. Clear the land.
    Axiom 2. Strip the topsoil (or bury it and haul in new if this saves one operation).
    Axiom 3. Provide a "workable" land profile (that is, as flat as possible).
    Axiom 4. Conduct all water to storm sewers (or else to the edge of the lot).
    Axiom 5. Build a good wide road—inexpensive but wide.
    Axiom 6. Set the house well back for a big front yard.
    Axiom 7. Keep the fronts even (this looks neat).
    Axiom 8. Hold to a minimum side yard.
    Axiom 9. Throw on some lawn seed.

By means of site reconnaissance and soil surveys the most productive land can be designated for lawns, gardens, or crop production or be preserved in its natural state. Areas of thin soil, poor or excessive drainage, or underlying rock are prime candidates for projected development. Homes, roadways, and cities belong on areas of low productivity.

The American suburbanite dream (as seemingly interpreted by the suburban builder and by our present building restrictions)
    A revised topography by courtesy of the bulldozer and carryall. The boulders are buried, the natural cover stripped, the brook "contained" in storm sewer or culvert. The topsoil is redistributed as a 4-inch skin over sand, clay, or rock.
    There sprouts a new artificial fauna of exotic nursery stock.
    This is our constructed paradise.

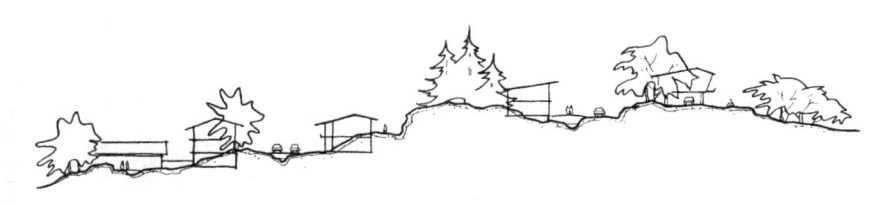

The natural ground forms are best accepted as givens. They are the resolution of myriad forces at work over a long period of time. To adapt to them is to harmonize with the forces and conditions by which they have evolved.

A better way is building with nature and in compression, which provides the human scale and charm we find so appealing in the older cultures, in which economy of materials and space dictated a close relationship of structure and landscape form.

Where, however, the uses imposed are unsuited, where they are awkward in plan or clumsy in execution, the result is distressing to both the eye and the intellect. Moreover, the disruptive consequences may be costly, even catastrophic. For the immutable forces of nature have a way of rejecting those built intrusions which violate the land.

Land 59

Each state, country, or municipality has as one of it's chief responsibilities a plan for the conservation and best use of the lands within its jurisdiction.

As long as I have the land . . . then I'm a rich man. Everything I need—my food, clothes, house, heat—it's all out there.
Alaskan Inuit, as quoted by John McPhee

If humankind is to thrive—yea, even survive—it is incumbent upon us to study and apply those principles by which we can bring our species and nature into symbiotic balance. The problems of encroaching civilization, the imperiled land, and the increasing need for its care have together become our heritage.

Land as a Resource

Land and the waters that lap its edges, flow across its surface, seep into its upper soil strata, and move within its deep aquifers are our ultimate resources. Mismanaged, they may be lost to us forever, and our national wealth and well-being proportionately diminished.

Before dividing our remaining land reserves into fragmented ownership parcels, it would be good to look at them in their wholeness to see what functions they now perform as farmland, forest, and open space. New patterns for their preservation, conservation, or thoughtfully considered development can then be devised. It is a matter of priorities, of seeing that each broad area of land is devoted to its most reasonable uses and that all land areas together are formed into logical systems.

Perhaps the most crucial function of our un-built-upon land areas is that of topsoil reservoir. This vital substance is the basis of all agricultural productivity. It occurs, where it still exists, as a thin layer of weathered rock intermixed with organic matter in depths ranging from a few inches to a few feet. This rich skim overlaying the subsoils and naked rock may be thousands of years in the making. Once lost, it is gone forever. We in the United States have dissipated in the span of five centuries well over one-third of our vital topsoil endowment. It has been scooped,

Severe soil erosion.

hauled, or washed and blown away to the rivers and thence transported to the sea. This is a loss no nation can afford. The disastrous consequences of misuse and waste of topsoil are to be observed in most of the arid regions of the world.

Productivity

All forms of life derive from the land and its cover of soil. There, in the chlorophyll of rooted plants, carbon dioxide and moisture are transformed by the energy of the sun into the basic sugars and starches of our food chain. This is a miracle of chemistry occurring only when the conditions are right. The resulting types of vegetation and animal life vary endlessly from patch to patch and from region to region. It is only recently that we have come to understand how closely all are interrelated.

When any area of land is disturbed, the delicate balances are shifted and the repercussions of change may be felt many miles away. This is not to imply that all natural or cultivated food-yielding land should be left unmodified. Often, with husbandry, its nutrient yield may be increased, and for many types of terrain there may be more important uses. It is, rather, proposed that in land planning and utilization the most productive areas are to be defined and protected. This is fully as true in the layout of a residential property as in the comprehensive planning of a state.

Habitat

The land is our terrestrial home not only for the human species but for all living organisms, which together constitute the biomass of the planet Earth.

Ecology has taught us that all organisms and creatures are interacting and interdependent; that all are contributors and have their necessary functions in the biologic scheme of things; that the mountains, forests, marshes, and rivers together form a community without definable limits; and that the integrity of the natural systems must somehow be preserved.

It is only within very recent times that members of the human race have seen fit to claim sole rights in land. This newly acquired compulsion to own land and take a permanent fix has become epidemic. Today, whole regions of the earthscape have been marked off by boundary posts and line fences, only to be further divided and subdivided, again and yet again.

Most such property ownership demarcations have been made on a wholly haphazard, geometric basis, without regard for topographic conformation.

Reason would tell us that if land must be parceled and subdivided (our entire culture seems now to be operating on this premise), new lines of

---

Conservation is a way of life which deals wisely with all natural resources, recognizing them to be . . . irreplaceable and essential to the welfare of mankind.
Warner S. Goshorn

An analogy: that in its land and resource planning each state be considered as a developing farmstead. An astute farmer would study the land until he or she came to understand it—its nature, constraints, and possibilities. The farmer would then so lay out (and continually adjust) the working components—living quarters, barn, pens, fields, orchard, and lines of connection—as to bring them into best relationship to each other an to the land-water holding. The farmer would plan the whole and each new element in such a way as to conserve and take full advantage of the land's best features: the ground forms, the woodlot, the spring, the drainageways, the soil, and the natural covers.
   Not only is such a farm (state) more productive,
   Not only is it more efficient,
   Not only is it more agreeable as a place to live and work,
   It is also the best possible investment for the farmer, the farmer's spouse, and their heirs.

A natural system is a co-related assemblage of topographic, climatic, or ecologic elements interacting in accordance with natural law.
   Watersheds, wetlands, coral reefs, meadows, and anthills are examples.

Land

All of North America was occupied, after a fashion, by Indians, whose home it was and who obtained their living from the land.

The Indian concept of landownership was completely different from that of the whites. The Indian regarded land as something to be used and enjoyed, even to be defended against trespassers, but not to be owned exclusively by one person, nor never to be bought and sold in the commercial sense.

When the white man sought to buy land from Indians, the latter might agree and accept a purchase price or gift, yet not understand what the white man meant. It was not simply that the white men drove sharp bargains or the Indians reneged on bargains accepted, though there was some of each; more importantly, there was never a genuine meeting of minds. . . .
Marion Clawson

The United States owned a great deal of land, public and private capital was in short supply, and the need for public improvement was great; why not make public land available to finance the construction of needed public improvements? This was a sound basic idea, which accomplished a great deal of good. . . .
Marion Clawson

The topsoil mantle is teeming with life. Scoop up a handful almost anywhere, and you are holding a cosmos of microscopic organisms and cells of regeneration.

ownership should be brought into consonance with the boundaries of functioning land and water systems.

Not only should our remaining undisturbed land be so apportioned as to express and accommodate the natural form order, but many of the presently fragmented landholdings should be reassembled and more logically defined. City and county limits are examples. Over the ensuing years, through the emerging techniques of surveying, land use planning, zoning, redevelopment, reclamation, and resource management, the mutilated landscape may be restored to fairer form and to a healthful wholeness.

Land Grants

In the United States, rights in land have flowed to individuals, corporations, and agencies mainly from government—from colonial powers in earlier times and later by acts of Congress.

Through the century following the Louisiana Purchase in 1803, the United States disposed of almost 1 billion acres of land held in public ownership. At first, the more important dispositions were those made to the states in support of public schools and the land-grant colleges. Then followed allotments for wagon roads, canals, and the building of railroads. In the last-named case the entrepreneurs were usually given alternate sections within a broad swath contiguous to the railroad right-of-way. The Homestead Act of 1862 extended rights in land to settlers. Military bounties, Indian rights, and grants to encourage such activities as timber culture, mining, irrigation, and reclamation were to swell the dispositions to date to almost half of the total land area of 50 states.

In Alaska today, the land-grant saga continues. From the time of the Alaska Purchase in 1867 until the Alaska Statehood Act of 1958, the federal government owned almost the whole of the territory.

It can be seen that from our country's beginnings to the present time the dynamics of land transfer, ownership, and use have had profound political, social, and economic implications. The story of land exploration, land hunger, land transactions, regulation, and use (and too often abuse) is the story of America. Land is our ultimate resource. We must plan for its conservation, regulation, and development on a more scientific basis. We must learn to use it more wisely.

Land Rights

Once in private ownership, land can be readily used or sold as a valued commodity. A factor of use or sale is, of course, the ability to define and

Almost imperceptibly the relationship of society to the land has changed, to a point at which the public good now largely transcends the rights of the individual.

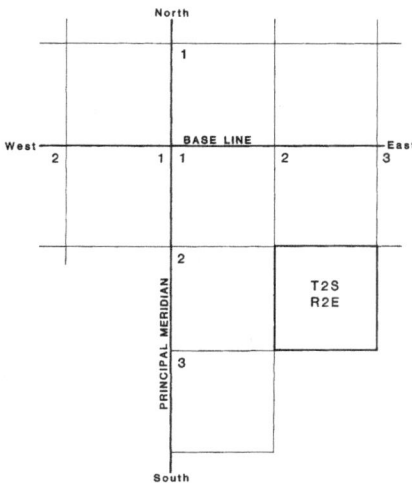

Within each region of the U.S. an east-west base line and north-south principal meridian have been established, and to these all subsequent land subdivision and title descriptions are related. Townships are numbered north and south of the base line, and ranges east and west of the principal meridian.

The principal units of land within counties are townships, six miles on a side, comprised of 36 sections, each approximately 1 mile square.

TOWNSHIP 2 SOUTH
RANGE 2 EAST

Sections are further subdivided as shown. Lots or parcels are described by bearings and distances or "metes and bounds" from stated reference points within a given area of the survey grid.

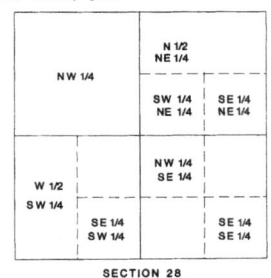

SECTION 28
(640 acres)

Diagrammatic system of land surveying.

prove rights of ownership by clear title to the property. Such proof presupposes a survey and the establishment on the ground of stakes, monuments, or other markings by which the property boundaries can be identified. Further, there must be a means by which a lot or parcel may be so described as to differentiate it from and relate it to all other landholdings. Finally, there is need for a systematic and orderly means of recording land descriptions and titles.

In the United States, by comparison, we are fortunate in our system. In many Latin American countries, for instance, few of these conditions pertain. There, accurate surveys seldom exist; rights in land are often clouded and in dispute, and the systematic recording of titles is not yet a fact of life. Much land has been preempted by squatters, now backed by traditional sentiment in favor of the pioneer and against those who own or believe they own superseding rights to the land. Such vague and chaotic conditions of property ownership lead to a lack of commitment, investment, and improvement by those not certain of established rights and give force to a growing movement toward massive land reform.

Surveying

The original land survey has left an indelible mark upon those parts of the United States to which it was applied. There was much to commend the system. As Marion Clawson has noted, we are a rectilinear country, divided into squares and oblongs like a haphazard checkerboard, with the lines running directly north-south and east-west.

Roads typically follow the surveyed section lines even though this means going up and down hills instead of around them. Farmers tend to lay out their fields parallel to the boundaries of their land even though this may mean cultivating up and down the slope rather than along the contours.

Land definition by transit and rod.

Land 63

Targets over random field stakes can be plotted by coordinates from an aerial photo grid.

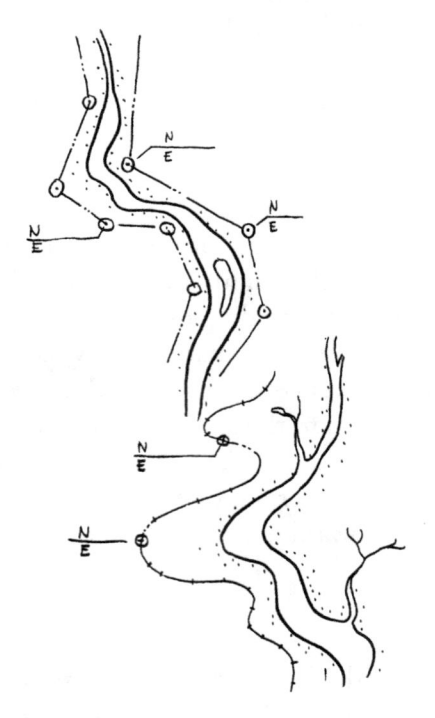

With photogrammetry even freely meandering lines can be plotted for property description and recording—with a trace of the line and coordinates on an aerial map for the record.

Only when all or part of the boundary line needs be staked or monumented is a field crew needed.

Meandering property lines are easily established.

We abuse land because we regard it as a commodity belonging to us. When we see land as a community to which we belong, we may begin to use it with love and respect....

That land is a community is the basic concept of ecology, but that land is to be loved and respected is an extension of ethics.
Aldo Leopold

The carrying capacity of land-water area is the population or level of activity that can be sustained for a given length of time without depletion of the resources or breakdown of the biological (natural) systems.

Much erosion has been caused or accelerated in this way. Some land experts, observing these types of bad land use, have been highly critical of the rectilinear land survey and argue for modification.

Perhaps the time has now come. The crude magnetic surveying instruments and need for range lines cleared through forest and swamps made the mechanical grid quite reasonable in its time. But now, with the advent of Geographic Information Systems (GIS), photogrammetry, laser sighting, computer techniques, coordinates, and electronic traverse computation, it is time for a whole fresh look at the process of land description and measurement. A gradual land resurvey to follow and respond to natural topographical conformation is clearly in order. Governmental regulation could now require that future land surveys and dispositions be based, as appropriate, on more logical parcel boundaries to meet sound land use criteria.

Use

We Americans, with a seemingly inexhaustible land reserve, have been extremely wasteful. We have claimed, cleared, and too often exploited, then moved on, to do it all over again. It is only now, with open land at a premium, that we have begun to understand the need for husbandry.

There are many examples of land well used—among them, New England villages fitted to the topography, the Amish farmsteads of Pennsylvania, Florida citrus groves, Wisconsin dairy farms, wheat and corn fields of the prairies, ranch lands of the plains, and bean fields, vineyards, and orchards along the west coast—and across the breadth of the land, well-tended homesites and gardens.

In the good examples, we may perceive these simple precepts of sound land management:

> Learn to read the landscape,
>   to comprehend the grandeur of its geologic framework,
>   to understand the vital workings and interdependence of the
>   land and water systems,
>   to discern in each form and feature the unique expression of
>   nature's creative process.
> Let the land's nature determine its use. And so address each
>   measure of the landscape as to evoke, through our planning, use,
>   and treatment, its highest qualities and potential.

When land passes from one ownership to another, certain legal rights are transferred with the property. Unless otherwise specified in the deed or governing regulations, these include the right to use, cultivate, mine, perform earthwork, remove the soil or vegetation from the land, or build upon it.

Plan to the land.

Landowners have the responsibility to use their property so as to protect its natural values and cause no harm to neighbors.

Running with the land are also certain responsibilities, many firmly established by our land law tradition. It is unlawful, for instance, to cause damage by directing an increased flow of storm-water runoff onto a neighbor's property. It is not lawful to alter grades significantly along a property line, or to create off-site earth slippage, erosion, or siltation, or to generate undue air, water, noise, or visual pollution. Other more recent restrictions dealing with such matters as wetland protection, beach access, erosion control, and unregulated grading are still to be fully tested in the courts.

Since most sites were acquired in the first place because they were attractive or had other positive qualities, it might well be proposed as a general rule that the less modification, the better. A fundamental principle of landscape design is to "plan to the site," letting the natural contours, conditions, and covers dictate the building and landscape forms.

Where for one reason or another it may be desirable to alter the grades, as to provide required use areas or to dispose of excavated materials, the topsoil on disturbed areas should first be stripped and stockpiled. The revised contours will then be reshaped to accommodate the proposed uses, to express the meld of natural and constructed elements, and to enhance the building-site composition.

Land

Reuse

Land is a finite resource. As usable land becomes scarcer, the need to reuse formerly abused land—or *brownfields,* as they have come to be known as—is clear. Brownfield sites are usually abandoned or underutilized former industrial areas that contain varying degrees of contamination by chemicals and other pollutants. Once these pollutants are removed, the land becomes suitable for other selective uses. These sites are often in close proximity to urban infrastructures, making their location highly desirable. In turn, for many instances, cleanup becomes cost-effective as a result of the increased land value. Examples in the United States include Gas Works Park in Seattle, Washington; Atlanta Station in Atlanta, Georgia; and Pittsburgh Technology Center in Pittsburgh, Pennsylvania.

Recycled brownfield site.

Topography

Topography is defined as the art of showing in detail on a major map the physical features of a place or region.

Land areas and the bottoms of water bodies are seldom level. They slope up or down; they undulate; they sometimes pitch precipitously to great heights or depths, and are often creased with streambeds, ravines, or seismic faults.

Contours can be thought of as edges of plateaus.

Representation by Contours

The shape, or relief, of the ground surface can be indicated by contours. These are lines of equal height above a fixed reference point, or *bench mark,* of known or assumed elevation. For some engineering projects of exceptional scope or precision, the bench mark will be a permanent monument with machined brass cap—its elevation recorded in hundredths of feet above mean sea level. Again, for a project of lesser scope the bench mark may be no more than the top of a rock or a driven pipe assigned an arbitrary elevation of, say, 100.0 feet.

Where the land gradient is mild, the contour interval or height differential may be reduced. Where the land is rugged, as in mountainous country, the interval may be increased to 10 feet, 100 feet, or more depending upon the need.

It can be seen that by contours alone the modulations of the Earth's surface can be graphically portrayed. In architectural or landscape planning a site plan prepared with a contour map as a base gives an invaluable feel for the land.

Land 67

Figure 1 is the plan of a small land area at scale of 1 inch = 100 foot. The dot represents a stone or stake, the top of which has an assumed elevation of 100.0 feet. The **X** is a spot elevation used to mark a high point, a low point, or some other spot of relevance. The curving contours are lines of equal height at 1-foot intervals above or below the level of the bench mark (BM). The closer together the contours (as along section A-A) the steeper the slope compared with B-B (a valley) or C-C (a ridge).

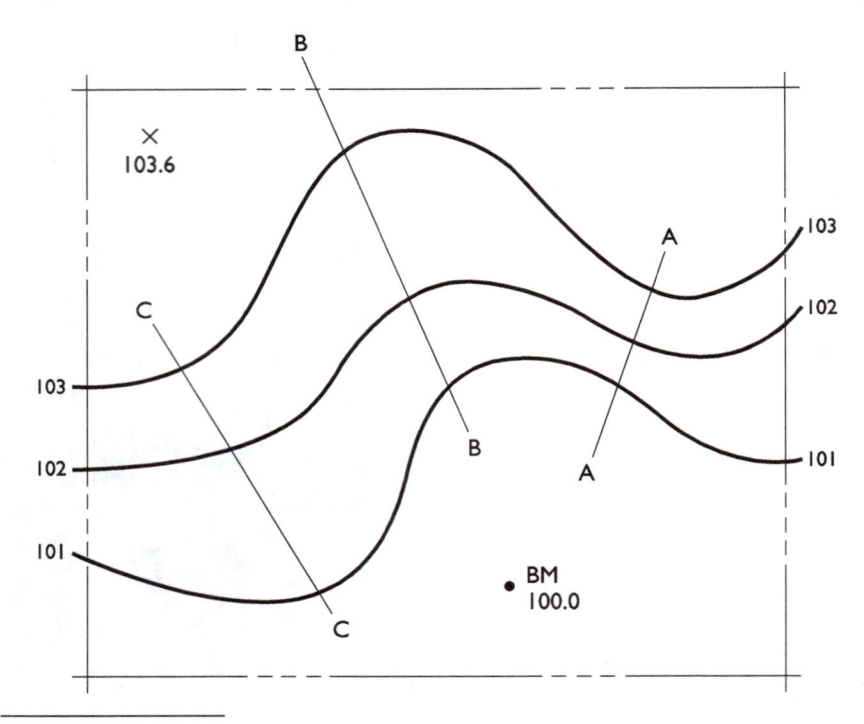

Figure 1.

Amphitheater seating on contour.

68   LANDSCAPE ARCHITECTURE

Illustrative section.

Sections

As a further aid, the contour map provides the opportunity to plot sections wherever an accurate land profile is needed. In Figure 2, for example, if section lines are drawn through any area of the map, as at lines A-A, or B-B, a profile can be plotted and enlarged or reduced to any useful scale.

Although Figure 2 shows a larger land area of more topographic diversity, the principle is the same as in Figure 1. A vertical measurement from the intersection of each contour with the baseline gives a series of points which, when connected, show the land profile at lines A-A and B-B.

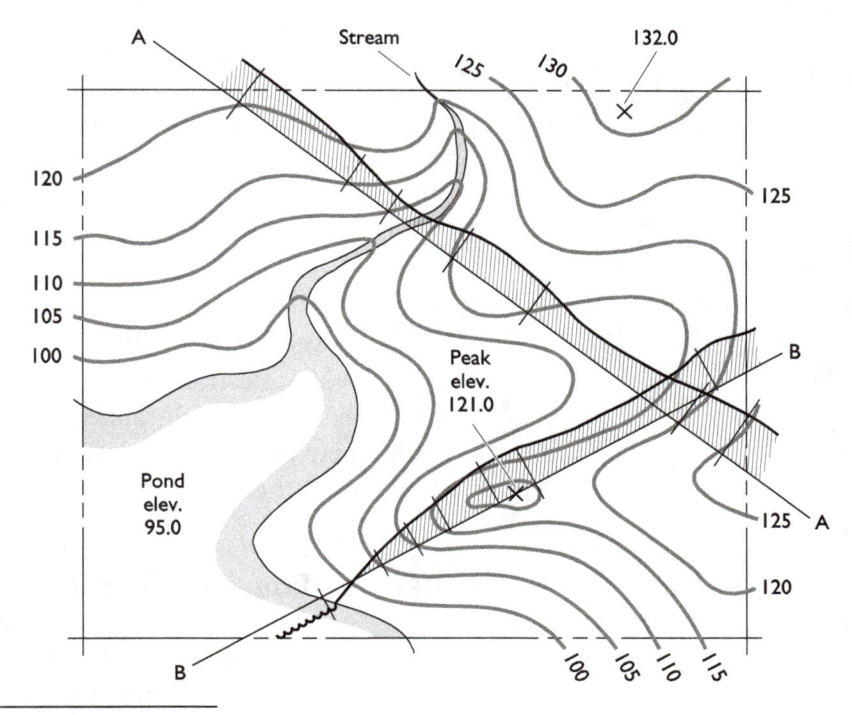

Figure 2.

Land 69

Models

Even more graphic than plans or sections is a model prepared by cutting and superimposing sheets of matboard, plywood, or plastic of the appropriate thickness along the contour lines. By means of such an exhibit the surface conformation or modeling of the entire property can be perceived at a glance. Aerial or perspective views of the model in photographic form are often used for ready reference.

Surveys

It is well to understand that surveying methods and maps are of many types and must be suited to their purpose. As for methods, the *compass and chain* is good enough for plotting logging roads but hardly suited to precision mapping. The *plane table survey* may be adequate for a limited site where precisely accurate property line descriptions and elevations are not needed. The *stadia survey* has long been the standard for accurate topographic mapping, but has recently been superseded by the *laser transit*. For larger-area coverage, a *photogrammetric survey* is usually prescribed. This involves the piecing together of overlapping aerial mosaics and the plotting of surface features by stereoptic projection. Commonly used in military reconnaissance, it yields a high degree of precision.

To utilize land for most purposes, a *topographic survey* is needed. Such a map will show not only the surface conformation by contours and spot elevations, it will also indicate the lines of property ownership, surface and subsurface features, and such other supplemental information as may be specified. Some surveys give no more information than a description in bearings and distances (metes and bounds) of the property perimeter. Often this is all that is required.

If contouring and spot elevations are needed they must be requested. With detailed site planning to be accomplished, the topographic survey specification may be expanded to include the location and description of specific surface and subsurface features. Core borings or test pits may be required and such elements as the adjacent roadway or the nearest off-site utility leads and projected capacities. When a topographic survey is needed, it is well to meet with the surveyor and review the requirements in detail. A specification and work order can then be drafted for execution. For an extensive or complicated development project, the survey specification may be many pages in length. For a typical residential homesite, however, the following sample specification should normally suffice.

Topographic Survey Specification

 Property: The property to be surveyed is marked on the enclosed location map (to be provided to the surveyor by the owner or landscape architect).

 General: Surveyor shall do all work necessary to determine accurately the physical conditions existing on the site.

Cardboard contour model.

Terrace edges simulate contour lines.

70 LANDSCAPE ARCHITECTURE

Datum: Elevations shall be referenced to any convenient and permanent bench mark with an assumed elevation of 100.0 feet. The bench-mark location shall be shown on the map.

Information required:

1. Title of survey, property location, scale, north point, certification, and date.
2. Tract boundary lines, courses, distances, and coordinates. Calculate and show acreage.
3. Building setback lines, easements, and rights-of-way.
4. Names of on-site and abutting parcel owners.
5. Names and locations of existing streets on or abutting the tract. Show right-of-way, type, location, width of surfacing, and centerline of gutters.
6. Position of buildings and other structures, including foundations, piers, bridges, culverts, wells, and cisterns.
7. Location of all site construction, including walls, fences, roads, drives, curbs, gutters, steps, walks, trails, paved areas, and so on, indicating types of materials or surfacing.
8. Locations, types, sizes, and direction of flow of existing storm and sanitary sewers on the tract, giving top and invert elevations of manholes and inlet and invert elevations of other drainage structures; location, ownership, type and size of water and gas mains, manholes, valve boxes, meter boxes, hydrants, and other appurtenances. Locations of utility poles and telephone lines and fire-alarm boxes are to be indicated. For utilities not traversing the site, show, by key plan if necessary, the nearest off-site leads, giving all pertinent information on types, sizes, inverts, and ownership.
9. Location of water bodies, streams, springs, swamps, or boggy areas and drainage ditches or swales.
10. Outline of wooded areas. Within areas so noted, show all trees that have a trunk diameter of 4 inches or greater at waist height, giving approximate trunk diameters and common names of the trees.
11. Road elevation. Elevations shall be taken at 50-foot intervals and at high or low points along centerlines of roads, flow line of gutter on property side, and tops and bottoms of curbs. The pertinent grades abutting street and road intersections shall also be indicated.
12. Ground surface elevations shall be taken and shown on a 50-foot grid system as well as at the top and bottom of all considerable breaks in grade, whether vertical, as in walls, or sloping, as in banks. Show all floor elevations for buildings. Spot elevations shall also be indicated at the finished grade of building corners, building entrance platforms, and all walk intersections. In addition to the elevations required, the map shall show contours at _-foot vertical intervals. All elevations shall be to the nearest tenth of a foot. Permissible tolerance shall be 0.1 foot for spot elevations and one-half of the contour interval for contours.

Supplementary Data

Aside from the basic topographic, or "topo," survey prepared by a professional surveyor or civil engineer and needed for most project design and construction, there are other sources of useful maps and reports available at nominal cost. Of these the U.S. Geological Survey (USGS) maps warrant special mention.[1] Several series are available, at different scales, but the one most often useful to the planner is the 7.5-minute series, in which each map (or *quadrangle,* as it is called) covers an area of about 60 square miles at a scale of 1 inch to 2000 feet. These survey maps show most of the pertinent topography of the area, including relief, wooded areas, all bodies of water, transportation routes, and major buildings.

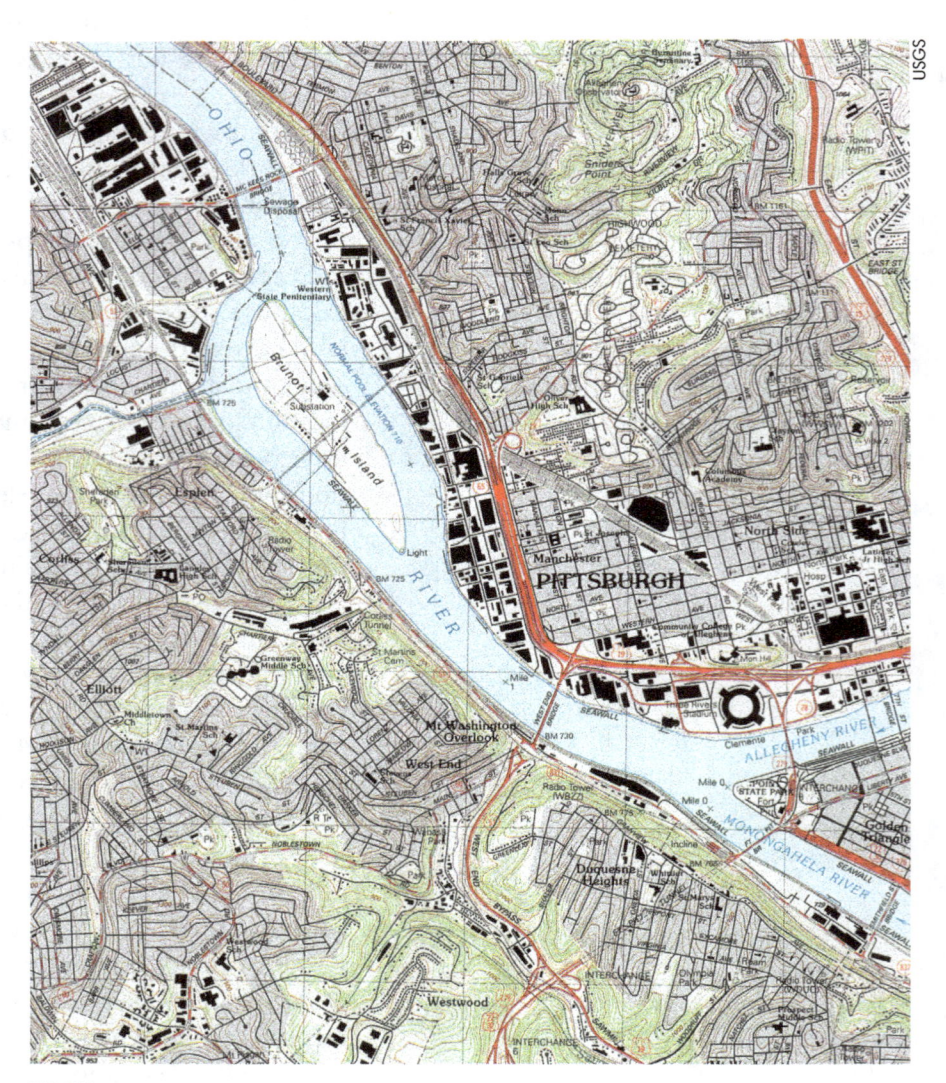

USGS map.

[1] U.S. Geological Survey maps may often be purchased locally at map or stationery stores, or they may be ordered directly from the main distribution center at USGS Information Services, Box 25286, Denver, CO 80225 (http://geography.usgs.gov/esic/to_order.html). If requested, an index map shows for each state the quadrangle to be ordered for a particular location.

For many counties the Natural Resources Conservation Service (formerly the U.S. Soil Conservation Service) has available published Soil Survey Reports, which include 11- by 14-inch field sheets of aerial photos on which soil types are delineated. These may be purchased at the nearest field office. For the areas covered, they can be most useful. Then there are the various types of coverage by satellite mapping and photography, which for certain localities show surface conditions with startling detail and accuracy.

Planning agencies and highway departments are often able and willing to provide survey information and reports for extensive metropolitan areas. This is especially useful in large-scale comprehensive planning, as for a campus, community, river basin, or park and open-space systems.

Other public agencies also can help with overall background mapping and data, which may be sufficient for site selection and preliminary land use diagrams. When it comes time, however, for detailed site planning and recording there is need for a certified topographic survey.

Digital maps in GIS format are a useful form of mapping used for supplementary data on a project. GIS maps, provided by most local governments through an online system, provide the basic topography, vegetation, waterways, transportation routes, buildings, soils, zoning, floodplains, utilities, easements, aerial photography, zoning restrictions or overlays, and individual lot information. More extensive data files are available from local, state, federal, and private agencies for everything from demographics to geographic and ecological data. Analytical GIS software helps the designer to process multiple layers of data and apply it in the design process.

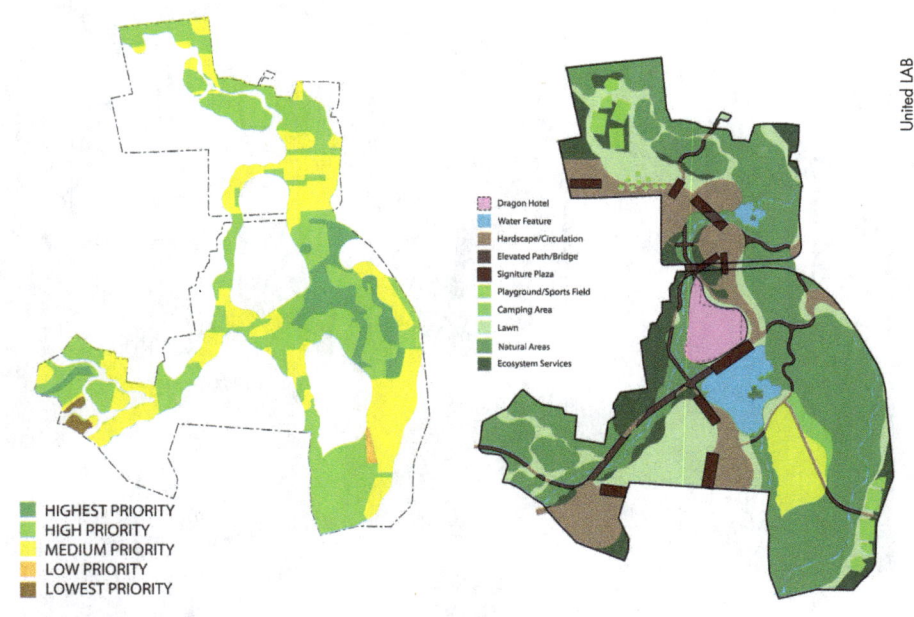

Data mapping used in the design process.

Land 73

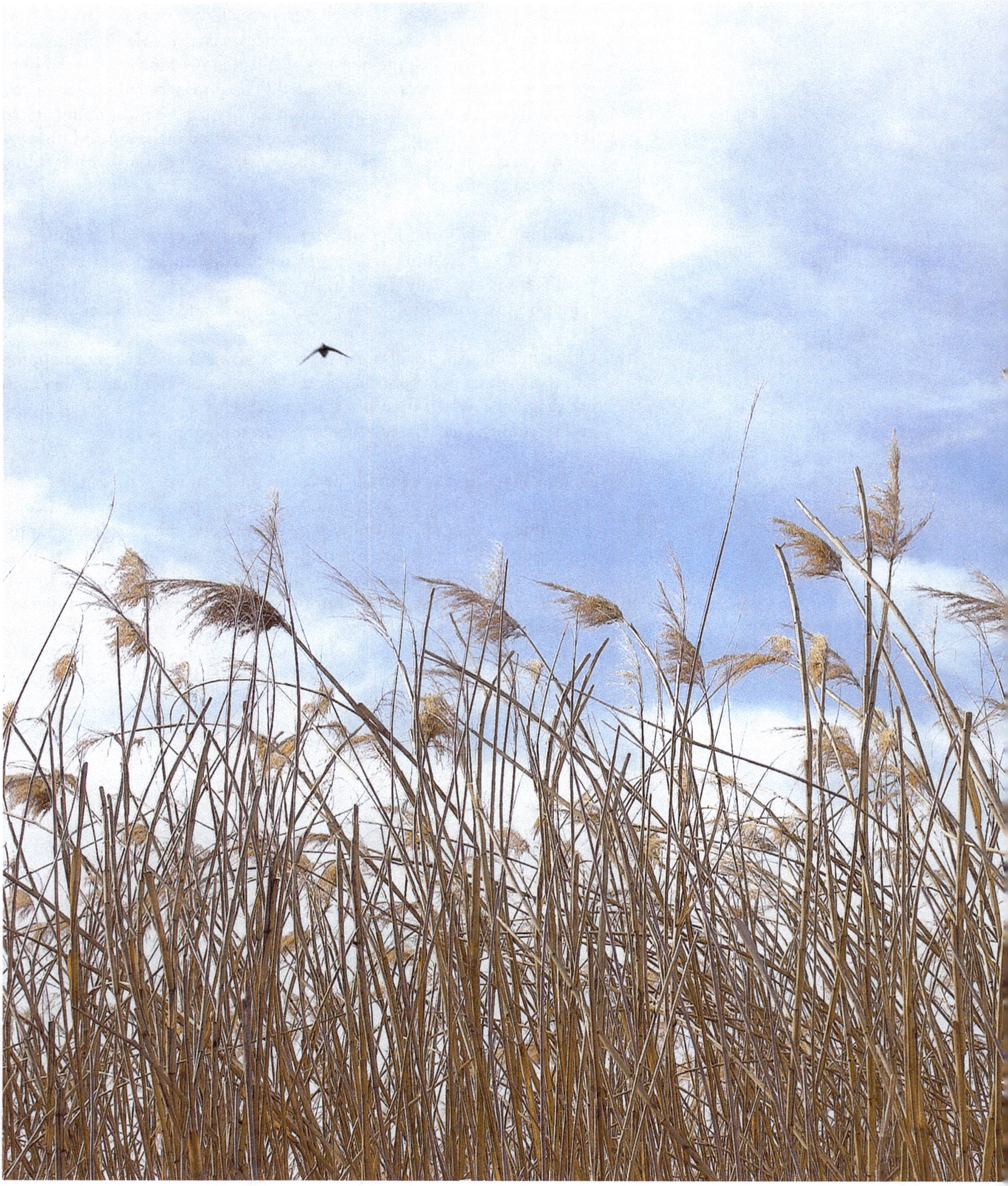

5 VEGETATION

Not many centuries ago, except for the water bodies and windswept deserts, the whole of planet Earth above the level of the sea was covered with vegetation. From the lichens, mosses, and sedges at the water's edge to the billowing grass of the prairies and plains. From the lush foliage of the swamp and marsh to the sparse fringe at the mountain timberline. In between, the dunes, rolling hills, and upland slopes were for the most part clothed with a dense growth of deciduous shrubs and trees or needled conifers.

Topsoil Mantle

In the Americas, until the migrations across the land bridge of the Bering Sea (the latest some 10,000 years ago), there were no living humans on either the North or South American continents to disturb or destroy this vegetative cover. As long as it remained intact, the fertile topsoil mantle, laid down by the ages, was secure and protected. This rich and loamy topsoil substance which overlays the weathered subsoils and rocky earth crust is the wealth of every nation, for only where it remains in place can food, fiber, or timber be produced. Where the vegetative growth has been destroyed by overgrazing, by unsound tillage, or by the clearing or burning of timberlands, the vital topsoil is soon washed or blown away to leave the vulnerable substrata or naked rock exposed. As noted, this has been the case in many countries of the Mideast, where much of the once forested land now resembles a deeply eroded moonscape.

In the United States we've not been immune to such wanton and destructive practices. Within the past century, with our power saws, earthmoving equipment, careless farming, and lax developmental regulations, we have lost a third or more of our topsoil heritage to the wind, storm-water erosion, and construction.

Aside from its protective function, the vegetation of the earth serves to catch and retain precipitation. Its foliage and roots absorb and transpire but a fraction of the falling snow or rain, the dew or drifting mist. Much of the rest is retained to filter through the soils to replenish the underlying freshwater tables or aquifer reservoirs.

Plants in Nature

The vegetal growth that covers most of our globe occurs in myriad forms that range from the towering redwoods of the Pacific coastal forest to the microscopic forms of algae and plant diatoms of our streams, freshwater bodies, and teeming saltwater seas. This wonder world of vegetation provides the habitat and basic food supply of all living creatures.

Plants in nature.

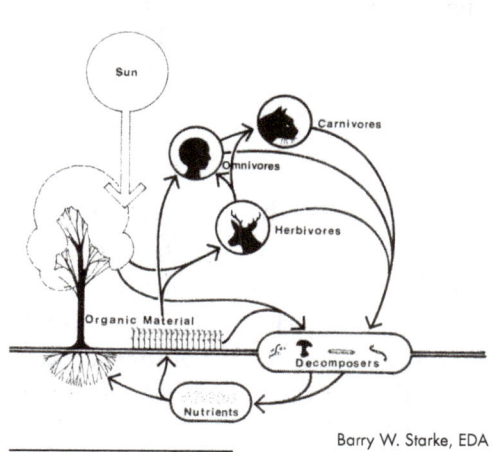

Food Chain

In the green chlorophyll cells of plants, and only there, the energy of the sun is transformed into the simple starches at the base of the biologic food chain. In this process of photosynthesis, plants draw moisture from the air and soil and in the presence of sunlight convert carbon dioxide into free oxygen and carbohydrates. It is in this vital miracle of chemistry that both the oxygen we breathe and the simple starches and sugars upon which all life depends are produced and replenished.

Some carbohydrates are consumed directly by humans, as in vegetables and fruits. Most reach our tables, however, through a complex spiral that begins with the lower forms of grazing organisms of land and sea and moves through a succession of increasingly larger and more complex herbivores and carnivores. Finally, they become our fare as fish, game, butchered livestock, or animal products. It can be seen that as plant life is diminished, life in all its varieties is thereby diminished, too.

Transpiration

It is not only the free oxygen produced by plants that refreshes the air. Water drawn by the plants from the soil and water table is given off by foliage as vapor through evapotranspiration. This cooling and moisturizing function contributes to the growing conditions for other plants and to creature comfort as well. Where it is lacking, arid desert conditions exist.

Climate Control

Plants ameliorate the climate in other ways also. They serve as buffers against a storm. Their foliage and mat of fallen leaves protect the soil against drying winds and sun. Even in wintertime their branches, twigs, and stems form a mesh to receive and transmit solar heat and help protect soils from freezing temperatures.

Water Retention

Plants store the moisture that falls as precipitation—in the crevices of their bark, in the fountain of woody yet aqueous cells that constitute their internal structure, and in the fibrous mat of detritus and roots that cover and penetrate the earth. Water retained is water allowed to cleanse the air or seep into the topsoil and subsurface aquifers. Runoff unchecked is erosion in the making, with siltation as a result.

Soil Building

In the cycle of living and dying, plants return to the earth their decaying fibers and cells to provide humus and deepen the film of topsoil. This slowly accreting and vital substance, if protected from erosion, increases available nutrients and moisture and the earth's fecundity.

Vegetation

The fallen leaves, fruits, stems, and rotting wood that are not retained by the soil as humus are washed away in the stream and river systems to enrich the broth of the tidal estuaries. This organic material in turn becomes food for aquatic plants and for oysters and spawning shell and fin fish.

Productivity

Long before our progenitors gathered their first handfuls of berries or dragged in the first game to their campfires, the forest, prairies, and waters had provided provender for a vast and voracious domain of insects, fish, reptiles, soaring birds, and roving animals. Today, natural conditions would be much the same as they were a million years ago were it not for the ascendancy of humankind. Human hands first stripped and stored nature's bounty, then harvested the grass, grain, and timber, and finally pushed back and destroyed the indigenous covers to make room for garden patches, fields, and settlements. Too often we humans have gained our abundance at the expense of the earth's other inhabitants, until the destruction of vegetative cover and wildlife has now reached devastating proportions. It is only within very recent times that we have paused to consider the consequences. More recently have we begun to understand the direct relationships that exist within the whole biologic realm of animals and plants.

Plant Identification

To work with plants, one must come to recognize them and be able to describe them in terms that others can comprehend. Botany, as a field of

Botanical prints.

scientific inquiry, has grown from the early classification of plants and their systematic study. Linnaeus,[1] sensing a need to better understand the relationships, established the botanical orders and introduced the concept of standardized nomenclature. With over 250,000 plant species now known to exist, it is doubtful that more than a few thousand yet remain unclassified. All plants (and other organisms) are given two scientific (Latin) names. One is for the group or genus; the second is for the species. The scientific names are generally descriptive of the plant characteristics or botanic significance. Latin is used because the meaning of Latin words is unchanging and universal. Were it not for scientific classification it would be impossible to identify a plant or describe it to others, since the common name or name commonly used in a given locality may differ from place to place—even within limited regions of the same country. In view of the international scope of plant study and use it can be seen that standardized plant names are a great boon, even if they are in Latin.

Plant Culture

The rambling sorties of the first botanists have given way to well-organized expeditions. In more recent times, plant explorers such as E. H. Wilson and David Fairchild have ranged the world, from the jungles of Africa to the Mongolian deserts and the peaks of the lofty Himalayas, in search of specimens for herbaria and botanic garden collections and for introduction to our gardens and farms.

Breeding

Early attempts at selective plant breeding and cross-pollination have led to more sophisticated techniques of hybridization. The pioneering feats of the plant breeder Luther Burbank excited enthusiastic interest and produced a tantalizing array of new and superior roses, potatoes, oranges, plums, and other improved plant varieties. Today, plant selection, plant crossing, and seed radiation are creating a veritable cornucopia of hardier, more disease-resistant grains, more luscious fruits, more nutritious vegetables, and more attractive ornamental plants.

Bioengineering

Over the past decade or so, the practice of bioengineering has emerged, which essentially involves combining the DNA of one living thing with that of another, thus creating a new organism. As pertains to plants, the object is to create new plants with enhanced characteristics such as drought resistance, frost tolerance, longer blooming, and so on. However, many fear the unintended consequences of this practice may threaten natural systems, and this debate is still being played out as of the writing of this edition.

---

[1]Carolus Linnaeus, Swedish botanist, 1707–1778, who was the first naturalist to classify the plants of the earth in an orderly arrangement.

Horticulture

The science of horticulture holds great promise. Yet, in our exuberant pursuit of new and improved plant varieties, we tend to ignore the vast and marvelous store of indigenous plants that surround us. They have evolved over countless centuries in nature's selective scheme of things. Each is a miracle of evolutionary adaptation and survival—the result of all natural forces. Each, where and as it stands, represents the highest form of plant life that the given situation can produce and for the time being sustain. We are only beginning to understand the essential functions of plants in our biosphere or the full extent of their contributions to the environment in which we work and live.

Santa Barbara Botanic Garden.

A Sunday afternoon visit to the botanical garden is usually sufficient to awaken an interest in plants. As a start in attaining a broader knowledge, it is well to learn to identify those plants within view of your residence windows—by their form, bark, twigging, buds, foliage, flower, and fruit. The range can then be extended to yard and to neighborhood. Beyond the town or city limits, in the field or woodland, lies a wealth of plants to be recognized and admired in all seasons of the year. Finally, for many enthusiasts the quest will eventually lead out along the streams and rivers and into the wilderness. There, in undisturbed nature, is to be found the realm of plants that were created. For those who understand what they see, it is a profoundly moving experience.

For the initiate, the simplest plant guide will suffice as a start on the trail of exploration, but think twice before scanning the pages; they may lead you a very long way.

Introduced Plantations

Who could it have been, in the dim and distant beginnings of human development, that on some daily food-gathering round first thought to dig and transplant a tuber? Or who consciously gathered and sowed the first seeds, to watch with impatience and then exclaim at the wonder of their sprouting? Whoever, whenever, these acts were the start of agriculture and, together with fire and toolmaking, the start of civilization. From that time, the culture of plants has become, in one way or another, an almost universal enterprise.

The propagation and cultivation of plants for food and fiber are a logical extension of the nomadic way of life. Nature's yield of forage, cereals, vegetables, nuts, and fruits was often sporadic and scattered. The farm field, orchard, and vineyard have increased the bounty manyfold, while barns, silos, storage cellars, and bins have sustained the supply.

The pioneer farms of the early settlers—those of the rail-splitter and horse-drawn plow—were fitted to the lay of the land. Streams, wetlands, and the surrounding forest were left undisturbed. As homesteading increased and the covered wagons rolled westward, the landscape changed with the impact—with rutted trails, line fences, cleared woodlands, plowed fields, and settlements. But the underlying topography remained for the most part intact. The air was clean, and the streams ran clear to debouch into pristine lakes.

As centers of trade were established to serve the farmlands, as ports and harbors were built, as first meandering rural roads, then sweeping high-

Agricultural land.

Vegetation

Disappearing farmland.

ways and transcontinental railways traced their paths across America and cities formed at their crossings, the landscape of nature gave way. It was a rapid and disheartening retreat.

It is disturbing to look about us at most of our developments—at the extent of the destruction of vegetation and the earth conformation, the degradation of lakes and waterways, the pollution of air and countryside. It is saddening to envision the landscape that once existed and to realize the superbly agreeable communities that, with intelligent planning, might have been brought into being.

It is mainly in nineteenth- and twentieth-century America, with our mechanized equipment and our pioneering "Clear the land! Drain the marsh!" complex that we have wrought so much damage to the natural landscape and ecological matrix. It need not be so. In the rural areas of Germany, England, and Scandinavia, we find instructive examples of agriculture, villages, and nature in symbiotic balance—with towns and cities contained, farmland intact, forests well-tended, and much of the wilderness preserved.

Invasive Species

The steady increase of world trade throughout the nineteenth and twentieth centuries into the globalized economy of today has resulted in the worldwide distribution of plant and animal species, both intentional and unintentional. For centuries, explorers and entrepreneurs have deliberately gathered plants and animals from one region and transported them to another region, generally for the commercial purposes of producing food, fiber, or ornamentation. Much of the intentional redistribution has served its intended purposes: to enhance agricultural production and to provide a wider variety of ornamentals, other types of plants, and so forth.

Kudzu vine.

Reestablished wetlands.

Both intended and unintended distribution also takes place as seeds, larvae, small plants and animals, and the like, are carried as stowaways in the transport of other products. Unintended redistribution has resulted in a new category of flora and fauna designated as *invasive species*. These species are considered invasive because of their aggressive growth and spread, to the detriment of indigenous species with which they compete.

Because invasives lack natural predators or herbivores in their new land, their growth and spread go largely unchecked, upsetting the natural ecological balance and, thus, threatening biological diversity. Well-known examples are the kudzu vine, which was imported into the United States to control erosion along highways, and the accidental introduction in the 1990s of the brown marmorated stinkbug.

Indigenous species may also become invasive if their natural controls are removed or become out of balance. Perhaps the best example of this is the explosive increase in the population of the native whitetail deer.

Vanishing Green

A new American landscape is taking form. There are encouraging signs. We find in our rural, suburban, and urban areas many examples of land well used and natural features preserved. Many farmsteads, homes, and communities have been planned in sympathetic response to their topographical settings, and extensive areas of open space have been acquired to conserve scenic mountain slopes, riverbanks, and shores. Unfortunately, however, the good examples are far outnumbered by the bad.

It is not a lost cause—far from it. We have learned that the wanton destruction of our earthscape can be precluded, that defilement and pollution can be stopped, that eroded land can be healed, that towns and cities can in time be rebuilt, and that the natural vegetation can be restored. Moreover, we are learning much about our ecology, we are developing a whole new science of resource management, and we are constantly increasing our knowledge of community and landscape planning. Within the next few decades it will be well within our capacity to preserve our natural systems and reshape our constructed environment more responsibly. In this endeavor, the preservation and creative use of plants will play an essential role.

Reestablishment

Many of those who have witnessed the slow degradation of the American landscape and the destruction of the vegetative covers have taken steps to reverse the trend.

Concern for the vanishing upland meadows, mountain and riverine forests, prairies, and coastal wetlands has resulted in the setting aside of millions of acres of state and national preserves. In addition, vast areas of cutover forest have been reestablished, and new plantations of trees (afforestation) have been installed on depleted or eroded lands as watershed protection, wildlife management preserves, and shelterbelt windscreens and for timber and grain production. These commendable programs have received and deserve wide public support and are to be expanded.

Community garden.

Urban Agriculture

Urban agriculture is the growing and distribution of food and other agricultural products within or in close proximity to urban areas. It has existed in one form or another since the beginning of civilization and agriculture itself. Although urban agriculture is not considered to be a replacement for traditional rural agriculture, it nonetheless provides urban residents with a valuable source for a larger variety of fresh products than they otherwise would have access to.

Gardening promotes community.

Urban agriculture is manifested in a variety of ways, ranging from "grow bags," used where no actual land area is available, to small garden beds in a townhouse environment, to community gardens of a half-acre or more in urban neighborhoods. Innovative planners and designers are increasingly looking at new ways to turn areas of underutilized open space, such as that on college and corporate campuses, into agricultural production. During the economic downturn and real estate bust of the recent past, some metropolitan areas demolished abandoned or dilapidated housing and converted the land to community gardens.

It's interesting to note that during World War II, the American Victory Garden movement produced almost half of U.S.-grown produce during that time. The potential of urban agriculture is far greater than is currently being realized; however, its popularity is quickly growing.

Agriculture on a college campus.

84   LANDSCAPE ARCHITECTURE

Urban Forestry

Seeking the cool shade of a tree might well be one of the most basic human reactions to the environment. The benefits of trees in an urban setting are many, including environmental and social benefits. Trees help mitigate the harsh microclimate created by increased building density and paved areas. They convert carbon dioxide into oxygen, mitigate the effects of increased urban runoff, and have many other benefits. Trees also make a significant contribution to the creation of social places and spaces in urban areas.

Although growing trees in an urban environment has many benefits, it also faces special challenges, including the effects of increased air pollution from automobiles, limited space and poor soil condition for root growth, limited sunlight resulting from building shadows, limited water supply, elevated temperatures, and competition with utility lines.

These considerations and the special requirements for the planting, care, and management of trees in urban areas have evolved over the years into what is now known as the practice of *urban forestry*. Urban forestry is practiced primarily by municipal governments, but in recent years non-profit organizations, such as the Friends of Urban Forests and Casey Trees, have joined the effort.

As the rate of urbanization of the world's population continues to increase, urban forestry will be one of the primary components of *green infrastructure*.

Future forest in an urban environment.

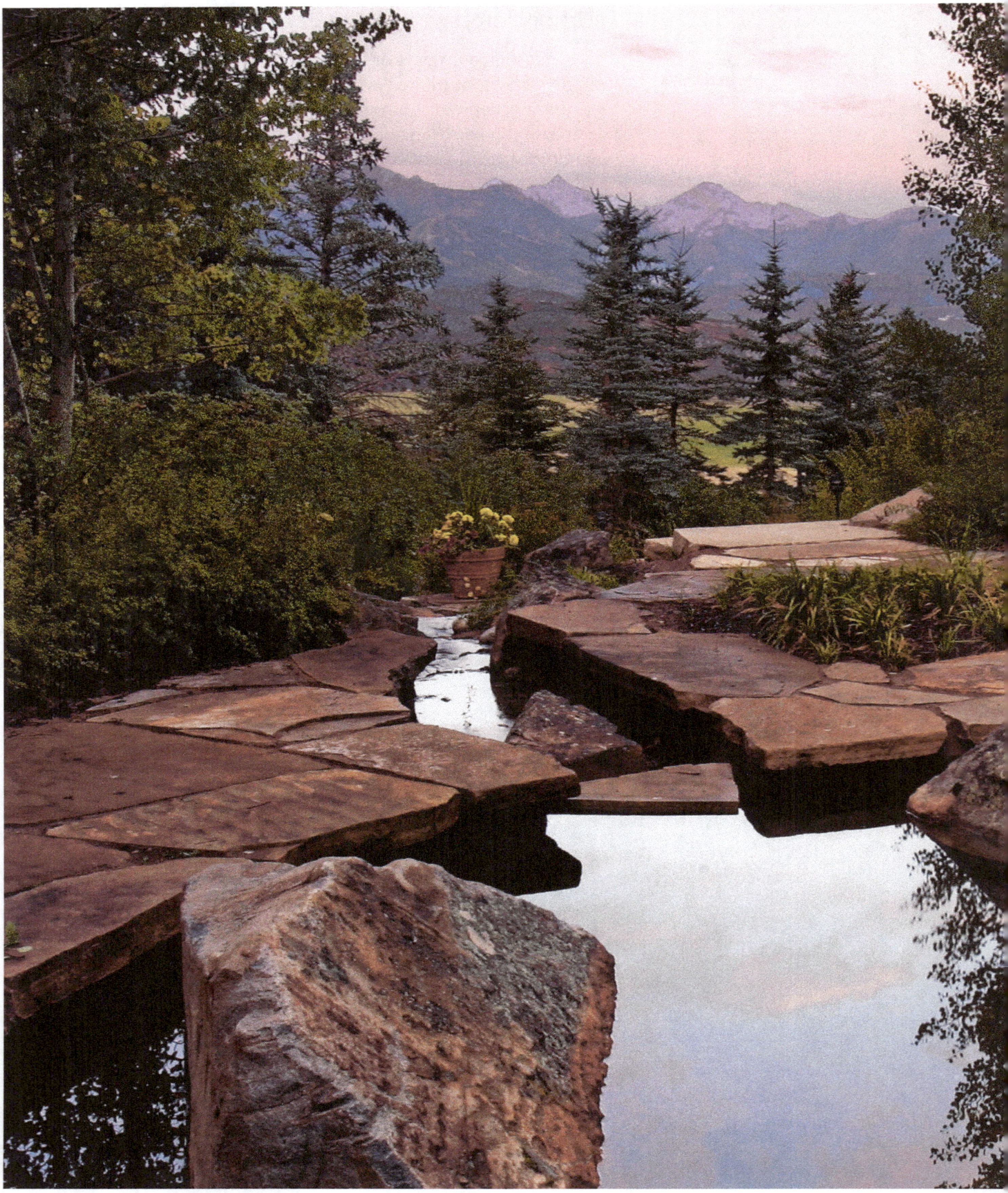

6
THE VISUAL LANDSCAPE

The View

A view is a scene observed from a given vantage point. Often an outstanding view is reason enough for the selection of a property. Once the site has been attained, however, the view is seldom used to full advantage. Indeed, the proper treatment of a view is one of the least understood of all the visual arts. A view must be analyzed and composed with keenly perceptive artistry to utilize even a fraction of the full dramatic potential. Like other landscape features, the view by its handling may be preserved, neutralized, modified, or accentuated. But before we attempt to deal with the view, we must learn more of its nature.

- A view is an evolving panorama of many blending facets.
- A view is a theme. Its proper realization resembles the musical creation of variations on a theme.
- A view is a constantly changing mood-inducer.
- A view is a limit of visual space. It transcends the boundaries of the site. It has directional pull. It may evoke a sense of expansive freedom.
- A view is a backdrop. It may serve as a wall of a garden or as a mural in a room.
- A view is a setting for architecture.

© D. A. Horchner/Design Workshop

87

Suitability as a Factor

To be enjoyed, a view must be related to people and to those areas and spaces used by them. We must be sure, however, that the use and the view are compatible. A scene of great activity or excitement, for instance, should hardly be introduced visually into an area of quiet repose.

How could the pupil concentrate in a classroom facing a ballpark or a river lock with its whistles, bells, shouting gatekeepers, straining tugs, and tows? Or how, cajoled by such a view, could the artist keep eyes on drawing or the librarian thoughts on the work at hand? Again, a scene of gentle pastoral tranquility may negate the effectiveness of a space designed to exhort combatants to action or inspire one to lofty thought. For such a purpose, the view should be lofty and awe-inspiring, vast and grand, or there should be no view at all. The invigorating qualities of a rocky chasm scene with craggy fir and the thunderous roar of rushing, tumbling water might destroy the serenity or passive atmosphere intended for an introspective space. A dynamic industrial scene of belching smoke, leaping flame, and switching freight cars has its design applications and its limitations, too. Even a sweeping night scene of a sprawling river city with its jewel-like constellations and patterns of light, its cubes and prisms of shadow and illuminated surface, its luminous vapors of smoke and steam, its crawling, beetlelike traffic glows, its arching river wakes and shooting beams, its trembling cloud reflections—even such a wondrous view as this may be unsuited to a number of use areas, while for many others it would be ideal.

The view is part of the design.

Design Treatment of a View

A view has landscape character. This will, of course, determine those areas or functions with which it should be combined. If the view is a dominant landscape feature, the related use areas and spaces should be developed in harmony with the view as it exists or as it may be treated.

A view need not be seen full front or be approached from a fixed direction. It is a panorama or a segment of a panorama to be seen from any or all angles. It may be viewed on the oblique, on the sweep, or broadside.

A view is an impeller. A powerful magnet, it will draw one far, and from one position to another, for the opportunity of better commanding its limits or seeing some part in a new and intriguing way. The skilled planner will let a view develop as the viewer moves across it, just as a mountain climber experiences more and more of a view in the ascent until it is seen in total.

A view may be subdivided. It may be appreciated facet by facet, with each bit treated as a separate picture and so displayed to best capture its special qualities. By design, a view may be deftly modulated as one moves from area to area. Each area will, by direction, foreground, framing, or by the function of the space, relate one to some new aspect of the scene until, at last, it is fully revealed.

If the view is to serve as a backdrop, the object placed against it must be in character.

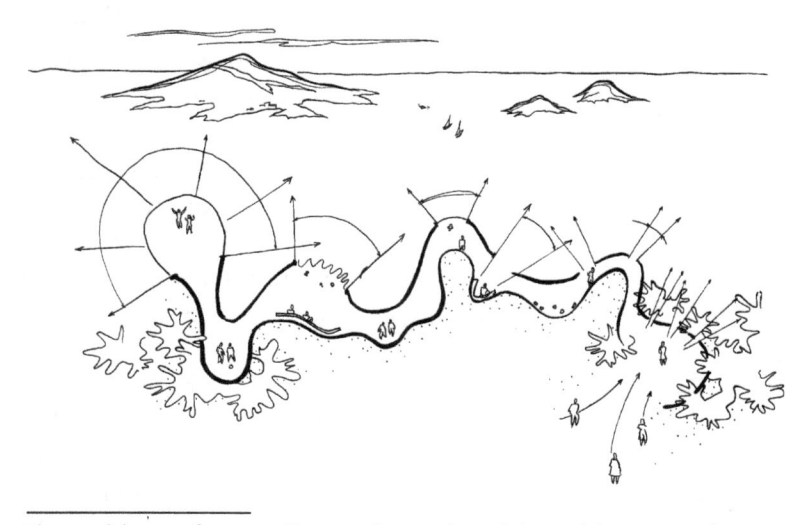

The modulation of a view. From a glimpse through loose foliage, to enframing slot, to wider sector, to reverse interest, to vista, to object seen against the view, to reverse interest, to objects placed against the view seen through a film of fabric, to concentration in a cavelike recess, to full, exuberant sweep.

Light or incongruous detail placed against a view may result in split interest and annoyance.

A view gains in effectiveness when certain plan areas are developed as a counterpoint or foil. If we stand for long at one vantage point, comprehending a view in its entirety, it begins to lose its first fresh appeal and strikes the senses with less impact. The interest of the open view may be sustained and much accentuated when certain plan areas are developed in balanced opposition. Such an area might be enclosed, with a narrow slot or a constructed aperture opening on some absorbing detail of the scenery. It might be a chaste volume kept simple and severe in form and neutral in tone, so that a colorful sector of view might glow more vividly. It might be a recessive area, leading one away from the view into some cavelike interior space for contrast, so that, emerging to the expansive-

The Visual Landscape 89

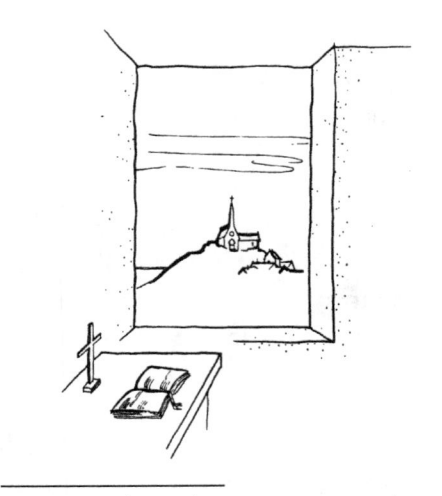

A view is a theme that may suggest and give added meaning to well-related functions.

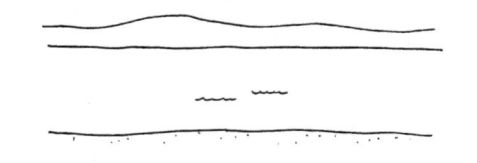

The best view is not always or often the full view.

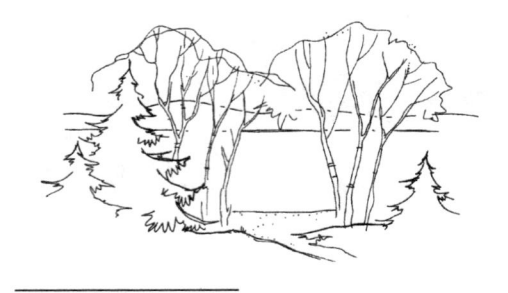

A view is usually better if enframed or seen through an appropriate screen.

ness of the view, one senses an emotional response of great release and freedom. A designed space may incorporate some feature subtly or powerfully related to the view: a ship relic related to a view of the ocean; hammered metal to a spectacle of blazing furnaces; a fruit bowl to an orchard view; a trout etching to a scene of splashing brook; a drawing of fox, grouse, or wild turkey or hunting accoutrements to a panorama of rolling game land; or a candle to a distant cathedral spire.

Some areas, to give respite, might best be planned without apparent relationship. For a heady view, like a heady drink, should be absorbed slowly and in moderation.

Split interest is a hazard in a treatment of a view. Light detail placed in front of a scene is usually lost or distracting—an element of annoyance. If the broad view is used as a backdrop, the object or objects placed before it must, singly or as a compositional group, either recede or dominate.

The Power of Suggestion

If a view or an object in the landscape is by design suggested only, the mind will multiply the possibilities of perception and thus expand the scope and richness of the suggested experience. The silhouette or shadow of a pine branch seen through a translucent panel or screen or projected upon it is often more effective than a direct view of the branch itself. The dim outline of a form seen at a distance or in half-light is thus often of more interest than the same form seen fully and in detail. And so it is with the view.

It has long been the belief of the Zen Buddhists, writes Kakuzo Okakura in *A Book of Tea,* that "true beauty could be discovered only by one who mentally completed the incomplete. It was this love of the abstract that led the Zen to prefer black and white sketches to the elaborately colored paintings of the classic Buddhist School."

Concealment and Revealment

A view should be totally revealed for fullest impact only from that position in the plan where this is most appropriate. It is not to be wasted in one first blast but conserved and displayed with perhaps more refinement, though certainly with no less feeling for suspense and timing, than shown by the striptease artist.

It has been told that, near the village of Tomo in Japan, a celebrated tea master planning to build a teahouse purchased, after much deliberation, a parcel of land with a startlingly beautiful view of the idyllic Inland Sea. His friends were most curious to learn how this great artist would exhibit his scenic prize, but during the time of construction they were, of course, too polite to investigate and waited to be invited.

Only when reaching the precise spot is the distant view revealed.

On the day when the first guests arrived at the entrance gate, they could hardly contain their eagerness to see the fabulous ocean view that would surely be eloquently revealed. As they moved along the narrow stone pathway toward the teahouse, they were aware that the sea was teasingly hidden from sight by the alignment of the path through thin bamboo clumps. At the door of the teahouse, they reasoned, the view would be opened to them in some highly sensitive enframement. They were more than a little perplexed to find the view there effectively concealed by a shoulder of lichened rock and a panel of woven straw fencing. As is the custom before entering a teahouse, they paused and bent over a stone basin brimming with water to rinse their hands. As they raised their eyes from this bowed position, they caught a glimpse, no more than a glimpse, between the great rock and a low, dark branch of ancient pine, of the shining sea below them. And as they looked, they sensed with tingling comprehension the relationship of the mother sea and the cool water at their fingertips.

Inside on the mats of the teahouse with the translucent screens closed around them they performed the simple ritual of the tea ceremony, still mindful of the lesson of the sea. Relaxed and refreshed at the ceremony's conclusion, the guests were half surprised when their host rose quietly to slide back the screens at one side of the room, revealing in its perfect completeness the overwhelming beauty of a seascape that stretched from the edge of the grass floor mats to the farthest distant limits of the sky.

The Vista

A vista is a confined view, usually directed toward a terminal or dominant feature. It may be a natural vista, as an allée opened through a grove

The view is a scene observed.

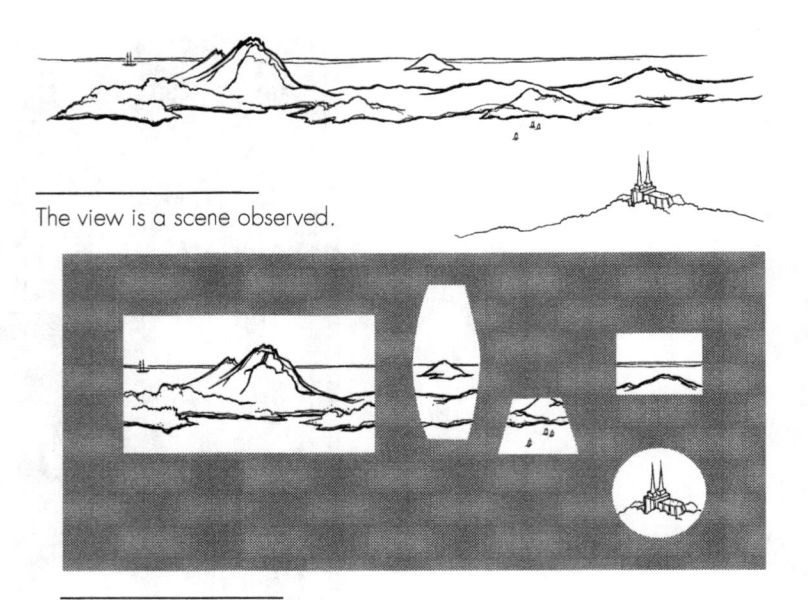

The vista is an enframed segment of a view.

Enframement and vista must be compatible.

of Japanese maples to give a view of Fujiyama; or it may be architectural, as the majestic vista from the Palace of Versailles toward the lavish Neptune Fountain. Each vista has, in simplest terms, a viewing station, an object or objects to be seen, and an intermediate ground.

The three together should make a satisfactory visual unit and are usually conceived as an entity. If one or more of the elements already exist and are allowed to remain, then the others must, of course, be designed in conformity.

Again, vista and the allied places and spaces must be compatible. If the vista is planned as an extension of a use area or space, the relationships of character and scale are important. For example, from the boardroom of a powerful bank the vista, if there is to be one, should hardly terminate at the roller coaster of an amusement park or the gates of the state penitentiary. Commanded by such a rarefied viewing box of marble, gilt, and paneled rosewood, the vista and its terminus should be equally impressive and richly conservative. The vista toward a national monument should hardly commence at a service station, drugstore, or factory. It might well be observed from another monument, a civic building, or a public gathering space. It is fundamental to the fine vista that the end justifies the beginning and the beginning justifies the end.

The terminus establishes the character of this space.

The Terminus

The terminal feature on which the vista is focused sets the theme to be developed. All other elements must fall into cadence, support the theme in harmony and counterpoint, and carry the work to a final satisfying crescendo. There is no room for discord, the superfluous, or the inappropriate; instead, the eye must see the right thing seen from the right place with just the right enframement.

Progressive Realization

The terminal feature may be displayed in progressive stages. If a vista can be seen from several stations along the approaches, the section seen from each station is to be treated separately. Sometimes a terminus may be viewed along an entire approach. In such a case, it should be revealed by its evolving spatial containment to exact the full potential of its changing perspectives. If the approach is long, the vista becomes tiring and should be divided into segments by changing the level, by expanding or contracting the frame of reference, or by altering the character of the spaces through which and from which it is seen. Often, in moving toward a distant focal point, one can at first discern no more than the outline of the terminal feature. As one continues, the feature reveals itself progressively: the component masses, the subcomponents, and finally the details.

Any vista may be satisfyingly staged in an infinite number of ways. It is only necessary that, from all viewing stations or lines of approach, there be developed a pleasing visual entity. A vista may induce motion or repose. Some vistas are static, to be enjoyed from one fixed viewing station, and are seen in their completeness from this point. Others, by the interest of their unfolding revelation or by the attraction of the terminus, draw one from point to point.

All vistas subject the observer to a compelling line of sight. A vista is insistent, a directional attraction to the eye. As such, a vista is a function of the axis.

The Axis

Essentially, the axis is a linear plan element connecting two or more points. In use it may be a court, a mall, or a drill field. It may be a path, a drive, a city street, or a monumental parkway. Always it is to be regarded as an element of connection.

In land planning, the axis has important applications. It has limitations also, for once an axis has been introduced, it generally becomes the dominant landscape feature. Established in a plan complex, it becomes so insistent that all other elements must be related to it directly or tacitly. Any area or structure impinging upon the axis, adjacent to the axis, or leading toward the axis must draw much of its use, form, and character from this relationship. Because it is a powerful landscape element, the axis tends to subjugate other landscape features. This can happen in more ways than one. It has been told that, in building the Palace of Versailles, King Louis XIV questioned the fact that the three approach avenues were unequally spaced on the drawings. When he was advised that the offending avenue was so aligned to miss a nearby village, Louis replied that he failed to understand the point. The plans were revised. To preserve a perfect symmetry, one axial approach was of necessity driven through the hapless village. Demolition crews set to work, and the hamlet was neutralized.

Almost as effective would be the driving of an axis through any established landscape area. Because the existing order of things would be disrupted, a new order would have to be devised, and this in relation to the intruding axial line, for there is little of polite gentility to the axis. It is forceful; it is demanding; and, as a result, things usually go its way.

> An axis is directional.
> An axis is orderly.
> An axis is dominating.
> An axis is often monotonous.

This is not to say that the axis is always best avoided. It is only to suggest that none of these attributes are conducive to relaxation, pleasant confusion, nature appreciation, freedom of choice, or many other such experiences that we humans tend to enjoy.

The axis.

Axial Characteristics

From a given use area, an axis is a dynamic plan line leading out and thus orienting the area outward. Such an area, both as a viewing point and as a source of axial movement, might well express this outward flow. How can this be accomplished? By shaping the space to induce movement outward. By constructing, in effect, a viewing box with its aperture well focused. By fanning the paving lines out and away or by sighting them accurately down the axial center line. By concentrating interest at the forward edge of the staging area, inducing flow to and past it. By directional forms. By use of concentric arcs circling outward, as from pebbles tossed into a pond.

Often, in an axial plan, the viewing stations and termini are interchangeable. It can be seen that the forms and lines and details that dispatch us from one station would, if we approached from the opposite direction, seem to beckon and receive us. This is fortunate, because most axial treatments allow for looking both up and down the line of sight and for moving from one end to the other and back again. We find that each transmitting area thus becomes, in turn, a receiving area. We may correctly conclude that when viewing points and terminal features are interchangeable, each must express the characteristics of the source as well as the terminus of axial view and movement.

The Visual Landscape

An axis, being a line of movement and use as well as vision, must satisfy all three functions. The axis, like the vista it creates, combines primary, intermediate, and terminal spaces in the same volume. It would seem only reasonable that all three need to be planned as integral parts of the whole. If the axial plan area is intended as a boulevard, it should, from start to finish, look like a boulevard and function as a boulevard. Every building at its flanks should belong to the boulevard. Every space projected or leading into its central volume should partake of the boulevard character.

Much lyrical praise has been heaped upon that prototype of all grand boulevards, the Champs-Élysées of Paris. Much criticism has also been leveled at its social and economic impact on the city at the time of its construction, for it cleared out a wide swath of living urban tissue. But, for the moment, let us dismiss from our minds such weighty implications and let ourselves rise up in our imagination until we can gaze down upon the whole stirring expanse of this magnificent axis.

Below us we see the grand Étoile, a wide traffic circle with forcefully radiating streets that disappear in the distance. The circle is massively defined by the stately trees and severe gray buildings at its sides. Its glistening pavement of clipped granite blocks is precise in pattern. The whole martial space has about it a stiffly proud and solemn air, as well it might, for there at its center looms the Arc de Triomphe, and at the arch's wreathlined base the Tomb of the Unknown Soldier, with its eternally glowing flame of tribute. The Étoile is a volume remarkably suited to its uses. As a focal point, the arch is seen fittingly framed for miles in all directions. The circle, a marshaling space and point of generation for, as well as the powerful terminus of, the Étoile, is also the head of the Champs-Élysées, and its archway commandingly rallies attention to the start of the wide boulevard.

The axial boulevard marches on, out to the east, still crisply military, progressing firmly in measured cadence of structures and trees until, almost imperceptibly, we note less of a military and more of a regal character, less of the coldly regimented and more of the ornately monumental; for now we approach the palace group. Here the Grand and Petit palaces flank the Avenue Alexandre III as it moves in grandeur from the Esplanade des Invalides across the Seine to join the boulevard. The transition is from palatial to civic as we continue along the Champs-Élysées to the Place de la Concorde, with its pretentious ministries and secretariats.

In our journey eastward from the Étoile we have passed resplendent apartments with silver entablatures, elite shops with high velvet curtains, proud restaurants with glittering chandeliers, and, finally, small cafés with their trim green awnings and crowded sidewalk tables, between which bustle the white-aproned garçons with trays poised lightly on fingertips. Here the boulevard takes on a lively air. Colors are gay, spirits are light, the smile is quick, and the heart is glad on the boulevard in Paris.

Courtesy French Embassy and Information Division, New York City

Arc de Triomphe and the Champs-Élysées.

The good life is not a matter of good gimmicks or of physical ease; it is a matter of things that uplift the spirit. High averages will not define it. The Arch of the Étoile and the tree-lined streets that come to it and depart are more important to the good life of the poorest Parisian than a tenth of one percent improvement in his substandard dwelling. I mean this rejection of the high average to apply to all elements of the good life—to the poetic life, to the political life, to the visual life, to the spiritual life. It is a life which occasionally though not too often because ecstasy can not be prolonged, as the readers of Dante's Paradisio *can discover. But a life without these high points is not the good life.*
John Ely Burchard

Today, we are more honest, more practical, and quite functional, but it has been at the expense of grace and gentility....
Pietro Belluschi

Yes, we have forgotten the simple courtesy of pleasing. What is true of architecture is even more so of city planning where the chief object seems to be to get the driver from A to B sitting down.
Henry H. Reed Jr.

What is the monumental? The word, by the way, in the architectural sense, is quite new. Ruskin a hundred years ago spoke only of power. Actually it is a recent borrowing from the French. "Monumental" they tell us is said of a building "qui a un caratére de grandeur et de majesté," for a monument is an "ouvrage d'architecture considerable par sa masse, son étendue, sa magnificence." Grandeur, majesty, magnificence!
Henry H. Reed Jr.

Beyond the ordered spaces of the Place de la Concorde we come to the Tuileries, the magnificent public gardens and park. At the garden's end, and handsomely framed, we behold the Palace of the Louvre, with its warm stone walls and rich ornamentation. Fronting the majestic Louvre we see the espaliered allées of sycamore, the gardens rolling with color, the screeching traffic, trim nursemaids, perambulators, barking dogs, and dodging children, the white-bearded, pink-cheeked old men in blue berets drowsing on benches in the sun, the well-scrubbed jaunty sailors and the *belles jeunes filles.* All that is in this whole exuberant space belongs to it—is of its very essence.

And where along the length of this great axis do we find the discrepancies in plan, the discordant notes? Some there must be, and many perhaps, but they are lost in the captivating and ringing experience of moving down through this evolving complex of boulevard volumes, the "elysian fields," from the hushed memorial solemnity of the arch at the Étoile to the palatial, then stately, governmental core to the splendid apartments, the chic shops, the lively café district, and on through the carefree expanse of the public gardens to the grandiose museum of fine arts. We feel ourselves to be, in turn, in one brief morning's stroll, the soldier, the courtier, the statesman, the person of wealth, the gay dilettante, the poet, the lover, the relaxed, free, and happy boulevardier, the stimulated observer, and finally the distinguished connoisseur.

If planned today, this Champs-Élysées would have a different mien. And so it should, for since its conception times have changed and conditions have changed, and plan concepts and forms have changed with them. The new boulevard would have less of the old despotic formality, less unbending symmetry. Retaining its hallowed monuments, it would be less monumental. It would open out and free the teeming residential districts at its sides. It would be less of the classifier and more of the synthesizer.

It would be more flexible and allow more flexibility. It would take its form from an empathetic understanding of individual Parisians and their emerging culture. It would express their new freedom, new ideas, and new aspirations. But let those who would change the present Champs-Élysées first study it long and thoughtfully because, in light of the times and the society for which it was built and its masterful handling of forms and space, there is no boulevard of its equal.

An axis has sometimes a negative, sometimes a positive effect on landscape elements within its field of influence. We have said that areas and objects adjacent to an axis are perforce related to it. Sometimes they suffer from the relationship because interest is less in the things themselves than in the thing-axis relationship. A fine linden tree, for example, if standing alone, is observed in terms of trunk and limbing structure, twigging, burgeoning foliage, sunlight and shadow patterns, and the beauty of its broad outline and delicate detail. If related to an insistent axis, however, the same tree is noticed primarily in that context. The subtle, the natural, and the unique are lost to the axial line.

Sometimes, by the fact of their relationship, axial elements may gain in interest and value. If as units they are dull, in pattern they may be striking. If by position they are inconspicuous, by axial frame of reference they may gain in significance.

The Axis as a Unifying Element

A terminal or intermediate station of one axis may function also as the terminal or intermediate station of another. Thus two or more plan areas may be focalized on a common point. Washington, D.C., whose plan diagram exemplifies this principle, has thereby developed one of the most cohesive metropolitan plans yet devised. Its long, radial, tree-lined avenues, converging on park, circle, structure, or monument, enframe handsome vistas and bind the city's complex, extensive, and heterogeneous parts into coherent unity. If we distinguish in the plan arrangement the outline of monumentality, this seems preeminently fitting.

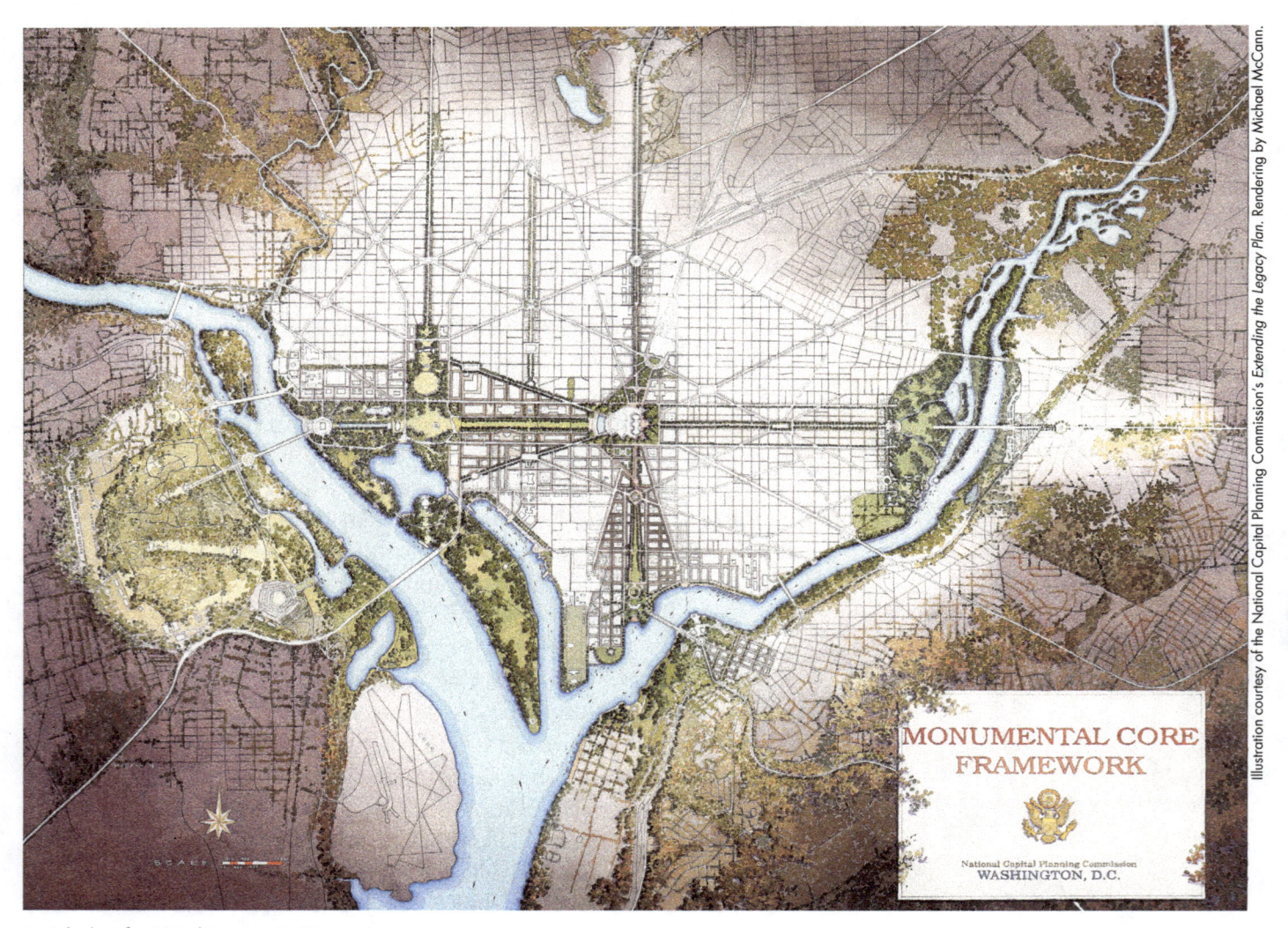

Axial plan for Washington, D.C.

98   LANDSCAPE ARCHITECTURE

Additional Characteristics

A powerful axis requires a fitting terminus. Conversely, powerful design features are often of such form or character as to require an axial approach. Such features are those best seen head-on.

> Or those best situated at the hub of converging plan lines
> Or those to be revealed in stages along a given line of approach
> Or those requiring controlled enframement and established viewing points
> Or those that gain through a direct relationship to other lineal plan elements

The axis presents the most imposing approach to a structure or other plan feature. The key word in this axiom is *imposing*, for the axis imposes a discipline upon spaces and forms as well as upon the viewer. The movement, attention, and interest of the viewer are imposed upon by axial composition and induced to alignment with the direction of its strong polarizing forces. An impressive, dogmatic design form, the axis expresses the supremacy of the human will over nature. It denotes authority, the military, the civic, the religious, the imperial, the classic, and the monumental.

To understand the significance of the axis when properly applied, we may well look to the ancient city of Peking (now Beijing), the northern capital of the khans. Kublai Khan, its founder, and the great city builders who followed him understood the power of the axis as have few before or since. Centuries ago, in the building of their city, they scrupulously avoided the use of the axis in those areas where its insistent lines were unsuited. The refreshing parks, marketplaces, and winding residential streets were relaxed and free in their forms and spaces.

In the whole fabulously delightful grounds of the Summer Palace, planned for sumptuous divertissement, there is scarcely a conscious axis to be found. But where the imperial presence was to be made manifest or the people were to be subjected to the concept of supreme deity, omnipotence, or military might, the axis was employed with sensitive understanding, as witness the military roads that stretch in broad grandeur from the city gates to the entrance of the once golden-roofed Forbidden City of the emperor—dynamic lines of force, subjecting the whole city to the will and authority of the all-powerful emperor.

Axial planning also highlights the Temple of Heaven, which lies on the plain to the south of the Imperial City. Here, each year at the time of the vernal equinox, the great khan rode in magnificent pomp and ceremony to welcome the coming of spring. The approach to this once sublimely beautiful temple was a wide causeway of white marble that commenced at a circular platform of noble proportions, rising in balustraded tiers. The spacious causeway, elevated above the level plain, extended to the gilded and deep-red-lacquered gates of the temple. Spaced out along the

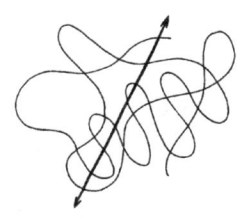

An axis imposed on a free plan area demands a new and related order.

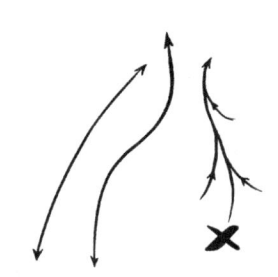

An axis may be bent or deflected but never divergent.

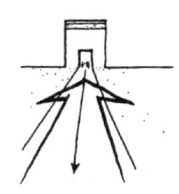

A powerful axis requires a powerful terminus.

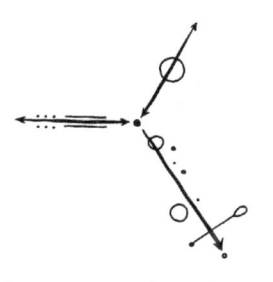

The axis is a unifying element.

The axis.

The Visual Landscape

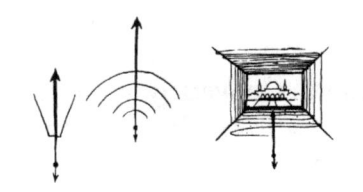

Terminus as a generator of axial movement.

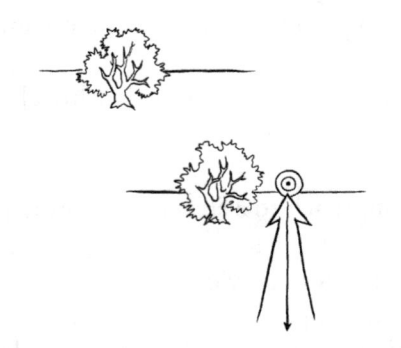

Often objects adjacent to a strong axis suffer in the relationship.

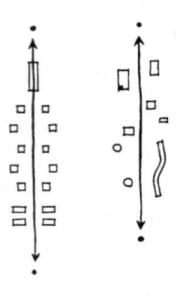

An axis may be symmetrical. But usually it is not.

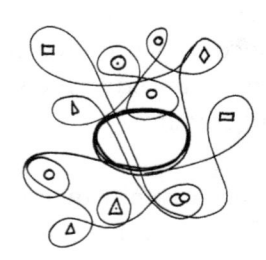

A small exhibit area may function well without a major vista or axis. Such a scheme permits a crowd to filter freely through the entire complex. In this case a powerful focal center is mandatory.

causeway sides, at regular intervals, were sockets to hold the standards of hundreds of waving banners, and between the standards were carved fire pits, in which pitch faggots were burned to illumine the long processions that moved past them in the night.

In the dark hours before the great annual event, the khan's subjects flocked through the streets of their city and out through the gates toward the temple, where they massed along the wooded edges of the plain to stand in watchful, wide-eyed wonder and respect. Then, through the gates, the foot soldiers came marching, division after bristling division of seasoned warriors, in dark helmets, chain breastplates, and padded felt boots, to mass in ordered formation along the causeway flanks. The courtiers and nobles followed in dazzling array, thousands upon thousands on horseback, each noble and mount in trappings of silk, gold, costly furs, and precious gems and each proudly taking his appointed place along the white marble pavement. The high priests, with smoldering incense pots, then moved in solemn procession, chanting, fur-capped, and in silken robes and gowns of unbelievable splendor. Slowly, with vast dignity, they took their august posts on the terraced platform, commanding the length of the ceremonial causeway.

Finally, as the first faint traces of light tinged the eastern sky with pink, the khan and his mounted retinue pranced through the golden gates of the Forbidden City and out through the throngs to the head of the causeway.

There, to the cadenced booming of drums and the crashing of brass and silver gongs the khan rode imperiously past the blazing fire pits, down the avenue of floating banners, on through the massed troops and kowtowing nobles, to the resplendent temple and the gleaming altar seen through its opened doors. Precisely at that hushed moment when he reached the high altar and bowed his head in grave salutation, the blazing red orb of the rising sun arched above the purple hills to the east, and every face and every eye and every thought in all Peking were focused down the length of that great axis to the sacred place where the exalted khan, their emperor, knelt to greet the spring.

The Symmetrical Plan

The use of the axis does not necessarily dictate the development of a symmetrical plan.

The elements of a symmetrical plan are the same and are in equilibrium about a central point or opposite sides of an axial line. The central point may be an object or an area, such as a fountain or the plaza that contains it.

The symmetrical axis may be a line or plane of use, such as a path, a broad avenue, or a mall. It may be a powerfully induced line of sight or movement, as through a series of imposing arches or gates, or between

100   LANDSCAPE ARCHITECTURE

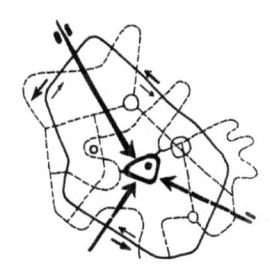

A diagrammatic and workable circulation plan for a large-scale exhibition area has the following features: main entrance, secondary entrances, major vista, minor vistas, strong focal point, major circulation loop, minor paths, and secondary focal areas and reference points for easy orientation.

Major and minor vistas need not be perpendicular.

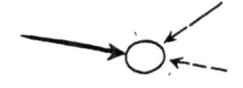

The terminus of a vista may be a space as well as an object.

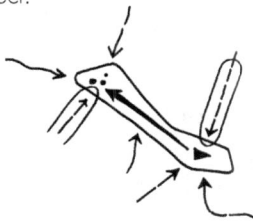

A major or a minor vista may be a function of an *area* or a *volume* as well as of a *line* of approach.

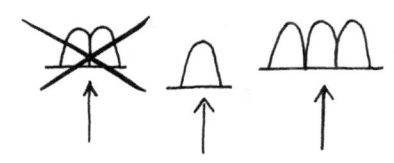

When the axis terminates in a structure that is to be entered, one or three openings are better than two since they provide a receptive element rather than an obstruction.

rows of rhythmically spaced trees or pylons, or toward an object or space of high interest. It may be a quiet vista across an open panel of turf on either side of which things appear to be equally balanced.

Symmetry may be absolute, as in the pillared and carved and polished perfection of the Alhambra's Court of the Lions. Or it may be loose and casual. Growing things, including humans, are often symmetrical, for the seed or the cell may be by nature symmetrical, and thus also are the shapes evolved through their development or growth. But in the natural landscape plan, symmetry is a rarity. Where observed, therefore, symmetry generally indicates an imposed system of order.

It is revealing to note that in the Western world the word *symmetrical* is often taken to be synonymous with beautiful and has the connotation of pleasant and handsome form. Perhaps this is because it implies an order to the scheme of things that is easily comprehended and thus enjoyed by humans. Perhaps it is because the word *symmetry* has come to be associated with plan clarity, balance, rhythm, stability, and unity, which are all positive qualities. Perhaps it is because we ourselves are symmetrical and take pleasure in the relationship.

Court of the Lions, the Alhambra, Spain.

The Visual Landscape 101

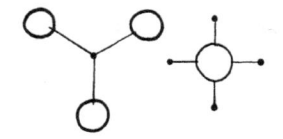

About a point or area

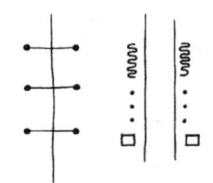

About an axis or plane

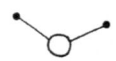

Bilateral—as the double wings of a maple seed

Trilateral—as the grappling hook

Multilateral—as the snowflake

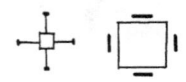

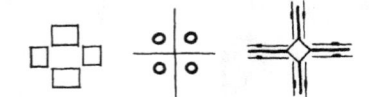

Quadrilateral—as by geometry

Symmetry: plan elements in equilibrium.

Dynamic Symmetry

When, by symmetry, two opposing elements or structures are seemingly held apart, an apparent attraction and tension develops between them. The two are strongly related, to the point that the opposing elements read as one, together with the intervening space and all that it contains.

The symmetrical plan has a quality of stability. Each pole generates its own field of force, and between these two fields is a field of dynamic tension. Each element within this field is at once in tension and in repose. By definition, every symmetrical composition must be in balance and, therefore, in repose. But the repose of symmetry is the more compelling for the fact that it bespeaks the resolution of myriad opposing forces held in equilibrium.

The Despotism of Symmetry

The symmetrical plan subjects plan elements to a rigid or formalized layout. Each feature must always be considered as a unit in the grand composition.

Sometimes a symmetrical plan may give added emphasis to objects. Such an object, for instance, might be featured as the terminus of a major or minor axis. Or it might be given greater importance through a progressively evolving sequence of approach or by its relationship to complimentary or complementary features. Usually, however, it may be said that the more powerful the total plan, the less potent the individual plan unit.

A symmetrical plan subjects a landscape to control. It systematizes the landscape. It organizes the landscape into rigid patterns. The natural environment is reduced to a setting or background for the plan composition.

A symmetrical plan subjects people to plan conformity. Not only are the landscape and all plan features subjugated to an organized plan of things, but so are we as well. We are held transfixed by a diagram of pattern. Our lines of movement are limited to the lines of the plan. The plan forms control our vision. We are consciously stirred or lulled by developing cadence, balanced repetitions, and the subjugation of all things to one concept. We are attuned subconsciously, as if by hypnosis, to the rhythmic symmetrical order of things and find ourselves in all ways conforming to the order of the plan. This conformity induces a sense of harmony, but if overworked it may often produce monotony and boredom.

It can be realized, however, that symmetrical plan forms, if skillfully handled, may be used to dramatize a concept and to evoke a sense of discipline, high order, and even divine perfection.

There is no such thing as "beauty by symmetry," with the exception of those cases where, because of the nature of the problem and its logical solution, the "balance" line of design happens to coincide with the middle line of symmetry. Only in such cases is symmetry logical and thus beautiful.

Eliel Saarinen

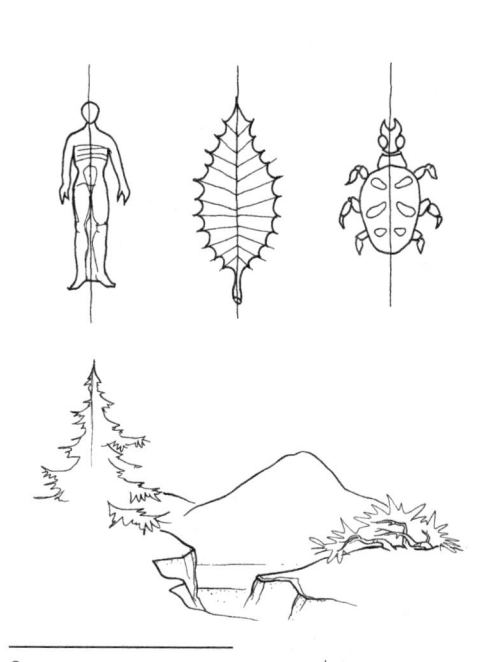

Symmetry in nature—growing objects in nature are often symmetrical because of the bilateral formation of their germ cell or seed; the natural landscape, a product of infinitely divergent forces, is rarely symmetrical.

The notion of identical figures to the right and left of an axis was not the basis of any theory in ancient (European) times.

Camillo Sitte

The Greeks used symmetry when appropriate, they did not use symmetry when not appropriate, and they never used symmetry in their (site) planning layouts.

Eliel Saarinen

The Nature of Symmetry

The symmetrical plan becomes a structural framework, compartmentalizing site features and functions. To be successful, such an arrangement must be an expression of the logical relationship of the features or functions so grouped. The rhythmically recurring elements of a symmetrical scheme divide the plan field into units. Each such unit, complete in itself, must still be related as a segment to the total plan.

Usually, the symmetrical plan has a strong relationship to adjacent structures. Often it is designed to extend such structures or to relate two or more of them. Such a plan is the familiar campus quad, an expanse of greensward crisscrossed with walks, flanked by dormitories and classrooms, and perhaps featuring on its long axis the library or chapel at one end and on the other the administrative center. College buildings symmetrically placed on their quadrangle may express a closely knit and well-balanced community of learning. Such a grouping is better suited to buildings of classic context and to areas where a sense of established order is to be engendered.

Symmetry is unsuccessful if it obviously forces unsymmetrical functions to a symmetrical plan arrangement. This is a common error in plan organization. It is painful to discover an important function balanced against the trivial. It is pathetic to find a plan area contorted beyond workability in order to achieve a visual balance with an area of dissimilar use. It seems dishonest to disguise a function or falsify a form to comply with the dictates of symmetry. If Keats was right in his observation that truth and beauty are one and the same, then such symmetry can never be beautiful, for not only must a plan be truthful to be beautiful, its truth must be evident.

Symmetry is a coordinator. It has application whenever it might be helpful in the comprehension of the whole of the plan or the relationship of the parts.

A symmetrical plan may be of crystalline form. This may be desirable if the function is by nature crystalline in its pattern of growth and expansion.

A symmetrical plan may be of geometric design. Such plan geometry may be excellent, but only if the function can be logically expressed in geometric line and form.

There are those who believe that geometry is the root of all beauty and that beauty of form and pattern can be consistently achieved by the application of mathematical formulas to the planning process. This thinking, they hold, gains support from the fact that people take pleasure in the comprehension of order. The writer contends, however, that the preference is generally for order over chaos rather than for symmetry over asymmetry.

The Visual Landscape

A plan that imposes geometry without reason may destroy desirable landscape character or may neutralize the inherent qualities of the areas or objects affected.

A geometric plan, direct and obvious, is quickly comprehended. It thus has the advantage of clarity. It has also the disadvantage of monotony if seen often or for long.

A geometric plan is not valid in the context of that which is natural or when it is intended that the human eye and mind and spirit be set free.

In far too many cases, symmetrical plans are conceived as a design expedient, a sort of geometric doodling. Such plans are repetitious and dreary, as uninspired as their authors. When geometric layouts are truly fitting, it is found that their symmetry is derived through clear logic and a conscious synthesis of all plan forms into symmetrical plan arrangement as the highest and best expression of the function. When appropriate and when intelligently applied in limited areas, symmetry is a plan form of compelling power.

Asymmetry

In nature, we can seldom find the elements of a landscape symmetrically balanced on either side of a line of sight. Yet visual balance is fundamental

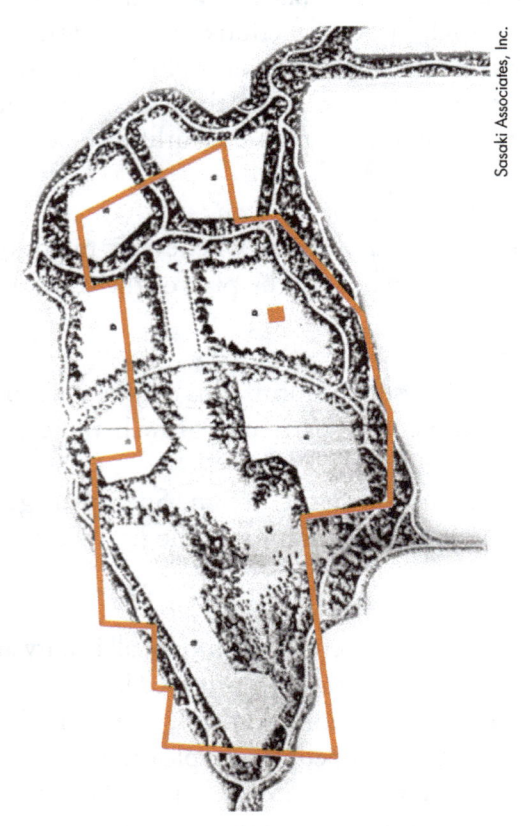

Olmstead plan (1865).

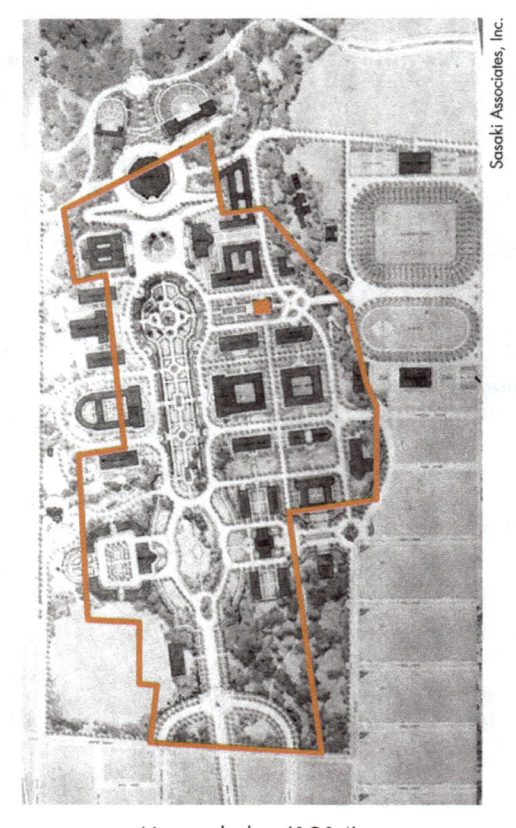

Howard plan (1914).

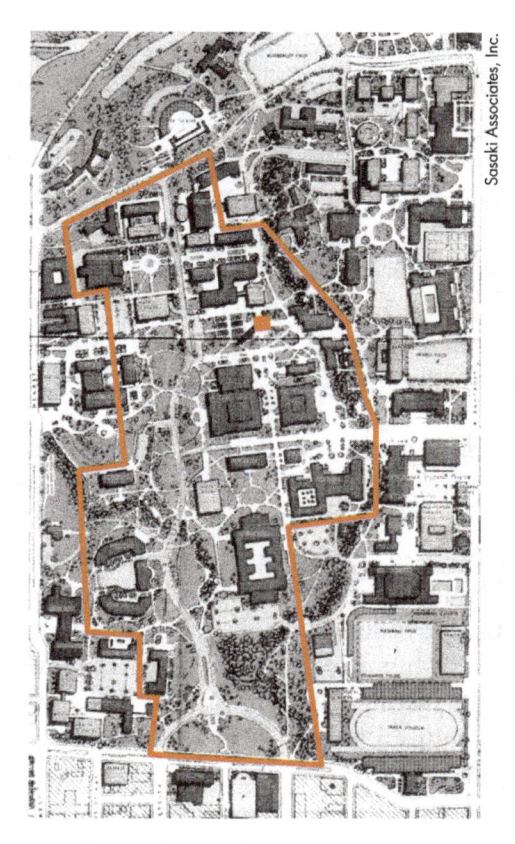

Church plan (1962). 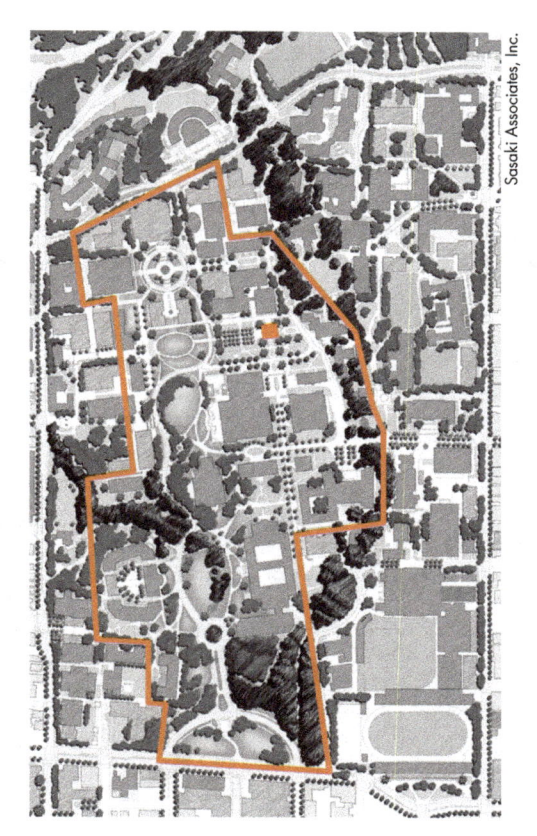   New Century plan (2002).
Plans for the University of California, Berkeley, displaying elements of symmetry and asymmetry.

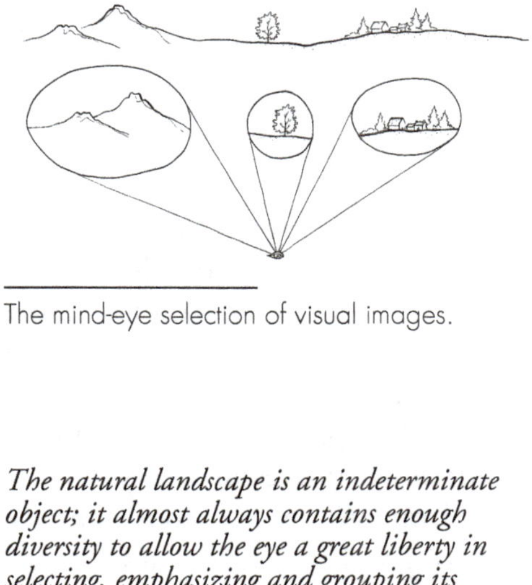

The mind-eye selection of visual images.

The natural landscape is an indeterminate object; it almost always contains enough diversity to allow the eye a great liberty in selecting, emphasizing and grouping its elements, and it is furthermore rich in suggestion and in vague emotional stimulus. A landscape to be seen has to be composed....
George Santayana

The eye, especially, demands completeness.
Johann Wolfgang von Goethe

to all satisfactory composition and to all art. It is generally conceded that any design, any picture, or any view or vista that lacks such balance is disturbing and unpleasant. Because we usually think of natural landscapes as being pleasant to look at, we might conclude that visual balance must somehow be inherent. This brings to mind two intriguing questions.

First, until an observer wanders along, how could there be visual balance? And then, does it not seem highly improbable that, from any given point of observation, the landscape should happen to balance visually on either side of a line of sight? Upon reflection it would seem, rather, that the eye must find or define in any landscape those vistas, views, or sight lines that produce a satisfactory visual balance. The trained eye is offended by the unbalanced and attracted to the balanced and tends constantly to seek out and bring into register those sections or portions of the visual landscape that provide a pleasant optical resolution of forces.

Visual Balance

The human eye is constantly darting about, probing and exploring a vague and luminous flux of evolving visual impressions. These are sensed subconsciously. At intervals, the mind permits or directs the eye to bring out of optical limbo and into conscious focus certain visual images. This

The Visual Landscape

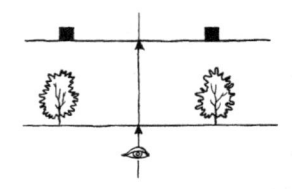

Symmetrical balance: equal and like masses balanced on either side of an optical axis or fulcrum.

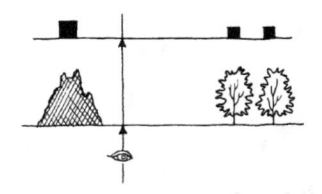

Asymmetrical occult balance: unequal and unlike masses balanced on either side of an optical axis.

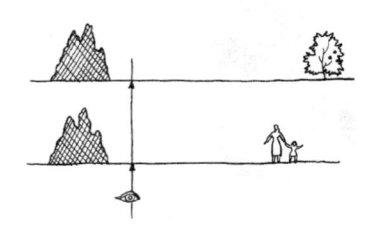

Asymmetrical occult balance: equilibrium achieved by mind-eye evaluation of form, mass, value, color, and association.

Occult balance.

We live in the midst of a whirlwind of light qualities. From this whirling confusion we build unified entities, those forms of experience called visual images. To perceive an image is to participate in a forming process; it is a creative act.
Gyorgy Kepes

Balance may also consist in a disposition of objects not similar nor similarly placed, but still so chosen and arranged that the sum of the attractions on one side of the vertical axis is equalled by the sum of the attractions on the other side. This kind of balance is called unsymmetrical or occult balance.
Henry V. Hubbard

is a creative effort. For the mind demands that the eye compose a visual image that is complete and in equilibrium. This is a joint mind-eye effort, for the acceptable equilibrium is not one of form balance, value balance, or color balance alone but one of associative balance as well. The mind-eye team may give little weight to a massive object that has no associative value, but it may give much weight to that which has strong associative value or immediate interest. A ripe apple swaying on a branch may thus outweigh the tree itself, or a chunk of rose quartz outweigh the mountain from which it was broken, or a solitary sunbather outweigh the immensity of a seascape.

Thus no two mind-eye combinations scanning a scene could ever bring into register an identical visual image or combination of images. For a scene has no limits, and the possibilities of selective composition are endless. But, by a vastly complicated series of instantaneous subconscious adjustments, each individual creates out of optical impressions visual images that for that particular observer are in equilibrium and, therefore, complete. The more sensitive and perceptive the mind-eye combination has become through instinct or training, the richer, the more delightful, and the more wondrous is the visual world that it reveals.

The child or the primitive perceives only objects in space. A more highly developed mind and a more selective eye perceive relationships. It can be seen that only rarely in nature would a sensed composition be balanced symmetrically on either side of a visual axis, but because equilibrium is required of all visual images, it must be possible to have balance without bilateral symmetry. This is indeed the case. Such asymmetrical, or *occult*, balance is the norm. Except in those cases in which bilateral symmetry has for some reason been contrived, it is by occult balance that we compose and comprehend the world about us.

Asymmetric Planning

Asymmetric planning brings us into closest harmony with nature. Freed of the rigidity of the symmetrical plan, each area may be developed with a fuller regard for its natural landscape qualities. Circulation is more free. Views are of infinite variety. Each object in the landscape may be seen and enjoyed for itself or its relationship to other landscape elements rather than for its relationship to a prescribed plan diagram. Such plan asymmetry is more subtle, casual, refreshing, interesting, and human. We are not led step by step along or through a rigid composition. We are, rather, set free to explore for ourselves and to discover in the landscape that which we may find to be beautiful, pleasant, or useful.

Asymmetric planning requires less disturbance of the natural or built landscape. Because it is developed in sympathy with the site, it normally requires less grading, screening, and construction. It is therefore more economical.

When for any reason the eye is to be habitually directed to a single point—as to an altar, a throne, or a stage—there will be violence and distraction caused by the tendency to look aside in the recurring necessity of looking forward, if the object is not so arranged that the tensions of eye are balanced, and the center of gravity of vision lies in the point which one is obliged to keep in sight.
George Santayana

In seeking now a reasonably solid grasp on the value of the word, organic, we should at the beginning fix in the mind the values of the correlated words, organism, structure, function, growth, development, form. All of these words imply the initiating pressure of a living force and a resultant structure or mechanism whereby such invisible force is made manifest and operative. The pressure, we call function—the resultant, form. Hence the law of form discernable throughout nature.
Louis H. Sullivan

The term organic design need not be an empty platitude. Biology has many valuable hints to offer the designer. . . . Indeed, there is much that could be said in support of a biological approach to the entire process of design, mainly in the sense that one broad biological field, known as ecology, undertakes to investigate the dynamic relations of all the organisms—both fauna and flora—in natural association with each other and with the other forces of the total environment in a given area of the surface of the earth.
Norman T. Newton

Architecture is not an art, it is a natural function. It grows on the soil like animals and plants. It is a function of the social order. Don't forget that.
Fernand Léger

Organic Growth

The jack pine growing on the mountain slope sends out its probing roots in search of soil pockets and moisture. Its trunk and limbs are braced against the winds, its needle clusters are held up and extended as a living mesh, to best soak in the cool, drifting morning fogs and to absorb the utmost vitality from the light and warmth of the sun. It shapes itself to the patch of ground—the furrow and ridge, the rivulet, the stump, the fallen log, the boulder. It responds to the encroachment and to the protection of its neighbors. When a tip is bent or broken, a new tip is formed. When a branch is smashed or torn away, the wound is healed and the gaping void is filled with new wood or with fresh twigs and needles. All positive qualities of the environment are utilized. All negative factors are overcome to the limits of possibility. The form of the pine is expressive of its development in harmony with its environment. This age-old process we know to be the process of *organic growth*.

Organic Planning

Organic planning, so widely touted and so seldom practiced, is fundamentally neither more nor less than the organic development of plan areas, volumes, and forms in response to all environmental constraints and opportunities. Symmetrical plan form can seldom be organic in this sense, except in those rare instances in which the essential quality of the use is such that, given unrestrained freedom and developmental conditions, its most logical plan expression would be symmetrical. It can be seen that even in such a case the impact of natural landscape features would tend to disrupt the symmetry.

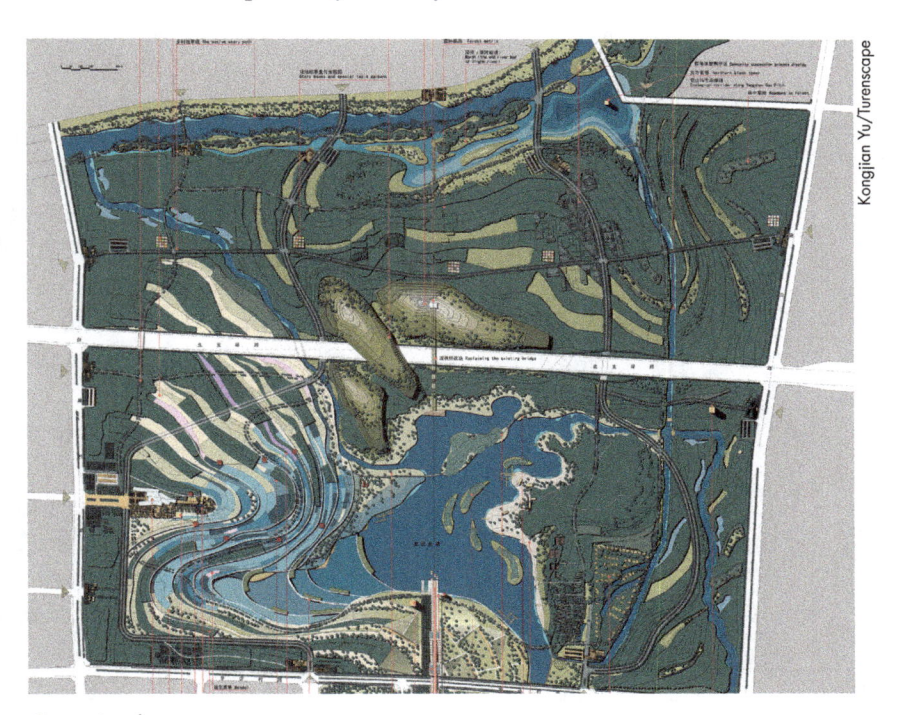

Organic plan.

The Visual Landscape

The basic law—in all fields of creation workers are striving today to find purely functional solutions of a technological-biological kind: that is, to build up each piece of work solely from the elements which are required for its function. But function *means here not a pure mechanical service. It includes also the psychological, social, and economical conditions of a given period. It might be better to use the term* organic *[functional] design.*
László Moholy-Nagy

Let me remind you of a famous passage in which Samuel Taylor Coleridge defined organic form. In a lecture on Shakespeare, given in 1818, he made a distinction between what he called mechanic form and organic form. "Form is mechanic," he said "when on any given material we impress a predetermined form, not necessarily arising out of the properties of the material." Organic form, on the other hand, is innate; shaping itself from within, as it develops, so that "the fullness of its development is one and the same with the perfection of its outward form."
Jacob Bronowski

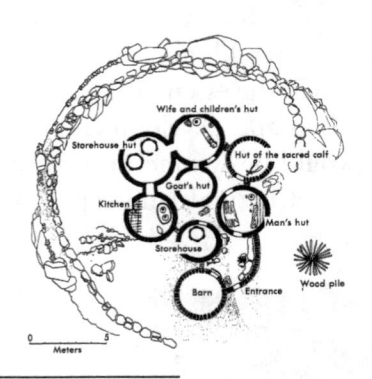

Organic planning: functional room arrangement of family dwelling. Cameroon.

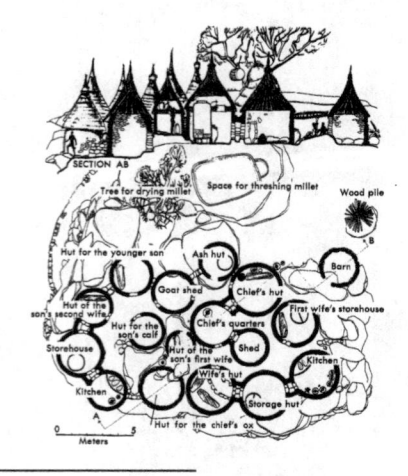

Organic cell cluster arrangement of rooms: residence of Cameroon chief.

It is abundantly apparent that, in the great preponderance of cases, the logical site-structure or site-project diagram will be asymmetrical. If the diagram expresses a use or a complex of uses well suited to a site, and if, in plan refinement, each function is developed in best relationship to other functions and to all positive and negative factors of the site, then such planning is truly organic.

Most things in nature, as well as most structures, are best appreciated when seen in the round. The asymmetric plan best provides such viewing. The approach of the observer to each plan element is meandering rather than fixed, giving a sense of modeling and third dimension. This plastic (sculptural) quality of an object, revealing its nature, shape, and detail, can be appreciated only if the observer moves around or past the object. Even the pictorial quality of a landscape is imbued with greater interest when observed from a constantly changing line of observation.

An axis may be developed asymmetrically. Such a treatment preserves the positive features of the axis while allowing greater plan flexibility. True, it precludes the controlled, measured cadence and hypnotic induction of bilateral symmetry—qualities which, we have found, are in some few cases highly desirable—but the asymmetrically treated axis has much more universal application.

The Use of Asymmetry

Asymmetry is well suited to large-scale urban planning. The most pleasant squares of Europe are asymmetrical. What a sad day it would be for San Marco in Venice if the piazza were to be reconstructed in rigid symmetry. The wonder and charm of such towns as Siena, Verona, and Florence would be lost to a symmetrical handling of their streets and buildings and spaces.

The most magnificent garden of history, the Yuan Ming Yuan, or Garden of Perfect Brightness, which today lies in ruin to the west of Beijing, was scrupulously asymmetric in plan, as attested to by Jean Denis Attiret, a French priest who many years ago found his way to the court of Emperor Ch'ien-lung. In 1743, he wrote to a friend in France describing its wonders (as quoted by Hope Danby in *The Garden of Perfect Brightness*):

> One quits a valley, not by fine straight allées as in Europe, but by meandering and circuitous routes—and on leaving one finds oneself in a second valley entirely different from the first as regards the form of the land and the structure of the buildings. All the mountains and hills are covered with trees, especially with flowering trees, which are very common here. It is a veritable paradise on earth.
>
> Each valley . . . has its pleasance, small in comparison with the whole enclosure, but in itself large enough to house the greatest

LANDSCAPE ARCHITECTURE

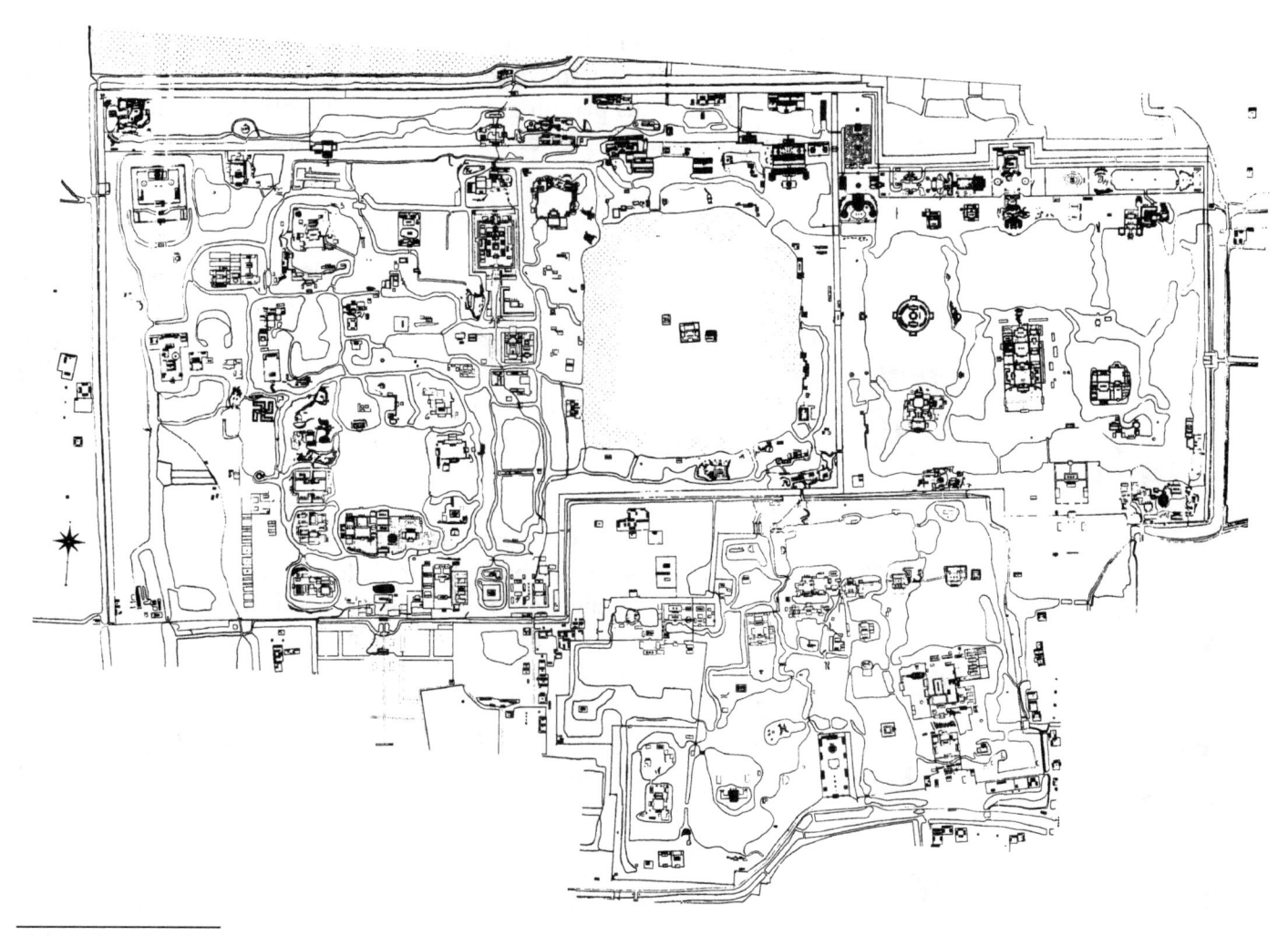

The Garden of Perfect Brightness.

I detest everything that is cold and academic. Only where the living purpose exists will new things be formed.
Eric Mendelsohn

Eighty-five percent of perception is based on sight.

of our European lords with all his retinue. But how many of these palaces would you think there are in the different valleys of this vast enclosure? There are more than two hundred.

In Europe, uniformity and symmetry are desired everywhere. We wish that there should be nothing odd, nothing misplaced, that one part should correspond exactly with the part facing it; in China also they love this symmetry, this fine order. The palace in Peking ... is in this style ... but in the pleasances there reigns a graceful disorder, an anti-symmetry is desired almost everywhere. Everything is based on this principle. When one hears this, one would think it to be ridiculous, that it must strike the eye disagreeably; but when one sees them one thinks differently and admires the art with which the irregularity is planned. I am tempted to believe that we [in eighteenth-century France] are poor and sterile in comparison.

The rash of symmetrical planning that marked the Renaissance in Europe had little reasonable basis. Far too often, it was symmetry solely for sym-

The Visual Landscape 109

metry's sake, a senseless forcing of the natural and built landscape into geometric patterns. No wonder our friend Attiret, like many others to follow, found this planning, by comparison with the freedom and rich variety of asymmetry, to be but "poor and sterile."

Visual Resource Management

Visual resource management is a relatively new, broad term describing planning and management practices directed toward preserving or enhancing the aesthetic quality of an area often referred to as a *viewshed*. The term is being applied by several public agencies to the technique of preserving and enhancing the nation's scenery. Innovative approaches are outlined in a number of well-prepared manuals that demonstrate a promising new concern.

Essentially, for any area or corridor of proposed for preservation, development or rehabilitation, both the scenic (aesthetically pleasing) and the blighting (visually incongruous) landscape features are inventoried and recorded by various graphic means and given a rating of their visual significance. Alternative proposals (e.g., for timber cutting, highway construction, extraction pits, reservoirs, or military installations) are then analyzed and evaluated for their relative benefits and negative visual impacts upon existing conditions. In deciding on the preferred route or course of action, the scenic considerations are shown to be telling, and often deciding, factors.

The procedures developed by the U.S. Forest Service are particularly sound, easy to understand, and effective. They are based on the premise that visitors to the national forests have an image of what they expect to see and that, insofar as possible, this expectation should be fulfilled.

They recognize and consider the numbers and types of viewers, the duration of viewing time, and the relative quality and intensity of the viewing experience. They assume that all lands are to be viewed on the ground, from passing roads or transitways, and from the air. They build upon the principle that all landscapes have a definable character and that those with the greatest dramatic power and/or variety have the greatest scenic value. They assess each potential view in terms of its foreground, midground, and background contribution. They give priority, in each scene, to the dominant elements in terms of line, form, color, and imagery. They consider the capacity of each landscape area to absorb alteration without loss of its visual character. Finally, they outline a systematic, step-by-step process of evaluation that makes good sense. Often, in the recommended procedures of some agencies, far too much emphasis is given to the numerical weighting and tabular mathematical rating of the various scenic elements. (How many points should be assigned, for instance, for a view of a historic church, an acre of mountain laurel, or a plummeting waterfall?)

Brochure promoting visual resource management.

110 LANDSCAPE ARCHITECTURE

Yosemite Falls.

It is suggested that in the assessment of scenic or any other values all quantifiable costs and benefits be computed and tabulated. The relative weight of these can be established with a fair degree of accuracy. Unquantifiable values, such as those of aesthetic, historical, or educational significance, can be reasonably evaluated only on a broad relative scale or on the basis of expert testimony in the presence of those who are to decide upon the merits of the alternatives.

The recent manuals on visual resource management are especially helpful as aids to untrained technicians and decision makers. Some provide the trained professional with welcome new insights and advanced approaches to the design of the visible landscape and have wide application.

Landscape Character

Looking down at the surface of our globe or moving in any direction across it, we find areas where there is an apparent harmony or unity among all the natural elements—ground forms, rock formations, vegetation, and even animal life. We may say of these areas that they possess a naturally produced landscape character. The more complete and obvious this unity, the stronger the landscape character.

The Natural Landscape

Let us imagine that we have been dropped into the uplands of Utah's great spruce forest. All about us rise wild and rugged slopes of rock bristling with tall evergreen spires that tower against the sky. The deep, shadowy ravines are choked with great boulders and fallen trees. Melting snow drips or trickles from the crevices or foams from high ledge to chasm, cascading toward the stillness of a mountain lake that lies below, deep blue at its center, shading to pale green along its gravelly edges.

Craggy coast.

Beach.

Dune.

112   LANDSCAPE ARCHITECTURE

Here all is in harmony, all is complete. Even the brown bear lumbering close to shore is clearly native to this place. The leaping trout, the wading tern, the caw caw of the flapping crow are part of this scene, part of its landscape character.

The blazing desert, the fetid mangrove swamp, the rockbound California coast—each has its own distinctive landscape character, and each evokes in the observer a strong and distinctive emotional response. No matter what the natural landscape character of an area and no matter what the mood it produces in us—exhilaration, sadness, eeriness, or awe—we experience a very real pleasure in sensing the unity and harmony of the total scene. The more nearly complete this oneness and wholeness, the greater the pleasure of the observer.

The degree of evident harmony of the various elements of a landscape area is a measure not only of the pleasure induced in us but also of the quality we call beauty. For beauty is "the evident harmonious relationship of all the sensed components." Natural landscape beauty is of many varying qualities, which include:

The picturesque	The bizarre	The delicate
The stark	The majestic	The ethereal
The idyllic	The graceful	The serene

Natural landscape character, too, is of many categories, including:

Mountain	Lake	Canyon	Pond
Dune	Sea	Forest	Desert
Prairie	Stream	River	Plain
Swamp	Hill	Valley	

Each of these and other types may be further subdivided.

A forest landscape character, for instance, might be one of the following subtypes:

White oak	Larch	Cypress
Scarlet oak	Spruce	Sabal palm
Beech	Hemlock	Mangrove
Ash	White pine	New Jersey coastal
Maple	Red pine	New Jersey river
Aspen	Jack pine	New Jersey barrens
Cottonwood	Loblolly pine	Rocky Mountain
Redwood	Pinon pine	Douglas fir
Eucalyptus	Live oak	Mixed hardwood

An area of land that has common distinguishing visual characteristics of landform, rock formations, water forms, and vegetative patterns is termed

The Visual Landscape

a *landscape type*. When the major type is broad or diversified, there may be defined within it landscape subtypes of significant differentiation.

Of the myriad examples that come to mind, each is distinctive. The more closely an area or any object within it approaches the ideal (or has the most of those qualities that we associate with perfection in a given type), the more intense is our pleasure.

The opposite of beauty we call ugliness. Ugliness results from a sensed lack of unity among the components or the presence of one or more incongruous elements. Since that which is beautiful tends to please and that which is ugly tends to disturb, it follows that a visual harmony of all parts of a landscape is desirable.

Modification

With only the visual aspects of site character in mind, it would seem that in developing a natural area we should do all that we can to preserve and intensify its inherent landscape quality. We should therefore eliminate objects that are out of keeping, and we may even introduce objects to increase or accentuate this native character.

The elimination of an incongruous element will usually effect an improvement.

Incongruous elements in the landscape.

Elimination of Incongruous Elements

In all planning, as in life, the elimination of an incongruous element usually effects an improvement. Let us suppose, for example, that we have wandered into a giant sequoia forest and stand in silent awe of the tremendous upward thrust of the redwood boles and their imposing, timeless grandeur. And then suppose that on the forest floor we should

114   LANDSCAPE ARCHITECTURE

happen to notice a neatly cultivated bed of pink petunias. The same petunias in a suburban garden bed might make quite a pleasant splash. But to find them here in the redwood forest would first surprise and then annoy us. They would annoy us because our experience would tell us that in this natural redwood grove petunias are not in keeping. They would set up unpleasant visual and mental tensions, and should we come often enough to this place, it is possible, even probable, that we would ultimately root them out with the toe of our boot. We would be eliminating an element that was in conflict with the natural landscape character.

An incident from the coauthor's own experience further illustrates this point. As a small boy he spent summers in a camp on Lake George in the backwoods of Michigan. At the lower end of this lake he found a spot that he came to consider his private bullfrog pond. It was a clearing in the cattails, jammed with mossy logs and stumps and closed almost tight with the pads of water lilies. When he waded quietly through the cattails, he would spy huge green-black bullfrogs floating among the pads or squatting dreamily on the logs. These he hunted for their saddles, which were most welcome at the family table. Every day he visited his pond, lying hour after hour on a log, motionless, with a whittled birch rod poised ready for a frog to surface. It was an idyllic world of cedar smell, sunlight, patrolling dragonflies, lapping water, and contentment.

Gravity is one of man's greatest enemies. It has shaped man himself, conditioned his body as well as his thoughts, and put its unmistakable stamp upon his cities. Thus in the narrow winding valleys of the world, life is a continual battle with gravity. One must live on the valley's bottom, or "fight the slope" until his dying days.

Grady Clay

One morning he found that a battered yellow oil drum had been washed into his frog pond by a storm. He pushed it outside the cattails. Next morning it was back. Again he pushed it from the pond, farther this time, but not far enough. Finding it once again floating jauntily among the lily pads, he shoved it out and went for a rowboat. With the anchor rope he towed the drum to the deepest part of the lake, bashed a jagged hole in its top with a hatchet and scuttled it. As he watched it slowly founder, he wondered why he had felt such anger at an old, rusty metal barrel. Years later, when he recollected the pond in terms of its landscape character, he realized at last why the drum had to go. It was a disturbing, inharmonious element in the miniature landscape, and it had to be removed. (Note: In later years he also came to realize that the lake bottom was no place to leave a barrel.)

Accentuation of Natural Form

If it is true that the elimination of certain elements from an area can improve its landscape quality, it follows that other elements might be introduced with the same result. To accentuate the landscape quality of a site within or abutting a cactus desert, for instance, we might remove an old tire that had been tossed there and replace it with a clump of fine native cactus plants gathered from the surrounding sandy draws. Or we might plant a single picturesque Joshua tree that

The Visual Landscape

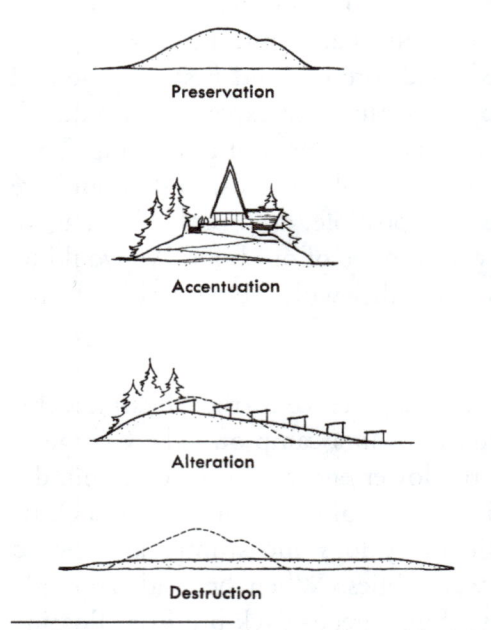

The four alternatives in the development of a hill.

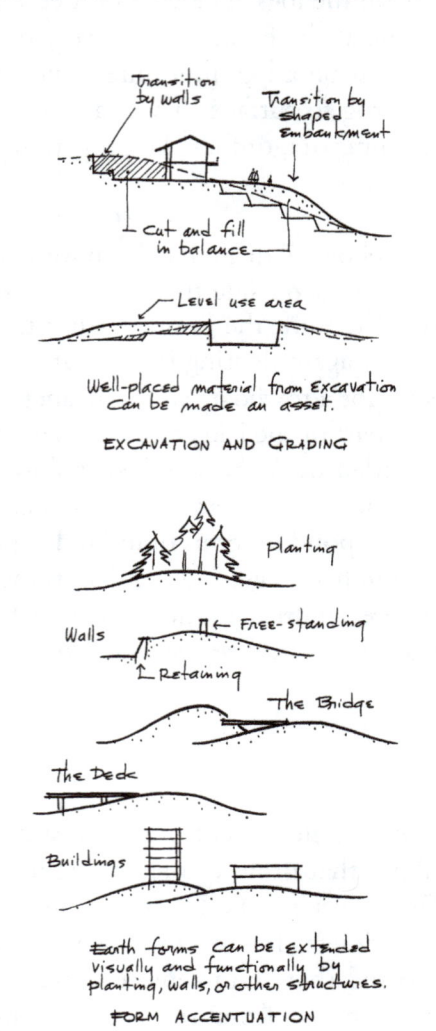

Red Rocks Amphitheater, Denver, Colorado.

would reflect and articulate the area's mood or landscape expression. To sum up, then, the landscape character of any area may be developed or intensified by eliminating any negative elements and by accentuating its positive qualities.

To improve a landscape or land area intelligently we must not only recognize its essential natural character but also possess knowledge that will enable us to achieve the optimum development of that character.

During the Ming dynasty in China this art was so highly refined that within a single garden of a few acres one might experience lofty mountain scenery, a misty lakeshore, a bamboo grove at the edge of a quiet pond, a pine-sheltered forest overlook, and a cascading waterfall. And, through the skill of the designer, the transition areas between viewing points were so masterfully contrived as to be fully as pleasant and dramatic as the major views themselves.

Major Features

There are dominant natural landscape forms, features, and forces that we can alter little, if at all. We must accept them and adapt ourselves and our planning to them. These unchangeable elements include such topographical forms as mountain ranges, river valleys, and coastal plains; such features as precipitation, frost, fog, the water table, and seasonal temperatures; and such forces as winds, tides, sea and air currents, growth processes, solar radiation, and gravity.

116   LANDSCAPE ARCHITECTURE

The natural site profile

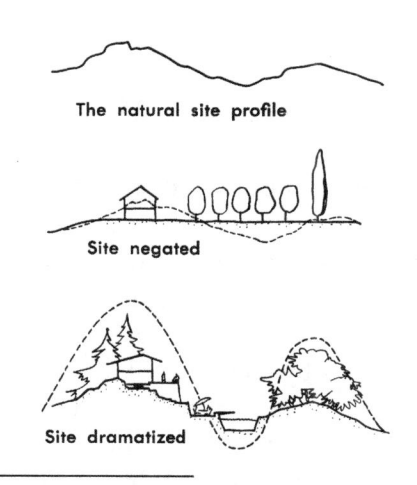

Site negated

Site dramatized

The essence of land planning for any project:
1. Seek the most suitable site.
2. Let the site suggest plan forms.
3. Extract the full site potential.

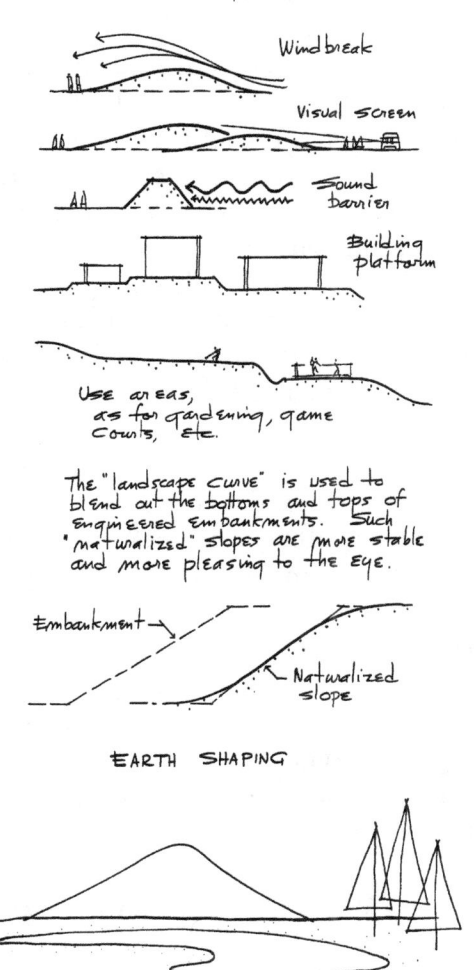

Windbreak

Visual screen

Sound barrier

Building platform

Use areas, as for gardening, game courts, etc.

The "landscape curve" is used to blend out the bottoms and tops of engineered embankments. Such "naturalized" slopes are more stable and more pleasing to the eye.

Embankment

Naturalized slope

EARTH SHAPING

In the natural landscape a human being can be an intruder.

These we analyze to the extent necessary to make an accurate assessment of their influence and effects. Then, if wise, we will shape our plans in full awareness of, and response to, the constraints and possibilities. Such considerations are fundamental to the placing of cities, the zoning of a community, the projected alignment of highways, the siting of industries, or the orientation and layout of a single home or garden.

The notable planning projects of any age demonstrate with clarity the adaptation of a structure or activity area to the landscape in such a way that the best qualities of each are made to complement the other. In such works, not only the constructed elements but the natural elements as well appear to have been designed by the planner, as in one sense they were, for all were considered together as integral parts of the total conceptual plan.

Minor Features

Taking a hill as an example, its landscape character may be such that its optimum yield or use is realized if it is carefully preserved from change. In its undisturbed state it might better produce its crop of timber, maple sap, nuts, or fruit. Throughout the United States we find huge tracts of land that have been set aside in their natural state as game preserves, parks, forests, or regional open space. In Japan many a village or town is nestled among hills or islands that have for centuries been left undisturbed by decree, in the best interest of the community.

Destruction of the Natural Form

A hill or knoll may be eliminated by grading; it may be split with a deep highway cut; it may be inundated by an impoundment; or it may be buried in construction. If any such treatment is proposed, its original landscape character need not be a consideration except as it poses a physical problem.

Alteration of the Natural Form

The native aspect of a hill may be altered or changed completely by modifying its shape through grading, construction, or other types of development. Such changes may be detrimental and result in a denuded, eroded, or hacked-up mound, or they may effect an improvement, as at the site of Chicago's Botanic Garden, where an eroded farm and polluted sump were converted to a whole new landscape of hills, sculptured slopes, freshwater lakes, streams, and lagoons as a receptive garden setting.

The Visual Landscape

Intensification

The essential landscape character of a hill may be intensified. Its apparent height and ruggedness may be increased to such a degree, for instance, that a small knoll may be made to appear precipitous.

Let us assume, for example, that we are the owners of a resort hotel in New Hampshire to which summer guests come each season for fresh air, rest, and exercise. We have noticed that many of the guests, for diversion, walk the easy path to the top of a nearby rise from which they can view the countryside. It occurs to us that the hill has become an important part of the resort life, and we decide during the off-season to improve this feature by giving it more interest and affording more of a climb to its top.

First, by transplanting a patch of hemlocks, we block off the easy path that led toward the hill and break a new path to a spring that bubbles from the rocks at its base. From this spring a view is opened up across the steepest face of the hill to a weathered old pine, which hides the hilltop beyond. A rough trail leads up through a pile of lichen-splotched rocks to a fallen tree trunk, on which the hiker can sit and rest. Already the hemlocks and spring and rocks have given a new perspective to the hill. Next the path winds easily down through a native birch clump to the far side of the hill, where the only way ahead leads steeply up the roughest, wildest part of the hillside. Up, down, and around the trail leads, from ferny ledge to fallen tree, to view, and finally to a point where it breaks out on top. There we place a rough stone slab for a seat, in the shelter of a granite outcrop.

Next summer, when our guests leave the porch and set out to walk to the hilltop, they find themselves hiking and climbing over a beautiful natural terrain they have never seen before. Through tangled wild-grape cover, around narrow ravines, pulling themselves from rock to rock, they carefully pick their way until they finally reach the summit. They have made it! Nothing, they may think as they rest, enjoying the view, is more exhilarating than mountain climbing. While 800 feet away and 200 feet below them, the oldsters sit rocking on the veranda, looking placidly out at the hill. For our purpose, we have eliminated the negative aspects of our hill and accentuated its positive qualities.

Any area of the natural landscape—pond, island, hillside, or bay—can be developed in this manner.

Early in his career the coauthor was engaged by the Michigan State Department of Parks in the planning of several campgrounds. His first assignment was to develop a site in northernmost Michigan as a state park for tourists, who would come to experience the joys of "wilderness living." Upon arrival at the park site, he found a large white "Public Park" sign at the entrance of a farm road that led in through a flat field of wild carrots to a trailer parking lot beside a muddy pond—not much of a wilderness campsite.

The planner's first step was to spend several weeks exploring the tract to become acquainted with all its natural features, good and bad. His aim was to utilize these features to the utmost. He proposed, in short, to intensify the native landscape quality of the site.

As a first step in the improvement program, the entrance road was moved from the open field to the thickest stand of balsam. Here a rough trail was carved through the rock and snaked up a ridge between the tree trunks, so that a camper's car or trailer could just ease through. The caretaker's sagging clapboard cottage with its red-and-white-painted window boxes was demolished and replaced with a rough-sawn slab cabin near the base of a towering pine. This change was made because the camper's first impression of the campsite would be of this venerable tree and the cabin in its shadow, and first impressions are usually the most lasting.

The site's main attraction, a spring-fed pond, was drained, scooped out, and developed as a natural swimming pool with a clean sand and gravel bottom. Above it, a large area of water was impounded to form a settling basin, and here the marsh birds, muskrats, and other wildlife could be seen from a timber bridge that was arched across the dam. At the lower end of the swimming pool a second bridge was built across the waterfall and spillway, where large speckled trout rolled and swam in the sparkling water of the pool below.

Trails were slashed through the densest cover and between the most jagged ledges. Every point of interest was strung on the new trail system like an offset bead.

In one of the more remote areas, a colony of beavers inhabited a stream, where they had built a dam. Much thought was given to the best way of displaying these shy creatures, a prize in any park. It was decided that to view them the hikers must find their way along an unmarked game trail as it threaded tenuously through a deep cedar swamp until, from the sloping trunk of a great fallen tree that overhung the pond, the hikers could look down to discover the beaver workings below them.

In the development of any land or water area, the landscape designer will focus on the essential effect to be conveyed (one inherent in the site). By emphasis, by articulation, and by the creation of progressive sequences of revealment, the observer will be led to discover the positive features of the locale and thus exact its full pleasurable impact.

Mont-Saint-Michel, France, surrounded by its rushing tides and reached only by causeway, is an ingenious and powerful adaptation of structure to natural forces and forms.

The Built Environment

Up to this point we have considered the natural landscape as something to be observed, as in some of our larger parks, for example, or along scenic parkways, or at the better resort hotels. In such cases a person becomes a microvisitor, permitted only to enter an area inconspicuously, observe respectfully, and leave unobtrusively. But there are relatively few areas that can be preserved in their pristine state or developed solely for the display of their natural beauty.

Use

We generally consider land in terms of use. At this point one is quite likely to ask: "What's all this talk about beauty and landscape character? What I want to know is, how can this property be used?"

But the hard, cold fact of the matter is that the most important factor in considering the use of land is a thorough understanding of its landscape character in the broadest sense. For the planner must first comprehend the physical nature of the site and its extensional environment before it is possible to:

- Recognize those uses for which the site is suited and that will utilize its full potential.
- Introduce into the area only those uses which are appropriate.
- Apply and develop such uses in studied relationship to the landscape features.
- Ensure that these applied uses are integrated to produce a modified landscape that is functionally efficient and visually attractive.
- Determine whether or not a project is unsuited and would be incongruous not only on the immediate site but in the surrounding environs as well and thus appear to be misplaced, unfit, and (by definition) ugly. Such an improper use would be disturbing not only aesthetically but practically, for an unsuitable use forced upon an unreceptive parcel of land generates frictions that may not only destroy the most desirable qualities of the landscape area but preclude proper function of the development as well.

Suitability

Since we are repelled by disorder, the discordant, and that which is ugly, since we are instinctively drawn to that which is harmonious and well formed, and since most artifacts and developments are designed to please, it follows that resultant beauty is a highly desirable attribute.

It is compatible; it seems well suited to its place. It works well; there is an efficient arrangement of all the parts. It looks good; it is beautiful; I like it.

Anything planned in the landscape affects the landscape. Each new plan application sets up a series of reactions and counterreactions not only about the immediate site but upon its extensional environment as well. This environment may extend a great distance in any direction and may include many square miles.

In considering the development of any area of the earth's surface, we must realize that this surface is a continuous plane. A project applied to this plane affects not only the specific site but all flow past it. Each addition or change, however minute, imposes upon the land certain new physical properties and visual qualities. It can thus be seen that the planner is engaged in a continuing process of landscape modification.

Harmony

The untouched landscape is in repose, a repose of equilibrium. It has its own cohesive, harmonious order in which all forms are an expression of geologic structure, climate, growth, and other natural forces. In the primeval forest or upon the open plain, the human is an intruder.

Esthetic impacts influence us at all moments. Consciously, or in most cases subconsciously, they provoke friendly or hostile reactions. . . . Their impacts on . . . decisions reach into even the most practical problems, into the shaping of things of daily use—cars, bridges—and above all, of our human environment.
Siegfried Giedion

Structure in harmony with surroundings. Crosby Arboretum, Picayune, Mississippi.

The Visual Landscape 121

If one penetrates the wilderness by trail or road, one may either roll with the topography and develop expressive harmonies or buck the terrain and generate destructive frictions. As human activity in an area increases, the landscape becomes more and more organized—agreeably if the organization is one of fitting relationships, disagreeably if the relationships are chaotic or illogical. The development of any area may entail a concentration of its natural landscape character, an integration of nature and construction, or the creation of a wholly built complex of spaces and forms. In any case, the commendable plans are those that effect a resolution of all elements and forces and create a newly unified landscape of dynamic equilibrium.

We are all familiar with humanized landscape areas in which everything seems to be working well together. We recall pleasant stretches of New England farmland, western ranch territory, or Virginia plantation country. In or near such areas, we experience a sense of well-being and pleasure. We say that a certain town or region is quaint, delightful, or picturesque. What we probably mean is that we subconsciously sense certain qualities of compatibility that appeal to us. These we like. Other places of disorder, confusion, pollution, bad taste, or poor planning, are disagreeable and bother us. If we were traveling, these would be bypassed. We would prefer not to live in or near them.

The negative qualities of such places are those we would attempt to eliminate in any replanning process; the positive qualities are those we would strive to retain and accentuate. It would seem to follow as a guiding principle that *to preserve or create a pleasing site character, all the various elements or parts must be brought into harmony.*

We make much of this word *harmony.* Do we mean to imply that everything should blend with or get lost in the landscape as through protective coloration or camouflage? No, but rather that the planner, in addressing a land-water holding, from small plot to vast acreage, will so integrate the structural and topographical forms as to produce the best possible fit. If the completed project seems to blend with the landscape, it is the happy result of an inspired design rather than the mistaken aim of an uninspired designer.

Contrast

It is known that the form, color, or texture of a handsome object can be emphasized through contrast. This principle applies as well to planning in the landscape and is exemplified by the bridges of the brilliant Swiss engineer Robert Maillart. All who have seen them marvel at the lightness and grace of the white reinforced-concrete arches that span the wild mountain gorges in Switzerland and Bavaria. Surely the lines and materials of these structures are foreign to the natural character of the craggy mountain

It is not yet conceivable that a well-designed and well-placed building, a bridge or road, can be an addition rather than a menace to the countryside?
Christopher Tunnard

background. Are they right for such a location? Or would the bridges have been more suitable if constructed of native timbers and stone?

In our national parks, bridges have usually been built of indigenous materials. Although some may quarrel with this policy, it has produced many bridges of high design quality and spared the park-using public from more of the typical fluted and fruited cast-metal or balustraded cast-stone monstrosities that clutter up so many of our American river crossings.

In his bridge design, however, Maillart has simply and forthrightly imposed a necessary function—a highway crossing—on the natural landscape. He has expressed with logical materials and refreshing clarity the force diagram of his structures. Moreover, by sharply contrasting his elegantly dynamic bridges and the rugged mountain forest, he has dramatized the highest qualities of each. The gorges seem more wild, the bridges more precise, more eloquent.

As another application of the principle of contrast, we may recall in color theory that to produce an area of greenest green, a fleck of scarlet may be brought into juxtaposition. To make a spot of scarlet glow with fire, an artist brings it into contrast with the greenest possible background.

It follows that before introducing contrasting elements into a landscape it would be well to understand the nature of the features to be accentuated. The contrasting elements will then be contrived to strengthen and

To me the quest of harmony seems the noblest of human passions. Boundless as is the goal, for it is vast enough to embrace everything, it yet remains a definite one.
Le Corbusier

Robert Maillart Bridge.

The Visual Landscape

Fallingwater, Bear Run, Pennsylvania. The precision and lightness of the concrete forms contrast bodily with the natural forms, colors, and textures of the site. Yet the structure seems at home here. Why? Perhaps because the massive cantilevered decks recall the massive cantilevered ledge rock. Perhaps because the masonry walls that spring from the rock are the same rock tooled to a higher degree of refinement. Perhaps because the dynamic spirit of the building is in keeping with the spirit of the wild and rugged woodland. And perhaps because each contrasting element was consciously planned to evoke, through its precise kind and degree of contrast, the highest qualities of the natural landscape.

enrich the visual impact of these natural features. Conversely, to emphasize certain qualities of the structure or component introduced, one will search the landscape and bring into contrasting relationship those features that will effect the desired contrast.

A further principle in the use of contrast, as illustrated by the work of Maillart, is that of two contrasting elements one must dominate. One is the feature, the other the supporting and contributing backdrop. Otherwise, with two contrasting elements of equal power, visual tensions are generated that weaken or destroy, rather than heighten, the pleasurable impact of the viewing experience.

We have said that to create a pleasing character for an area all components must work together in harmony. We find striking examples that seem to violate this precept: Maillart's bridges, for instance, and Frank Lloyd Wright's Fallingwater at Bear Run. At first appraisal, these structures would seem to be completely alien to their surroundings. Yet with study, one senses in each a quality of fitness—of spirit, purpose, material, and form.

Lines of movement give shape to the built environment.

The Visual Landscape 125

Construction

We have considered natural landscape elements and their importance in the planning process. Constructed forms, features, and lines of force are major planning factors, too.

As we look at any road map, we find it crisscrossed with lines of various kinds and colors that we recognize as highways, minor roads, streets, railroads, ferryboat routes, and even subways. These lines seem innocuous enough on paper. But those of us who have zoomed along with the streaming traffic of a turnpike, or stood by the tracks as the *Limited* roared by, or tried to maneuver a catboat through the churning wake of a ferry will agree that the map lines tracing their path indicate powerful lines of force. Such lines are essential to the movement of people and goods, but unfortunately they may also be disruptive, sometimes lethal. Every few minutes someone in the United States is killed by a moving vehicle, and the incidence of serious injury is much higher. It must occur to us, if we ponder these facts, that we planners have as yet failed to treat transportation routes with the proper respect, or else we have not yet learned to design them with foresight and imagination.

There are countless other features of the built environment that, if perhaps less dominant, still have great effect on our planning. To understand their importance we might list a few that deserve investigation in project siting. For openers the list will include:

> Peripheral streets
> Walkway access
> Adjacent structures to remain
> Structures to be demolished
> Subsurface construction
> Energy sources and supply
> Utility leads and capacities
> Applicable zoning
> Building code and regulations
> Easements
> Deed restrictions

This sampling may in itself seem formidable, but it does not include such additional considerations as neighborhood character, general site aspects, mineral rights, amenities, public services, and so forth. Any one of these features might well spell the failure or success of an enterprise. The list will differ considerably, of course, with projects of such varying types as a residence, school, shopping mall, or marina.

If our plans are to respond to a wide variety of contrived and natural givens, how do we proceed? It is proposed that, starting down the list,

The ultimate principle of landscape architecture is merely the application and adjustment of one system to another, where contrasting subjects are brought into harmonious relationship resulting in a superior unity called "order."

Stanley White

Site character preserved and enhanced.

Development compatible with landscape character.

The Visual Landscape   127

each item in turn will be studied with regard to where the problems and possibilities lie. We will then maximize all possible benefits and reduce or eliminate, insofar as is feasible, any negative aspects. An ingenious solution has often converted liabilities into assets.

Compatibility

The most constant quality of the landscape is the quality of change. Aside from the processes of growth and the changing seasons, we are forever tugging and hauling at the land, sometimes senselessly, destroying the positive values and sometimes intelligently developing a union of

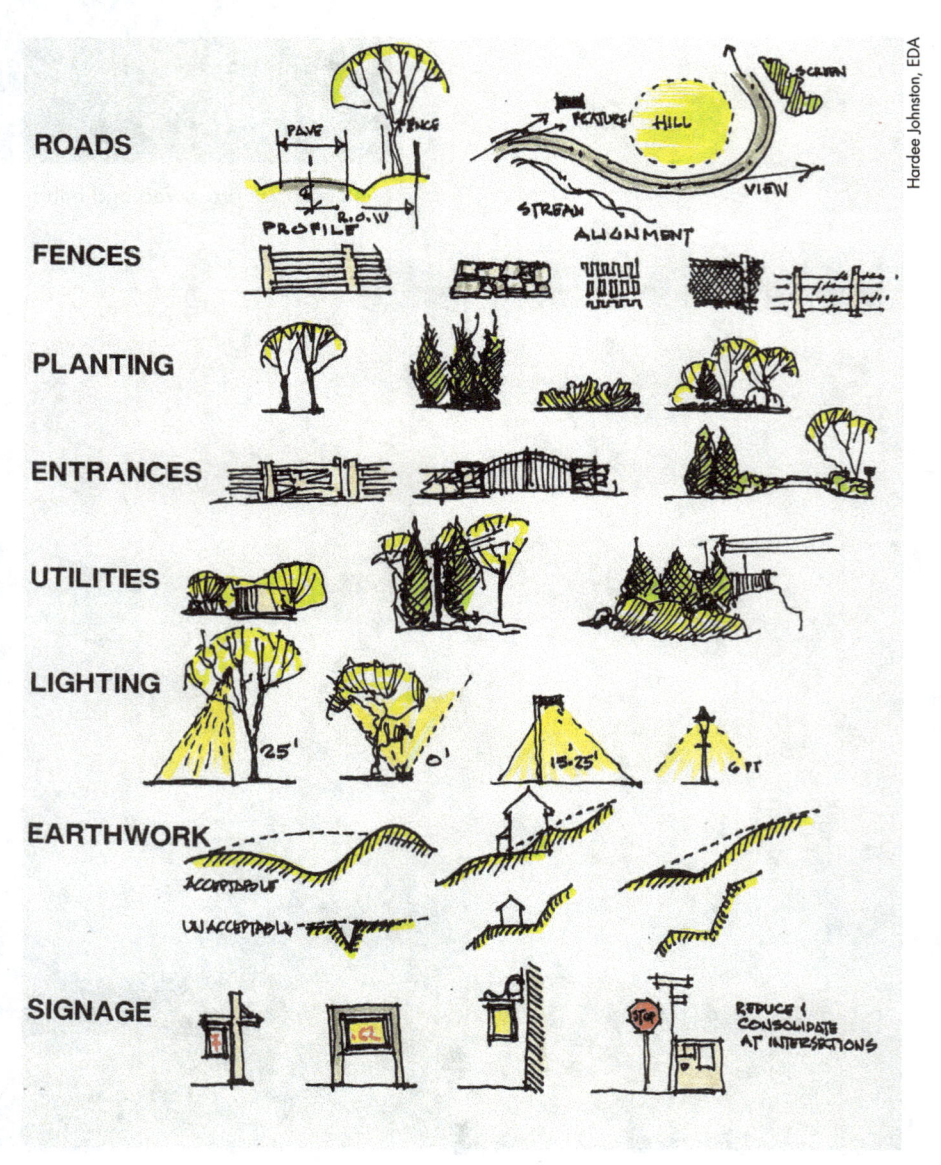

Elements of design in rural landscape.

128   LANDSCAPE ARCHITECTURE

function and site with such sensitivity as to effect an improvement. Whenever constructions are imposed on a site, its character is thereby modified.

Landscape evolution is a continuing process. At its best it is an ongoing exercise by which compatible uses are brought into harmonious interaction with our natural and built environs.

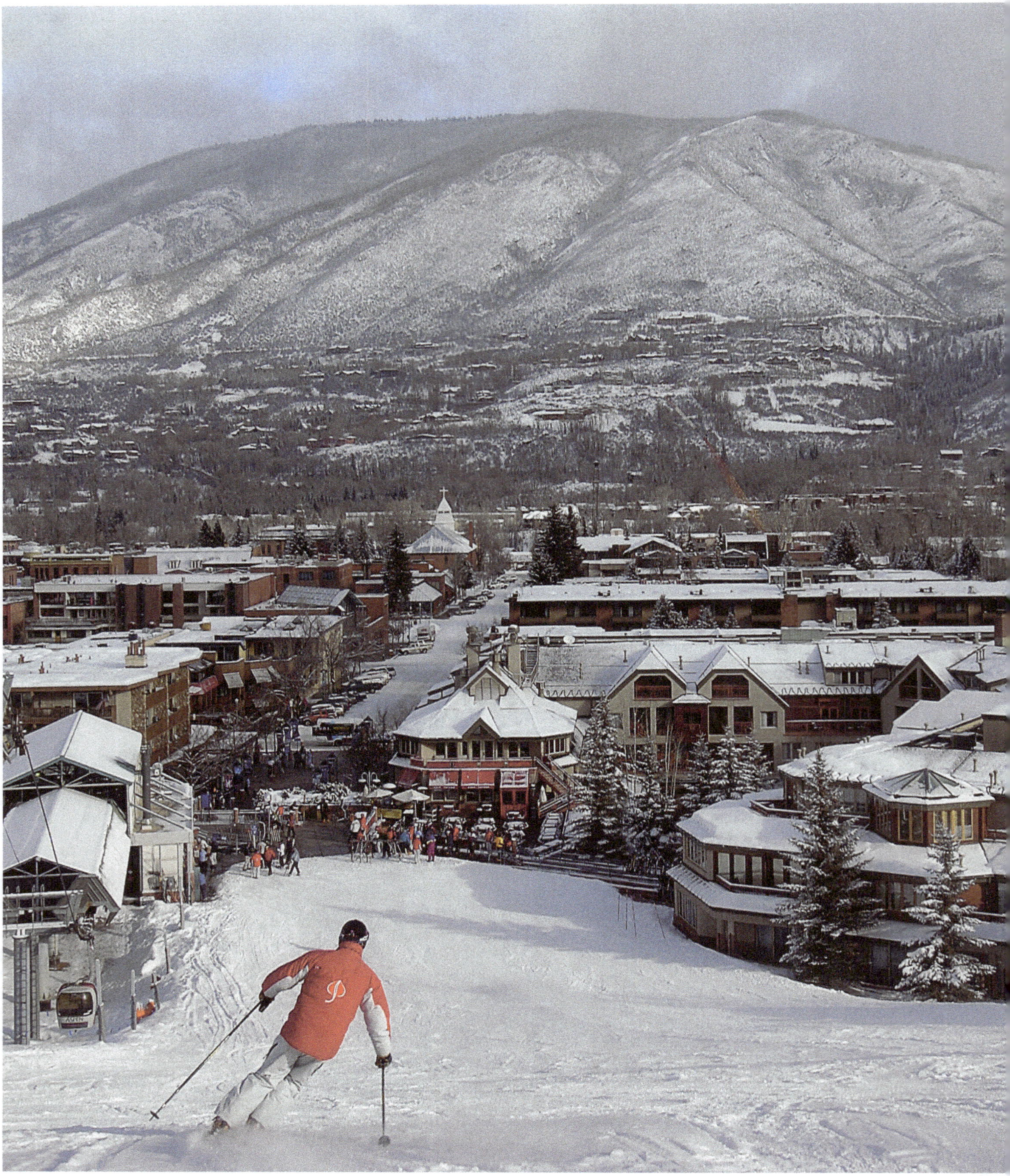

7
THE PLANNED ENVIRONMENT

Our country has passed, or perhaps is still passing, through a pioneering stage. Until very recently, one of our rugged freedoms has been our freedom to do with our land whatever we might wish. In the exercise of this dubious right we have voraciously exploited our natural wealth and ravished the land.

We have reduced millions upon millions of acres of forested watershed to eroded gullies and ruin. We have gouged enormous tracts of fertile land into barren wastes in our strip-mining operations. We have watched billions of cubic yards of rich topsoil wash out, irretrievably, to the sea. We have grossly polluted our streams and rivers with sewage and industrial waste. We have plundered our natural environment to a degree unprecedented in other civilizations. We have erred, and grievously. Now, late but at last, we have come to recognize the error of our ways.

In seeking to curb the waste and destruction, our present planning philosophy has been mainly one of restriction and prohibition. It has been, to a large degree, negative. No doubt such constraints have been helpful, but they are not enough. It is high time now that we reappraise our whole physical planning process, so that we may devise a positive approach more in keeping with our new understanding of land use.

© D.A. Horchner/Design Workshop

By proven planning techniques and legislative measures, the presently scattered urban components can be gathered up and regrouped into activity nodes of various types—each fitted harmoniously to the land, each more self-sufficient and complete, and each connected by parkways and aerial glideways to an intensified city-regional core.

Much of the new thinking falls under the category of dynamic conservation. This concept has its roots in the emerging realization of the need for stewardship, of caring for the earth, and of providing a sustainable living environment. All point to the need for comprehensive land use planning. Not a stance for the status quo, which is impossible to achieve. Not a negative approach of uncompromising opposition, block and delay, and endless litigation. Not a stubborn resistance to growth, which in the present scheme of things is in most areas destined to occur for the foreseeable future. But rather a cooperative approach by the public agencies and private enterprise working together to outline a long-range evolving land use plan by which orderly regional growth and development may best be accommodated.

A Conservation Credo

For what does the conservation movement stand?

- A long-term strategy for the wise and sustainable use, restoration, and replenishment of our natural resources
- The preservation of our ecologic, historic, and scenic superlatives
- Public access to beaches, shores, and open-space lands for compatible use and enjoyment
- The provision of scenic parkways, hiking and biking trails, and cross-country greenway corridors
- Controlled-access highways that sweep around, not through, plant and animal communities and human settlements
- The logic of carrying capacity in land use management, rather than (superficial) area zoning
- Communities fitted to and around the best features of the landscape
- An end to urban sprawl and the scourge of scatteration
- More compact and efficient cities and towns spaced out within a protected open-space frame of productive farmland, forest, and nature preserves
- The fostering through education of a caring concern for the well-being of planet Earth

Environmental Issues

We've heard much in recent years of environment concern. The concern is worldwide. Among the more knowledgeable, it often extends to the dimension of human survival. For many, the term *environment* is so vague and general that it has come to have little meaning. Yet while the term with its problems and possibilities has become so complex, the issues to be addressed are clear. Since they all affect or are affected by land planning, they are listed as follows, with brief comments suggesting proven solutions.

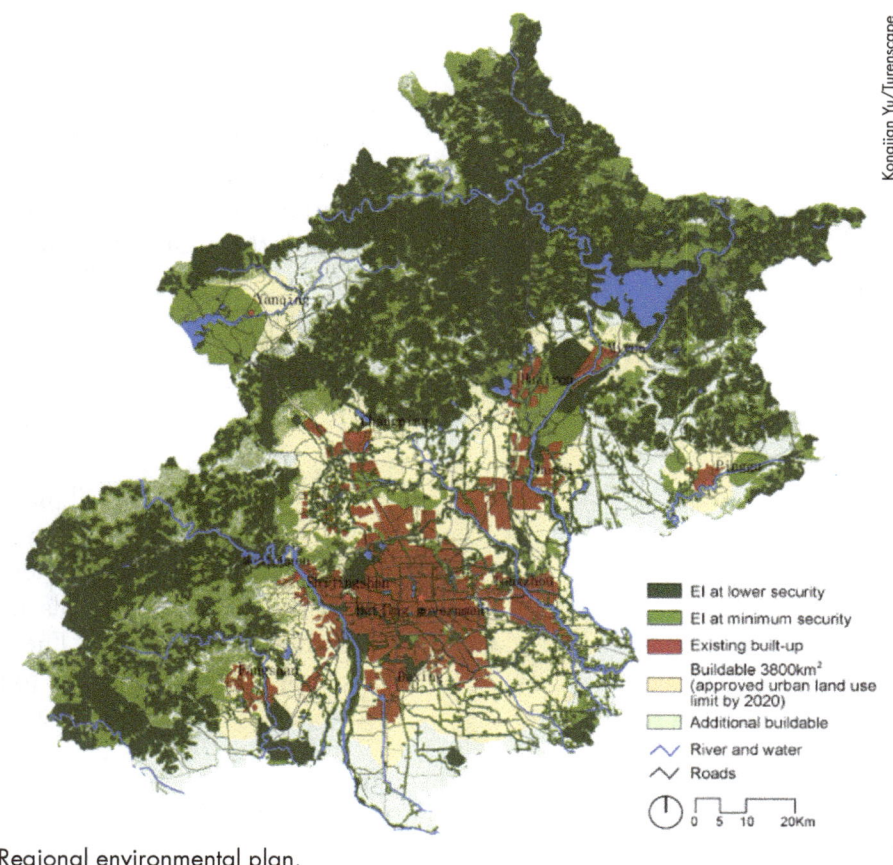

Regional environmental plan.

Growth Management

Growth management implies and requires the long-range planning by a regional planning or metro government agency. Development of any kind is approved only when in consonance with an adopted regional land use plan. Occupancy or use is permitted only when all required services are in place and operational.

Regional Planning

The number of people in an area is often less important than the way in which their centers are arranged. There is a common misconception that the more people to be attracted to live or work in a given jurisdiction, the more income and tax benefits. Under most existing conditions of uncontrolled land use and scatteration, the reverse is true. Costly road and utility extensions combined with schooling, welfare, fire and police, and other services soon overtake the overall tax yield. Moreover, increased traffic and disruption usually drive the original owners away.

The officials and staffs of individual jurisdictions tend to work for the local good rather than the long-range good of the larger regional community. There are many highly successful examples of officially designated

At the dawn of civilization, say 5,000 years ago, the population of the world cannot have numbered much more than 20 million. Today the yearly increase in world population is nearly twice this amount. Self-multiplying, like money at compound interest, world population reached the billion mark in the 1850's and the 2 billion mark in the 1920's. Even more disquieting the rate of increase has also been steadily increasing. At the present rate, today's population will double itself in less than fifty years.

Julian Huxley

The Planned Environment

regional councils devoted to the long-range regional well-being. Why are there not more? It is simply that local governments are reluctant to relinquish their sovereignty, and their officials their position, to grant favors to constituents and friends. One proven solution to this dilemma is an areawide petition to the county or state government to charter a regional planning agency with specifically limited powers and full authority to enforce them. Such powers might well comprise those beyond the capability of a single jurisdiction—such as long-range planning of land use, transportation networks, utility systems, water resource management, and recycling.

As to land use, an evolving long-range regional plan should designate only generalized zones for residential, institutional, commercial, and recreational centers—all placed where there is need, adequate water, and other required resources—and where they would fit compatibly into the natural and built environment. Within the generally defined zones, local governments and officials would still have their continuing rights to subdivide and regulate. They would retain their other functions as well, as long as they conformed to the official regional plan and its overriding ordinances.

Metro Government

A further step, with glowing examples, is the metro form of government. With metro government, several contiguous counties are granted a charter by the state. Although wide general authority is granted, only specific major duties of regional scope are assigned. Otherwise, local governments are assured their continued offices and sovereignty. The efficiency and effectiveness of such a government—one unified government over a multiplicity of jurisdictions—is soon apparent.

The community gets involved.

Civic Action

Where political favors and patronage have become an environmental threat, a civic action group may be needed. The Allegheny Conference of Western Pennsylvania is an example. Over a period of more than 50 years it has transformed this once desolate landscape into one of the most livable cities in America.

Essentially, the conference was founded by several businessmen who returned from the Second World War to find living and working conditions intolerable and corruption rife. They formed a nonpolitical council of civic leaders. It meets once a year to propose priority needs for improvement and to hear of progress. It has a small executive committee and staff, raises funds from private individuals and foundations, and, project by project, is transforming the region.

Civic action groups may be of many sizes and forms. They need only be composed of one or more dedicated citizens. Sometimes their membership is numbered in the thousands. Such examples as the Sierra Club and the American Conservation Foundation are making an immense contribution to our living environment.

Conservation Easements or Gifts of Land

One promising means of preserving the integrity of the landscape is by lease or sale of conservation easements. This limits the use to that which

Landscape integrity can be protected by conservation easements.

The Planned Environment

exists. A farmer may thus maintain full use of a farmstead while enjoying a one-time easement profit and continuing tax relief.

Significant unused portions of a property may also be sold or donated, with restrictions, to a conservation group for profit or tax benefits. Permanent open space is thereby built into the regional plan.

Water Resource Management

Planners have been slow to recognize the shortage of freshwater. In many regions this has reached crisis proportions. Along both coasts the well fields and water tables of urbanizing centers have been drawn down to a level where saltwater is intruding. Upland rivers, already stressed by deforestation and irrigation, have been further depleted to supplement the huge and wasteful demands. Some of our inland rivers, studded with reservoirs, have been reduced to a trickle or seasonal mudflat.

Clearly, our national freshwater consumption must be reduced and controlled. We can no longer afford millions of acres of sprinkled lawn or the washing of streets with freshwater. Nor can irrigation, with potable water, of millions of acres of marginal farmland be afforded. Soon, irrigation for the most part will be by treated wastewater. Communities will have separate potable water and treated wastewater systems. Advanced water management will work to restore, replenish, and sustain fresh-

Natural stream system restored.

136 *LANDSCAPE ARCHITECTURE*

water reserves. It will regulate the draw from sources to meet demonstrated area needs. It will promote regional and open-space planning, reforestation, and wetland protection. The natural flow of major streams and drainageways will be restored and maintained. River basins will be studied and planned from source to outfall as integrated units.

Soil Loss

The basic wealth of a nation is its fertile topsoil mantle. Our entire food chain is utterly dependent upon it. Without topsoil we would have no vegetation to retain precipitation and transpire it in the fresh air we breathe and upon which life depends. Nor would it retain the falling moisture to gradually seep into the underlying water tables. The desert countries, or vast areas thereof, are examples of erosion in the extreme. They were once forested or grasslands with flowing streams and abundant water. Shipbuilding, lumbering, and the clearing of land for vineyards, orchards, and farms allowed the soil to erode in deep gullies and wash irretrievably to the sea. Barren Greece, Israel, Syria, and Spain were once entirely green.

In our short history, and mostly within the past century, America has lost one-third of its precious topsoil to erosion by wasteful farming practices, deforestation, and construction. Needed is education and the recognition

America has lost one-third of its topsoil to erosion.

The Planned Environment   137

of the topsoil value, coupled with strictly regulated and enforced excavation and grading controls by which all topsoil is replaced or stockpiled.

Of near equal concern to the loss of soil by erosion is the dissipation of farmland. A major reason is that an owner is tempted or forced to sell because of high tax assessments based on land value determined by rezoning or the sale of neighbors' land for other than agricultural use. Only with assessments based on productivity, and with regional land use planning and zoning, can needed croplands be preserved and essential farming be ensured.

Pollution

Our once pristine living environment is now polluted shamefully. In many districts the air we breathe is so polluted that health is affected. People die, livestock dies, wildlife and vegetation die from noxious fumes and acid rain. Even the global climate is adversely affected by the sheath of carbon dioxide which is increasingly enveloping planet Earth. It will take time, public outcry, legislation, and immense funding to reduce and, hopefully, eliminate these problems.

Our water is polluted, too. Contaminated runoff and seepage from surrounding lands has so polluted our streams, aquifers, and water bodies that it is no longer safe to eat fish in quantity if taken from even the farthest reaches of the Great Lakes. Farming and development must be so controlled as to ensure that contaminated surface runoff is intercepted and filtered.

Even the seemingly inert soil is being polluted—as by absorption of airborne fumes, fertilizing, insect and weed control, misnamed sanitary fills, and the disposal of atomic waste.

The public views pollution with varying degrees of alarm and is demanding governmental action and relief. We are beginning to realize that pollution abatement and control lie at the very heart of environmental planning.

Safety

Safety at home, at work, or in travel is dependent upon thoughtful design. Vehicles, be they autos, trains, boats, or barges, are undergoing constant changes and improvements. So, too, must our land planning and routes of interconnection. Designated traffic-free walkways and bikeways will soon thread through our cities and across the countryside. Limited access parkways and freeways with no roadside intrusion will link our centers. On-grade street and highway crossings will be all but eliminated. Interarea transit routes, elevated or depressed at crossings, will swerve not through but around communities, with ramp approaches at the sides.

Design for the disadvantaged will be universally mandated. In all planning, the elimination of hazard will be a fundamental. Crime and the new threat of terrorism are spreading darkening and dangerous shadows on the American scene. The planned elimination of unkempt districts, obsolescence, and vacant lurking places will do much to abate the blight. More than that. Our revitalization of towns and cities must provide employment and recreation for those who seek it. There is much that can be done under trained professionals to help clean up and revise the region. All would benefit. The original Civilian Conservation Corps (CCC) or later youth and adult volunteer groups with modifications would serve as excellent examples.

Auto-free bikeway.

Climate

Some like it hot, some like it cool or cold. A first consideration in planning is that the prospective builder make an early choice. For climate affects not only temperature, but plan location, orientation, materials, and form.

Climate is more than high or low, wet or dry, or ranges on the thermometer. It involves qualities of light (from desert glare to forest glimmer) and marked differences in humidity. The seasons and their characteristics are dramatic climatic factors.

Weather, breeze, wind force and direction, fog, precipitation, flood, and drought—all are functions of climate.

Natural Disasters

Cyclones, hurricanes, earthquakes and floods are a fact of life. We can only avoid them to the extent possible. That extent has been significantly

The Planned Environment

increased in recent years by improved detection and monitoring capability. Untold thousands of lives have been saved by early warnings and the evacuation of threatened settlements.

The present dangers are alarming. As an example, the teeming cities of Los Angeles and San Francisco both lie astride the San Andreas fault, which will predictably experience violent quakes and volcanic eruption at any time. Some settled there in spite of the risk; others unknowingly. This daily risk of their lives is increasingly a matter of choice, as our scientists become able to trace and record fault lines, fire- and flood-prone areas, and the paths of high-velocity storms.

New Orleans Flood, 2005. A disaster directly attributable to poor land use planning.

War

War is the ultimate environmental disaster. Villages and cities are shelled into stinking ruin. Regions are blasted, gouged, and denuded. Populations are decimated, and combatant cultures demeaned and demoralized. Combatants and noncombatants alike are mutilated or killed. War is sheer hell.

Wars won or lost have never ended war and never will. They are the result of the human condition—overcrowding, hunger, poverty, inequalities, greed, and national yearning for freedom, expansion, or power. Only by addressing and curing wrongs in the human condition can war be averted.

No single mind or nation will ever be able to find the solution. This suggests an evolving super, multinational civic action group comprised of recognized nonpolitical leaders. Call it "The International Council for Humanity" or the like. Membership would be one of a nation's highest honors.

Council membership of admired and influential world leaders would be by invitation only and limited to one per nation. The exception would be a small executive committee with staff, which would work year-round. Its purpose would be to gather background information for use of the members and for presentation at the annual conference. Governmental officials might be called upon but would have no voice or vote in the annual report recommendations. Such a council would meet once a year for an intensive conference to discuss world problems and alternative solutions. Each conference would end with a report of recommendations for priority action by governments, existing or newly created agencies, private foundations, or other groups able to make a difference.

The council would have no authority or power of enforcement, yet its annual report and recommendations, being the concerted opinion of international leaders and their supporters, would have tremendous influence for good.

Conservation

Although addressed elsewhere in this volume, conservation as an issue of the environment is worthy of repetition. In tending to human needs, we cannot afford to neglect or despoil the setting in which all life is lived.

Experienced landowners and developers have learned the value of land appreciation. A property is first surveyed for its positive on-site and off-site features.

These are to be preserved, protected, and built into the plan. Where possible they are to be shared with adjacent properties. Every project when completed should add to, rather than detract from, the desirability of the site and its surroundings.

Without exception, site reconnaissance should take detailed account of the notable features. These may be such natural features as a single tree, a grove, spring, pond, or scenic view of river, lake, forest, or mountain. It may be a drift of rare plants or the nest of an endangered species of bird. Perhaps it may be a historic place or monument. All are to be conserved and built into the plan for the enjoyment and uplift of the users.

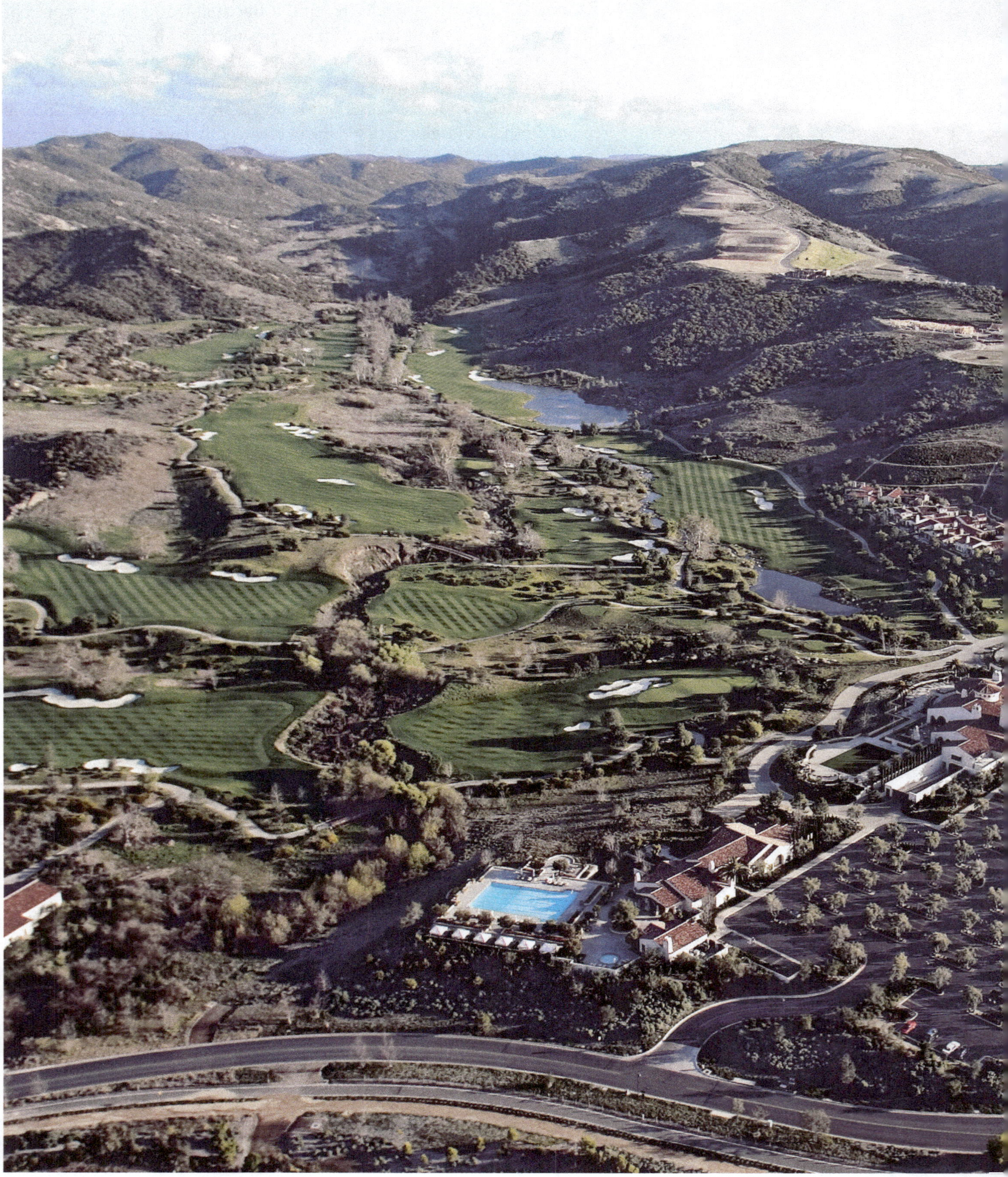

8
COMMUNITY PLANNING AND GROWTH MANAGEMENT

Tom Lamb, Lamb Studio

The word *community* has many connotations, most of them favorable. For people, like plants and animals, seem to flourish in shared and supportive groupings. What is the nature of such planned community groupings, and how are they best formed?

The Group Imperative

Historically, people have banded together for some compelling reason, as for protection within the gated walls of the medieval city or the palisade of the fort. They have formed communities to engage in farming, commerce, or industry or to pursue their religious beliefs. In the opening up of America, settlements grew spontaneously around harbors and river landings, at the crossings of transportation routes, and wherever natural resources were concentrated or abundant.

Within communal aggregations, friendships have been made mainly on the basis of propinquity. Dwellings were built in the most favorable and affordable locations, and then families moved in to make friends or sometimes to feud with the folks next door. Social groupings and working alliances were for the most part accidental. Homes were permanent, and neighborhoods were relatively stable. Towns and cities proliferated—too often in patterns of squared-off streets. Residential districts became impacted, often without schools, conveniences, or open-space relief. As densities and traffic increased, time-distances became greater,

Any consideration of the future of open space, such as exists between our urban centers, requires a thoughtful appraisal of one of our most voracious consumers of land: housing. Man's preference in housing, especially in urban fringe areas, results in the sprawl of single detached units in an awesome continuum across the countryside.

What is the origin of the desire for this type of shelter expression—this compulsion to flee the city and to build cube on cube across the open land? Is it a desire for tax relief? Vested equity? Breathing space? Contact with the land? Or the poetics of "Home Sweet Home"? Regardless, is the solution largely that of better design within the acceptance of this preference? Or change from separated horizontal forms to unified collective density patterns? Perhaps as space between units decreases, space between our urban centers may be preserved, or may increase.

Walter D. Harris

The subdivision as we know it is a typical United States invention, with few counterparts in Europe or Asia.

pollution often became intolerable, and surrounding fields and woodlands melted inexorably away.

With the coming of the twentieth century and the advent of the automobile, the farm-to-city movement was suddenly reversed. Initially a few of the wealthy fled the industrial city to build romanticized farmsteads and rusticated villas such as those along the Hudson River. They were soon joined by many members of the middle class, to whom social reform was bringing an improving standard of living and newfound mobility. These families shared the beckoning dream of a better, more fulfilling life out beyond the city outskirts, where they could live amid forest, fields, and gardens in communion with nature. As they surged outward in ever-increasing numbers, the new suburbia was born. It was to become an American phenomenon. New types of dwellings would be designed, and innovative community patterns would be created. The subdivision tracts, planned communities, and new towns gradually evolved and are still evolving. If they fall somewhat short of the vision, it is because they have destroyed too much of the nature that they sought to embrace. It is because they have carried along with them from the city too many of the urban foibles—the bad habit of facing homes upon traffic-laden streets instead of pleasant courts or open-space preserves, of inexplicably lining schools, churches, and factories haunch to haunch along the roaring highways. It is because we have allowed the interconnecting roadways to become teeming thoroughfares along which has coalesced mile after mile of crass, traffic-clogging commercial-strip development. It is because we still have much to learn about the basics and intricacies of group living, of land use, and of transportation planning.

Problems

Without controls, unsuitable uses infiltrate residential areas. Widened streets and highways draw to their sides commercial-strip coagulations that reduce their carrying capacity and restrict the traffic flow. Deterioration and blight are rampant. Vacant structures are vandalized. Property values plummet, and the solid citizens of the original homes move out if they can. Sadly, wherever they go to start anew, without better planning and regulation, the cycle will be repeated. It need not be so.

Monotony

Too often in suburban development a well-wooded site is leveled, the trees and cover destroyed, the streams and drainageways encased in massive storm sewers or open culverts. Look-alike houses are then spaced out in rows along a geometric checkerboard of streets. A new flora of exotic plants is installed in the hard-packed ground. The native fauna—the furred and feathered creatures of the wood and meadow—take off to seek a more livable habitat.

Variety, the antitheses of monotony, can be preserved and attained by sensitive land and community planning, with far more resident appeal and at far less initial and continuing cost.

Inefficiency

The well-planned neighborhood or community—urban, suburban, or rural—should function as an efficient mechanism. This is to say that energy and materials are to be conserved and frictions eliminated. Energy conservation suggests that things and services needed—schools, shopping, and recreation—should be convenient, easy to reach, and close at hand. Yet in some neighborhoods many blocks must be traveled and many streets crossed in order to buy a quart of milk or a loaf of bread. Playgrounds and even elementary schools can be reached only by braving a grid of rushing trafficways. As we know from reading the papers, some children and adults never make it.

Most contemporary shopping centers are inaccessible by foot.

In a planned community, by comparison, dwellings of all types are clustered around the activity centers. Access by foot, bicycle, or electric cart is via traffic-free greenways. Safer. More pleasant. Far more efficient.

The alignment of homes and apartment buildings along roadways and streets was for years the accepted procedure. It is no longer considered desirable. Few families would opt for a home that faced upon a busy trafficway if offered the alternative of off-street courtyard living. Offset residential groupings not only provide more salable and rentable housing, they do so more economically. Further, the efficiency of the passing street is increased by the elimination of curbcuts at every driveway, with the intrusions that these imply.

Community Planning and Growth Management 145

With clustered off-street housing, the high cost of street and highway construction with its trunkline sewers and utility mains can be shared by many more dwellings. Single- and double-loaded streets are not only uneconomical, they are fraught with all sorts of problems.

The common practice of constructing sewers, utility mains, and energy distribution systems within the street right-of-way is another source of recurrent difficulties. Power poles and overhead wires interfere with street tree plantings which must then be periodically mutilated to keep the lines clear. Beyond that, it is patently impractical to tear up a section of pavement and close a lane, if not the whole street, for the installation of each new service lateral—or for the seemingly endless repair or enlargement of in-street water, gas, or sewer mains. Far better that a utility easement be reserved along rear property lines to leave the streetscape unscathed.

In many unplanned communities the greatest waste is in uncalled-for and destructive earthwork and unneeded storm-sewer construction. These costs are incurred because the site layout runs counter to the topography. Natural covers protect and stabilize the soils and slopes. Natural drainageways and streams carry off the excess precipitation. But with the vegetation destroyed and the drainageways blocked, the heavy expense of resultant drainage structures and soil stabilization must be factored into the cost of each dwelling. Not to mention replacement plantings.

Radburn, New Jersey, 1928. This revolutionary concept of community living was devised by its planners, Henry Wright and Clarence Stein, as an answer to living with the automobile. Homes were grouped in superblocks with automobile access from cul-de-sac streets precluding high speed through traffic. Pedestrian walkways, free of automobile crossings, provided access to large central park areas in which and around which were grouped the community social, recreational, and shopping centers.

In this plan concept were sown the seeds of ideas that have sprouted in most of the superior neighborhood and community plans of succeeding years.

In the home-building and community development industries—profit motivated and highly competitive as they are—it is indeed fortuitous that the most successful entrepreneurs have learned that well-conceived and well-built projects are not only more efficient, they are more environmentally sound, more people-friendly, more salable or rentable, and more profitable.

Unhealthful Conditions

Mens sana in corpore sano. A sound mind in a sound body. What has community planning to do with the state of one's health?

If we are, as it is said, largely the product of our heredity and our environment, then let us hope that we come of hardy stock, for living in neighborhoods that are obsolescent, polluted, and/or traffic-fraught is hardly conducive to health.

Mental well-being derives from rational order and behavior. When living conditions are clearly unreasonable; when the daily experience is one of frustration, anxiety, or disgust, it is hard to maintain a positive state of mind.

As to behavior, we live in a revved-up society that our parents could not have imagined. In our crowded lives everything is done at double speed and driven intensity. Between spates of whizzing about to keep up the pace, we spend long hours in sedentary occupations. Much of the working day is spent hunched over the desk, counter, or machine—or staring into computers. We are detached from the wholesome reality of the field and furrow, the woodlot, the vineyard, the creatures of the barn and dooryard that kept our forebears sane and healthy. Can our planned communities of the future provide the antidote, the counterpoint, to such mechanistic living? Can we find in our new neighborhoods the opportunities for healthful outdoor exercise and recreation, for group activities and fulfilling communal life? It is believed so.

Danger

Who could deny that our present communities, as most of us experience them, pose danger to life and limb?

> The street crossings and trafficway intersections
> The mix of people and vehicles
> Overhead power lines
> Toxic levels of soil and water contamination
> The polluted air that we breathe . . .

In addition, there's the increasing threat posed by crime in our streets and alleys—the weekly muggings, break-ins, or drive-by shootings. These are endemic to obsolescence and vacancies, to unlighted lurking places—and as well to the lack of better places to be and better things to do.

All these potential and very real dangers are subject to planned improvement.

Possibilities

As we set out to plan the more salubrious neighborhoods of the future, wherein lie the possibilities? It is proposed that they will have:

>   A better fit of construction to the land
>   A better fit of homes to related trafficways
>   A better fit of homes to homes and homes to activity centers
>   A rich variety of things to see and do
>   Freedom of individual expression and innovative improvement
>   A shared sense of true community, of compatible living together.

Building Arrangements

Why do houses face upon streets? "Because," some might say, "they always have." Probably such respondents are right, for we humans are slow to accept any change, even when the advantage is obvious. Until recently, in the United States it was uniformly a legal requirement that all platted homesites be dedicated with frontage upon a public right-of-way. As a consequence, homes sprouted row upon row along streets and highways across the countryside. This posed few serious problems as long as the roads were used by horses and horse-drawn carriages, wagons, and carts.

Then came the automobiles. They came, and came, and they keep on coming. The roadways are overwhelmed. They have been widened and lengthened until today the trafficway network covers most of the landscape like a coarsely woven mesh. Meanwhile, buildings continue to crowd alongside the pulsing motorways. Communities are thus cut apart—divided and subdivided again by lines of fast-moving traffic. This makes little sense for either the residents or the motorists.

In seeking solutions to the dilemma, land planners have sought to have the frontage requirement rescinded. Where this has been accomplished it has produced building-road relationships that hold much promise.

One fairly recent advance is that of *planned unit development,* or PUD as it is now commonly called. A PUD ordinance, where enacted, provides that in the planning of sizable residential tracts, incentives are given for creative site planning. While the types of permitted land uses and the total land coverage and density limits are fixed, the more restrictive provisions of long-obsolete codes no longer govern. New mixes of housing types and traffic-free neighborhoods are encouraged. Clustering and shared open space are consistent features, together with built-in convenience and recreation centers. The resulting communities and new towns have demonstrated the many benefits of off-street residential groupings and pointed the way to new concepts of true community living.

Separation of pedestrian and automobiles in planned community.

Access and Circulation

If the new residential areas are to be traffic-free, what of the automobile? It is to be assumed that driver-operated vehicles in one form or another will long be a favored form of transportation. This will be even more so when the paths of vehicular movement are freed of the myriad pedestrian crossings and hazardous intersections, when arterial roads and circulation drives are designed as free-flowing parkways with no on-grade intersections and widely spaced points of access or egress.

Communities will no longer be cross-hatched with roads and streets but will instead be planned as a series of sizable pedestrian domains of various types, fitted to the topography. Each will be bounded and interconnected by nonfrontage circulation drives. Each neighborhood, and the larger community, will be accessed by vehicles from the outside with inward penetration to residential parking courts and service compounds. Pedestrians and vehicles will thus be separated—each with their own specially designed areas of operation. Neighborhood living will then be safer and more pleasant, and vehicles can move at sustained speeds without interference.

Activity Centers

Schools, shopping, and recreation centers are the main community destinations. In many of the early planned communities they were intentionally isolated from single-use residential groupings. In one area were placed the look-alike single-family homes, at another the look-alike town houses, and elsewhere the look-alike apartments. In such sanitized residential conclaves there was little of interest to see or do—except at the distant school, playground, or shopping mall. As a result, the housing neighborhoods were overly quiet to the point of being boring.

In the more recent mixed-use planned communities, housing units of varying types are grouped closely around the activity centers. Not only is access more easy, but this lively, more democratic mix affords welcome variety and increased opportunity for neighbor-to-neighbor meetings and friendships.

In such freely composed, more compact, and focalized residential groupings the activity hubs and nodes get more use, as do the interconnecting paths of pedestrian movement. Especially if the places are made more attractive with plantings, lighting, and such furnishings as fountains, sculpture, and banners. And if the ways are pleasantly aligned and enhanced with mounding, trees for shade, benches, and perhaps here and there a bike rack or a piece of child's play equipment.

In most of the more PUD developments, homes and apartments are arranged in compact groupings or clusters to squeeze out wasted separation space around and between the buildings. This is not only more land- and cost-efficient, but also, with the same overall densities, yields an increased measure of shared open space.

This compaction is evident also in the better activity centers. Both at the neighborhood and community levels, compatible uses are combined. Examples include the elementary school and park; the high school, game courts, and athletic field; the shopping, business, and professional office complex; the community building, church, library, and performing arts assemblage; or the museum and center for arts and crafts. In all such cases the intensification is beneficial. Moreover, the gathering together of once dispersed uses into more vibrant nucleii also provides in the overall community plan additional open area.

Open Space

Why community open space? Because without it there can be little sense of community. It is mainly in the outdoor ways and places that communal living takes place.

Community park and open space.

Open space equates with many forms of recreation. Some, like lacrosse or field hockey, require expansive areas. Others need only limited space. A child's slide or a basketball backstop, for instance, will fit almost anywhere. Baseball fields and basketball courts need precise orientation and construction, while more passive kinds of recreation—picnicking, kite flying, or playing catch—take little more than an open field. Lineal spaces, as for jogging paths, health trails, or bikeways, must be carefully woven into community plans to ensure continuity.

Open space has other values, too. If it follows and envelops the drainageways and streams, it serves to preserve the natural growth and define buildable areas with lobes of refreshing green. It also provides cover for birds and small animals that contribute much delight to the local scene, not only in the suburbs but in the inner city as well.

Where does such open space come from? As noted, it is a natural product of the PUD planning approach which, with fixed densities, features clustered building arrangements. Available open spaces include the unpaved areas of the street rights-of-way—or the whole of utility easements. They are acquired in part as segments of park and recreation systems. Unbuildable areas such as floodplains, marshes, steep slopes, and narrow ridges make their contributions, as do the open areas of business office parks, the university campus, and institutional grounds. Some highly desirable open space may be derived from the reclamation of extraction pits, landfills, strip-mining operations, cutover timberlands, or depleted farms. Public agencies such as the Department of Transportation, water management districts, or the military may transfer excess or vacated holdings. Again, prime lands may be donated by foundations or by private citizens,

Community Planning and Growth Management 151

with or without the incentives of tax abatement. And there are, too, the possibilities of scenic and conservation easements.

Piece by piece, parcel by parcel, an open-space system can in time be fitted together for the good of all concerned—provided that for each community there is a program and a plan.

New Ethic in Community Planning: P-C-D

Preserve the best of the natural and historic features.
Conserve, with limited use, an interconnecting open-space framework.
Develop selected upland areas with site-responsive building clusters.

By this approach the project site is thoroughly analyzed by a team of qualified planning experts and scientific advisers. Then on the topographic surveys a line is drawn around those areas of high scenic, historic, or ecological value (P). These areas and features are to be preserved intact, without significant disturbance. Around them, as protective buffers, are then described conservation swaths of lesser landscape value. The conservation (C) areas may be devoted to limited open space or recreational uses that will not harm their natural quality. Development (D) or construction areas are only then allocated on the receptive higher

Many conservationists who would protect and assure the best use of our lands and waters have yet to learn that cooperative, large-scale, long-range planning is more effective than the common no-growth tactic of "block and delay."

A planned community using the P-C-D approach (Pelican Bay, Collier County, Florida). Beach, dunes, and tidal estuary *preserved*. Wetlands, waterways, and native vegetation protected (*conserved*). Clustered *development* on the upland, within an interconnected open-space frame. All work well together.

152   LANDSCAPE ARCHITECTURE

A planned community with golf course as open space.

ground. Here the structures are usually clustered in more compact and efficient arrangements within the blue and green open-space framework. Here, without inflicting negative impacts, people can live and work at peace with their natural surroundings.

Planned communities are prime examples of sound economic development coupled with conservation. Yet even the most glowing examples have come into being only after long years of battle with outmoded codes and with self-styled environmentalists, who by all reason should be the greatest advocates. For mile after mile of beachfront and thousands upon thousands of acres of prime forest and wetland have already been set aside and preserved intact, voluntarily, by comprehensive community planning.

Much can be accomplished when this process comes to be carried forward in full cooperation with local citizens, dynamic conservation groups, and contributing public agencies. It can be seen that such P-C-D planning applies not only to residential development, but to every type of use and parcel—to whole regions and to the larger state.

Community Planning and Growth Management

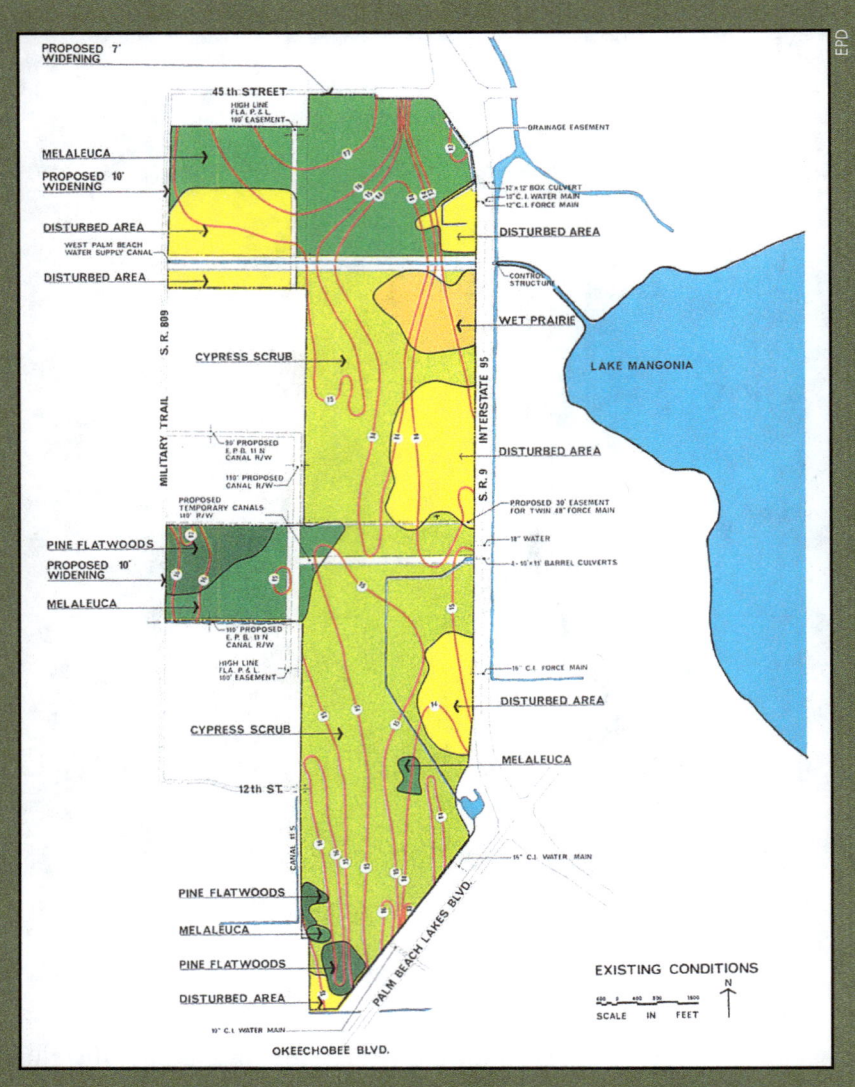

Existing site conditions.

THE PLANNED COMMUNITY

As in much of Florida, West Palm Beach has experienced unprecedented growth. This has provided an expanding economic base, many public facilities, and other benefits. It has also brought with it the usual problems which accompany rapid and piecemeal development.

Recognizing the opportunity and need for the comprehensive planning of unified neighborhoods, the city early on adopted an innovative *planned community development,* or PCD, ordinance. The following proposal was one of the first to prove its effectiveness.

Conceptual community planning studies
(Villages of West Palm Beach, Florida)

The planned community.

154   LANDSCAPE ARCHITECTURE

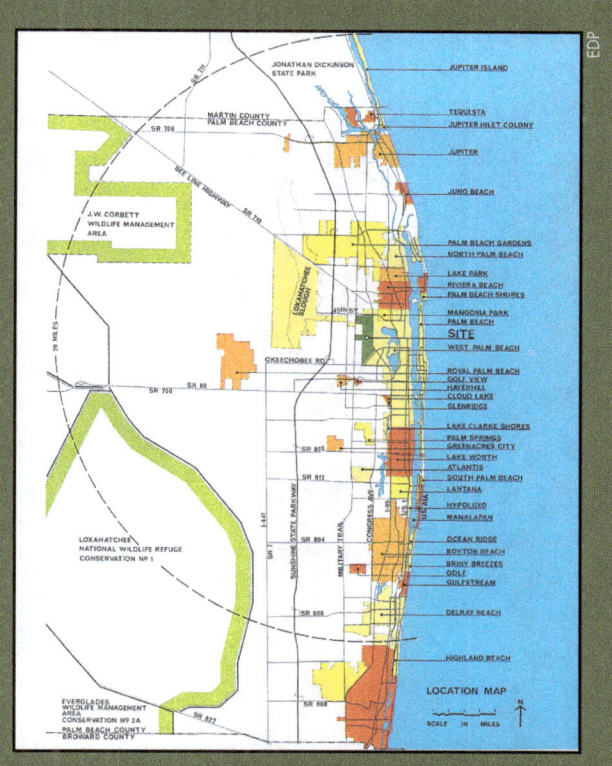

Regional framework.

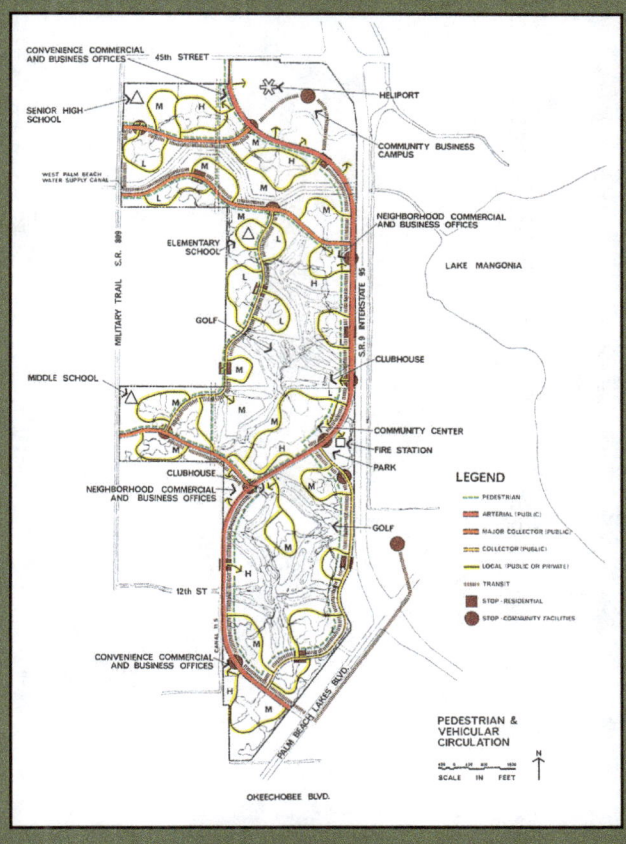

Circulation patterns.

Community Planning and Growth Management 155

Conceptual community plan.

156 LANDSCAPE ARCHITECTURE

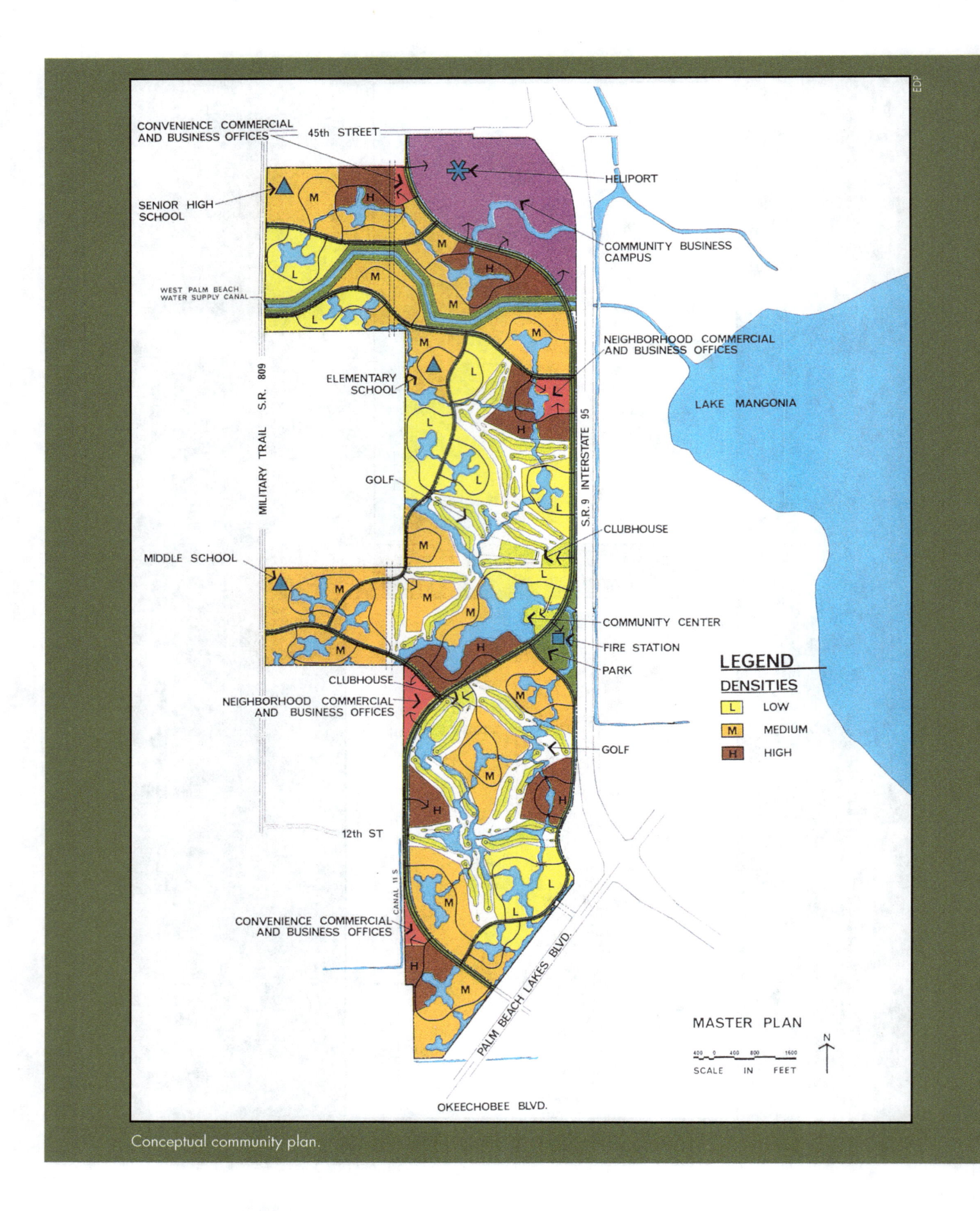

Flexibility: Possible plan adjustments.

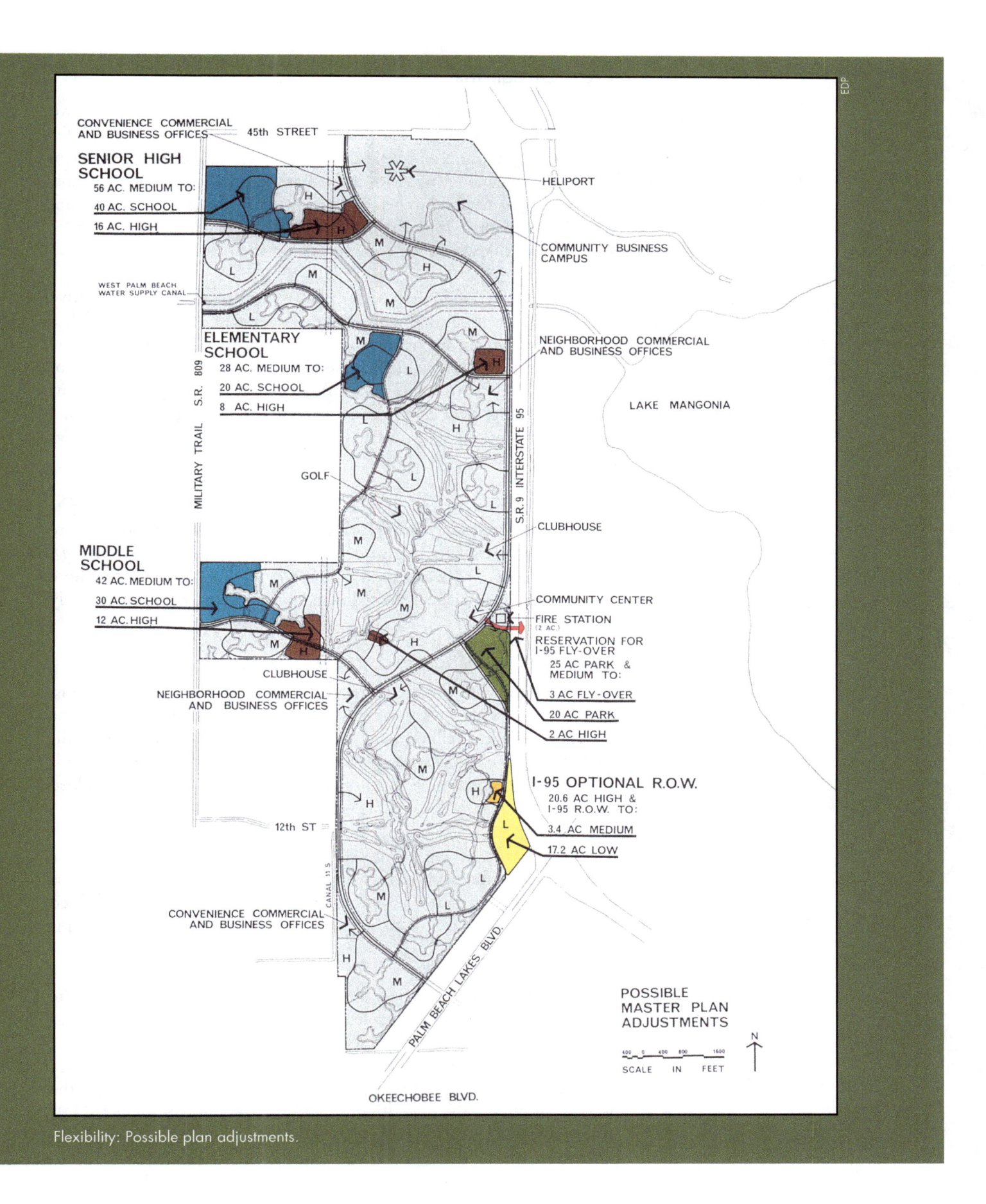

Community Planning and Growth Management 157

All good planning must begin with a survey of actual resources: the landscape, the people, the work-a-day activities in a community. Good planning does not begin with an abstract and arbitrary scheme that it seeks to impose on a community; it begins with a knowledge of existing conditions and opportunities . . .

The final test of an economic system is not the tons of iron, the tanks of oil, or the miles of textiles it produces: The final test lies within its ultimate products—the sort of men and women it nurtures and the order and beauty and sanity of their communities.
Lewis Mumford

New Directions

In appraising the better examples of recently planned communities we find many promising features. Some planning concepts, like the transfer of development rights and flexibility zoning, were unheard of even a few years ago. Some have met with immediate acceptance, others have not, and still others have yet to be adequately tested. While some approaches have failed in their initial application, they may contain the seeds of ideas that will flower in the communities of the future.

With the transfer of development rights, owners of ecologically sensitive or productive agricultural land may negotiate with planning officials a trade-off by which the right to develop the prime landholding is forfeited in exchange for the right to develop a similar, or different, type of project at an alternative location. Often by such an arrangement a valuable community asset can be preserved and extensive tracts of marginal or depleted property transformed into highly desirable real estate. Everyone thus benefits.

Fine communities seldom if ever just happen. They must be thoughtfully and painstakingly brought into being. Improved approaches are continually emerging and give new meaning to such words as *housing, health, education, recreation,* and *community.* In the shaping of our more advanced residential areas the following principles are being successfully applied.

Apply the PUD approach. Planned unit development (PUD) is a rational framework for the phased development of community plans. Essentially, it establishes at the start the types of uses to be included, the total number of dwellings, and a conceptual plan diagram. The traditional restrictive regulations are waived, and each successive phase as it is brought on in detail is checked against the conceptual plan and judged solely on the basis of foreseeable performance.

Request flexibility zoning. For larger tracts, this permits within the zone boundaries the free arrangement and progressive restudy of the land use and traffic-flow diagrams as long as the established caps are rebalanced and not exceeded and as long as the plan remains consistent with community goals.

Consider the transfer of development rights (TDR). In recognition of the fact that for reasons of their ecologic, scenic, or other values certain areas of land and water should be preserved in their natural state, TDR provisions allow and encourage a developer to transfer from the sensitive area those uses originally permitted by zoning. Although the relocation of the uses or dwelling units to another property is sometimes provided, TDR is most effective when the densities of contiguous building sites in the same ownership are increased to absorb the relocated units.

Relate all studies to water resource management. The fourfold purpose is to prevent flooding, protect water quality, replenish freshwater reserves, and provide for wastewater disposal.

Provide perimeter buffering. As supplementary or alternative open space, a band of land in its natural state may well be left around the borders of larger development sites. This provides a screen against adjacent trafficways or other abutting uses and offers a welcome backdrop for building construction.

Create a community portal. One of the best ways in which to engender a sense of neighborhood or community is by the provision of a cohesive circulation system and an attractive gateway.

Ensure regional access. Thriving communities need connection to the shopping, cultural, and recreation centers and the open spaces of the regions which surround them. Aside from paths and controlled-access roadways, linkage may be attained by bikeways, by boat if on water, and by rapid transit in one or more of its many forms.

Preclude through-community trucking. Although local streets must be used on occasion by heavy trucks (by permit) and for daily deliveries by smaller vehicles, a direct truckway link to the community storage and distribution center has many advantages. Here heavy loads may be broken down for home or commercial delivery and bulk and private storage space provided for seasonal equipment, boats, and recreation vehicles.

Plan an open-space framework. As an alternative to facing homes and other development directly upon trafficways, many communities now wisely provide for the reservation of variformed swaths of land, in public or private ownership, as preferred building frontage. Vehicular approach to buildings, parking, and service areas is from the rear. The open-space system, which usually follows streams and drainageways, may also include walks, bicycle and jogging paths, and wider recreation areas.

Plan a hierarchy of trafficways. Even in smaller communities a clear differentiation between arterial, circulation, and local-frontage streets ensures more efficient traffic movement and safer, more agreeable living areas.

Limit roadside frontage. Insofar as possible, the facing of buildings upon arterials and circulation streets is to be precluded, with intersections to local frontage streets spaced no closer than 660 feet.

Make use of three-way (T) street intersections. They reduce through traffic, increase visibility, and make pedestrian crossing much safer.

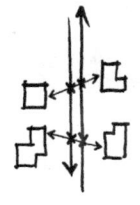

Home-to-home relationships across a busy street or highway . . .

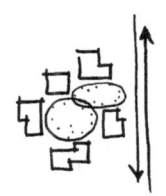

should give way to roadside clusters around a shared court.

Community Planning and Growth Management

Provide for rapid transit. Sheltered bus and minitransit stops and attractive community rapid transit stations, where appropriate, do much to stimulate transit use and reduce vehicular traffic.

Integrate paths of movement. Only when streets, walkways, bicycle trails, and other routes of movement are planned together can their full possibilities and optimum interrelationships be realized.

Vary the housing types. A well-balanced community provides not only a variety of dwellings, from single-family to multifamily, but also accommodates residents of differing lifestyles and a broad income range.

Vary housing type.

Include convenience shopping.

Encourage community programs.

Systematize the site installations. All physical elements of a community—buildings, roadways, walks, utilities, signage, and lighting—are best planned as interrelated systems.

Cluster the buildings. The more compact grouping of individual dwellings and the inclusion of patio and zero-lot-line homes yield welcome additional open space for neighborhood buffering and recreation use.

In Great Britain a charitable organization called the Learning Through Landscapes Trust has transformed nearly 10,000 school yards into imaginative learning gardens.
Landscape Architecture magazine, October 1994

Feature the school-park campus. The combining of schools with neighborhood and community parks permits much fuller use of each at substantial savings.

160   LANDSCAPE ARCHITECTURE

Include convenience shopping. While regional shopping centers fill the largest share of family marketing needs, they usually require travel by automobile. Neighborhood and community centers, with access by walks and bikeways, are needed to provide for a lesser scale of convenience shopping and service.

Provide employment opportunities. Bedroom communities—those planned for residential living only—require the expenditure of time, income, and energy just to get to and from work. Integral or closely related employment centers add vitality and convenience.

Relate to the regional centers. The larger business office campus, industrial park, or regional commercial mall is best kept outside, but convenient to, the residential groupings. Such centers are logically located near the regional freeway interchanges and accessible to the interconnecting circulation roads.

Plan for transient accommodations. When highway-related motel, hotel, or boatel accommodations do not otherwise fulfill the traveler's needs, a community inn is a welcome addition.

Consider a conference center. In addition to the auditorium and meeting rooms of the school-park community centers, a conference facility related to the commercial mall, business office park, cultural core, marina, golf course, tennis club, or inn is a popular amenity and asset.

Make recreation a way of life. Aside from private recreation opportunities and those provided at the neighborhood and community school parks, there is usually need for swimming, golf, and racquet clubs, a marina and beach club if the community is on water, a youth center, and access to hiking, jogging, and bicycle trails. The broader the range of available recreation, the more fulfilling is community life.

Encourage community programs, activities, and events. Although many do not require special space or site areas, no development program could be complete without consideration of all those social activities that contribute so much to community living. These include worship, continuing education and health care programs, children's day care, a craft center and workshop, a little theater, game and meeting rooms, a newspaper, service clubs, Little League, dances, contests, and parades. Some start spontaneously; others may require encouragement and guidance.

Build out as you go. Scattered or partially finished building areas are uneconomical and disruptive. In the better communities, construction proceeds by the phased extension of trafficways, utilities, and development areas. They are completed as examples. Construction materials and equipment are brought in from the rear, and the prearranged staging areas and access roads retreat as the work advances.

Honor historic landmarks.

Establish nature preserves.

Ensure a high level of maintenance. A maintenance center and enclosed yard, perhaps combined with a water storage or treatment plant, is best located inconspicuously at the periphery, with ready access to trucking and the areas to be served. It is to be well equipped and phased in advance of development to provide complete maintenance from the very start.

Honor the historic landmarks. When features of archaeological or historical significance exist, they are to be cherished. Their presence extends knowledge of the locality, its beginnings, and traditions and gives depth of meaning to life within the community.

Establish nature preserves. Every locality or site has in some degree its prized natural features. Be they subtle or dramatic, they add richness and interest and are to be protected, interpreted, and admired.

Name a scientist advisory council. In both initial and ongoing planning much can be gained by the naming of a team of scientist advisers. Convened periodically to bring their expertise to bear on the evolving plans and proposals, they are especially helpful in the study of large, complex, or ecologically sensitive holdings.

Appoint an environmental control officer. In the phased construction of each new parcel the responsibility for environmental protection is best centralized in one trained person who is present during all phases of planning, design review, and field installation.

Form a design review board. The plans for all buildings and major site improvements are best subjected from the start to a panel of qualified designers for review and recommendation as to acceptance, rejection, or modification. An architect, a landscape architect, and the environmental control officer would be appropriate members.

Prepare a development guideline manual. As the basic reference document for all planning, design, and continuing operation of the community, an expanding loose-leaf manual is essential. As it evolves, it will contain:

- The community goals and objectives
- The conceptual community plan
- Each phased neighborhood or parcel plan as it is brought into detailed study
- A section and flowchart describing plan review procedures
- Plan submission requirements and forms
- Architectural design guidelines
- Site design guidelines
- The master planting plan and policy and recommended plant lists
- A section on environmental quality control
- A section on energy conservation
- A section on solid waste disposal and recycling
- Homeowners' association covenants

As the need arises or is foreseen, supplementary sections will be added and the manual kept updated and complete. To be fully effective, its provisions must be equitably and uniformly enforced.

Establish a means of governance. It is important from the start of planning to have in mind the type of political entity that the community is to be or to become a part of. This will be a key factor in the determination of the type and level of public services to be provided and of responsibilities for planning reviews and permitting, for the installation of utilities, streets, and other improvements, and for taxation and decision making.

Create a homeowners' association. The developer, builders, and final homeowners all benefit by the early formation of a permanent organization in which the owner of each lot or home has a pro rata responsibility and vote and to which assessments are paid. The purpose of the association is to provide the mechanism for the formulation and implementation of continuing community maintenance and improvement policies.

Ensure flexibility with control. The most successful American communities have been guided in their development by policies that accomplish the following:

- Establish the broad outlines of compatible land use and routes of movement
- Provide the guidelines required to ensure flexibility, design quality, and environmental protection
- Encourage individuality and creativity

Unmanaged growth is a cancer on the land.

Growth Management

In the coming decades one of the most important aspects of land planning will be that of growth management. On the face of it, the regulation of population expansion and distribution might seem an impossibility. How, for instance, can the awesome burgeoning of our population be brought under control? Yet this is imperative, for by present projection it will double and then double again within the next 100 years. One can imagine the stress on buildable land, farmsteads, food production, freshwater reserves, and roadway capacities.

Or how can the constant shifting or tidal flows of population migration within our borders be managed? These vexing and critical problems are at last being addressed by our institutions and government. Pending effective solutions nationally, there are many means by which our planning professions can improve the local situations and prospects.

The Guideline Plan

To manage growth and ensure sound development within a given locality it is essential that each community, city, and/or region have a clear understanding of existing conditions and what they might better be in the future.

Growth management is a search for the best relationships of people to land, water, other resources, and to routes of travel.

This implies the need for a planning committee, council, or commission, depending upon the size of the area concerned. Ideally such groups represent the best of the local leadership aided by a professional planner and staff. Their task is the preparation of a guideline plan and action program. This will define the types, locations, and limits of development foreseen to produce the most desirable conditions for living and working. It will preserve and protect the best of the natural features including forest and farmland. It will provide a protective framework of open-space lands, around which development is to occur. It will allocate areas for all types of uses deemed necessary to produce in time a balanced and stable community. It will provide for interconnection of the various activity centers with a system of free-flowing paths, streets, parkways, and freeways. It will be general in outline with flexibility to meet changing conditions.

This guideline plan and improvement program is to be constantly updated and revised for use in reviewing all future development proposals.

Project Review

Wherever uncontrolled development is permitted, it will in time occur—most often causing an unwelcome incursion. Road and utility capacities are exceeded, natural features destroyed, farmland eliminated, and school systems overloaded. Pleasant communities are disrupted and changed beyond redemption. Often their very nature is so changed that existing homeowners move to more agreeable surroundings.

How is such disruption to be prevented? It is easier than might be supposed. Where a planning committee or council exists and where a development plan and guideline program have been prepared, each new development project must meet the test of phased review to meet approval or be rejected.

The first phase is a determination that the proposed project meets the spirit and conditions of the guideline or can be amended to do so. If tentative approval is granted, the development is carried through a series of further stages, which include a detailed impact statement, cost/yield analysis, and posting of performance bonds if called for. Only with such a strict review process and presentations in public meetings can the citizens and their leadership be assured of orderly growth and transition.

Required Services

Having satisfied the suitability and project review phases, the final key to growth management is the assurance that all public services are in place and operation before the first occupancy is permitted. Such services include required approach-road improvements, all off-site utility leads, adequate fire and police protection, school facilities (in the case of residential development), open space, and recreation. Who pays for their provision? It only makes sense that the speculator/developers—not the existing citizens—pay for the costs involved.

Even well-planned development is not always good—especially when it throws established systems out of kilter. Uncontrolled development is seldom desirable because of its disruptions and costs to the members of the existing community. Unmanaged growth results in that cancerous American form of land use and development known as urban sprawl.

Much of what needs to be done in the way of environmental planning falls within the category of growth management. This goes beyond the obvious need to stabilize the doubling, redoubling, overwhelming, and shifting populations. It deals essentially with bringing people, land, and other resources into balance. In this endeavor it can directly affect the future of every region.

There are some—yea, many—localities where a desirable equilibrium has already been attained; where land is preserved or built out to capacity in its "highest and best use"; where trafficways, utilities, schools, and other amenities are working well together and where further growth would be disruptive. Again, there are areas of scenic splendor, ecologic sensitivity, or high agricultural productivity where the existing condition is best left largely undisturbed. In every region, however, there can be found potential sites for well-planned communities or other enterprises if and when it can be established that they belong.

Unless or until our exploding population growth is checked, more and ever more construction is inevitable. We can no longer, however, allow the uncontrolled development of our prime remaining natural or agricultural lands. We must first explore and maximize the possibilities of renewal and redevelopment. We must reclaim, redefine, reuse, and often reshape our obsolescent or depleted urban, suburban, and rural properties. We can and must create a whole new re-formed landscape within the grand topographical setting of protected mountain slopes, river basins, shores, desert, forest, and farmland.

Implicit in long-range planning is the concept of sustainable development. For unless continuity is planned into the system, the term "long-range" has little meaning. Ideally, the supply of land, water, and other resources would be inexhaustible. Since this is not a fact of life, our planning must be the formulation of strategies for restraint, wise use, replenishment, and restoration.

It involves such broad and diverse concerns as the efficient use of energy. It deals with such finite matters as limitation on consumption, land use controls, and recycling. As to land and landscape planning, it soon leads to the realization that urban sprawl and scatteration must be curbed and reversed—replaced with concentrated and interconnected centers of

Golden Gate National Recreation Area.

human activity within protected and productive open-space surrounds. It demands, in short, comprehensive regional planning.

In our planning and replanning, we must preserve intact such significant natural areas as are necessary to protect our watersheds and maintain our water table, to conserve our forests and mineral reserves, to check erosion, to stabilize and ameliorate our climate, to provide sufficient areas for recreation and for wildlife sanctuary, and to protect sites of notable scenic, ecologic, or historic value. Such holdings might best be purchased and administered by the appropriate federal, state, or local agencies or conservancy groups.

We must ensure the logical development of the existing landscape. Such thinking points to a national resource planning authority. Such an authority would be empowered to explore and determine, on a broad scale, the best conceivable use of all major land and water areas and natural resources. It would recommend the purchase of those that should be so conserved. It would encourage, through zoning, enabling legislation, and federal aid, the best and proper development of these and all remaining areas for the long-range good of the nation. It would constantly reassess and keep flexible its program and master plans and engage for this work the best of the trained physical planners, geographers, geologists, biologists, sociologists, and experts in other related disciplines. Regional, state, and federal environmental advisory boards composed of distinguished scientists and thinkers might well be consti-

Community Planning and Growth Management

tuted, with participants nominated to this post of high honor by their respective professional groups.

Further, we must consciously and astutely continue the evolution toward a new system of physical order. This may be one of improved relationships, as of people to people, people to their communities, and all to the living landscape. Since we have now become, in fact, world citizens, the new order may stem from a philosophic orientation that borrows from and incorporates the most positive driving forces of the preceding and contemporary cultures.

While the Athenians, as has been noted, faced their homes inward to family domains of privacy, while the Egyptians expressed a compulsion for lineal progressions, while the Chinese designed their homes and streets and temples as incidents in nature, and while the Western predilection was for a continuum of flowing space, perhaps the new universal philosophic guidelines may be a felicitous blending.

The value of the secure, private contemplative space may come to be generally recognized. The appreciation of lineal attainment may be translated into the design for pleasurable and rewarding movement along transitways, parkways, and paths. Whole cities and regions may be harmoniously integrated with natural landscape, in which interconnecting open space may provide a salubrious setting for our new architectural and engineering structures.

For the first time in the long sweep of history, environmental protection is becoming at last a world concern. The wise management of our land and water resources and the earthscape is becoming a common cause. Fortunately, when the problems are nearing crisis proportions, the essential technology is at hand. Perhaps we can pull it all together in time, and sooner than many suppose, with enlightened, creative planning.

Significant environmental improvement does not necessarily require a monumental effort. It is sometimes achieved at a massive scale, as by

Small urban improvements.

168   LANDSCAPE ARCHITECTURE

effective and far-reaching flood control programs, clean air legislation, or the scientific management of regional farmlands, wetlands, or forest. For the most part, however, it is accomplished on a far lesser basis. It is the sum of an infinite number of smaller acts of landscape care and improvement. It is:

- The advent of a well-designed park or parklet
- The placing underground of power distribution and telephone cables in a new community
- The cleanup and water-edge installation of paths and planting along a forgotten stream
- Neighbors caring for their street
- A linden tree installed beside the entrance of an urban shop
- A vine on a factory wall
- A scrap of blowing paper picked up by a child in the school yard

Each act generates others. Together, they make the difference.

Scatteration and Urban Sprawl

It is believed that there is no greater threat to our cities and outlying countryside than the blight of urban sprawl. The subject is given place

Rampant sprawl followed World War II.

Community Planning and Growth Management 169

Growth management is not a door slamming shut, as some might think—as some might wish. It is more of a regulating valve by which flow and capacities are brought into optimum balance.

Pittsburgh Point, circa 1990.

in this text because most readers with such an interest are those best suited by training and experience to deal with and solve this problem.

The early towns and cities of America were compact and self-contained. Compact for convenience. Streets were muddy. Horses, the only means of locomotion, had to be harnessed and hitched to buggy or wagon. The hostile forest closed in around. Self-contained because the only goods and foodstuffs available were to be gathered from the forest or garden or bought at the general store.

When towns and cities grew by accretion, their centers were strengthened by the growth that crowded around them. As new roads and highways were built, comparable settlements formed as nodes along the way, soon to be surrounded by farmsteads. When the railroads came, new settlements coagulated at railroad or river crossings or natural harbors. In time, transportation routes also found their way to remote centers of agriculture, mining, lumbering, or to notable scenic attractions.

This congenial land use pattern prevailed until after the Second World War. Then, with rampant industrialization and the rapid extension of our road and highway networks, the urban centers, with their frictions and fumes, had less appeal and the open countryside beckoned. Existing homeowners or builders moved out from the towns and cities to outlying homesites or the evolving suburbs, which were an American invention. Stores and factories followed—to leave the hemorrhaging cities with ever-increasing vacancies, dilapidation, and taxes. An influx of lower-income families and welfare recipients exacerbated the problems.

Not only the cities were faced with the resulting dilemmas—for wherever new development occurred in the rural landscape, the adjacent farm- and forestlands were taxed, not according to their use, but as potential development acreage. A swelling tide of farmers were tempted, or forced, to sell their farmsteads and add to the scatteration.

And so we find ourselves today. Almost without exception our towns and cities are burdened with debt, pocked with obsolete or vacant structures, woefully polluted and crime-ridden. In the surrounding outlands, thriving family-owned farms are becoming a rarity. The once unspoiled "America the Beautiful" is cluttered with a maze of poorly maintained roadways and unplanned scatteration. In time, the owners of outlying dwellings demand paved access, utilities, and such public services as schooling and busing. It is hard to imagine a less efficient or more destructive pattern of development. It has come to be known, and vilified, as urban sprawl.

Restoration

Fortunately, there are today those with a compelling vision of a better way—and the knowledge by which troubled neighborhoods and cities

Urban revitalization is a major weapon against sprawl.

can be restored to health and more rational cities and metropolitan regions planned into being. Each of the antidotes which follow describes a tried and proven approach to land use planning that has produced an environment for living that is more comfortable, convenient, efficient, and fulfilling.

Individually or in sum they point the way to the end of urban sprawl and the comprehensive planning of far more desirable living and working centers.

The City

Urban sprawl is for the most part flight from the city. When a city is grossly polluted, poorly maintained, crime-ridden, and heavily in debt; when the beckoning countryside is largely unzoned; and when a network of unrestricted roads leads outward—this exodus is understandable.

What would it take to stop the outflow and reverse the trend—to bring the entrepreneurs and home builders back? One answer, of course, is to renovate the city and make it safer and more attractive. In city after city this has proven to be not only feasible but an accomplished fact.

Activity Centers

Activity nodes—such as those of communities or commercial, business, research, medical, university, or recreational centers—are working enti-

Community Planning and Growth Management

ties. They can be unplanned and awkward, or they can be designed or redesigned to function like a well-tuned machine.

To better things for any type of center, it is well to list those components necessary to make it complete—including housing for the workers—and then designate areas for them to be constructed phase by phase for optimum performance.

Each activity node is to be connected to others and the center city by parkway or rapid transit. Such complete and functional centers planned within the cities, or (if needed) beside controlled access highways, provide a highly desirable alternative to urban sprawl. In addition, they greatly reduce place-to-place travel time and traffic. They are more pleasant and convenient. They are more profitable and successful for all concerned.

Fixed Boundaries

Scatteration or urban sprawl is the creeping dispersion of the more successful enterprises and more desirable housing into the surrounding countryside. All sorts of support services follow along. Not only does this weaken vital centers, it infiltrates the outlying agricultural, forest, and wetlands with a network of incompatible roadways and ill-matched types of development.

How can this hemorrhaging of the city and the disruption of the surrounding region be precluded? Only by the imposition of fixed boundaries and development controls to check the outward pressures.

Where strong metropolitan or regional planning commissions are in place, such confining limits can be accomplished by strictly enforced zoning. There will be opposition by speculators, but the benefits of the confined cities and centers are overwhelming. With land area at a premium, vacant lots and obsolescence are rare; maintenance, land values, and tax yields are high and the economy thrives. Moreover, the center is complete, convenient, and in balance.

Open Space

What constitutes open space? It is unpaved, un-built-upon land or water bodies. Within a metropolitan area, the best possible open-space system is comprised of recreational parks or parklets aligned along the natural streams and drainageways. The latter, preserved to the 50-year flood level, form an interconnected swath of green where the soils are richest and the foliage and tree cover most luxuriant. Here, within or beside the swath, is the preferred route for parkways, bikeways, and walking/jogging paths. They belong in the public domain. Even where presently enclosed in concrete culverts or built upon, waterways can in time be reopened and restored to their natural flows. Urban open space can also

Open space comes in countless forms.

be provided by planted parkway medians and berms, by institutional grounds and in-city forests. Street trees supplement open space by serving as windbreaks in the trafficway channels and by providing welcome shade and cooling.

The urban pattern of the future will be one of compact and confined centers surrounded by park and recreation lands, gardens, agricultural

Community Planning and Growth Management 173

fields, nature preserves, or forest. Internally and externally, nature will always be close at hand, with urban sprawl precluded.

Roadways

Presumably, highways are designed to move motorists safely, efficiently, and pleasantly from place to place. Yet, except for national parkways, turnpikes, and interstate highways, there are few trafficways without buildings fronting upon them, together with driveway openings—sometimes 100 or more per mile. Every car slowing down to turn off or to allow another to enter reduces the capacity of the highway and flow of traffic—often to a standstill. By what right are abutting property owners permitted to convert highways built with public funds into highly valuable private building frontage? Highway engineers know the hazard and friction of roadside intrusion and would opt for development-free borders along all major roadways. By all reason, new through highways and arterials should be designed with limited access—with off- and on-ramps no closer than one-quarter mile on each side. Privileged landowners would no longer gain at others' expense; the traveling public would have the free-flowing highways they paid for and deserve. Thus, too, could be eliminated mile after mile of sordid strip commercial and unplanned sprawl.

Land Value Appreciation

Developers are often blamed for our woes. Sometimes rightly so. But in fact, the better developers are a key to salvation. Given an enlightened governmental and planning framework that encourages sound and creative development, the large-scale, long-range landowner developer is the hope of the American landscape.

Alone, or in a consortium, only the heavyweight developer has the financial depth and staying power to:

- Assemble sizable tracts of buildable property
- Produce a community or other activity center in accordance with a comprehensive plan that addresses all pertinent considerations and includes all needed components
- Build in phases, toward long-term completion
- Reserve and dedicate large stretches of the most scenic, sensitive, or productive open-space land
- Engage experienced planners and top scientific advisers
- Coordinate fully with such public agencies as the transportation authority, school district, water resource management district, park/recreation/open-space board, and regional planning authority

The large-scale, long-range developers have a reputation to gain and protect. Proven, high-quality performance makes everything easier. With a

Two key provisos of growth management policy are that entrepreneurs contribute their fair share of the funds needed for off-site improvements and that all required services be in place before occupancy is permitted.

very significant investment at stake, they well know that any blighting uses or construction would be harmful to their reputation and relationships—and also to their investment. The goal of all experienced landowners or developers is land value appreciation. In simplest terms this means that everything built or changed adds value to the remaining land.

Recentering

Almost without exception, the dispersed elements of uncontrolled sprawl cause stress and disruption. The problem is not only that of disturbing the intruded land but mainly that of connecting those elements to shopping, schools, and other destinations—all at public expense.

Where in time their location is found to be unfavorable—as by reason of climate, topography, lack of conveniences, friends, or employment—they are usually sold for lesser uses or abandoned as a total loss. Many of the isolated homesteaders or owners of other enterprises soon miss the advantages of planned communities or the renovated city and opt to return or move on.

What can be done to heal scatteration and restore the integrity of rural lands? There are many possibilities. Among them:

- The scattered parcels can be assessed and taxed to cover the cost of the required services and off-site improvements. This, in most cases, would soon make remote living prohibitive.
- Acquisition by purchase of an unsuitable property is the direct approach. Often it costs less for a jurisdiction to buy the home or development than to provide the road improvements, maintenance, and schooling. A condition of purchase can be the granting of lifetime tenancy for the owners.

When the perceived advantages of dispersed living are outweighed by those of new or replanned centers, the owners will gravitate to the more attractive locations. The gradual regrouping of the scattered elements into well-defined and balanced activity centers—each with its supporting services and adjacent worker housing—creates a much more desirable environment for living the good, full life.

Zoning

Zoning cannot be a substitute for planning, and planning cannot be a substitute for design—the three must work together.

Conventional zoning as it is commonly practiced is as harmful as it is archaic. In traditional zoning practice, large areas of land are set aside and restricted to a single type of use, as for detached single-family homes, row houses, or apartments, or, again, as for commercial development, business office, light or heavy industry, institutional, recreational, or open space.

Community Planning and Growth Management

The zoned areas are often delineated without thought of topography, the transportation network, or even abutting land uses. Usually they are oversized "to be sure of sufficiency," and in response to political pressure by landowners who buck for the highest potential sales value of their property. Such overzoning results in large un-built-upon tracts within the metropolitan area—increasing the costs of interconnection by road and utilities and encouraging, rather than discouraging, scatteration even within the city.

An advanced, and highly successful, form of zoning is that of planned unit development (PUD), which is especially designed for complete and balanced community or activity center planning. In each case, for a given parcel or tract, existing zoning restrictions are relaxed and creativity is encouraged. Homes and other buildings may be arranged freely. They need not face upon a public street. They may instead front upon off-street courts, plazas, or dedicated walkways—with parking bays or compounds located beside or underneath. They may be designed with a mix of low to high-rise buildings and with such supporting uses and services as may be needed to make the community or center complete.

Such PUD-designed activity centers are in all ways superior to the traditional pattern of structures lined out along streets and highways, with their danger, fumes, and noise, and without ready access to recreation, schools, or convenience shopping. With such attractive in-city communities and educational, commercial, or other centers as can be produced under PUD zoning procedures, there is far less incentive to flee the city and follow the highways to somewhere out beyond.

Construction Regulations. One of the common inducements to urban sprawl is the lack of siting and building regulations in the outlying districts. While some may have zoning and building codes, they are usually loosely enforced, if at all. This invites an invasion of those who seek a place in the woods or beside a stream or along some country farm road, where they may clear and grade out a level spot and build a cabin, shack, or house, or haul in and hook up a trailer. It is to be noted that throughout the countryside there are many attractive mobile home parks that show the multiple advantages of grouping isolated units into thriving communities. Even the most modest rural intrusion causes disruption, but when extensive clearing and grading is involved the result may be a neighborhood disaster. In less than one day, the gung-ho operator of a bulldozer or chain saw can trash a whole hillside and subject it to ever-deepening erosion—or cause miles of stream pollution and siltation in the drainageway below.

Needed is a mandatory statewide land use and construction code that is strictly enforced. The provisions will vary with the geographic location—as for coast, prairie or plain, mountains, river basins, or wetlands. In each case, however, the following subjects should be among those addressed:

The frontiers of waste management are yet to be explored. Beyond the exclusion of trash landfill mountains and offshore refuse reefs are the possibilities of massive topsoil replenishment. A blend of salvaged wood fiber, pulverized plastic, and glass mixed with processed sewage could in time restore to vast areas of eroded land a productive soil mantle.

A positive planning approach. Beach and wetlands are preserved; residential clusters, from single-family neighborhoods to towers, are confined to the uplands; there is raised beach access for all.

- Land use
- Impact statement
- Slope protection
- Clearing of natural vegetation
- Earthwork (excavation, filling, and grading)
- Topsoil conservation
- Drainage of wetlands
- Blocking of natural drainageways
- Water supply
- Road frontage

Without such regulation, the blight of sprawl is bound to spread. With enforced legal controls, urban sprawl can be stopped and its ravages healed.

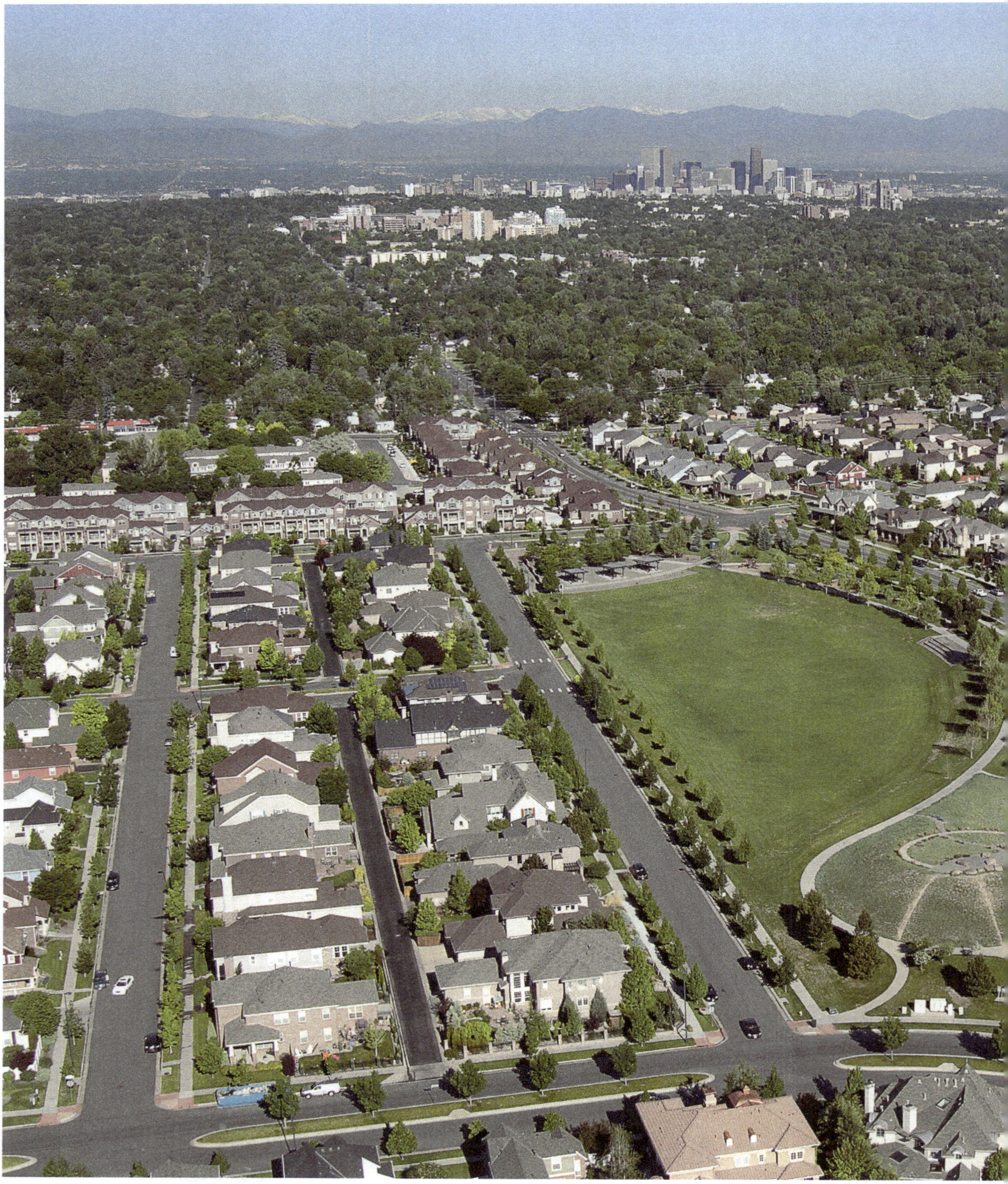

9
THE REGIONAL LANDSCAPE

Rational land use planning can stop at no property line or jurisdictional boundary. Streams flow, trafficways must interconnect, and polluted air, for example, is wafted wherever the winds may blow it.

Every land or water holding abuts other properties and should respect the relationship. Every downstream property is influenced by all that transpires in the watershed above. Each habitation, community, and municipality affects and is affected by conditions within its surrounding social, economic, political, and physical region. Since these are not synonymous, what should the regional boundaries be? They will vary, depending upon the nature of the study.

Interrelationships

For too long the city has been considered a circumscribed entity. By tradition we have thought of the city versus the farmland, the city versus the suburbs, the city versus the townships or counties in which the city lies. Many serious and often needless conflicts have resulted from a lack of coordinated planning. There have been costly duplications of administration and facilities. Animosities have been generated that will for years preclude intelligent cooperation on even the simplest of inter-area issues. There is, however, a wise and growing tendency to plan for the development of the city and its surrounding matrix as a unified region.

I would beg my fellow conservationists, as I would beg my fellow farmers, to realize that we must quit thinking of our countryside piecemeal, in terms of separate products or enterprises: tobacco, timber, livestock, vegetables, feed grains, recreation, and so on. We must begin to think of the human use of each of our regions or localities as one economy, both rural and urban, involving all the local products.

Wendell Berry

The problem of the landscape architect—even as of the architect, the town planner, the engineer, and indeed all men of good will—is now, and will be more acutely every day, the development of ways and means for bridging the gap between town and country, the antithesis between urban and rural life—more specifically between the masonry, the asphalt, and the dingbat construction of the town and the quiet greenery of meadow, forest, and shore. How to open up the town to the country, how to bring the town culturally to the country—that is our primary problem. . . .

Garrett Eckbo

Concurrent with the trend to broaden the scope of planning from an urban to a regional basis is the drive to structure or restructure residential districts into more self-sufficient neighborhoods. These, surrounded by greenbelts and connected by freeways to the manufacturing complexes, the urban cores, and the outlying hinterlands, give promise of a more humanized living environment.

Our homes, neighborhoods, and cities are telltale physical expressions of the way we think and live. Their plan layout and form are in a state of continuous evolution to reflect our changing ideas about living, as we constantly seek a better fit with our natural and built environment. With this in mind, it might be well to study the broad outlines of our present patterns of social and land use organization. Perhaps with better understanding we can improve the relationships and our way of life.

The Family

In our democratic society, as in most cultures of the past, the family is the smallest and yet most significant social unit.

Family lifestyles as we know them today are far different from those of the log cabin, the working farm, or the plantation. The free and rigorous life of the pioneer has given way to the more ordered routine of the farmers on their acreage or the conformity of confined city dwellers. Parental attitudes have changed. The discipline of once paternal- or maternal-dominated family living has become more relaxed and casual. Salons, grand balls, and great dinners are almost a thing of the past, as are the chambermaid, the cook, and the well-trained staff of servants.

Life has become so automobile-oriented that many families have taken their cars into their homes or parked them at the front door. Homes and gardens are less pretentious, less ornate. They are mechanized, less cluttered, more open. Front and rear porches have disappeared along with the stable and alley. The wide front lawn has been replaced by the walled garden courts of patio homes and town houses. Exterior house walls have been opened up to let in more air and sunlight and to enframe the views of garden, sky, and landscape—to provide more contact with nature and with the stone, water, and plants of the earth. As concepts of family living have changed, the forms of our dwellings have changed to reflect them.

The Cluster

It has been learned that from 3 to 12 families constitute the optimum interfamily social group. If their dwellings are clustered in a convenient plan arrangement, kaffeeklatsches, parties, children's play and games, and "get-togetherness" on a first-name basis are natural and spontaneous. Neighbors borrow cups of butter or sugar and exchange views and form friendships at the parking compound; children share toys and

To see the interdependence of city and country, . . . to appreciate that there is a just and a harmonious balance between the two—this capacity we have lacked. Before we can build well in any scale we shall, it seems to me, have to develop an art of regional planning, an art which will relate city and countryside. . . .
Lewis Mumford

As long as man's activities are in sympathy with nature, or are on so small a scale that they do not interfere with nature's self-renewing cycle, the landscape survives, either in a predominantly natural form or as a balanced product of human partnership with nature. But as soon as the growth of the population or its urban activities are sufficient to upset nature's balance, the landscape suffers, and the only remedy is for man to take a conscious part in the landscape's evolution.
Sylvia Crowe

Any architect worth his salt knows that a building is not designed by putting together a series of rooms. Any building that is good has an underlying design concept that binds all the parts together into a whole. Without this it is not architecture. Nor does a designed neighborhood consist of a series of "projects" that are strung together. There must be an underlying design plan that binds together the pieces and makes the neighborhood an entity.
Edmund N. Bacon

The physical plan can seldom if ever, create a "neighborhood" except in the most abstract use of the word. It can, however, very materially assist other forces in fostering a true neighborhood feeling.
Henry S. Churchill

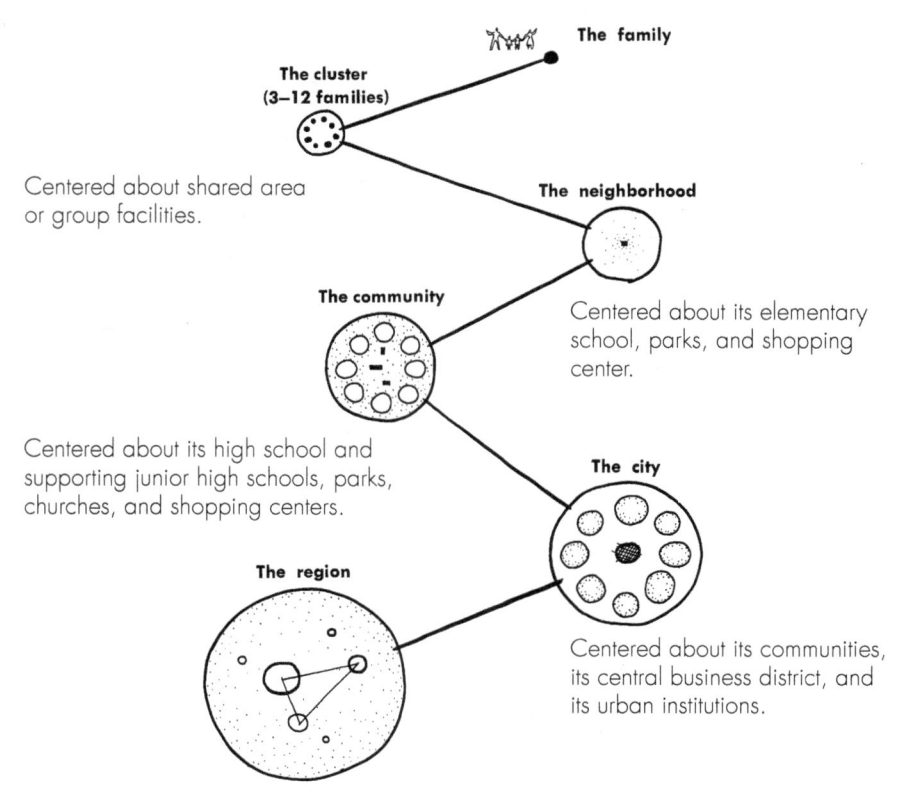

The family

The cluster (3–12 families)
Centered about shared area or group facilities.

The neighborhood
Centered about its elementary school, parks, and shopping center.

The community
Centered about its high school and supporting junior high schools, parks, churches, and shopping centers.

The city
Centered about its communities, its central business district, and its urban institutions.

The region
Centered about its towns and cities, its regional parks, its agricultural and industrial centers and regional shopping centers.

turf. Ideally, the families in such a cluster would have the same general goals and standards but a diversity of individual status and interests.

As a group exceeds 12 to 16 households in number, it becomes unwieldy, tends to lose its cohesion, and automatically breaks up into smaller social alliances.

The most desirable plan arrangements for the cluster will afford an off-street parking compound, freedom from the noise and danger of passing traffic, pedestrian interaccess, and a focal place or feature such as a central lawn panel or a children's play court. The grouping will have a harmonious site and architectural character and physical separation from adjacent clusters or structures. Compactness and the sharing of party walls are the mark of many successful clusters, where the normally unusable side-yard space is squeezed out and aggregated for group use and enjoyment.

The Neighborhood

A neighborhood is at best a grouping of residential clusters around shared open space. It should be small enough to encourage participation of all families in group activities and large enough to contain a convenience-shopping center, playfields, and buffering. An enduring neighborhood plan and one that has accommodated changing concepts of social behav-

The Regional Landscape   181

ior and education is one formed around and providing safe walkway access to an elementary school. In size and population it is shaped to yield or contribute to the approximate number of students required for a balanced school facility. It is not essential, however, that either the school, shopping, or other shared amenities be centered within the single neighborhood confines. It is often more desirable that they be placed outside or between subneighborhood enclaves of varying character and size and be laced together with interconnecting greenways, walks, and bicycle trails.

In the well-conceived neighborhood, peripheral roads will provide access and vehicular connection to free-flowing regional parkways. Through traffic will be precluded. Ideally, the neighborhood will be composed of planned tracts grouped around and between lobes of semiprivate park that open into the larger community school-park system. Each such tract, developed as an entity, would be freed of all arbitrary lot restrictions. On the PUD model its proposed layout would be subject to review by the planning agencies solely on the basis of livability. Land use patterns and densities, as approved, would then be fixed by covenants between the landowners and the municipality.

The Community

A planned community, as differentiated from the neighborhood, would at best comprise two or more neighborhoods separated by greenbelt

Fort Detrich

Valley Springs

East Hills

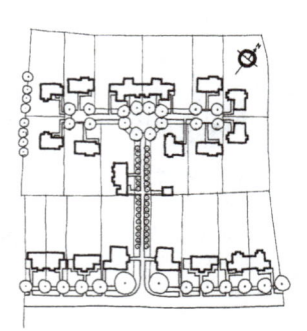

Welwyn Garden City

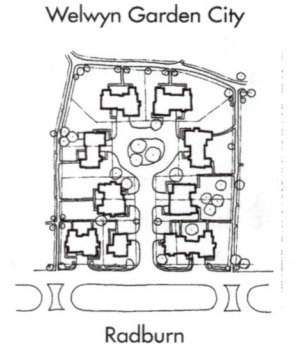

Radburn

Five cul-de-sac arrangements that provide a cluster of family dwellings.

Planned communities with regional character.

182   LANDSCAPE ARCHITECTURE

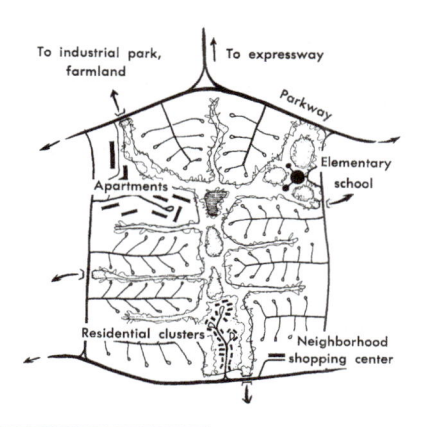

Neighborhood plan diagram number 1: approximately 1200 families (one-third in multifamily units).

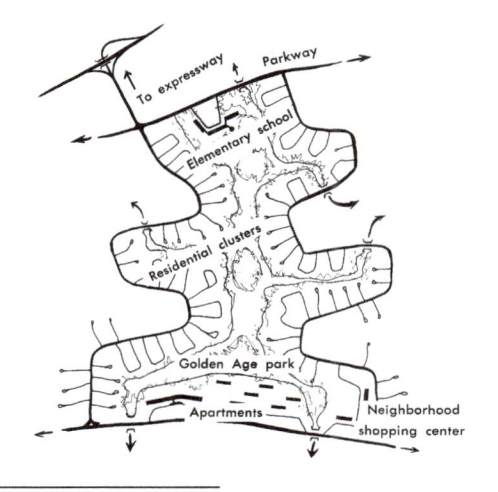

Neighborhood plan diagram number 2: approximately 1200 families (one-third in multifamily units).

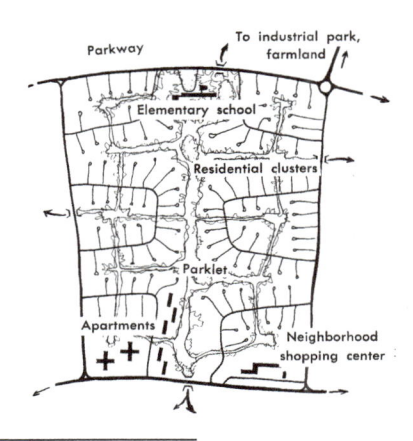

Neighborhood plan diagram number 3: approximately 1200 families (one-third in multifamily units).

spaces. It will be interconnected with controlled-access parkways and oriented to the more important communal features and nodes. It need not be contained within the limits of a city. Satellite communities, or the larger new towns, spaced out in the open countryside and served by freeways and rapid transit, have many advantages.

Being more self-sufficient, they reduce the number of external vehicular trips required and thereby conserve fuel and energy. They are less disruptive of neighboring trafficways, land uses, and established systems than if developed within or immediately contiguous to other residential areas. All planned communities, whether perforce impacted or formed more freely as satellites, have the great advantage of being brought on area by area and stage by stage in accordance with a balanced overall conceptual diagram. The ultimate capacities of roadways, schools, parks, and freshwater supply mains, for example, can be predetermined and facilities phased in without the need for costly periodic enlargement or reconstruction.

The land use patterns, traffic-flow diagrams, and population cap will be determined initially. There will be defined flexibility zones (the more extensive the better) within which the approved uses and number of

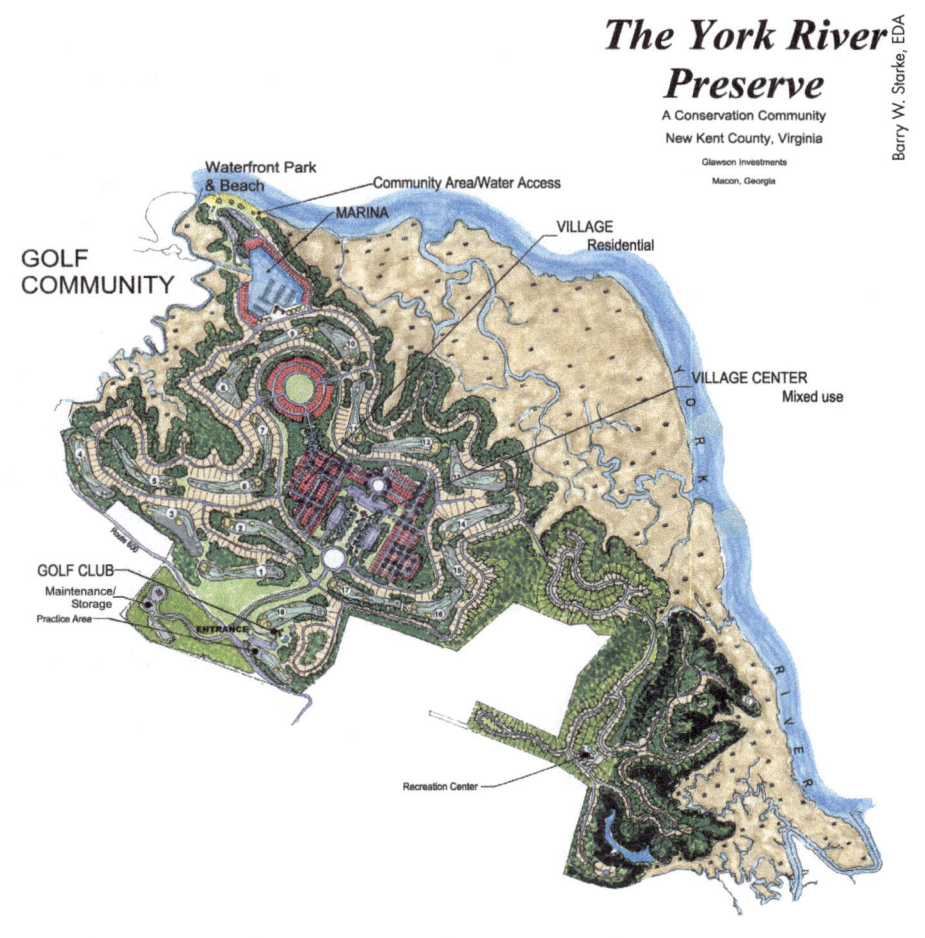

The York River Preserve
A Conservation Community
New Kent County, Virginia
Glawson Investments
Macon, Georgia

Planned community with conservation as the organizing element.

The Regional Landscape 183

dwellings may be freely arranged on the basis of subsequent and more detailed study and changing long-range needs. Environmental protection covenants, performance standards, and design guidelines are to be formulated and enforced from the start. Such planned communities, having clearly demonstrated their many benefits, are the promise of the future. There can be no better answer to regional growth and resource management.

Theoretically, the ideal community will be composed of several to many interrelated neighborhoods of diverse social, architectural, and landscape character. Each neighborhood, while separate and unique, will share common pathways, amenities, and open space. When fully built out, in a process which may take several decades, a community will usually include and support a high school and one or more junior high schools, each within a school-park campus and community center, with game courts, sports fields, meeting rooms, auditorium, and library. There will be a community shopping and business office mall as well as the deployed neighborhood convenience centers. A transit station and light manufacturing or business campus are normally planned, and a wide range of cultural, recreational, and employment opportunities afforded.

Since we are creatures of our environment, better communities will follow as new and better concepts of community living, land ownership, and land use evolve. The superior community, as we envision it today, will be distinguished by the following features:

- A natural periphery demarcated by highway, greenbelt, river, ridge, cliff, ravine, or other physical barrier.
- Community identity. Orientation to a symbol, such as a high school, church, shopping center, or park that gives it focus and meaning.
- Provision for outdoor communal activities in clean, sunlit, and shaded spaces uninterrupted by vehicular traffic flow.
- Minimum friction and danger in use of the automobile, coupled with maximum convenience. Free-flowing trafficways, with no on-grade crossings.
- A community open-space framework, around which the buildings are grouped.

The City

A city is a large and densely populated center of economic, social, and political activity, having a relatively fixed geographic position and specific governmental powers granted to it in charter form by the state. It is the center of an urban culture.

Our cities can be only as good as enlightened public opinion permits or demands them to be. This education and persuasion toward civic action and progress is an often neglected phase in contemporary urban planning.

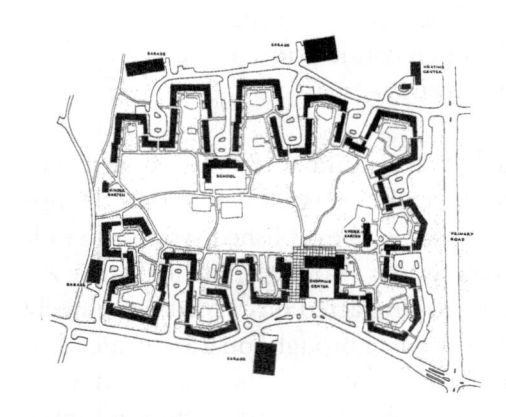

A neighborhood of apartment dwellings, each related to an exterior approach and an interior social court and to a large central park area. The relatively high density of the apartment groups yields large open space where it counts.

Every community needs a symbol of its existence. Much of modern community frustration has come into being because a symbol of the visual meaning for its life is missing. Because no symbol is found, there is no center on which to focus life.
Ralph Walker

The city in its regional context: Waikiki.

The city in its complete sense, then, is a geographic plexus, an economic organization, an institutional process, a theatre of social action—and an esthetic symbol of collective unity. On the one hand it is a physical frame for the commonplace domestic and economic activities; on the other, it is a consciously dramatic setting for the more significant actions and the more sublimated urges of human culture.

Lewis Mumford

In the city . . .
  People go where people are,
  sit where there is place to sit,
  look when there are things to see,
  and like face-to-face encounters.

The form of a city will be, at best, the three-dimensional expression of its varied functions working well together. A good city is expressive of our times, our technology, and our ideals. It is an evolving organic entity, with its roots in the past and its orientation to the future.

The thriving city must be a growing, functioning organism, requiring and capable of providing light, air, water, food, circulation, elimination of waste, and regeneration, or else it will wither and die. Desirable city features include:

- The most of those high qualities that civilization has attributed to urbanity; the least of those evils that the ages have condemned
- A harmonious fit with the natural landscape setting and surroundings
- A cohesive and comprehensible metropolitan diagram
- A well-designed, compact, and intensive central business district (CBD) with outlying satellite subcenters—all interconnected with rapid transit
- A differentiation of zones—the center city, inner city, outer city, and suburbs—each with its own development codes and regulations
- A circumferential freeway and parkway system with radial boulevards to the CBD bypass ring road

The Regional Landscape

In every historical epoch except our own, the cultivated and influential person, the civilized, polite and urbane citizen, inevitably lived within the city. . . . Indeed the classical names for the city express these very virtues: civis—*city;* civilized, civilization; urbs— urbane; polis—*polite and elegant.*

Ian L. McHarg

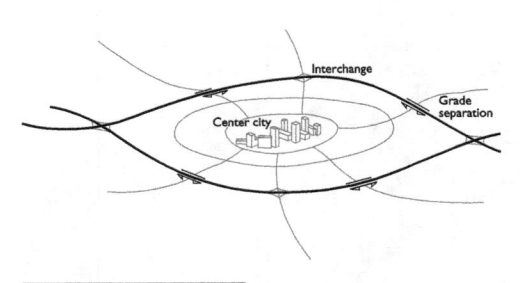

Freeways should surround rather than penetrate the center city, with collector-distributor highways providing interarea movement. The construction of freeways through an urban center where traffic is already at a saturation point can only result in chaos.

Regional planning is the conscious direction and collective integration of all those activities which rest upon the use of earth as site, as resource, as structure. . . .

Lewis Mumford

The new regional pattern will be determined by the character of the landscape: its geographical and topographical features, its natural resources, by the use of land, the methods of agriculture and industry, their decentralization and integration; and by human activities, individual and social in all their diversity.

Ludwig K. Hilberseimer

A regional plan that pieces together the disparate plans of the various member jurisdictions and blankets the whole with a layer of further restrictions does more harm than good.
  Worthy regional planning starts with an understanding of human needs and the landscape.

- Separation, by alignment and level, of vehicular accessways and transportation routes
- Traffic and parking accommodated but made incidental to the higher aspects of city life
- An expression of the city dweller's gregarious nature—congregating places where people can meet to exchange goods, services, and ideas—the marketplace, the shopping mall, the park, the square, and the plaza
- Human scale, so that city dwellers, workers, and visitors feel themselves in agreeable proportion to what they see and hear and so that they share a sense of being pleasantly related to the city and thus to the ambient world
- Handsome architecture and landscape architecture enriched with sculpture, murals, and fountains
- Order, efficiency, beauty, and a milieu conducive to the development of the full human powers
- Clean and healthful surroundings
- A free-flowing and easy transition between urban, suburban, and rural areas

The Region

A region is a large and generally unified, but loosely defined, geographical area that provides the supporting base for one or more centers of population concentration. To simplify the complex problems of regional planning almost to the point of naïveté, it might be proposed that each region should be analyzed and planned for its highest and best use in relation to the land and its resources.

Planning on a regional basis, whether in terms of geographic, political, social, or economic regions, provides a more comprehensive and effective frame of reference than the consideration of any community, town, city, or county alone.

Regional planning agencies are at best nonpolitical and service-oriented. They provide planning coordination, regional information, and technical assistance to the member jurisdictions. Their primary functions are:

- Data gathering, analysis, storage, and distribution
- The preparation and updating of a comprehensive regional plan
- The conduct of studies for various planning elements such as housing, transportation, and open space
- The provision of liaison with state, federal, and local jurisdictions
- The processing of state and federal grants-in-aid to local governments
- The recording and coordination of all proposals relating to the protection, alteration, or development of salient land and water areas
- Recommendations as to the significance of regional environmental impacts

186   *LANDSCAPE ARCHITECTURE*

The gridlocked metropolis (hypothetical), still all too common in urbanizing America. Negative features:
- Building frontage on trafficways
- Central business district (CBD) transected
- Traffic friction and congestion
- Commercial strip coagulation
- Sprawl and scatteration
- Resulting vacancies and obsolescence
- Lack of facile interconnection between activity centers
- Disorganization and inefficiency
- Unconsolidated land use districts
- No open-space system or preserves
- Lack of coastal and waterway protection
- Little response to topography

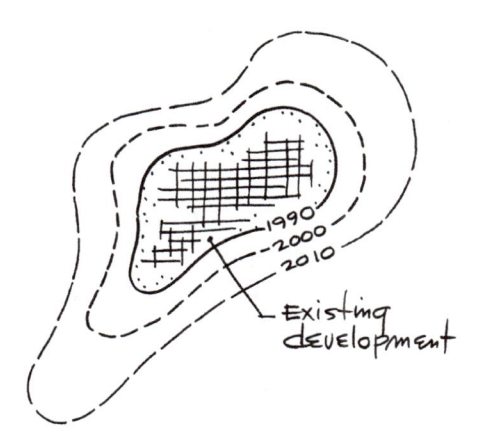

Urban service lines. As a device to ensure infill and protect open-space lands, some municipalities are including as an element of their comprehensive plans a map of urban service lines showing by year the limit to which public services are to be extended. Within the period noted, development will not be permitted beyond the designated line.

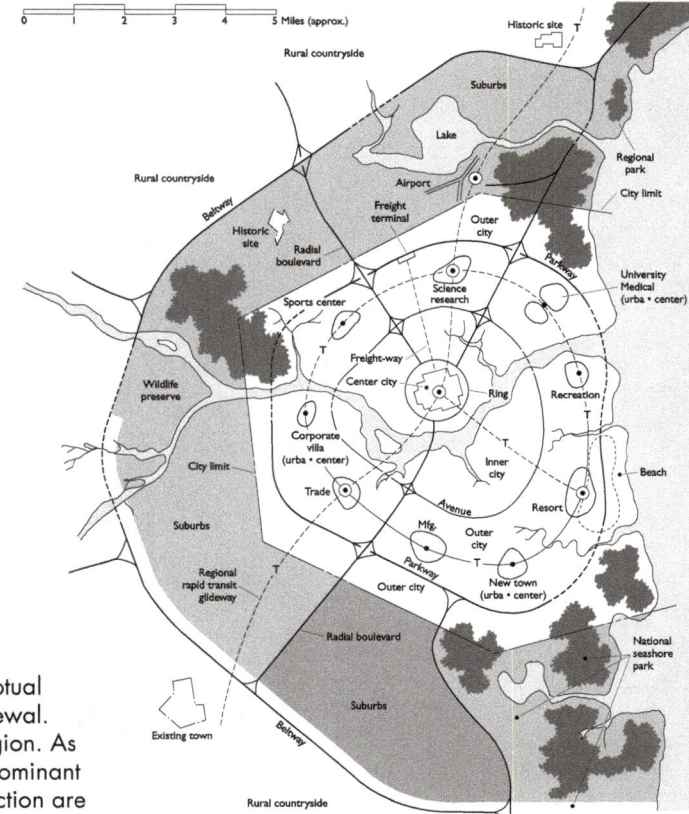

A city for the twenty-first century (hypothetical). A prototype conceptual plan for phased long-range development, redevelopment, and renewal. Shown is a conceptual plan, or model, for a typical urbanizing region. As can be seen, it preserves and conserves (protects) the best of the dominant topographic features. Development areas and routes of interconnection are fitted compatibly with the natural landscape enframement.

The Regional Landscape 187

The goal of regional planning is to develop through intergovernmental cooperation the best possible *diagrammatic framework* of land uses and trafficways, to provide the evolving *performance standards* required to ensure environmental integrity, and then to *encourage the free and creative expression of private enterprise.*

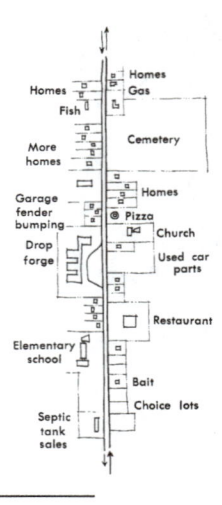

The highway and adjacent uses. A highway almost anywhere in almost any state: fifty driveway entrances per mile; unplanned, unzoned, unintelligent—a study in friction, confusion, inefficiency, and chaos.

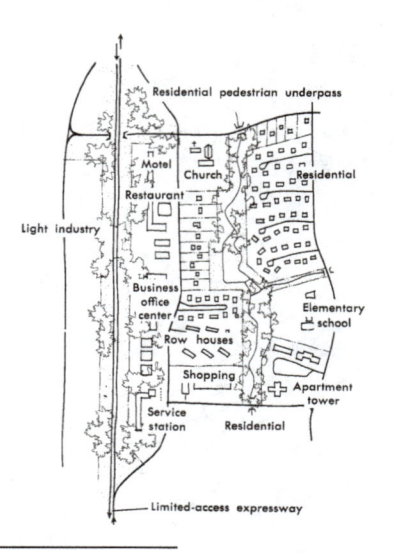

Planned, zoned, intelligent: highway traffic flows freely; functions are grouped; homes orient to park; school, church, and shopping areas have access.

Regional Form

The land use and trafficway patterns of each region, if well considered, will respond to the "want to be" of the land. They will preserve the scenic superlatives, protect areas of ecological sensitivity, and ensure the integrity of the natural systems. They will recognize and adjust to the natural land and water forms. They will avoid the delays and hazards of on-grade trafficway crossings. They will provide economies in travel time and distance and in construction, operation, and maintenance costs. They will provide a setting within which and around which development may take place freely and creatively as the direct expression of human needs.

Desirable features of the region will include:

- Compact and thriving, off-highway neighborhoods, communities, and cities within an open-space surrounding
- Phased development contours precluding the uncontrolled growth and sprawl of urbanizing areas
- The "land banking," in public or tax-adjusted private ownership, of all holdings not foreseeably needed or desirably suited for development
- Wide, free, uninterrupted preserves allocated for farmsteads, forest, recreation, wildlife management, and conservation
- The location of all new activity centers in optimum relationship to land and water resources, topographical features, and other planned uses

Regional development should respond to the "want to be" of the land.

188   *LANDSCAPE ARCHITECTURE*

Regional planning agencies can be effective only if
- The state officially prescribes the boundaries of each region.
- Regions are defined along county lines, since socioeconomic data are normally acquired on a countywide basis.
- County membership in, and support of, the regional agency is mandated by the state.

Most municipalities and regions have zoned development land far in excess of foreseeable needs. Not only does this encourage scattered parcel-by-parcel construction, it results in tax assessments disproportionate to productivity and drives homeowners from their properties and farmers from their farms.

New construction would be better accommodated by the infill of existing centers until they were built out and unified. When additional land might then be needed for development, new cohesive communities could be defined through the process of comprehensive planning.

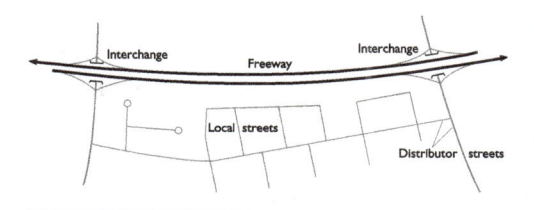

The limited access concept of freeway development should be extended where feasible to all through or distributor roads within the metropolitan region. While building frontage would not be permitted on these thoroughfares, connections to local streets would be encouraged and facilitated.

- Nonfrontage expressways and circumferential and radial roadways with parkway characteristics providing free-flowing regional access to urban centers and satellites
- Direct rapid transit interconnection of the regional hubs with subsurface or overhead approaches to the station plazas
- Separate, consolidated transmission-truckway corridors linking major production, processing, and distribution centers
- The programmed provision and strategic allocation of all basic service centers and amenities needed for living the good, full life
- A unified park, recreation, and open-space system
- Arterial parkways, with scenic-historic byway loops traversing areas of natural and historic significance
- A long-range land and water management program based upon ongoing ecological studies and a regional resource inventory
- Development based on the highest and best use of the land and performance standards, rather than blindsided conventional zoning

Wildlife habitat preserved: Santa Monica Mountains Conservancy.

Open-Space Frame

The regional open-space frame will embrace and separate the various land uses and activity nodes. It will provide background, base, and breathing room, and when so arranged as to preserve the best of the landscape features, it will give each region its unique landscape character.

Perhaps the most important task of regional planners is to define and help to bring into being a spacious, interconnecting, and permanent open-space preserve as the framework for ongoing development.

The Regional Landscape

The open-space preserves of a region should be so designated and landbanked. Only those agricultural and recreational uses that would cause them no significant harm should be permitted, and land should be taxed accordingly.

When and only when adequate public services can be assured through the economic *extension* of existing trafficways or mains (or by a centralized installation, in the case of satellite communities) should "preserve" land be rezoned and development be allowed to proceed.

As a counteraction to urban sprawl with its destruction of wildlife habitat—many landowners are establishing their own on-site habitats and wildlife preserves.

It is foolish to permit satellite shopping malls to be built if they reduce the vitality of existing commercial centers.
New regional shopping nodes should be permitted only as their need can be demonstrated.

Greenways and Blueways

Greenways are paths of movement for vehicles, pedestrians, and migrant wildlife. Ways because they are paths; green because they are enveloped in foliage. They may vary in scale from a woodland trail to a national parkway through mountainous terrain.

Blueways trace the flow of surface runoff—from rivulets to streams, to broad and sometimes raging rivers. Like the veins and arteries of the human body, they tend to serve as an interconnecting system. They transport nutrients from the uplands, and feed and drain the bottoms. Within the flow ways are to be found the most verdant foliage and abundant bird and wildlife populations of each region. In all seasons they ameliorate the climate and add interest to the landscape. They are best preserved in their natural state.

Greenways and blueways.

By a single regulation, and without cost, the most rational of all open-space diagrams could be established by and for each region. To wit:

> From this date neither unauthorized construction of any type, nor the destruction of natural vegetation shall be permitted within the 50 year flood limits of a stream or waterbody.

The result would be a protected flow way of privately and/or publicly owned lands that would reduce the surface runoff of precipitation, reduce erosion and siltation, conserve water, moderate the extremes of climate, and enhance the landscape. As a border to tillable or buildable lands it would provide windscreen and flood control.

A complete regional recreation system provides insofar as feasible the whole range of opportunities, from the child's play lot within the residential cluster to the state or national park.

On the ascending order of social groupings—i.e., home, cluster, neighborhoods, community, etc.—each may be expected to provide for its own particular recreation needs. Beyond these, two or more groups or jurisdictions may jointly provide additional facilities such as public swimming pools, tennis centers, or golfing that perhaps neither could provide alone.

Larger installations such as zoos, botanical gardens, or major marinas require areawide support, as do expansive regional parks and forest preserves.

On an even grander scale, state and national parks provide for recreation within the context of scenic or historic superlatives.

Zoning as commonly practiced is not workable.

In the creation of healthy environment nature's collaboration is not only important, but also indispensable.
Eliel Saarinen

When by reason of public ownership, or by easement, a greenway can be aligned through or contiguous to a blueway corridor, the benefits are manifold.

The Essentials

It is believed that the evaluation of sound regional development can be reduced to four simple tests:

1. *Does it belong?* Is the use of the land or water area consistent with federal, state, and regional plans and with community goals?
2. *Is it sustainable?* Can it be built without exceeding the carrying capacity of the land? The use should not be permitted if it would impose significant long-term stress on the natural ecological systems. Should there be question, the filing of an environmental impact assessment might well be required.
3. *Would it be a good neighbor?* Is the proposed use complementary and complimentary to the existing and proposed uses in the neighborhood? Or would it have harmful physical or visual effects? Would it reduce property values? Would it destroy, or preserve, cherished landmarks? A well-conceived, well-designed project should enhance, not harm, its environs.
4. *Are adequate levels of public service in place?* At all stages of project construction and use, the proposed improvement should have available all public services required, without overloading of trafficways, power or water supply systems, storm sewers, waste treatment plants, fire and police facilities, and (in the case of residential development) schools and recreation areas. Not only should all such facilities be online when needed, but the local government should also be assured that the developers and users will bear their fair share of the cost.

If these four conditions can be satisfied, there should be no cause to oppose the project, for it should become a welcome regional asset.

Regional Planning

There are three approaches to regional planning—four, really. The fourth is the do-nothing course of just letting things drift—to watch the landscape disintegrate area by area, until it comes apart at the seams. Scatteration, traffic glut, and loss to the many for the gain of the few are the inevitable consequences.

In a more rational approach, the regional jurisdictions form a voluntary association comprising selected local officials as representatives. With a small paid staff, they undertake studies and make recommendations to the various responsible agencies. Such an association has the advantage of political clout, but the disadvantage of political jousting.

The Regional Landscape

A more effective advisory group is civic in nature. In form it may well be a citizen's committee or council initiated by one or more public-spirited individuals who assemble a team of nonpolitical but highly respected leaders in various aspects of regional life. Representatives of business, educational, financial, scientific, social, labor, and agricultural interests are among the potential participants. Again, with a small but well-trained staff they define the goals and objectives and set about on a comprehensive course of phased studies. The council may meet as a body no more than once a year, but their consensus recommendations, when adopted, carry impressive weight with the officials and agencies concerned.

A third means of addressing regional issues is the formulation of an official regional planning commission with responsibility for certain metropolitan programs. Such a metro commission receives its charter from the state, with well-defined powers and provisions. The commission members are elected by the regionwide constituency. A professional director and staff are appointed. In the areas of assignment, the focus is on coordinated planning, and construction and operation in the best interest of the entire metropolitan region and all of its citizens.

Governance

The citizens of each locality and jurisdiction like to handle their own affairs—and should, within reason. It is reasonable that they have their own school boards, committees, councils, and elected officials to keep an eye on things and respond to local needs and aspirations.

It is unreasonable, however, that within a cohesive metropolitan region such common and overriding concerns as transportation, transit and transmission, regional land use planning, resource management, law enforcement, and recycling should be handled in such a fragmented and inefficient manner as is usually the case. Most cities, towns, and boroughs now do their own independent thing—in disregard and often defiance of what goes on just across their borders. Those responsible for essential regional services are thus confounded by the need to patch together a host of disparate local programs rather than put into operation coherent, regionwide plans. It can be seen that the multitudinous duplications of staff, administrative overhead, and equipment—let alone the resolution of conflicts—is costly and wasteful in the extreme.

By all reason, most (though not all) regional planning, construction, and implementation procedures should be systematized and centrally controlled. This calls for a metro form of government. Where this has been most successful, several basics have applied:

- The metro government concept was voted into being by all citizens affected, after an educational campaign and series of public forums.

The *carrying capacity* of a land-water area or a natural ecological system is the limit of its ability to support a population without significant degradation or breakdown.

Town and country must be married and out of the union will spring a new life, a new hope, a new civilization.

Ebenezer Howard

- The enabling legislation and charter delegate broad powers, but limit the initial responsibilities to a few well-defined programs that are clearly of regionwide scope. Responsibilities can be expanded from time to time on the basis of proven performance.
- Certain powers and tasks are reserved to the local jurisdictions and officials to ensure their independent authority and support.
- The metro council membership is composed of elected leaders representing the various interests of the region.

Generally it can be stated as observable fact that whatever is good for the region as a whole is good for the whole of its people.

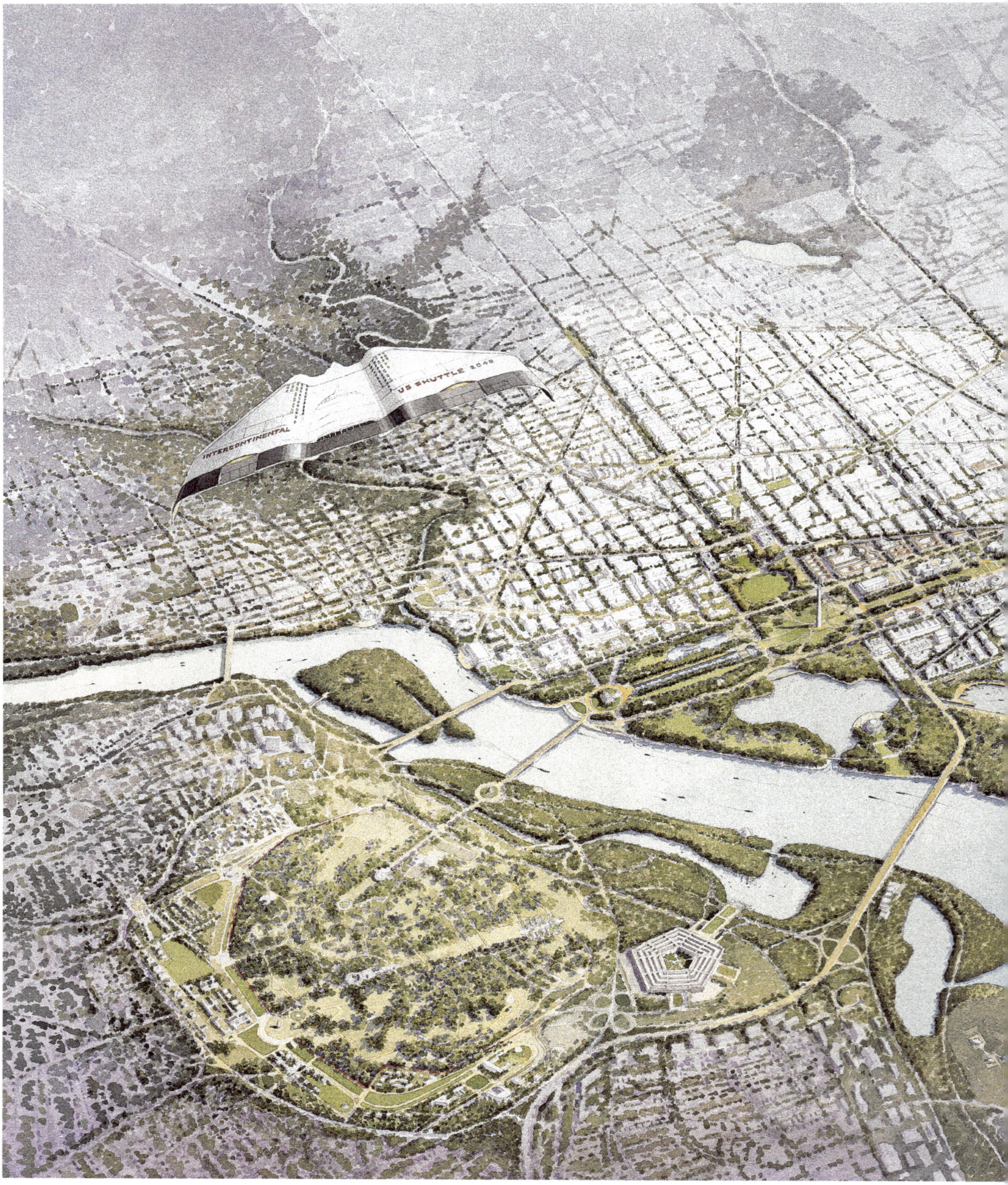
INTERCONTINENTAL
US SHUTTLE 2048

Illustration courtesy of the National Capital Planning Commission's *Extending the Legacy Plan*. Rendering by Michael McCann.

10 URBAN DESIGN

It sometimes seems that our contemporary planning is an unholy game of piling as much structure or as much city as possible in one spot. The urban areas to which we point with pride are often merely the highest, widest, and densest piles of brick, stone, and mortar. Where, in these heaps and stacks of masonry, are the forgotten, stifled people? Are they refreshed, inspired, and stimulated by their urban environment? Hardly, for in our times, too often a city is a desert.

Cityscape

To be bluntly truthful, our burgeoning American cities, squared off and cut into uncompromising geometric blocks by unrelieved, unterminated trafficways, have had more of this arid desert quality than those of other cultures past or present.

If we compare a map of Rome as it was in 1748 with a recent aerial photograph of New York, we marvel at the infinite variety of pleasant spaces that occurred throughout the Eternal City. Of course, as Rasmussen has pointed out in *Towns and Buildings*, "Great artists formed the city, and the inhabitants, themselves, were artists enough to know how to live in it." We wonder why such spaces are for the most part missing in our contemporary city plans.

Traditionally, the urban spaces of America have been mainly corridors. Our streets, boulevards, and sidewalks have led past or through to

Our contemporary landscapes are characterized by immense metropolitan airports, zig-zag patterns of high-voltage power lines and disturbed historical sites. Our familiar landscapes are not small farmsteads and dirt roads, rather they are the yawning expanses of urban development.
Patricia C. Phillips

According to a recent poll, most Americans (56 percent), if given the choice, would now prefer a rural life; 25 percent would opt for the suburbs, and only 19 percent for an urban living environment.

Large cities seen from an altitude of several hundred feet do not present, as a whole, an orderly facade. Their vastness is their most striking feature; whatever quality they possess is lost in sheer quantity. Areas that give evidence of planning occupy but a small surface. Disorder predominates. Buildings are piled up near the center and scattered haphazardly towards the outskirts. The few green spots and other places of beauty known to the tourist, seem hidden in a maze of grey and shapeless masses that stretch toward the surrounding country in tentacular form. The very borders of the city are undefined, junk and refuse belts merging with the countryside. If on beholding this sight we pause to contemplate modern cities and consider what they could have been if planned, we must admit in the end that, in spite of their magnificent vitality, they represent one of man's greatest failures.
José Luis Sert

something or somewhere beyond. Our cities, our suburbs, and our homesites are laced and interlaced with these corridors, and we often seek in vain to find those places or spaces that attract and hold us and satisfy. We do not like to live in corridors; we like to live in rooms. The cities of history are full of such rooms, planned and furnished with as much concern as were the surrounding structures. If we would have such appealing outdoor places, we must plan our corridors not as channels trying to be places as well but as free-flowing channelized trafficways. And we must plan our places for the use and enjoyment of people.

The City Experienced

The old cities of Europe, Latin America, and Asia had, and still have, to their credit and memorable charm, their plazas, piazzas, courts, squares, and fountains and their distinctive, indefinable, uplifting spirit of joie de vivre. These cities were conceived as three-dimensional civic art and in terms of meaningful patterns of form and open spaces. Our cities, with few exceptions, are oriented to our traffic-glutted streets.

Whom are we to blame for this? Aristotle, in his *Rhetoric,* states, "Truth and justice are by their nature better than their opposites, and therefore if decisions are made wrongly, it must be the speakers who (through lack of effective powers of persuasion) are to blame for the defeat." For our purpose, this passage might well be paraphrased: "Facility, interest, and beauty are by nature better than chaos, the dull, and the ugly, and therefore if decisions are made wrongly, it must be we planners who, through lack of effective powers of persuasion (or more compelling concepts of urban living), are to blame."

In searching for a more enlightened approach to urban planning we must look back and reappraise the old values. While recognizing the fallacies of the "city beautiful" in its narrowest sense, we must rediscover the age-old art of building cities that inspire, satisfy, and work. And surely we will, for we are disturbed by the vapid nature of the cities we have planned or, worse, have allowed to grow unplanned in sporadic, senseless confusion.

Evident Needs

We, in contemporary times, have lost the art of, and feeling for, overall plan organization. Our cities lack coherent relationships and plan continuity. With our automobiles as the symbol and most demanding planning factor of our times, we have found the meandering streets, places, and plan forms of the ancient cities to be unsuitable. We have rejected (with good reason) the synthesizing device of the inexorable "grand plan" but have found, for the most part, few substitutes save the mechanical grid and other patterns of uninspired geometry. The transit,

The essential thing of both room and square is the quality of enclosed space..
Camillo Sitte

The basic tenet of urban design is disarmingly simple: the best city is that which provides the best experience of living.

From Giovanni Battista Nolli's map of Rome.

For the most part, it is proposed that those cities have proven most agreeable that are the most expressive of and responsive to their time, place, and culture; that are functional; that afford convenience; and that are rational and complete.

The corridor canyons that are New York City's streets stretch on interminably without relief, without focal point, and without the welcome interruption of useful or meaningful space.

Urban Design

The unit of measurement for space in urban society is the individual....
Arthur B. Gallion

A city plan is the expression of the collective purpose of the people who live in it, or it is nothing.
Henry S. Churchill

The first step in adequate planning is to make a fresh canvas of human ideals and human purposes.
Lewis Mumford

From cradle to grave, this problem of running order through chaos, direction through space, discipline through freedom, unity through multiplicity, has always been, and must always be, the task of education, as it is the moral of religious philosophy, science, art, politics and economy.
Henry Adams

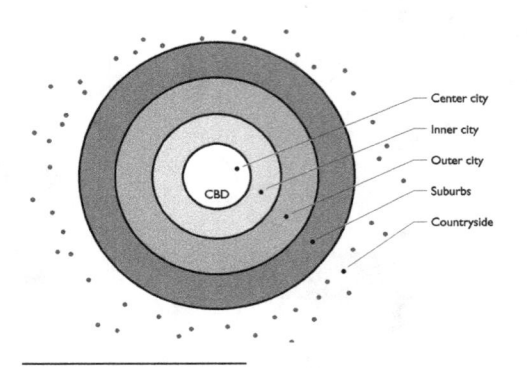

In thriving cities, each component district is well defined and fulfills its contributing functions.

Will the city reassert itself as a good place to live? It will not, unless there is a decided shift in the thinking of those who would remake it. The popular image of the city as it is now is bad enough—a place of decay, crime, of fouled streets, and of people who are poor or foreign or odd. But what is the image of the city of the future? In the plans for the huge redevelopment projects to come, we are being shown a new image of the city—and it is sterile and lifeless. Gone are the dirt and noise—and the variety and the excitement and the spirit. That it is an ideal makes it all the worse; these bleak new Utopias are not bleak because they have to be; they are the concrete manifestation—and how literally—of a deep and at times arrogant, misunderstanding of the function of the city.
William H. Whyte Jr.

the protractor, and the compass have delineated for us a wholly artificial pattern of living areas and spaces. We must and will develop new types of plan organization better suited to our way of life. In future urban planning considerations, the significant space is bound to return, and we will again have ways and places as important as the structures.

The desert character of our cities is concentrated in the downtown core. Here the average cityscape is a conglomeration of metal, glass, and masonry cubes set on a dreary base plane of oil-splattered concrete and asphalt. It is bleak, chill, and gusty in wintertime, and in summer it shimmers and weaves with its stored-up, radiating heat. Within view of its naked towers, the open countryside beyond is often many degrees warmer in winter and cooler in the summertime.

Such an oppressive and barren cityscape falls far short of the mark. Our cities must be opened up, refreshed, revitalized. Our straining traffic arteries must be realigned to bypass the city cores, to pass under or around the perimeter of unified pedestrian areas or levels in which offices, shops, and restaurants are planned together in close proximity and in which people may move about without on-grade crossings of trafficways. In contrast with the stark masonry canyons and roaring avenues, the new pedestrian domains will provide a garden-like setting for freely composed groupings of towers and terraced structures, variformed courts, and walkways—providing the welcome relief of foliage, shade, splashing water, flowers, and bright color. Like oases, such intensified multiuse plazas will transform the city into a refreshing environment for vibrant urban life. Many exemplary prototypes are appearing in America and abroad.

The City Diagram

To understand how a city works (or why it doesn't work) and plan toward its improvement, it is helpful to dissect it into its various parts and to examine each part separately. Such an approach reveals the surprising fact that in few cities have such components been planned, or even considered, as functioning entities. As to components, for the purpose of this examination it is proposed that we consider, first separately and then together, the center city, the inner city, the outer city, and the suburbs.

The Center City, or Central Business District (CBD)

The center city serves a double purpose. It is not only the core of the urban metropolis, it is as well the polarizing and dynamic core of the whole surrounding region. Here one expects to find the centers of government, commerce, and trade; the principal financial institutions; and the corporate headquarters of industry, manufacturing, and communications. Here, too, are most often found the cultural superlatives—the cathedral, performing arts center, central library, museums, and galleries, and as well the theaters, stadium, and sports arenas.

198 LANDSCAPE ARCHITECTURE

There are, certainly, ample reasons for redoing downtown—falling retail sales, tax bases in jeopardy, stagnant real-estate values, impossible traffic and parking conditions, failing mass transit, encirclement by slums. But with no intent to minimize these serious matters, it is more to the point to consider what makes a city center magnetic, what can inject gaiety, the wonder, the cheerful hurly-burly that make people want to come into the city and to linger there. For magnetism is the crux of the problem. All downtown's values are its by-products. To create in it an atmosphere of urbanity and exuberance is not a frivolous aim.

Jane Jacobs

The central business district, in compression, will grow upward instead of out; obsolescence will disappear; densities will increase, and the core will regain its dynamic intensity.

Our present troubled, largely obsolescent, and woefully inefficient urban centers are spilling out over their boundaries and messing up their countryside. Such uncontrolled sprawl can and must be stopped. Not only for the good of the cities, which are losing their focal dominance and vitality, but as well for the farmlands, forests, and rural American landscape, which are rapidly going to pot.

An arcade or mall of shops and restaurants that never close helps keep the streets safe and the downtown vital. Occupants of upper-story apartments in office and commercial buildings add to the evening street life, and round-the-clock surveillance.

The best way to promote security in a downtown area is to ensure that the streets are alive with responsible urban residents who come out to enjoy the evening sites and activities. In such an atmosphere, restaurants and theaters thrive, shops stay open, and people can linger or stroll about in relative safety.

Central Park, New York City, was the first public park built in America. A competition for its design was held in 1858; the winners, Frederick Law Olmsted and Calvert Vaux, were the first American landscape architects. This magnificent urban open space of 843 acres has attracted to its sides much of the prime residential, commercial, and cultural construction of the city. Its effect on real estate values, its inestimable contribution to the city, its ineffable meaning to all who see and sense and use it—these lessons should never be forgotten by the urban planner.

With each complex a small empire in itself, there is reason to allocate for each its own distinctive segment of the center. Since all segments share the need for shopping, dining, and hotels, a centralized superplaza is suggested, around which the various building groupings can take form. With few exceptions, parking, storage, distribution, and mechanical systems are to be relegated to subsurface plaza levels.

Within the CBD, through streets should be eliminated—phased out in time and replaced by circulation loop drives around and between the traffic-free plaza islands. These surface drives, bridged at the plaza-to-plaza crossings, will provide for the free circulation of cabs, buses, emergency vehicles, and a limited number of private cars by special permit.

On the linked plaza islands of the revitalized center will rise a new urban architecture. The freestanding megaliths of the present need to be replaced by interconnected complexes of high and low structures with flying terraces, roof gardens, inset patios, open courts, domed conservatories, and galleries. Aloft, boxed window ledges, balconies, and terraced setbacks will become the private gardens of the center city. Rooftop restaurants and illu-

Urban Design 199

The memorable cities of the world—London, Amsterdam, Paris, Copenhagen, Madrid, Athens, Rome, Montreal, New York, New Orleans, San Francisco—are those in which people live where they work. Civic and business centers are interspersed with town houses, apartments, and cafés, with bakeries and boutiques, with wine, cheese, fruit, and florist shops, and with artists' studios.

minated recreation courts and pools will add sparkle and animation to the skyline. At pedestrian levels, buildings will open out upon a labyrinth of landscaped courts and meandering walkways. Passageways from place to place and level to level will be weather-protected. They will be flanked with seasonal exhibits, displays, and plantings—with flower stalls and book marts; candy, nut, and pizza shops; pretzel, fruit, and popcorn stands . . . and provision for sidewalk bazaars with paintings, carvings, crafts, antique jewelry, mechanical toys, entertainers, and all those divertissements that add excitement and pleasure to shopping.

Utilize rooftops.

Revitalize existing open space.

Redevelop the waterfront.

With surface traffic and parking restricted within the city center, rapid transit will flourish. (Such cities as Stockholm, Toronto, and Paris are telling examples.) Multilevel transit hubs, centrally located, are major regional destinations and points of transfer. Linked, computerized cars arrive and depart at swishing speeds through illuminated subsurface transitways or by aerial monorail.

It is proposed that the CBD of the future will be confined, and constricted, by a tight and inflexible ring to preclude its "leaking out" and

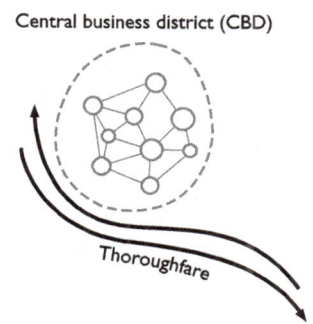

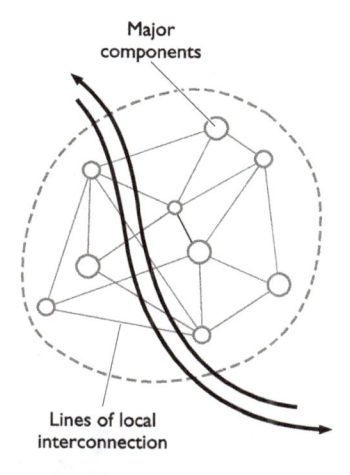

Within a theoretical central business district (CBD), the circles represent major destinations such as banks, department stores, civic centers, regional sports facilities, or entertainment districts. The lines represent paths of pedestrian circulation. A closely knit set of CBD elements is mutually sustaining. A compact center makes for easy connections in terms of time, distance, and friction. Dispersion of the CBD negates the advantages of "downtown."

Patterns of mix are important. The vibrant centers are those in which the old is intermixed with the new, the low with the high, the simple with the elaborate.

When rows of shops and homes are interrupted by blocks of stark office towers or by blank building walls, evening street life is diminished. To sustain street appeal and nighttime activity, office and apartment towers are best grouped around off-street plazas or courts. Business, residential, and commercial relationships are all thereby intensified.

The *layering* of shops, apartments, and offices is proving to be a successful means of keeping the evening streets alive, with people at hand to enjoy them.

Planned CBD: Shanghai, Huangpu River.

ensure its intensity. Access by automobile via radial boulevards will be intercepted at the center-city perimeter by a decked distributor ring road within a spacious right-of-way. Vehicles arriving at the ring can either circumvent the CBD entirely if this is desired or enter by well-spaced ramps into the parking and transport levels of the plazas. The ring is more than a free-flowing trafficway. Its wide swath of space can accommodate ample open-air parking compounds as well as water management holding ponds and recreation areas. Here too, available to center-city visitors, can be located such attractions as elements of the zoo, botanic garden, and aviary. Or perhaps the annual art fair or ethnic festivals.

Housing? The more successful cities have proven the value of devoting the upper stories of buildings and towers to in-city apartments for executives and higher-salaried workers, who then in the evenings throng into the pedestrian ways and places to keep them alive and thriving.

The Inner City

Outward of the ring lies the area best described as the "inner city." It is the band containing the bulk of housing and service facilities that

Urban Design 201

Eminent domain is the authority by which a government or public agency can appropriate, with due recompense, private property for public use or benefit. To make the exercise of eminent domain more acceptable, its application may be conditioned by such provisions as:

1. Use only after open negotiation has been tried and failed.
2. Use only for the final 10 percent of the land required when a holdout has blocked acquisition.
3. When long-range acquisition is in the public interest, grant the owner tenancy for a stated period of time.
4. Purchase, with leaseback for conditional uses.

provide the necessary support of the CBD and adjacent urban satellite communities. Commonly, in its present form, it is mostly obsolescent—left behind in the exodus of the previous residents who followed the expanding trafficways into the lands beyond. In its dilapidated state it is pocked with abandoned structures and vacant properties. Here and there are the remnants of once-thriving neighborhoods. Here too, one finds start-up businesses in reclaimed buildings and blocks of homes restored and renovated by enterprising newcomers.

Available Opportunities

Here in the inner city, with its frequent stretches of boarded-up buildings and rubble-strewn land, there is opportunity to acquire at affordable cost the sites for clustered housing enclaves or whole new communities. Until recently this was not possible because of absentee or holdout parcel owners. Now, however, with innovative redevelopment techniques providing the powers of eminent domain, the sizable sites required can be assembled and cleared by a redevelopment authority.

World Trade Center Memorial, New York City.

In city after city, such reclaimed tracts of inner-city wasteland are now sprouting with well-planned, mixed-use, residential developments. Dwellings range in type from single-family homes to multistory apartments. Residents, many of whom are employed nearby, may be workers of low to moderate income or high-salaried executives.

The inner city offers the greatest opportunity for urban renewal and redevelopment, for with overall planning and self-help incentives it can provide not only the housing but also a wide spectrum of the service and supply facilities needed to support the adjacent CBD and the outer city. With unemployment and the lack of housing two of the major urban problems, the inner city teems with latent solutions.

Examples of inner-city housing.

There is a truism to the effect that in every problem and seeming disaster are to be found the seeds of opportunity. In many ways our present cities are little short of disasters. Where then do the opportunities lie?

The inner city, where the problems seem most hopeless, may become the promised land. In this deteriorated band are to be found many sound homes and start-up business structures inviting rehabilitation. Here too are endless opportunities for employment in the demolition of obsolete structures, clearing of land, reconstruction of streets and utility lines, and for privately refinanced redevelopment and planned communities.

Housing

It is in the inner city that low- to moderate-income housing will make its most telling advances. While the tower apartments of the CBD (on costly land and with elevators required) will be designed mainly for residents with the higher incomes, the mixed-use neighborhoods outside the ring will include the full range of housing types for those of all income levels, including the displaced and presently homeless.

At the upper end of the housing scale will be zero lotline homes, town houses, garden apartments, and low-rise multifamily apartments resembling horizontal condominiums. The separated single-family homes facing on local streets or culs-de-sac (with front yards devoted to display and side yards unused) will no doubt persist, but there will be a preponderance of dwellings with common walls and fenced or walled outdoor living areas.

Town houses are a long-standing tradition—from Boston and Philadelphia to San Francisco. Georgetown in Washington, D.C., surely one of the most delightful residential areas of our country, has narrow brick homes set wall to wall along its narrow, shaded streets. Its brick walk pavements, often extending from curb to facade, are opened here around the smooth trunk of a sycamore or punched out there to receive a holly, a boxwood, a flowering tree, or a bed of myrtle. In this compact community, where space is at such a premium, the open areas are artfully enclosed

Urban Design 203

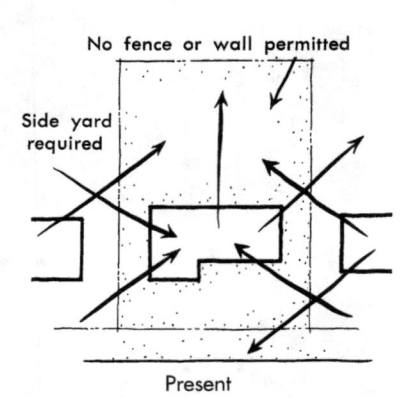

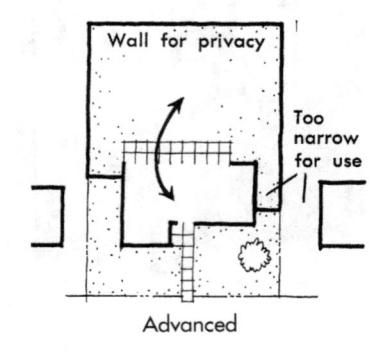

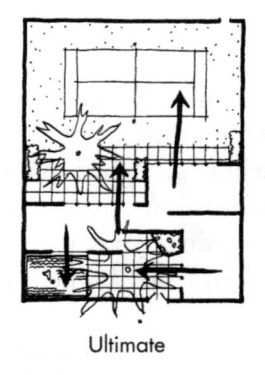

Relaxation of side-yard, setback, and enclosure restrictions will permit full use of lot, privacy, and indoor-outdoor transitions.

by fences, walls, or building wings to give privacy and to create a cool and pleasant well of garden space into which the dwelling opens.

Mid-to-lower-scale dwellings will also be designed in compact arrangements within open-space surroundings—with schools, child care centers, and convenience shopping close at hand. Again, some residential buildings will resemble horizontal habitats, with common laundries, storage spaces, gardens, and even kitchens. New concepts will be evident also in modular and prefab construction.

While the construction framing members and panels will be of uniform dimensions, the room shapes and arrangements can be of infinite variety—as can panel materials and finishes. Fixtures, equipment, and furnishings will be standardized but freely arranged within the living spaces. (This will be a modernized version of the age-old, economical, and delightfully varied Japanese modular approach to residential construction.) With wide front and side yard setbacks consolidated into shared usable space, the building groupings can be diverse and compact, with things to see and do close at hand. For most homeowners and tenants, this will be a desirable feature.

In working with urban renewal and model cities programs, we have discovered that the openness of newer communities was at first the thing with greatest appeal to families relocated from older neighborhoods or from cramped and aching slums. But the residents soon became dissatisfied with the severe buildings, the wide grass areas, and the play equipment set out on flat sheets of pavement. One would hear the officials ask, "What's wrong with these people? Why aren't they happy? What did they expect? What more do they want?"

What they wanted, what they missed, what they unconsciously longed for, were such congregating places as the carved and whittled storefront bench, the rear-porch stoops, the packed-clay, sun-drenched boccie courts, the crates and boxes set in the cool shade of a propped-up grape arbor or in the spattered shadow of a spreading ailanthus tree. They missed the meandering alleys, dim and pungent, the leaking hydrants, the hot, bright places against the moist, dark places, the cellar doors, the leaning board fences, the sagging gates, the maze of rickety outside stairs. They missed the torn circus posters, the rusting enameled tobacco signs, the blatant billboards, the splotchy patches of weathered paint. They missed the bakery smells of hot raisin bread and warm, sugared lunch rolls, the fish market smells, the clean, raw smell of gasoline, the smell of vulcanizing rubber. They missed the strident neighborhood sounds, the intermittent calls and chatter, the baby squalls, the supper shouts, the whistles, the "allee, allee oxen," the pound of the stone hammer, the ring of the tire iron, the rumbling delivery truck, the huckster's cart, the dripping, creaking ice wagon. They missed the shape, the pattern, the smells, the sounds, and the pulsing feel of life.

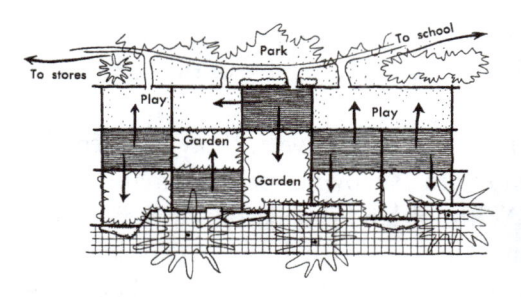

Minimum homes for maximum living.

What they missed, what they need, is the compression, the interest, the variety, the surprises, and the casual, indefinable charm of the neighborhood that they left behind. This same charm of both tight and expansive spaces, of delightful variety, of delicious contrast, of the happy accident, is an essential quality of planning that we must constantly strive for. And one of the chief ingredients of charm, when we find it, is a sense of the diminutive, a feeling of pleasant compression. Private or community living spaces become a reality only if they and the life within them are kept within the scale of pleasurable human experience.

Mixed use is nothing new.

A further error of our planning has stemmed from the lingering compulsion to force our cities into lots and blocks of uniform size and use. Such "ideal" cities of monotonous conformity are gray in tone. If we examine most recent plans, we find that one zone is designated for single-family homes, another zone for town houses, and another for high-rise apartments; an isolated district is set aside for commercial use; a green area will someday be a park. May we place in this residential area an artist's studio? It is not allowed! An office for an architect? A florist shop? A bookstall? A pastry shop? No! In a residential area such uses are usually not permitted, for that would be "spot zoning," the bureaucratic sin of all planning sins. These have too often been the rules, and thus the rich complexities that are the very essence of the most pleasant urban areas of the world are even now still being regulated out of our gray cities. London, after the Blitz, was replanned and rebuilt substantially according to this antiseptic planning order. The first new London areas were spacious, clean, and orderly, and all would have seemed to be ideal except for one salient feature: they were incredibly dull. Nobody liked them. Our zoning ordinances, which to a large degree control our city patterns, are still rather new to us. They have great promise as an effective tool

Urban Design

and a key to achieving cities of vitality, efficiency, and charm when we have learned to use them to ensure these qualities rather than preclude them.

The Outer City

In the replanned, far more efficient city diagram, the limits of the revitalized inner city will be defined by a circumferential parkway that provides external vehicular access, as well, to the satellite centers of the outer city.

In the expanding rings of previous outward growth, those districts farthest removed from the city center are usually newer, with many sound neighborhoods yet remaining. Without land regulation, however, most outer residential areas have been infiltrated by such incompatible uses as repair shops, used car lots, and truck stops, to name a few. These disparate uses are to be phased out—gathered into their own unified compounds, where they can operate more efficiently without disrupting their neighbors or the landscape.

It is in the outer city also where new satellite centers—as for health, education, business offices, manufacturing, and recreation—can take form at receptive sites surrounded by the communities of their employees. Such satellites connected center to center with intercity rapid transit and at the peripheries by the regional freeway and parkway circumferentials will attract those enterprises seeking togetherness in more conducive surroundings. Thus will be achieved far more efficient activity centers, with the advantage of nearby housing and optimum regional access. Such "centering" is believed to be the only means of ending the all-American scourge of urban sprawl.

Suburban sprawl.

Disastrous urban sprawl can be effectively preempted by investing in the fundamental systems that protect and nourish a healthy urban environment.
Dylan Todd Simonds

The Suburbs and Beyond

It would seem that suburban living has become the American dream. The early abandonment of the industrialized city in search of greener pastures gained momentum until it became a rout. The migration was given impetus by the coming of the automobile and the expansion of highway networks. Moreover, as families and businesses pulled up stakes, city taxes were raised to compensate for the loss, while property values declined. The outward flight has continued until now many who work in the city and live in exurbia must spend hours a day in bucking traffic as they drive to and fro. It is only recently that the balance is beginning to tip. As suburban communities become commercialized and lose their appeal, and as revitalized cities become more attractive, there is an increasing back-to-the-city movement. As a result, the agricultural lands and forest beyond are less threatened. With the stemming of scatteration and the emerging acceptance of regional planning and redevelopment, we can in time have the best of all worlds—thriving cities, attractive suburbs, and a protected regional matrix of productive farmsteads, forest, and wilderness preserves.

Freeway sculpture.

The Ubiquitous Automobile

Even more than the Industrial Revolution, even more than our threatening population explosion, even more than electronic technology, the automobile has been the chief determinant in American land planning for the past many years. In the foreseeable future this will probably yet be the case. Without a drastic change in our thinking, the automobile will continue to dominate our cities, our communities, and our lives. The challenge is to segregate and improve our trafficways while at the same time devising the means by which cohesive living and working areas may be freed of through-traffic intrusions.

Urban Design   207

The drivers and passengers of motorized vehicles are safest and happiest when the travel experience is one of flow through pleasant and variformed corridors. Street crossings and on-grade intersections are anathema to fast-moving traffic. They are to be avoided. By realigning expressways and arterial highways around, not through, residential and activity centers, the major causes of interruptions and accidents can be eliminated.

People Places

Where do city people like to be? Not where they feel intimidated by rushing traffic or the blank walls of massive office towers. Not where getting from here to there entails a long walk, wait, or tiresome climb. Not in a blazing or frigid windswept expanse of paving. Not where there is little of interest to see or do. People prefer instead to be in or move through ways and places of comfort, interest, and delight. They enjoy the meandering walk through contracting and expanding spaces. They enjoy the charm of diminutive nooks and passageways—of places where they can rest, to talk or people-watch. Such experiences are seldom happenstance; they must be thoughtfully planned.

With passage by Congress of the Americans with Disabilities Act (ADA), there is now a national mandate to shape and reshape our living environment with the disadvantaged in mind. All people will benefit from such sensitive planning.

Well-designed ways and places, especially those intended for public use, accommodate everyone—not only the spry, but, as well, all who by reason of age or disability have special needs or problems. All of us in our lifetimes—from stroller days to the times of crutches, the cane, the walker or wheelchair—are "disadvantaged" to some degree in terms of mobility or cognizance.

Only in recent years have our public agencies and physical planners come to recognize the needs and possibilities, and take positive action. Now most building codes and regulations incorporate requirements designed to make life safer, more comfortable and convenient.

In general it can be said that in reviewing the merits of any architectural or landscape architectural proposal it should be tested vicariously by the experience of all potential users.

Among the more helpful innovations are well-marked, well-lighted pedestrian street crossings. Curbs at street corners are depressed and tapered. Ramped platforms are provided at bus stops to allow for the loading and unloading of passengers at the conveyance floor level. In parking courts, stalls are reserved near the entranceways for the use of the handicapped. Steps to public buildings and areas are being eliminated or alternative ramps installed with easy slopes and with handrails. Often entrance gates and doors are fully automated. Since many persons cannot read, or have language difficulties, the use of internationally standardized symbols has become a welcome feature of informational and directional signs.

The starkness of once-hostile downtowns has been relieved with shade tree plantings, miniparks, seating, fountains, and floral displays. Gradually our evolving metropolitan areas are taking form around interconnected, traffic-free business, shopping, and residential centers. On these well-furnished islands the experience of getting about, or being, in safe, attractive, and refreshing surroundings gives new meaning to town and city.

Urban Green, Urban Blue

Few would deny that cities would be more pleasant if less bleak and more gardenlike. Is that asking too much of the system? Not when we can witness many examples of downtown transformation. Everywhere across the nation once-barren streets are now a-greening and a-blooming. Flower-bedecked planters, window boxes, and hanging baskets enframe store windows. Recessed bays and setbacks are converted to miniparks with raised planting beds and seating. Concrete boulevard medians are converted to seasonal showpieces. Vacant lots in the inner city are cleared of trash by citizen groups and with the help of civic groups or clubs made neighborhood gardens and gathering places.

The local embellishments are heartening signs of new attitudes. At the larger, citywide scale, publicized and aided tree-planting programs have clothed mile upon mile of streets and drives with burgeoning foliage. Polluted streambeds and riverbanks have been cleared of debris and restored to verdant waterways. Lakeshores and waterfronts have become a focus of public improvement and the focal points and pride of many cities.

Building upon such successes, sentiment is growing for open-space programs that will in time incorporate or consolidate large swaths and small bits and pieces of public land into integrated systems. Under the centralized guidance of expanded departments of parks, recreation, and open

Urban green/blue.

Urban Design

Hyatt City Center.

space, our contemporary cities might well in time come to approach the ideal of "an all-embracing garden-park within which buildings, travelled ways and gathering places are beautifully interspersed."[1]

But, one might ask, with urban real estate being sold by the square foot instead of the acre, how can such open space be afforded and assembled?

In the center city the vacating of through and selected local streets would yield more than enough area for the ring-road bypass with its buffering parkland. The elimination of the divisive existing parking lots and structures can free up another 10 percent of the average CBD, as can the razing of half-used obsolete buildings. Reclaimed vacant or tax-delinquent lands can be added to park and recreation holdings. If within the city there are cliffs, steep slopes, or arroyos, so much the better. Where there are in-city streams or a waterfront, the possibilities are expanded.

Throughout the greater metropolitan confines, the evolving processes of reclamation, rehabilitation, and redevelopment will create extensive open-space reserves. To these can be added the gifts of property by public-spirited donors and the essential links and fill-in parcels acquired with bonds or budgeted capital improvement funds. The lands are there in various conditions ready to be put together into an open-space system and framework for ongoing development.

The New Urbanity

The needs of the human beings who would work and live in our cities must come to have precedence over the insistent requirements of traffic, over the despoiling demands of industry, and over the callous public acceptance of rigid economy as the most consistent criterion for our street and utility layouts and for the development of our boulevards, plazas, parks, and other public works.

What are the human needs of which we speak? Some have been so long ignored or forgotten in terms of city planning and growth that they may now seem quaint or archaic. Yet they are basic. We human beings need and must have once again in our cities a rich variety of spaces, each planned with sensitivity to best express and accommodate its function; spaces through which we may move with safety and with pleasure and in which we may congregate. We must have health, convenience, and mobility on scales as yet undreamed of. We also must have order. Not an antiseptic, stilted, or grandiose order of contrived geometric dullness or sweeping emptiness but a functional order that will hold the city together and make it work—an order as organic as that of the living cell, the leaf, and the tree. A sensed cohesive and satisfying order that permits

[1]Kublai Khan, in outlining the plan for his new capital city, Tatu, the present-day Beijing.

New urban area.

the happy accident, is flexible, and combines the best of the old with the best of the new. An order that is sympathetic to those structures, things, and activities that afford interest, variety, surprise, and contrast and that have the power to "charm the heart." We humans need in our cities sources of inspiration, stimulation, refreshment, beauty, and delight. We need and must have, in short, a salubrious, pollution-free urban environment conducive to the living of the whole, full life.

Such a city will not ignore nature. Rather, it will be integrated with nature. And it will invite nature back into its confines in the form of clean air, sunshine, water, foliage, breeze, wooded hills, rediscovered water edges, and interconnected garden parks.

Gradually, but with quickening tempo, the face of urban America is taking on a new look. It is a look of wholesome cleanliness, of mopping up, renovation, or tearing down and rebuilding. There is a sense of urgency, directness, nonpretense, and informality. There is a new group spirit of concerted actions and of people enjoying the experience of making things happen, of coming and being together in pleasant city surroundings. There is a freshness, sparkle, and spontaneity as American as apple pie. The movement was born partly of desperation—of the need by property owners to "save the city" and protect their threatened investments. It responds to the need for energy conservation and the contraction of overextended development patterns. It stems from revulsion at pollution, filth, decay, and delapidated structures. It is a strengthening compulsion to clean house, repair, and rebuild, mainly by private enterprise. There is a new vitality. There is a sense of competition, too, marked by inventiveness. Fresh winds are astir in our cities.

Urban Design

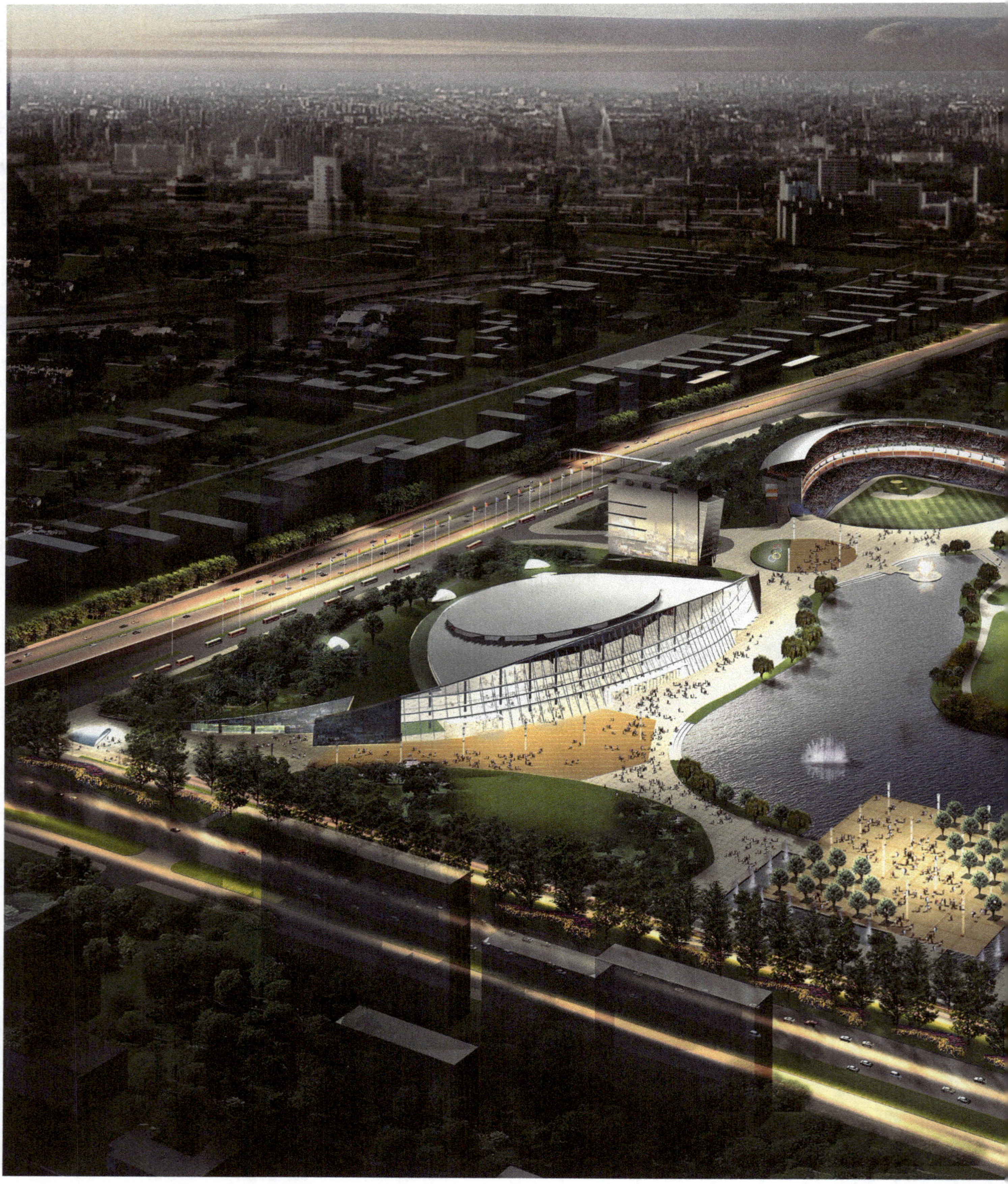

11
SITE PLANNING

Sasaki Associates, Inc.

For every site there is an ideal use. For every use there is an ideal site.

Program Development

A first step in the design of any architectural, landscape architectural, or engineering project is to have a clear understanding of just what is being designed.

Many a completed installation functions poorly or actually precludes the very uses for which it was planned. Perhaps it was doomed because it was forced upon an unsuitable site or because it was not well designed, not clearly expressive of its purpose. Or its operation may be hampered by the frictions it generates. Most often, however, the root of failure lies in the fact that a program was never fully considered; the complete project with all essential relationships and impacts was never envisioned or thoughtfully conceived.

It is our tacit responsibility as planners to help carry each work to successful conclusion. To accomplish this aim, to plan a project intelligently, we must first understand its nature. It is essential that we develop a comprehensive program. By research and investigation we must organize a precise and detailed list of requirements on which we can base our design. To this end we might well consult with all interested persons and

In defining the program for a project we are at this point less concerned about what it will look like and more concerned about what it will be.

To dream soaring dreams is not enough. To have value, dreams and ideas must be translated into the hard reality of feasible proposals.

Design as a form-giving process is the creation of places, spaces, or artifacts to serve a predetermined purpose.

In every area of human endeavor, the most successful projects are those best planned and designed.

The responsibility of the planner is to guide those involved to the best solution and to help ensure in all ways possible the project's success.

Any plan is essentially the scheduling of specific means to definite ends. . . . Any kind of planning implies conscious purpose. . . .
Catherine Bauer

draw freely upon their knowledge and views—with the owners, with potential users, with maintenance personnel, with planners of similar undertakings, with our collaborators, with anyone who can contribute constructive thought. We will look to history for applicable examples. We will look ahead to envision possible improvements based on newly developing techniques, new materials, and new concepts of planning.

We will try to combine the best of the old with the best of the new. Since the completed work will be the physical manifestation of this program, the program itself must be designed thoroughly, imaginatively, and completely.

Site Selection

If we as planners are concerned with wedding a proposed structure or use to a site, let us first be sure that the parties are compatible. We have all seen buildings or groups of buildings that seem foreign to their location. No matter how excellent these structures or how well contrived their plan, the total result is disturbing.

It would seem obviously foolish, for instance, to situate:

> A school fronting on an arterial trafficway
> A roadside restaurant with zero approach-sight distance
> A shopping center without adequate parking space
> A farm without a source of potable water
> A tavern near a city church
> A fabricating plant with room for neither storage yard nor expansion
> A new home at the end of a jet landing strip
> A meat-packing plant upwind of a suburb
> An apartment building 30 feet above a mined-out seam of coal

Each would seem, on the face of it, doomed to failure. Yet each, to the coauthor's knowledge, has been attempted. It is reassuring to those of logical mind to note that in the due course of events each enterprise has been subjected to disrupting strains, scathing antipathies, bankruptcy, or collapse—all rooted in the choice of an inappropriate site for the given use.

In far too many cases, a project has started with the unquestioned acceptance of an unsuitable location. This is a cardinal planning error. An important, if not the most important, function of a planner is the sometimes delicate, sometimes forceful task of guiding an entrepreneur to the selection of the best possible location.

Alternative Sites

As advisers, we should be capable of determining the requisite site requirements for any given venture and be able to weigh the relative merits of alternative situations. First we must know what we are looking for. We must thoughtfully, perhaps even tediously, list those site features that we consider necessary or useful for the proposed project, be it a power dam, a new town, or a frozen yogurt stand. Next we should reconnoiter and scout out the territory for likely locations. For this task we have a number of helpful tools, such as U.S. Geological Survey (USGS) maps, aerial and remote-sensing photography, road maps, transportation maps, planning commission data, zoning maps, chamber of commerce publications, plat books, and city, county, township, and borough plans.

The purpose of the game is to improve the environment whenever you do anything to change it.

Garrett Eckbo

If a client makes the wrong planning decision in site acquisition or otherwise, and has first advised the planner, the fault lies not so much with the client as with the planner, who has failed to present a persuasive case.

Given the facts and a full understanding of the alternatives, reason tends to prevail.

With maps or other materials as a guide, we will visit the most likely places and explore them. Such scouting parties may be launched by automobile or plane or, even better, helicopter, which not only offers immunity from barbed-wire fences, cockleburs, and no-trespassing signs but also gives an ideal overall perspective of likely properties. Much can be noted from an automobile, especially the relation of proposed sites to adjacent development patterns and approaches. But sooner or later, to be effective, we must get up off the seat cushions and cruise about the property on foot.

Having narrowed our choice to several alternative tracts of land, we will then analyze them in detail. The favorable and unfavorable aspects of each will be carefully noted and assayed. Sometimes we will discuss the comparative analysis of the various parcels informally with the client. Again, we may prepare a well-documented report for presentation, as to a board of directors, an authority, or a city council. Such a report, oral or graphic, may list the sites in order of suitability. Often, however, it is bet-

Site Planning 215

ter to present only the relative merits of the alternative sites, in clear, concise terms, and leave to the decision makers the business of discussing pros and cons and making the selection.

The Ideal Site

We all know of planned developments that seem to be natural outgrowths of their sites: a home terraced down to a fronting beach; a subdivision artfully fitted to the contours, vegetation, and other topographical features of a pleasant valley; a school with its playground in a parklike setting placed at the community center and approached along safe and inviting pedestrian paths; a factory with ordered production units, tanks, storage areas, and shaded parking space all planned in admirable relationship to approach roads, trackage, or piers.

We must determine those landscape features, natural and built, best suited to our needs and then search for a site that provides them. The ideal situation is the one that, with least modification, most fully meets the project requirements.

> Our primary work as planners is to help fit human activities to the "want to be" of the land.

Site Analysis

Now that we have selected the location, what is our next concern? At the same time that the program requirements are being studied and

Existing off-site features may guide or even dictate how the site is developed.

refined we must gain a thorough understanding of the site and its surroundings: not only the specific area contained within the property boundaries, but the total site, which includes the environs to the horizon and beyond.

Graphic survey information and supporting reference data are essential, but they must be supplemented by at least one, and preferably repeated, visits to the site. Only by actual site observation can we get the feel of the property, sense its relationship to the surrounding areas, and become fully aware of the lay of the land. Only in the field can we gain an understanding of the site's bounding road, the lines of pedestrian approach, the arc of the sun, the prevailing breeze, the good views, the ugly views, the sculptural landforms, the springs, the trees, the usable areas, those features to be preserved if possible, and those to be eliminated. In short, only on the ground can we come to know the site and its character. We must climb from hollow to hill, kick at the sod, dig into the soil. We must look and listen and fully sense those qualities that are peculiar to this specific landscape area.

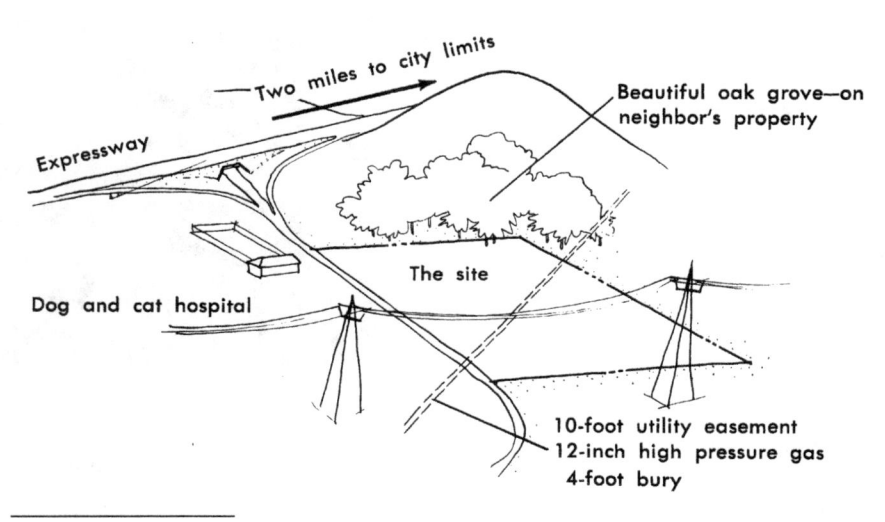

The extensional aspects of a site.

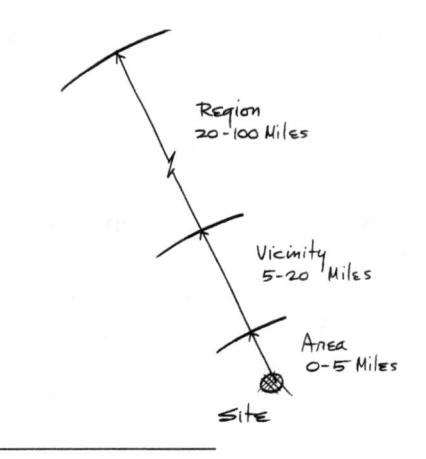

The site and its extensional environs.

Whatever we can see along the lines of approach is an extensional aspect of the site. Whatever we can see from the site (or will see in the probable future) is part of the site. Anything that can be heard, smelled, or felt from the property is part of the property. Any topographical feature, natural or built, that has any effect on the property or its use must be considered a planning factor.

In our present power-happy and schedule-conscious era, this vitally important aspect of developing a simpatico feeling for the land and the total project site is too often overlooked. And too often our completed work gives tragic evidence of our haste and neglect.

Site Planning

In Japan, historically, this keen awareness of the site has been of great significance in landscape planning. Each structure has seemed a natural outgrowth of its site, preserving and accentuating its best features. Studying in Japan, the coauthor was struck by this consistent quality and once asked an architect how he achieved it in his work. "Quite simply," said the architect. "If designing, say, a residence, I go each day to the piece of land on which it is to be constructed. Sometimes for long hours with a mat and tea. Sometimes in the quiet of evening when the shadows are long. Sometimes in the busy part of the day when the streets are abustle and the sun is clear and bright. Sometimes in the snow and even in the rain, for much can be learned of a piece of ground by watching the rainfall play across it and the runoff take its course in rivulets along the natural drainageways.

Site features can be the reason for the project.

"I go to the land, and stay, until I have come to know it. I learn to know its bad features—the jangling friction of the passing street, the awkward angles of a windblown pine, an unpleasant sector of the mountain view, the lack of moisture in the soil, the nearness of a neighbor's house to an angle of the property.

"I learn to know its good features—a glorious clump of maple trees, a broad ledge perching high in space above a gushing waterfall that spills into the deep ravine below. I come to know the cool and pleasant summer airs that rise from the falls and move across an open draw of the land. I sense perhaps the deliciously pungent fragrance of the deeply layered cedar fronds as the warm sun plays across them. This patch I know must be left undisturbed.

"I know where the sun will appear in the early morning, when its warmth will be most welcome. I have learned which areas will be struck

Therefore, let us build houses that restore to man the life-giving, life-enhancing elements of nature. This means an architecture that begins with the nature of the site. Which means taking the first great step toward assuring a worthy architecture, for in the rightness of a house on the land we sense fitness we call beauty.
Frank Lloyd Wright

Thus we seek two values in every landscape: one, the expression of the native quality of the landscape, the other, the development of maximum human livability. . . .

Site planning must be thought of as the organization of the total land area and air space of the site for best use by the people who will occupy it. This means an integrated concept in which buildings, engineering construction, open space and natural materials are planned together at one time. . . .
Garrett Eckbo

by its harshly blinding light as it burns hot and penetrating in the late afternoon, and from which spots the sunset seems to glow the richest in the dusky peace of evening. I have marveled at the changing dappled light and soft, fresh colors of the bamboo thicket and watched for hours the lemon-crested warblers that have built their nests and feed there.

"I come to sense with great pleasure the subtle relationship of a jutting granite boulder to the jutting granite profile of the mountainside across the way. Little things, one may think, but they tell one, 'Here is the essence of this fragment of land; here is its very spirit. Preserve this spirit, and it will pervade your gardens, your home, and your every day.'

"And so I come to understand this bit of land, its moods, its limitations, its possibilities. Only now can I take my ink and brush in hand and start to draw my plans. But in my mind the structure by now is fully visualized. It has taken its form and character from the site and the passing street and the fragment of rock and the wafting breeze and the arching sun and the sound of the falls and the distant view.

"Knowing the owner and his family and the things they like, I have found for them here a living environment that brings them into the best relationship with the landscape that surrounds them. This structure, this house that I have conceived, is no more than an arrangement of spaces, open and closed, accommodating and expressing in stone, timber, tile, and rice paper a delightful, fulfilling way of life. How else can one come to design the best home for this site?"

There can be no other way! This, in Japan as elsewhere, is in simplest terms the planning process—for the home, the community, the city, the highway, or the national park.

A thorough understanding of the site is necessary for a successful design response.

Site Planning

Comprehensive land plan.

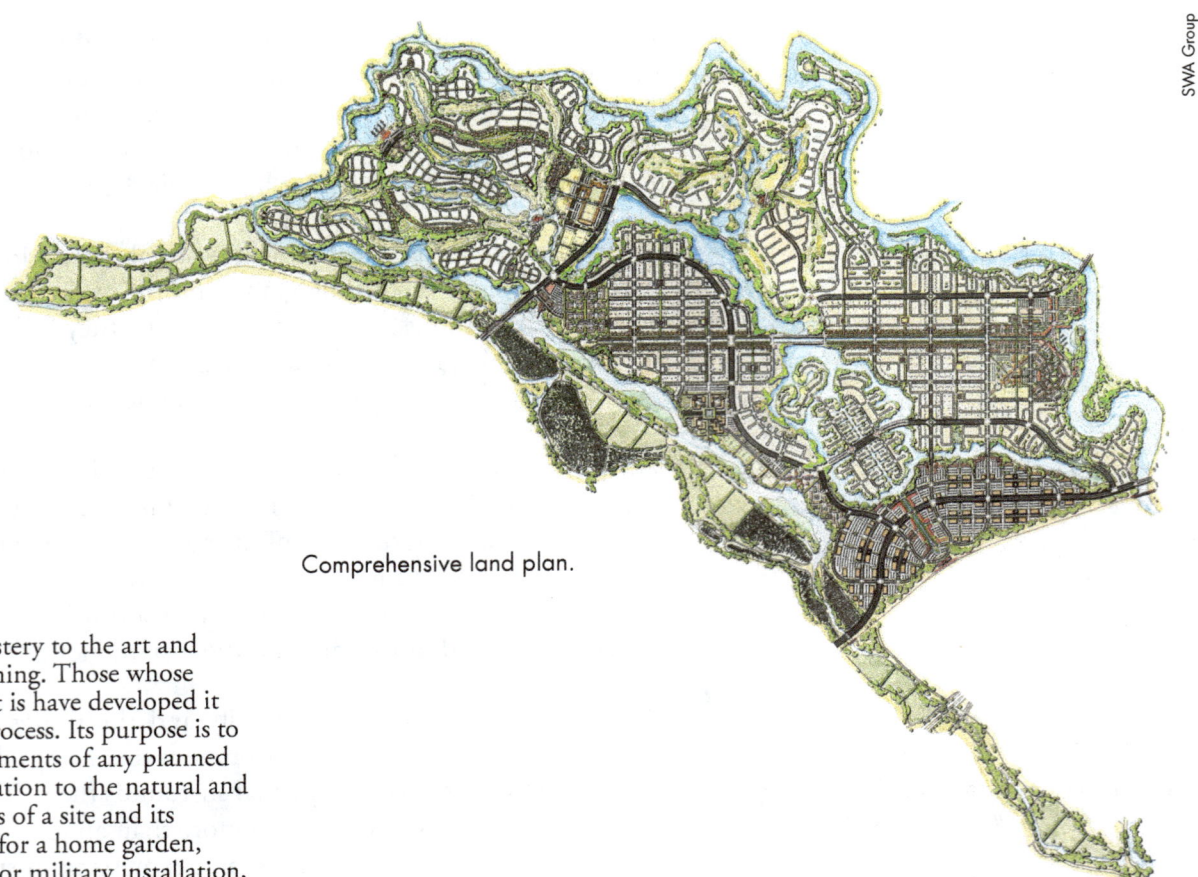

There is a little mystery to the art and science of site planning. Those whose professional work it is have developed it into a systematic process. Its purpose is to best arrange the elements of any planned development in relation to the natural and constructed features of a site and its environs. Whether for a home garden, university campus, or military installation, the approach is essentially the same.

The site-planning procedure normally involves the following ten steps, several of which may take place concurrently:
1. Definition of intent (scope, goal, and objectives)
2. Procurement of topographic survey
3. Program development
4. Data gathering and analysis
5. Site reconnaissance
6. Organization of reference plan set and file
7. Preparation of exploratory studies
8. Comparative analysis and revision of studies, leading to an approved conceptual plan
9. Development of preliminary development plans and estimate of costs
10. Preparation of construction plans, specifications, and bidding documents

The comprehensive planning process is a systematic means of determining where you are, where you want to be, and how best to get there.

In America, we planners approach our problems in a less contemplative frame of mind. We are "less sensitive" (of which fact we are proud) and "more practical" (a pathetic misnomer). We are rushed by the pressures of time, economics, and public temperament. The planning process is accelerated, sometimes to the point of frenzy. But the principle remains the same: to realize a project on a site effectively, we must fully understand the program, and we must be fully aware of the physical properties of the site and of the total environs. Our planning then becomes the science and art of arranging the most fitting relationships.

Comprehensive Land Planning

Traditionally, most land and landscape planning has been done on a limited scale and with limited objectives. Given a proposed project description, the planner has been expected to fit it onto a given site to the maximum advantage of the owner. Sometimes the effects on the neighboring lands and waters were considered. Sometimes they were not. In our emerging environmental and land-use ethic it is believed that they should, and must be.

Regional influence.

In building a cabin in the forest the native instincts of the pioneers as they felled the trees and cleared the land may have been good enough. In contemporary times however, with land reserves receding so rapidly and with building sites under such stress, every development is subject to new planning factors. The larger and more intensive the project, the greater the consequences and the greater the need for care and concern. This has led to a process known as comprehensive land planning. It is a systematic approach especially suited to developments of greater scope or sensitivity.

Even in single-home construction it is incumbent upon the planner to organize a file of background information. This will include the governing zoning maps, codes, and other pertinent regulations. City plans and street maps will show the location of community schools, parks, shopping areas, and other amenities to which the residence will relate. Needed also is a thorough investigation of all that transpires on, contiguous to, or beneath the building site—including such potential subsurface surprises as mine workings, high-pressure fuel transmission lines, or buried cables.

The best source of design criteria is field observation.

Site Planning 221

Comprehensive land planning is usually initiated with an investigation of the region embracing the project site. The immediate vicinity and its interrelationships with the property to be developed is given more thorough study. Finally, the project site itself is analyzed to gain the full understanding so essential to landscape planning.

Site Analysis Guidelines

The following procedure is suggested as a guide to systematic site analysis:

Regional Influences. The site analysis process most often begins with the location of the project site on a regional map and a cursory investigation of regional, vicinity, and area planning factors. From such documents as U.S. Geological Survey maps, road maps, various planning reports, and the Internet, much useful insight can be gained about the surrounding topographic features, land uses, roadway and transporta-

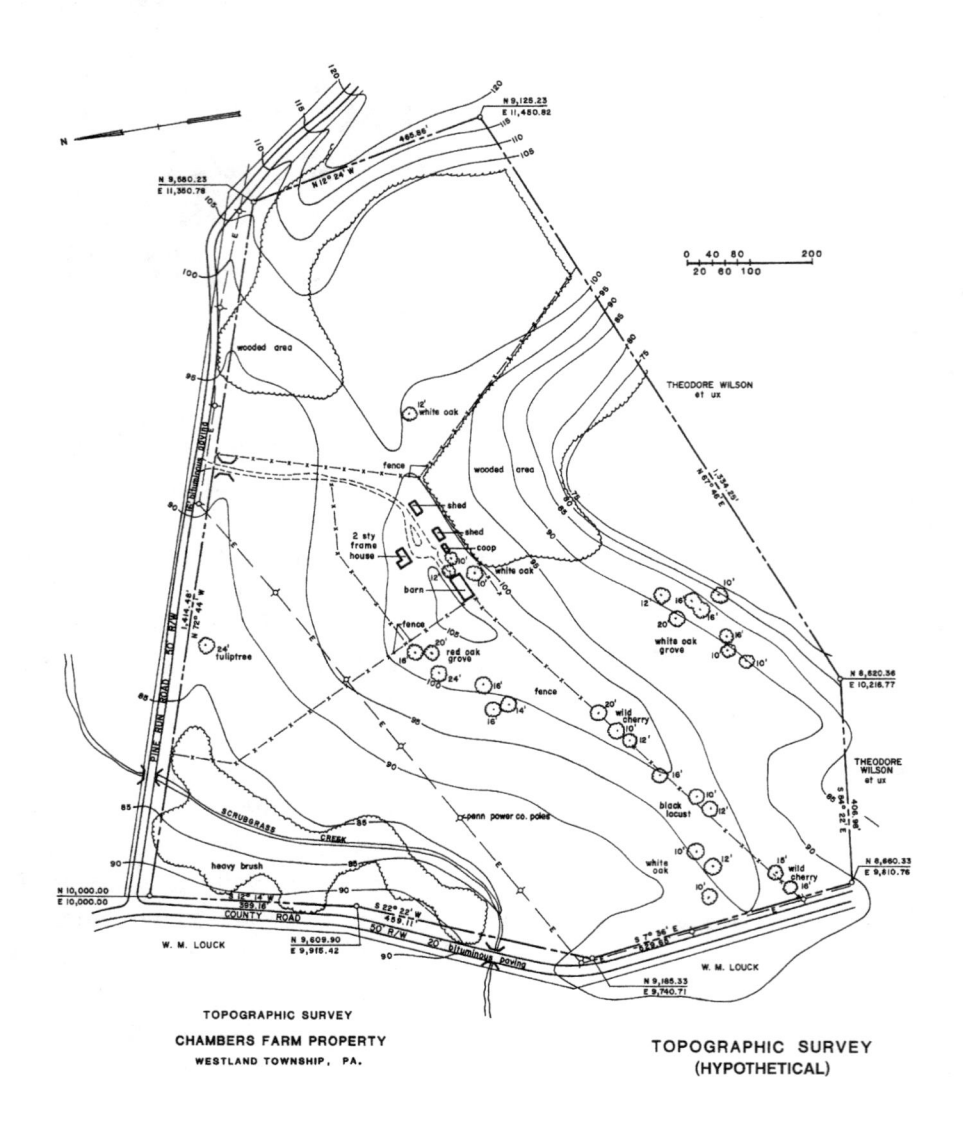

TOPOGRAPHIC SURVEY
CHAMBERS FARM PROPERTY
WESTLAND TOWNSHIP, PA.

TOPOGRAPHIC SURVEY
(HYPOTHETICAL)

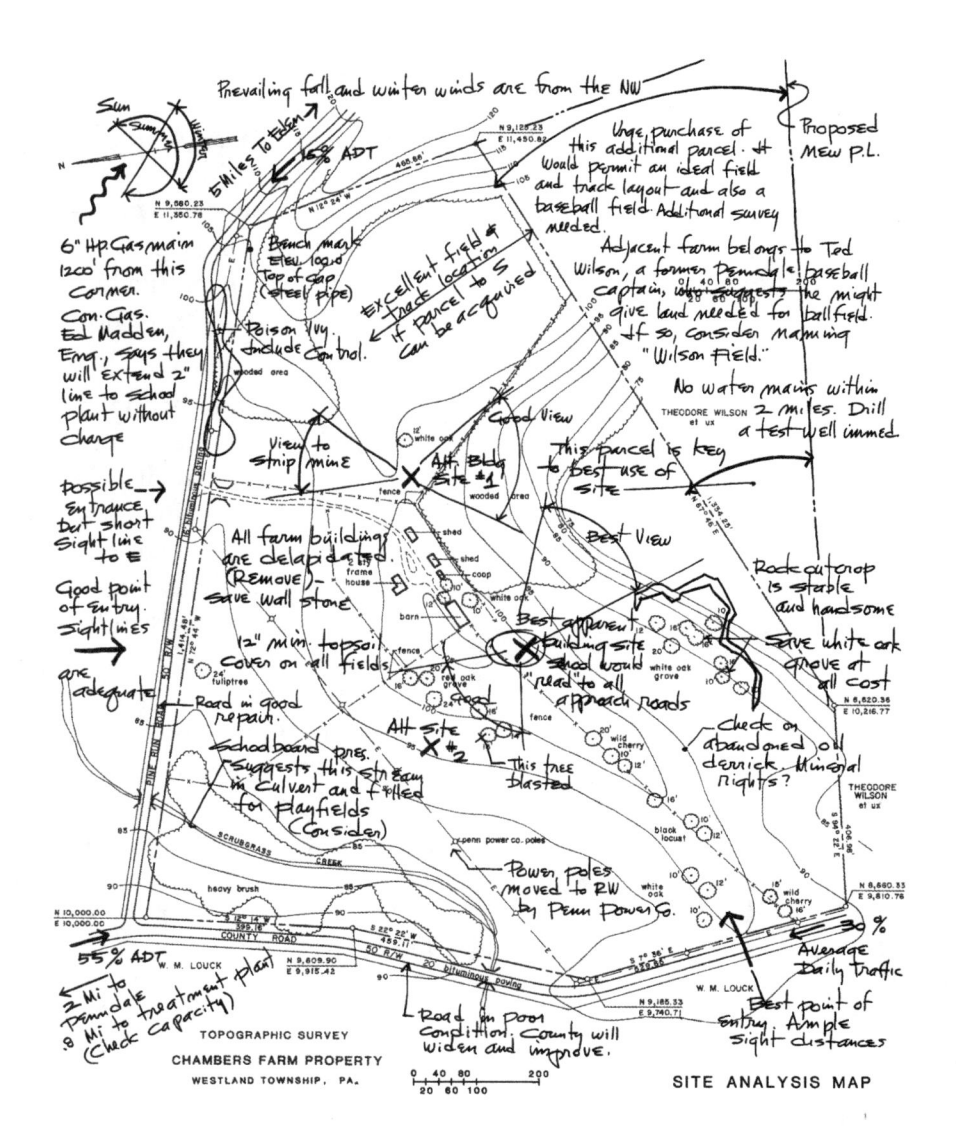

tion network, recreational opportunities, and employment, commercial, and cultural centers. Together these establish the extensional setting to which the proposed project will relate.

The Project Site. Before design studies can be initiated, the planner must be fully conversant with the specific nature of the site—its constraints and possibilities. This knowledge is obtained mainly by means of a topographic survey and site visitation.

Topographic Survey. The basic topographic survey is customarily prepared by a registered surveyor at an engineering scale (1 inch = 20 feet, 50 feet, or 100 feet, etc.) This scale is predetermined to be the one best for the project's planning studies. A survey specification describing the information to be provided by the surveyor and the form of presentation is the responsibility of the planner.

Site Planning   223

Site Analysis Map. One of the most effective means of developing a keen appreciation of the property and its nature is the preparation of a site analysis map. A print of the topographic survey furnished by the surveyor is taken into the field, and from actual site observation additional notes are jotted down upon it in the planner's own symbols. These amplify the survey notations and describe all conditions on or related to the site that are pertinent in its planning. Such supplementary information might describe or note:

- Outstanding natural features such as springs, ponds, streams, rock ledges, specimen trees, contributing shrub masses, and established ground covers, all to be preserved insofar as possible
- Tentative outlines of proposed *preservation, conservation, and development* (PCD) areas
- Negative site features or hazards such as obsolete structures or deleterious materials to be removed, dead or diseased vegetation, noxious weed infestation, lack of topsoil, or evidence of landslides, subsidence, or flooding
- Directions and relative volumes of vehicular traffic flow on approach roads; points of connection to pedestrian routes, bikeways, and riding trails
- Logical points of site ingress or egress
- Potential building locations, use areas, or routes of movement
- Commanding observation points, overlook areas, and preferred viewing sectors
- Best views, to be featured, and objectionable views, to be screened, together with a brief note describing each
- Direction of prevailing winter winds and summer breezes
- Exposed, windswept areas and those protected by nearby topographical forms, groves, or structures
- Off-site attractions and nuisances
- An ecological and microclimatic analysis of the property and its environs
- Other factors of special significance in the project planning

In addition to such information observed in the field, further data gleaned from research may be noted on the site analysis map or included separately in the survey file. Such information might include:

- Abutting landownerships
- Names of utility companies whose lines are shown, company addresses, phone number, engineers
- Routes and data on projected utility lines
- Approach patterns of existing roads, drives, and walks
- Relative abutting roadway traffic counts
- Zoning restrictions, building codes, and building setback lines

- Mineral rights, depth of coal, mined-out areas
- Water quality and supply
- Core-boring logs and data
- Base map

It is helpful early on in the planning process to prepare a base map which sets the format for all sheets to follow. Drawn on drafting film or stable translucent paper to give clear reproduction, it sets the trim lines and title block with project name and location, owner's and planner's identification, north point, scale, and dateline. Aside from the property lines and coordinates, it will show only that information to be carried forward to all derivative sheets.

Most site and architectural studies, conceptual plans, and working drawings will be prepared on reproducible prints of this base map.

Plan Set and Reference File. As the surveys, base sheets, overlays, site analysis map, and other background data are developed, they are assembled as a coordinated reference file—together with supporting plans, reports, and correspondence. All are to be kept complete and updated throughout the planning process. With the application of computer techniques, the preparation, maintenance of, and access to the reference files can be streamlined and expedited.

The material in the reference file will vary for each project depending upon its size and complexity. For more extensive planning—as for a hospital, stadium, or new community—the file may include such background data as:

- Regional and local master plans
- Zoning and subdivision regulations
- Projected highway network
- Regional water management program
- Airfields and flight zones
- Transmission lines and stations
- Utility systems
- Fire, police, and ambulance services
- Flood and storm records
- Air and water pollution sources and controls
- Demographic data and user profiles
- Schools
- Recreation facilities
- Cultural amenities
- Economic statistics and trends
- Tax rates and assessments
- Governance

Perhaps the planning process can best be explained as a series of subconscious conversations. . . . —the question posed, the factors weighed, and then the recorded conclusion. The more lucid the thinking, the more coherent the powers of idea communication . . . the better is the plan.
B. Kenneth Johnstone

Site Planning

There is an area of the conceptual and forming process that is common to the four major physical planning disciplines and often to others as well. This is the formulation of the basic plan concept by which, in sketch or diagram, the use areas and plan forms are conceived in harmony with the natural and constructed forms, forces, and features of the total project site. Usually the plan concept is best arrived at through a collaborative effort in which all participants contribute freely of their experience and ideas.

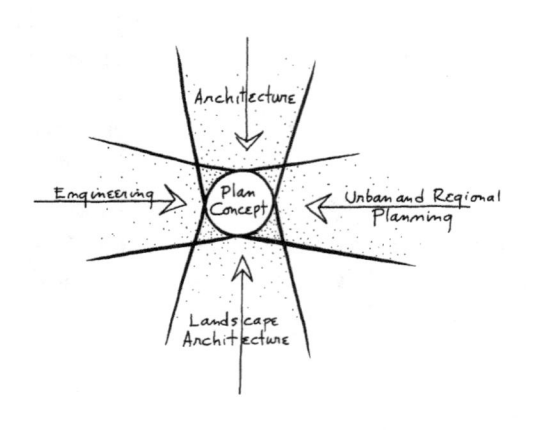

On larger commissions the landscape architect often serves as a member of a closely coordinated professional team, which includes architects, engineers, planners, and scientist-advisors. A generalist, the landscape architect brings to the planning-design process specialized training in the physical sciences—such as physiography, geology, hydrology, biology, and ecology—and a feeling for the land, human relationships, and design.

The Conceptual Plan

A seed of use—a cell of function—wisely applied to a receptive site will be allowed to develop organically, in harmonious adaptation to the natural and the planned environment.

We have by now developed a comprehensive program defining the proposed nature of our project. We have begun to sense its resonance within the total environs. Up to this point, the planning effort has been one of research and analysis. It has been painstaking and perhaps tedious, but this phase is of vital importance because it is the only means by which we can achieve full command of the data on which our design will be based. From this point on, the planning process becomes one of integration of proposed uses, structures, and site.

Plan Concepts

If structure and landscape development are contemplated, it is impossible to conceive one without the other, for it is the relationship of structure to site and site to structure that gives meaning to each and to both.

This point perhaps raises the question of who on the planning team—architect, landscape architect, engineer, or others—is to do the conceiving. Strangely, this problem, which might seemingly lead to warm debate, seldom arises, for an effective collaboration brings together experts in various fields of knowledge who, in a free interchange of ideas, develop a climate of perceptive awareness and know-how. In such a climate, plan concepts usually evolve more or less spontaneously. Since the collaboration is arranged and administered by one of the principals (who presumably holds the commission), it is usually this team leader who coordinates the planning in all its aspects and gives it expressive unity. It is the work of the collaborators to advance their assigned tasks and to aid in the articulation of the main design idea in all ways possible.

Site-Structure Diagram

When planning a project or a structure in relation to a land area, we first consider all the various uses to be fitted together and accommodated. For a high school, for instance, we would determine the approximate architectural plan areas and their shapes—the general plan areas required for service, parking, outdoor classrooms, gardens, game courts, football fields, track, bleachers, and perhaps future school expansion. Over a point of the topographic survey (or site analysis map) we would then indicate, in freehand line, use areas of logical size and shape in studied relation to each other and to the natural and built

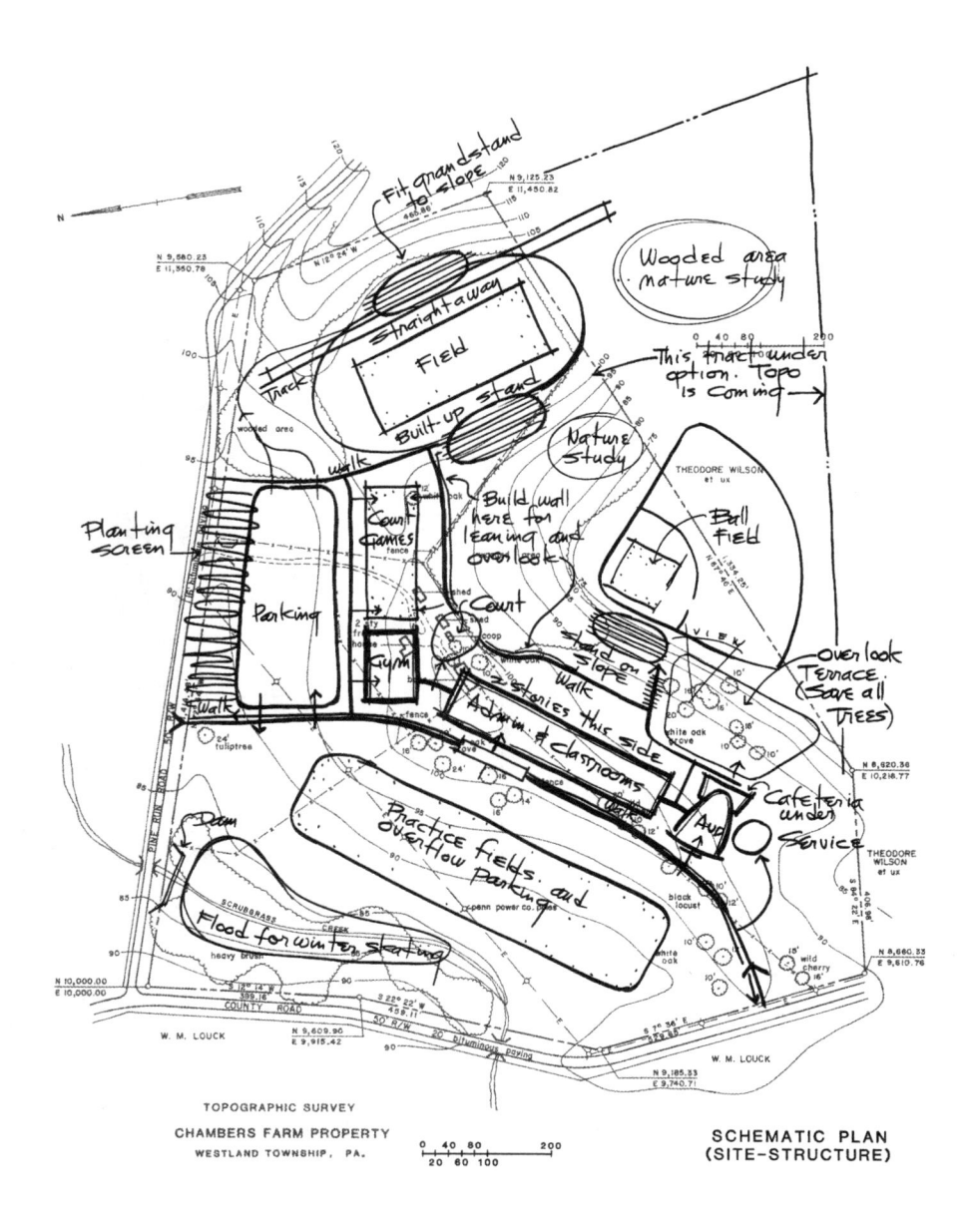

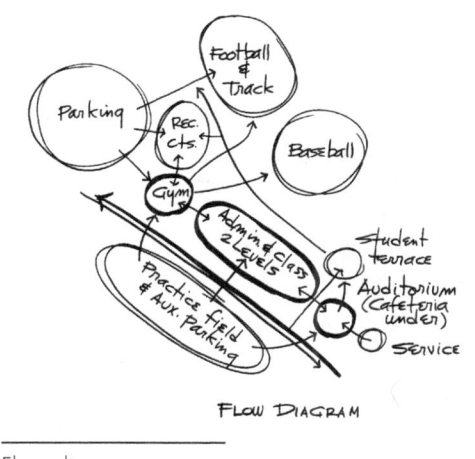

TOPOGRAPHIC SURVEY
CHAMBERS FARM PROPERTY
WESTLAND TOWNSHIP, PA.

SCHEMATIC PLAN
(SITE-STRUCTURE)

Flow diagram.

landscape features. Having thus roughed in the site use areas, we may at last block in the architectural elements of the project. The result is the site-structure diagram.

Conceptual Site Plan

The balance of the planning process is a matter of comparative analysis and refinement of detail—a process of creative synthesis. A good plan, reduced to essentials, is no more than a record of logical thought. A dull plan is a record of ineffectual thinking or of very little thinking at all. A brilliant plan gives evidence of response to all site factors, a clear perception of needs and relationships, and a sensitive expression of all components working well together.

Site Planning 227

SITE PLAN
(CONCEPTUAL)

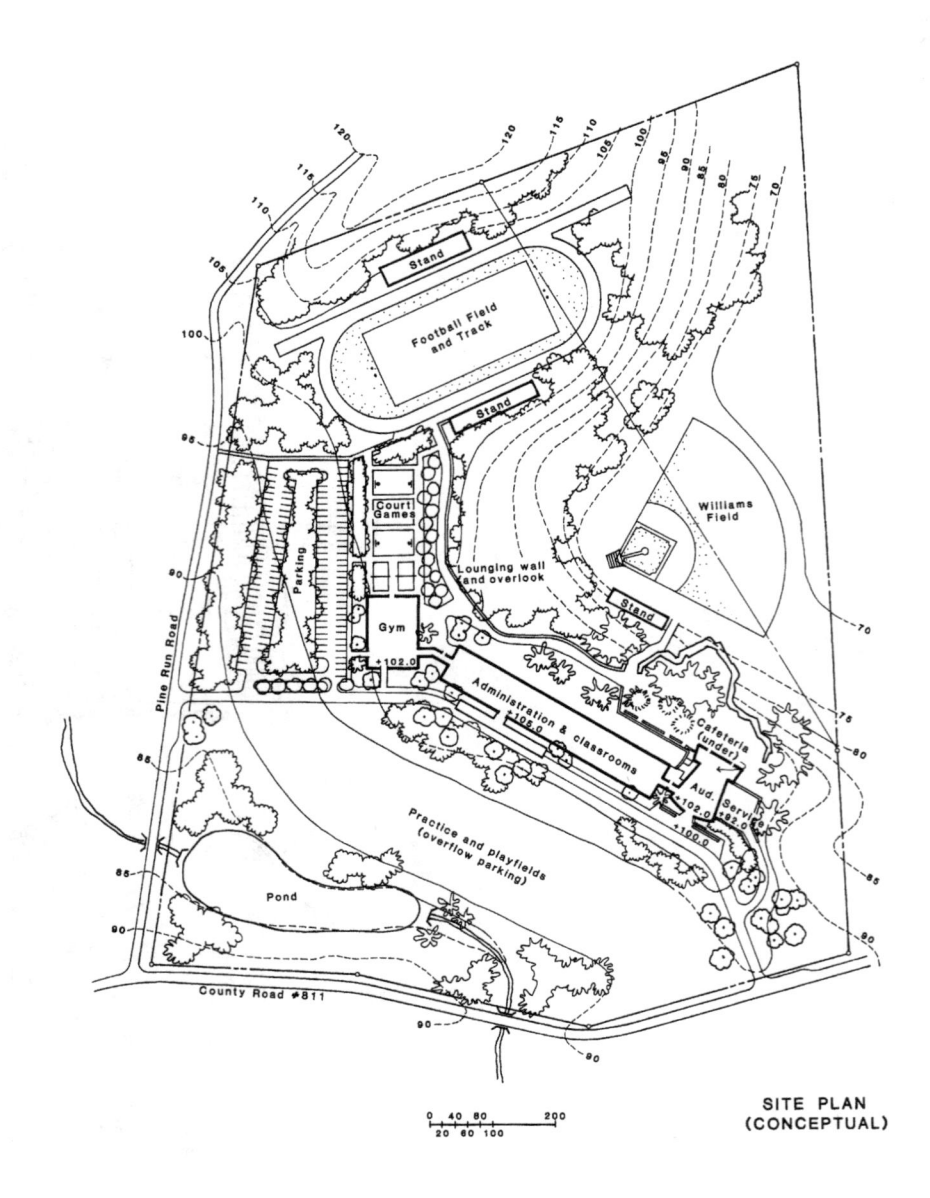

The Planning Attitude

In his admirable treatise *On the Laws of Japanese Painting,* Henry P. Bowie has written:

> One of the most important principles in the art of Japanese painting—indeed, a fundamental and entirely distinctive characteristic—is that of living movement, *sei do* . . . it being, so to say, the transfusion into the work of the felt nature of the thing to be painted by the artist. Whatever the subject to be translated—whether river or tree, rock or mountain, bird or flower, fish or animal—the artist at the moment of painting it must feel its very nature, which, by the magic of art, he transfers into his work to remain forever, affecting all who see it with the same sensations he experienced when executing it.

It is not the thing done or made which is beautiful, but the doing. If we appreciate the thing, it is because we relive the heady freedom of making it. Beauty is the byproduct of interest and pleasure in the choice of action.
Jacob Bronowski

Meaningful design is far from an exercise in graphic exposition. It is an empathetic process—a creative act of the intellect.

Design begins with a conceptual determination of the desired nature of space or object. This "what shall it be" aspect may be focalized by a flash of intuitive genius, by a methodical analysis of possibilities, or by logical extension and improvement upon past examples.

The visual aspects of superior design are marked by a clear and direct expression of idea, time, place, materials, and technology, coupled with a fine instinct for three-dimensional form.

And again:

> Indeed, nothing is more constantly urged upon his attention than this great underlying principle, that it is impossible to express in art what one does not feel.

And so it is with planning. We can create only that for which we have first developed an empathic understanding. A shopping mall? As designers, we must feel the quickening tempo, the pull and attraction, the bustle, the excitement of the place. We must sense the chic boutique displays, the mouthwatering sights and smells of the bakery shop; we must see in our mind the jam-packed counter of the hardware store and the drugstore with its pyramids of mouthwash, perfume, nail polish, hot-water bottles, and jelly beans. We must see in the market the heaps of grapefruit, oranges, rhubarb, brussels sprouts, bananas; whiff the heady fragrance of the floral stalls; picture the shelf on shelf of bargain books, the bolts of cotton prints, the sloping trays of peppermints and chocolate creams. We must feel the brightness of the sunshine on the sidewalks and the coolness and protection of shaded doorways and arcades. We must feel crowds and traffic and benches and trees and perhaps the sparkle and splash of a fountain or two. And then we can start planning.

A children's zoo? If we would design one, we must first feel like one of the flocking children, the gawking, clapping, squealing kids; we must appreciate the delight, the laughter, the chatter, the confusion, and the rollicking thrill of the place. We must feel the diminutive, squeaky cuteness of the mouse town, the bulk and immensity and cavelike hollowness of the spouting whale with its dimly illumined interior. We must know the preening strut of the elegantly wandering peacocks, the quack, quack, quacking of the waddling ducks, the soft furry whiteness of the lop-eared rabbits, and the clop, clop, clopping and creaking harness and the awed delight of the pony ride. As we make our plans, we must, in our minds, be at the children's zoo, and we must see it, hear it, feel it, and love it as a child would love it.

Are we to design a parkway, hotel plaza, terminal, or bathing beach? If we would create them, we must first have a feeling for their nature. This self-induced sensitivity we might call the *planning attitude*. Before we mature as planners, it will be intuitive.

Impact Assessment

It has been proposed that no development should be permitted if, all things considered, it were to do more harm than good. But how is this to be ascertained? Until recently this might well have been a matter of hotly debated opinion. With the advent of the federally mandated *Environmental Impact Statement,* however, there is now the means of making a fairly rational appraisal.

The chart that follows provides a checklist of environmental and performance factors to be considered in large-scale, comprehensive planning.

Site Planning

Environmental impact assessment checklist

1. Identify all proposed uses or actions that would have a significant impact upon the environment.
2. In the appropriate frame of the matrix place a square for a negative impact and a circle for one that is seen to be beneficial.
3. Within each square or circle place a number, from 1 to 10, to represent the magnitude and importance (local to regional) of each impact: 10 represents the greatest effect, 1 the least. While the arithmetic sum is not to be considered an absolute indication of the project's worth, it is a telling decision factor.
4. In text to accompany the completed chart discuss any unusual, potent, hazardous, or lasting impact or impacts inherent in the project.
5. In separate sections describe those means by which in the project planning and design the negative consequences have been mitigated and the benefits increased.

Proposed land use, project, or action:

1. Destruction of habitat
2. Modification of habitat
3. Alteration of surface drainage
4. Change in stream or river flow
5. Effect on freshwater reserves
6. Excavation, filling, or grading
7. Dredging
8. Mining or extraction
9. Forestry
10. Agricultural uses
11. Home and garden
12. Residential communities
13. Recreational uses
14. Institutional uses
15. Commercial uses
16. Industrial uses
17. Urbanization
18. Transportation; transit
19. Transmission
20. Utilities
21. Impoundments
22. Harbors, piers, or marinas
23. Blasting, drilling and explosions
24. Energy generation
25. Other (list)

Earth
- Landform
- Soils
- Mineral resources
- Geologic features

Water
- Surface conformation
- Visual appeal
- Quality
- Supply

Atmosphere
- Quality (gases; particulates)
- Climate (macro; micro)
- Temperature

Processes
- Flooding
- Erosion
- Sedimentation
- Stability (slides and slumps)
- Air movement
- Solar penetration (sunlight; cast shadow)

Flora
- Ecological systems
- Visual continuity
- Trees
- Shrubs
- Ground covers
- Crops
- Habitat
- Rare plant species

Fauna
- Birds
- Land animals and reptiles
- Fish and shellfish
- Rare or endangered species
- Food chains

Land use
- Wilderness
- Wetlands
- Forestry; grazing or agricultural uses
- Recreational uses
- Residential uses
- Institutional uses
- Commercial uses
- Industrial uses
- Urbanization
- Open-space preserve

Visual and human interest
- Scenic quality
- Landscape character
- Views and vistas
- Parks and recreation
- Conservation areas
- Archaeological or historical interest
- Unique physical features
- Inappropriate uses
- Pollution

Social factors
- Health
- Safety
- Cultural patterns (lifestyle)
- Employment
- Population density and distribution
- Public services
- Cultural amenities

Built environment
- Buildings
- Engineering structures
- Landscape development
- Community integrity
- Urbanization patterns
- Transportation network
- Utility systems
- Waste disposal facilities

Other
- List

An official Environmental Impact Statement (EIS), as is required on most federally aided projects, is governed by a pro forma set of instructions. Essentially the statement is to describe:

- All significant negative impacts to be expected from the proposed development, and the means by which the planners have ameliorated them as far as feasible.
- All positive values created by the project, and the means by which they have been enhanced in the planning process.
- The rationale for proceeding with construction. Only with rare exceptions is approval justified unless the long-term negative factors are outweighed by the benefits.

When such environmental considerations are defined and explored early, they become not only a useful test but also a sound basis for the evolving studies and resulting planned solution. The negative impacts of the project can thus be reduced and the attributes significantly increased during the planning process. The many benefits of such a systematic approach cannot be overemphasized.

Computer Application

The advent of the computer, the Internet, and other cyberspace-related advances has altered the planning/design process immensely—yet fundamentally has changed it not at all. The goals and procedural steps of planning remain the same. As a means of attaining the goals, however, the computer has opened up an intriguing range of possibilities. Together with its accouterments it has provided a whole new array of bright and radiant tools. It is important that in our fascination with the tools we are not distracted from the task to be accomplished.

Capability

The function of computer technology is to access, store, manage (manipulate), and display information. As to access, once the planner has developed the project program and decided upon the background material needed, the computer can search the vast Internet storehouse of facts and graphic examples and file them for easy reference. Even surveys, plans, and photographs can be scanned and computerized—to be recalled on the screen and enlarged, reduced, or edited at will.

As schematic studies progress, they too can be recorded for comparative analysis and optimization. The evolving schemes and resulting conceptual plan can be projected three-dimensionally for viewing from various angles. If so desired, the images may be modified by the planner to effect

Computer visualization.

The skill of drawing, that beautiful coordination between the hand, eye, and mind, is as crucial to making good use of computer graphics as it has always been to the design professions.
William J. Johnson

improvement. Or they may be supplemented with overlays showing perspective views of the actual project site and environs, along with design features such as walls, paving, lighting standards, ancillary structures, or planting. Concurrently with the visual comparison, the computer can provide running data on land and building coverage, area of various types of paving or ground covers, cubic yardage of masonry, soil, and so on—and thus the basis for comparative costs.

The advantages of computer use are manifold: not only in time-cost savings but as well in the scope of research material made available and the ability to organize and store it for rapid retrieval; not only in the ability to project, compare, and modify the schematic studies, but to test them for relative cost; not only to display the various proposals by screen, but to select the viewing points and to visualize the plans and spaces as by sequential movement through them.

In the recording of survey information and in the dimensioning of construction drawings, the use of coordinates for property corners, outlines, and locations saves endless hours of calculation and drafting. Computer imagery precludes the need for slide preparation and projection—and makes obsolete the clumsy presentation boards and easels set up at public meetings. The printout of plans and text in various sizes and forms, with ease of revision, is another obvious advantage. As if these advantages weren't enough, new capabilities and refinements are constantly becoming available.

Limitations

What, then, are the limits to design by computer? The fact is that the valued computer cannot design at all. It is incapable of either perception or deduction. It cannot discern the personality of the client, cannot sense the character of the site, cannot know the feel of stone, wood, or water, cannot apprehend the wonder of a view. It cannot learn from experience or apply to the planning process the lessons of travel and observation.

Some would-be planners have become enslaved by computer technology. For them to sit before screen or keyboard is to go into a rapturous trance. It is to be hoped that with time they will recognize the computer's role for what it is—the esteemed and highly efficient servant, but never the intuitive master.

Site Development

The product of the site planning process is a conceptual plan. This is, in effect, a diagram of fitting relationships—of areas to structure, of area to area, and of all to the lay of the land. The land uses and their relationship have grown out of the program and site analysis. They have been explored in a number of quick schematics until the best fit is achieved. The plan has been tested and adjusted to minimize its negative impacts and to provide the most of those features that are desired.

The conceptual plan is a preliminary drawing—the concept without details or fixed dimensions, intentionally so, for in its detailed development, perhaps in phases, it is subject to change, refinement, and improvement.

Upon its approval by the client or other decision makers, it becomes the reference guideline in the preparation of detailed (working) site development plans and specifications.

Site-Structure Expression

If to design a project or a structure in harmony with its total site is a valid objective, it follows that the design expression would vary from site to site in accordance with the variation in landscape character.

To illustrate, let us consider a summer weekend vacation lodge. If built on a sheltered, rock-rimmed inland lake in northern Maine, its abstract design form would vary greatly from the form it would have if located anywhere along the wind-whipped coast of Monterey, California, in the smoky Ozark Mountains, on Florida's shell-strewn Captiva Island, or along the lazily winding Mississinewa River in central Indiana. Forgetting for the moment the implications of a specific property, we can see that each of the varying locations suggests its own intrinsic design response.

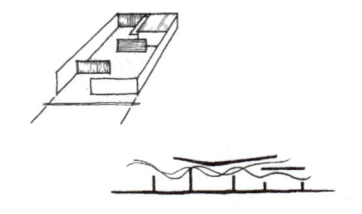

Interplay of horizontal and vertical spaces.

Rigid property lines may be softened to relieve the sense of tight enclosure.

Consider carefully the scale of objects introduced.

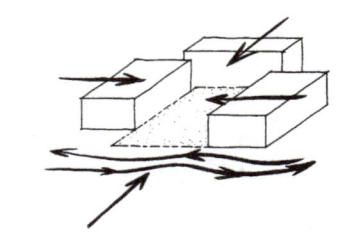

The feel of the city lot.

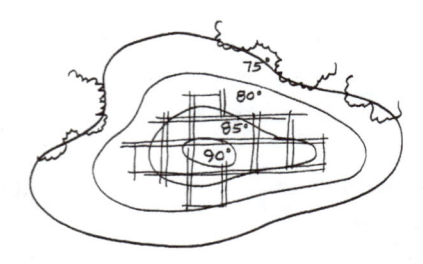

Cities, with their concentration of masonry and paving, are hotter in summer and colder in winter than the suburbs and countryside. The "desert" climate can be ameliorated by the provision of open-space preserves, parks, street planting, and private gardens.

It might therefore be a helpful procedure to classify a site according to type and determine the design characteristics suggested. Let us consider four typical building sites and the design features that they elicit.

A City Lot

Area is at a premium. The plan will be compact, of necessity. Space is limited. Plan forms will probably be contrived to expand the apparent space by the multiple use of areas and the interplay of volumes. Through ingenious plan arrangement even the smallest structures are made to feel spacious.

The city environs impose a sense of confinement and oppression. Perhaps here embattled city dwellers will wish to entrench, dig their cave, or build their fort and feel secure. But more likely they will seek relief and release from pressure. If so, in their dwellings and gardens the hard, the rigid, the confining forms will give way to the light, the nebulous, the transparent, and the free.

Areas and spaces are minute in scale. Scale, both induced and inductive, is an important design consideration. An object well suited to the open field could be overwhelming in the cityscape. A giant tree, for example, might dwarf an urban complex, while a dwarf tree could give it increased and more desirable visual dimension.

City site.

234   *LANDSCAPE ARCHITECTURE*

In the city, a rock, a tree, or a single potted plant may represent all of nature.

A city should be built to give its inhabitants security and happiness.
Aristotle

City streets and pedestrian walks are dominant lines of approach, observation, and access. They are elements most strongly relating the dwelling to the community. The driveway throat and front entrance will normally be designed to convey a receptive cove quality. The relationship of the structure to the insistent lines of the city street becomes an important consideration.

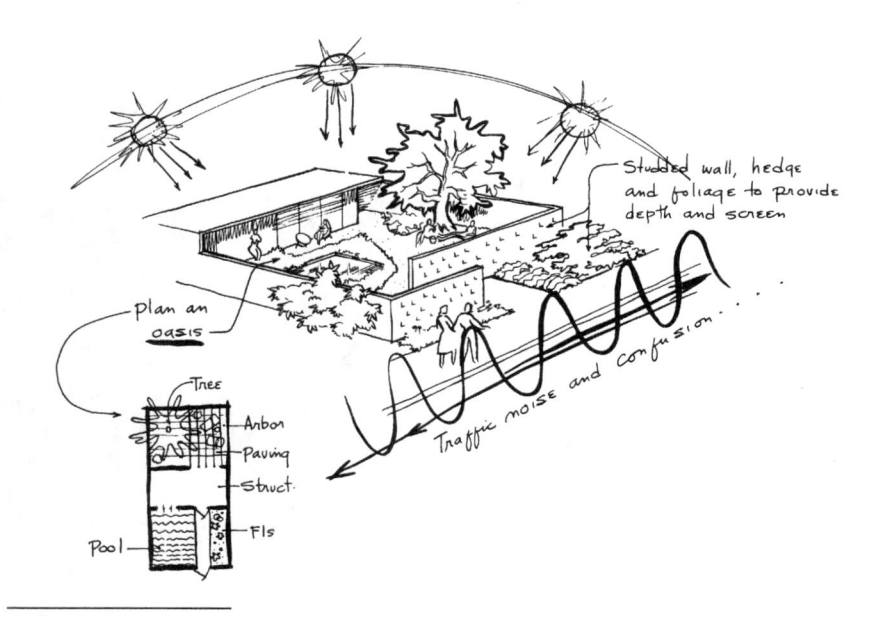

Design for depth adjacent to street.

The city street is a source of noise, fumes, and danger. Plan elements adjacent to the street may well be contrived to provide noise abatement, depth, privacy, and security. Perforated visual screens or studded sound barriers have useful application.

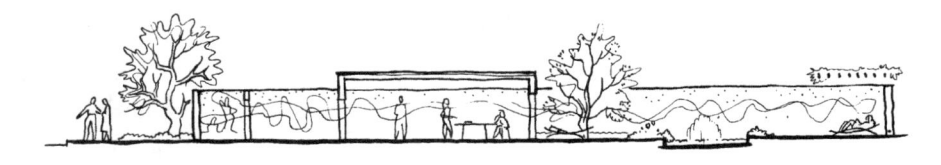

Living space in the city may extend from property line to property line.

The city is, climatologically speaking, a desert of pavement and masonry. A city is often many degrees hotter in the summertime than the surrounding countryside. Design an oasis; make maximum use of breeze, shade, shadow patterns, sunscreens, and the refreshing qualities of water in fountain, pool, or jet spray. The climate may be further modified by air movement fanned or directed through pierced or baffled screens or across moist fabric, gravel, or other evaporative surfaces. In cool weather, heat may be introduced in radiant elements or by warm water circulated in fountains or pools.

Site Planning 235

Natural features—trees, interesting ground forms, rocks, and water—are scarce and therefore have increased value and meaning. They are no longer part of the natural scene but are now isolated objects to be treated in a more stylized way. Utilize natural features to the full, design them into the scheme, orient to them. Earth, plants, and water in the city may well be treated as sculptural or architectural elements. Since in the city all materials appear to be introduced, exotic plants and materials are appropriate.

City materials tend to be less rustic and more sophisticated. Because sizes and quantities are limited, richness of material and refinement of detail gain in importance.

Courtyard garden.

Surrounded by neighbors, one becomes an integral part of the community, a unit in a group of related units, an important part of the whole. Neighborhood character cannot be blithely violated without social repercussions. We are tacitly obliged to conform. To achieve a measure of conformity while designing a residential complex of individuality and distinction is a difficult art, mastered long ago by the Japanese. Their modular homes of stone, wood, tile, and woven mats are arranged tightly along their city streets with an artistry that produces patterns of infinite variety yet great harmony.

From the street to the farthest limits of the city lot, there is little room for the necessary transitions from the din of the passing street to areas for quiet family living. Designed transitions are a mark of the successful city house. The Japanese admire a quality called *wabi* that has application here. This quality may be exemplified by a black walnut with its rough, splotched, gray-green outer husk. With husk removed, the exposed walnut shell is seen to be a handsome, rich brown case of hard ridges in structural pattern. Cracked open, the shell reveals the walnut kernels encased in a membrane of delicate veining and fitted to the smooth interior chambers. Finally, the ivory-white kernel itself is a marvel of beautiful sculptural form. We may see in this example an inward progression from the unostentatious to the highly refined.

A city property has a fishbowl quality resulting from the proximity of neighbors. Privacy is a tacit design requirement in a city dwelling. A logical orientation of such structures is inward, to private gardens, patios, or courts.

Rural Site

Land area is plentiful. The plan is more open, free, and "exploded." Although the specific site may be circumscribed by property boundaries, the visual limits may include extensive sweeps of the landscape far beyond. The scope of planning considerations is increased, since fence-line geometry, orchards, paddocks, even a mountaintop miles away may become design factors and elements. Our scheme must be planned to the horizon.

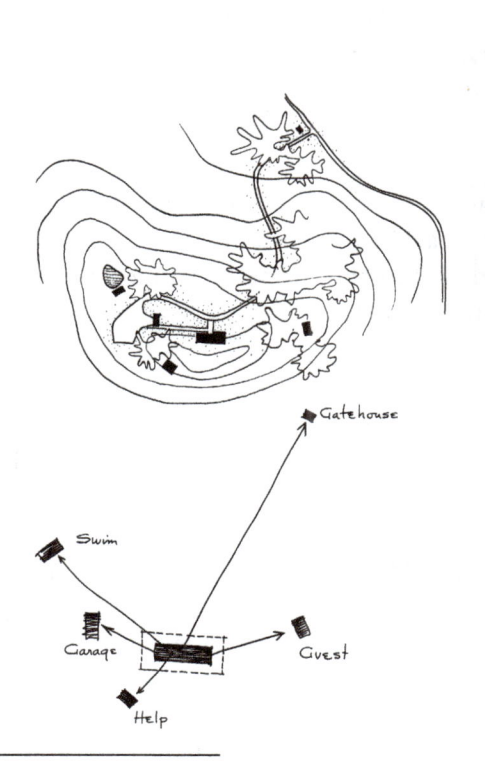

Rural site.

Ample area permits an exploded plan, each element being related to the most compatible topographic features.

Freedom, with open view of fields, woods, and sky, is the essential landscape quality. We may logically orient our plan outward to embrace the total site's best features and to command the best views.

The choice of a rural site would indicate a desire to be at one with nature. Make nature appreciation a design aim and theme. Insofar as possible, the natural environment will be disturbed or modified only to improve it.

The major landscape features are established. Build to them, feature the best, screen out and de-emphasize those that are less desirable, and contrive structural forms in best relation to the natural forms.

Site Planning 237

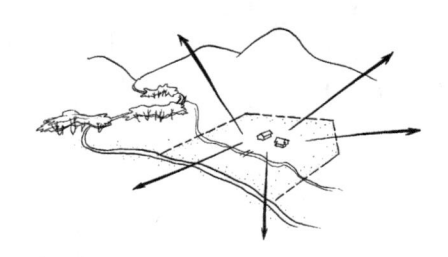

Rural property has an expansive feel. Streams, groves, distant hills, all features of the landscape that can be seen or sensed, are a part of the extensional site.

Major landscape features are established; build to, around, and among them.

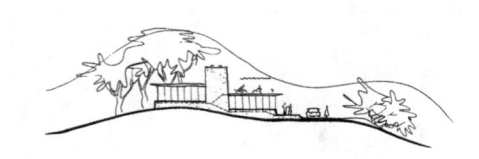

Structural forms conceived in sympathy with ground forms borrow power from and return power to the landscape.

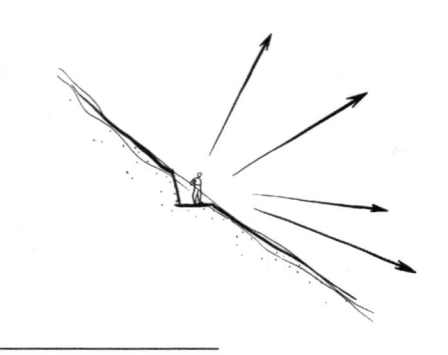

On the sloping plane, orientation is outward.

The landscape is dominant (in character and mood). Presumably the site was selected because of its qualities. If the existing landscape character is desirable, it may be preserved and accentuated by the site-structure diagram. If alterations are required, we may modify or completely change the site aspect, but only in such a way as to take fullest possible advantage of the existing features.

Earth and ground forms are strong visual elements. A structure conceived in studied relation to ground forms gains in architectural strength and in harmony with the topographical features.

The pleasant landscape is one of agreeable transitions. In the planning of transitions between structure and site, intermediate areas relating structure to the land are of key importance.

Structures become elements imposed on the landscape. Either the site is considered basically a setting for a dominant structure, or the structure is conceived as subordinate to the landscape and designed to complement the natural contours and forms.

The rural landscape is a landscape of subtleties—of foliage shadings, sky tints, and cloud shadows. Our planning will recognize these qualities and treat them sympathetically, or they will be wasted.

In a rural site, one is more exposed to the elements and weather—rain, storms, sun, wind, snow, frost, winter cold, and summer heat. The site-structure diagram and architecture should reflect a thorough understanding of adaptation to the climate.

A rural site implies increased land area and greater maneuverability. The automobile and pedestrian approaches, important elements in our design, may often be so aligned within the property boundaries as to reveal the best site and architectural features.

The indigenous materials of a rural site—ledge rock, fieldstone, slate, gravels, and timbers—contribute much to its landscape character. The use of such natural materials in buildings, fences, bridges, and walls helps relate structures to their surroundings.

The essential quality of the landscape is the natural and the unrefined. Our structural materials may well reflect this naturalness and forgo high refinement.

Steeply Sloping Site: Unobstructed Inclined Plane

Contours are major plan factors. Contour planning (the alignment of plan elements parallel with the contours) is generally indicated.

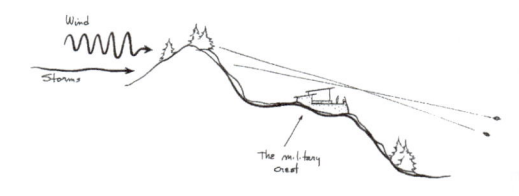

Use of the slope for protection.

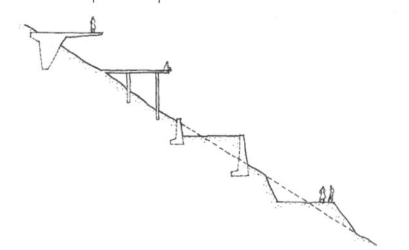

On a sloping site the level plane is achieved by terracing, retaining walls, the supported platform, or the cantilever.

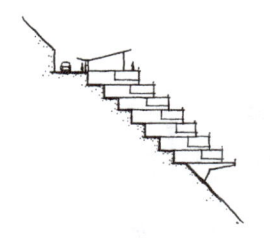

Imposed structures may hug the slope,

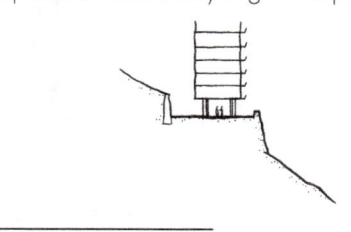

rest on a platform,

or stand completely free.

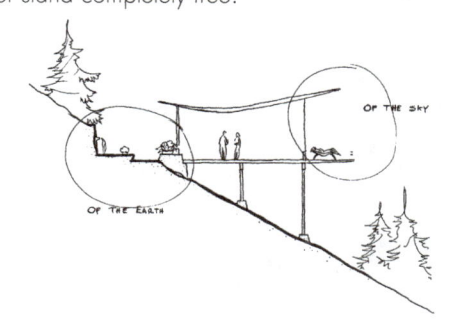

A structure imposed on a sloping site belongs to the sky as well as to the earth.

Slope stabilization.

The areas of relatively equal elevation are narrow bands lying perpendicular to the axis of the slope. Narrow plan forms such as bars or ribbons are suggested.

Sizable level areas are nonexistent. Where required, they must be carved out of or projected from the slope. If they are shaped of earth, the earth must be retained by a wall or by a slope of increased inclination.

The essence of slope is rise and fall. A terraced scheme is suggested. Levels may separate functions, as in split-level or multideck structures.

The slope is a ramp. Ramps and steps are logical plan elements. The slope grade is perhaps too steep for wheeled traffic. Access is easiest along contours. This fact dictates a normal approach from the sides.

The pull of gravity is down the slope. Our design forms not only must have stability, they must express stability to be pleasing. An exception, of course, would be those structures in which a feeling of daring or conditioned exhilaration is desired.

The sloping site has a dynamic landscape quality. The site lends itself to dynamic plan forms. The dramatic quality of a slope is its apparent

Site Planning   239

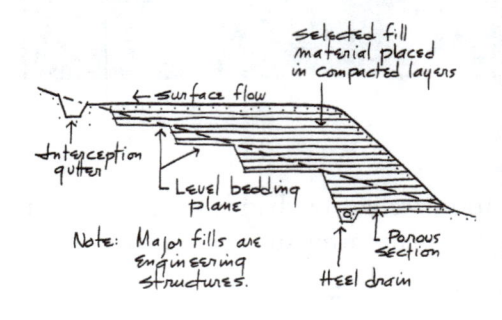

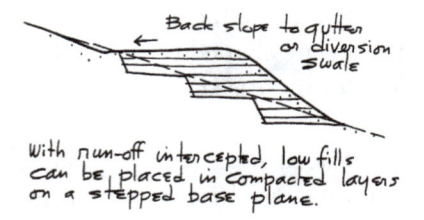

change in grade. Natural grade changes may be accentuated and dramatized through the use of terraces, overlook decks, and flying balconies.

A slope inherently emphasizes the meeting of earth and air. A level element imposed on a sloping plane often makes contact with the earth or rock at the inner side and is held free to the air at its outer extremity. Where the element makes contact with the earth, the jointure is to be clearly expressed. Where the leading edge flies free, this airy union of structure and sky should also be given design expression.

The top of the slope is most exposed to the elements. The planner may exploit or create a land profile similar to the military crest of the artillery manual—an adaptation or modification of the slope to preserve or enhance the view while affording increased protection from winds and storm.

A sloping site affords interest in views. Site development to create richness of landscape detail may be minimized, for when a sloping site commands a fine view, little else is required.

Development of steep slopes.

240   LANDSCAPE ARCHITECTURE

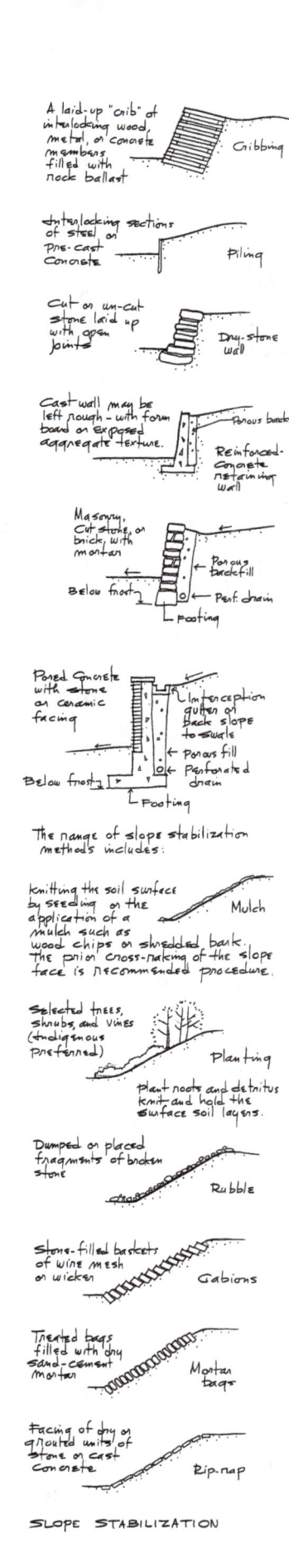

Helipad created on steep site.

The slope is oriented outward. Plan orientation is normally outward and down. Since the view side is exposed, the plan relation to sun, wind, and storms is of increased consideration.

A sloping site has drainage problems. Groundwater and surface runoff from above must be intercepted and diverted or allowed to pass freely under the structure.

A slope brings out many of the most desirable qualities of water. The play of water in falls, cascades, spouts, trickling rivulets, and films is an obvious plan opportunity.

Level Site

A level site offers a minimum of plan restrictions. Of all site types, the level site best lends itself to the cell-bud, crystalline, or geometric plan pattern.

A level site has relatively minor landscape interest. Plan interest depends upon the relationship of space to space, object to space, and object to object.

A flat site is essentially a broad-base plane. All elements set upon this plane are of strong visual importance, as is their relation one to the other. Each vertical element imposed must be considered not only in

Site Planning 241

Water provides the most level site.

Horizontal walls accentuate the level site.

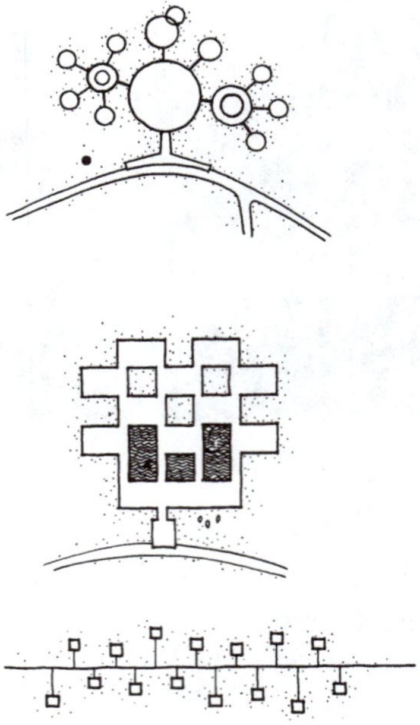

The level site adapts itself to the cell-bud, crystalline, or geometric plan.

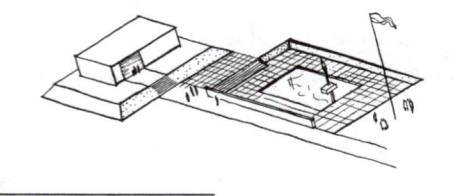

On the level site, the pit, the mound, and the vertical assume telling significance.

terms of its own form but also as a background against which other objects may be seen or across which shadow patterns may be cast.

A flat site has no focal point. The most visually insistent element placed on this site will dominate the scene.

Lines of approach are not dictated by the topography. The possibility of approach from any side makes all elevations important. Lines of exterior and interior circulation are critical design elements since they control the visual unfolding of the plan.

The dome of the sky is a dominant landscape element of infinite change and beauty. We may well feature the sky through the use of reflecting basins, pools, courts, patios, and recessed openings.

The sun is a powerful design factor. We may use it as a sweeping beam or flood and design in terms of light and shade. We may explore the myriad qualities of light and utilize the most effective in relation to our forms, colors, textures, and materials. We may dramatize cast shadow—solid as from a wall, moving as from water, sculptural as from objects, dappled as from foliage, or as a dark background and foil for luminous objects displayed against it.

242   LANDSCAPE ARCHITECTURE

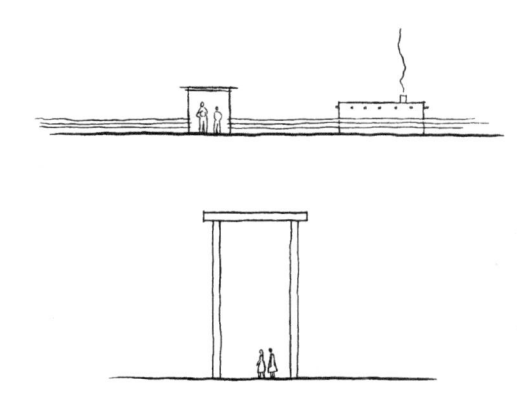

On the scaleless level plain, scale is what one makes it.

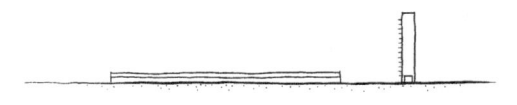

The horizontal in harmony, the vertical in dramatic contrast.

A level site has a neutral landscape quality. Site character is created by the elements introduced. Bold form, strong color, and often exotic materials may be used here without apparent violation of the native landscape.

The site offers little privacy. The creation of privacy is a function of the plan orientation. Privacy may be attained by the focus of spaces toward screening elements, inward to enclosed courts or outward to infinity from viewing points on the periphery.

Third dimension is lacking. Third dimension in the ground plane may be achieved through the creation of earth or architectural platforms or pits. Slight rises, drops, and steps assume exaggerated significance on the level site.

The flat site offers no obstruction to lateral planning. An expanded scheme with connective passageways or elements is a logical plan expression.

A flat site tends toward monotony. Since interest is in structure rather than in the natural landscape, the structure should be enhanced and dramatized in all ways possible.

The horizon is an insistent line. Striking effects may be achieved through the use of low, horizontal forms (complementary) or incisive verticals (contrasting).

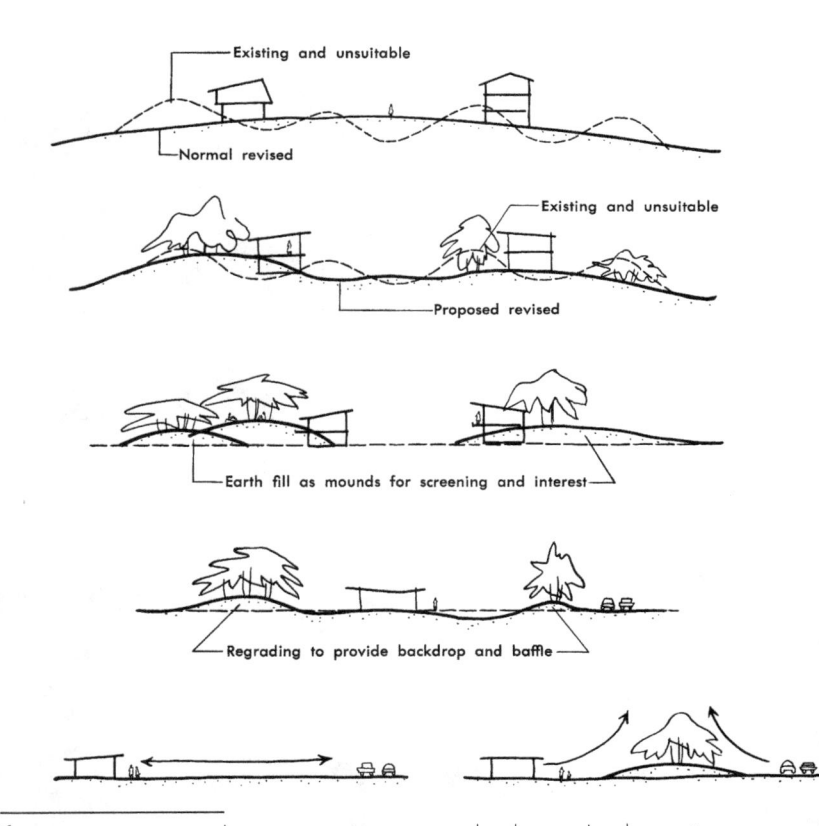

If we must use our earthmovers to create a new landscape (and sometimes we must), let us use them to create a landscape of topographical interest and pleasant and useful forms.

Site Planning 243

Flat landscape under the open sky is often oppressive and lacking in human scale. Scale is therefore easily controlled, from the intimate to the monumental. Human scale, if it is to exist, must be consciously created.

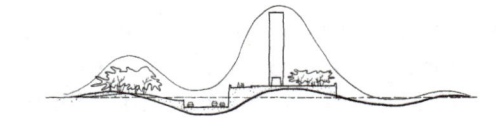

Where flatness equals monotony, maximize every topographical opportunity.

Other Sites

This same procedure of determining (by perception and deduction) the abstract design characteristics suggested by a given landscape type may, of course, be applied to sites of many varieties, including:

The mountainous	The lakeshore
The windswept	The island
The snow-covered	The estuarine
The forest	The oceanfront
The streamside	The resort
The boulder-strewn	The suburban
The pastoral	The institutional campus
The pond	The business district
The waterfall	The industrial park
The river edge	The heavy industrial

In planning any development or designing any structure in relation to a given site, it is helpful first to deduce the general design characteristics dictated by a thoroughgoing analysis of the existing landscape.

The inner city.

The mountain resort.

The urban waterfront.

The lakefront.

The forest.

244　LANDSCAPE ARCHITECTURE

Site-Structure Plan Development

It can be seen that the forces, forms, and features of the total site exert both a powerful and often subtle influence on the schematic plan. In the refinement of the plan and the design of each component, their relationship to all aspects of the environs is to be further studied.

Outward and Inward Plan Progression

We must consider each function from the innermost point of generation to the off-site terminus. In the design of a home, for example, we would be concerned with the route of the small-fry not only from bed to bathroom to breakfast table but also from breakfast table to the nearest door, to play areas, to pathway, to school—all in a natural and pleasant progression. Or, in more prosaic terms, we would plan the route of refuse from kitchen to service area to refuse truck to street—all with inconspicuous convenience. The relationship of dining table to window to view involves enframement and development of the view to the property limits and, in most cases, beyond.

Conversely, each element or area must be designed as the logical conclusion of a function originating at the extremities of the site environs. Anyone approaching your property to make a delivery is subtly directed to the service drive, the parking space for the delivery truck, the service walk, the service entrance, and the storage compartment. By design, guests arriving for the evening are alerted and invited in, welcomed to the approach court, directed to the parking bay, and guided to the entrance door, where they enter to the vestibule and the hospitality of the inner home. This same inward and outward progression is applicable to the planning of any project, be it a sawmill, a recreation park, or a world's fair exposition.

Expansion-Contraction of Plan Concept

Most site-planning problems can be fully solved only by expanding the areas of consideration to the farthest extensional aspect of the site and by contracting each problem to the minutiae of human experience and irreducible detail. For although it is true that an object or element must be judged in relation to all other elements with which it is allied, it is also true that objects can be fully appreciated only when they are experienced one at a time, in depth, and at the living moment.

Satellite Plan

As a total structure is conceived in harmony with the total site, so must each element or area of the structure be conceived in harmony with related site areas. In an elementary school, for instance, we would plan the kindergarten, its outdoor play lot, garden, and entrance gate all as one. The gymnasium we would coordinate with the game courts, equipment areas, and playfields. We would consider the boiler plant together with its service and storage areas. The auditorium with its approaches and parking compound, the classrooms with their related outdoor spaces, each element with its extensional site areas would be treated as an integrated plan complex. The overall scheme in diagram would thus resemble a solar system with sun, planets, and satellites.

Integral Planning

When a structure is imposed on a site, certain changes in landscape character are effected. It is important that these changes be controlled by the planner. Our elementary school is not just plunked down in a city block or in the midst of a suburban community. Rather, ideally, it is fitted to the property and conceived in harmony with the community with such skill that the new landscape created is an improvement over the original.

Integrated plan.

The best site plan is that which yields the greatest long-term benefit with the least total cost and stress.

For a lesson in relating architecture to site we may well look to the Renaissance planners. In the building of the magnificent Piazza San Marco in Venice, the architect commissioned to design the cathedral, or the campanile, or the Doge's Palace, or the memorial columns at the water gate never conceived of his building or columns as design entities solely. Instead, he instinctively considered his works as integral parts of the piazza in terms of his proposed structure, which he conceived, from broad plan to most minute detail, in terms of its impact on the piazza and vice versa. Each planner not only designed that for which he was commissioned but redesigned the entire piazza and, in doing so, his city of Venice. Thus, and only thus, was he fulfilling his obligation to his client and his city. The secret of much of the charm and great beauty of European towns and cities lies in the conscious application of this planning axiom. Much of the hodgepodge and helter-skelter appearance of the American scene results from planning with seeming ignorance of and indifference to the existing environs.

Proving the Plan

How do we know whether our proposed installation is well related to its site? There is one sure test we can apply. We can experience it vicariously through the senses of those who will see and use it. At any stage in the creative process, from rough sketches to final drawings or model, we can by our imagination lift ourselves up and look down at the project with a fresh perspective. We can bring it alive in our mind's eye. We can say, in effect, as we look down at the plans for a church:

> "I am the minister. As I drive by my church or approach it, does it express those inspirational qualities to which I have dedicated my life? As I enter my study, do I sense that this space is remote enough to give me privacy for study and meditation, yet accessible enough to attract to its doors those who need help or counsel or those who come on church business? As an office, is it so located that I can direct and oversee church activities? Does this church that I am to administer have an efficiently organized plan?"
>
> "I am the janitor. As I come to work in the morning, where do I park my car? How do the barrels of cleaning compound get moved from the service dock to the storage area? Where do I store my ladders and snow removal equipment? Did someone in their planning think about me and my work?"
>
> "I am a Boy Scout coming to troop meeting. Are the walks planned to take me where I am going, or do I cut across the lawn? Some friends of mine are waiting outside. Do we have a place where we can rip around and blow off steam and maybe shoot a few baskets? Where do we put our bikes? Where do we set up practice tents? Where do we . . . ?"
>
> "I am a member of this church, and I am coming to worship. Does my church invite me in? Am I able to drive close to the entry on a cold, rainy day? Where do I park? Is there ample room? After the service, is there a pleasant space adjacent to the doors where we may linger and greet our friends and welcome visitors?"

All these things are a part of church life and need to be arranged for in its planning. The function of any project and the relationship of building to site may thus be tested by an imaginary introduction to and walk-through by people typical of those who will see, service, and/or use it.

The process of site-structure plan development is a search for logical progressions and best relationships.

Site-Structure Unity

We have discussed the importance of developing responsive site-project relationships. Let us now consider other means by which we may achieve site-structure unity.

Rikiu was watching his son Shoan as he swept and watered the garden path. "Not clean enough," said Rikiu, when Shoan had finished his task, and bade him try again. After a weary hour the son returned to Rikiu: "Father, there is nothing more to be done. The steps have been washed for the third time; the stone lanterns and trees are all well sprinkled with water; moss and lichens are shining with a fresh verdure; not a twig, not a leaf have I left on the ground." "Young fool," chided the teamaster, "that is not the way a garden path should be swept." Saying this, Rikiu stepped into the garden, shook a tree and scattered over the garden gold and crimson leaves, scraps of the brocade of autumn.

Kakuzo Okakura

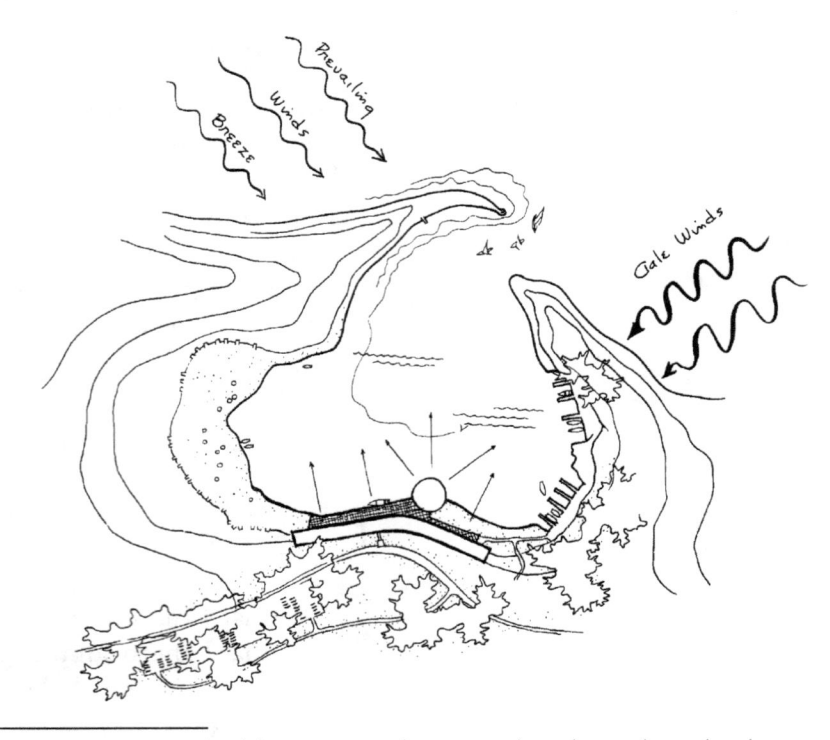

Site-structure unity: yacht club, terrace, and restaurant have been planned to the natural ground forms, which overhang and command the bay. Boat slips are fitted to the protective ridge. The beach area extends the soft receptive wash of the harbor. Cabanas follow the natural bowl. The breakwater and light extend the existing rocky shoulders of the point. The parking areas are "hidden" in the shade of the existing grove. Such a simpatico feeling for the existing topography ensures a plan development of fitness and pleasant harmonies of aesthetics and function.

Where site and structure meet we may well "structure" the site and at the same time "wash" the landscape over and into the structure.

Hideo Sasaki

We may design the structural elements to utilize and accentuate landforms. A lighthouse, for example, is an extension of the jutting promontory. The ancient fort or castle extended, architecturally, the craggy top of a hill or mountain. Our modern municipal water tanks and transmission or relay towers rise from and extend the height of a topographical eminence. These applications are obvious. Not so obvious is the location of a community swimming pool to utilize and accentuate the natural bowl configuration of a landscape basin or valley. More subtle yet may be the conscious planning of a yacht club to utilize and emphasize the structural protective shoulders of a point or the soft receptive forms of a quiet bay.

Terraced ski lodges stepping down the snowy slope of a mountain, floating structures on water, light, airy structures fixed against the sky, massive structures rooted in rock—each draws from its site a native power and returns to the site this power magnified. Whole cities have been imbued with this dynamic quality—Saigon overhanging its dark river and slow-flowing tributaries, Lhasa braced proudly against its mountain wall, Darjeeling extending its timbered mountain peaks and towers into the clouds.

A structure and its site may be strongly related by architectural treatment of site areas or elements. Clipped allées and hedges, water panels, precise embankments and terraces, all extend the limits of design control. Many of the French and Italian villas of the Renaissance were so architectural in their treatment that the entire property from wall to wall became one grand composition of palatial indoor and outdoor rooms. These grandiose garden halls were demarcated by great planes or arches of sheared beech, of masonry and mosaic, rows of plinths, and elaborate balustraded walls. They embraced monumental sculptured fountains and parterre gardens of rich pattern or mazes of sharply trimmed box hedges. The integration of architecture and site thus became complete.

Unfortunately, the results were often vacuous: a meaningless exercise in applied geometry—the control of nature for no more reason than for the sake of exerting control. Many such villas, on the other hand, were and still remain notable for their great symphonic beauty. In these, without exception, the highest inherent qualities of the natural elements of the site—plants, topography, water—were fully appreciated by the planner and given design expression. Seldom, for instance, has water as a landscape element been treated with more imaginative control than at Villa d'Este in Tivoli, where a mountain torrent was diverted to spill down the steep villa slopes through the gardens, rushing, pouring, gushing, foaming, spurting, spewing, surging, gurgling, dripping, riffling, and finally shining deep and still in the stone reflecting basins. Here at Villa d'Este, water, slopes, and plant materials were handled architecturally to enhance both the structure and the site and superbly unite the two.

Alternatively, the landscape features of the site may be embraced by the dispersion of structural or other planned elements into the landscape.

Ingenious water displays—Villa D'Este.

Site Planning 249

Satellite

Buckshot

Finger

Checkerboard

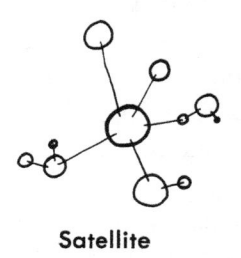

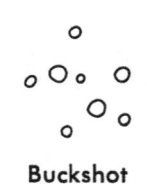

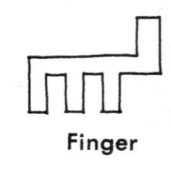

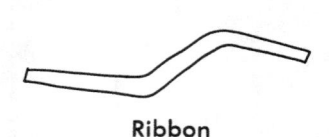

Ribbon

Exploded

Dispersion of plan elements.

The satellite plan, the buckshot plan, the finger plan, the checkerboard plan, the ribbon plan, and the exploded plan are typical examples.

Just as the early French and English explorers in North America controlled vast tracts of land by the strategic placement of a few forts, so can the well-placed elements of a scheme control a given landscape. Such is true of our national parks with their trails, lodges, and campgrounds sited to unfold to the user the most interesting features of the park. Such is true, in *linear* plan expression, of any well-planned scenic drive or highway extended into the countryside. Our military installations are often, in plan, scattered over extensive land areas, each function—be it rifle range, officers' quarters, tank proving ground, tent sites, or artillery range—relating to those topographical features that seem most suitable. For this same purpose, many of our newer schools are exploded in plan. Unlike the old three-story monumental school set *on* the land, the newer schools of which we speak are planned *to* the landscape, embracing and revealing its more pleasant qualities with such success that school and landscape are one.

The site and the structure may be further related by the interlocking of common areas—patios, terraces, and courts, for example. A landscape feature displayed from or in such a court takes on a new aspect. It seems singled out. It becomes a specimen held up to close and frequent observation under varying conditions of position, weather, and light. A simple fragment of rock so featured acquires a modeling and a beauty of form and detail that would not be realized if it were seen in its natural state. As we watch it from day to day—streaming with rain, sparkling with hoarfrost or soft snow, glistening in the sharp sun and incised with shadow, or glowing in subdued evening light—we come to a fuller understanding of this landscape object and thus of the nature of the landscape from which it came.

The landscape may be even more strongly related to structure by the orientation of a room or an area to some feature of the landscape, as by a vista or a view. A view or a garden may be treated as a mural, a mural of constant change and variety of interest, extending the room area visually to the limits of the garden (or to infinity for a distant view). It can be seen that, to be pleasant, the scale, mood, and character of the landscape feature viewed must be suited to the function of the area from which it is observed.

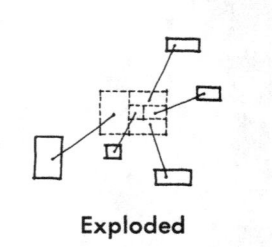

To the foreign visitor in a traditional Japanese home, one of the most appealing features of many is the use of smoothly sliding screens of wood and paper by which the entire side of a room may be opened at will to bring into the space a cloudlike flowering plum tree, a vigorous composition of sand, stone, and sunlit pine, a view through tiered maple branches to the tiered roof of a distant pagoda, or a quiet pool edged with moss and rippled by lazily fanning goldfish. Each feature viewed is treated with impeccable artistry as part of the room, to extend and unite it with the garden or landscape. The Japanese would tell us that they have a deeper purpose, that what they are really trying to do is to relate people and nature completely and make nature appreciation a part of their daily lives.

To this end they introduce into their dwellings the best of those objects of nature that they can find or afford. The posts and lintels of their rooms, for instance, are not squared and finished lumber but rather a trunk or limb of a favorite wood shaped, tooled, and finished to bring out its inherent form and pattern of grain and knotting. Each foundation stone, each section of bamboo, each tatami (woven grass mat) is so fashioned by the artisan as to discover, and reveal in the finished object, the highest natural quality of the material that is being used. In the Japanese home one finds plants and arrangements of twigs, leaves, and grasses that are startling in their beauty. Even in their art forms the Japanese consciously, almost reverently, bring nature into their homes.

In such ways we, too, may relate our projects and structures to their natural setting. We may use large areas of fenestration. We may devise our approaches and paths of circulation to achieve the most desirable relationships. We may recall and adapt from the landscape colors, shapes, and materials. We may make further ties by projecting into the landscape certain areas of interior paving and by extending structural walls or overhead planes. We may break down or vignette our structures from high refinement to a more rustic quality as we move from the interior outward. This is a reverse application of the quality *wabi* mentioned before. This controlled transition from the refined to the natural is a matter of great design significance.

If a building or plan area of any predetermined character is to be imposed on a landscape of another character, transition from the one to the other will play an important role. If, for example, a civic plaza and art museum are to be built at the edge of a city park, all plan elements will become more "civic" and sophisticated as one leaves the park to approach the plaza. Lines will become more precise. Forms will become refined and architectural. Materials, colors, textures, and details will become richer. The natural park character will give way gradually, subtly, to an intensified urbane character consonant with the planned expression of the museum. Conversely, if a park or wooded public garden is planned in a highly developed urban district, plan forms will relax and be freer and more natural as one approaches the open space. Such controlled intensification, relaxation, or conversion of plan expression is the mark of skilled physical planning.

Site Systems

As a logical extension of the principles of site-project unification the concept of *site systems* deserves special attention. The term implies simply that all site improvements are conceived to be constructed and function in a systematic way.

Drainage

With few exceptions the natural site provides for storm runoff across its surface without causing erosion. The ground-stabilizing roots and tendrils of living plants knit the soils and absorb precipitation. The fallen twigs and leaves also form an absorptive mat to keep the soil moist and cool the air. The natural swales, streambeds, and river gorges of the undisturbed landscape provide for the most efficient storm-water flow, while marshes, ponds, and lakes provide the ultimate storage and recharge basins. Any alteration to this established network is both disruptive and costly. When the movement of materials is required, new storm drainageways must be shaped, and often extensive artificial storm-sewer systems. Usually, with the installation of roofs, paved areas, and sewer pipe, the amount and rate of runoff is increased to the detriment of the project site and downstream landowners.

Experience would suggest that artificial drainage devices be minimized and that the natural drainageways be preserved and utilized to the utmost

The least disruption of the natural drainage system should be the cardinal rule in developing land; however, some disturbance and change to the natural system are unavoidable. Nevertheless, the resulting changes in runoff and drainage patterns must be managed to "return" them to the natural condition in the surrounding downstream area as expediently as possible in terms of both time and distance, thus minimizing erosion and flooding. This practice, referred to as *stormwater management,* has become mandatory in many parts of the United States for most land-disturbing activities.

Much of what the profession of landscape architecture and this book are about is an approach to the planning, design, and use of land that produces the least possible impact on the land. Over the last several decades, this practice has gradually been embraced by the larger planning and design community and, increasingly, has become recognized by regulators, who have incorporated some of the practices into land-use codes and ordinances. As these practices have become more widespread, they have become known as *low-impact design* (LID)

While LID practices can include anything that reduces the effects of development on the land, the most common practices focus on the biological—or natural—systems approach to stormwater management, which is done by simulating conditions in nature. This includes the use of bioswales, bioretention or rain gardens, green roofs, and permeable paving, to name a few of the options. All of these devices are intended to slow and temporarily store runoff water, filter sediment and pollutants, and recharge groundwater in a more effective, efficient process than conventional stormwater management techniques.

riverfront treatment train

green roofs

wetland purification system

streetside swales

greenhouse

tree nursery

community garden

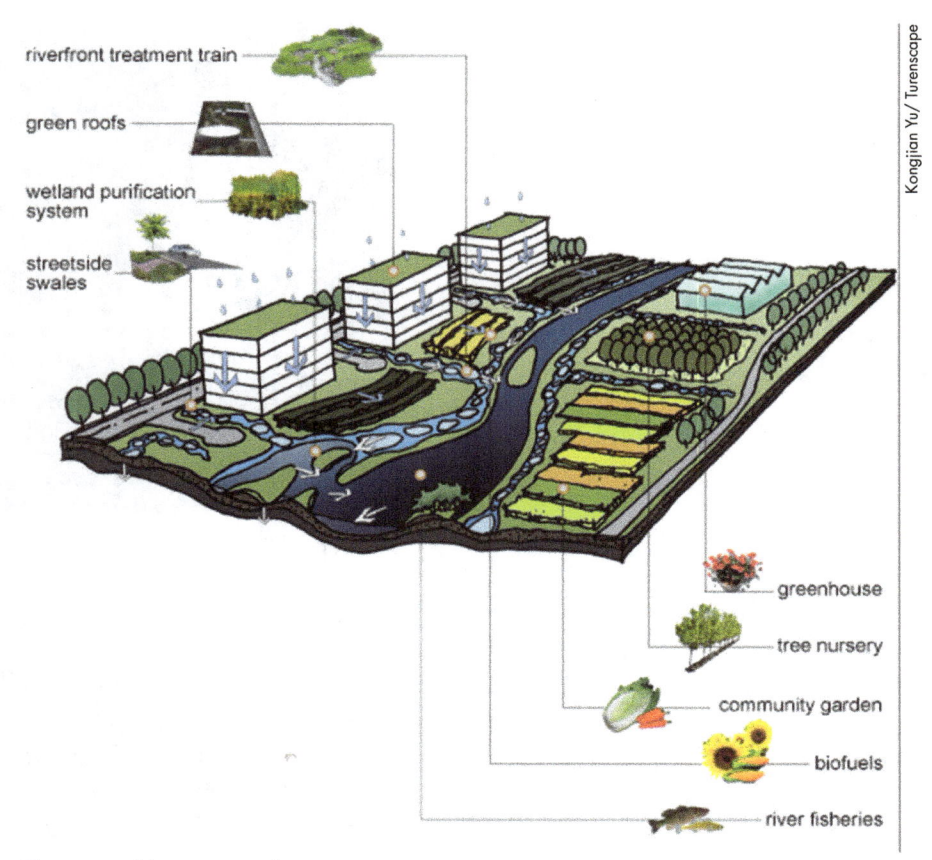

biofuels

river fisheries

Kongjian Yu/Turenscape

Elements of low-impact design.

Movement

Planned paths of pedestrian and vehicular movement that oppose the existing ground forms generate the problems and costs of earthwork, slope retention, interception gutters, storm-sewer connections, and the establishment of new ground covers. When such routes are aligned instead to rise and fall with the natural grades, to follow the ridge lines and ravines, or to trace a cross-slope gradient that requires no heavy cuts or fills, they not only are more economical to build but are also better to look at and more pleasant to use.

Well-designed walks, bicycle trails, and roadways also provide interconnecting networks of movement that ensure regional continuity; they are particularly suited to the type of traffic to be accommodated and take into account factors such as safety, efficiency, and landscape integrity. Materials, sections, profiles, lighting, signing, and planting are coordinated and designed as an integrated system.

Lighting

Site illumination does many good things. It provides safety in traffic movement and crossings, it warns of hazards, and it serves to increase

Site Planning 253

Proper lighting enhances the design.

security and reduce vandalism. It interprets the plan arrangement by giving emphasis to focal points, gathering places, and building entrances. It demarcates and illumines paths of interconnection, serving as a guide-on. With accent lighting, fine architecture or site areas of exceptional significance or beauty can be brought into visual prominence.

Well-conceived lighting gives clarity and unity to the overall site and to each subarea within it. However, poorly conceived lighting can be discordant with a design, become a source of light pollution, or even create hazardous conditions.

Improper lighting is offensive and hazardous.

254 *LANDSCAPE ARCHITECTURE*

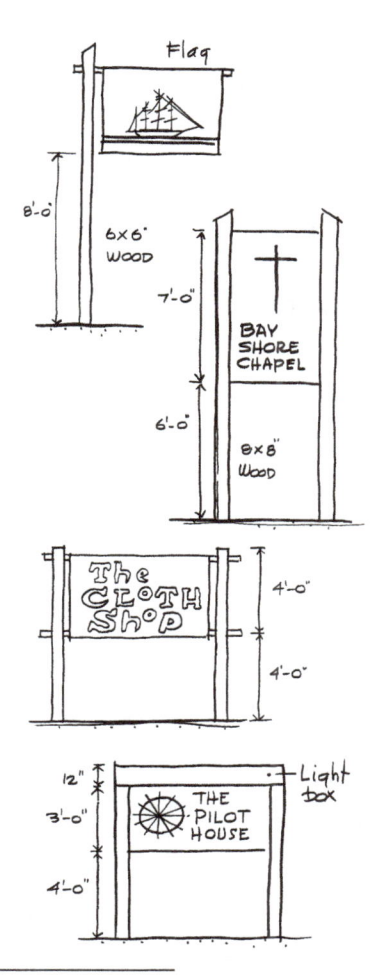

Unity with diversity is the key to identification signs. Shapes, sizes, and letter forms may vary with the information to be conveyed. Materials, mountings, and colors are usually standardized.

Signs

Graphic informational systems are closely allied with site illumination, since the two are usually interdependent and complementary. Street and route lighting obviously must be planned together with the positioning of related directional signs. Often, light standards provide support for signs and informational symbols. Signs, like lighting, are best developed as a hierarchy, each sign being designed in terms of its size, color, and placement to best serve its particular purpose and all existing together as a related family. When the system is kept simple and standardized, the signing gives its own sense of order and clarity to the trafficway pattern and the landscape plan.

Planting

Planting excellence is also systematic. It articulates and strengthens the site layout. It develops an interrelated pattern of open, closed, or semi-enclosed spaces, each shaped to suit its planned function. Planting extends topographical forms, enframes views and vistas, anchors free-standing buildings, and provides visual transitions from object to object and place to place. It serves as backdrop, windscreen, and sunshield. It checks winter winds. It catches and channels the summer breeze. It casts

Plantings articulate and strengthen site layout.

Site Planning

shadow and provides shade. It absorbs precipitation, freshens the air, and modifies climatic extremes.

Aside from serving these practical functions, plants in their many forms and varieties are also pleasing to the eye. But even their beauty is increased if there is an evident reason behind their selection and use.

Fine plantings, like any other fine work of design, have a fundamental simplicity and discernible order. Many experienced landscape designers limit their plant lists to a primary tree, shrub, and ground cover and one to three secondary trees, shrubs, and supplementary ground cover—grasses, herbs, or vines, with all other supporting and accent plants comprising no more than a small fraction of the total.

Except in urban settings, the large majority of all plants used will be native to the region and will therefore fit and thrive without special care.

Essentially, each plant used should serve a purpose, and all together should contribute to the function and expressiveness of the plan.

Materials

Just as the palette of plant materials is limited in the main to those which are indigenous, so is it also with the materials of construction. Wall stone from local quarries seems most appropriate. Crushed stone and gravels exposed as aggregate, bricks made of local clays, lumber from trees that grow in the vicinity, and mulches made of their chipped or shredded bark all seem right in the local scene. Even the architectural adaptation of the natural earth, foliage, and sky colors relates the constructions to the regional setting.

The reduction of the number of materials used to a small and selective list lends simplicity and unity to the planned development.

Operations

All projects must be planned to work and work efficiently. Each building and each use area of the site must operate well as an entity, and all together as a well-organized complex. This can be achieved only if all components are planned together as an integrated system.

Maintenance

To be effective maintenance must be a consideration from the earliest planning stages. This presupposes that all maintenance operations have been programmed. It also assumes that storage for the required materials and equipment is provided, that access points and ways are strategically

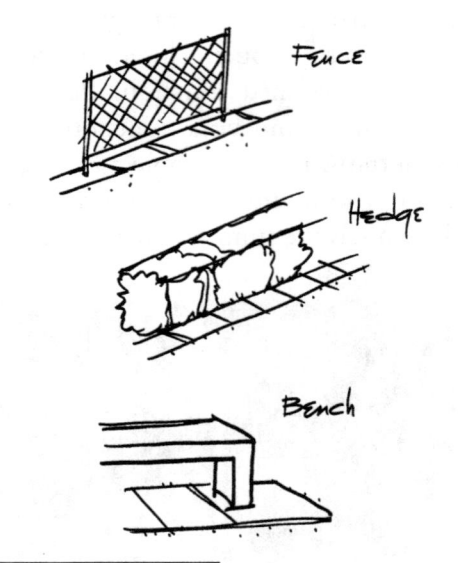

Edging strips.
Paved mowing strips of concrete, set brick, or stone at lawn edges carry the wheel of an edger and eliminate hand trimming.

From small-home grounds to campus, to park, to large industrial complex, site installation and maintenance costs can be reduced and performance improved by the standardization of all possible components, materials, and equipment. Use only the affordable best; therein lies quality and economy.

located, that convenient hydrants and electrical outlets are installed, and that maintenance needs are reduced insofar as practical.

It also means that the number of construction materials and components and thus the replacement inventory of items that must be kept stocked are reduced to a workable minimum. This requires standardization of light globes, bench slats, anchor bolts, sign blanks, curb templates, paint colors, and everything else. Usually, a reduction in the quantity of items stocked can result in improved quality at significant savings. This is possible only if the maintenance operation is planned from the start as an efficient system or is converted to one.

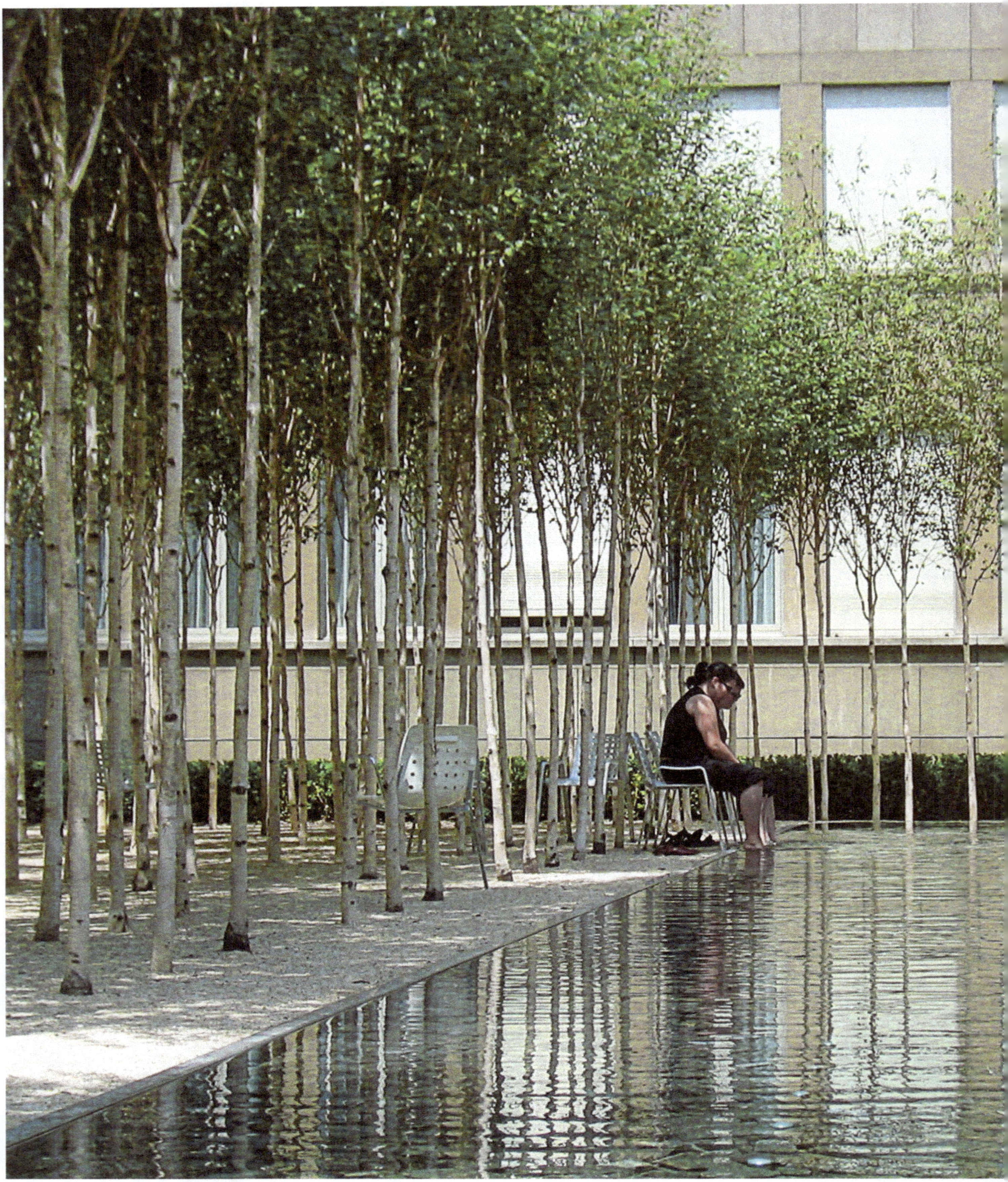

12
SITE SPACES

In two-dimensional site planning we are concerned with defining use areas and their relationship one to another and to the total site. In further developing the conceptual plan, attention is centered upon the translation of the areas into functioning volumes. Each volume or space is conceived in size, shape, material, color, texture, and other qualities to best accommodate and express its purpose. It can be said that planning is two-dimensional; three-dimensional thinking takes us into the realm of design.

Spaces

Much of the art and science of land planning is revealed to the planner when it is first realized that one is dealing not with areas but with spaces. As an example, the playground composed of play equipment set about on a dull base plane has little child appeal, while the same apparatus arranged within a grouping of imaginative play spaces can provide endless hours of delight. It is a matter of designing the volumetric enclosure and spatial interconnections to suit the use.

In the same vein, a highway is more than a ribbon of pavement traversing the base plane. A properly designed highway is conceived also in terms of volumes—open where safe vision and pleasant views so dictate, closed for screening, varied in its spatial conformation to provide interest and relief from fatigue, and modulated to reveal the embracing landscape in the best possible way. The superior highway will be a scientifically contrived, expanding and contracting, variformed volume

PWP Landscape Architecture

through which motorists may move speedily, safely, and freely while enjoying a highwayscape designed to keep them relaxed and happy and, at the same time, alert.

A city is not at best a heterogeneous conglomeration of buildings lined out in a rigid grid pattern; a well-planned city is perceived as an evolving composition of structures and interrelated spaces. More than the buildings, it is the form and character of the open spaces they define that give a city its essential quality. Perhaps the most disturbing fact of our disturbing American cities is that most structures are arranged as in a wall along constricted city streets rather than grouped around traffic-free courts, squares, and plazas.

The creation of well-organized interior and exterior spaces for uses of any type and scope is our goal as environmental designers.

Space is defined by the base, vertical, and overhead planes.

People live on the earth, on the land, but in three-dimensional air-space, the atmospheric volume, immediately above this land surface. Plans and land-use maps may be measured diagrammatically and abstractly in square footage and acreage, but space for living is measured in cubage, in volumes of air-space enclosed or organized with tangible physical elements....

The experience of being within fine three-dimensional spatial volumes is one of the greatest experiences of life.

Garrett Eckbo

Spatial Impact

Volumes have been designed for the intended purpose of torturing the occupants. It has been said that during the Spanish Civil War an architect was ordered to devise such a chamber. He developed a translucent polyhedron of sharply intersecting planes—an insidious enclosure in which a locked-in victim found himself unable to lie, sit, stoop, or kneel without tilting or tumbling the cubicle. The surfaces were slippery, burning hot in the sun, and frigid in the cold of night. In any light, the colors were distressing if seen alone; seen together, in their discordant clashing, they soon became maddening.

If it is possible to devise distressing volumes, then, conversely, it should also be possible to create volumes that yield an experience of pleasure. We may recall a favorite golf course fairway as such an agreeable space.

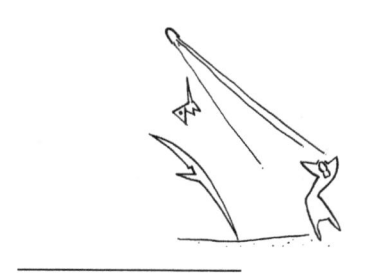

Tension.

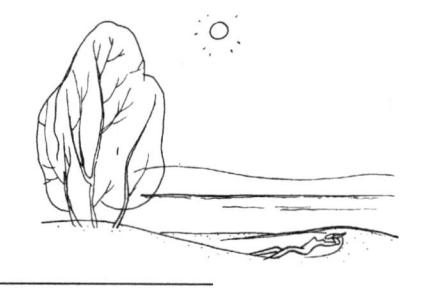

Relaxation.

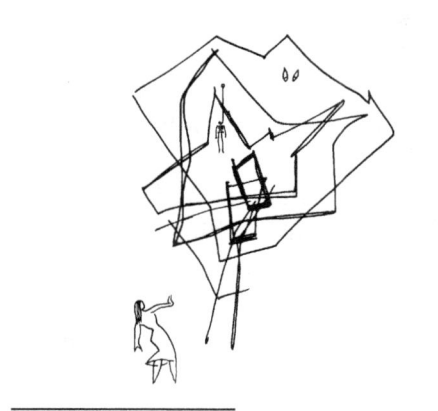

Fright.

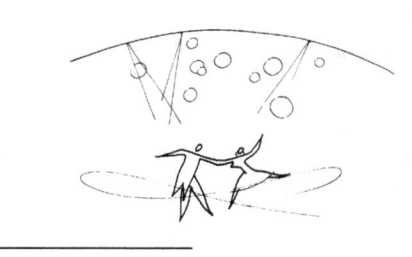

Gaiety.

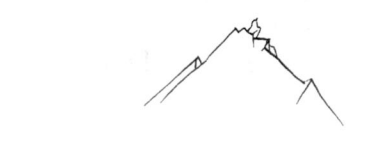

Contemplation.

Expansive, free, and undulating, it is open to the sky, enclosed with foliage, and carpeted with turf.

An outdoor space of far different mien is the cascade approach and plaza of New York's Rockefeller Center. It is walled by a canyon of metal, masonry, and glass and has a base of cut stone and terrazzo; its overhead plane is a tower-framed segment of sky, relieved by the tracery of foliage and the moving color of waving flags. Here is a space artfully planned to attract, refresh, and excite us and condition us for entry into the elegant restaurants, shops, and offices at its sides. Not far away, we can find yet another outdoor space of high design refinement. The garden of the Museum of Modern Art is an urbane volume eminently suited as a backdrop and visual extension of the adjacent galleries or as a place in which to wander through sunlight and dappled shade, viewing the pools and sculpture.

There will come to mind, upon reflection, many other similarly pleasant site spaces—a picnic spot on some lakeshore, a stadium, a public square, a residential swimming pool and garden. By analysis, we find that all are pleasant because, and only because, in size, shape, and character they are manifestly suited to the purposes for which they were intended.

As an instructive exercise, we might list the abstract qualities or spatial characteristics of a series of varying volumes, each designed to induce a predetermined response:

> *Tension.* Unstable forms. Split composition. Illogical complexities. Wide range of values. Clash of colors. Intense colors without relief. Visual imbalance about a line or a point. No point at which the eye can rest. Hard, polished, or jagged surfaces. Unfamiliar elements. Harsh, blinding, or quavering light. Uncomfortable temperatures in any range. Piercing, jangling, jittery sound.
> *Relaxation.* Simplicity. Volumes varying in size from the intimate to the infinite. Fitness. Familiar objects and materials. Flowing lines. Curvilinear forms and spaces. Evident structural stability. Horizontality. Agreeable textures. Pleasant and comfortable shapes. Soft light. Soothing sound. Volume infused with quiet colors—whites, grays, blues, greens. "Think round thoughts."
> *Fright.* Sensed confinement. An apparent trap. A quality of compression and bearing. No points of orientation. No means by which to judge position or scale. Hidden areas and spaces. Possibilities for surprise. Sloping, twisted, or broken planes. Illogical, unstable forms. Slippery, hazardous base plane. Danger. Unprotected voids. Sharp, protruding elements. Contorted spaces. The unfamiliar. The shocking. The startling. The weird. The uncanny. Symbols connoting horror, pain, torture, or applied force. The dim, the dark, the eerie, the brutal. Pale and quavering or, conversely, blinding garish light. Cold blues, cold greens. Abnormal, monochromatic color.

Site Spaces

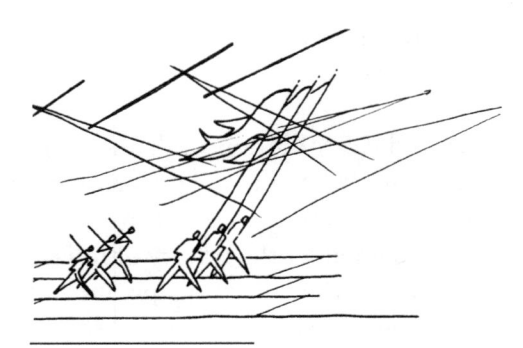

Gaiety. Free spaces. Smooth, flowing forms and patterns. Looping, tumbling, swirling motion accommodated. Lack of restrictions. Forms, colors, and symbols that appeal to the emotions rather than to the intellect. Temporal. Casual. Lack of restraint. Pretense acceptable. The fanciful applauded. Warm, bright colors. Sparkling, shimmering, shooting, or glowing light. Exuberant, lilting sound.

Contemplation. Scale not important since subjects will withdraw into their own sensed well of consciousness. Total space mild and unpretentious. No insinuating elements. No distractions of sharp contrast. Symbols, if used, should relate to subject of contemplation. Space providing a sense of isolation, privacy, detachment, security, and peace. Soft, diffused light. Tranquil and recessive colors. If sound, a low muted stream of sound to be perceived subconsciously.

Dynamic action. Bold forms. Heavy, structural cadence. Solid materials such as stone, concrete, wood, or steel. Rough, natural textures. Angular planes. Diagonals. The pitched vertical. Concentration of interest on focal point of action, as to rostrum, rallying point, or exit gate through which the volume impels one. Motion induced by sweeping lines, shooting lights, and climactic sequences of form, pattern, and sound. Strong, primitive colors—crimson, scarlet, and yellow-orange. Billowing banners. Burnished standards. Martial music. Rush of sound. Ringing crescendos. Crash of brass. Blare of trumpets. The roll and boom of drums.

Sensuous love. Complete privacy. Inward orientation of room. Subject the focal point. Intimate scale. Low ceiling. Horizontal planes. Fluid lines. Soft, rounded forms. Juxtaposition of angles and curves. Delicate fabrics. Voluptuous and yielding surfaces. Exotic elements and scent. Soft, rosy pink to golden light. Pulsating, titillating music.

Sublime spiritual awe. Overwhelming scale that transcends normal human experience. Soaring forms in contrast with low horizontal forms. A volume so contrived as to hold one transfixed on a broad base plane and lift one's eyes and mind high along the vertical. Orientation upward to or beyond some symbol of the infinite. Complete compositional order, often symmetry. Highly developed sequences. Use of costly and permanent materials. Connotation of the eternal. Use of chaste white. If color is used, the cool detached colors, such as blue-greens, blue, and violet. Diffused glow with shafts of light. Deep, full, swelling music with lofty passages.

Displeasure. Frustrating sequences of movement or revelation. Areas and spaces unsuited to anticipated use. Obstacles. Excesses. Undue friction. Discomfort. Annoying textures. Improper use of materials. The illogical. The false. The insecure. The tedious. The blatant. The dull. The disorderly. Disagreeable colors. Discordant sounds. Uncomfortable temperature or humidity. Annoying lights. That which is ugly.

Dynamic action.

Sensuous love.

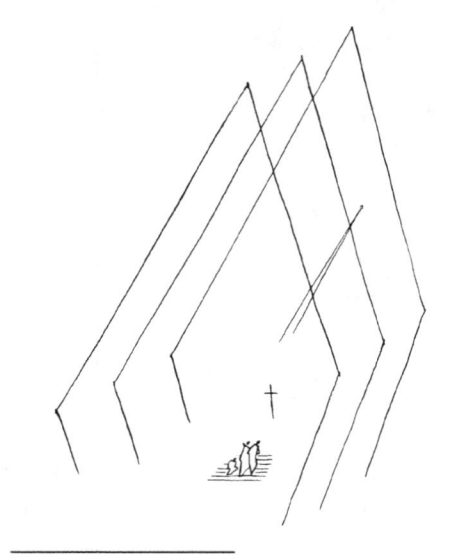

Sublime, spiritual awe.

We must create pools of stillness, areas of entrancement; and the purpose of these is not to escape from life—even the vibrant life created by the new sources of energy that characterize our modern civilization—but to enjoy life in its profoundest essence.
Sir Herbert Read

From its hollowness arises the reality of the vessel; from its empty space arises the reality of the building.
Lao-tzu

A creation in space is an interweaving of parts of space . . .
László Moholy-Nagy

Architecture . . . is the beautiful and serious game of space.
Willem Dudok

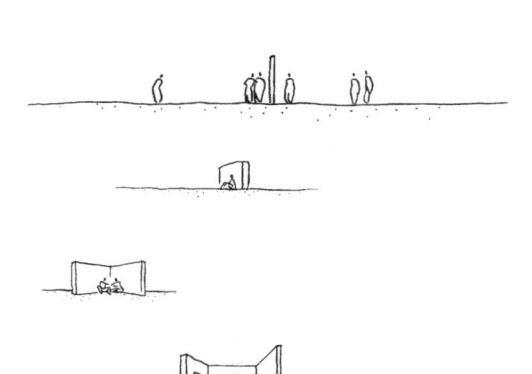

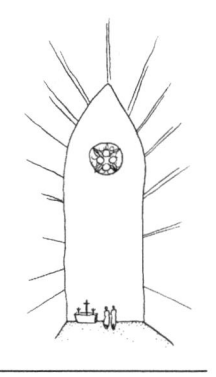

The qualities of space.

Pleasure. Spaces, forms, textures, colors, symbols, sounds, light quality, and odors all suited to the use, whatever it may be. Satisfaction of anticipations, requirements, or desires. Sequences developed and fulfilled. Unity with variety. Harmonious relationships. A resultant quality of beauty.

If we were to list the requisites of the ideal space for each of a series of varying uses, we might be amazed at the variety of suggested spatial characteristics and at the degree of precision with which the characteristics can be defined. A child's play lot, for example, would be designed as a Lilliputian wonderland of induced action, shrieks, and squeals. Intriguing forms, a rich variety of textures, and bright splashes of color would be right, for children have an acutely developed tactile sense and a love of shapes and primitive hues. Their play space might well be variformed with tunnels, obstacles, baffles, movable objects, and things to climb over, under, and through. It should be a place of strong contrasts; sun to shadow, smooth to rough, bright to dull, open to closed, and high to low. A well-designed play lot for a child gives full play to imagination. It is in itself a plaything conducive to excitement and rollicking delight.

A space for private outdoor dining would have an entirely different set of criteria. As a volume it should be simple in shape, intimate in size, and refined in texture and detail. It should be shaped to invite repose. It should create a serene and pleasant atmosphere conducive to conversation. For the point of highest interest, it might well focus on the surface of the table and the faces of the diners poised above it. It should be a casual space of studied subtleties. As can be imagined, if the child's play activities were to be transposed to a space such as has been described for dining, the child would soon become restive. If, on the other hand, the diners were moved to the space designed as a play lot, we could in time expect no less than nervous collapse or chronic indigestion.

Spatial Qualities

The essence of a volume is its quality of implied containment.

A confined space may be static, inducing repose. It may direct and concentrate interest and vision inward. The whole spatial shell may be made seemingly to contract and bear down, to engender a feeling of intensity or compression.

Alternatively, a space may open out. It may direct attention to its frame and beyond. It may fall away or seem to expand. It may seem to burst outward. It may impel outward motion to its perimeter and to more distant limits.

A space may be flowing and undulating, suggesting directional movement. A space may be developed to have its own sufficient, satisfying

Site Spaces

qualities. It may appear complete within itself—or incomplete, a setting for persons or objects.

A space may be in effect a vacuum.

A space may have expulsive pressure.

A space may dominate an object, imbuing the object with its particular spatial qualities. Or it may be dominated by the object, drawing from it something of its nature.

A space may have orientation inward, outward, upward, downward, radial, or tangential.

A space may be developed as an optimum setting for an object or environment for a given use.

A space may be designed to stimulate a prescribed emotional reaction or to produce a predetermined sequence of such responses.

Active public space.

Passive private space.

264 LANDSCAPE ARCHITECTURE

A space may relate to an object or another space and gain its very meaning from the relationship. It may relate to vista or view, the rising or setting sun, a sunlit slope, the starlit sky, or the welcome evening breeze.

A complex space assumes to a degree the qualities of its component volumes and should relate them into a unified entity.

Spaces may vary from the vast to the minute, from the light and ethereal to the heavy and ponderous, from the dynamic to the calm, from the crude to the refined, from the simple to the elaborate, and from the somber to the dazzling. In their size, shape, and character they may vary endlessly. Clearly, in designing a space for any given function, we would do well first to determine those qualities most desirable and then to do our best to provide them.

The Japanese, in their landscape design, have learned to develop spatial volumes of such intrinsic human scale and personalized character that the spaces can be satisfied only by the presence of the person or persons for whom they were conceived. The Abbot's Garden of Nikko, for instance, is complete only when the abbot and his followers are seated sedately on the low, broad terraces or are wandering comtemplatively among the gnarled pine trees or beside the quiet ponds. The imperial Shinjuku Gardens, once sublimely beautiful and faultlessly groomed, seemed somehow incomplete except in the emperor's presence. The contemporary American family home and garden as a well-designed unit to provide a balanced composition of interior and exterior spaces needs for its fulfillment the family members and friends for whom it was created.

Spatial Size

Planned spaces are usually considered only as they relate to humans. Paddocks, corrals, dog runs, canary cages, and elephant traps are exceptions, but even these are best conceived with more than fleeting attention to the habits, responses, and requirements of the proposed occupants. Take the elephant trap, for instance. Few architects approach their planning with a keener awareness of their client's traits than the native builder who directs the construction of the stout timber and rattan enclosure for the trapping and training of wild elephants. The canary cage, too, with its light enframement, seed cups, swinging perches, and cuttlebone, is a volume contrived with much thought for the well-being of the canary. In planning spaces for people, it seems plausible that their accommodation and happiness should be of as great a concern to the planner as those designed for the bird and the pachyderm.

It is well known that the size of an interior space in relation to people has a strong effect on their feelings and behavior. This fact may be illustrated graphically in the accompanying diagrams.

Squat.
Eat.
Yak.
Rock 'n' roll.
The yodeling three.
Growl at the price of fish.

Sit.
Dine.
Talk.
Fox-trot.
Light opera.
Compare car mileages.

Be seated.
Banquet.
Converse.
Waltz.
Symphony.
Discuss world trade relations.

Site Spaces **265**

Exterior spaces have similar psychological attributes. On an open plain, timid persons feel overwhelmed, lonesome, and unprotected; left to their own devices, they soon take off in the direction of shelter or kindred spirits. Yet, on this same plain, bolder persons feel challenged and impelled to action; with freedom and room for movement they are prone to dashing, leaping, yahooing. The level base plane not only accommodates but also induces mass action, as on the polo field, the football field, the soccer field, and the racetrack.

If, upon this unobstructed surface, we set an upright object, it becomes an element of high interest and a point of orientation for the visible field. We are drawn to it, cluster about it, and come to rest at its base. No small factor in this natural phenomenon is the human atavistic tendency to keep one's flanks protected. A vertical plane or wall gives this protection and suggests shelter.

Increased protection is afforded by two intersecting upright planes. They provide a corner into which our subject may back and from which he or she can survey the field for either attacker or quarry. Additional vertical planes define more corners and spaces that may be further controlled by the introduction of overhead planes. Such spaces derive their size and shape and degree of enclosure from the defining planes, acting together and counteracting.

A volume may be stimulating, or it may be relaxing. It may be immense, suggesting certain uses, or it may be confining, suggesting others. In any event, we are attracted to those spaces suited to our purpose, be it hiking, target shooting, eating grapes, or making love. We are repelled by, or at least have little interest in, those spaces that appear to be unsuited to the use we have in mind.

Whatever we perceive as "beauty" in nature is never, and in no way, an addition to what we perceive as "utility." All organic shape and detail depend clearly upon structure itself, and never can they be looked upon as decorative adjunct.

Richard J. Neutra

Spaces can be created by the aura of people or activities.

266 LANDSCAPE ARCHITECTURE

The man was perceived to be a fool who . . . seriously inclines to weigh the beautiful by any other standard but that of good. . . . The useful is the noble and the hurtful is the base.
Plato

I shall define beauty to be a harmony of all the parts, in whatsoever subject it appears, fitted together with such proportion and connection, that nothing could be added, diminished or altered, but for the worse.
Leon Battista Alberti

Blue and green are the colors of the heavens, the sea, the fruitful plain, the shadow of the Southern noon, the evening, the remote mountains. They are essentially atmospheric and not substantial colors. They are cold, they disembody, and they evoke impressions of expanse and distance and boundlessness. Blue . . . always stands in relation to the dark, the unillumined, the unactual. It does not press in on us, it pulls us out into the remote. An "enchanting nothingness" Goethe calls it in his Farbenlehre.

Blue and green are transcendent, spiritual, nonsensuous, colors . . . yellow and red, the classical colors, are the colors of the material, the near, the full-blooded. Red is the characteristic color of sexuality—hence it is the only color that works upon the beasts. It matches best the phallus symbol—and therefore the statue and the Doric column—but it is pure blue that etherealizes the Madonna's mantle. This relation of colors has established in every great school as a deepfelt necessity. Violet, a red succumbing to blue, is the color of women no longer fruitful and of priests living in celibacy.

Yellow and red are the popular colors, the colors of the crowd, of children, of women, and of savages. Among the Venetians and the Spaniards high personages affected a splendid black or blue, with an unconscious sense of the aloofness inherent in these colors. . . .
Oswald Spengler

Some spaces are person-dominated, controlled in size by such factors as the reach of one's arm or the turning radius of one's car. Other spaces dominate us. The visitor to the Grand Canyon is brought into relation to the dizzying heights and yawning depths in such a way as to thrill at their maximum impact. On the Blue Ridge Parkway in Virginia we are intentionally brought to the precipice edge. Again, on some narrow passageway one is thrust like an ant against the vast, empty dome of the sky. Mysterious Stonehenge in England, a great circle of space carved out of the moors with massive stone posts and lintels, is a dramatic reminder that even neolithic people knew the power of the space to inspire and humble humans. It would seem that they must have sensed that one's soul is stretched by the feeling of awe and one's heart revitalized by the experience of abject humility.

Between the micro- and macrospaces we may plan spaces of an infinite range in size. The volumetric dimensions should never be incidental.

Spatial Form

It has been said that, ideally, in design, form follows function. This statement is more profound than it seems. It is open to argument unless we assume that aesthetic and intellectual considerations are an inherent aspect of function. What all this means is that any object, space, or thing should be designed as the most effective mechanism for doing the job at hand; moreover, it should look it. If the designer can achieve an actual and apparent harmony of form, material, finish, and use, the object should not only work well but also be pleasant to see. Let us take a simple example. An ax handle has for its purpose the transmission of the full power of the wielder's stroke to the cutting edge of the blade. A superior handle, by long tradition, is made of selected straight-grained, seasoned ash with just the right degree of toughness and flexibility. It is shaped to the grip and butted to prevent slipping. From the grip it swells in a strong force-delivering, shatter-resistant curve of studied thickness and length. When the tapered helve is fitted and wedged at precisely the right angle to the head, the ax is in perfect balance, lies well in the hands, and is good to use. It is also good to look at. To the experienced user it is truly an object of beauty.

If shown a new ax with a handle made of plastic, the wooden ax–handle user would probably be incredulous; a shaft that had no grain and looked like glass surely couldn't be trusted. It would appear incongruous and ugly. If, however, one came to learn by experience that the new handle was in all ways superior, it would come in time to be admired, and no ax with a wooden handle could ever seem quite as admirable again.

A sloop is a vessel designed to utilize the driving force of the wind. In the superior sloop the hull is fastidiously shaped to cleave the waves, slide buoyantly through the water, and leave a smoothly swelling wake; the

Site Spaces 267

deep keel extends the conformation of the hull as a streamlined stabilizer; the spars are so fashioned as to carry the optimum areas of sail; the humming stays are of finest stainless-steel cable; the halyards, sheets, and sails are of nylon; the cleats are so formed as to fairly reach for the lines; tiller and rudder are precisely fitted and balanced to sweep and bear. Such a sloop, heeled and scudding, is a miracle of shapes, materials, and forces all working together in harmony. Here again, form is designed for function, and the form is a beautiful thing. As the poet Keats has aptly proposed, "Beauty is truth, truth beauty."

Spatial Color

In passing, it is of interest to note an early Chinese theory of volumetric color design. According to this theory, we have become so accustomed to the color arrangements of nature that we have an aversion to any violation of the accepted rule. It follows that in selecting colors for any space, interior or exterior, the base plane is treated in earthy colors—the hues and values of clays, loams, stones, gravels, sands, forest duff, and moss. The light blues and blue-greens of water, recalling its unstable surface, are rarely used on base planes or floors, and then only in those areas where walking is to be discouraged. The structural elements of wall and overhead, when they are visually apparent, are given the colors of the tree trunk and limb—blacks, browns, and deep grays. The receding wall surfaces adapt their hue from the recessive planes of the landscape—

Corridor spaces.

268 LANDSCAPE ARCHITECTURE

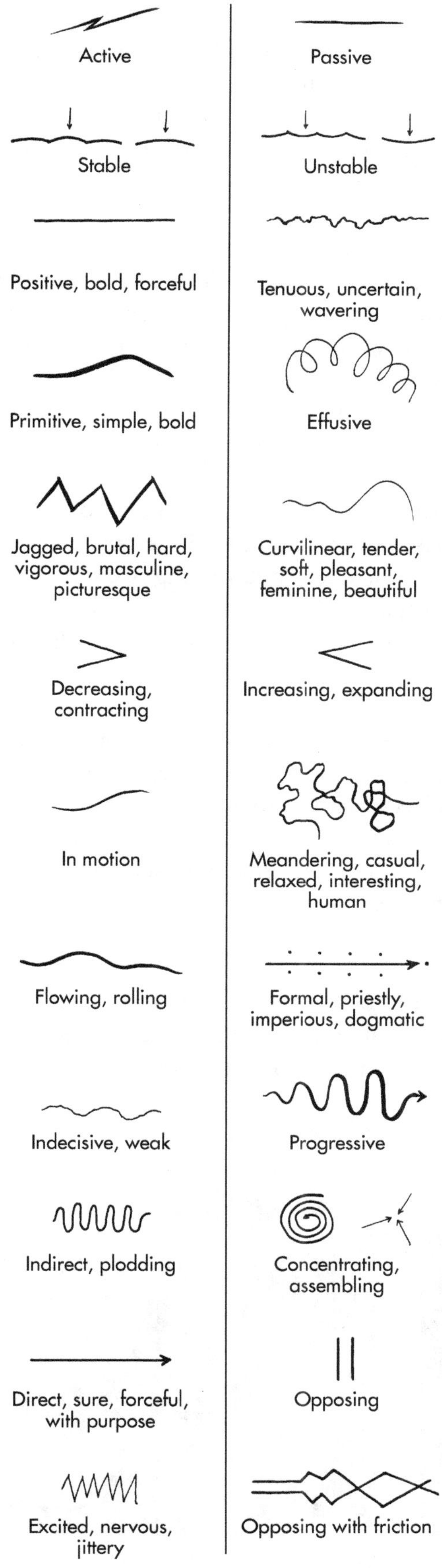

such as sunlit foliage, distant hills, or the sky as it nears the horizon. Ceiling colors recall the airiness of the sky and range from deep cerulean blue or aqueous greens to misty cloud whites or soft grays. Landscape architects found that this tested theory of nature adaptation applies as well to the use of materials, textures, and forms.

There are, of course, many other theories and systems of color application. One would keep the volumetric enclosure neutral, in shades of gray, white, or black, and let the objects or persons within the space thus glow with their own subtle or vivid colors. Another calls for infusing a space or coloring a form with those hues and values that, alone or in combination, produce a prescribed intellectual-emotional response. Given a basic color theme, this approach modulates harmonious overtones to soothe, contrasting ones to give interest and emphasis. Another system manipulates spaces and objects within those spaces by the studied application of recessive and dominant values and hues.

A familiar and sound practice of interior designers is to use a dominant graphic, weaving, or other object as the chromatic theme piece of a space and select all colors, vivid or pale, to recall and accentuate it.

Yet another would determine for any given area or structure one appropriate color which, running through the whole, could be used as a unifying trunk. All other colors would be, to this trunk, its branches, twigs, leaves, flowers, and fruit. Such a scheme can be likened to the overall coloration of the willow tree, the oak, or sassafras—or to the blending hues of the clouded mountainside or river valley. All features or scenes observed in nature have, without exception, their own harmonious system of coloration. In the creation of meaningful spaces, the knowledgeable handling of color is essential.

Abstract Spatial Expression

We have learned that just as abstract design characteristics may be suggested by a given landscape type, so may they be suggested by a proposed use as well. The spatial requirements of a cemetery, for instance, would hardly resemble those of an amusement park. We come to the amusement park for a laugh, for a shock, for a change, for relief and escape from ordered routine. We want to be fooled, and we delight in confusion and distorted, contorted, ridiculous shapes. We seek the spectacular, the spinning, tumbling, looping, erratic motion. We love the roller coaster's flash and roaring crescendo, the brassy clash of cymbals, the jarring sock-ring-a-ling-ting of the tambourines, the rap of the barker's hammer, and the raucous honky-tonk. We thrill to color as gaudy as greasepaint, as garish as scarlet and orange tinsel, as raffish as dyed feathers, gold sequins, and rainbow-hued glitter. We expect the scare, the boff, the flirt, the come-on, the tease, and the taunt. All is gay tumult; all is for the moment; all is happy illusion. We accept materials as cheap and as temporary as bunting and whitewashed two-by-fours. Everything is a surprising, attracting,

Abstract line expression.

diverting, winding, expanding, contracting, arresting, amusing, tumultuous carnival atmosphere. If we want a successful amusement park, this atmosphere is created. We must create it with all the planned whoop-de-doo and spatial zis-boom-bah that we can conjure into being. This is not only desirable; it is indispensable. Here, order and regimentation are wrong, and the stately avenue or the handsome mall would be in fatal error.

How different are the spatial requirements of a cemetery! Here we would expect the volumes to be serenely monumental, spacious, and beautiful. We would expect enveloping enclosure to provide protection and imply detached seclusion. The entrance gates, like the prelude to an anthem, would give theme to the spaces within, for these are the earthly gates to paradise. We enter here in our moments of most poignant sorrow, to bury the dead in solemn ceremony, as from time's beginning.

We come in grief, seeking that which will give solace and comfort. The spatial character might well suggest peaceful quietude in terms of subtle harmonies of form and texture. Troubled and questioning, we seek here reassurance and order. Order as a spatial quality is effected by evidence of logical progressions, visual balance, and a regular cadence of plan or sequential revelation.

Humbled and distraught by the presence of death, we would orient ourselves to some superior power. The presence of divine power may be suggested in plan form and by symbol. A sensitive variation of the classic axial treatment that so compellingly relates humans to the concept has no better application than here. There may also be breathtaking vistas and sweeping views, as long as vistas and views are in keeping with the sacred and the sublime.

At those thoughtfully selected plan areas where an inspirational quality is to be concentrated or brought to culmination we might use the verticals that effect an uplift of the spirit. A simple cross of white marble lifted

Arlington National Cemetery.

Vietnam Veterans Memorial.

270   LANDSCAPE ARCHITECTURE

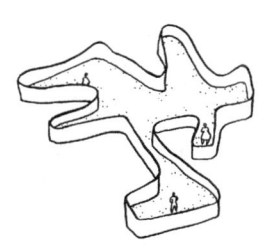

Complex for excitement, diversion, curiosity, surprise, induced movement.

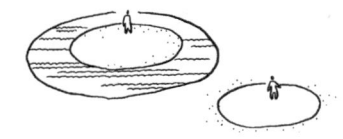

Enclosure may be effectively *implied* by strong demarcation of the base plane.

Simple enclosure for concentration on idea, form, and detail.

Confined for relaxation and induced repose.

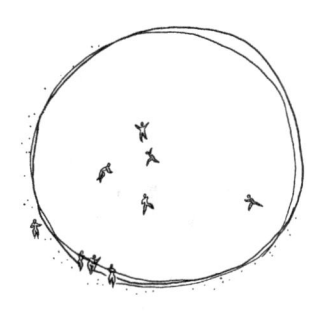

Open and free for induced action and exuberance.

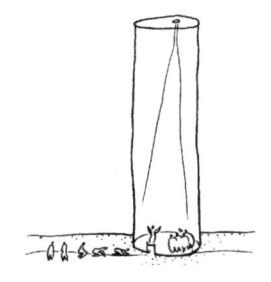

Volumes may be contrived to impart specific predetermined emotional and intellectual impacts.

Functions of vertical enclosure. Induced human responses vary with the type and degree of enclosure.

against the clouds may evoke in the viewer an emotional response of great satisfaction and spiritual meaning.

We seek here a fitting and final resting place for those whom we have loved. In design, this concept is translated into terms of the eternal and the ideal. The eternal may be suggested by the timeless features of the landscape—the moss, the fern, the lichened rock, the sun, the grove of gnarled and venerable oaks, the gently sloping summit of a hill. Materials such as marble, granite, and bronze will be selected to endure.

Idealism may be expressed through the creation of those spaces and those high art forms that will instill the conviction that here in this sacred place the living and the dead are truly in the presence of their God.

In like manner, any such functional places and spaces we may name—the shopping center, the summer camp, the amphitheater—will immediately bring to mind desirable spatial characteristics. These, it should be apparent, are fundamental to the design.

Elements of Containment

In a large measure, all spaces acquire their being and character from the elements that contain them. Because each element so used will imbue the space to some degree with its own qualities, it must be well related not only to all other such elements but also to the essential resultant character desired for the space.

Lines, forms, colors, textures, sounds, and odors all have certain predictable impacts on the human intellectual-emotional responses. If, for example, a certain form or color says or does things to the observer, this is reason enough to employ such a form or color in the shaping of those structures, objects, or spaces that are to convey this message. Surely, if the abstract expression of a given line violates the proposed expression of structure, object, or space, it should be used only with studied intent. Every line evident in the form or planes has its own connotation. This must be in keeping with the intended nature of the space.

Definition of Volumes

Asian cultures have long understood that to have significant spaces you must have definitive enclosure and that the size, shape, and character of the enclosure determine the quality of the space. Openness, void, and mere expanse are not enough; they may be only emptiness.

Outdoor volumes may be of infinite scope, limited only by the horizon, or they may be as finite as the space between two cedar fronds. In shaping outdoor volumes the designer is not as limited as in architectural or engineering construction by materials, forms, or sizes. One may employ not only the full range of fabricated materials but also all the materials of nature. A seaside volume may be formed naturally of shell-strewn beach, a wind-battered tangle of wild seagrape, rolling surf, and luminous sky. A sophisticated urban park space framed by apartment towers on the avenue may be further defined by a pavement of sawed slate in a pattern, clipped yew, tubbed oleanders, spun-brass fountain bowls, glazed tiles, and illuminated water.

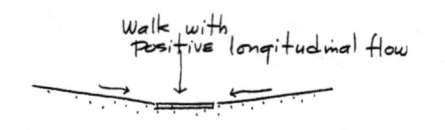

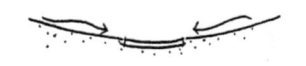

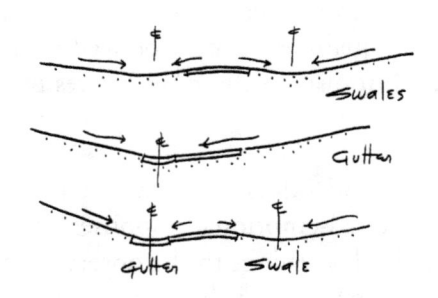

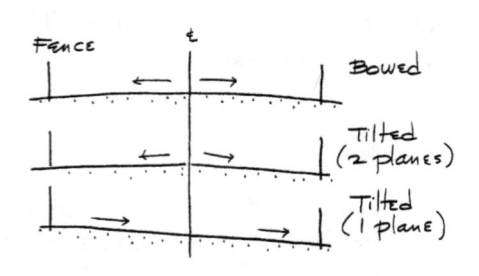

Exterior space may be as loosely defined as by sand, the open sky, and the foliage of quaking aspen. Or an outdoor space may be tightly controlled by terrazzo mosaic pavement, polished marble walls, carved mahogany panels, tinted glass, ceramic murals in rich patterns, and gaily colored canopies of fabric. All exterior volumes, controlled or free, are formed of three volumetric elements: the *base plane*, the *overhead plane*, and the *vertical space dividers*.

The Base Plane

The base plane is closely related to the arrangement of use areas, for it is on this volumetric floor that we are most concerned with use. What we see when we look at a project plan is what will be laid out on the base plane. It will establish not only the kinds of use but also the plan relationship of each use to all others.

The base plane surface is often the natural surface of the earth. With its topsoil strata, ranging from thin to deep, its soil moisture and fertility, and its cover of plants, this plane is veritably the base of all life. The wise planner will never disturb or modify the natural ground surface without reason. Any modifications made will be those that implement the proposed use while protecting the quality of the project site.

The general composition of the earth plane is mineral, ranging in hardness from granite, limestone, and shale to the clays, loam, and sand. The supporting strength and stability of the soil strata depend not only on the nature of each but also on its angle of inclination, the presence of water, and its relation to the other strata and the surface. Appearances are deceptive; deceptions are often disastrous. When the degree of support and stability are of consequence, the soil types and load-bearing capacities are to be determined by test pits or core borings.

Soils and the moisture and frost they retain are powerful eroders and corroders. From the structural point of view, extreme care must be taken in the selection of materials that are placed on or make contact with the earth. In considering outdoor spaces, we associate with the ground plane such natural construction materials as rock, gravel, and sand and such constructed materials as brick, concrete, asphalt, and ceramic tile. These seem compatible. Most other materials, including untreated wood or uncoated metals, are subject to rapid decay or rust.

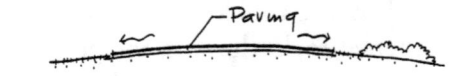

The base plane establishes the volumetric *area*.

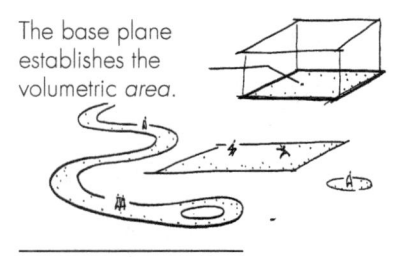

The size, shape, and texture of the base are designed to express the *use*.

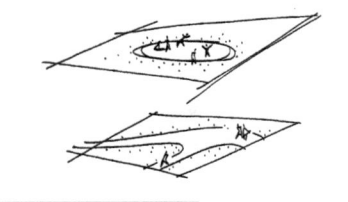

Within a given area surface materials, patterns, and colors define the appropriate use.

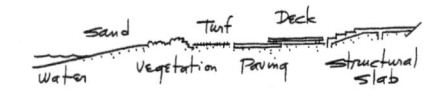

Base surfaces range from fluid to rigid.

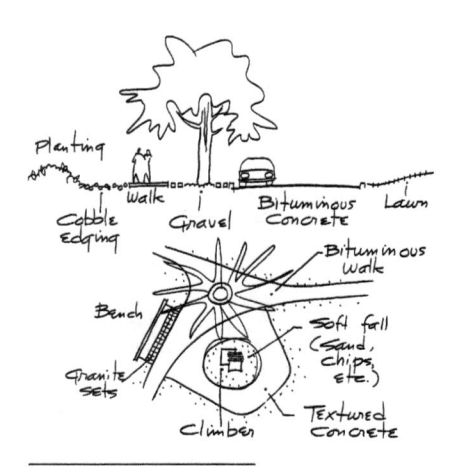

Uses suggested by differentiation of surface materials.

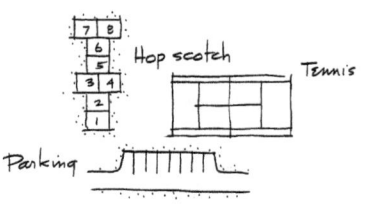

Uses defined by delineation.
THE BASE PLANE IS THE PLANE OF *USE*.

It is on the base plane that we establish our trafficways. They are best aligned in compliance with the earth's natural conformation. To violate the land is to incur expensive cuts and fills and require costly drainage structures. Moreover, on the disturbed surface areas a tight-knit cover must be reestablished for the sake of appearance and to preclude devastating erosion. The most stable and beautiful drives and highways of the world are those that follow the ridges and valley floors and rise or fall across the side slopes where the cross gradient is most suitable. Perhaps such drives are pleasant because they are basically lines of dynamic force flowing in harmony with the natural forms and forces of the earth. Our friend Plato, if we could question him on this point, would nod in sage agreement.

Every object existing on the base plane has plan significance. If the object is to be preserved, its relation to other elements of the plan must be thoughtfully considered. If the object is to be moved, the ease and means of moving warrant study. If the object is to be modified, the degree and type of modification must be analyzed.

The base plane, in a world governed by the law of gravity, gets the most use and wear. It requires the most care and maintenance. The planner must recognize, as does the caretaker, that all materials and textures applied to this plane should be selected with concern for their permanence and appearance during all phases of their projected use.

Site Spaces 273

Site activities are generally associated with level planes. Except when porous, these must be tilted or shaped to provide for surface drainage.

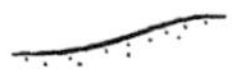

In site usage the warped plane most often connotes passive areas or buffer zones.

Ramps, perrons, or steps are used to provide transition from level to level.

Terraces are designed to fit level use areas to sloping ground and to separate site functions.

THE BASE PLANE MAY BE LEVEL, WARPED, RAMPED, STEPPED, OR TERRACED.

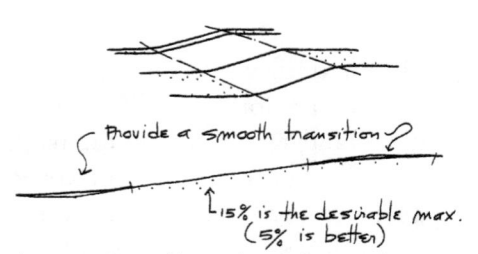

Provide a smooth transition

15% is the desirable max. (5% is better)

As a connector of base planes, the ramp has several advantages over steps. A ramp is:
- Easier to ascend/descend
- Less formidable for wheeled vehicles
- More of a unifier than divider
- More economical to construct

THE RAMP (An inclined path or plane)

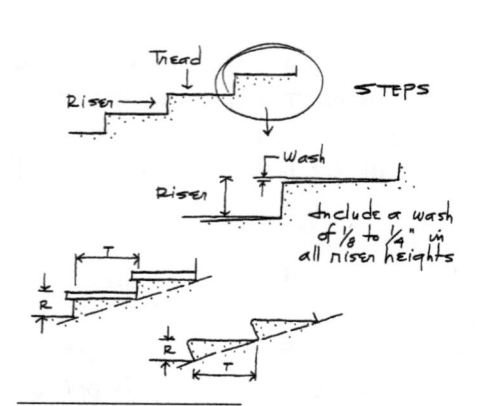

Tread
Riser
STEPS
Wash
Riser
Include a wash of ⅛ to ¼" in all riser heights

Tread-Riser Relationships

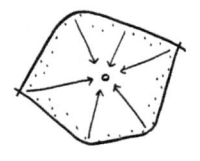

Where areas are drained to a central inlet, the fall is computed from the farthest points.

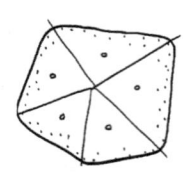

If smaller subarea drain inlets are used, consider the patterned placement of the inlets and construction joints.

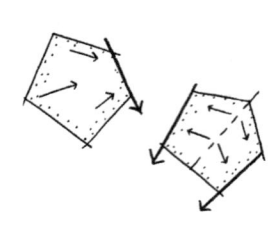

Paved surfaces may be warped or tilted to conduct runoff to a gutter or outfall at one or more sides.

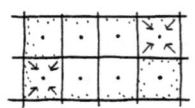

In modular areas a coffered grid can relate drainage and paving patterns.

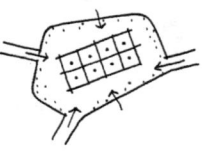

Geometric drainage grids can be incorporated in irregular paving shapes.

Base Plane Surface Drainage

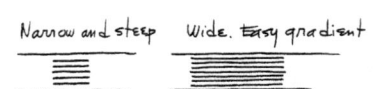

Narrow and steep   *Wide. Easy gradient*

Narrow steps increase the apparent height and separation of levels. Broad steps unite the planes visually.

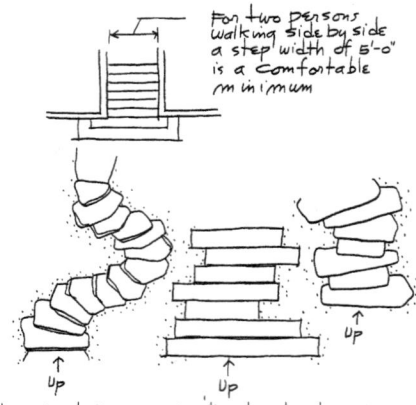

For two persons walking side by side a step width of 5'-0" is a comfortable minimum

Up   *Up*   *Up*

In natural sites or naturalized embankments, steps need not be of uniform size, shape, height, or depth.

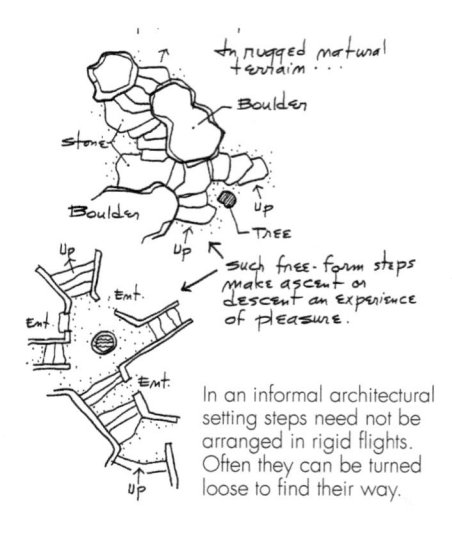

In rugged natural terrain
Boulder
Stone
Boulder
Tree
Up   *Up*
Ent.
Such free-form steps make ascent or descent an experience of pleasure.
Ent.
Up

In an informal architectural setting steps need not be arranged in rigid flights. Often they can be turned loose to find their way.

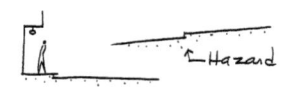

Hazard

Never use a single riser except at a building platform.

Ht 2'-10"
Height of HR = 2'-10" ±

In flights of six or more risers a handrail is recommended.

Stair Characteristics

274   LANDSCAPE ARCHITECTURE

The art of manipulating levels is a large part of the art of townscape.

Gordon Cullen

Sidewalks and pavings traversed each day can be transformed into a hard-surface mural or community quilt—a participatory and collective artifact engaging people in making their turf.

Karen Bergmann

The earth plane—level, warped, sloped, or terraced—is the base for all construction. This is the plane on which, in which, and around which all things are placed. On this plane are established the primary plan forms of the project. The treatment of the ground plane is important to the accomplishment of proper transitions. The shapes and patterns of the base, if well handled, may subtly or powerfully relate a structural element to the site and to all other components. Through the sensitive design treatment of the ground surface we may coordinate, accentuate, and integrate all elements placed thereon.

Various functions of the base plane.

The Overhead Plane

In the shaping of outdoor spaces we come to think of the overhead plane as being free, extending to the tree canopy or the sky. Seldom, if ever, have the most accomplished designers been able to devise anything as beautiful. Even the open sky, however, has its limitations. We sometimes require shelter; and further, we know that often our site spaces and volumes must have height control. To realize this we need only hold one hand palm upward and the other palm downward over it, and slowly bring the two together. We can at once, by this exercise, sense the spatial importance of the overhead plane. We will remember, as children, our pleasure in crawling under a porch floor or, as adults, sitting under a low

Overhead space definition. The form, height, pattern, density, solidity, translucence, reflectivity, sound absorbance, texture, color, symbolism, and degree of overhead enclosure all have a telling effect on the spatial quality.

Overhead canopy defines pedestrian space.

porch roof or an arbor. Even in a large open area, a suspended or supported overhead surface may provide this psychological, and perhaps physiological, function.

When open blue infinity is appropriate as a ceiling, we accept it and perhaps rack our powers of ingenuity to best feature the sky with its moving cloud forms and opalescent colors by day and its glorious show of constellations in the night. It has been said that if we were permitted to view the sky but one day and night of our life, we would count it our most memorable earthly experience.

When the sky is not suitable as a ceiling, we contrive overhead controls. The form, character, height, and extent of overhead enclosures will have a telling effect on the character of the volumes they help to define.

The new overhead plane may be as light as translucent fabric or foliage; it may be as solid as beams, plank, or reinforced concrete. It may be perforated, pierced, or louvered. If solid, it controls not only the sun and rain but also, by its degree of translucence or limit of overhang, the amount and quality of light. To appreciate the effect of light on a given

To grasp space, to know how to see it, is the key to the understanding of building.
Bruno Zevi

Every field of design today—architecture, industrial, graphic, landscape and urban—operates on the common basic premise of functionalism; i.e., that the ultimate form of the object designated must flow from an objective analysis of its function.
James Fitch

The sky often forms the overhead plane of exterior spaces.

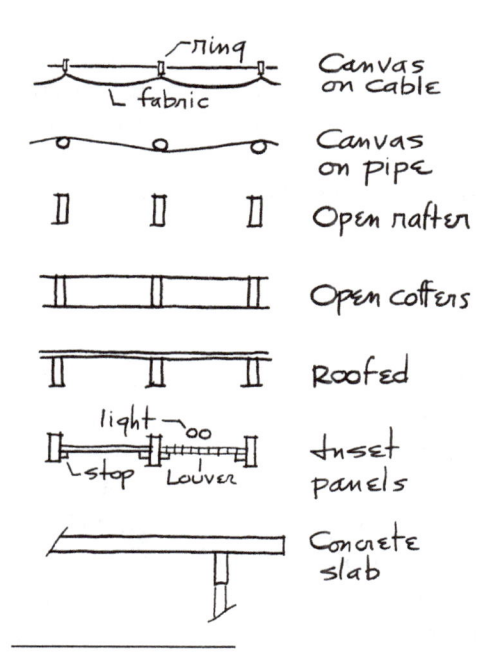

Overhead sunscreens.

space we need consider but a few of its unlimited qualities. In color, light may be pearly, milky, amber, cobalt, lemony, aqueous, inky, sulfurous, or silvery. In intensity, it may range from pale, soft, or limpid to brilliant, blazing, dazzling, or blinding. Light has motion—as in shooting, piercing, quivering, dancing, scintillating, creeping, flooding, or streaming light. It has distinctive character—as in dappled, splotched, or mottled light; subdued, harsh, or glaring light; searching, glinting, shadowy, gleaming, or glowing light. Light has mood—as in gloomy, haunting, or mysterious light; cozy, inviting, or exciting light; relaxing, refreshing, or cheering light. These are but a few of its qualities and effects that have design application.

The solid overhead plane may serve as a shield or modifier of natural light, or it may act as a source of direct or reflected illumination. If pierced or partially open, the overhead cover may not in itself be as important visually as are the shade and shadows it casts. We may consider such a plane as a disk or patterned screen held up between the sweeping orbit of the sun and the textured surfaces upon which its shadows fall and over which they move. Generally, the spatial ceiling is kept simple because it is to be sensed more often than seen.

The Verticals

The vertical elements are the space dividers, screens baffles, and backdrops. Of the three volumetric planes, the vertical is the most apparent and the easiest to control. It also has the most important function in the creation of outdoor spaces. The verticals contain and articulate the use areas and may tightly control and enclose them, as with masonry walls, or more loosely define them, as with vegetation.

Site Spaces **277**

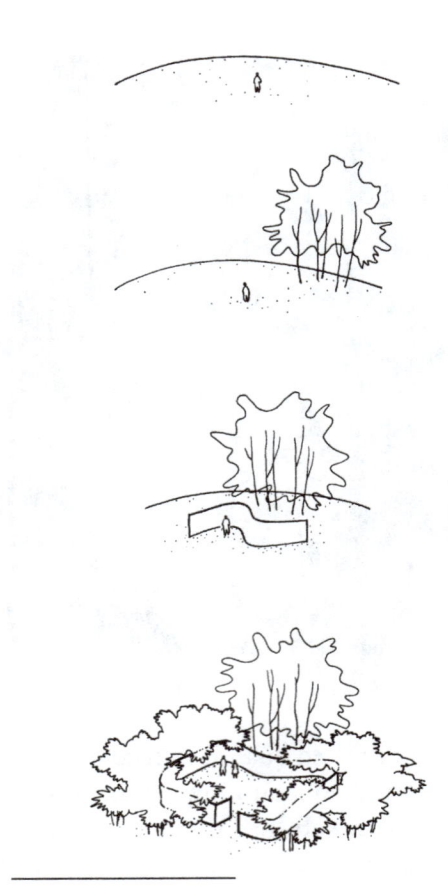

Site volumes: degrees of vertical enclosure.

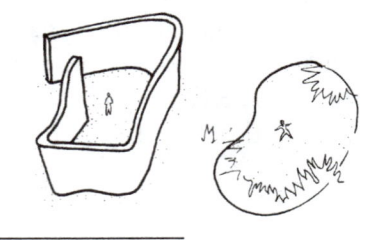

Enclosure may be light to solid.

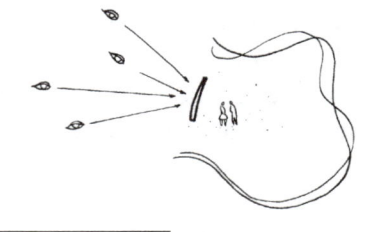

An arc of enframement may give adequate privacy.

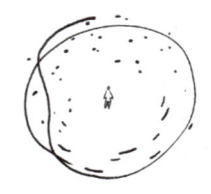

Enclosure by dispersed plan elements.

The vertical plane.

By plan manipulation, the vertical elements may extend and expand the use areas to apparent infinity, by screening out the near or obtrusive features of the landscape and by revealing such receding or expansive features as the distant view, the horizon, or the limitless spaciousness of the open sky.

Enclosure for Privacy

Neither enclosure nor openness is of value in itself. The degree and quality of enclosure has meaning only in relation to the function of a given space. Enclosure is desirable when privacy is desired. The orientals have a faculty for creating their own privacy by mentally blocking out those things they find to be distracting or disturbing. They seem able to bring into sensed focus a volume suited to their pleasure or their needs. This ability enables them to enjoy a degree of privacy even in a crowded marketplace. For occidentals this is more difficult, and such privacy as we may require must usually be sought out or achieved by design.

It has been said that, in our contemporary civilization, privacy is at once one of the most valuable and rarest of commodities. We may readily observe this lack of privacy by walking down almost any city street.

We are only now beginning to realize again the advantages of private living and working areas that are screened from the public view and focused upon the enclosed court or garden. In Egypt, Pompeii, Spain, Japan, and all mature cultures, such walled residences, palace courts, and temple grounds were, and still are, the most functional and pleasurable of all planned spaces.

Privacy has long been recognized as essential to the cultivation and appreciation of those things of highest human value. Enclosure for privacy need not be complete. It may be achieved by no more than a strategically placed screen or by the dispersed arrangement of standing elements.

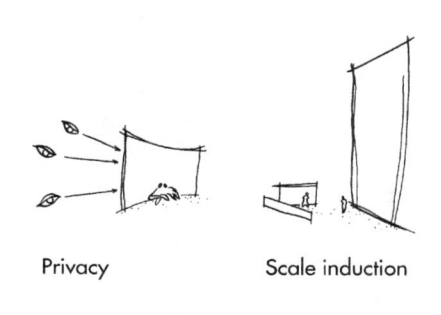

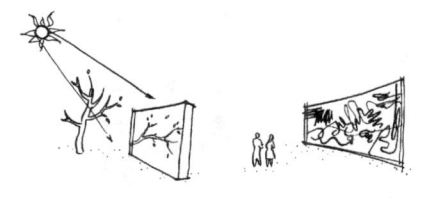

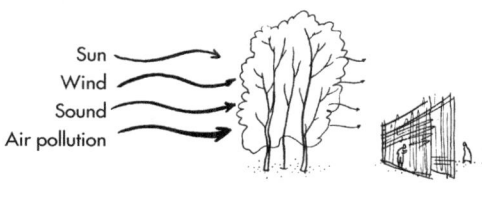

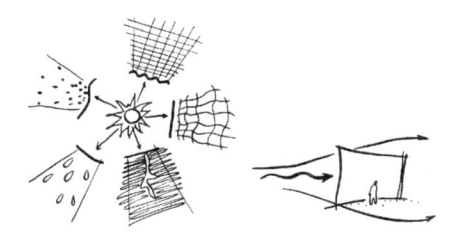

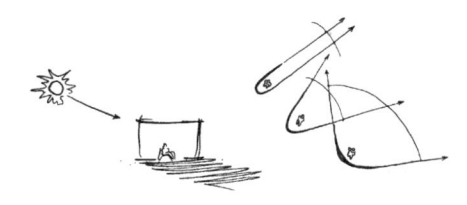

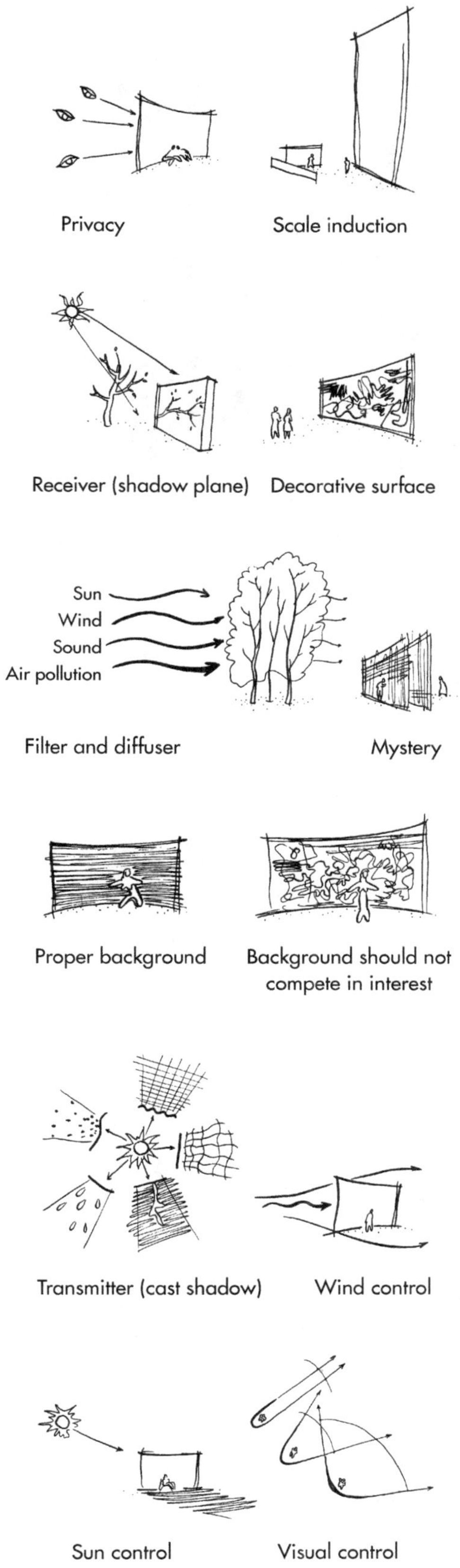

Qualities of Enclosure

Again, vertical enclosure may be as rugged as the rocky face of a cliff or a wall of piled-up fieldstone. It may be as sophisticated as a panel of etched glass—or light as a tracery of blossom or foliage. The range of form and materials is limitless. But whether the enclosure is massive or delicate, crude or refined, the essential business is to suit the enclosure to the use of the space or the use of the space to the predetermined enclosure.

Visual Control

All things seen from a space are a visual function of the space. Not only the extent and nature of the enclosure but also the nature of the revealment must be in keeping with the use. Anything that can be seen from a space is visually in the space and must be taken into account. Often, an object far removed may be introduced to the space by opening to, enframing, and focusing on the object. A far-off mountain peak or a nearby tree may thus be brought into a garden. The bustle and clamor of a sprawling city and its harbor may, for its interest and therapeutic value, be brought into the convalescent spaces of a military hospital grounds. A distant cathedral campanile may thus be transported to a churchyard, or a quiet pond to a garden terrace.

Enclosure is desirable for those spaces in which an internal object is to be featured. It is evident in such cases that distractions should be eliminated and interest concentrated on the object to be viewed. It would be difficult, for instance, in viewing a piece of sculpture to appreciate those subtle nuances of light and shade that reveal the modeling of a torso if the sculpture were to be seen against a line of flapping laundry or a stream of moving traffic. Even against a vista of regal magnificence, much of the loveliness of an individual rose, for instance, would be lost to the observer. The backdrop of anything to be observed in detail should rarely compete in interest.

Spatial enclosure, when doubling as a backdrop, should be devised to bring out the highest qualities of the object seen against it.

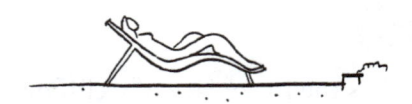

Edging

Stand

Seat

Safety barrier

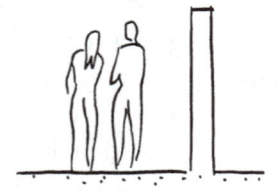

Enclosure for privacy (wall height determined by function)

Vertical definition.

The vertical plane provides space enclosure and visual control.

In general, it may be stated that when interest is to be directed to an object within a given area, the elements of containment must focus attention inward. When interest is to be directed outward to object or view, the enclosure is pierced or opened to accentuate and frame that which is to hold our attention.

Elements within a Space

Vertical planes provide not only containment, screen, and backdrop but often become the dominant spatial feature as well. Other vertical elements may include furniture set about on the base plane, a specimen magnolia of striking branching habits and flower, a cool jet of rising and falling water, or a children's slide or climbing structure of welded metal tubing. Such freestanding objects assume a sculptural quality. In scale and form they must satisfy the hollowness of the volume, enrich it, and pick up and accentuate its character. The shape and color of freestanding objects may counterplay with the shape and color of the space, may be visually apparent against the backdrop. If the object is to dominate, the backdrop plane is subdued to serve as a foil. If the spatial plane is to dominate, as in a mural or a building facade, the standing object is placed or designed to heighten the visual impact.

When an object is placed within a space, the object and enclosure may be perceived as an entity, but often more important is the expanding, contracting, evolving relationship of the spaces between the two. As an example, the roundness or squareness of an object may best be accentuated by placing it off center in a variformed volume to develop dynamic spatial relationships between it and the enclosing planes.

280 LANDSCAPE ARCHITECTURE

Post and rail

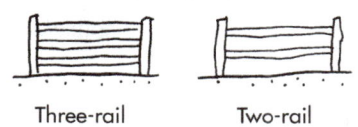

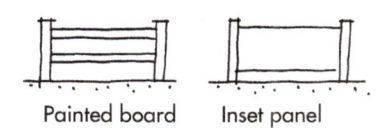

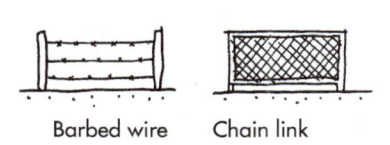

Three-rail   Two-rail

Painted board   Inset panel

Barbed wire   Chain link

Vertical boards

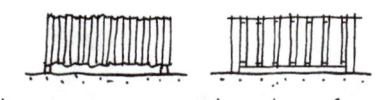

Chestnut, cypress, or cedar poles on frame

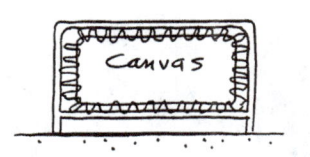

Pipe frame with canvas and grommets

Fences.

Concentration of interest

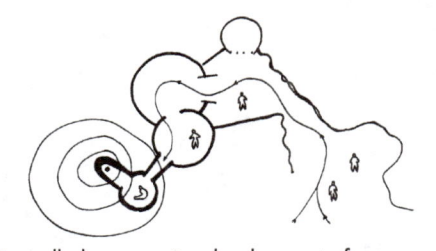

Controlled progressive development of a concept

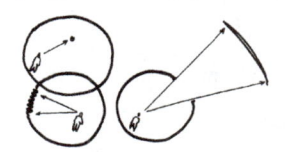

Visual control

Functions of enclosure.

An object that of itself has complex form or intricate lines is usually best displayed in a volume of simple shape so that the spatial relationships enhance the object rather than confuse or detract.

When several objects are placed in a volume, the interacting spaces between objects, as well as between objects and the enclosing planes, are of design importance.

Structures as Vertical Elements

Often, buildings are the dominant features within or surrounding a space. If within, they may be treated as sculptural elements to be experienced in the round. Within or without, the space is developed to focalize attention on the major facades or components and to impel movement toward the entrances.

The external spaces may be designed to serve as foreground or setting, as an anteroom, or as an external building compartment. The function of the building may even be concentrated in the exterior space and the building itself be incidental. Such structures may serve primarily as spatial enclosers, dividers, and backdrops.

Vertical objects within a space.

Public squares, courts, or plazas flanked by structures pose a complex problem in design, for they and the people who use them must all be in scale. Which has priority? St. Peter's clearly dominates its piazza and the assembled crowds. New York's Central Park rules as verdant queen over the edifices at her sides. The tiny town squares of Capri, Italy, and Taxco, Mexico, on the other hand, are in effect no more than charming stage sets for the lounging, dining, parading townsfolk and tourists who gather there from early sunup to the late, cool hours of the evening. People, spaces, or structures—which?

Site Spaces 281

There is no rule except that each, in turn and together, must be taken into full account and all relationships made pleasant through a sense of fitness.

The Vertical as a Point of Reference

In planning an area for any purpose, except when mystery, bewilderment, or confusion might be intended, it is well to set up enough visual "guide-ons" to give orientation to the users. Often such points of reference serve also to provide the theme for their related spaces. A revolving

While providing a theme for this public space, this water feature is a vertical reference.

Precise control of form, materials, light, acoustics, temperature.

Elimination of distractions.

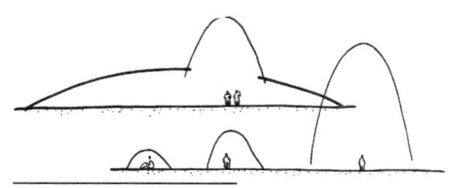

Emotional implications of varying spatial volumes.

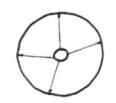

No spatial variety—static. 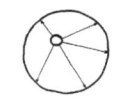 Variety—dynamic.

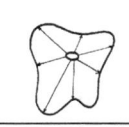

Increased spatial variety and interest. 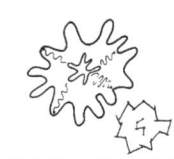   Form clarity lost by improper enframement.

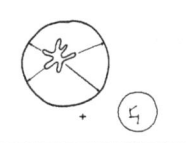

Complex form interest heightened by simple enframement. 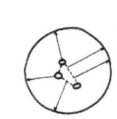   Several objects placed in a volume relate to the enclosure not only singly but also as a group.

ferris wheel, for example, draws one to, and becomes the symbol of, the amusement park. A venerable beech tree on a rise, the library campanile, or the ceremonial flagstaff of the parade ground may so "explain" and guide one through a campus, just as one is led around the golf course from green to numbered green.

In the treatment of sizable areas, we have discovered an intriguing planning phenomenon that has many useful applications. We have found that a freestanding vertical element or panel brought near a small use area within the larger space may have such a strong visual relationship to the user that it imparts its own scale. A great plaza, for example, may be overwhelming to a person who enters or wanders through. If, say, a small bench were to be placed within the space, the volume by contrast would seem even more overpowering. A person seated on the bench would sense only the relationship to the total plaza. If, however, near the bench, we were to place a honey locust tree, a stone fountain, or a decorative screen, our intimidated friend would first sense being seated under the tree, beside the fountain, or near the screen and only incidentally would sense the dimensions of the greater volume. One would relate oneself to the scale of the introduced objects.

Within a large space, many such human reference points may be placed, and, indeed, these must be furnished if pleasure is intended. (We recognize, of course, that historically the primary objective of many great public spaces has been to humble and sometimes even humiliate the crowds that mill about within them.) When awe, wonder, or humility is to be instilled by spatial impact, the human reference points are removed or distorted. When comfort and assurance are desirable, a human scale must be made evident. Generally, the steps, doorways, or windows of adjacent buildings suffice to establish a sense of scale; if not, such human reference points are to be otherwise provided.

The Vertical in Relation to Pix

In spatial design, the verticals generally have the greatest visual interest. Since, either moving about or seated within a volume, we are face-to-face with the verticals, we are usually more conscious of them than of either the base or the overhead plane. We may rightly assume, therefore, that such standing surfaces or objects present the most telling design possibilities. Features of greatest interest or refinement are normally placed or incorporated on the verticals and at eye height—*pix*. It would seem obvious that pix for a seated person is lower than pix for a person who is standing, but because this critical design factor is too often ignored, the point is emphasized. One of the most distressing of all visual experiences is to have a vertical plane terminate at or near eye level, particularly in the case of a fence, wall, or balcony rail. The top of such a vertical element seems to do violence to the eyes of those who pass or see it.

Site Spaces

Objects at pix (eye level) command attention.

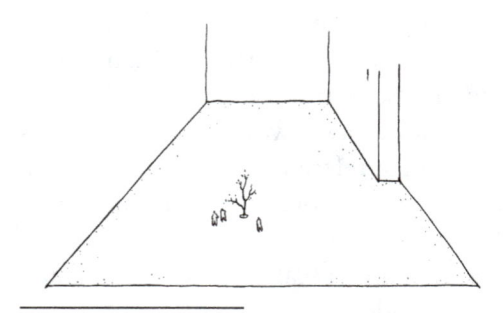

An object introduced within a large space may impart, within the area of its influence, its own lesser scale.

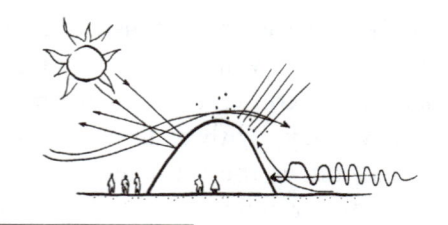

Privacy, shelter, protection.

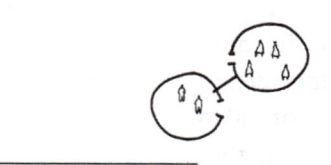

Classification of interest.

One of the most pleasant of visual treats, on the other hand, is to have the eye come comfortably to rest upon an object or plane so placed that it falls into pleasing perspective and focus. If, moreover, in the thing observed the viewer discovers subtle and fitting relationships to the space, the use, and the user, the pleasure is intensified. Such relationships may sometimes be accidental, but more often they must be consciously planned.

Verticals as Articulators

Verticals reinforce and explain the traffic and use patterns of the base plane. Just as the gate piers of a driveway say "Enter," the sweeping curbline says "Follow me," and the entrance platform says "Come to rest and alight here," so must the verticals of any space elucidate the plan. They must attract, deflect, direct, detain, receive, and accommodate the planned use as the area demands. The plan pattern of the base plane most often sets the theme of a space, and the verticals most often modulate this theme and produce those variations that develop the rich harmonies.

Verticals as Controlling Elements

The verticals, providing as they do the degree and kind of spatial enclosure, are important in the control of wind, breeze, sunlight, shadow, temperature, and sound. The wind may be diverted, checked, or blocked. Desirable breezes may be directed to play across moist cooling

284   LANDSCAPE ARCHITECTURE

Vertical articulation.

surfaces or used to give motion and sound by activating flags, foliage, mobiles, or those delightful oriental divertissements, wind-flutes or wind-bells. Sunlight may be intercepted, filtered, diffused, or admitted in its full glorious, healing, life-giving splendor.

Like the overhead, the verticals may serve an important function in casting shadows to wash across a paving, dapple a wall, dance, creep, flicker, tremble, stretch, blank out a space in dim coolness, or incise a bold architectural pattern onto a receiving plane.

Plant Materials

Much of the earth's land surface, as it were, is subdivided into variformed volumes by trees—freestanding, in rows, in clumps, or in masses. Often, proposed use areas may be sited to take advantage of spaces already tree-enframed. Again, partial tree or shrub enclosure may be supplemented by additional planting or by grading and construction. In such cases the native growth provides the ideal transition from development to the nat-

Vertical incises the ground plane.

ural scene and ensures landscape continuity. If we cannot use existing trees for full or partial volume control, in most localities we may draw upon an extensive palette of plant materials that range from the wildly free to the stiffly architectonic in their native or manicured forms.

Effective Enclosure

It must be remembered that the vertical space enframers are not usually seen alone from within the volume but in the round as well. They, together with the spaces they enclose, become in total a unified landscape element to be related to all other landscape features.

Vertical objects form spaces within spaces.

An Axiom

Lack of effective enclosure is the key to most unsatisfactory spaces or places. We cannot stress too strongly the need for the proper type and degree of vertical definition. All good site development is marked by the organization of vertical (and overhead) planes to provide both optimum enclosure and optimum revealment.

By such means, it can be seen, we must synthesize not only the microlandscape but the extensional landscape as well.

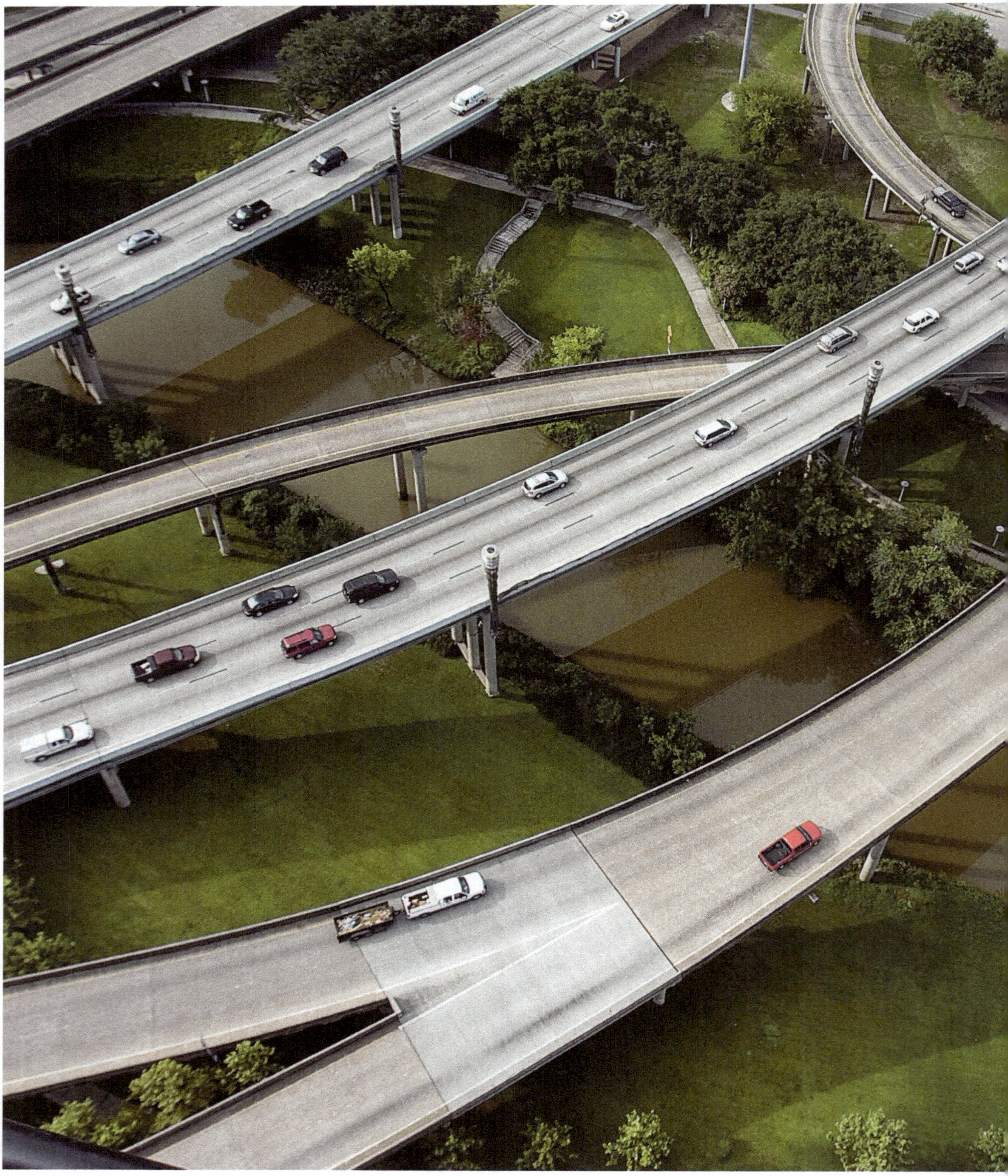

13 CIRCULATION

Bill Tatham, SWA Group

Most constructions have meaning only to humans, and only as we experience them. They are revealed by lines or patterns of circulation that lead us to, through, over, under, or around them, on foot or on horseback, by plane, train, automobile, or any other means of locomotion or conveyance. We thus realize that the circulation pattern is a major function of any planned development because it establishes the rate, sequence, and nature of its sensed realization or visual unfolding.

Every object as a perceptible entity exists in time as well as in space. This is to say that an object cannot be comprehended in its entirety at any one instant or from any one point of observation. It is perceived, rather, through a flow of impressions. When in motion, one sees a series of images blending into an expanding visual realization of an object, space, or scene. Perception is not a matter of sight alone. All the senses may be involved—sight, taste, smell, touch, and hearing. The rate, order, type, and degree of perception are a matter of design control. Much of this control is effected by planned patterns of circulation.

Motion

Experience is rarely static; almost always, motion is involved in the person or in the thing experienced. A structure is seldom seen from a fixed point of view or in direct elevation but usually by people on the move. Its three-dimensional form and modeling are therefore often as important as its facade. The plan pattern of a site is also usually realized from an infinite number of viewing points by people moving through it. The more fluid the circulation pattern, the more points of view and, therefore, the more interest and enjoyment in viewing.

Motion Impelled by Form and Concept

One afternoon, some time ago, the coauthor entered the National Gallery in Washington to join a group of sightseers who were starting out with a guide. The group stood in the great rotunda, at the base of the towering black marble columns that support the lofty dome. "Do you know," asked the guide, "what the architect of this great edifice has planned as an introduction? He has directed you here to give you the theme—the magnificence of all history—to make you feel ant-high and insignificant before all the greatness that lies behind and ahead. You are awed by new, strange shapes and sizes and the astonishing opulence. But the architect doesn't want to scare you away, as most of us are by strange and unfamiliar things. So, as we approach the Mercury Fountain at the rotunda's center, he wants to make us feel at ease. And how does he accomplish this? By the size of things, by scale.

"The figure of Mercury is less than life-size. The steps leading up to the fountain are broad and low rather than high and forbidding. The water play is subdued to a splash and burble rather than a rush. The architect gives us also a concept with which we are familiar, not a terrible war god but one of the more kindly gods, Mercury, who speeds and flashes about on winged feet. We, who know the legends, want to walk closer to this figure. Here in this lofty dome of light and space is held out to us that which makes us want to come near, makes us feel pleased and relaxed.

"And so the architect has piqued our curiosity, impressed us, and humbled us. He has pleased us. Now he wants to get us moving out into the exhibit rooms. How is this accomplished? You will notice that he starts a centrifugal movement with a dominant spiral theme. The lines of the figure of Mercury are spiral in diagram. The subject of the sculpture, appropriately, is 'flight.' Motion is further suggested by the movement of the water as it ripples toward the fountain brim. All lines move outward. Above us, even the carved eagles on the architrave seem ready to soar away. Even the coffers of the tremendous dome sweep in a great spiral pattern. By sound, motion, and induced ideas, by strong urging of architectural form and line, we are compelled to outward motion."

The Kinematics of Motion

Without reference to the cause of movement, it is interesting to dwell for a few moments on the various characteristics of pure motion. By design, the line or trajectory of induced movement may be meandering, discursive, circuitous, looping, zigzagging, ricocheting, ascending, descending, hyperbolic, or centripetal; it may be an arc or a direct straight shot. In

Motion implied by form.

290   LANDSCAPE ARCHITECTURE

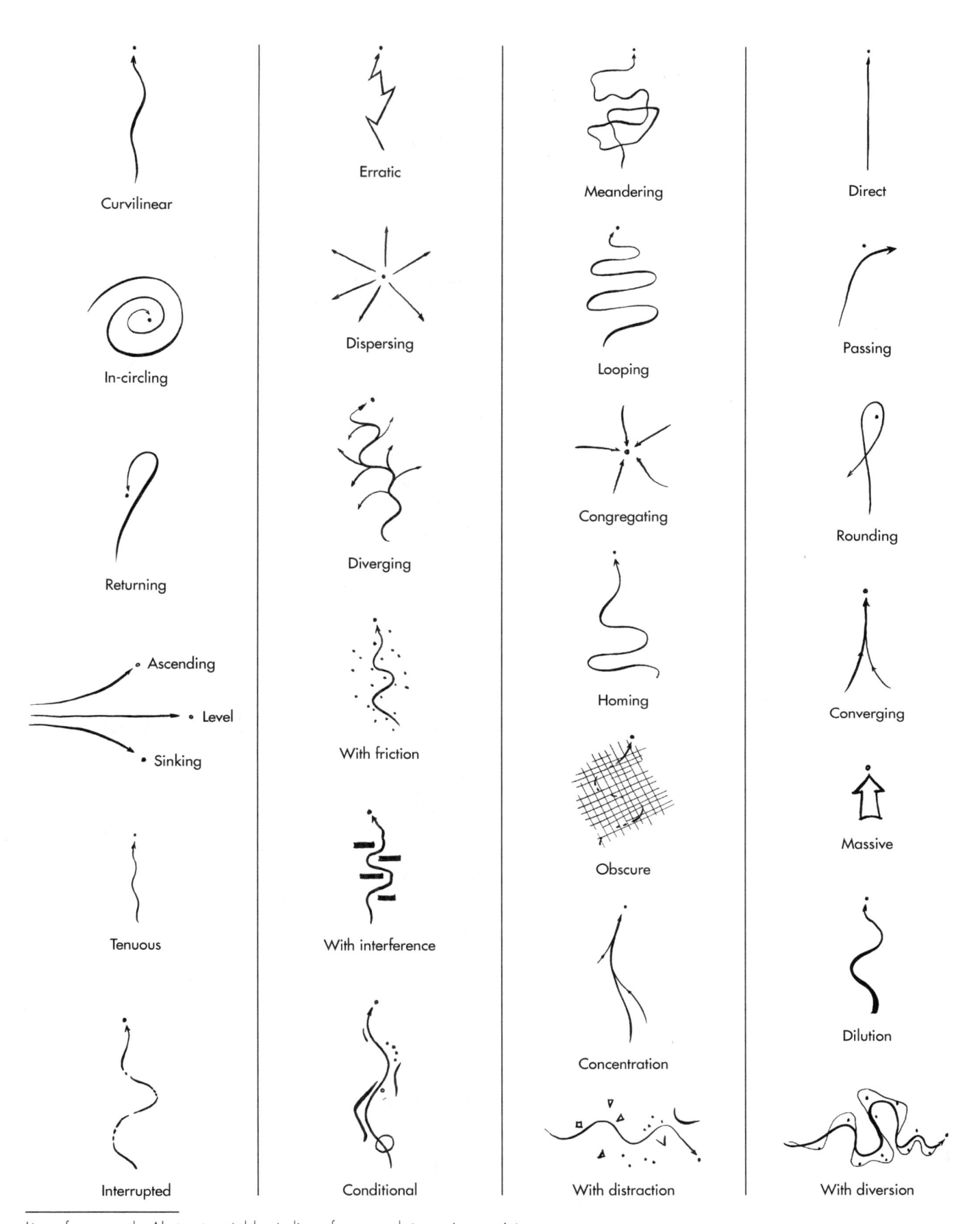

Curvilinear	Erratic	Meandering	Direct
In-circling	Dispersing	Looping	Passing
Returning	Diverging	Congregating	Rounding
Ascending / Level / Sinking	With friction	Homing	Converging
Tenuous	With interference	Obscure	Massive
Interrupted	Conditional	Concentration	Dilution
		With distraction	With diversion

Line of approach. Abstract variables in line of approach to a given point, area, or space.

Circulation 291

speed, the motion may range from the creeping-crawling to the whizzing-whistling. The nature of induced motion may be soothing, startling, shocking, baffling, confusing, exploratory, logical, sequential, progressive, hieratic, linear, wavelike, flowing, branching, diverging, converging, timorous, forceful, expanding, contracting, and so on, ad infinitum.

The alignment, speed, and nature of motion produce in a moving subject a fairly predictable emotional and intellectual response and must therefore be carefully considered. The abstract qualities of the path or line by which an object or space is approached must also be controlled with care. Motion that is induced must be accommodated and satisfactorily resolved. This fact is also obvious, but, like so many obvious things, it is too often overlooked in our planning.

Impelling Factors

The observant planner soon learns that one is impelled to motion horizontally, vertically, downward—when it gives ease and pleasure of motion and satisfaction in alignment. Our sense of sight, hearing, taste, touch, and smell are often compelling factors in the subconscious plotting of our courses and the determination of our actions. Physical comfort is a powerful factor, too.

We are attracted to:

That which is impressive

The unusual

The admirable

Pattern

That which is necessary

We tend to move:

In logical sequences of progression
In lines of least resistance
Along easiest grades
In lines suggested by directional forms, signs or symbols
Toward that which pleases
Toward things wanted
Toward things that have use
Toward change; from cold to warm, from sun to shade, from shade to sun
Toward that which has interest
Toward that which excites curiosity
Toward the beautiful, the picturesque
For the pleasurable sensation of motion
For the experience of space modulation
Toward exposure, if adventurous
Toward protection, if threatened

Toward points of entry
Toward the receptive
Toward points of highest contrast
Toward points of richest texture or color
To attain a goal
By pride of height attained, distance traveled, friction overcome
In haste, via the direct; with leisure; with leisure, via the indirect
In harmony with circulation patterns
In harmony with abstract design forms
Toward and through pleasant areas and spaces
Toward order, if tired of confusion
Toward confusion, if bored with order
Toward objects, areas, and spaces that suit our mood or needs

LANDSCAPE ARCHITECTURE

Repelling Factors

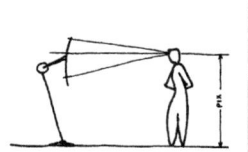

We are repelled by:

Obstacles	The obvious
Steep grades	The undesirable
The unpleasant	The uninspiring
The monotonous	The forbidding
The uninteresting	The demanding
The dull	Danger
The ugly	Friction
The unsuitable	

Motion Directors

We are directed or guided by:

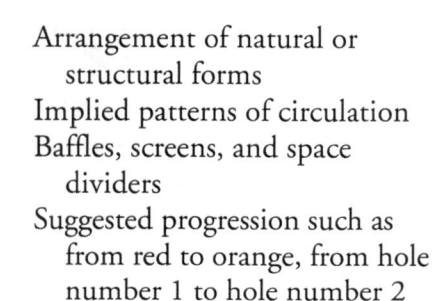

Arrangement of natural or structural forms	Signs
	Symbols
Implied patterns of circulation	Mechanical controls such as gates, curbs, and barriers
Baffles, screens, and space dividers	Dynamic plan lines
	Spatial shapes
Suggested progression such as from red to orange, from hole number 1 to hole number 2	

Repose Inducers

We are induced to repose by:

Conditions of comfort, enjoyment, or rest	Opportunity for concentration
	Restriction of movement
Opportunity for privacy	Inability to proceed
Opportunity for fuller appreciation of view, object, or detail	Imposed indecision
	Functions related to rest and repose
Pleasant arrangement of forms and space	Attainment of optimum position

Horizontal Motion

We are affected by horizontal motion in the following ways:

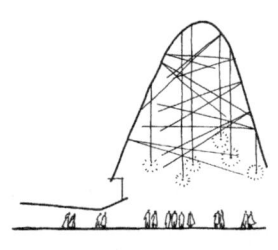

Movement is easier, freer and more efficient in horizontal planes.	Visual interest is in the vertical planes.
Movement is safer.	Most functions are better suited to horizontal surfaces.
Change of direction is easier.	Movement is easier to control.
Choice of direction is greater.	Vision of moving objects is easier to control.

Circulation 293

The weird 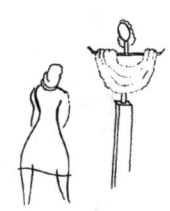 | *The elegant*

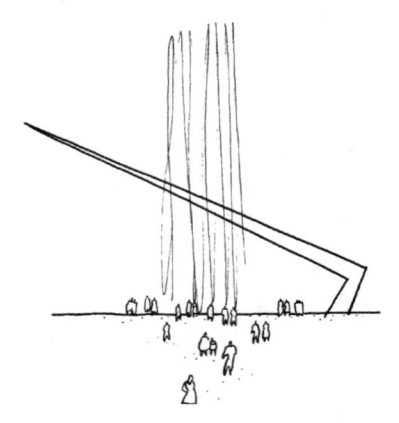

That which is bold

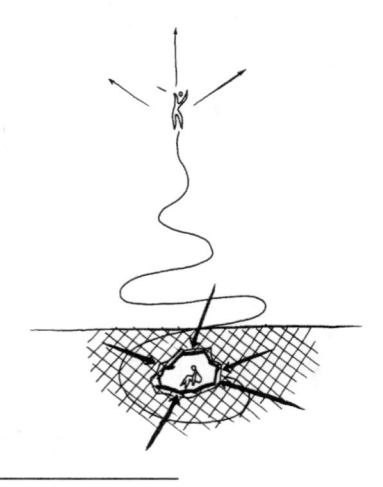

Height connotes attainment, inspiration, the sublime and release.
Depth connotes regression, concentration, confinement, shelter, the profane, and the weight of pressure.

Downward Motion or Decline

We are affected by downward motion in the following ways:

Effort is minimized, but elevation must be regained.

Safety depends on checks and on texture.

Downward motion gives a sense of refuge, hiding, digging in.

It gives a coasting, swooping sense of being in harmony with the forces of gravity.

Vision is oriented to the base plane.

Interest is increased in things of the earth—in plants, water, and minerals.

It offers relatively effortless movement, most welcome in the home stretch when energies flag.

It gives a sense of increased confinement, protection, and privacy.

It suggests the coalpit, the swamp, the fertile valley.

It embodies the rathskeller concept.

It embodies the bargain basement concept.

Downward movement and depth are accentuated by deep earth colors, solidity and simplicity of form, natural materials, and falling or quiet water.

Upward Motion, Rise, or Climb

We are affected by upward motion in the following ways:

Upward motion requires force of lift to overcome gravity.

It adds a new dimension to motion.

It is exhilarating.

It gives a sense of accomplishment, of conquest of gravity.

It gives a sense of going up in life.

It offers detachment from the things of the earth.

It embodies the concept of man or woman against the sky.

It epitomizes increased concern for safety and stability and for texture of the base plane to provide necessary traction and grip.

It imparts a moral implication of exaltation, of being close to God.

It gives a sense of being closer to the sun, of being rarefied.

It offers detachment from the crowd, supremacy, command.

It implies military advantage.

It means attainment of the pinnacle.

It offers expanding views and vistas.

It offers visual interest in the overhead plane, using sun and sky to full effect.

All the above are increased in proportion to the angle of inclination.

294   LANDSCAPE ARCHITECTURE

Induced Response

We respond by:

Relaxing in the familiar, becoming aroused or excited by the unfamiliar

Finding pleasure in unity, variety, and that which is fitting

Ossifying and decaying physically, mentally, and spiritually amid the rigid and fixed

Finding security in order

Finding amusement and divertissement in the strange, in the lively, and in change.

On the street, in crowded shopping districts, and perhaps even more particularly in exhibit areas, we are invited, cajoled, badgered, seduced, preached to, begged, teased, blasted at, or otherwise attracted by a constantly evolving, rolling barrage of visual persuaders. Sometimes falteringly, sometimes unerringly, we follow our eye-mind impellers toward that which is:

Meaningful	Dominant	Dramatic
Animated	Spectacular	Sample
Contrasting	Subtle	Clean
Unusual	Associative	Natural
Beautiful	Inspiring	Weird
Varied	Strange, amid the familiar	Plausible
Near pix, or eye level		Colorful
Decorative	New	Lively
Necessary	Pleasing in pattern	Pleasantly shocking
Desirable	Pleasing in form	Bright
Restful, when weary of tumult	Pleasing in scale	Familiar, amid much that is strange
	Safe	
Startling	Stable	In motion against a fixed background
Vigorous	Suitable	
Bold	Convenient	Charming
Interesting	On course	Subdued, when weary of the bright
Exciting	Educational	
Abstract	Curious	
Select	Exotic	Awesome
Successful	Extraordinary	Symbolic
Distinguished	Appropriate	Fresh
Sophisticated	Stimulating	Excellent
Comprehensible	Admirable	Useful
Superlative	True	Logical
Supreme	Diverting	Sequential
Impressive	Amusing	Progressive
Surprising	Suggesting	Human
Ingenious	Satisfying	Appealing

Circulation

Our senses of sight, hearing, taste, touch, and smell are often compelling factors in the subconscious plotting of our courses and the determination of our actions. Physical comfort is a powerful factor, too.

Distance as Friction

In moving about by any means, distance is considered an obstacle to be overcome, area that must be traversed, and space that must be bridged, with energy expended. When speed and economy are factors, it is incumbent upon the planner to select or devise a route that is as direct as practicable and that provides a minimum of deterrent to smooth and rapid travel.

Such a route would be of suitable grade and alignment. The speed and volume of traffic would be accommodated. Traffic of various types and velocities would be classified and separated. All obstacles would be removed. Grade crossings would be eliminated. Safety would be assured in all ways possible. All objects and elements along the route would facilitate and express a freedom of movement because such trafficways must not only be direct and free but must also suggest efficiency.

Positive Qualities of Distance

Distance is a function of area, and area is a function of space. Both area and space are usually at a premium. In our world of expanding population and increasing pressures, we often yearn for more room and seek to extend our constricting boundaries. When boundaries are fixed, as is usually the case, we attempt to expand them by some plan device. We increase perceived distances. This high art was long ago mastered by the planners of those cultures that lived in compression—on the fortified island or hilltop or within the city wall. It is an art that we, in the increased planning concentrations and population densities of the near future, must relearn and develop.

Space Modulation

It is an established planning fact that we seek in an area that quality of harmony, oneness, or unity that is the mark of any well-conceived work of science or art. We are attracted to such places and rebel at the intrusion of the incongruous element—for example, a claptrap hotdog stand in a beautiful natural gorge.

In addition, we seek a harmonious sequence of transition from one space to another. In going from club terrace to the swimming pool below, a detour through the parking lot would be disturbing. When driving the family from home to a picnic spot, we would avoid the business districts and prefer a parkway route, river road, or country lane, to sustain or heighten the anticipated mood and provide a pleasantly evolving transition.

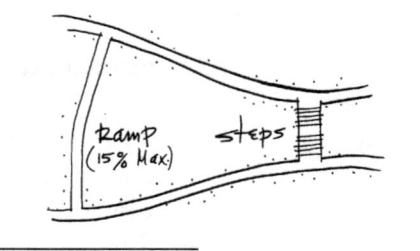

Often a ramp is planned as an alternative to nearby steps in order to accommodate the handicapped, wheeled vehicles, and equipment.

People in motion take pleasure in the sensation of change—change of texture, light quality, temperature, scent, visual patterns, expanding or contracting vistas, and the fluid visual impressions of objects, spaces, and views.

We take pleasure in an area arranged in shape, line, color, and texture to accommodate and express the use for which it was intended. We have learned also that our pleasure is increased when the area is further developed into a volume or series of volumes that, by degree and type of enclosure, further articulate the planned use. We enjoy moving to and through a space and around or past an object. We also enjoy moving from one space to another, the experience of sequential space-to-space transition.

Sometimes the transition is subtle. One may be led through a sequence of varying spaces that provide a complete change in use and mood in such a way that the transition is almost imperceptible. Sometimes the transition is powerful. One may, by planned intent, be so compressed into a low, tight, dark space that release into a lofty, dazzling, free space is startling and dramatic. In any event, the skilled planner, by spatial manipulation, can play upon human emotions, reflexes, and responses as surely as does the skilled musician with the harp or flute or drum.

In one of the Summer Palace groups near the Jade Fountain to the west of Beijing, there once existed a walled enclosure known as the Court of the Concubine. Here, many years ago, lived the favorite concubine of

Spaces of passage.

Circulation

one of the imperial princes. At one end of the courtyard stood her handsome residence of lacquered wood, tile, soft mats, and woven screens, and at the other end a light, airy pavilion, where she and her maids whiled away the summer afternoons. By legend, she had been brought from the open plains of Szechuan (Sichuan) Province, and she longed for its lakes, woods, meadows, and far mountains and for the wide spaces and the freedoms she had known there. And here, in the Summer Palace, this confining courtyard had now become her world.

The prince and his planners, wishing to please her, set out to create, within the limits of this space, an expansive paradise of freedom and delight. From her residence, to give the illusion of distance, the walls of the courtyard were stepped both inward and down to increase the apparent distance to the facing pavilion. Furthermore, to reduce the effect of rigid enclosure, the far plantings extended on either side of, and beyond, the lines of the converging walls. Even the size of the paving slabs was reduced from near to far. Moving outward, all textures changed imperceptibly from the rough to the refined, and colors varied from the warm scarlets, reds, oranges, and yellows to the soft, cool, muted greens and lavenders and evanescent grays. Trees and plants in the foreground were bold in outline and foliage; those near the fragile pavilion were dwarfed and delicate. Water in the near fountain gurgled and splashed, while in the far ponds it lay mirrorlike and still. By such manipulations of perspective alone, the views from the concubine's quarters were made to seem expansive and the pavilion remote.

As the mistress left the terrace of her residence to move out in the courtyard, she passed through a pungently aromatic clump of twisted junipers to come upon a curiously contorted "mountain stone" that rose serenely from a bed of moss. On the stone wall behind it was incised a pattern of stylized cloud forms with the poetic inscription "Above the plains of Szechuan the clouds rest lightly on the lofty mountain peaks." Here, 10 steps from her terrace yet hidden from view, she could be, in her thoughts, again among her mountains.

Just beyond, and angling temptingly out of sight, was a wall of emerald tile with an embossed tile dragon that seemed to writhe in splendid fury toward an open gateway. Inside the gate was a low stone bin spilling over with blooming peonies that laced the sunlit space with their pastel colors and delicious spicy fragrance. The sound of trickling water was meant to lead her eye to a cool and shadowy recess where a teakwood bench was placed near the light spray of a waterfall. From overhead, the branches of weeping willow cascaded down until the tips dipped into the water, where gold and silver fantails drifted languidly among the floating willow leaves. A meandering line of stepping-stones led across the pond to disappear into the tracery of a bamboo grove where swaying finches trilled and filled the light air with soft and tremulous melody. The thin pathway led out beyond to a ferny opening beside the farthermost lobe of the pool, which here lay deep and silent. At its edge, a carved soapstone table and cushioned seats were arranged in the shade of a feathery smoke pine near the steps of the pavilion.

From the raised pavilion platform, looking back, a surprising new vista met the eye. For, by forced perspective, the residence seemed startlingly near. The path that led from it was ingeniously concealed, and another route of return invited one to new garden features and spaces.

This masterful courtyard was designed as an evolving complex of spaces, each complete in itself. And each transition, space to space and element to element, was contrived, with a deft assurance born of long centuries of practice, as a harmonious progression.

Space modulation! We in America have yet to learn the meaning of the words. But we will learn it in the crowded years ahead, for indeed we must; and we will develop it, without a doubt, to new heights of artistry.

Conditioned Perception

Experience has taught us that what a thing is, is often of less importance than how we relate to it. The tree unseen or unremembered for us does not exist. The tree on the distant hilltop may be for the moment only an object that marks our path. As we approach, we see it to be a pear tree with many pleasant connotations. Coming close, we may be tempted to pick its fruit. Or perhaps in the noontime heat of an August day we may welcome the chance to lie in its shade, hang a child's swing from one of the lower branches, or spread a picnic at its base. In every case the tree is the same, but our impression of it changes with our sensed relationship. This being so, it would seem that should we place a tree or any other object in a space, we must consider not only the relationship of the object to the space but also the relationship of the object to all who will use the space. We must program the user's perception of the object by a sequence of planned relationships that will reveal its most appealing qualities.

Our impressions of an object or a space are conditioned by those we have already experienced or those anticipated. A bright, sunlit court is the more pleasant because we have just left the leafy coolness of an arbor. The splash and spray of a fountain are the more appreciated when we have approached it by way of the hot, dry sunbaked court. The birch clumps have more meaning when we sense that the river lies just ahead. The wide, free space is wider and freer to us when we realize that behind or beyond it we have known or will know the compression of confined spaces.

We plan, then, not a single experience alone but rather a series of conditioned experiences that will heighten the interacting pleasurable impact of each. The Chinese epicure would understand this procedure, for to him or her the well-conceived banquet is a balanced succession of sensory delights. The thin, bland shark-fin soup, the brittle wafer of salt seaweed, the glutinous pungency of jellied egg, mealy water chestnuts with almond bits, the sweet astringent bite of crab-apple preserves, light, fluffy fried rice, steaming sweet-sour fish in persimmon sauce, bitter tea, crisp vegetables braised in light peanut oil, tender chewy bits of mushroom and meat, soft noodles in broth with pigeon eggs, the rich custard of ripe durian, mouth-cleansing tea, the cool acidulous mango and more tea, and finally the lightest and driest of wines. Each such meal is designed as an artistically balanced sequence of gustatory, tactile, visual, and intellectual experiences. Should we be satisfied with less artistry in planning the places and spaces of our living environment?

Experience, we may see, is compounded of that which we have perceived, that which we are perceiving, and that which we expect to perceive. As we move through a space or a complex of spaces, we subconsciously remember that which we have passed or sensed. We thus orient backward in time and space, as well as forward, and find that each orientation gives meaning to the other and to all.

Sequence

Sequence, in terms of planning, may be defined as a succession of perceptions having continuity. Sequences have no meaning except as we experience them. Conversely, all experience is sequential.

In nature, sequences are casual and free. Sometimes, but not always, they are progressive. Such a progression may be one of ascent, as in the expe-

The Franklin Delano Roosevelt Memorial is a sequence of outdoor spaces interpreting the four terms of his presidency.

300 LANDSCAPE ARCHITECTURE

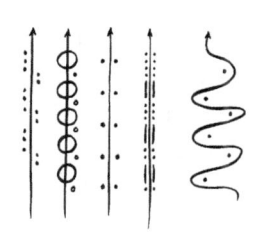

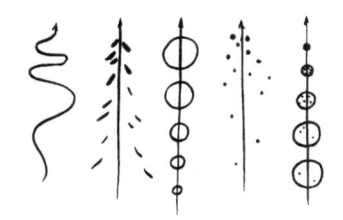

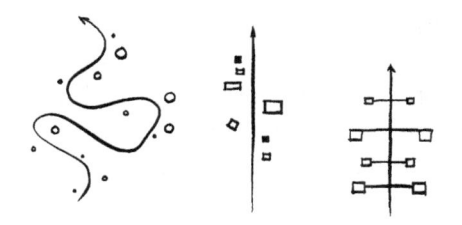

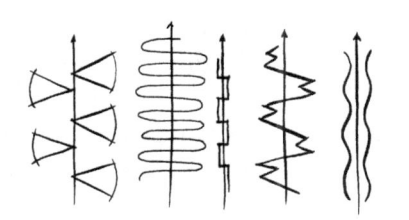

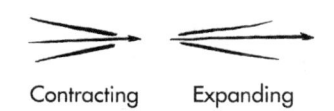

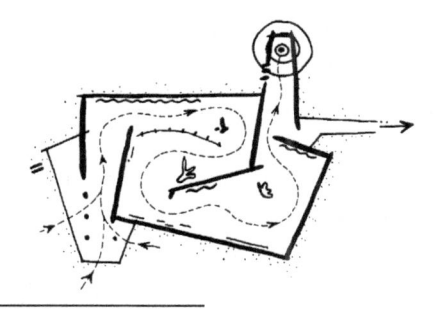

rience of climbing from lowland to mountain peak; one of direction, as westward from the central plains across the desert, over the mountains, through the valleys, and to the ocean; one moving inward, from the sunlit edges of a forest to its deep, shadowy interior; or a progression of enclosure, complexity, intensity, convenience, or comprehension.

Sometimes the sequences of nature are revealed with no more order than in the haphazard impressions of an adult or a child wandering lackadaisically through the landscape, along a lonely stretch of seashore, or among the shallow pools of a tidal flat.

The planned sequence may be casual or disciplined. It may be rambling and intentionally devil-may-care, or it may, to achieve a purpose, be contrived with a high degree of order. The planned sequence is an extremely effective design device. It may induce motion, give direction, create cadence, instill a mood, or reveal or explain an object or a series of objects in space.

A planned sequence is a conscious organization of elements in space. It has a beginning and an end that is usually, but not always, the climax. Indeed, there may be several or many subclimaxes, each of which must satisfy its supporting sequence. Through its suggestion of motion and momentum, one feels compelled to move from the start of a sequence to its completion. Once initiated, sequence and induced movement are to be brought to a logical, or at least a satisfying, conclusion.

It can be seen that all planned spaces are experienced by a progressive order of perceptions or events. It can also be appreciated that such sequences are subject to design control. A well-conceived plan determines not only the nature of climaxes but also their timing, their intensity, and the transitions by which they are evolved.

A sequence may be simple, compound, or complicated. It may be sustained, interrupted, varied, or modulated. It may be focalizing or diversifying, minute or extensive; and it may be subtle or powerful.

A sequence in its abstract beat or meter may, like the varied rhythms of a jungle drum, instill a feeling of excitement, warning, fear, frenzy, mystery, wonder, awe, pleasure, happiness, exultation, power, anger, belligerence, challenge, temptation, regret, sadness, uncontrollable grief, or comfort.

Woe be to the designer who, by plan sequence, induces in the observer a mood or expectation not in keeping with the functions of the plan. In contrast, how superbly effective is that sequential order of spaces and form that develops and accentuates an induced response in consonance with the preconceived experience.

If a sequence is marked with a rhythmic recurrence of one or more spatial qualities—size, shape, color, lighting, or texture—a cadence soon

Circulation 301

becomes evident. Depending upon its nature, intensity, and rate of incidence, such a cadence has a slight to very considerable emotional impact upon the moving observer. Sometimes the effect is desirable, sometimes disastrous. Suffice it to note that, in the planning of any spaces through which people are to move on foot or by vehicle, an understanding of both spatial modulation and space cadence is essential.

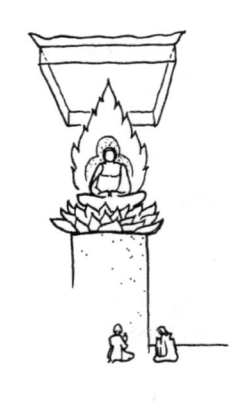

The Ordered Approach

When in motion, we are acted upon by the physical environment through which we pass. It would seem, therefore, that when moving toward a goal we could be prepared, by design, for that goal, or when moving toward an anticipated experience, we could be prepared for that experience. This is, in fact, the case.

As an example of the reverse effect, let us consider the members of a family on their way to a city church that fronts upon a busy commercial highway. As they drive along, they feel hurried and then perhaps a little alarmed when they must swing sharply out of the rushing traffic into the tight entrance of the church drive. It is narrow and jammed with idling cars that are waiting to discharge passengers. After a lurching and nervous advance, the driver finally stops to let his wife and children out near the entrance door, only to find soon after that the church parking lot is filled. Frantically, he crosses the highway to park in the lot of a nearby supermarket, then jogs back up the hill to the church, where he squeezes into the pew beside his family just as the service begins. He and his wife and children are ruffled and tense, and the service is over before they regain their composure. Obviously, for these people and for great multitudes like them, a presumably pleasant experience of going to church has never been properly planned.

In the same community, let us say, another church has been sited to front on a quiet residential parkway. On Sunday mornings, as the families make their way to church by car or along the pleasant approach walks, the church is seen set back, framed by trees, and serenely inviting. Driveways, entrance loop, and the parking areas are easily reached and adequate. Connecting walks lead to a wide and spacious court, from which the entrance doors open. Here, pausing before entry, one is prepared by form, by symbol, by the very quality of the space, for the services inside. Here, after the service, families and friends can meet and visit in appropriate surroundings. The approaching, attending, and leaving of this church are all planned as conducive, meaningful aspects of worship.

In Asian cultures, such approaches are designed with admirable sensitivity. As one moves, for example, down the roadway toward the entrance gate of temple grounds, the very street assumes an air of reverent dignity. By tradition, walls and gates close out the temporal world and enclose a garden space of tranquil peace, a symbolic paradise. From far down the road to

Progressive sequential realization of a concept or conditioned attainment of a goal.

the innermost altar, the approach is designed as a superbly modulated transition, from the crude to the refined, from the crass to the rich, from the distracting to the introspective, from the temporal to the sublime.

By similar means, we may be conditioned for any planned human experience. And, by all odds, we should be.

Pedestrian Movement

The characteristics of pedestrian traffic can best be understood by comparing them with those of a stream or river. Foot traffic, like flowing water, follows a course of least resistance. It tends toward the shortest distance, point to point. It has a pressure of momentum. It has force. It erodes. Swift movement requires a straight, smooth channel with increased width at the curves. If not provided, such a channel will be forced. Just as in the swift river jutting points are worn away, rock ledges are undercut, and the oxbow is "strung," so does the force of pedestrian traffic grind away at impinging or constricting forms or leap the channel to shape a new and freer course.

Just as a canal establishes the route, rate, and maximum volume of its boating traffic, so constructed walks can fix the path and control the movement of pedestrians. Again, as with the meandering stream on a level plain, the course of such traffic may be governed by unpredictable variables. Sometimes, in campus planning particularly, where lines of pedestrian force are so difficult to predetermine, only the major walks are constructed with the buildings, and the crosswalks or meandering pathways are laid down later along those unconscious and natural lines of movement worn thin in the campus turf.

Pedestrians move in sequence through zoological display.
Adam Jones, Jones & Jones Architects and Landscape Architects, Ltd.

An obstacle in a traffic stream, as in a stream of water, produces turbulence. Turbulence is friction. Where directional traffic or rapid flow is desirable, islands in the path or walkway are best streamlined or shaped to divert and direct flowing traffic.

Intersections are points of maximum turbulence. In pedestrian trafficway planning, such turbulence is often a positive quality, as in those

Circulation 303

The planner of an exhibition attempts to foresee people's behavior and predict where they will hurry, stop, look, or drift on. His aim is to control the flow and arrest it where he wants; but controlling the flow does not mean that people are to be moved along predestinate grooves like trams or shuffled around hurdles like sheep. Ideally the planner is aiming to direct people's movement in such a way that they see what there is to see with ease and in their own time. He must also ensure that the public does not get lost, tired, or bored with the whole affair.
James Gardner and Caroline Heller

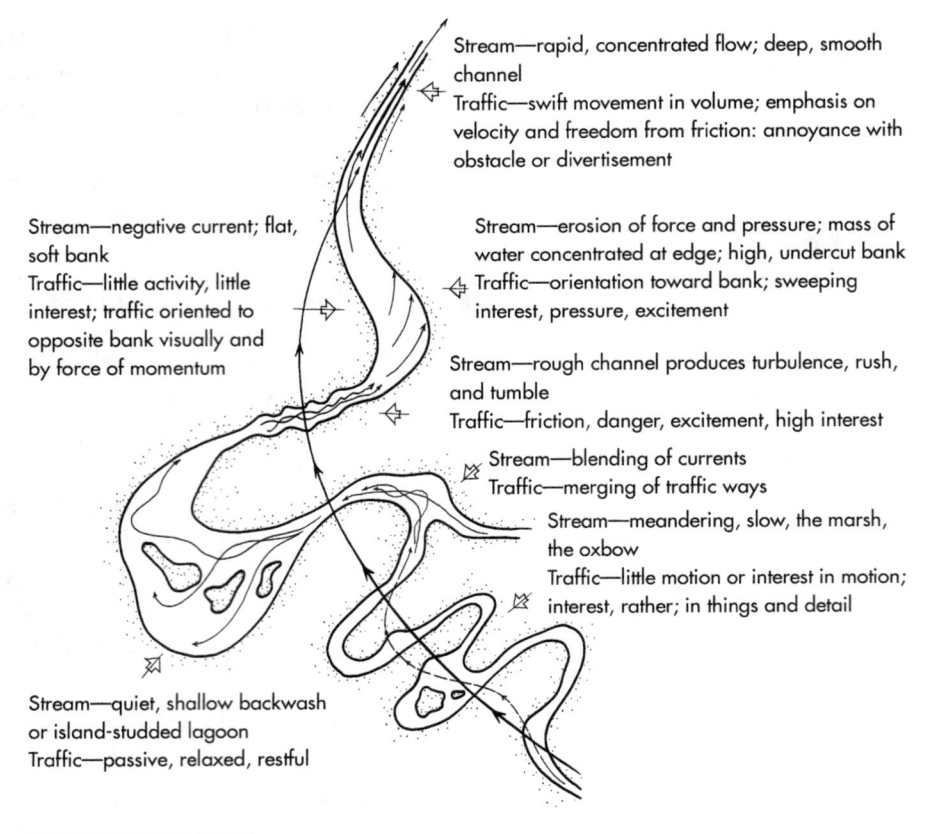

Stream—rapid, concentrated flow; deep, smooth channel
Traffic—swift movement in volume; emphasis on velocity and freedom from friction: annoyance with obstacle or divertisement

Stream—negative current; flat, soft bank
Traffic—little activity, little interest; traffic oriented to opposite bank visually and by force of momentum

Stream—erosion of force and pressure; mass of water concentrated at edge; high, undercut bank
Traffic—orientation toward bank; sweeping interest, pressure, excitement

Stream—rough channel produces turbulence, rush, and tumble
Traffic—friction, danger, excitement, high interest

Stream—blending of currents
Traffic—merging of traffic ways

Stream—meandering, slow, the marsh, the oxbow
Traffic—little motion or interest in motion; interest, rather; in things and detail

Stream—quiet, shallow backwash or island-studded lagoon
Traffic—passive, relaxed, restful

Pedestrian traffic as a moving stream. An analogy.

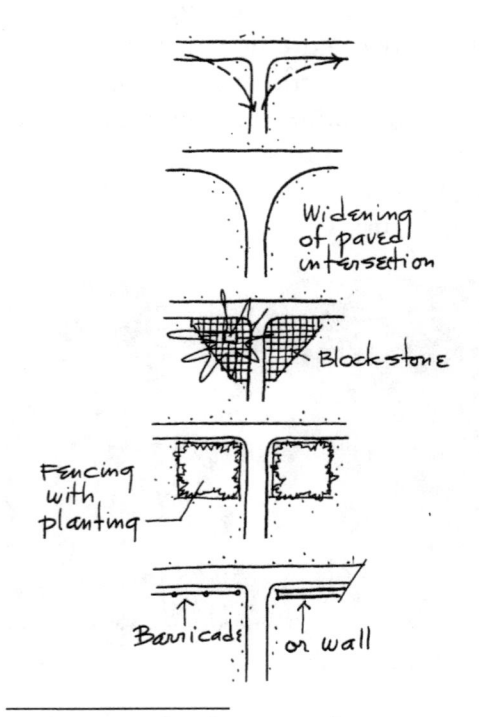

Reinforcement of walk curves and intersections. Short-cutting, with its consequent wear and erosion, can be precluded.

places where excitement, activity, or high interest is desirable, or where perforce the flow of traffic is to be decelerated, or where, by plan intent, people are made to mill and churn and jostle about. The degree and nature of such ebullient hurly-burly may be planned, as in the marketplace, the trade show, the amusement park, or the country fair. When two or more intersecting streams of traffic are to be merged into one fast, free-flowing stream, the area of juncture must be widened and shaped to provide a smoothly swelling transition and an uninterrupted flow.

An intersection must accommodate and express the functions induced by the fact of intersection. Geographically, the place of the meeting of streams or rivers is strategically important. For here not only are the watersheds of two valley systems merged, but also the life and trade and culture that flow down with the streams. In Pittsburgh, for example, the Golden Triangle is centered for good reasons at the point where the Allegheny and Monongahela rivers meet to form the start of the Ohio. Here, as in most such instances, many interacting forces are engendered by the fact of convergence. The conjunction, whether of water, trade, culture, transportation, motor traffic, or pedestrian movement, introduces considerations that must be resolved or developed in the related land planning.

Casual foot traffic, like a quiet stream, takes a meandering course. Traffic that is passive by nature or preference is found where quiet water on a river would be found, in the lagoon or island-studded backwash and out of the mainstream or current. This sheltered lagoon character, with all its design implications, is germane to those many plan functions that are related to, yet out of, main pedestrian traffic streams. In the same way, the swift freedom of the channel or the sweep of the bend is clearly analogous to many planned landscape areas.

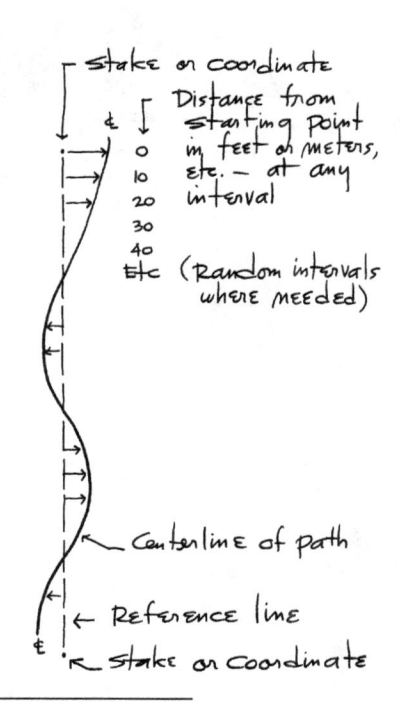

Things Seen

Since walking is still the most frequent means of locomotion, most places and spaces are seen by the circulating pedestrian and from eye level. As we have learned, the line of movement may be fixed, or it may be undirected and free, allowing a number of alternative routes and a variety of viewing experiences. Slow movement engenders interest in detail. When we are in a hurry, we tolerate few delays, but if moving leisurely, we welcome deflection and distraction. We have little interest in motion and take pleasure instead in things seen or experienced.

The Base Plane

Pedestrian traffic moving on the base plane is sensitive to its textures, which determine the type and speed of foot traffic. A given texture not only accommodates a certain classification of use but may attract it as well, as in the following examples:

Texture	Traffic
Natural granite, rough sandstone	The hobnailed boot
Packed earth, the field, the forest duff	The hiking shoe, the moccasin
Snow	The ski, the snowshoe
Ice	The skate, the crampon
Sand	The clog, the sandal, bare feet
Turf	The spiked or crepe-soled shoe, the cleated football boot
Bituminous paving	The tennis sneaker
Flagstone	The loafer
Cut stone, concrete brick	The business shoe
Polished marble	The dancing pump

Distance and Grade

Moving under our own power, we are conscious of distances to be overcome and the effort of climbing a grade. When these are negative factors, they are reduced insofar as possible by the arrangement of the plan. Apparent distances and grades can be reduced by route alignment, by screening, and by space modulation. Paths, for instance, can loop up or down a long, steep slope to reduce the apparent height, for the straight, unbroken climb to the top is in all ways more tiresome than gradual ascent from station to station along a path that angles up the contours.

Random path layout
To describe or field-stake meandering paths, measurements to the centerline can be made by offset distances along a reference line.

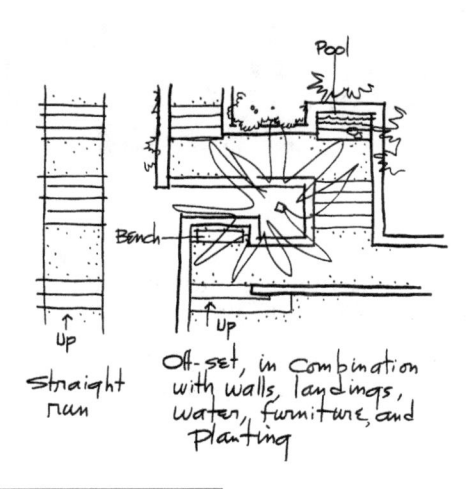

Changes of grade requiring steps provide design opportunities.

Circulation 305

Variations in the ground plane.

Often, as we have noted, within a constricted complex it becomes desirable to increase apparent distances and heights. This again may be achieved in large measure by the manipulation of trafficways and sight lines or by the viewing of a peak from a pit, a pit from a peak, and a far corner from the longest diagonal.

Pedestrian traffic, being earthbound, is more of a flow than a trajectory. This flow may be induced, arrested, divided, pooled, channeled, directed, diverted, or accelerated by skillful planning.

The Automobile

Highways, streets, and even driveways, as plan elements, must be considered as lethal lines of force. These lines and their intersections are lines and points of smashups, crippling accidents, and death. If a high-tension line crossed a community with its wires stretched low or sagging within reach of children, there would be a storm of citizen protest. Yet unprotected highways slice freely through the landscape, and our cities and our suburbs are cut into senseless squares by murderous boulevards and streets. Why? In the name of all reason, why?

There is, in the light of unprejudiced analysis, not one valid reason for our present checkerboard system of streets except for the obvious ease of laying them out. This seems a sorry excuse indeed. Our street and property patterns were, in fact, devised in the era of the horse and buggy and for the convenience of the surveyor. Because they so profoundly affect the patterns of movement, the quality, and very safety of our daily lives, it is high time for a change.

With our omnipresent automobiles we have found traffic friction increased from mere annoyance to a deadly phenomenon. In self-defense we have devised wider roads, separated roads, the overpass, the underpass, freeways, skyways, and multitiered interchanges. Engineers, in solving the very practical problem of moving people and automobiles through space, have created sweeping forms of awesome grandeur. Yet ever-new types of vehicles, trafficways, and communities must be developed if we are to domesticate the roaring, fuming, four-wheeled monsters that we have created.

Traffic Flow

In the planning of our highways and streets, we must conceive them as friction-free paths of vehicular movement. This is their primary purpose. Yet if we were to plot a typical street or highway as a force diagram, we would wonder how a more friction-studded, danger-laden, chaotic trafficway could possibly be imagined. We know, for instance, that each point at which the paths of two vehicles merge is a point of potential conflict and that each point at which they cross is a point of hazard. Obviously, the fewer such points, the better. Yet, with rare exceptions, our present trafficways are so laced and interlaced with mergings and crossings that their very function is precluded. How blind we have become in our conditioned complacency!

In our trafficways of the future, the grade intersection will be eliminated in every possible instance. Roads will be planned for fast, safe, uninterrupted traffic flow. Turning radii will be greatly increased. Rights-of-way will be widened and shaped to accommodate and contain all foreseeable and compatible roadway functions. Vehicular traffic of various types and

---

When the horse was discarded, the winding roads and streets over which he jogged were not discarded with him. The automobile inherited them. Some of them have been "improved" from time to time, but their basic features have remained unchanged. The result of pushing motor cars out over these old roads was at first simply a mild havoc and runaway horses, but later, "the traffic problem." Today we are still rebuilding old roads that were constructed for another vehicle, instead of special roads for the special needs of the automobile. This simple fact is the key to the whole present-day traffic problem.
Norman Bel Geddes

The street system of our cities and the road system of the region follow archaic patterns which go back to a time of beast drawn vehicles. The needs and practices that created the old thoroughfares are entirely alien to the auto. The old road necessarily ran through the villages, which provided resting places for passengers, a stage where horses could be fed and exchanged. Today those old regional routes—have become highways, and motor vehicles speeding along them carry traffic danger into every village and town.
Ludwig K. Hilberseimer

We spend more and more hundreds of millions of dollars to build more and more super highways to more and more remote distances so that more and more people may drive more and more rapidly until they come to the place where they must stop and wait and wait longer and longer—to get into the district where it is harder and harder and harder to move around at all!
Frederick Bigger

There will be in the future no roads or tracks which must be crossed at grade. Transportation and transit lines will be depressed or buried as free-flowing tubes—or lifted up above the earth that the goods or traffic they carry may glide along swiftly, safely, almost without friction.

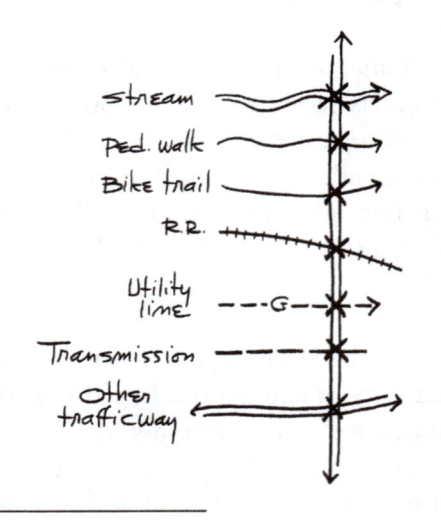

In the interest of safety, efficiency, and economy the crossing of transportation routes by any other line of flow or trafficway should be avoided insofar as feasible.

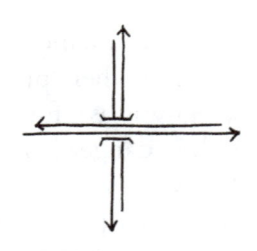

Grade separation without interconnection is often desirable.

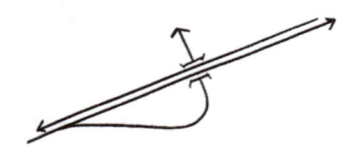

The left-turn underpass (or overpass) Highway crossing provided without hazard or interruption of traffic flows.

speeds will be segregated and given separate and specially planned routes. Marginal intrusions will be eliminated. Innovative safety controls and devices will be planned with and built into the highways. High-speed transcontinental motorways will weave through the open country between our towns and cities rather than threading them center to center. Our residential, commercial, and industrial districts will be planned off to the side, protected and entered by widely spaced, free-flowing parkways or designated truckways. Multimodal systems of movement will be devised to interconnect polarized city centers and new satellite communities.

A highway, road, or driveway is in itself a unified whole. It must be complete. It must be safe. It must be efficient. It must work well as a route of circulation and interconnection. It should also provide a pleasant experience of movement from point to point through the landscape. This useful and pleasurable quality is most evident when the right-of-way is aligned in harmony with the topography and is wide enough to accommodate all required physical and visual functions. How pleasant is the parkway with limits that extend to the rim of the valley through which it winds or with right-of-way widened to protect the sight lines from a sloping grade or ridgetop!

It can be reasonably expected that highways, roads, and driveways will long continue to be designed as the major means of access to most project sites. Each landscape area will be considered in relation to its accessway, and, conversely, each line of access will be conceived as an integral part of the thing or place toward which or away from which it leads.

In the Landscape

The contemporary highway with its adjunct approaches and structures is not only the most dominant feature of our landscape, it is also the most salient factor in our land and community planning. Once established in any landscape, a roadway becomes a potent feature and imme-

Pedestrian and auto separation.

Have you ever conceived of a road which would allow no car to approach your own—which would hold you to your course without the danger of being struck or striking any object—where you could decide in advance how fast you would like to drive, and by maintaining that constant, effortless pace, arrive at your destination on scheduled time? It sounds impossible? But you can have such a road. The means of bringing it about are available. The idea is thoroughly practical. It can be built to work in conjunction with an automatic control installed in your car. The highway you use can be made as safe and pleasant at all times as it would be if your car were the only automobile upon it.
Norman Bel Geddes

diately changes the character of the land areas through which it makes its way. In most site-structure diagrams the roadway is the most dynamic line to which use areas can be related. Without doubt, the most telling advances in our future planning will be the diagramming of more reasonable relationships between our teeming trafficways, communities, cities, and the surrounding landscape. The automobile has rendered obsolete all prior concepts of land planning.

This much cannot be denied the automobile: it has given us exhilarating freedoms of distance and time. We move about more readily than ever before. The automobile has, however, invaded our living and working areas, disrupted cherished pedestrian ways and places, and imposed a distressing double visual scale.

Far too much of our landscape is presently experienced at the same time by persons in speeding automobiles and by people moving about on foot. These two forced relationships are incompatible. This omnipresent dilemma has hardly as yet been recognized, let alone resolved. Ignoring it has caused us increasing and sometimes insurmountable problems; perhaps its study and resolution may bring the first plan forms and patterns fully expressive of our automotive age.

In the new landscape for living, all motor and pedestrian traffic will be segregated. Our living and working areas will be readily approached and serviced by the automobile, but they will be oriented to, and interspersed with, attractive, refreshing pedestrian spaces unpenetrated by roadways. Walking will again be a pleasure when it is freed from the sound, sight, fumes, and danger of rushing traffic and when it leads us through places and spaces designed for walking and congregating. And our motorways, designed solely and specifically for free vehicular movement and riding pleasure, will seem a dream on wheels.

The relationship of land use areas and buildings to trafficways is discussed in other sections of this book. In considering vehicular circulation, however, it would be instructive at this point to list the key principles to be applied in the location and design of roadways, approach drives, motor entrance courts, and parking compounds.

The Roadway

Every roadway, be it a rural drive or an urban expressway, is a unique work of design and will have its own regional and functional characteristics. In planning trafficways of any type or magnitude, however, the following principles will pertain.

Determine the most rational alignment. This implies efficient connection. The roadway will weave between and provide access to activity centers and areas of population concentration. It will follow existing boundary lines and borders insofar as feasible. It will

Circulation 309

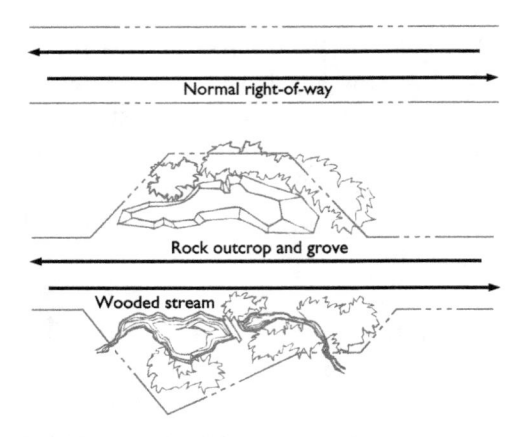

Even within urban areas the legally prescribed right-of-way should be widened to include and preserve such natural features as ponds, streams, ravines, or groves of trees, as "furnishings" to the freeway.

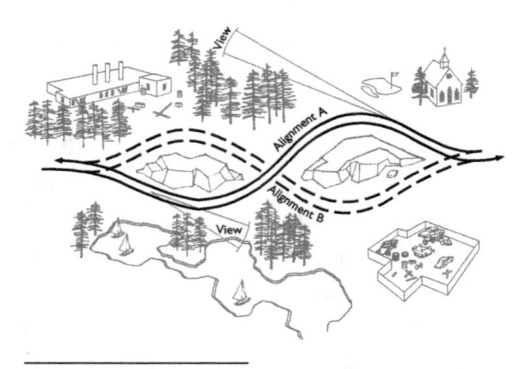

In considering alternate highway locations, weight should be given to that one which provides the best scenic attributes. Here alignment A has a visually pleasant path. Alignment B does not.

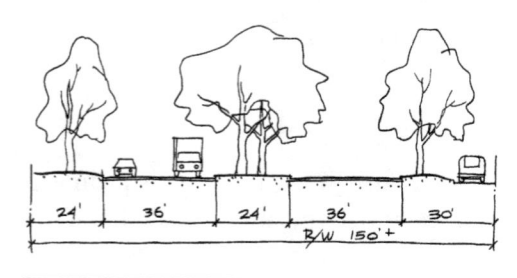

Arterial: six-lane divided. Six-lane divided arterials carry massive volumes of high-speed traffic. They interconnect and provide access to the large metropolitan communities and districts. While pedestrian walks are not compatible, minitransit and reserved bus lanes may share the right-of-way.

respond to the topographical forms and vegetative growth and fit into the landscape.

Accommodate the traffic. The eventual carrying capacity is based on the best possible projection of development within the service area of the roadway corridor. If the full facility is not to be constructed initially, the right-of-way should be adequate for all future needs.

Preserve the natural systems and scenic superlatives. A first requisite in this regard is a right-of-way of ample and variable width. It will allow for all foreseeable lanes, shoulders, side slopes, and drainageways without crowding. It will expand in places to include such natural landscape features as streams, ponds, groves, and rock outcrops. It will also provide buffering to screen unsightly uses and to protect and enframe desirable views.

Provide the optimum cross section. Lane widths and their number will depend upon projected traffic types and volumes. When traffic volumes are high, the topography is rough, and if existing conditions and land values permit, it is usually desirable to plan for separated roadways. Earthwork and construction costs can often thus be reduced to more than recoup the additional land taking. The advantages include the reduction of the roadway scale, the elimination of headlight glare, the reduction of side-slope height and width, and a more natural landscape fit.

Adjust the horizontal curvature. Major high-speed roads are designed with radius curves and interconnecting spirals. Lesser roads are often designed with tangents connected by radius curves at their points of intersection. Minor roads and woodland trails usually just feel their way along the land and between the trees and other obstacles without benefit of geometry. The important point is that in every case the planned centerline is to be field-staked and adjusted to avoid unforeseen obstructions and problem areas and to take full advantage of the topographical setting and views.

Adjust the vertical profiles concurrently. The best vertical alignment rolls with the contours to require a minimum of clearing, grading, and erosion control. It must provide clear sighting of oncoming vehicles and points of roadway entry from the sides. It must also ensure the positive drainage of the roadbed and the adjacent swales or gutters. The degree of rise or fall is an important safety factor in inclement weather.

Design for stability. A well-built road like a well-built structure starts with a solid foundation. In the construction of any roadway it is essential that the base be stable and well drained and that the successive courses laid thereon be interlocked and well compacted. The total section, including slab or wearing course, is designed as a unit to best withstand the local climate and support the anticipated loadings.

Provide a suitable driving surface. In texture, the surface will give grip under adverse weather conditions. In color it will be at once heat-reflective, easy on the eyes, and differentiated from the hues of the road-edge soils and materials to give visual definition. On

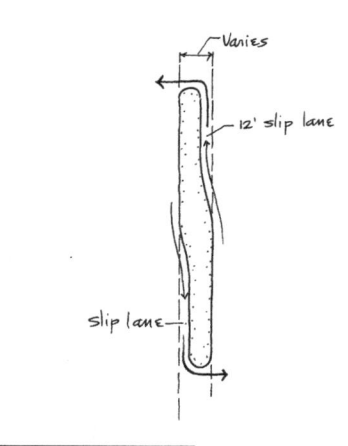

Slip lane in the arterial median.

Every highway is bordered by an idle strip as long as it is; keep cow, plow and mower out of these idle spots, and the full native flora, plus dozens of interesting stowaways from foreign parts, could be part of the normal environment of every citizen.

Aldo Leopold

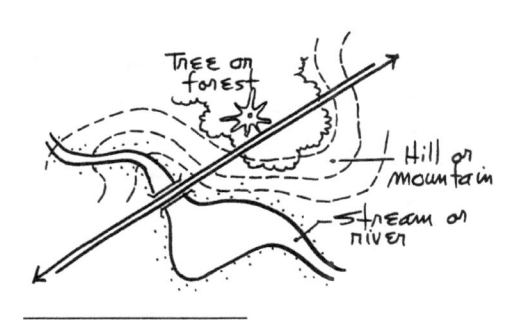

Whenever a roadway transects a natural landscape form, disruption and/or costly construction is the result.

major roads this definition of the traveled roadway can also be achieved by edge and centerline striping. The use of native crushed stone, coral, or gravels as surface aggregate is always appropriate.

Build in the safety features. Reduced gradients, wider curves, controlled access, and elimination of on-grade crossings are all conducive to safety. Other protective features include guardrails, reflectors, and clear directional signage. At special nodes such as major off-ramps or interchanges, roadway illumination by nonglaring light sources can be helpful.

Keep the structures simple. The best highway structures—bridges, overpasses, underpasses, retaining walls, and culverts—are usually direct expressions of their purpose, the locality, and the materials of construction. In some local situations, as in parks, rough-dressed native stone and rough-sawn timbers may be used effectively. Usually, and especially on highways, unadorned concrete and structural steel are more appropriate.

Coordinate the informational system. Good directional signage is easily visible and complete. It gives the right information at the right place and in a clearly comprehensible form consistent with the character and design speed of the roadway.

Use indigenous plant materials. The best planting of any roadway is achieved by the preservation of all possible existing native vegetation. Selective thinning is usually needed to articulate the road edges, enframe the views, and create a pleasantly modulated volumetric enclosure. Supplementary seeding and planting are in the main installed for slope protection and erosion control.

In the open, uncultivated countryside a highly effective procedure is to seed all disturbed roadside areas with a hardy strain of wild grass. An undulating border is then mowed with a sickle bar, while the naturalized area is left uncut to receive a crop of windblown seeds from the adjacent meadows and woodlands. Trees, shrubs, vines, weeds, and wildflowers combine in time to produce a maintenance-free roadside of indigenous beauty.

Maximize the landscape values. In every case a well-designed roadway will be aligned through the landscape in such a way and be so constructed as to preserve and display the best features and views while attaining a harmonious fit. A good roadway provides comfort, interest, and pleasure to the traveler. A good roadway is also a good neighbor.

The Approach Drive

In the selection of a proposed site for any project, the off-site approaches are a primary consideration. What one experiences in coming or going may be a decisive factor. If, for example, the approach to an office center or residential community required passage through a freight yard or deteriorating neighborhood, one would look for other choices. Conversely, if the traveled route would lead through a forest preserve or past an attractive shopping court, this would be a positive factor.

The psychology of arrival is more important than you think. If it is not obvious where to park, if there is no room to park when you get there, if you stumble into the back door looking for the front entrance, or if the entrance is badly lighted, you will have subjected your guests to a series of annoyances which will linger long in their subconscious. No matter how warm your hearth or how beautiful your view, the overall effect will be dimmed by these first irritations.

Thomas D. Church

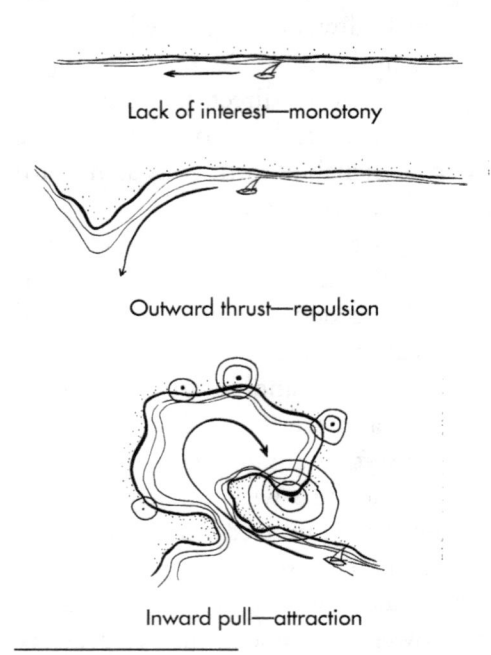

Lack of interest—monotony

Outward thrust—repulsion

Inward pull—attraction

The pull of the harbor. The successful drive approach and forecourt will suggest a receptive cove. Usually the most attractive point on the cove periphery will be the entrance door or gate.

Most residential streets (forced to comply with rigid subdivision standards) are grossly oversized and by their width destroy the livability so much to be desired.

Increased street width means increased speed, hazard, cost, and disruption.

On-street parking is a principal cause of traffic-related accidents.

In locating a project on any site, the line of approach will influence or dictate not only the position of the structural elements but will probably also determine the relationships of the site use areas as well. Assuming that an approach drive is to be developed between an existing circulation drive or street and a proposed building, let us consider the design requirements. All else being equal, it should:

Announce itself at the passing roadway. The driveway entrance is best located where it wants to be. This is at the point of the most logical penetration or highest visual interest along the fronting property line. The driveway should be well identified by street number or appropriate entrance sign. It should be considered in relationship to adjacent driveway entrances and nearby landscape features.

It will invite one in with recessive forms, as in a cove or harbor. In plan layout and site treatment, it will set the theme for all that lies ahead. Often it will introduce at the gateway the materials and architectural theme that will be used throughout the site development.

Provide safe access and egress. The driveway entrance is set at a point which will ensure safe sighting distance up and down the passing street or roadway. It is not to be located just below a steep crest or around a sharp curve. Abrupt turning movements are avoided, and, where possible, a glide-in entry with a generous turning radius is planned. On larger projects a deceleration lane is often provided if traffic volumes are heavy. A right-angle roadway entrance connection is best for two-way sighting.

Develop a pleasant transition. We design an attractive space and theme sequence from driveway throat to building entrance to parking court and return. The drive width may vary, swelling at the drive entry, at the curves, and at the forecourt, always suggesting traffic flow.

We devise a transition from the character of the highway to the character of the project and structure, be it a residence, an apartment tower, a business office, a shopping mall, or a school. We move from the scale of the passing road to the scale of the building entrance court, from high velocity to repose. At one instant, for example, a person may be whisking along the trafficway at whistling speed; two minutes later the same person may be standing contemplatively at the building entrance. Between the two conditions are telling changes in mental attitude that must somehow be agreeably resolved. By the design of the driveway, the visitor must be prepared for the experience of arrival.

Be logical. The approach should present the driver with a minimum number of decisions. It is to be remembered that traffic tends to the right but also to the easier fork and to the easier grade. The pathway should be obvious but restrained. This is to say that it must read clearly to the driver while intruding as little as possible on the natural landscape.

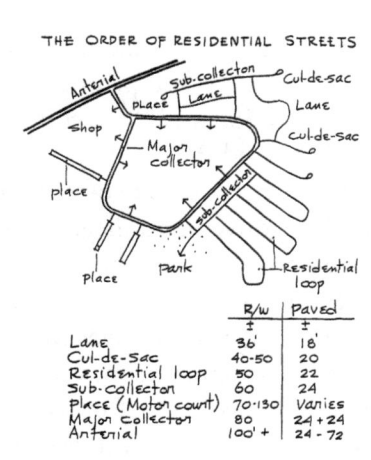

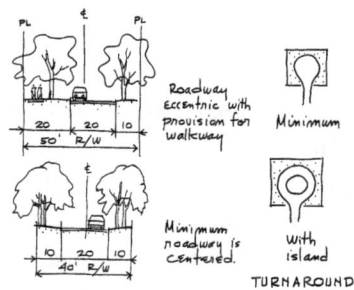

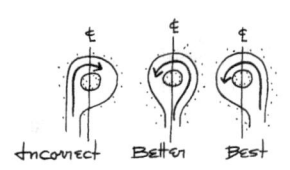

Take full advantage of the site. The alignment of the driveway presents an excellent opportunity to plan for the visual unfolding or realization of the site—its topography, cover, vistas, views, and better landscape features. It should be aligned to reveal the pleasantly undulating edge of a woodlot or planting, the modeling of ground forms, and the counterplay of tree trunk against tree trunk, mass against mass, texture against texture, and color against color as one moves along.

Move with the contours. To preclude unnecessary disruption, the drive should flow with or angle easily across the contours. Often it may follow a broad ridgeline. Again, it may move up a drainageway to the side of and preserving the natural flow line, thus gaining positive drainage at one side while enjoying a degree of protection and concealment. Because a driveway and its gutters often provide for the storm-water flow from large areas of the property, the grades should permit surface flow without undue erosion. It should also provide for the gravity flow of any contiguous storm or sanitary sewers.

Avoid splitting the property. The driveway alignment will be such as to reserve as much land as possible in an undisturbed condition. The planner will strive to retain the best landscape features while defining cohesive use areas.

Be economical in layout. The driveway will be kept short for economy of construction and ease of maintenance. Other considerations include the relative ease of excavation, a balance of cut-and-fill materials, and the alternative costs of drainage structures or bridges.

Be safe. Avoid crossing other drives, walks, bicycle trails, or active use areas.

Be consistent. Keep the quality of the approach drive consonant with that of the site, the proposed project uses, and the structures.

Reveal the structures gradually. Design the approach road to make the first impression of the property and buildings attractive. A building is usually more interesting if seen from a curving drive approach, to show its form and extent before attention is centered on detail. Much of the nature of a structure is thus revealed by a planned exposition of its sculptural qualities from a drive that leads past or around it. Open successive views to the structure, each from the optimum distance and position and with the best attainable enframement.

The Entrance Court

The entrance court is an integral part of both the approach drive and the building. It terminates the one, introduces the other, and unifies the two.

The driveway should never appear to collide with a building but should rather sweep toward and past it.

Circulation 313

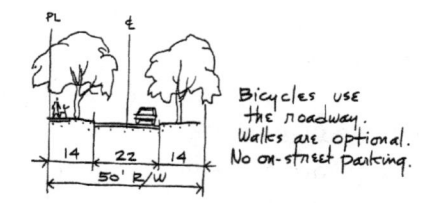

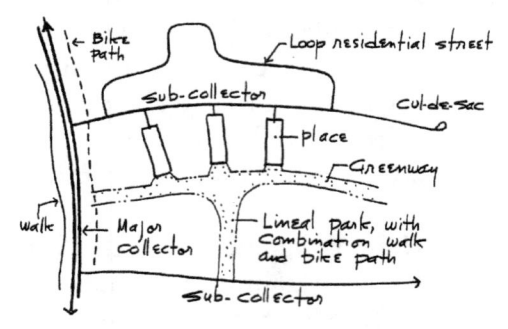

Approach from the right. Since in the United States a car moves in the right lane of traffic, we have developed taxicab and private car conditioning that tells us, as we near a destination, to chart a course that will bring the right side of the vehicle toward the building entrance. This right-curb approach is valid mainly because of two-way streets, which make pulling to the left curb inconvenient, illegal, or dangerous and usually all three. Where possible, plan a one-way loop. One-way traffic at a building entrance is always preferable. It is safer. There is also a psychological advantage, for a driver with right wheels to the curb feels superior and, for some reason, very clever.

Accommodate the left-hand approach where necessary. On some sites an approach from the left is the only way possible. If this is planned, we try to arrange sufficient depth to permit the driver to swing past the entrance and circle back to achieve the favored position. If, however, the drive must perforce lead in from the left, we do what we can to make this feasible by making the point of discharge obvious, by providing a landing platform opposite the building entrance, or by planning for discharge within a paved forecourt.

Consider the climatic conditions. The approach court and building entry are planned for all conditions of weather, darkness, and light. Visitors are to be protected from storm winds, rain, and glaring sun. Since paving is hot in the summer and cold in the winter, the building is not to be planned as an island in a sea of paving. We avoid the long walk or the long view across paving toward the building entrance.

Avoid the need for backing. The backing of vehicles near entranceways, especially in areas where children may be congregated or playing, is to be scrupulously avoided.

Complete Streets

In the mid-twentieth century, the focus of highway and street design in the United States was on moving automobiles and commercial motorized vehicles from one place to another as quickly as possible. The unwritten code for other forms of transportation using streets and highways, such as pedestrians and bicycles, was "User beware—use at your own risk." Many localities around the country even gave automobiles, rather than pedestrians, the right-of-way at intersections.

Beginning in the 1960s, planners and designers recognized that the focus of the living, working environment on the automobile was neither healthy nor desirable. They began to examine the possibility of reintroducing pedestrian traffic, as well as other modes of transportation, into streets and roadways as a means of creating better, more "livable" communities.

Street, highway, and transportation design had long fallen under the purview of bureaucrats who were resistant to change, so progress in this

Proposed streetscape accommodates multiple modes of transportation and low-impact design.

area was slow. However, with renewed interest in more livable communities and movements such as New Urbanism, Smart Growth, and Traditional Neighborhood Development, public opinion has brought about some change in the attitudes of the transportation and engineering community. Today the design of streets to be used by multiple forms of transport, including motorized vehicles, bicyclists, and pedestrians, in a safe, aesthetically pleasing way is known as *complete streets*.

Components of complete streets include bicycle lanes, traffic-calming devices, street trees, medians, reduced lane widths for motorized vehicles, mass transit pullouts, sidewalks, well-defined crosswalks, pedestrian signals, appropriate lighting, and measures for accommodating disabled travelers. Evidence is mounting that, if designed properly, complete streets are safer, promote better health, and increase adjacent land values.

Beginning in the early 1970s, many state and local governments enacted laws and regulations that require or encourage complete-street policies. Such policies are also now encouraged by the U.S. Department of Transportation.

Parking Compounds

Parking compounds provide an essential link between vehicular circulation ways, approach drives, and their termini. They are designed for the safe and efficient storage of cars. When space and site conditions permit, they are usually located beyond the building entrance as one approaches by car. Sometimes, however, they may serve in themselves as the approach court to one or more buildings. Whatever the planned function, it is to be accommodated and clearly expressed.

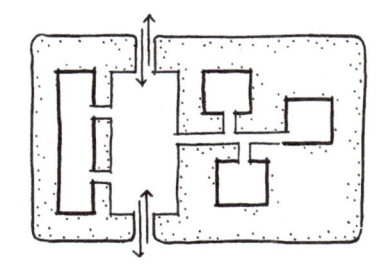

Provide off-street parking. Single and clustered buildings are benefited by the provision of internal parking courts.

Circulation 315

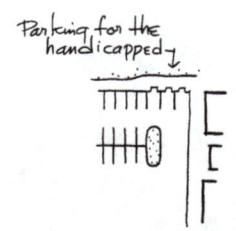

Consider the handicapped
Reserve stalls of extra width, with depressed curb, near the destination.

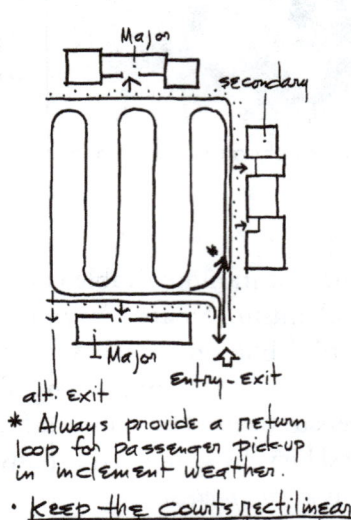

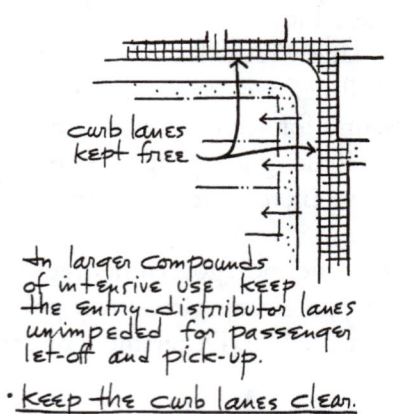

* Always provide a return loop for passenger pick-up in inclement weather.
- Keep the courts rectilinear and the traffic pattern simple.

In larger compounds of intensive use keep the entry-distributor lanes unimpeded for passenger let-off and pick-up.
- Keep the curb lanes clear.

Nighttime illumination of the entire compound is essential to security and safety.
- Mark the entry-exit clearly with sign and illumination.

Accessibility must be incorporated into circulation planning.

Test all plan possibilities. The siting of parking areas is best achieved by the study of alternative shapes and flow lines in relation to the building and topographical features. The most prevalent parking layouts are easily diagrammed for adaptation and testing.

Approach, pass, and park. Ideally, a driver will approach with the building to his or her right, discharge the passengers, continue to the parking space, and return on foot by a pleasant and convenient route to the doorway. Ideally, too, upon departing the driver would be able to pick up the car and circle back to passengers at the building entrance.

Screen the parking areas. A direct view from the entrance court into the parking area is not usually desirable. Except for commercial or business office projects, a well-placed parking or service compound is convenient but incidental to and secluded from the building.

Consider multiple use. A parking compound may be located for shared use by several buildings or activity areas concurrently. Or it may serve one purpose in daytime and another for evening or off-peak hours. Parking areas, when not in use for their primary purpose, may also serve other functions such as recreation, assembly, or temporary storage. Accommodate the vehicle. Since the parking court is planned for the efficient storage of automobiles, it must be designed with full understanding of the maneuvering require-

LANDSCAPE ARCHITECTURE

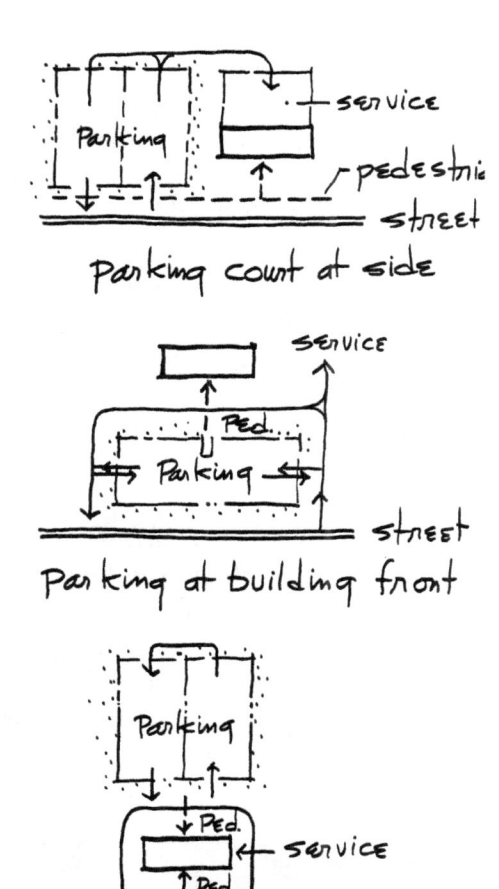

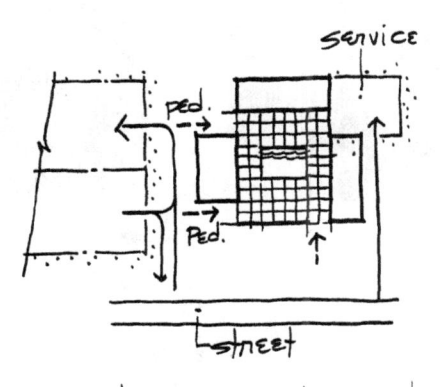

ments of the car. These dictate gradients, turning radii, aisle and stall widths, and paving textures, which may well vary to differentiate lanes of movement and areas for parking storage.

Consider the disabled. The parking compound with its backings and turnings is an area of special hazard for pedestrians with impaired vision, hearing, mobility, or other handicap. For them, bays with widened stalls are to be reserved near building entrances. Moreover, as an added safety precaution and to preclude the random movement of vehicles, the traffic flow pattern is to be kept simple and well defined, with the entire area illuminated. Those with parcels to carry, strollers to wheel, or children in tow will be grateful.

Segregate service traffic. Service vehicles range in size from small motorized carts and pickups to larger delivery and refuse trucks. They require convenient access to building entrances, collection stations, mechanical rooms, utility vaults, and similar locations. When practical, service vehicle circulation and parking areas are separated from passenger automobiles and are designed to accommodate the larger turning radii, maneuvering space, and holding patterns required.

Plan for emergency access. Fire trucks, ambulances, police cars, and utility service vans require building access. The site plan must ensure that these vehicles can get where they need to go. If direct road access cannot be provided, walks and other paved areas may be utilized, provided they are designed with this purpose in mind.

Travel by Rail, Water, and Air

Aside from the automobile, the traditional means of transporting people and goods have been trains, planes, and waterborne vessels. Their routes, crossings, and points of convergence have set the locations of our towns and cities and provided their outlying regions with the essential outlets for agricultural products and manufactured goods.

The railroads, ships, and airlines have served their purpose well. Recently, however, they have experienced increasing problems in their stubborn insistence, and sometimes forced requirement, that they maintain their original all-purpose role of moving goods and people concurrently. The two functions are incompatible. As new forms of conveyance by rail, water, and air emerge, the carriers will be highly specialized, as will be their routes, equipment, and terminals. Improved means of transit, transportation, and distribution will change established concepts of land use, community, and city and require a whole new planning approach.

Travel by Rail

Passenger travel by rail in its most recent forms is known as *rapid transit*. Some types are streamlined versions of the old interurban or commuter trains. They move on fixed rails on grade, underground, or elevated.

Circulation 317

Some vehicles are equipped with steel wheels, some with wheels that are coated. All are highly automated and can be computer-controlled. Other types use linked cars which are suspended from or propelled along a single or multiple glideway. All systems have been improved to a point at which they are light, bright, environmentally sound, and highly efficient. They can move people in groups from point to point within a region far more rapidly and at less cost per mile than the passenger car or bus. Why, then, hasn't rapid transit been more widely accepted?

First, it does carry many more people to more places each day than is generally realized. The advanced systems of San Francisco, Toronto, Montreal, and Washington are promising examples, as are the guided systems of Disneyland and Disney World. Where rapid transit has not succeeded or has failed to realize its full potential, there are common causes at the root of the failure. For instance:

> *The dwellings within the communities served are too widely dispersed.* In the typical single-family-home suburb, it often takes longer to drive to or be driven to the station than to ride from station to destination.
> *The transit connections are not direct.* At the downtown end of the line, the station is often blocks away from the office, shopping, or cultural centers.

Multiple modes of transportation.

318 LANDSCAPE

The stations are inadequate. They are often grim. Old railway stations or other obsolete structures are sometimes converted to the new use without remodeling or thought for the convenience, comfort, or pleasant relaxation of the waiting passengers.

The passing scenery is ugly. Some routes, using the old railroad trackage or right-of-way, provide the most extensive slumming excursions extant. By established railroad custom, the public must ride the same route as the tank cars, flatcars, crated chickens, and bawling calves, past the rear doors of the soap factory, junkyard, and slaughterhouse. It is not a good way to attract or hold would-be commuters.

The Transit Potential

The mass movement of people at high velocities between areas of residential concentration and regional activity centers has manifest advantages. Among these are predictability, safety, and savings in time, land area, and energy. The era of transit is at hand, perhaps as much by necessity as by reason. It will come into its own as a flourishing travel mode when, but only when:

The transitway is planned as a means by which to structure or restructure the region and new types of residential communities and urban activity cores.

The experience of travel by rapid transit is conceived in terms of safe, efficient, and pleasurable movement from center to center.

The transit facility is programmed and planned as a complete and interrelated whole. In other words, communities, stations, vehicles, routes, and termini are planned together as a smoothly operating system.

Travel by Water

When we think of a boat in motion, we think of a smoothly gliding hull, a curving wake of tumbling water, and dancing light. The course of a boat, like the water through which it moves, is fluid and undulating. Having no fixed track or roadway, it curves in wide arcs and must be given ample space for maneuvering. Even at rest at its mooring, a boat seems mobile. All plan lines relating to boats at rest or in motion should suggest this streamlined fluid mobility. In every way possible, smooth flow should be encouraged and obstructions eliminated. The heavy, the rough, the jagged, the sharp are out of place. They are destructive and impeding in fact and disturbing by connotation.

Being exposed to the elements and the tides, a boat requires for its mooring a sheltered harbor or a protective pier. Harbor and pier provide such shelter by topography, structure, or a combination of both. They are points of transition between the water and the land, where the

---

The solution to public transit is the planning of activity centers to which people can ride together.

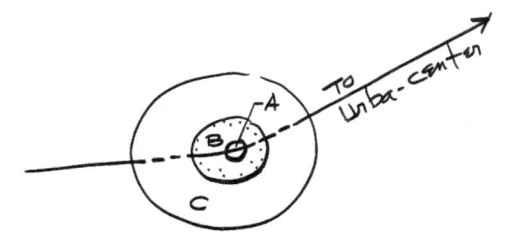

Transit node community. A—Station with minicar storage and recharge. Multifamily dwellings and convenience center.
B—Dwellings within walking distance.
C—Minitransit access by all-weather golf carts or electric bus.

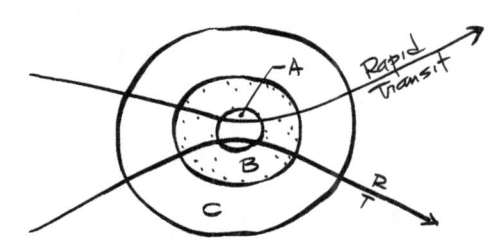

Urba-center. A—Multilevel transit terminal. B—Primary urban activity zone. Terraced pedestrian domain. Movement by elevators, escalators, and moving walks. C—Supporting urban activities. Movement by minibus or minirail. Decked parking but no surface automobile traffic. Goods distributed by tubes and beltways from peripheral transport terminals.

Regional rapid transit. Energy conservation (economic necessity) may soon force us to do what reason so far has not.

Circulation 319

mobile and free meet the static. The fact of this meeting might well be developed and expressed in all plan forms. Indeed, no great stretch of the imagination is required to understand that any structure related to water and boatways gains when the full drama of the relationship is exploited.

A summer cottage on a lake or bay, for example, is best conceived as a planned transition from land to water. It relates the solid to the fluid, the mineral to the aqueous, the confined to the expansive, and strong-cast shadow to shimmering light. Often it provides also a transition from car to yacht, yawl, or rowboat. It is terraced down; it overhangs, overlooks; it screens off and then subtly or dramatically reveals; it embraces, ramps or steps into, invites view or movement from land to water and water to land. It accentuates, by lucid structural relationships, the highest qualities of land and water. At the land approach, it is of the land; at the water's edge, it is of the water.

A riverside restaurant, if worthy of its site, will orient to the river and its traffic and display it in all its motion and color. On the landward side, it will take its form from the features of the land and from the passing walk or street or highway. On the riverside, it will be shaped to the line of the river's flow and to the curve of approaching craft. It is a rewarding experience to dine in such a waterside restaurant, with its glass-walled dining room projected and elevated to catch the flowing river view, or at shaded tables set on a terrace or deck beside the river wall, or at tables spaced out on the pier beside the bobbing boats and lapping water. In the same way, with the seaside hotel, the waterfront park, the bridge, the pier, the harbor, and the lighthouse, our site plans and structures will express the land-and-water meeting.

Water travel.

Illustration courtesy of the National Capital Planning Commission's *Extending the Legacy Plan*. Rendering by Michael McCann.

Boatways and waterways, when well conceived, have few detrimental characteristics and many attractive features. Large bodies of water ameliorate the climate, enliven the landscape, and provide a direct and inexpensive means of travel and transportation. Rivers follow the valley floors. Usually, their easy gradient encourages travel along their banks as well as upon their surface. They, together with their feeding streams and rivulets, promote a lush growth of vegetation and the most pleasing landscape environment of the regions through which they pass. All waterways attract industrial, commercial, and residential development. How can they all be accommodated? Which should have preference? The solution here is not usually one of blanket prohibition, for such prohibitions tend to dam up overriding pressures, but is rather one of planned relationships. Lucky the region or city that is empathetically related to its rivers, lakes, canals, or waterfront.

Travel by Air

The view from a plane unfolds a modeled and checkered landscape of towns, hills, lakes, rivers, valleys, farmland, field, and forest moving slowly under the wings. We are impressed with the continuity of the landscape. We sense, perhaps for the first time, that every object in the landscape is related to the whole. Sight distances are great. Visible areas are enormous. Objects, to be seen, must be simple, bold, and contrasting in colors or textures. They are most often read from the air by their shadows. All essential plan forms or objects requiring recognition from the air, and especially at the airports and their approaches, must be so emphasized.

Travel by plane is flight and is seemingly effortless while one is airborne. This smooth, flashing speed accentuates the frictions and delays of the airport and cross-country travel beyond it. The frictions of port transfer and of port-to-city distance must be drastically reduced by improved land and transportation planning. The competitive port of the future will have fast and easy access to other transportation centers and to central discharge points. There are other problems to be overcome. Among them, the deafening din at the airport aprons is mounting, decibel by decibel, to a point at which it will soon become unbearable. Sometime before that critical point or very shortly after, the pressure of economics and the advance of science will have reduced the ear-shattering roar to a pleasant whistling hum.

An airport should rightly be planned as a port. Here again, in this air harbor the land meets an opposite. This meeting and all induced transitions are to be analyzed and expressed. All current or foreseeable requirements and characteristics of planes, at rest or in flight, are to be accommodated. Further, the joint use of airfields by cargo and passenger planes with their varying speeds, needs, and capabilities will no longer be tolerable. Transport planes will be related to industrial and distribution centers. Passenger planes and ports will be linked to centers of population and urban activity. From the surrounding towns and cities new exclusive or classified approach roads will be necessary, as will a system of strategically placed air taxi stations. In this light, we can consider an airport primarily in terms of a continuing and ultimate experience of travel in which passengers can arrive by car, park, check baggage, and enplane (or, conversely, arrive by plane, pick up baggage, and leave by car, limousine, or tramway) in one swift, pleasant, uninterrupted swoop. There are, of course, many other considerations in the planning of an airport.

Airports require large areas of flat topography or land that can be readily modified to give long, level runways. Because such areas are often of necessity remote, the tendency of airports is to bring to the spot as many port facilities as possible. Hotels, theaters, conference rooms, libraries, and even recreation, amusement, and shopping centers have been planned into the airports as revenue producers. In the interest of increased efficiency, all extraneous uses must be limited in the future.

A municipal airport is no longer a landing strip, a windsock, and a ticket booth. The modern airport is an extremely intricate complex of myriad related functions. These must be studied to determine their optimum relationship to the cities and the region that the airport serves. Like all projects planned in the landscape, the airport must be studied in terms of minimizing its negative impacts and increasing its benefits.

People mover.

Exterior escalator.

322   LANDSCAPE ARCHITECTURE

People Movers

The need for increasing numbers of persons to get from here to there, usually in a hurry, has given rise to a whole array of vehicles and devices that have been grouped together in the category of transportation and circulation systems. Without them, many of our newer governmental, business office, commercial centers, and even zoos and botanic gardens could no longer function. In type and size they vary according to the distance and height to be traveled, the number of passengers to be carried, and the rate of speed required.

> *Moving walkways, chairways, and escalators.* These are a low-speed, step-on-and-off means of movement that can be used alone or in combination, indoors or out.
>
> *Automated cars.* Electronically controlled automated cars that move on rails or guideways are, in effect, horizontal elevators. Used singly or linked, they can transport groups of people at moderate speeds for distances ranging from several hundred yards to several miles. They are smaller campus and in-town adaptations of the longer-range and faster subway, glideway, and monorail transit vehicles.
>
> *Small bus trains.* Jeeps with trailers may be open to the sky or provided with full, all-weather protection. Bus trains are used frequently in recreation or exhibition areas and are often equipped with public address systems.
>
> *Minibuses.* Small buses of all sizes and shapes have longer ranges, higher speeds, and greater maneuverability than bus trains. Some minibuses, used to link airport waiting rooms with distant plane pods, are of "maxi" proportions, carrying many dozens of passengers and hoisting them by hydraulic lifts to the level of the plane door.
>
> *Long-range buses.* Long-range buses on separate busway routes are an increasingly popular form of suburban-urban transportation. They make stops at strategically located community waiting shel-

High-speed monorail.

Cable cars traverse steep slopes and rugged terrain.

ters or at one or more peripheral parking fields and then provide express linkage on reserved lanes to downtown centers.

Cable cars. Traversing steep slopes or mountainsides (as in Bogotá and Caracas) or skimming high overhead on suspended aerial cables (as at Cologne in Germany), cable cars can leap chasms, rivers, and ranges with safety and ease.

Bicycles, tricycles, and mopeds. While self-propelled, these vehicles are not to be overlooked as people movers. It is only recently that, for the first time in many decades, the annual sale of bicycles in the United States has exceeded that of automobiles. Where off-road, off-sidewalk paths and trails are provided, especially as lineal parklike connectors to community and regional centers of attraction, bicycles and electric carts blossom into use.

The electric cart. The modified golf cart on three to four wheels, with all-weather provision and carrying from one to a dozen passengers, is becoming popular. It will provide the ideal future link between home and transit station, where it can be easily stored and recharged while awaiting the transit rider's return. The use of such carts, together with cycles for intracommunity travel, would reduce the need for internal roads and reliance on the more costly, more space-demanding automobile.

Integrated Systems

It might be thought that the proliferating assortment of people conveyers would lead to utter chaos in their weaving in and out, up and down, and back and forth on crisscrossing routes and trajectories. Far from it. These vehicles provide, at last, the components needed to fit together a rational system of multimodal transportation. They provide the key to the structuring or restructuring of the regions and metropolitan areas around intensive multilevel transit-transportation hubs. These concentrated activity centers, freed of automobile traffic and the divisive interchanges, streets, and parking lots, can become again urbane and delightful pedestrian domains.

The sterile vehicular trafficways and parking lots will be replaced by terraced plazas, garden courts and malls, and refreshing in-city parks through which people can move about on foot or be transported from level to level and center to center in year-round comfort.

Automobiles will swish through the open countryside on controlled-access parkways, freed of trucks and buses. They will provide safe and pleasant alternative means of connection between the urban and regional nodes, where they will be stabled at the periphery.

New integrated systems of circulation give promise of innovative and vastly superior concepts of land and community planning.

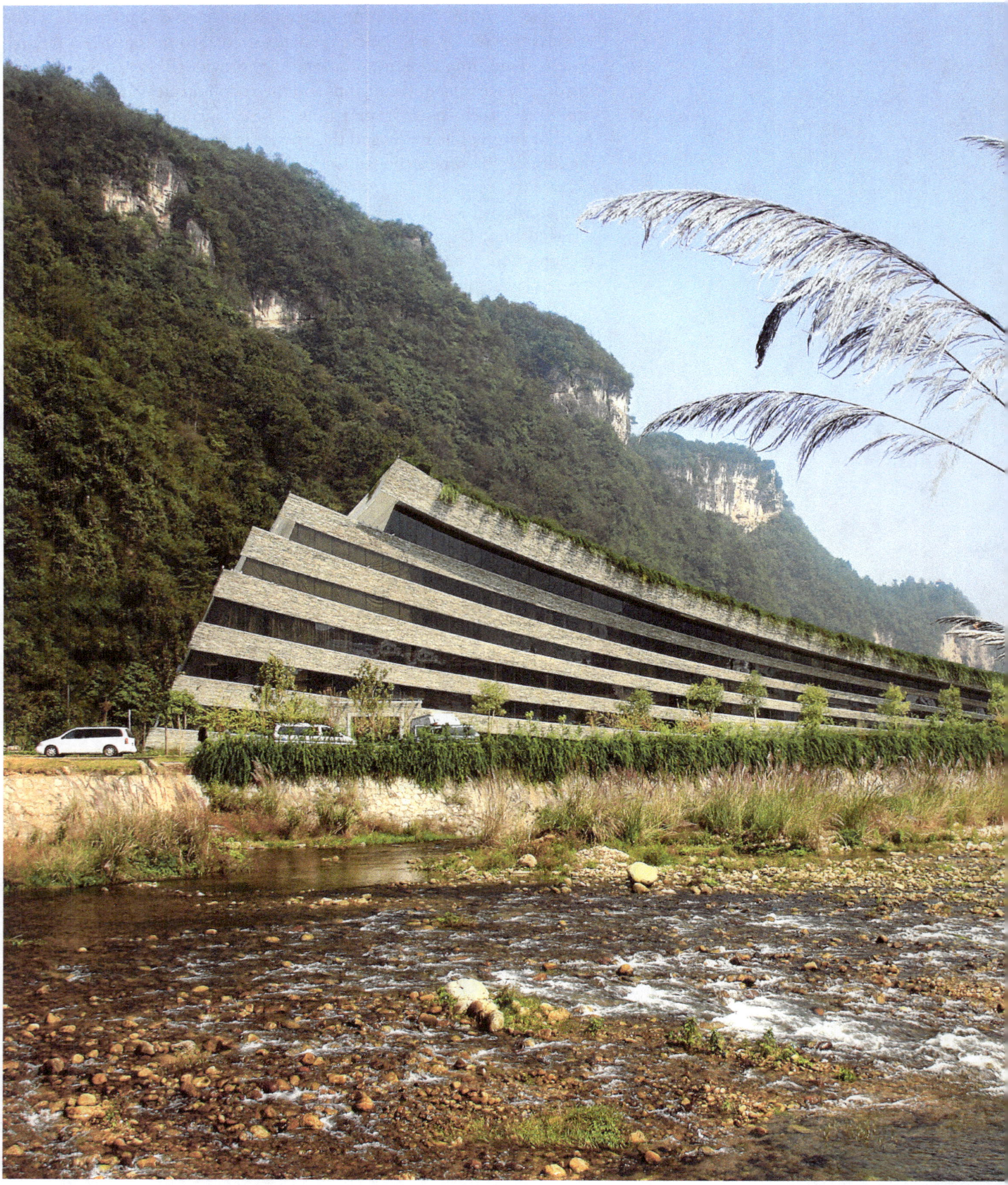

14 STRUCTURES

In theory, architectural and engineering structures are conceived by their designers as the ideal resolution of purpose, time, and place. When this is achieved, the resulting structure—be it a cabin or cathedral, an aqueduct or amphitheater, a windmill, barn, or suspension bridge—is memorable for its artistry. The cities and landscapes of history are studded with such masterworks, many surviving as cherished cultural landmarks. It is fortunate that in contemporary times we may travel to study and learn from them—to understand their admirable traits and qualities.

What qualities, then, are common to the great examples?

Common Denominators

It can be observed that, with few exceptions, at the time of their building, notable structures:

- Fulfilled and expressed their purpose—directly and with clarity.
- Reflected the cultural mores of their time, location, and users.
- Responded to the climate, the weather, and the dictates of seasons.
- Applied or extended the state-of-the-art current technology.
- Fitted compatibly into the built environs and the living landscape.

Kongjian Yu/Turenscape

327

We contemporaries proceed in blithe disregard of the truths and lessons of history. If we, proud spirits that we are must learn our truth firsthand, there need be no problem, for we are surrounded by examples of the good and the bad and need only develop a discerning eye to distinguish art from error.

A building is a thing in itself. It has a right to be there, as it is, and together with nature, a compensation of contrasts.
Marcel Breuer

Architecture subtly and eloquently inserts itself into the site, absorbing its power to move us and in return offering to it the symphonic elements of human geometry.
Le Corbusier

Purpose

We have proposed that the adage, "Form follows function," is valid only when it is understood that the term *function* transcends the delimiting connotation of "utilitarian." The term *function* in the context of expressive design is comprehensive and includes such considerations as traditional values, ethics, aesthetic quality, feasibility, acceptability, and fitness. Only if all such requisites are satisfied can it be said of a structure or form that it truly fulfills its intended function or purpose.

Culture

The culture of a community or nation is an evolving state of being or communal mind-set. It implies, sometimes overkindly, a certain level of civilization. As such, it is at any given time the manifestation of a people's beliefs and aspirations—those ideas or things that are acceptable and those that are not. This cultural litmus test is by custom applied not only to dress, foods, and works of music, literature, and art—but perhaps most particularly to buildings and other structures.

Cultural approbation allows for obvious improvement and some innovation—but rejects vociferously, and sometimes violently, that which seems out of place or offensive. This being so, it would follow that the architect, engineer, or landscape architect in the planning stage might well take pains to ensure, insofar as possible, public approval and acceptance.

Successful structures and planned landscapes not only conform to discerning public taste; they serve to upgrade and refine it.

Locality

Masterful structures are an expression of place. They respond to and grow out of their site. They accentuate its positive qualities. At best, the design of structures is a highly developed exercise in creative synergy. Sensitive design reflects, distills, and often makes more dramatic the indigenous landscape character. It utilizes every favorable aspect of the topography. It is aware of and braces for the directional winds and storm. It opens out to the breeze and favorable views. It traces the orbit of the sun. It designs into and composes with the adjacent built environment. The mark of a well-conceived structure is that it enhances, rather than degrades, its site and surroundings.

Technology

Architecture, engineering, and landscape architecture are at the same time an art and a science. The art has to do mainly with visual qualities—craftsmanship, composition, and the appearance of things. Science entails the organization of structural and mechanical systems and the satisfaction of human needs, all in accordance with the timeless laws and principles of nature.

Technology in recent years has advanced with astounding rapidity. In the design of structures, for example, it was not long ago that prestressed concrete was unknown, as was steel reinforcing, electronics—or even electricity, for that matter. Now, with a broad range of new materials and construction techniques, the possibilities have expanded manyfold. With the emergence of computer technology the design of physical structures has taken on new dimensions.

Environs

What have these advances contributed to the betterment of our environment? Not much that is evident. Not yet at least. We can get around faster, build higher, and communicate with the speed of light. But many would hold that the net results of our building in this age of mechanical marvels has been to trash and grievously pollute not only our immediate living environment, but the greater continental land masses, the depths of the seas that surround them, and the atmosphere as well. Clearly, our technical and structural capabilities have outstripped our ability to envision and realize a world in which structures are conceived and built in full awareness of nature's forms and forces—and in harmony with the living Earth. A critical change of course is the challenge of our times.

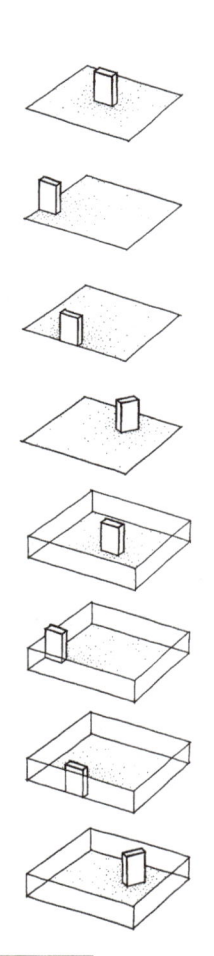

This rage for isolating everything is truly a modern sickness.

Camillo Sitte

Building composition forms outdoor space.

Composition

We physical planners like to think of ourselves as masters of space organization, yet in truth we are often baffled by the simplest problems of spatial arrangement and structural composition. What, for instance, are the design considerations in relating a building to its surrounding sea of

Composition of structures. When a structure is to be related to a given area or space, both the shape and the character of the area or space will be affected by the positioning of the structure.

Structures 329

We need desperately to relearn the art of disposing of buildings to create different kinds of space: the quiet, enclosed, isolated, shaded space; the hustling, bustling space pungent with vitality; the paved, dignified, vast, sumptuous, even awe-inspiring space; the mysterious space, the transition space which defines, separates and yet joins juxtaposed spaces of contrasting character.

We need sequences of space which arouse one's curiosity, give a sense of anticipation, which beckon and impel us to rush forward to find that releasing space which dominates, which climaxes and acts as a magnet, and gives direction.

Paul Rudolph

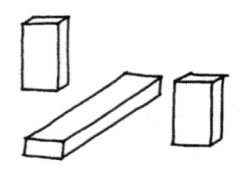

Composition of structures. Often the form of the structures themselves is not as important as that of the spaces they enclose. A single structure is perceived as an object in space. Two or more structures are perceived not alone as objects but also as related objects, and they gain or lose much of their significance in the relationship.

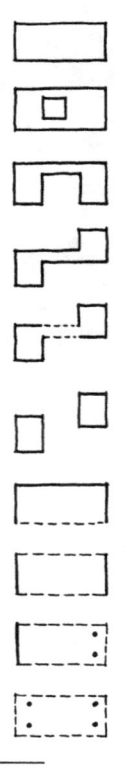

Spatial penetration of structure.

space or to its fronting approaches, or two buildings facing each other across an intervening mall, or a group of structures to each other and the spaces they enclose? Let us start from the beginning.

Buildings and Spaces

If we were to place a building on a ground plane, for instance, how much space should we allow around it? First, we will want to see it well from its approaches. The spaces about it should not only be large enough or small enough but also of the right shape and spatial quality to compose with the structure and best display it. We want to be sure that enough room is allowed to accommodate all the building's exterior functions, including approaches, parking and service areas, courts, patios, terraces, recreation areas, or gardens. Such spaces are volumetric expressions of the site-structure diagram. We want to be certain that the structure and its surrounding spaces are in toto a complete and balanced composition. Just as all buildings have purpose, so should the open spaces that they define or enclose. Such spaces must be clearly related to the character, mass, and purpose of the structures.

Often the form of a building itself is not as important as the nature of the exterior space or spaces that it creates. The portrait painter knows that the outline of a figure or the profile of a head is sometimes secondary to the shape of the spaces created between figure or head and the surrounding pictorial enframement; it is the relationship of the figure to the surrounding shapes that gives the figure its essential meaning. So it is with buildings. Our buildings are to be spaced out in the landscape in such a way as to permit full and meaningful integration with other structures and spaces and with the landscape itself.

Groups of Structures

When two or more buildings are related, the buildings, together with the interrelated spaces, become an architectural entity. In such a situation, each structure, aside from its primary function has many secondary functions in relation to the assemblage.

The buildings are arranged to shape and define exterior volumes in the best way possible. They may be placed:

    As enclosing elements
    As screening elements
    As backdrop elements
    To dominate the landscape
    To organize the landscape
    To command the landscape
    To embrace the landscape
    To enframe the landscape
    To create a new and controlled landscape

> To orient the new landscape outward or inward
> To dramatize the enclosing structures
> To dramatize the enclosed space or spaces
> To dramatize some feature or features within the space

They are placed, in short, to develop closed or semienclosed spaces that best express and accommodate their function, that best reveal the structural form, facade, or other features of the surrounding structures, and that best relate the group as a whole to the total extensional landscape.

We have seen too often in our day a building rising on its site in proud and utter disdain of its neighbors or its position. We search in vain for any of those relationships of form, material, or treatment that would compose it with the existing elements of the local scene. Such insensitive planning would have been incomprehensible to the ancient Greeks or Romans, who conceived each new structure as a compositional element of the street, forum, or square. They did not simply erect a new temple, a new fountain, or even a new lantern; they consciously redesigned the street or square. Each new structure and each new space were contrived as integral and balanced parts of the immediate and extensional environment. These planners knew no other way. And in truth, there can be no other way if our buildings and our cities are again to please and satisfy us.

An isolated city dwelling, suspended as it were in space, is but a Utopian dream. City dwellings should always be considered as the component parts of groups of structures, or districts.
José Luis Sert

For as there cannot be a socially healthy population consisting only of egotistic individualists having no common spirit, so there cannot be an architecturally healthy community consisting of self-sufficient buildings.
Eliel Saarinen

Building dominates the urban landscape.

Each building or structure as a solid requires for its fullest expression a satisfying counterbalance of negative open space. This truth, of all planning truths, is perhaps the most difficult to comprehend. It has been comprehended and mastered in many periods and places—by the builders of the Karnak Temple, Kyoto's Katsura Palace, or the gardens of Soochow (Suzhou), for example. We still find their groupings of build-

Structures 331

ings and interrelated spaces to be of supremely satisfying harmony and balance; each solid has its void, each building has its satisfying measure of space, and each interior function has its exterior extension, generation, or resolution of the function.

What do we contemporary planners know of this art or its principles, which have been evolved through centuries of trial and error, modification, reappraisal, and patient refinement? The orientals have a highly developed planning discipline that deals with such matters in terms of tension and repose. Though its tenets are veiled in religious mysticism, its plan applications are clear. It is a conscious effort in all systems of composition to attain a sense of repose through the occult balance of all plan elements, whether viewed as in a pictorial composition or experienced in three dimensions:

>   The near balanced against the far
>   The solid against the void
>   The light against the dark
>   The bright against the dull
>   The familiar against the strange
>   The dominant against the recessive
>   The active against the passive
>   The fluid against the fixed

In each instance, the most telling dynamic tensions are sought out or arranged to give maximum meaning to all opposing elements and the total scheme. Though repose through equilibrium must be the end result, it is the relationship of the plan elements through which repose is achieved that is of utmost interest. It is the contrived opposition of elements, the studied interplay of tensions, and the sensed resolution of these tensions that, when fully comprehended, are most keenly enjoyed.

A group of structures may be planned in opposition both to each other and to the landscape in which they rise, so that as one moves through or about them, one experiences an evolving composition of opposing elements, a resolution of tensions, and a sense of dynamic repose. A single tree may be so placed and trained as to hold a distant forest or group of smaller trees in balanced opposition and give them richer meaning. A lake shining deep and still in the natural bowl of a valley may, by its area, conformation, and other qualities, real or associative, hold in balanced repose the opposing hills that surround it. A plume of falling water at the lake's far end may balance the undulations of its points and bays.

Walter Beck, long a student of oriental art and composition, has said of the superb gardens that he planned at Innisfree: "On a wall, at the lake edge, is a rock which I call the dragon rock; it is the key in a grouping of stones whose function is to hold in balance the lake and nearby hills; whose function is to cope with the energies of the sky and the distant

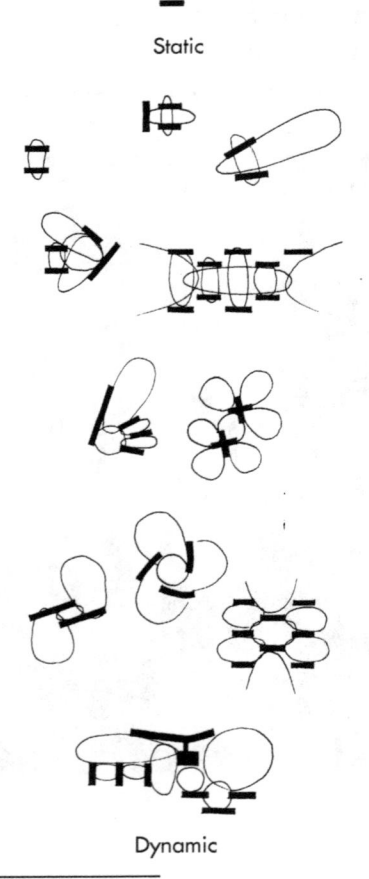

Opposing structures generate a field of dynamic tension.

landscape."[1] It can be seen that tremendous compositional interest and power can be concentrated in such key objects—rocks, sculpture, structures, or whatever you will—that by design may hold a great system of elements in balanced tension and thus in dynamic repose.

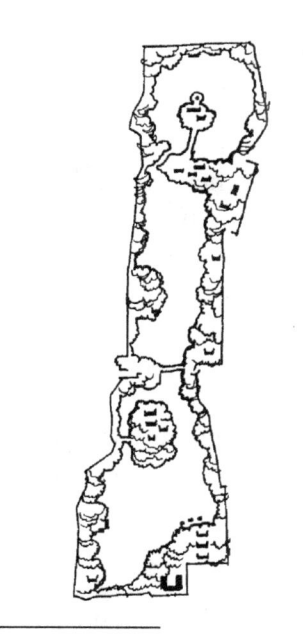

It would seem, from a comparison of the European and oriental systems of planning, that the Western mind is traditionally concerned primarily with the object or structure as it appears in space, while the Eastern mind tends to think of structure primarily as a means of defining and articulating a space or a complex of spaces.

In this light, Steen Rasmussen, in his book *Towns and Buildings,* has made a revealing graphic comparison of two imperial parks, that of King Louis XIV at Versailles and the Sea Palace Gardens in Beijing. Both were completed in the early 1700s, both made use of huge artificial bodies of water, and both were immense; but there the similarity ends. A close study of these two diametrically opposed planning approaches, illustrated here, will lead one to a fuller understanding of the philosophy of both occidental and oriental planning in this period of history.

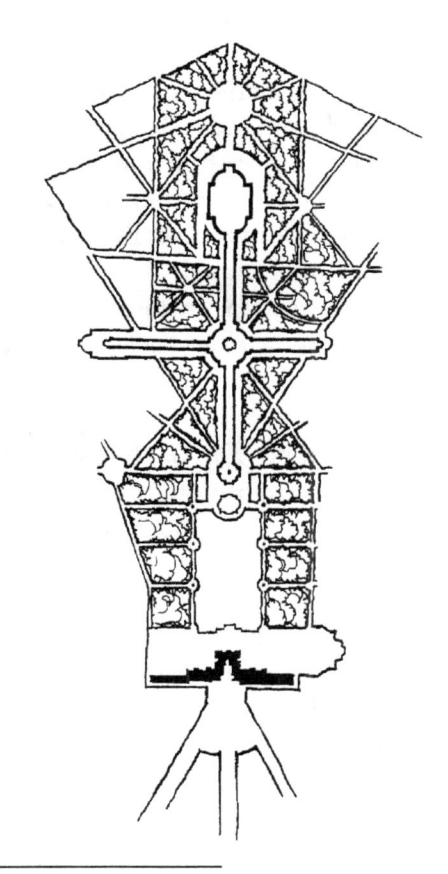

Too often, when placing or composing structures in space we revert to cold geometry. Our architectural libraries are bulging with building plans and diagrams laid out in crisp, abstract patterns of black and white that have little meaning except in the flat. It is small wonder that buildings that take their substance from such plans are destined to failure, for they were never conceived in terms of form in space or of spaces within form. The world is cluttered with such unfortunate travesties. The intelligent planning of buildings, parks, and cities is a far cry from such geometric doodling. A logical plan in two dimensions is a record of logical thinking in three dimensions. The enlightened planner is thinking always of space-structure composition. His or her concern is not with the plan forms and spaces as they appear on the drawings but rather with these forms and spaces as they will be experienced in actuality.

Many Renaissance squares, parks, and palaces are little more than dull geometry seen in the round. One clear, strong voice crying out against such puerile design was that of Camillo Sitte, a Viennese architect whose writings on city building first appeared in 1889 and whose ideas are still valid and compelling today. It was Sitte who pointed out that pre-Renaissance people used their public spaces and that these spaces and the buildings around them were planned together to satisfy the use. There were market squares, religious squares, ducal squares, civic squares, and others of many varieties; and each, from inception through the numerous changes of time, maintained its own distinctive quality. These public places were never symmetrical, nor were they entered by wide, axial streets that would have destroyed their essential attribute of enclosure. Rather,

Peking, Sea Palace gardens.

Versailles Park.

[1]From *Painting with Starch* by Walter Beck (Van Nostrand, Princeton, N.J., 1956).

they were asymmetrical; they were entered by narrow, winding ways. Each building or object within the space was planned to and for the space and the streams of pedestrian traffic that would converge and merge there. The centers of such spaces were left open; the monuments, fountains, and sculpture that were so much a part of them were placed on islands in the traffic pattern, off building corners, against blank walls, and beside the entryways, each positioned with infinite care in relation to surfaces, masses, and space. Seldom were such objects set on axis with the approach to a building or its entrance, for it was felt that they would detract from the full appreciation of the architecture. Conversely, it was felt that the axis of a building was seldom a proper background for a work of art.

Sitte discovered that such important buildings as cathedrals were rarely placed at the center of an open space, as we almost invariably place them today. Instead, they were set back against other buildings or off to the side to give a better view of facade, spires, or portals and to give the best impression from within the square or from its meandering approaches.

Rules of Composition

Down through the centuries, much thought has been given to the establishment of fixed formulas or rules that might govern building proportions, or the relationship of one building to another, or the relationship of a building to its surrounding volumetric enclosure.

The location of the equestrian statue of Gattamelata *by Donatello in front of Saint Anthony of Padua is most instructive. First we may be astonished at its great variance from our rigid modern system, but it is quickly and strikingly seen that the monument in this place produces a majestic effect. Finally we become convinced that removed to the center of the square its effect would be greatly diminished. We cease to wonder at its orientation and other locational advantages once this principle becomes familiar.*

The ancient Egyptians understood this principle, for as Gattamelata *and the little stand beside the entrance to the Cathedral of Padua, the obelisks and the statues of the Pharaohs are aligned beside the temple doors. There is the entire secret that we refuse to decipher today.*

Camillo Sitte

There have long been those who believe that mathematics is the all-pervading basis of our world of matter, growth, and order. To them, it has followed naturally that order, beauty, and even truth are functions of mathematical law and proportion. The *golden rectangle,* for example, has long been a favorite of mathematicians, perhaps because of the fact that if a unit square is subtracted from each ever-diminishing rectangle, a golden rectangle each time remains. This "ideal" rectilinear shape (whose sides have a ratio of 1:1.618, or roughly 3:5) has appeared again and again, in plan and in elevation, in the structures and formed spaces of the western world.

Miloutine Borissavlievitch, in his absorbing work, *The Golden Number,* has explored its application to architectural composition. He proposes that although the golden rectangle considered by itself is, both philosophically and aesthetically, the most beautiful among all horizontal rectangles, "when considered as a part of a whole, it is neither more beautiful nor unattractive than any other rectangle. Because a whole is ruled by the laws of harmony, by the ratios between the parts and not by a single part considered by itself." He notes that "Order is indeed the greatest and most general of esthetic laws," and then suggests that there are only two laws of architectural harmony: the law of the same and the law of the similar.[2]

[2]Though Borissavlievitch is speaking here only of proportions, it is to be noted that the laws of the same and the similar apply as well to materials, colors, textures, and symbols.

Pistoia

Verona

Verona

Nuremberg

Salzburg

Ravenna

Perugia

Verona

Cologne

Modena

Strasbourg

Lucca

Amiens

Geneva

Gattamelata

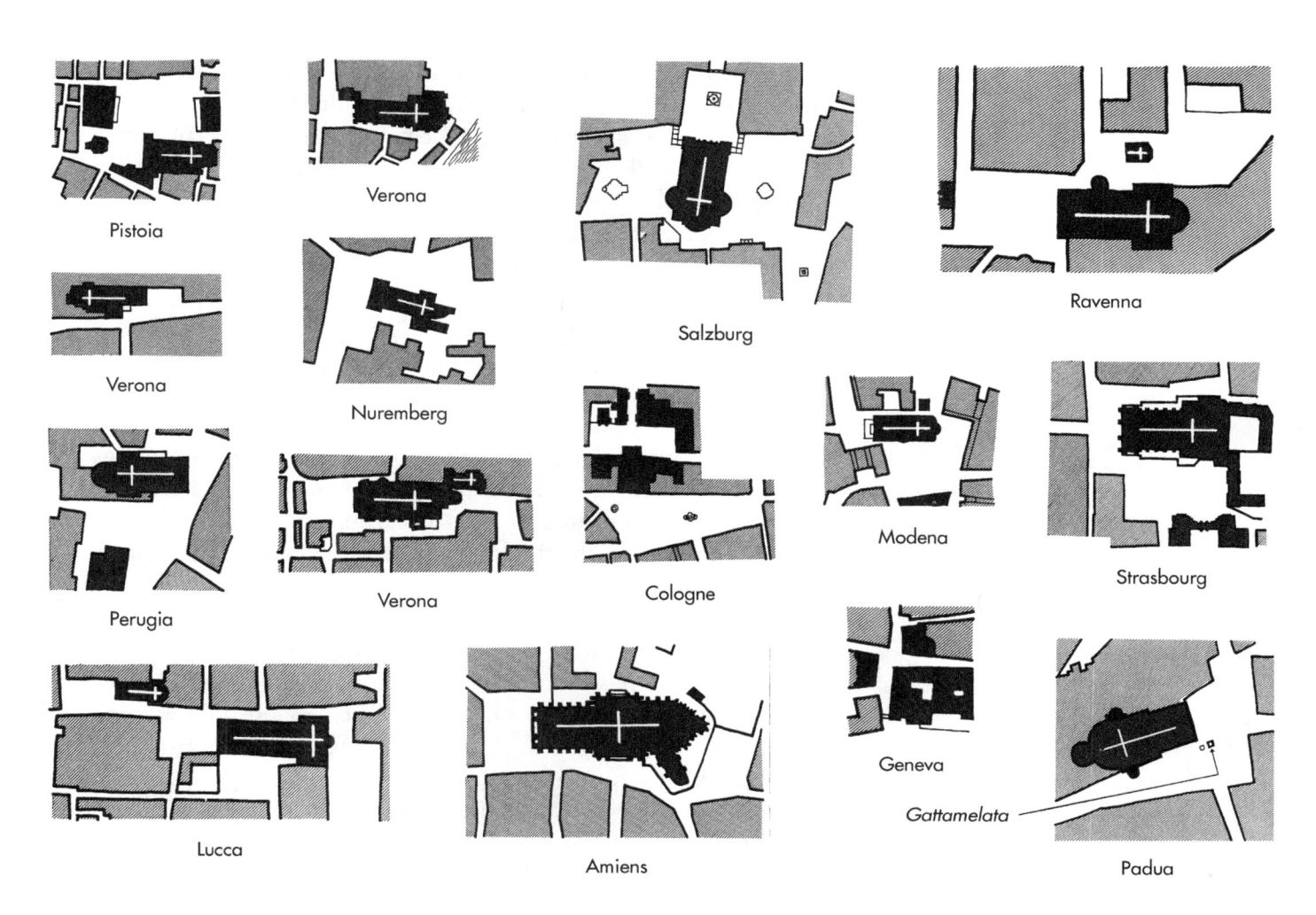

Padua

The law of the same. Architectural harmony may be perceived or created in a structure or composition of structures that attains order through the repetition of the same elements, forms, or spaces.

The law of the similar. Architectural harmony may be perceived or created in a composition that attains order through the repetition of similar elements, forms, or spaces.

Borissavlievitch notes that "whilst the Law of the Same represents unity (or harmony) in uniformity, the Law of the Similar represents unity in variety." He wisely notes also that "an artist will create beautiful works only in obeying unconsciously one of these two laws. Whilst we create, we do not think about them, and we follow only our imagination and our artistic feeling. But when our sketch is made, we look at it and examine it as if we were its first spectator and not its creator, and if it is successful we shall know, because of our knowledge of these laws why it is successful; if it is not, we shall know the reason of the failure."

"The beautiful," said Borissavlievitch, "is felt and not calculated."

Leonardo Fibonacci, an Italian mathematician of the thirteenth century, discovered a progression that was soon widely adapted to all phases of

Structures

planning. He noted that starting with units 1 and 2, if each new digit is made the sum of the previous two, there results a progression of 1, 2, 3, 5, 8, 13, 21, 34, and so forth, which, translated into plan forms and rhythms, is visually pleasing. It was later discovered that the progression approximates the growth sequence of plants and other organisms; this, of course, added to its interest and confirmed in the minds of designers the notion that this progression is "natural" and "organic."

Marcus Vitruvius, a Roman architect and scholar who lived in the first century before Christ, set out to formulate a system of proportion that he could apply to his plans and structures. In his search he undertook an exhaustive study of the architecture and planning of ancient Greece. In the course of his work he produced a book setting forth his findings and expounding his theories on the *anthropomorphic module,* a unit of measurement based on the proportions of the human body. This was to have a profound effect on the thinking and planning of the Renaissance.

Leonardo da Vinci, the creative giant of his time, analyzed and tabulated his own system of mean proportions of the component parts of the human figure in relation to its total height and then derived a table of classic proportions and ratios from which he developed for each project a suitable modular system. As architect-engineer-sculptor-painter, he translated his findings into all his works and through them demonstrated to posterity his conviction that, to achieve order and beautiful proportion in any work, the major masses or lines and the smallest detail must have a consistent mathematical relationship.

The conviction that architecture is a science and that each part of a building has to be integrated into one and the same system of mathematical ratios may be called the basic axiom of Renaissance architects. Today, we physical planners are still searching for the modular system most applicable to our contemporary work. One of the distinguishing marks of Japanese planning and architecture is a fundamental order, or mathematical relationship, of the elements. This stems, at least in part; from the use of the *tatami,* or woven grass mat (approximately 3 by 6 feet), as a standardized unit of measurement. Traditionally, a modular grid system based upon this unit has been the foundation of most building plans and surrounding spaces. By this system, a room is a given number of mats in length and width, and a building plan is so many mats in area. In their planning, the Japanese make use also of the 12-foot dimension, which is divisible by 1, 2, 3, 4, and 6.

If a unit such as a closet or a case requires less than the full module, it is not distorted to fill the module; rather, it is set free within the module and composed within the modular framework. The fact that an object is smaller or larger than the module is not concealed but is artistically revealed and elucidated. This approach would seem to be clearly superior to our American modular systems by which components are designed

Vitruvian Man: A study by Leonardo da Vinci from one of his notebooks illustrating his principle, "The span of the man's outstanding arms is equal to his height."

The Vitruvian figure inscribed in a circle and square became a symbol of the mathematical sympathy between macrocosm and microcosm.
Rudolph Wittkower

(or forced) to fit precisely within a given structural grid. The Japanese form order also differs significantly from the rigid geometric planning of Europe's Renaissance, which worshiped insistent symmetry rather than such a free and flexible system of modular organization.

Structures in the Landscape

We have seen how the ancients struggled with the *visual* aspects of architectural composition, of trying to create a fairer world in their own rational image. They found within the mathematical context no universal rules except those of order, proportion, and scale. Could it be that in their compulsion to measure, compare, and debate they overlooked the ultimate truth so evident in all of nature's structures? This is the *law of fitness*. The law of fitness would reveal to us that the optimum structure, of any type, is that which for its time and place and with the most economical use of materials best fulfills its purpose.

Without exception nature has fashioned, in the mast-and-spar construction of each tree, the skeleton of each animal or bird, each eggshell, and each weed stalk, a structure of utmost simplicity, strength, and resilience. Each as a form is eminently suited to its function. Each is designed and engineered without concern for aesthetics, yet each, in its absolute fitness, is intrinsically beautiful. Could it be that a dogma of rules and formulas could preclude rather than foster meaningful design? Could it be that a preconceived notion of plan form and structural shapes could produce archaic buildings? Could it be that, as in nature, our most ingenious and handsome structures will be derived in a forthright search for ever more expressive form? It could be. The unselfconscious architecture of the New England farm, the Greek hill town, and the African council house all share nature's direct approach, and all, in their ways, are eloquently expressive.

As with structural forms and objects, nature has much to teach us, as well, in the plan layout of our homes and cities. We have yet to see an axial anthill or a symmetrical plan arrangement of a beaver colony. The creatures of the wild have learned to fit their habitations to the natural land conformation, to established patterns of water flow, to the force and direction of the winds, and to the orbit of the sun. Should not we be as responsive?

Yet we have all seen towers with expanses of metal and heat-absorbing glass focused into the rays of the sun. We are all too familiar with broad avenues aligned to receive, unchecked, the full blast of prevailing winter winds. We recall groupings of campus buildings which have completely destroyed the natural character of the hills and ravines upon which they have been imposed. We know of checkerboard communities laid out in utter disdain of contours, watercourses, or wooded slopes, or geology, storm, or view.

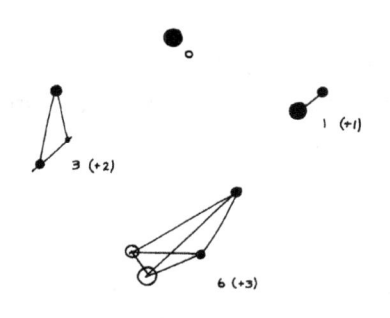

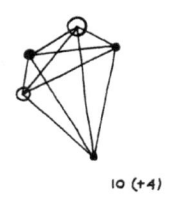

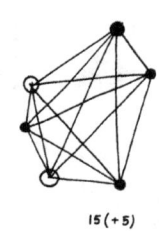

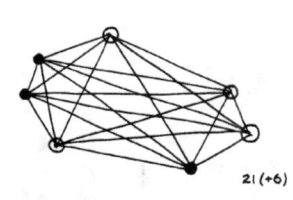

Composition of structures. The number of polar relationships increases arithmetically with the addition of each unit to a complex of structures. Since each new unit modifies the composition, its relationship to all other units is a matter of design and planning concern.

Structures 337

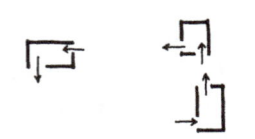

Three disconnected plan elements

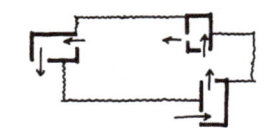

Addition of connective linkage

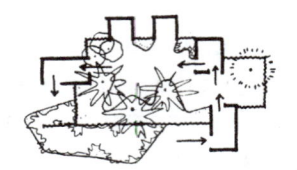

Further articulation of plan circulation

Integration of structures.

Classification by the addition of structural elements plus definitive circulation ways.

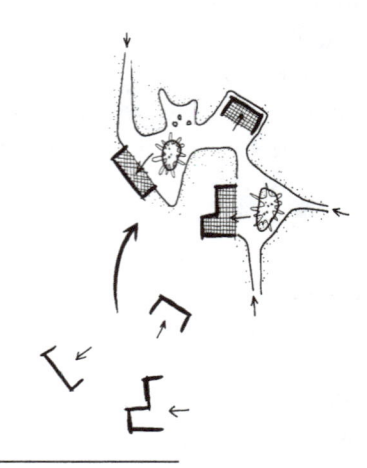

Diverse plan elements related by circulation patterns.

If there be a lesson, it is this: *Architecture by formula and site planning by sterile geometry are equally doomed to failure.*

Individual buildings are sometimes spaced out as deployed units of a greater architectural composition. It can be seen that such structures and the spaces they define combine to give a more telling impact than would be possible for any single structure of the group. Sometimes this is desirable; sometimes it is not. Such an arrangement of structures seems most reasonable when each building not only *appears* but also *functions* as a part of the total complex. In every case in which a building serves as a unit of an architectural group, the entire group is treated as a cohesive and unified composition, and each structure owes allegiance to the whole.

Buildings may be arranged freely in the landscape as individual units. In such cases, when they need not be planned as part of a complex, they and the spaces around them may be designed with much more freedom. Their relationship is not one of building to building but rather one of building to landscape, with all that this implies.

Buildings of similar character may be dispersed, even at considerable distances, in such a manner as to dominate a landscape and unify it—as in a university campus or military installation. Though a great variety of uses may be given to the intervening landscape areas, each element within the visual field must be compatible by association.

Planned building composition.

Structures are often composed in relation to natural or constructed elements of the landscape, such as a water body, a railroad siding, or a highway. In such cases, the buildings, singly or in composite, may be given their form and spacing to achieve the best possible relationships. A resort

338   LANDSCAPE ARCHITECTURE

complex and its fronting lake are in effect composed as an interrelated unit, in which the lake adds much to the resort and resort, in turn, adds to the ambience of the lake.

A factory and its receiving and shipping yards are designed *to* and *with* the railroad. A roadside restaurant is planned as one with the highway in terms of landscape character, sight distances, approaches, resolution of momentums, and composition of spaces and forms.

It is to be remembered that a building complex, as much as a natural forest grove, has its own landscape character. This must be recognized if it is to be accentuated by the planned relationships and supporting site treatment.

Some buildings are static. They stand aloof and are complete in themselves. Such structures are no doubt valid when the intended architectural expression is that of detachment, grandeur, the austere, or the monumental. They require that their setting and site development be in keeping.

Other building groupings, by their very plan layout, seem to express human freedom and interaction. They form a responsive relationship with nature and the constructed landscape. It can be seen that not only the structures themselves but also their abstract arrangement determine to a large degree their character and the character of the larger landscape area that they influence or embrace.

Often, scattered buildings may be brought into a more workable and visually satisfying relationship by connecting them with paved areas or by well-defined lines of circulation. Again, this integration may be accomplished by the addition of structural elements such as walls or fences. Sometimes tree rows or even hedges may suffice to bind them together. The elements that unite such structures may at the same time define for each the most fitting volumes of related space.

The Defined Open Space

Open spaces assume an architectural character when they are enclosed in full or in part by structural elements. Such a space may be an extension of a building. Sometimes it is confined within the limits of a single building or enclosed by a building group. Sometimes such a space surrounds a structure or serves as its foreground, as a foil, or as a focal point. Each such defined open space is an entity, complete within itself. But more, it is an inseparable part of each adjacent space or structure. It can be seen that such related spaces, structures, and the landscape that surrounds them must all be considered together in the process of design.

A defined outdoor volume is a well of space. Its very hollowness is its essential quality. Without the corresponding void, a solid has no mean-

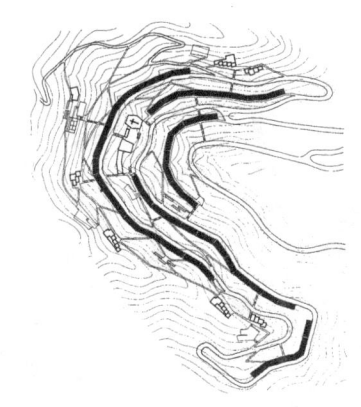

Ribbon pattern in free alignment, to flow with the topography. Site-structure harmony is pleasantly evident.

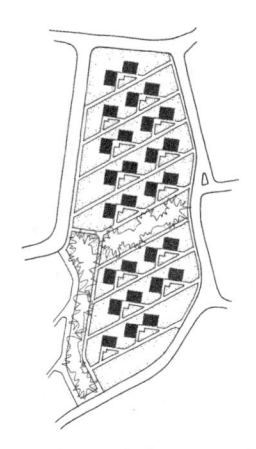

A T-square and triangle layout: order without reason, monotonous in the extreme.

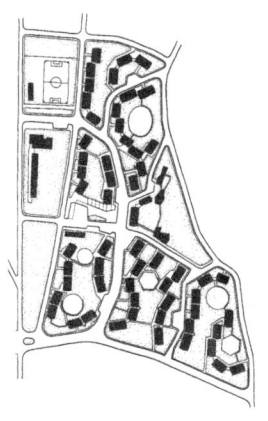

Buildings arranged in a free compositional pattern. Note the pleasant variety of defined spaces and building relationships. Such groupings provide a more relaxed and pleasant environment for living.

Various compositional arrangements of apartment structures.

Architecture defines open space.

ing. Is it not then quite evident that the size, shape, and quality of the negative space will have a powerful retroactive effect upon the adjacent positive masses? Each structure requires for its fullest expression a satisfying balance of mass and void. The same void may not only satisfy two or more solids and relate them to each other, it may also relate them as a group to some further structures or spaces beyond.

Whatever its function, when the hollowness of a volume is a quality to be desired, this concavity is to be meticulously preserved and emphasized by letting the shell read clearly, by revealing enclosing members and planes, by incurving, by belling out the sides, by the use of recessive colors and forms, by letting the bottom fall away visually, by terracing or sloping down into and up out of the base, by digging the pit, or by depressing a water basin or reflective pool and thus extending the apparent depth of the space to infinity. A cleanly shaped space is not to be choked or clogged with plants or other standing objects. This is not to imply that the volume should be kept empty, but rather that its hollowness should be in all ways maintained. A well-placed arrangement of elements or even a clump or grove of high-crowned trees might well increase this sense of shell-like hollowness.

The defined space, open to the sky, has the obvious advantages of flooding sunlight, shadow patterns, airiness, sky color, and the beauty of moving clouds. It has disadvantages, too, but we need only plan to minimize

340   LANDSCAPE ARCHITECTURE

these and to capitalize on every beneficial aspect of the openness. Let us not waste one precious yard of azure blue, one glorious burst of sunshine, or one puff of welcome summer breeze that can be caught and made to animate, illuminate, or aerate this outdoor volume that we plan.

If the volume defined by a structure is open to the side, it becomes the focal transition between the structure and the landscape. If open to the view, it is usually developed as the best possible viewing station and the best possible enframement for the view seen from the various points of observation.

Abstract composition. The garden of Ryōanji, Kyoto, surely one of the 10 outstanding gardens of all time, is an abstract composition of raked gravel simulating the sea. The walled space expands the limits of the related monastery refectory and terrace. Designed as a garden for contemplation, it owes its distinction to its simplicity, its perfection of detail, its suggestion of vast spaces, and its power to set free the human mind and spirit.

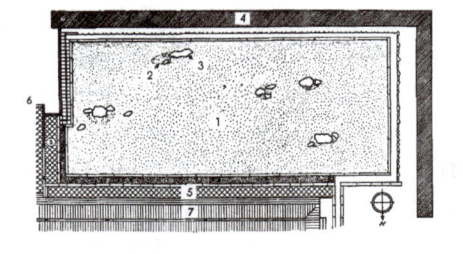

(1) Sanded ground, (2) moss, (3) stone, (4) earth wall, (5) tile pavement, (6) ornamental gate, and (7) veranda.

The defined open space is normally developed for some use. It may extend the function of a structure, as the motor court extends the entrance hall or as the dining court extends the dining room or kitchen. It may serve a separate function in itself, as does a recreation court in a dormitory grouping or a military parade ground flanked by barracks. But whether or not it is directly related to its structure in *use*, it must be in *character*. Such spaces, be they patios, courts, or public squares, become so dominant and focal in most architectural groupings that the very essence of the adjacent structures is distilled and captured there.

Habitations

What does a dwelling want to be? Shelter? Family activity center? Base of operations? All three, no doubt, and each of these functions is to be expressed and facilitated. But in its fullest sense a habitation is much more. It is our human fix on the planet Earth, our earthly abode. Once accepted, this simple philosophic concept has far-reaching implications.

In the planning of their homes and gardens, Asians not only adapt them with great artistry to the natural landscape but also consciously root them in nature. Constructed of materials derived from the earth (with varying degrees of tooling and refinement), these homes and gardens are humanized extensions of earth form and structure and are fully attuned to the natural processes. Like the nest of the bird or the beaver's lodge, they are nature particularized.

Dwelling-Nature Relationships

It is proposed that each human habitation is best conceived as an integral component of the natural site and landscape environs. The extent to which this can be accomplished is a measure of the dwelling's success and the occupant's sense of fitness and well-being.

This integration of habitation with nature is an exacting enterprise. How is it to be achieved? As a beginning:

Explore and analyze the site. Just as the bird or the animal scouts the territory for the optimum situation, just as the farmer surveys the holding and lays out fields and buildings to conform to the lay of the land, just so must the planner of each home and garden come to know and respond to the unique and compelling conditions of the selected site.

Adapt to the geological structure. The conformation of every land area is determined largely by its geologic formation—the convolutions, layering, upheavals, erosion, and weathering of the underlying strata. These establish the stability and load-bearing capacity of the various site areas and the ease or difficulty of excavation and grading. They determine as well the structure, porosity, and fertility of the subsoil and topsoil, the presence of groundwater, and the availability of freshwater reserves. Only with the knowledge of subsurface conditions, gained by test holes or drilling or the keen eye of experience, can one plan to the site with assurance.

Preserve the natural systems. Topography, drainageways, waterways, vegetative covers, bird and wildlife trails and habitat all have continuity. One test of good land planning is that it minimizes disruption of established patterns and flows.

Adjust the plan to fit the land. In the recomposition of solids and voids the structural elements are usually designed to extend the hill or ridge and overlook the valley. Well-conceived plan forms honor and articulate the basic land contours and water edges. The prominence is made more dominant, the hollow and cove more recessive.

Reflect the climatic condition. Cold, temperate, hot-dry, or warm-humid, each broad climatic range brings to mind at once planning

Take advantage of natural site characteristics.

problems and possibilities. Within each range, however, there are many subarea variations of climate or site-specific microclimate that have direct planning implications.

Design in response to the elements. Protect from the wind. Invite the breeze. Accommodate the rain or snow. Avoid the flood. Brace for the storm. Trace and respond to the arcing sun.

Consider the human factors. On- and off-site structures, trafficways, utility installations, easements, and even such givens as social characteristics, political jurisdictions, zoning, covenants, restrictions, and regulations may have a telling influence.

Eliminate the negatives. Insofar as possible, all undesirable features are to be removed or their impacts abated. The undesirables include pollution in its many aspects, hazards, and visual detractions. When they cannot be eliminated, they are mitigated by ground forms, vegetation, distance, or visual screening.

Accentuate the best features. Fit the paths of movement, use areas, and structures around and between the landscape superlatives. Protect them, face toward them, focus upon them, enframe them, and enjoy them in all conditions of light and in all seasons.

Let the native character set the theme. Every landscape area has its own mood and character. Presumably, these were among the chief reasons for the site selection. Only if the indigenous quality is not desirable or suited to the project use should it be significantly altered. Otherwise, design in harmony with the theme, devising pleasant modulations, light counterpoint, and resonant overtones.

Integrate. Bring all the elements together in the best possible dynamic relationships. This is the lesson of nature. This is the primary objective of all planning and design.

Whatever the type of dwelling, be it a single-family home, a townhome unit with garden court, or a tower apartment . . . whatever the location, be the site urban or rural, mountain or plain, desert or lakeside . . . the planning approach is the same.

Human Needs and Habitat

What would the ideal garden home be like? As a clue, observation will teach us that at least the following requirements of most home dwellers should be satisfied.

Shelter

The contemporary home, like all before it, is first of all a refuge from the storm. With the advent of sophisticated heating devices, climate controls, diversified construction materials, and ingenious structural systems, the concept of shelter had been brought to a new high level of refinement. But architecturally this basic function of shelter is to be served and given clear expression.

Primitive. Shelter is main consideration.

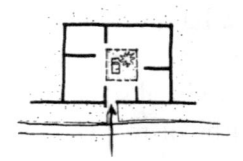

Greco-Roman. Protection and privacy are of prime value.

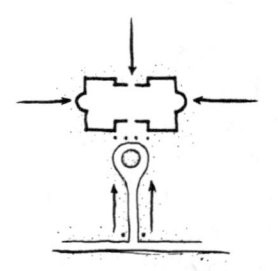

Renaissance. Each structure is an idealized object in space.

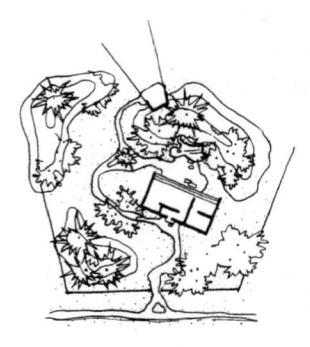

Oriental. Nature is revered, privacy is demanded; structures are related to lot and total landscape.

Evolution of a way of life.

Protection

This implies safety from all forms of danger, not only from the elements but from fire, flood, and intruders as well. Although the nature of potential threats has changed through the centuries, our instincts have not. Safety must be implicit.

Today, an ever-present hazard is that of the moving vehicle with its backings and turnings. It does not belong within our living areas and should not be admitted. The automobile should be stabled within its own service area or compound.

Utility

Each dwelling should be a lucid statement of the various purposes to be served. Not only is each use to be accommodated, it is to be conveniently related to all others. And what are these uses? They are those of food preparation, dining, entertaining, sleeping, and (perhaps) child rearing. These uses are supplemented by the library, correspondence corner, workshop, laundry . . . and supported by storage spaces, mechanical equipment, and waste disposal systems. Often, much of the home entertainment and relaxation takes place on the balcony, lawn, or terrace. The outdoor spaces also provide healthful exercise and satisfy our agricultural yearnings. Even the pot of chives or the parsley bed has its important symbolic meaning.

Utility connotes "a place for everything, and everything in its place," all working well together. While a home is far more than a machine for living, it must function efficiently.

Amenity

It is not enough that a dwelling works well. It must also be attractive and pleasant. It must satisfy the human bent for display and our love of beautiful objects. Beauty is not, however, to be confused with decoration, ornamentation, or the elaborate. True beauty is most often discerned in that which is utterly simple and unpretentious—a well-formed clay pot, a simple carpet of blended wools, handsomely fitted and finished wood, cut slate, handcrafted silver—always just the right form, material, and finish to serve the specific purpose, always the understatement, for less is truly more.

In considering dwellings and display, mention should be made of the *tokonoma* of the traditional Japanese home. Constructed of natural materials of elegant simplicity, the tokonoma is a place reserved for the sharing of beautiful objects. These objets d'art are selected from storage cabinets or gathered from the garden or site and brought out, a few at most at one time, to mark the season or a special occasion. They may include hangings, paintings, a bowl, sculpture, or a vase or tray to receive

Buildings as part of the landscape.

a floral arrangement. Our Western homes and gardens and their displays could well be distinguished by such artistry and restraint.

Privacy

In a world of hustle and hassle, we all need, sometimes desperately, a place of quiet retreat. It need not be large—a space in the home or garden set apart from normal activities where one can share the enjoyment of reading, music, or conversation or turn for quiet introspection. It is very human to feel the need for one's own private space.

A Sense of Spaciousness

Just as we feel the need to retreat, we feel also upon occasion the need for expansive freedom. With dwelling and neighborhoods becoming more and more constricted, such spaciousness inside property limits is almost a rarity. But we can learn from those cultures in which people have lived for centuries in forced compression that space can be "borrowed."

Living spaces may be so arranged and interrelated that common areas may be shared to make each component space seem larger. Apparent spatial size may be increased also by the subtle use of forced perspective and by miniaturization. Again, by the studied arrangement of walls and openings, views can be designed to include attractive features of the site or neighboring properties or extended to the distant hill or horizon. Even

Spring rides no horses
    Down the hill
But comes on foot
    A goosegirl still
And all the loveliest
    Things there be
Come simply,
    So, it seems to me.
Edna St. Vincent Millay

The spirit of a garden is its power to charm the heart.
Kanto Shigemori

Structures

The earth is our home and the ways of nature our paths to understanding.

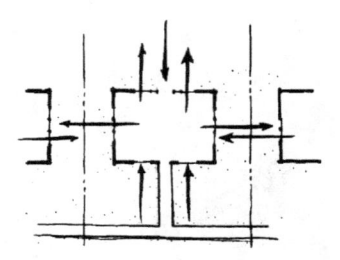

Present American showcase (vestigial renaissance). Nature ignored. Outward orientation. Privacy is lost. Little use of property. A product of side-yard, setback, and no-fence restrictions.

Future American-trend home. Total use of site as living space. Privacy regained. Indoor-outdoor integration. Natural elements introduced. Compact home-garden units grouped amid open park and recreation areas which preserve natural-landscape features.

The most obvious place to put the house is not always the right one. If there is only a small area of land, you'll be tempted to use it for the house. It probably should be saved for arrival, parking or garden. . . .

Is there one particular spot on the property that seems just right in every way? Have you picnicked there and found it idyllic? Have you spent long winter evenings planning a house there? Has it occurred to you that if you build your house there the spot will be gone? Maybe that's where the garden should be.
Thomas D. Church

within the walled garden or court the ultimate spaciousness can be experienced by the featured viewing of the sky and clouds and the evening constellations. It is no happenstance that in crowded Japan a favorite spot on the garden terrace is that reserved for the viewing of the moon.

Nature Appreciation

Deeply ingrained in all of us is an instinctive feeling for the outdoors—for soil, stone, water, and the living things of the earth. We need to be near them, to observe and to touch them. We need to maintain a close relationship with nature, to dwell amid natural features and surroundings, and to bring nature into our homes and into our lives.

A distinguishing mark of the recent American dwelling is the trend toward indoor-outdoor living. Most interior use areas now have their outdoor extensions—entryway to entrance court, kitchen to service area, dining space to patio, living space to terrace, bedroom to spa, game room to recreation court, and sunroom to garden. In the well-planned habitation, especially in milder climes, it is often difficult to differentiate between indoors and out.

It has been theorized that, ideally, each home and garden should be conceived as the universe in microcosm. If this idea seems abstruse, let it pass. Perhaps in time, upon further reflection, you may find it to have deep meaning.

Residential Components
Existing Site Features

Often a residential site is selected because of some outstanding attribute. It may be a venerable oak or an aspen grove. It may be a spring, a pond, or a ledge of rock. It may be an outstanding view. All too often those things most admired when the site was acquired are ignored or lost in construction. It only makes sense that such distinctive features be preserved and dramatized in the homestead planning.

Area Allocation

By custom in the United States, and almost uniquely among worldwide homesteads, the area fronting on the passing street has usurped a large part of each residential property for the sole purpose of home display. Traditionally, the foreground of open lawn has been bordered by shrubs, the house garnished with foundation planting for public approbation. Side yards, too, have been treated mostly as unused separation space—leaving only the backyard for family use and enjoyment. It is only recently that the unified house-garden concept has gained popularity and that indoor-outdoor living has come into its own.

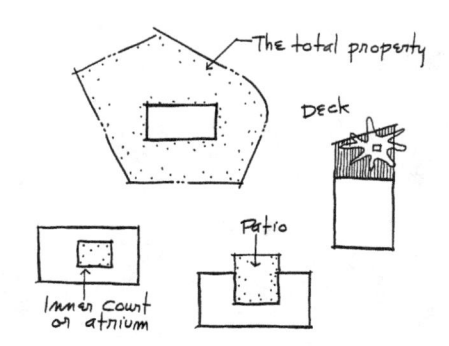

RESIDENTIAL OUTDOOR OPEN SPACE (some possibilities).

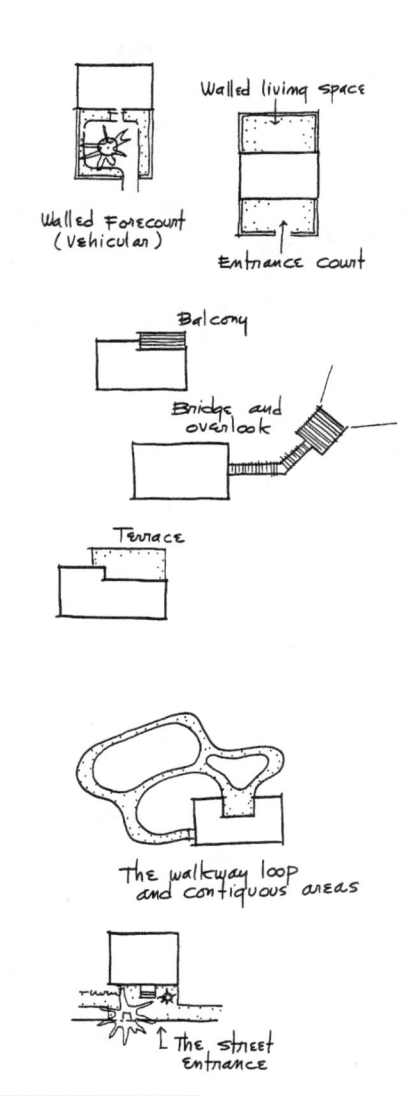

Outdoor living areas are designed to:
- Provide useful and pleasant spaces for all activities
- Integrate with and complement the architecture
- Fit into the site in such a way as to preserve and reveal its best features

Some costly sweeps of irrigated and manicured lawn will long be with us, as will many dollhouse and castle homes designed primarily for display. Increasingly, however, the greenswards are being reduced in size, homes opened up to patios, courtyards, and open recreation space. Most of the natural ground forms and vegetation are being preserved, and family life more outwardly oriented.

The Dwelling

The residence is the centerpiece of the homestead—within which and around which everything happens. What happens depends upon the type of residence selected and the kinds of home life planned for. If there is truth to the saying that in time dog owners come to resemble their canine pets, then it can likewise be observed that much of what homeowners are and do can be judged by their choice of dwellings.

The dwelling itself is a structural framework for living the good, full life. In some cases, the good life may be confined to the walled enclosure of a residence standing proud, aloof, and self-contained. Other homes may open outward, serving as a multifaceted viewing box and staging base for a host of outdoor activities.

Be it an urban apartment, suburban residence, a farm homestead, or wilderness retreat—each has its limitations and possibilities in terms of indoor-outdoor relationships.

In the city high-rise, the outdoor experience may be provided by no more than a sunny window ledge with potted plants or a balcony with seating, a view, and perhaps a hanging basket or two. With good fortune there might even be a private or shared roof garden. An on-grade town house may have its doorstep planting and a rear courtyard with expanded opportunities—as for dining space under a tree or arbor, a pool, a fountain, or patch of herbs or flowers. The suburban home or farmstead, with more area, can open out to a wider array of outdoor living and working spaces. So, too, with the remote cabin or cottage whose owners may choose to leave the natural woodland surrounds unchanged.

Outdoor Activity Spaces

Every outdoor activity needs its measure of usable space. This space may be as small as that required for a child's sandbox or kitchen herb garden—or as large as for a tennis court, swimming pool, vegetable garden, orchard, or even a putting green. No matter what the anticipated uses, if they are to be realized and enjoyed they must be designed into the plans.

The patio or terrace, embraced by the dwelling, extends its interior spaces and relates them to all outdoors. The area between home and

Structures 347

Outdoor activity areas can be:
- Depressed
- Raised
- Filled
- Excavated
- Terraced
- Decked
- Cantilevered
- Built over water on piling
- On floated

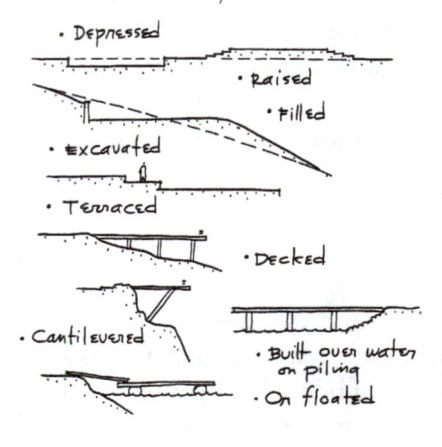

Decks may be stepped.

Extend the structure.

Built around trees.
Secure anchor
Beam
Telephone poles
Fitted to a steep slope

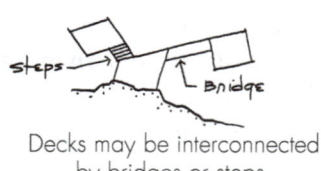

Steps
Bridge
Deck

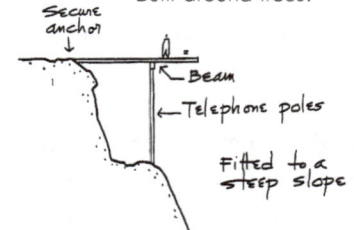

Decks may be interconnected by bridges or steps.

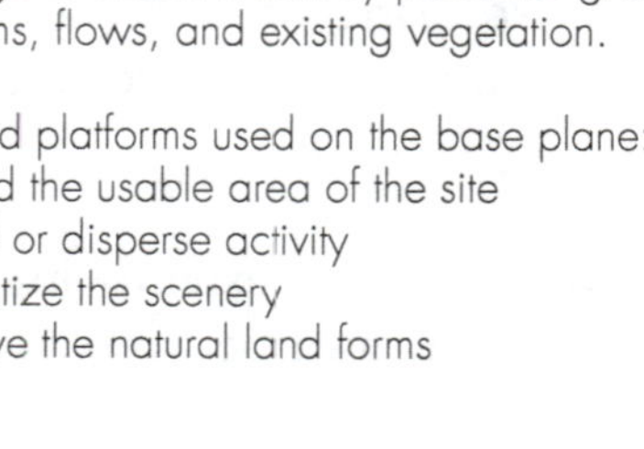

The bridge or raised walkway preserves ground forms, flows, and existing vegetation.

Decks and platforms used on the base plane:
- Expand the usable area of the site
- Extend or disperse activity
- Dramatize the scenery
- Preserve the natural land forms

Outdoor activity space.

garage, open or enclosed, may serve as an entrance court or outdoor living room—with paving and planting and perhaps a wall fountain or other water feature.

Bordering the patio or terrace may be the game court or lawn, cultivated garden, or natural vegetation. The cultivated garden may be no more than a scattering of selected shrubs, clumps of iris, a swath of crocus and narcissus, a bed of lilies, or patch of native grasses. It may consist of a specimen evergreen or a flowering crab apple in a planter with an edging of myrtle or ivy. It could be no more than a square of tulips within an area of paving or a raised bed of peonies surrounded by gravel mulch. A tubbed fig tree. A cactus garden. Or an extensive outlay of well-tended borders and beds.

A single pot of geraniums on the table is a garden in itself, as is a poolside grouping of containers spilling over with blossoms. Some of the most beautiful garden spaces remembered could be encompassed by the outreach of one's arms.

The service area—open, walled, or partially screened—is most often associated with the garage and parking court. Here space is to be provided for deliveries, car storage, and turnabout. Here too will be provision for the temporary storage of refuse and recyclable materials waiting for collection and for the compost station.

348 LANDSCAPE ARCHITECTURE

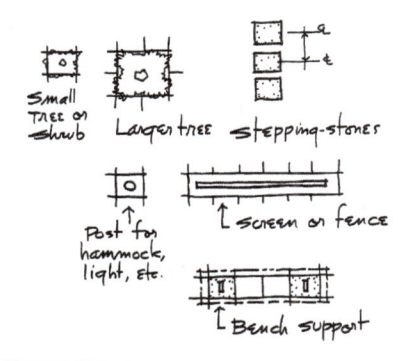

The deletion of one or more modular units provides space for post and bench settings, pools, plant bins, plants, etc.

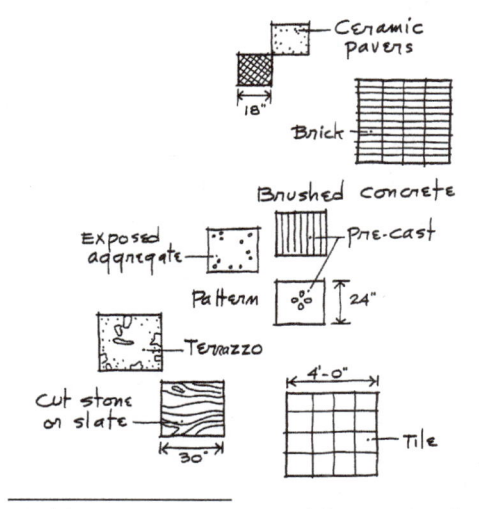

Modular paving units vary widely in size and type.

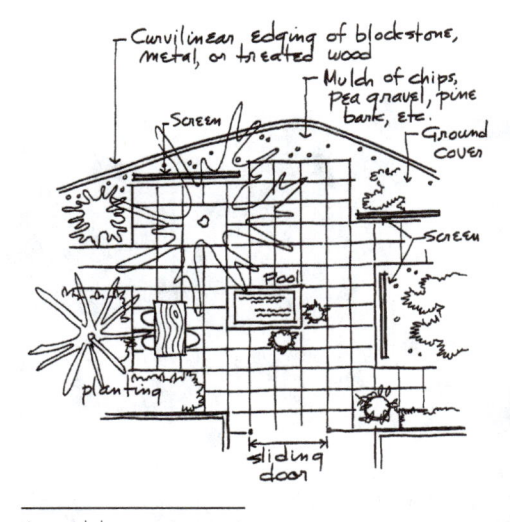

A modular paving system
- Is flexible
- Helps achieve design unity
- Reduces installation and replacement costs

MODULAR PAVING

As an adjunct there may be an offset storage shed for equipment and supplies. It may serve as well to house the meters and valves of utility systems and to hang the hose reels.

The service court border is a convenient location for the kitchen garden and for the entryway to a possible greenhouse, potting shed, or vegetable garden. Here, if there are screen walls, arbor, or fencing, is an opportune place for the growing of flowering vines or grapes or such espaliered fruits as oranges, lemons, pears, figs, peaches, or apples.

Service courts often double as a paved recreation area, with net-post sockets, line markings, and perhaps a basketball backstop. At one side there may be a gated entry to the children's play space, with swings and play equipment—overseen, if possible, from the adjacent kitchen windows.

Supplementary Structures

As noted, many site-related spaces can be planned into the dwelling or attached thereto by extension. Again, a garage, guesthouse, or studio may be detached and designed as an architectural counterpoint. So, too, with the smaller workshop or toolshed. Supplementary structures may be intentionally varied in character—more related to the site than to the domicile, and suited particularly to the intended use. Such might be

Supplementary structures.

Structures 349

poolside dressing rooms or an overlook shelter. Sometimes, living quarters are incorporated in a recreation structure such as a weekend ski lodge or a boathouse with its related slips and dock.

Furnishings

No homestead is complete without its outdoor equipment and furnishings. A well-organized storage wall or shed complete with maintenance machinery and tools is a must.

Recreation supplies and equipment—the nets, paddles, and racquets; the quoits, stakes, and hammock; the archery target and chest of toys—are all to have their ordered place. Then too there will usually be benches, chairs, tables, and other such outdoor equipage. Paving, ground covers, and planting—which may or may not be considered furnishings—are treated in other chapters of this book.

Besides the basics, there may be as well such decorative accouterment as planters, window boxes, and a variety of wooden or ceramic containers. Mosaic murals or panels add interest and color, as do canopies and awnings. Sculpture is always an attribute, as are flags and seasonal decorations for the holidays. Then there are such animating features as windbells, birdbaths, and feeders.

Not to be overlooked are the enhancements of water and lighting. Water in some form—brimming basin, rivulet, trickle, spray, or splash—has a place in every garden. Lighting, too. A post light to mark the walk entrance, trace lighting along the drive and paths, floodlighting of the game court, uplighting of trees, and the highlighting of sculpture, mural, floral display, or moving water—all add much of pleasure and sparkle to the evening.

Site furnishings can be built in like this seat wall or freestanding.

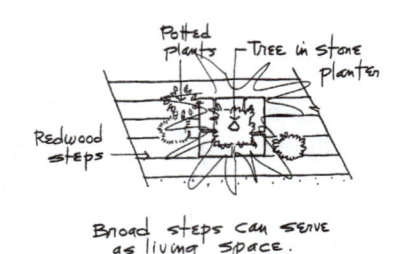

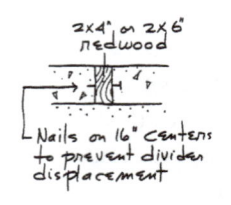

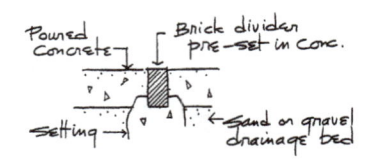

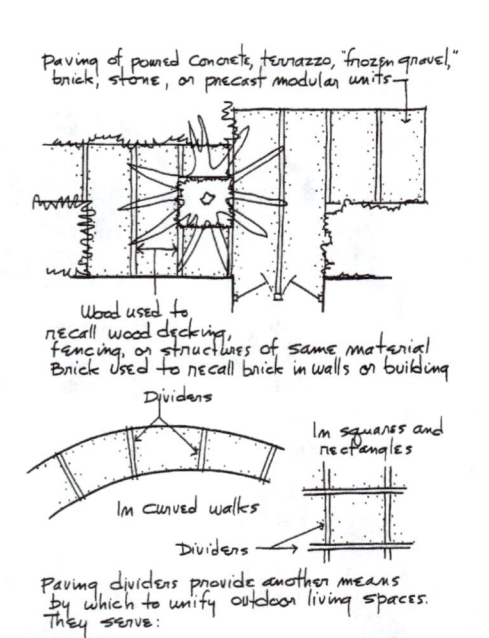

350 LANDSCAPE ARCHITECTURE

Effective lighting of water feature.

Water, actual or implied, has a place in every garden.

The cost of exterior furnishings is but a fraction of the overall domicile outlay. Often these outdoor fittings are the things most seen and used and thus most experienced. This is reason enough to acquire and enjoy the best. In large measure, the quality of the homestead is gauged by the quality of the furnishings.

Variations on a Theme

When in our planning we ignore the natural processes or violate the land, we must live with the distressing consequences. When, however, we truly design our structures and living spaces in response to the forces, forms, and features of the host landscape, the lives of the occupants will be infused with a sense of well-being and pleasure.

The accompanying photographic examples have been selected to illustrate the means by which homes and gardens may be planned together, in harmony with their site and landscape environs—and responsive to the needs and desires of the users.

Structures 351

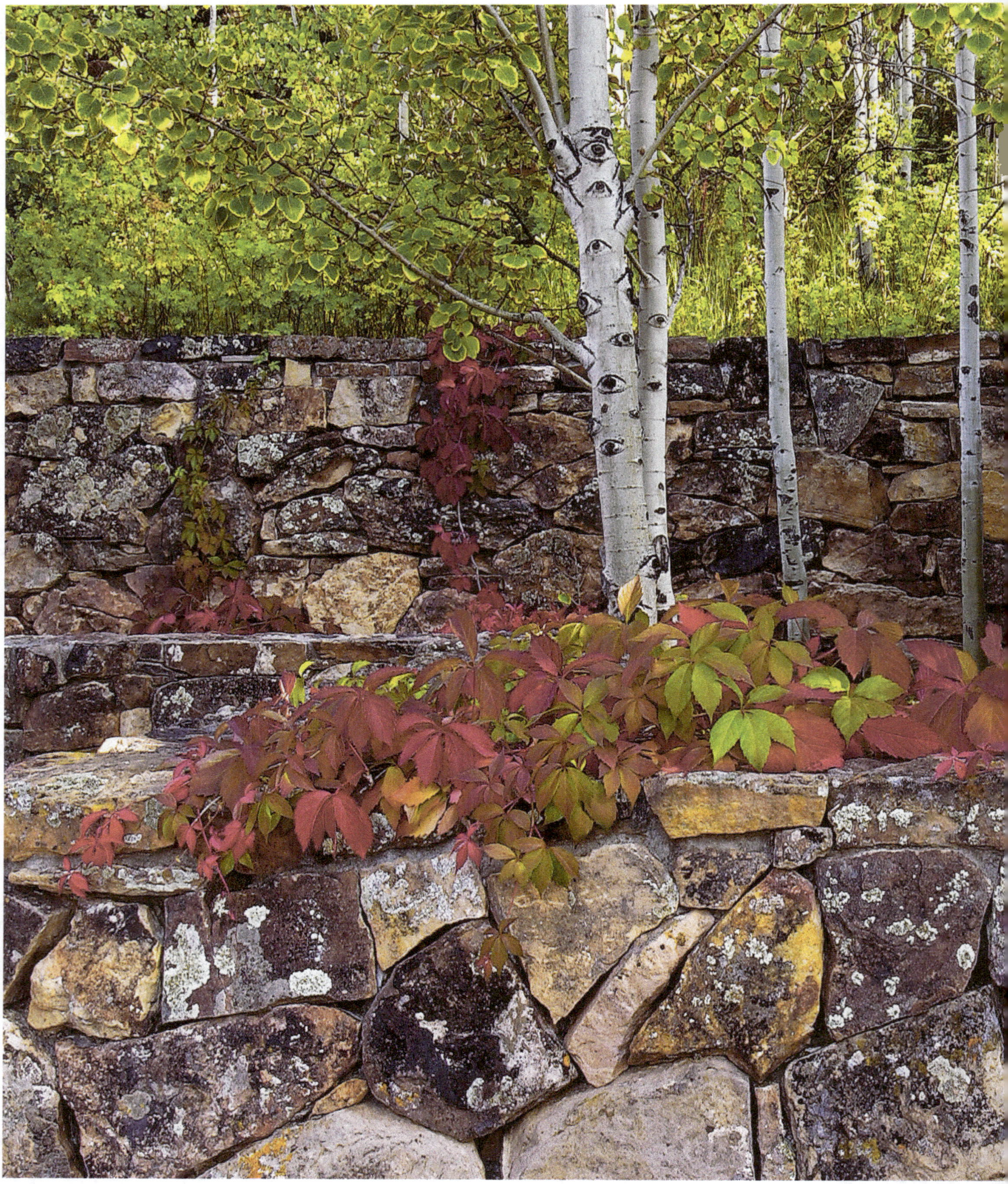

15
LANDSCAPE PLANTING

When the settlers beached their rough landing boats on our eastern shores, they brought with them the carefully tended seeds, roots, and cuttings of our first gardens. Our gardens now stretch from sea to sea. For most Americans, the love of plants and gardening is inherent.

Those of us whose work it is to help plan our living environment can learn from this. It is our hope that this feeling for plants and their care may extend to the care of all vegetation and the waters and soil which support it; that the best of our wilderness and wild rivers may yet be preserved; that our vulnerable watersheds may be reforested and protected; that essential marshes may be restored and reflooded; that our remaining dunes may be replanted to bearberry and juniper, to fox grape and pine, or reseeded to their cover of sea oats; that our clustered communities can be planned within and around an all-embracing open-space framework of farmland and forest; and that our homes and schools may be planned as gardens and our cities as garden parks.

Purpose

Many involved in land planning think of plants as no more than horticultural adjuncts to be arranged around construction projects which are otherwise complete. Nothing could be further from the truth. Vegetation and existing ground cover are in fact one of the primary considerations in the selection and planning of most properties. To a large extent they establish

© D. A. Horchner/Design Workshop

the site character. They hold the soils, modify the climate, provide windbreak and screen, and often define the conformation of use areas.

Plants in the landscape are either those existing in their natural habitat or those which have been introduced. Since established plants by the very fact of their existence have proved themselves to be suited to the site, it would seem logical to preserve them, at least until the need for their removal has been thoughtfully determined. Persons who have had occasion to replace vegetation, often carelessly destroyed, know the problems and costs involved.

When, however, new plantings are prescribed, they are to be given careful consideration, for a single inappropriate plant can alter or destroy the visual quality of a landscape or disrupt its ecological balance.

Conversely, well-conceived plantings can do much to transform an otherwise dull and barren site into a more useful, comfortable, and pleasant place to be.

Process

Each and every plant installed should serve a predetermined purpose. It is to be selected as the best of the available alternatives to suit the specific growing conditions and the precise design requirements, for planting design of excellence is a blending of science and art.

Base Map

For overall landscape planting, as for a residential site, school ground, or hospital, a base plan at the scale of 1 inch to 10 feet, 20 feet, or 30 feet is recommended, with 1 inch to 40 feet as a maximum. For detailed or limited areas, as for a flower bed or kitchen garden, a scale of 1 inch to 1 or 2 feet may be more workable. The plan should bear the owner's name and address, graphic scale, date, and a fairly accurate north point. It should also show building outlines, fenestrations, and any such topographical features as walls, fences, lampposts, driveways, walks, or other paved areas, and existing plants to remain.

Plant Selection

With a print of the base map in hand, one is ready for plant listing and allocation. As a start, it is suggested that the first plan be a rough study, with notes, diagrams, and a tentative listing of plant types desired. Even in this first trial listing one should have in mind the characteristics of each plant considered—its shape, height, spread, foliage, color and texture, season of bloom and fruiting, and so forth. Essential, too, is a general knowledge of its cultural requirements, including its hardiness, preferred soil type, acidity range, and moisture content; its tolerance for sun, shade, and exposure; or its need for protection.

Slope and watershed protection.

Windscreen.

Overhead space definition and canopy.

Enframement.

Backdrop.

Some gardeners have an intuitive feel for such things, but for most the green thumb comes only with years of hands-on experience.

In plant selection, guidebooks and catalogs are useful, but there is no substitute for visits to a nursery or sales lot. A drive round the neighborhood is helpful, too, for it shows what does well and looks best in various locations. Fortunate are those who have gardening friends to whom they may turn for counsel.

Installation

With or without a planting concept in mind, if the initial installation is to be sizable it is usually wise to call upon the services of an experienced professional gardener or landscape architect for a detailed layout. There are then several courses of action. The owner may do the planting at his or her leisure, or it may be installed in one or more phases by a gardener or selected landscape contractor. If the installation is to be let out to bid, as in sizable operations, a complete set of plans, details, specifications, and bidding documents will be needed.

Guidelines

In preparing the planting layout for garden, campus, industrial park, or new community, the approach is much the same. The aim is to enhance in all ways possible the routes of movement and the usable areas of the site. The following time-tested principles are offered as a guide.

Preserve the existing vegetation. Streets, buildings, and areas of use are to be fitted amid the natural growth insofar as practicable. The landscape continuity and scenic quality will thus be assured; the cost of site instal-

Shade.

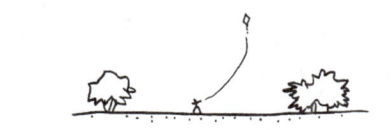

Ground space definition.

Plan reinforcement.

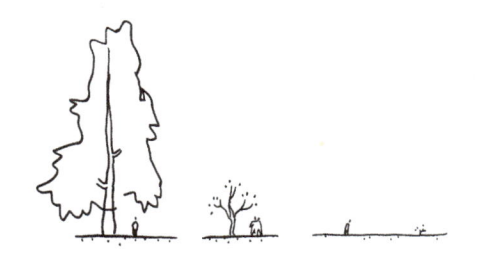

Scale induction.

Ornamentation.

Preserving natural vegetation.

Landscape Planting 355

CANOPY TREES

These include the taller, shade and forest species that, alone or together, form a high foliage crown.

Use indigenous canopy trees to:
- Filter the sun
- Soften architectural lines
- Set the landscape theme
- Unify the area
- Provide the spatial ceiling

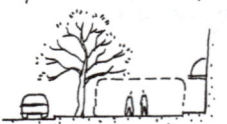

Trees help establish pedestrian scale.

INTERMEDIATE TREES

Lower deciduous and coniferous species with foliage extending from near the ground plane to at least eye height.

Install intermediate trees in the open or understory for screening, backdrop, and visual interest.

A sparse grove of well-placed trees can unify and give refreshing relief to a building group or compound.

Trees can define a space or frame a view.

lation and maintenance will be reduced; and the structures, paved surfaces, and lawns will be richer by contrast.

Select each plant to serve its intended function. Experienced designers first prepare a rough conceptual planting diagram to aid in making detailed plant selections. The diagram is usually in the form of an overlay to the site construction drawings. On it are sketched out, area by area, the outlines, arrows, and notes to describe what the planting is to achieve, as for example:

Light shade here.
Screen unsightly billboard.
Cast tree silhouette on wall.
Reinforce curve of approach drive.
Use ground cover and spring bulbs in foreground.
Plant specimen magnolia against evergreens.
Enframe valley view.
Shield terrace from glare of athletic field lights.
Provide enclosure and windscreen for game court.

The more complete the conceptual diagram and notes, the easier the plant selection, and the better the final results.

Trees are the basics. If tree selection and placement are sound, the site framework is well established. Often, little additional planting will be needed.

Group trees to simulate natural stands. As a rule, regular spacing or geometric patterns are to be avoided. Trees in rows or grids are best reserved for limited urban situations where a civic or monumental character is desired.

Use canopy trees to unify the site. They are the most visible. They provide the dominant neighborhood character and identity. They provide sun filter and shade and soften architectural lines. They provide the spatial roof or ceiling.

Install intermediate trees for understory screening, windbreak, and visual interest. They are the enframers, particularly suited to the subdivision of a larger site into smaller use areas and spaces. As a category they include many of the better accent plants and ornamentals and may be used as individual specimens.

Utilize shrubs for supplementary low-level baffles and screens. They serve as well to provide enclosure, to reinforce pathway alignments and nodes, to accentuate points and features of plan importance, and to furnish floral and foliage display. They can also be used (sparingly) for hedges.

Treat vines as nets and draperies. Various types can be planted to stabilize slopes and dunes, to cool exposed walls, or to provide a cascade of foliage and blossoms over walls and fences.

Install ground covers on the base plane to retain soils and soil moisture, define paths and use areas, and provide turf where required. They are the carpets of the ground plane.

In all extensive tree plantings, select a theme tree, from three to five supporting secondary trees, and a limited palette of supplementary species for special conditions and effects. This procedure helps to assure a planting of simplicity and strength.

Choose as the dominant theme tree a type that is indigenous, moderately fast-growing, and able to thrive with little care. These are planted in groups, swaths, and groves to provide the grand arboreal framework and overall site organization.

Use secondary species to complement the primary planting installation and to define the site spaces of lesser magnitude. Each secondary tree type will be chosen to harmonize with the theme tree and natural landscape character, while imbuing each space with its own special qualities.

Landscape Planting 357

SHRUBS

Shrubs are woody perennial plants, usually smaller than a tree, with multiple stems branching from on near the ground.

Utilize shrubs for supplementary low-level screening and for their interest of form, foliage, flowers, and fruit. They may also be used as natural and (sparingly) as trimmed hedges.

Plants and grasses may be augmented with mulches such as shredded bark, wood chips, or gravel.

VINES AND GROUND COVERS

Plants vary from woody to herbaceous, from deciduous to evergreen, from succulents to grasses.

Select those ground covers which will provide superior:
- Erosion control
- Soil moisture retention
- Naturalized foregrounds
- Lawns and playing surfaces
- Maintenance reduction

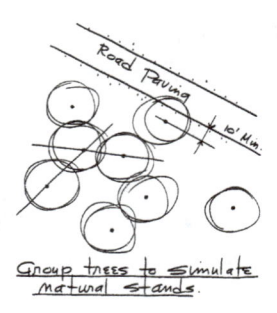

Avoid regular spacing—or the placement of more than two trees in a line. Distances depend upon tree types and whether free-standing specimen or an inter-laced canopy is desired.

NEW PLANTING INSTALLATIONS

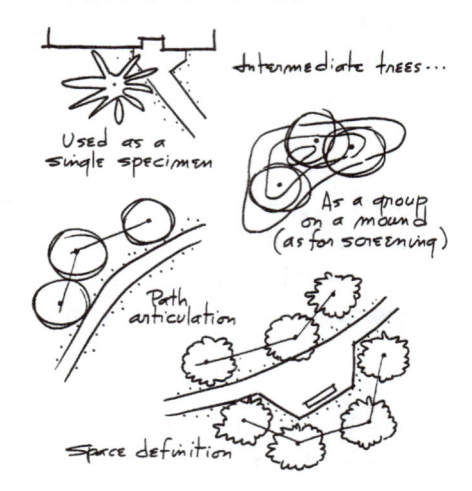

Intermediate trees (and shrubs) are the place, plane, and alignment definers. Use them to reinforce the lines and forms of the plan.

Trees provide shade and interest along walks and bikeways.

Install screen plantings adjacent to trafficways to reduce noise and glare.

Supplementary tree species are used as appropriate to demarcate or differentiate areas of unique landscape quality. The uniqueness may be that of topography, as ridge, hollow, upland, or marsh. It may be that of use, as a local street or court, a quiet garden space, or a bustling urban shopping mall. It may be that of special need, as dense windscreen, light shade, or seasonal color.

Exotic species are to be limited to areas of high refinement. They are best used only in those situations in which they may receive intensive care and will not detract from the natural scene.

Use trees to sheathe the trafficways. An effective design approach is to plant the arterial roads or circulation drives with random groupings of trees selected from the secondary list. Local streets, loop drives, and cul-de-sacs are transitioned in, but each is given its own particular character with supplementary trees (and other plants) best suited to the use, the topography, and the architecture.

Give emphasis to trafficway nodes. The intersections of circulation routes are often given added prominence by the use of modulated ground forms,

Background.

Shadow.

Silhouette.

Foreground.

358   LANDSCAPE ARCHITECTURE

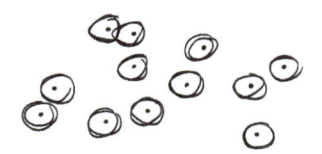

The random spacing of trees is suited to the naturalized landscape—as for park and recreation areas and reforestation. Often a blend of indigenous, nursery, and permanent species produces the best stand.

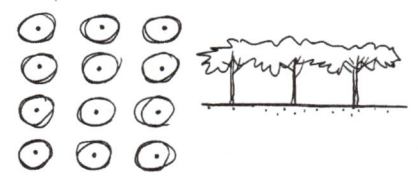

The geometric spacing of canopy trees creates spacious architectural rooms. This is more appropriate in level, geometric courtyards of civic-monumental character.

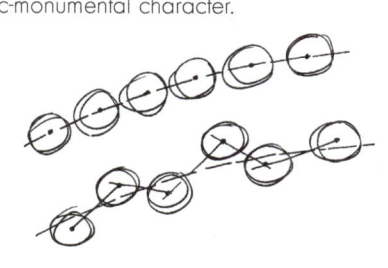

Trees in a single or double row have strong visual impact. This arrangement is therefore best reserved for the urban or built environment.

In the more natural landscape an offset, irregular tree line is usually preferred.

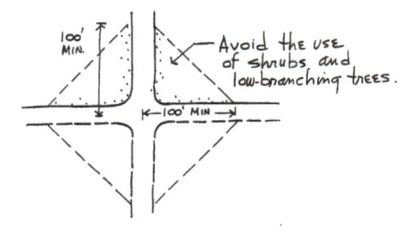

Keep the sight lines clear at trafficway intersections.

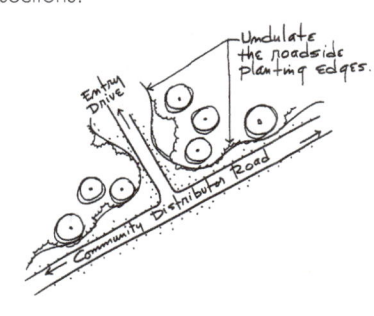

Create a harbor-like entrance portal to each neighborhood.

Texture.

Form.

Color.

Line.

walls, fences, signing, increased levels of lighting, and supplementary planting.

Keep the sight lines clear at roadway intersections. Avoid the use of shrubs and low-branching trees within the sighting zones.

Create an attractive roadway portal to each neighborhood and activity center. The entrance planting should be arranged to provide a welcoming harbor quality.

Arrange the tree groupings to provide views and expansive open spaces. Plants are well used as enframers rather than fillers.

Close or compress the plantings where the ground forms or structures impinge. This sequential opening and closing and increasing or decreasing the height, density, and width of the planting along any route of movement give added richness and power to the landscape.

Expand the roadside plantings. Where space is limited, the initial landscape plantings and often site construction may occur outside the right-of-way. A landscape or planting easement may be required.

Landscape Planting 359

Plants combined with mounding can hide parking and service areas.

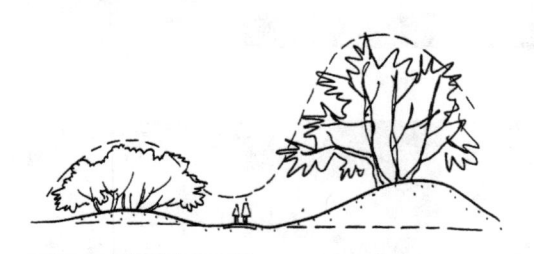

Combine planting with earth shaping to create landscape interest.

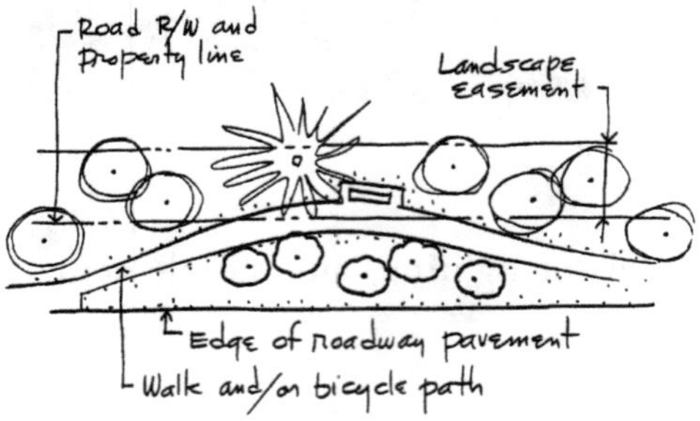

Landscape construction and planting can occur outside of the street right-of-way (R/W) where space is limited and a "Landscape Easement" provided.

FORM AND SPACE MODULATION

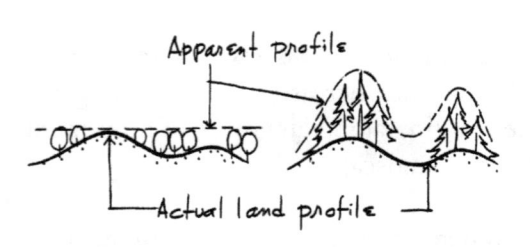

Plants are well used to accentuate land forms and intensify landscape power.

Use plantings to reinforce the alignment of paths and roadways. They can help to explain the plan layout and give clear direction.

Provide shade and interest along the paths and bikeways. If made attractive, they will be used.

Conceal parking, storage, and other service areas. Trees, hedges, or looser shrubs may be used alone or in combination with mounding, walls, or fencing to provide visual control.

Consider climate control in all landscape planting. Plants can be used to block winter winds, channel the breeze, temper the heat of the sun, and otherwise improve the microclimate.

Complement the topographical forms. By skillful planting, the visual impact of the landscape can be greatly enhanced.

Use plants as space definers. They are admirably suited to enclose, subdivide, and otherwise articulate the various functional spaces of the site

EXAMPLE BY REGION

	Northern Michigan	West Coast Bay Area	Central Arizona	Southwest Florida
	Resort	University	Urban Park	Community
Theme Tree	White Pine	Cal. Live Oak Eucalyptus	Washingtonia Palm	Live Oak Slash Pine
Secondary	Ash Basswood Am. Beech Sugar Maple Aspen	Olive Monterey Pine White Alder Pistache	Canary Pine Arizona Ash Stone Pine Cypress	Tree Wax Myrtle Cabbage Palm Mahogany
Supplementary	Shadblow White Birch Hemlock Am. Cedar Striped Maple Pin Cherry	Fl. Cherry Hawthorn Vine Maple Ironwood Plum	Fruitless Mulberry Sour Orange Evergreen Pear Crape Myrtle	Black Olive Weeping Fig Royal Poinciana Mangrove Silver Buttonwood

A similar listing is made for shrubs, vines, and ground covers. Together they should constitute a compatible family of plants expressive of the site character desired.

LANDSCAPE ARCHITECTURE

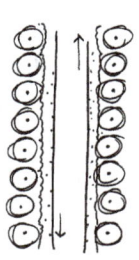

Avoid monotonous edges in roadside and other plantings.

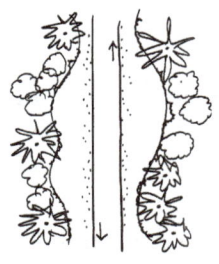

Undulation in both the horizontal alignment and vertical profile add landscape appeal.

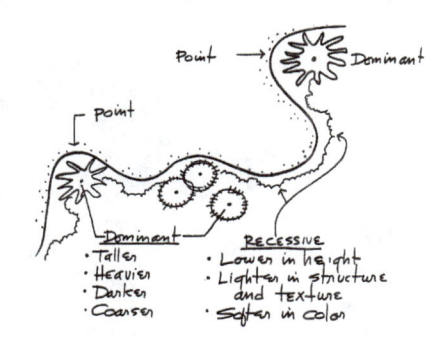

In mass plantings emphasize the points with dominant plants and make the bay recede.

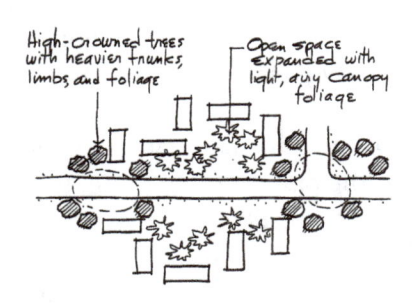

Strengthen the building closures and trafficway modes with trees of more structural character.

Plants soften the ground plane.

Trees create outdoor rooms.

and the passageways that connect them. They convert use areas into use spaces. By their associative nature and their color, texture, and form, they can endow each space with qualities appropriate to the use or uses intended.

Plants used for backdrop, screening, shade, or space definition are generally selected for strength, cleanliness of form, richness of texture, and subtlety of color. Plants to be featured are selected for their sculptural qualities and for ornamental twigging, budding, foliage, flowers, and fruit.

Stress quality, not quantity. One well-selected, well-placed plant can be more effective than 100 plants scattered about at random.

Advances

Within the past few years landscape planting at all levels has undergone a remarkable change. This is a direct reflection of several cultural transitions such as:

- A general change in the American lifestyle from the ostentatious to the casual, from the formal to the informal

Landscape Planting

- Two working-parent families with little spare time for gardening
- Smaller homesites and lack of garden space, especially in urban areas
- A drastic reduction in the number of available caretakers, gardeners, and maintenance personnel
- Depletion of freshwater reserves and limitations to irrigation

All of these trends have led to a reduction in the size of lawn and garden areas. One appealing result has been the expanding practice of container gardening. Instead of cultivated garden beds, the trend is now toward planted containers—ceramic pots, either free standing or in window boxes, raised stone bins, planters, or hanging baskets.

The advantages of container plantings are many:

- They require less time, effort, and expense for installation and upkeep.
- Far less irrigation is needed.
- The floral display can be placed at strategic accent points (e.g., patios, entrances, or pathway intersections).
- Many floral or foliage containers can be taken indoors for table or window display and appreciation.

Container plantings.

Once-barren city streets, now tree-lined, have come alive with plants and floral color. There may be fewer plants than in the traditional public gardens, but they are placed where they count.

With less area and time for gardening, the once-familiar vegetable plot in urban areas is now nearly a thing of the past. For one thing, it is hard to surpass or equal the quality of commercially grown vegetables so temptingly displayed in our markets. Also, it is usually hard for the homeowner to find space to plant even a row of lettuce. Containers planted with parsley, thyme, and other herbs are welcome attributes beside the kitchen door.

Xeriscape.

Native, or indigenous, plants are those growing naturally on the site and historically characteristic of the region.

Naturalized plants are those introduced accidentally or by intent that have accommodated themselves to the growing conditions and become part of the local scene.

Exotic plants are those foreign to the natural site and locality.

Our lawn areas are also shrinking. Not only has their maintenance become an extravagance and a chore—the use of our diminishing supply of freshwater for irrigation has come into question. Even when the use of treated wastewater for irrigation has been made mandatory, it is predicted that in time the broad sweeps of lawn (an American phenomenon) will become a rarity.

There are three favored alternatives to the mowed lawn. The first is paving or more construction—which is reasonable only if it serves a good purpose. The second is the so-called Xeriscape treatment—using plants that require little if any irrigation. Such plants, ranging from cacti to a wide selection of tough perennials or ornamental grasses, may be supplemented with mulches of gravel, shells, chips, or bark to create remarkably attractive compositions. A third alternative to the mowed lawn is the preserved natural setting, with or without minor modification. In suburban or rural settings with thriving natural growth this is often much to be preferred. It is relatively maintenance-free, and it is less expensive to establish. It "belongs" to the site and is obviously compatible. It provides refreshing coolness in summer and a welcome windbreak in winter.

In all these ways and more will the landscape plantings of the future differ.

Landscape Plantings in Low-Impact Design
Green Roofs

Although roofs covered partly or completely with living plants, called *green roofs,* have been around for centuries, the concept has been embraced and expanded as part of the conservation and sustainability movement in design and building today. Even though the design and installation of green roofs offer many structural and watertight integrity challenges, the benefits are many. In addition to benefitting the environment by reducing stormwater runoff, mitigating climate change, converting and absorbing carbon dioxide, and many other effects, rooftop

Landscape Planting

vegetation provides insulation, extends the life of the roof, and reduces energy consumption.

Theoretically, almost any landscape planting that can be installed on a conventional site can be part of a green roof installation; however, most green roofs are limited to relatively shallow soil to reduce the overall weight of the roof, and, therefore, the size of the planting materials used is limited.

Green roofs.

Because the world's population is expected to continue to become more and more urbanized, the use of green roofs will no doubt increase as a means of mitigating the environmental effects of higher population density while at the same time allowing for more open space to be preserved.

Bioswales, Bioretention Areas, and Rain Gardens

Since the 1990s, landscape plantings have assumed a much larger role in the practice of stormwater management (SWM). The primary new features in SWM that employ landscape plantings are bioswales, bioretention areas, and rain gardens. All three features are similar in that they use plants to slow the rate of runoff and to filter sediments and pollutants.

Bioswales are used in areas where water is moving across the surface of a site after being collected from, say, a parking lot to a bioretention area or stormwater management pond. The plants in the swale physically slow the flow of the water, which causes sediments to settle out as plant roots absorb pollutants.

Bioretention areas are generally basins that receive and hold runoff. They are designed to hold and slowly release runoff into the groundwater while filtering it in the process. Here, the landscape plantings serve as filters, absorb pollutants, and enhance wildlife habitat.

Rain gardens perform the same function as bioretention areas, but they generally operate on a smaller scale.

Rain garden.

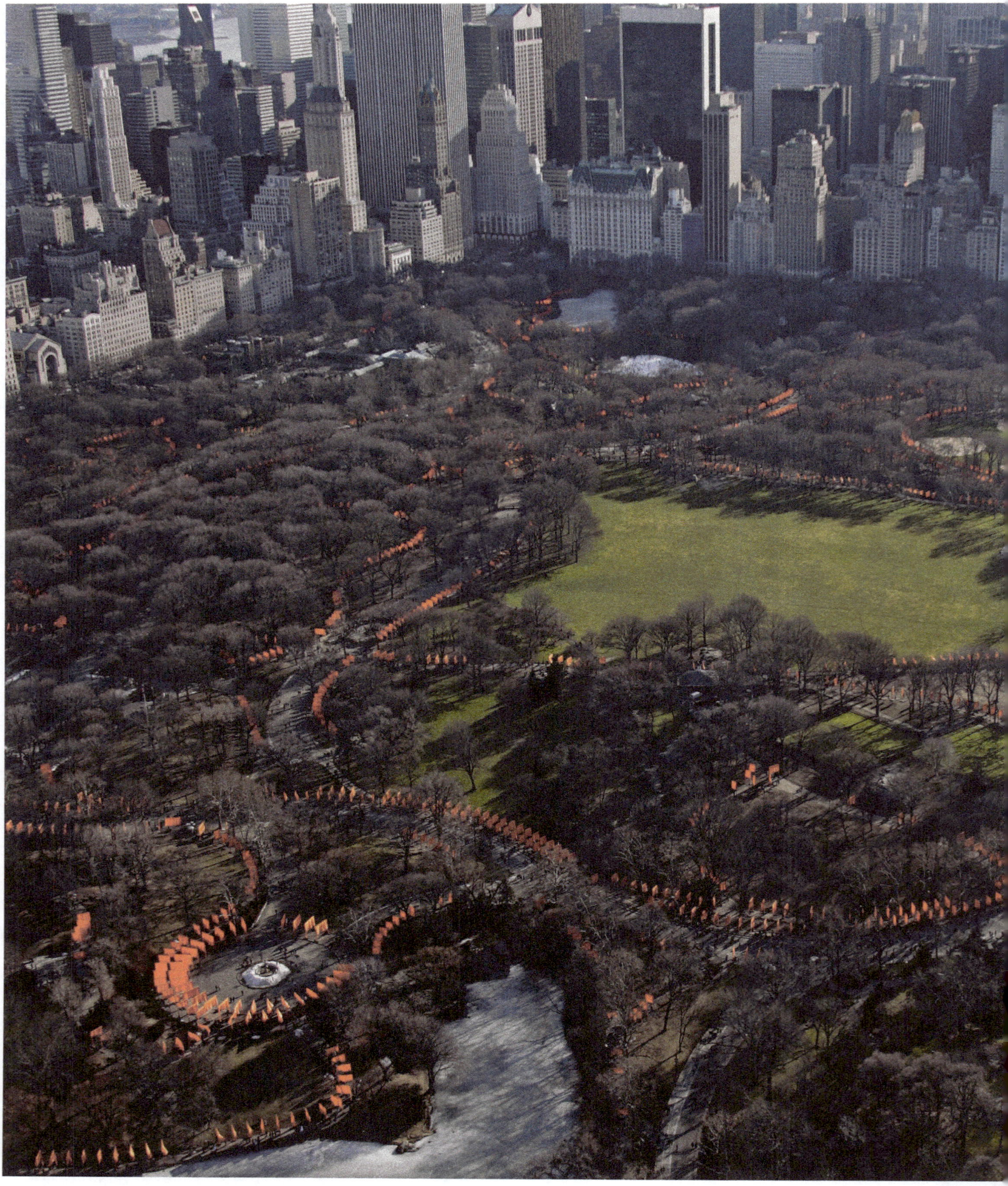

Christo and Jeanne-Claude. The Gates, Central Park, New York City, 1979–2005. Photo: Wolfgang Volz. Copyright Christo and Jeanne-Claude 2005.

PERSPECTIVE

Looking back, I feel fortunate to have been in the Harvard Graduate School of Design during the period 1936–1939, in the tumultuous years of "the rebellion." At the time, I was somewhat puzzled and disappointed at first, for I had come to the school following the bright Beaux Arts star. Its particular brilliance in those times was perhaps like the last blazing of a meteor ending its orbit, for the Beaux Arts system[1] was soon to wane. But blazing or waning, it was gone by the time I arrived there.

Disavowal and Quest

Dean Joseph Hudnut, one of the first of the architectural educators to read the signs, soon brought to the school three prophetic and vital spirits, Gropius and Breuer, late of Germany's Bauhaus, and Martin Wagner, a city planner from Berlin. They came as evangelists, preaching a strong new gospel. To the jaded Beaux Arts student architects, wearied of the hymns in praise of Vignola, beginning to question the very morality of the pilaster applied, and stuffed to their uppers with pagan acanthus leaves, the words of these new professors were both cathartic and tonic. Their vibrant message with its recurring and hypnotic text from Louis Sullivan, "Form follows function," was strangely compelling. We began to see the glimmer of a beckoning light.

---

[1] A system of architectural and design instruction that held almost complete sway over American schools from the beginning of the century to the early 1940s.

A fervor almost religious in quality seemed to sweep the school. As if cleansing the temple of idols, Dean Hudnut ordered the Hall of Casts cleared of every vestige of the once sacred columns and pediment. The egg-and-dart frieze was carted away. The holy Corinthian capital was relegated to the cobwebs and mold of the basement. We half expected some sign of God's wrath. But the wrath did not come, and the enlightenment continued. The stodgy Hall of Casts became an exciting exhibit hall.

As the architects sought a new approach to the design of their structures, the landscape architects sought to escape the rigid plan form of the major and minor axis, which diagram, inherited from the Renaissance, had become the hallmark of all polite landscape planning. Inspired by the example of our architectural colleagues, we assiduously sought a new and parallel approach in the field of landscape design.

Through the resources of Harvard's great library of planning we peered into history. We pored over ancient charts and maps and descriptions. We scanned the classic works of Europe and Asia for guidance. We searched for inspiration in the related fields of painting, sculpture, and even music.

Our motives were good; our direction excellent. But, unknowingly, we had made a fatal error. In searching for a better design approach, we sought only to discover new forms. The immediate result was a weird new variety of plan geometry, a startling collection of novel clichés. We based plan diagrams on the sawtooth and the spiral, on stylized organisms such as the leafstalk, the wheat sheaf, the fern frond, and the overlapping scales of a fish. We sought geometric plan forms in quartz crystals. We adapted "free" plan forms from bacteria cultures magnified to the thousandth power. We sought to borrow and adapt the plan diagrams of ancient Persian courtyards and early Roman forts.

We soon came to realize that new forms in themselves weren't the answer. A form, we decided wisely, is not the essence of the plan; it is rather the shell or body that takes its shape and substance from the plan function. The nautilus shell, for instance, is, in the abstract, a form of great beauty, but its true intrinsic meaning can be comprehended only in terms of the living nautilus. To adapt the lyric lines of this chambered mollusk to a schematic plan parti came to seem to us as false as the recently highly respectable and generally touted practice of adapting the plan diagram of say, the Villa Medici of Florence to a Long Island country club.

We determined that it was not borrowed forms we must seek, but a creative planning philosophy. From such a philosophy, we reasoned, our plan forms would evolve spontaneously. The quest for a new philosophy is no mean quest. It proved as arduous as had been that for new and more meaningful forms. My particular path of endeavor led in a search through history for timeless planning principles. I would sift out the common denominators of all great landscape planning. At last, I felt sure, I was on the right track.

Findings

In retrospect, I believe this particular pilgrimage in search of the landscape architectural holy grail was not without its rewards, for along the way I met such stalwarts as Lenôtre, Humphry Repton, Lao-tzu, Kublai Khan, Pericles, and fiery Queen Hatshepsut. Many of their planning concepts so eagerly rediscovered (some to be set forth in this book) have served, if not as a planning philosophy, at least as a sound and useful guide.

Like good Christians who, in their day-by-day living are confronted with a moral problem and wonder, "What would Christ do if he were here?" I often find myself wondering at some obscure crossroads of planning theory, "What would Repton say to that?" or "Kublai Khan, old master, what would you do with this one?"

But back to our landscape classes and our student revolution. Sure that we had found a better way, we broke with the axis. According to Japanese mythology, when the sacred golden phoenix dies, a young phoenix rises full-blown from its ashes. We had killed the golden phoenix, with some attending ceremony, and confidently expected its young to rise, strong-winged, from the carnage. We had never checked the mythological timing. But we found that, in our own instance, the happening was not immediate.

In lieu of the disavowed symmetry, we turned to asymmetrical diagrams. Our landscape planning in those months became a series of graphic debates. Our professors moved among our drafting tables with wagging heads and stares of incredulity. We had scholarly reasons for each line and form. We battled theory to theory and principle to axiom. But, truth to tell, our projects lacked the sound ring of reality, and we found little satisfaction in the end result of our efforts.

Upon graduation, after seven years' study in landscape architecture and a year of roaming abroad, and with a hard-earned master's degree, I seemed to share the tacit feeling of my fellows that while we had learned the working techniques and terms of our trade, the indefinable essence had somehow escaped us. The scope of our profession seemed sometimes as infinite as the best relating of all mankind to nature, sometimes as finite as the shaping of a brass tube to achieve varying spouting effects of water. We still sought the poles to which our profession was oriented. For somehow it seemed basic that we could best do the specific job only if we understood its relationship to the total work we were attempting. We sought a revealing comprehension of our purpose. In short, what were we, as landscape architects, really trying to do?

Like the old lama of Kipling's Kim, I set out once again to wander in search of fundamentals, this time with a fellow student.[2] Our journey

---

[2] Lester A. Collins, later chairman of Harvard's department of landscape architecture.

took us through Japan, Korea, China, Burma, Bali, and India and up into Tibet. From harbor to palace to pagoda we explored, always attempting to reduce to planning basics the marvelous things we saw.

In the contemplative attitude of Buddhist monks, we would sit for hours absorbed in the qualities of a simple courtyard space and its relationship to a structure. We studied an infinite variety of treatments of water, wood, metal, plant material, sunlight, shadow, and stone. We analyzed the function and plan of gardens, national forests, and parks. We observed people in their movement through spaces, singly, in small groups, and in crowds. We watched them linger, intermingle, scatter, and congregate. We noted and listed the factors that seemed to impel them to movement or affected the line of their course.

We talked with taper-fingered artists, with blunt-thumbed carpenters, with ring-bedecked princes, and with weathered gardeners whose calloused hands bore the stains and wear of working in the soil. We noted with fascination the relationship of sensitive landscape planning to the arc of the sun, the direction and force of the wind, and topographical modeling. We observed the development of river systems and the relation of riverside planning to the river character, its currents, its forests and clearings, and the varying slopes of its banks. We sketched simple village squares and attempted to reduce to diagram the plan of vast and magnificent cities. We tested each city, street, temple group, and marketplace with a series of searching questions. Why is it good? Where does it fail? What was the planner attempting? Did he achieve it? By what means? What can we learn here? Discovering some masterpiece of planning, we sought the root of its greatness. Discovering its overall order, we sought the basis of order. Noting unity in order, we sought the meaning of unity.

This consuming search for the central theme of all great planning was like that of the old lama in his search for truth. Always we felt its presence to some degree, but it was never clearly revealed. What were these planners really seeking to accomplish? How did they define their task? How did they go about it? Finally, wiser, humbled, but still unsatisfied, we returned to America to establish our small offices and be about our work.

Insights

Years later, one warm and bright October afternoon I was leaning comfortably in the smooth crotch of a fallen chestnut tree, hunting gray and fox squirrels, the timeless sport of the dreamer. My outpost commanded a lazy sunlit hollow of white oak and hemlock. The motionless air was soft and lightly fragrant with hay fern. Close by, beyond a clump of dogwood still purple with foliage and laced with scarlet seed pips, I could hear the squirrels searching for acorns in the dry, fallen leaves. An old familiar tingling went through me, a sense of supreme well-being and an indefinable something more.

Ryoanji.

Silver Pavilion.

I half recalled that the same sensation had swept through me years ago, when I first looked across the city of Peking, one dusky evening from the Drum Tower at the North Gate. In Japan it had come again in the gardens of the Katsura Detached Palace, overlooking the quiet water of its pine-clouded pond. And again I recalled this same sensation when I had moved along the wooden-slatted promenade above the courtyard garden of Ryoanji, with its beautifully spaced stone composition in a panel of raked gravel simulating the sea.

Now what could it be, I wondered, that was common to these far-off places and the woodlot where I sat? And all at once it came to me!

The soul-stirring secret of Ryoanji lay not in its plan composition but in what one experienced there. The idyllic charm of the Silver Pavilion was sensed without consciousness of contrived plan forms or shapes. The pleasurable impact of the place lay solely in the responses it evoked. The most exhilarating impacts of magnificent Peking came often in those places where no plan layout was evident.

Architecture is again in transition. This time in a knee-jerk reaction to the bombastic excesses of later postmodernism to a time of searching introspection. A turning from buildings conceived principally as design objects to simpler, less pretentious, and more humane structures. From those designed to dominate their sites to those fitted compatibly to ground forms, drainage patterns, vegetation, and the arc of the sun. From showpiece mechanisms to environment-friendly, indoor-outdoor habitations conducive to living the good, full life.

What must count, then, is not primarily the designed shape, spaces, and forms. What counts is the experience! The fact of this discovery was for me, in a flash, the key to understanding Le Corbusier's power as a planning theorist. For his ideas, often expressed in a few scrawled lines, dealt not so much with masses or form as with experience creation. Such planning is not adapted from the crystal. It is crystalline. It is not adapted from the organism. It is truly organic. To me, this simple revelation was like staring up a shaft of sunlight into the blinding incandescence of pure truth.

With time, this lesson of insight (perception and deduction) becomes increasingly clear. One plans not places, or spaces, or things; one plans experiences—first, the defined use or experience, then the empathetic design of those forms and qualities conceived to achieve the desired

Perspective 371

Landscape art is not to be confused with landscape architecture. In the former context, natural elements such as water, stone, or plant materials are used to create a pictorial design or aesthetic experience.

Landscape architecture differs in that it is the art and science of preserving or creating compatible relationships between people and their activities and the natural worlds about them.

At every turn in the progressive development of our profession there is need for experimentation and innovation. There is need, too, for a constant infusion of new ideas from the world of art and from artists on the leading edge. It is essential, however, that we differentiate between the timely and welcome contributions of landscape artists and the timeless and far broader mission of the landscape architect.

results. The places, spaces, or objects are shaped with the utmost directness to best serve and express the function, to best yield the experience planned.

Evolution and Revolution

That was long ago. Now, with more than 50 years of practice and teaching behind me, I look back with widened perspective to the days of the student rebellion, and the subsequent years of search and application. In that time there have been other revolts in the fields of architecture and landscape planning. The first was a counterrevolutionary movement against the stark geometric forms and overutilitarianism of the Bauhaus, Gropius and "Corbu" and their fervent disciples, myself among them.

This mellowing phase of the raw post-Bauhaus evolution added a welcome warmth and richness. It produced what many believe to be the finest designs of the century. Not only in architecture, but in the related arts and sciences as well. While the direct fulfilling of need remained a given, and while "styles" and ornamentation were taboo—the hard lines were softened; textures and colors were given full play; and sculptors, weavers, and artists were welcomed back into the fold. Buildings were opened up to the sun, the breeze, and the view. Nature was rediscovered.

In landscape planning the trend veered abruptly away from the formalism of the European Renaissance—to one of respect for topographical form and features. Hillocks, ravines, and wooded slopes were left intact to be admired—as were rock outcroppings, springs, streams, dunes, and tidal estuaries. It seemed a near return to Olmstedian times, with echoes of Thoreau. One could hear Aldo Leopold calling.

Then came postmodernism, the "full flowering" of the revolution. In the name of free expression, it elaborated. It distorted. It fantasized. In its heyday it created some of the most bizarre, flamboyant structures and artifacts yet foisted on the public. True—banks, office buildings, and private homes no longer resembled the Beaux Arts Greek temples, Tudor palaces, or Georgian countinghouses. Nor the sometimes brutal concrete and glass constructions of Bauhaus times. Instead, the postmodern "blossoming" brought on a fantasyland of utter nonfunction. Office towers built in regions of blazing summer heat and winter chill, for example, were conceived as glittering Valhallas—with cooling and heating loads that sank their sponsors financially. No matter, the creations "made a powerful statement." Too often, however, the only statement was, "Look at me. Look at me. Look at me."

In the extreme, some landscape architects as well came to violate the natural sites to which, by rights, their projects should have responded. Self-conscious "landscape art" was "designed" for its shock value. Human needs, natural systems, and ecologic factors were blithely ignored and, by some, even ridiculed.

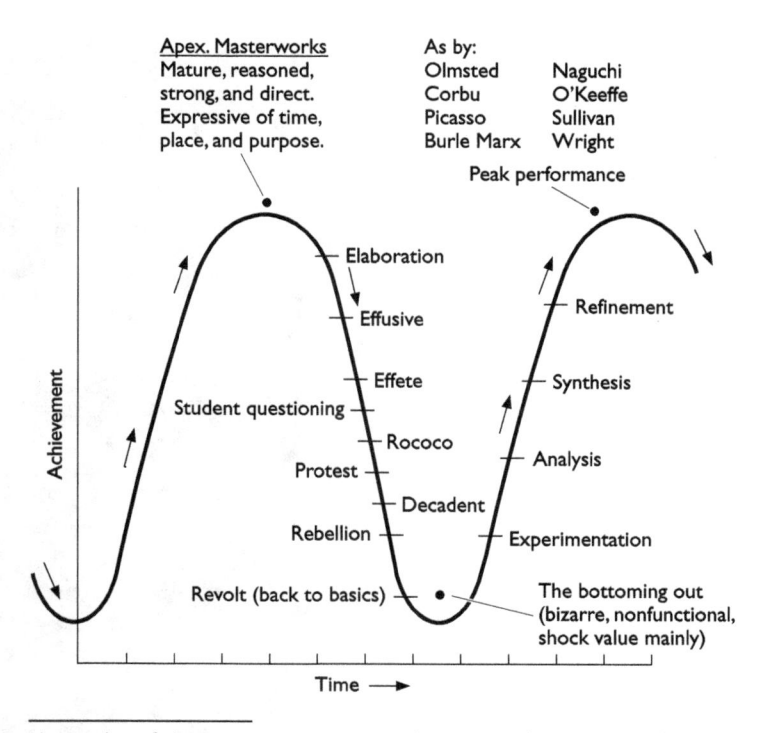

```
Apex. Masterworks          As by:
Mature, reasoned,          Olmsted    Naguchi
strong, and direct.        Corbu      O'Keeffe
Expressive of time,        Picasso    Sullivan
place, and purpose.        Burle Marx Wright
```

The cycles of design expression, as in the arts, architecture, and landscape architecture.

Some years ago Henry Elder, a brilliant architectural historian, shared with his students his concept of the cyclical nature of design. By a simple looping diagram, with examples, he traced through recent history the periods of creative innovation, the maturing toward the classic ideal, and then the decline into the fanciful and effete. Elder noted that well before the bottoming out there always appear the dissenters who, in revulsion, buck the system in protest and start the next upward loop. In their own rebellious ways they seek a new direction—a fresh start in which design, lean and clean, once again leads the way to expressive and meaningful form.

It may well be time for another revolt, this time with an environmental thrust and an ecological spin. A time when once again "form follows function," but in which the context of "function" is expanded to include the accommodation of all human needs and aspirations.

Viva la revolution!

The Planned Experience

One plans not places, spaces, or things; one plans experiences.

By this criterion, a highway is not best designed as a strip of pavement of given section, alignment, and grade. A highway is properly conceived as an experience of movement. The successful highway is planned, in this light, to provide for the user a pleasant and convenient passage from point to point through well-modulated spaces with a maximum of satis-

Essentially, the best living space, indoors and out, is that best suited to the needs and desires of the users.

To understand life, and to conceive form to express this life, is the great art. . . . And I have learned to know that in order to understand both art and life one must go down to the source of all things: to nature. . . .

Nature's laws—the laws of "beauty," if you will—are fundamental, and cannot be shaken by mere esthetic conceitedness. These laws might not always be consciously apprehended, but subconsciously one is always under their influence. . . .

The more we study nature's form-world, the more clearly it becomes evident how rich in inventiveness, nuances, and shiftings nature's form-language is. And the more deeply we learn to realize, in nature's realm, expressiveness is "basic."

Eliel Saarinen

One plans not places, or spaces, or things. . . . one plans experiences.

faction and a minimum of friction. Many of the serious failures of American roadways stem from the astounding fact that, in their planning, the actual experience of their use was never even considered.

The best community, by this test, is that which provides for its habitants the best experience of living. A garden, by this standard, is not designed as an exercise in geometry; it is not a self-conscious construction of globes, cubes, prisms, and planes within which are contained the garden elements. In such a geometric framework the essential qualities of stone, water, and plant materials are usually lost. Their primary relationship is not to the observer but to the geometry of the plan. Final plan forms may be, in some rare cases, severely geometric, but to have validity, a form must be derived from a planned experience rather than the experience from the preconceived form.

A garden, perhaps the highest, most difficult art form, is best conceived as a series of planned relationships of human to human, human to structure, and human to some facet or facets of nature, such as the lichen-encrusted tree bole of an ancient ginkgo tree, a sprightly sun-flecked magnolia clump, a trickle of water, a foaming cascade, a pool, a collection of rare tree peonies, or a New Hampshire upland meadow view.

374   LANDSCAPE ARCHITECTURE

A city, also, is best conceived as an environment in which human life patterns may be ideally related to natural or constructed elements. The most pleasurable aspects of cities throughout history have not derived from their plan geometry. Rather, they have resulted from the essential fact that, in their planning and growth, the life functions and aspirations of the citizens were considered, accommodated, and expressed.

To the Athenian, Athens was infinitely more than a pattern of streets and structures. To the Athenian, Athens was first of all a glorious way of life. What was true of Athens should be no less true of our "enlightened" urban planning of today.

The design approach then is not essentially a search for form, not primarily an application of principles. The true design approach stems from the realization that a plan has meaning only to people for whom it is planned, and only to the degree to which it brings facility, accommodation, and delight to their senses. It is a creation of optimum relationships resulting in a total experience.

We make much of this matter of relationships. What then is an optimum relationship between a person and a given thing? It is one that reveals the highest inherent qualities of that which is perceived.

Unplanned experience.

For to live, wholly to live, is the manifest consummation of existence.
Louis H. Sullivan

In the final analysis, in even the most highly developed areas or details one can never plan or control the transient nuances, the happy accidents, the minute variables of anything experienced; for most things sensed are unpredictable and often hold their very interest and value in this quality of unpredictability. In watching, for instance, an open fire, one senses the licking flame, the glowing coal, the evanescent ash, the spewing gas, the writhing smoke, the soft splutterings, the sharp crackle, and the dancing lights and shadows. One cannot control these innumerable perceptions that, in their composite, produce the total experience. One can only, for a given circumstance or for a given function, plan a pattern of harmonious relationships, the optimum framework, the maximum opportunity.

The perception of relationships produces an experience. If the relationships are unpleasant, the experience is unpleasant. If the relationships sensed are those of fitness, convenience, and order, the experience is one of pleasure, and the degree of pleasure is dependent on the degree of fitness, convenience, and order.

Fitness implies the use of the right material, the right shape, the right size, and the right volumetric enframement. Convenience implies facility of movement, lack of friction, comfort, safety, and reward. Order implies a logical sequence and a rational arrangement of the parts.

The perception of harmonious relationships, we learn, produces an experience of pleasure. It also produces an experience of beauty. What is this elusive and magical quality called beauty? By reasoning, it becomes evident that beauty is not in itself a thing primarily planned for. Beauty is a result. It is a phenomenon that occurs at a given moment or place when, and only when, all relationships are perceived to be harmonious. If this is so, then beauty as well as usefulness should be the end result of design.

All planning of and within the landscape should seek the optimum relationship between people and their living environment and thus, per se, the creation of a paradise on earth. Doubtless this will never be fully accomplished. Humans are, sadly, too human. Moreover, because the very nature of nature is change, such planning would be continuing, without possible completion, without end. And so it must be. But we may learn from history that the completion is not the ultimate goal. The goal for all physical planners is an enlightened planning approach. Again, for instruction on this point, we may turn to the wisdom of the East. Because of the dynamic nature of their philosophies, the Zen and Taoist conceptions of perfection lay more stress upon the process through which perfection is sought than upon perfection itself. The Zen and Taoist art of life lies in a constant and studied readjustment to nature and one's surroundings, the art of self-realization, the art of "being in the world."

Plan not in terms of meaningless pattern or cold form. Plan, rather, a human experience. The living, pulsing, vital experience, if conceived as a diagram of harmonious relationships, will develop its own expressive forms. And the forms evolved will be as organic as the shell of the nautilus; and perhaps, if the plan is successful, it may be as beautiful.

And so we come full circle.

What, again, is the work of the landscape architect?

It is believed that the lifetime goal and work of the landscape architect is to help bring people, the things they build, their communities, their cities—and thus their lives—into harmony with the living Earth.

John O. Simonds
January 1, 2005

Nautilus.

Retrospective

John Ormsbee Simonds 1913–2005

Born in Jamestown, North Dakota, in 1913, John Simonds was the fourth of five sons of a circuit-riding minister, the Reverend Guy Wallace Simon, and his wife, Marguerite Ormsbee Simon. Recalling the words he heard at his father's knee, John learned the principle that would guide him throughout his life: "Son, the most important thing in life is to leave the world a better place because you have traveled through it." Years later, John would reflect, "In trying, I've come to believe that no other profession affords a better opportunity than landscape architecture."

In 1920, at age seven, John moved with his family to Lansing, Michigan. On graduation from high school, urged by the owner of a nursery for whom he had worked during the summers, John enrolled in Michigan State University to study landscape architecture. In his junior year he learned, from a missionary friend, of the possibility of temporary work with the British North Borneo Timber Company. Fascinated from childhood by stories of the "wild men" of Borneo, John made a bold, almost unheard-of step for a young man of only 20 years. Taking leave from his studies, he traveled by steamer on a solo trip around the world. The journey would turn out to be a career-defining experience and confirmation that travel should be a cornerstone of a landscape architect's education.

With a bus ticket to Seattle, a third-class passage on the Dollar Line, and $200, he headed for Borneo. The route of the voyage included brief stops in Shanghai, Tokyo, and Yokohama. He would write in his journal, November 12, 1933: "Japan is a garden! Beautiful! I *must* come back." In Borneo, "work" would have required of him a three-year contract. However, he decided to remain there until his money ran out. Through a chance meeting with a young native man, John was virtually adopted by the family and experienced the life of Borneo, not the life of the British planters. He titled his unpublished memoir of those months "Headhunters and Cannibals I Have Known."

After six months, money gone, he reluctantly headed for home, this time as a common seaman on the Dollar Line. A kindly bosun helped him to jump ship in Italy, where he acquired a bicycle and pedaled his way from Naples to Florence. He enjoyed the people, the scenery, the art and sculpture, and the wine but was not overly impressed by the classical architecture. He arrived in New York in September in time for his final year at school.

Graduation in the spring of 1935 promised few if any available jobs. The one opportunity suggested by the dean was that of foreman in the Civilian Conservation Corps (CCC) camp in Big Bay in far northern Michigan. John seized it. During the following year he would lead a crew of unskilled young men from the cities of Michigan in building a state park for Marquette—roads, bridges, shelters. His first park.

He knew well that he wanted and needed more study, and application to the Harvard Graduate School of Design brought a scholarship that made it possible. Thus it was that he joined Garrett Eckbo, Dan Kiley, and James Rose in the class of '39, often dubbed the class of "modernist rebels." It was a time when the old paradigms of the profession no longer answered the needs at hand. In 1991, John amusingly recalled the period in a letter to Stuart Dawson:

> These were the deep Depression years. If ever there was a flock of poor little lambs who had lost their way, it was we, our friend Garrett Eckbo among us. (The coming of apostles Haag, Halprin, and Saint Hideo had been foretold by the constellations—but they had yet to make their appearance.) As students of landscape architecture, we had strayed off the glittering Beaux Arts avenue and the imperious Renaissance axis. We were lost in the thorny underbrush somewhere between Haffner Woods, Walden Pond, and the Bauhaus.

Although "rebel" might seem an inappropriate term to describe such a gentle man, in fact, John was a rebel among rebels. While Eckbo and Kiley were infatuated with new modernist form and would launch careers that would see them vie for the deanship of landscape architectural modernism, Simonds, already anointed with Eastern thought, set out to pursue not only new design and form but, in the tradition of Frederick Law Olmsted, embrace the big picture—people and the environment, man and nature—making the world a better place.

On graduation from Harvard, the vow to return to Japan became a reality. With introductory papers from Harvard to the Japanese Cultural Trust and with adequate funds, John set out with his close friend Lester Collins, once again to circle the globe. They were privileged to visit the best of Japan under the best possible circumstances. Eastern teachings about the relationships of man and nature would form the basis for his own philosophy of design—and of life. "To so address each person, place, and thing as to discover and reveal its highest quality."

The travelers' journey was to take them to Thailand, Cambodia, Bali, India, and just over the pass into Tibet but was cut short by the outbreak of World War II in Europe. They returned home by the way they had come.

Faced with the decision of making his start in the practice of his profession, John recalled a conversation with Harvard Dean Hudnut. When the dean had asked him where he might be considering "setting up shop," John had told him that he had a possible residential job or two in Pittsburgh, where his elder brother lived, but he really liked the Pacific Northwest. The dean's advice: "John, in the Pacific Northwest, God will be your competition; in Pittsburgh you are needed." So off to Pittsburgh it was, where his younger brother, Philip, who had completed engineering studies at Harvard, joined him to form the firm of Simonds and Simonds (later to become The Environmental Planning and Design Partnership.) As with many landscape architects of the day, the early focus was on military housing, which was soon replaced by larger municipal projects and revitalization. As the firm grew, John and Philip together, convinced of the benefits of travel, gave each of the key staff members one month off each year expressly for that purpose.

In 1942 John met his bride-to-be, Marjorie Todd. Filled with fond memories, Marj recalled the circumstances of their meeting: "We had a mutual friend, Paul Johnston, who kept saying, 'John, you've got to meet Marj Todd' and 'Marj, you've got to meet J. O. Simonds.' One Sunday afternoon I thought I had a date with Paul, who drove up in his convertible. Another girl was in the front seat and John in the back. The rest is history." They married the next spring and went on to raise four children, sharing life together for 63 years. In Marj's words: "For all those years, he taught me design and I taught him music and how to dance. John was a devoted father and family man and never neglected his family for his work."

During the next 20 years, John's work and influence would expand rapidly with projects ranging from the Chicago Botanical Garden (one of John's favorite designs) to major new communities and new towns in Florida. Concerned with the degradation of the environment by insensitive and poorly planned growth, John became a pioneer in conservation-oriented communities, creating places for human habitats that were indeed compatible with the environment. He led the early way in creating multidisciplinary teams to solve the complex problems of bringing people and the land together while protecting and enhancing resources. In 1965, John was commissioned by the legislature of the Commonwealth of Virginia to lead a multidisciplinary team in the creation of a statewide environmental protection plan and to draft legislation to implement the plan. *Virginia's Common Wealth*, as the plan is titled, was cutting-edge environmental planning of its day and is still in use.

Although John was not an avant-garde designer and form was not his focus, the need for good-quality design was firmly implanted in his philosophy and methodology. John believed "form must take its shape from the planned experience, rather than the experience from the preconceived form.... The living, pulsing, vital experience, if conceived as a diagram of harmonious relationships, will develop its own expressive forms. And the forms evolved will be as organic as the shell of the nautilus; and perhaps, if the plan is successful, they may be as beautiful."

John's success in planning and designing environmentally compatible development earned him the respect of state and national leaders. He was an adviser to then-governor Robert Graham of Florida and advised President Lyndon Johnson as a member of the President's Task Force on Resources and the Environment.

In view of all his other activities, John was a remarkably prolific writer. His writing talents extended not only to landscape architecture, but he wrote extensively about his travels and his time in the Civilian Conservation Corps, about humor, and he even plied his hand successfully to children's books. His professional publications, including the classic text *Landscape Architecture,* have shaped generations of landscape architects.

Marj Simonds said John wrote *Landscape Architecture* because "he felt compelled to get the word out about the comprehensive profession of landscape architecture." She recalled that while spending summers on Lake Charlevoix in Michigan, John would set aside several hours a day, drive to a remote wooded spot on the lake, and write. *Landscape Architecture* was first published in 1961, and many believe it was his crowning professional achievement.

John was a man of great presence but also one of the most unpretentious, selfless, and self-effacing people one could ever meet. He always had great respect for his peers and treated them with admiration and the utmost courtesy, even though he might not agree with their view or direction. In a letter to *Landscape Architecture* magazine following the death of his former classmate Dan Kiley in 2004, John wrote:

> At Harvard's Graduate School of Design, Dan was one of the rebels, along with Garrett Eckbo, James Rose, and myself, who were looking for ways to make landscape architecture meaningful again. During his long career, he also made architects conscious of the role of the landscape architect. Dan believed that by using a grid, you related structures to landscape. You can't argue with that. If I thought he moved too far toward geometric concepts, I could tease him about that.... Dan Kiley was a great man and a good friend.

John loved children and loved to help shape their lives and futures. He was a mentor and teacher of people of all ages, including not just landscape architects, but people from all walks of life. John taught site planning at Carnegie Mellon University in Pittsburgh for over 12 years and was the mentor of scores of landscape architects, architects, and planners throughout his career.

Perhaps more than any twentieth-century landscape architect, John was broadly focused and comprehensive in his work and contributions to the profession. He understood the importance of a strong membership organization to the future of landscape architecture. The tireless work on the part of John and a small band of forward-looking members grew the American Society of Landscape Architects (ASLA) from a small insignificant group of landscape architects to the highly effective organization it is today.

As a part of its 100th-year anniversary celebration in 1999, ASLA created a one-time Centennial President's Medal to recognize a living landscape architect who, through achievement, excellence, and service to the profession, stood out among his or her peers. In selecting John Simonds for this high honor, the ASLA noted:

> John has done it all—exemplary public service, a leading private practitioner, a major contributor to the literature of our profession, an outstanding teacher and unsurpassed service as ASLA President and Co-Founder of the Landscape Architecture Foundation. He has done all of this unselfishly with grace and humility for over 50 years, leading by example and never tooting his own horn.

When notified of his selection, John responded in his typical modest, self-effacing and humorous manner:

> Your letter announcing the award of the ASLA "Centennial President's Medal" is overwhelming.
>
> My first reaction was to make a mental list of those who deserved it more. On second thought I have decided never to record the list in case others might see it and agree.
>
> It was enough to realize what the profession and the ASLA have become. To be so honored for my dedication to the drive is more than could be imagined. You must know the glow of such an honor.

John died May 26, 2005, leaving an unsurpassed landscape architectural legacy.

Project Credits

Position on page is indicated as follows: T = top; B = bottom; M = middle; L = left; R = right.

Page and Position	Project	Location	Landscape Architect/Designer
12	Banyan Tree Bintan Resort	Bintan Island, Indonesia	Belt Collins
17	South San Francisco Bay Salt Pond Restoration	San Francisco, California	AECOM
24	Traditions, a Festival Marketplace	Budaghers, New Mexico	Design Workshop
25	Casa Morada	Islamorada, Florida	Raymond Jungles, FASLA
26	Anchorage Museum Common	Anchorage, Alaska	Charles Anderson, Atelier, PS
27	Pennsylvania Residence	St. Davids, Pennsylvania	Stephen Stimson Associates, Landscape Architects, Inc.
28	Miami Beach Botanical Garden	Miami Beach, Florida	Raymond Jungles, FASLA
29	The Gateway to the McDowell Sonoran Preserve	Scottsdale, Arizona	Phil Weddle, AIA, Weddle Gilmore Architects and Christopher Brown, FASLA, JJR|Floor
30 TR	Fiesta Americana Grand Los Cabos Resort	Los Cabos, Baja California, Mexico	EDSA
30 TL	Park Avenue Redevelopment	South Lake Tahoe, California	Design Workshop
31	Jamison Square	Portland, Oregon	PWP Landscape Architecture
32	Tanner Fountain, Harvard University	Cambridge, Massachusetts	PWP Landscape Architecture
34	Village of Woodbridge	Irvine, California	SWA Group
34 ML	Gap Headquarters, Embarcadero Building	San Francisco, California	OLIN
34 MR	Stanford University	Stanford, California	SWA Group
34 BL	Folk Art Park	Atlanta, Georgia	Robinson Fisher Associates
34 BR	Creekfront	Denver, Colorado	Wenk Associates, Inc.
35 ALL	Civic Plaza	Reno, Nevada	PWP Landscape Architecture
41 T	Montage Resort and Spa	Laguna Beach, California	Burton Landscape Architecture Studio
42 B	Tianjin Qiaoyuan Wetland Park	Tianjin, China	Kongjian Yu/Turenscape
43	Surry County Waterfront Access Study	Surry County, Virginia	Earth Design Associates, Inc.
48	Glenlyon Foreshore Wetland	Burnaby, British Columbia	Phillips Faarevaag Smallenberg
49	Rio Grande Botanic Gardens	Albuquerque, New Mexico	Design Workshop
51	The Red Ribbon Park	Qinhuangdao, Hebei Province, China	Kongjian Yu/Turenscape
52	Buffalo Bayou Promenade	Houston, Texas	SWA Group
53 R	Holon Park	Holon, Israel	M. Paul Friedberg
54 TL	Star River	Panyu (Guangzhou), China	Belt Collins
54 TR	The Rain Garden, Oregon Convention Center Expansion	Silverton, Oregon	Mayer/Reed
54 ML	Star River	Panyu (Guangzhou), China	Belt Collins
54 MR	North Shore Riverfront Park	Pittsburgh, Pennsylvania	AECOM
54 BL	Water Culture Square in Dujiang Yan, Sichuan Province	Sichuan Province, China	Kongjian Yu/Turenscape
55	Maymont Japanese Garden	Richmond, Virginia	Earth Design Associates, Inc.
56–57	Private Residence	Grand Tetons; Jackson, Wyoming	Design Workshop
58	The Gateway to the McDowell Sonoran Preserve	Scottsdale, Arizona	Christopher Brown, FASLA, JJR|Floor and Phil Weddle, AIA, Weddle Gilmore Architects
65	River Islands	San Joaquin Valley, Lathrop, California	SWA Group
66	Menomonee River Valley Industrial Center and Community Park	Milwaukee, Wisconsin	Wenk Associates
68	Les Jardins de l'Imaginaire	Terrasson-Lavilledieu, France	Kathryn Gustafson, Jennifer Guthrie and Shannon Nichol, Gustafson Guthrie Nichol Ltd.

Page and Position	Project	Location	Landscape Architect/Designer
69	Deck Overlook, Compton Park	Alexandria, Louisiana	Moore Planning Group, LLC
70 T	Landscape Restoration Plan for Menomonee Valley Phase II	Menomonee Valley	Landscapes of Place
70 B	Woodland Home	Sherborn, Massachusetts	Stephen Stimson Associates, Landscape Architects, Inc.
73 ALL	The Regeneration/ Yongsan Park	Seoul, Korea	United LAB
74–75	Clark County Wetlands	Las Vegas, Nevada	Design Workshop
76 TR	Private Residence	Aspen, Colorado	Design Workshop
76 BL	Buttercup Meadow, Crosby Arboretum	Picayune, Mississippi	Andropogon Associates, Ltd.
80	Santa Barbara Botanical Garden	Santa Barbara, California	Dr. Frederic Clements
83 BL	Southport Broadwater Parklands	Gold Coast, Australia	AECOM
84	Daybreak Community	South Jordan, Utah	Design Workshop
84 TL	Gary Comer Youth Center	Chicago, Illinois	Hoerr Schaudt
84 BL	Shengyang Jianzhu University Campus	Shengyang, China	Kongjian Yu/Turenscape
85	Atlanta City of the Future	Atlanta, Georgia	AECOM, and Praxis3 Architecture
86–87	Private Residence	Aspen, Colorado	Design Workshop
88	Tupelo Farm	Albemarle County, Virginia	Nelson Byrd Woltz Landscape Architects
91	Private Residence	Aspen, Colorado	Design Workshop
93	George "Doc" Cavalliere Park	Scottsdale, Arizona	Christopher Brown, FASLA, JJR|Floor
95 TL	Ashley Farm	Delaplane, Virginia	Earth Design Associates, Inc.
95 BR	Haven Meadows	North Haven, New York	Hollander Design
98	Extending the Legacy: Planning America's Capital for the 21st Century	Washington, DC	Pierre Charles L'Enfant, Original Design, National Capital Planning Commission, AECOM
105 R	Campus Plan, University of California, Berkeley	Berkeley, California	Sasaki Associates, Inc.
107	Forest Park and Central Section of Olympic Park, Beijing City	Beijing, China	Kongjian Yu/Turenscape
121	Pinecote Pavilion, Crosby Arboretum	Picayune, Mississippi	Andropogon Associates, Ltd./Fay Jones, Architect
123	Salginatobel Bridge	Schiers, Switzerland	Robert Maillart, Architect
124	Fallingwater	Bear Run, Pennsylvania	Frank Lloyd Wright, Architect
125 L	Overtown Pedestrian Mall	Miama, Florida	Wallace Roberts Todd, LLC
125 R	Campus Green, University of Cincinnati	Cincinnati, Ohio	Hargreaves Associates
127 T	Hither Lane	East Hampton, New York	Reed Hilderbrand
127 B	Rancho Viejo	Santa Fe, New Mexico	Design Workshop
130–131	Little Nell	Aspen, Colorado	Design Workshop
133	Growth Planning for Beijing	Beijing, China	Kongjian Yu/Turenscape
134	Baldwin Hills		Mia Lehrer + Associates
136	The Qian'an Sanlihe Greenway	Qian'an Hebei Province, China	Kongjian Yu/Turenscape
139	Cedar Lake Park	Minneapolis, Minnesota	Jones & Jones Architects & Landscape Architects, Ltd., Richard Haag Associates, Affiliated Designers, Master Plan Phase; Darrel Morrison, FASLA, Sub-Consultant, native plant design, master plan phase; Kestrel Landscape Architects, post-construction prairie grassland establishment
142–143	Shady Canyon	Irvine, California	SWA Group
149	The Woodlands	Athens, Georgia	Robinson Fisher Associates
151	Refugio Valley Community Park	Hercules, California	SWA Group
152	Pelican Bay Cluster Development	Collier County, Florida	EPD
153	Shady Canyon	Irvine, California	SWA Group
154	Villages of West Palm Beach	West Palm Beach, Florida	EPD
155 ALL	Villages of West Palm Beach	West Palm Beach, Florida	EPD
156	Villages of West Palm Beach	West Palm Beach, Florida	EPD
157	Villages of West Palm Beach	West Palm Beach, Florida	EPD
160 TL	Arbolera de Vida Redevelopment	Albuquerque, New Mexico	Design Workshop
160 BL	Seibert Circle	Vail, Colorado	Design Workshop

Project Credits

Page and Position	Project	Location	Landscape Architect/Designer
160 R	WaterColor	Walton County, Florida	Nelson Byrd Woltz Landscape Architects
162 R	The Gateway to the McDowell Sonoran Preserve	Scottsdale, Arizona	Phil Weddle, AIA, Weddle Gilmore Architects and Christopher Brown, FASLA, JJR|Floor
167	Golden Gate National Recreation Area	Marin County, California	SWA Group
168 L	Tide Point Promenade, Digital Harbor	Baltimore, Maryland	W Architecture and Landscape Architecture
168 R	Emery Barnes Park Public Art	Vancouver, British Columbia	Stevenson & Associates Landscape Architects
170	Pittsburgh Point	Pittsburgh, Pennsylvania	Griswold, Winters, Swain and Mullin
171	Zhongshan Shipyard	Zhongshan City, Guangdong, China	Kongjian Yu/Turenscape
173 TL	Wildcat Ranch	Aspen, Colorado	Design Workshop
173 TR	Broken Sound Planned Community	Boca Raton, Florida	SWA Group
173 ML	Rincon Park	San Francisco, California	OLIN
173 MR	Clark County Wetlands	Las Vegas, Nevada	Design Workshop
173 BR	Clemente Park	Pittsburgh, Pennsylvania	EPD
178–179	Crescent Park, Lowry Redevelopment	Denver, Colorado	Design Workshop
182 TL	Rancho Viejo	Santa Fe, New Mexico	Design Workshop
182 TR	Park Avenue Redevelopment	South Lake Tahoe, California	Design Workshop
182 BL	The Woodlands of Athens	Athens, Georgia	Robinson Fisher Associates
182 BR	Lowry Redevelopment	Denver, Colorado	Design Workshop
183	York River Preserve	New Kent County, Virginia	Earth Design Associates, Inc.
188	Harbour Ridge	St. Lucie County, Florida	EDSA
189	The Big Wild Greenbelt, Santa Monica Mountains Conservancy	Southern California	Community Development by Design
190 TL	Buffalo Bayou Promenade	Houston, Texas	SWA Group
190 TR	Cedar Lake Park	Minneapolis, Minnesota	Jones & Jones Architects & Landscape Architects, Ltd; Richard Haag Associates, Affiliated Designers: Master Plan Phase; Darrel Morrison, FASLA: Sub-Consultant, native plant design, master plan phase; Kestrel Landscape Architects: post-construction prairie grassland establishment
190 BL	Cedar Lake Park	Minneapolis, Minnesota	Jones & Jones Architects & Landscape Architects, Ltd; Richard Haag Associates, Affiliated Designers: Master Plan Phase; Darrel Morrison, FASLA: Sub-Consultant, native plant design, master plan phase; Kestrel Landscape Architects: post-construction prairie grassland establishment
190 BR	Gene Coulon Memorial Beach Park	Renton, Washington	Jones & Jones Architects & Landscape Architects, Ltd.
194–195	Extending the Legacy: Planning America's Capital for the 21st Century	Washington, DC	National Capital Planning Commission, AECOM
199	Central Park	New York, New York	Frederick Law Olmsted and Calvert Vaux
200 TL	False Creek North, Concord Pacific Place	Vancouver, British Columbia	Don Vaughan Associates/Phillip Wuori Long
200 BL	Bryant Park	New York, New York	OLIN
200 R	Baltimore Inner Harbor	Baltimore, Maryland	Wallace Roberts & Todd, LLC
201	Planned CBD	Shanghai, China	Sasaki Associates, Inc.
202	World Trade Center Memorial	New York, New York	PWP Landscape Architecture
203 TM	Old Harbor Park	Boston, Massachusetts	Carol R. Johnson Associates
203 TR	Emery Barnes Park	Vancouver, British Columbia	Stevenson & Associates Landscape Architects
203 BL	The Residences on Georgia	Vancouver, British Columbia	Phillips Farevaag Smallenberg
203 BM	888 Beach Avenue	Vancouver, British Columbia	Phillips Farevaag Smallenberg
203 BR	The Crestmark	Vancouver, British Columbia	Harold Neufeldt
207 L	Uptown Rocker, Hope Street Overpass	Los Angeles, California	Lloyd Hamrol, Sculptor
207 R	Uptown Rocker, Hope Street Overpass	Los Angeles, California	Lloyd Hamrol, Sculptor
209 TL	Seattle City Hall Plaza	Seattle, Washington	Gustafson Guthrie Nichol Ltd.
209 TR	Maguire Gardens, Los Angeles Public Library	Los Angeles, California	Office of Lawrence Halprin, FASLA/Campbell & Campbell/Jud Fine, Sculptor
209 BL	The Fullerton Hotel	Republic of Singapore	Belt Collins

Project Credits

Page and Position	Project	Location	Landscape Architect/Designer
209 BR	Tokyo Museum of Science and Innovation	Tokyo, Japan	Hargreaves Associates
210	Hyatt City Center	Chicago, Illinois	Peter Lindsay Schaudt Landscape Architecture, Inc./Pei Cobb Freed & Partners
211	The Commons	Denver, Colorado	Design Workshop
212–213	Wukesong Cultural and Sports Center, 2008 Beijing Olympic Green	Beijing, China	Sasaki Associates
216	Vietnam Veterans Memorial	Washington, DC	Maya Lin, Architect
218	Mount St. Helens National Volcanic Monument	Washington	Charles Anderson, Atelier, PS and EDAW
219	Weyerhaeuser Headquarters	Tacoma, Washington	PWP Landscape Architecture
220	River Islands	Lathrop, California	SWA Group
221	Xochimilco Ecological Park	Xochimilco, Mexico City	Mario Schjetnan/Grupo de Diseño Urbano, S.C.
232	Los Angeles River Revitalization	Los Angeles, California	Mia Lehrer + Associates, Wenk Associates, Civitas Inc., Tetratech Inc.
234	Upland Road	Cambridge, Massachusetts	Reed Hilderbrand
236	La Posada	Santa Fe, New Mexico	Design Workshop
237	Blue Ridge Farm	Upperville, Virginia	Earth Design Associates, Inc.
239	Hotarumibashi Park	Yamanashi Prefecture, Japan	Tooru Miyakoda, Keikan Sekkei Tokyo Co., Ltd.
240 T	Mary Kahrs Memory Garden	University of Georgia	Robinson Fisher Associates, Ecological Planning & Design
240 B	Oconee River Greenway	Athens, Georgia	Robinson Fisher Associates
241	J. Paul Getty Museum	Los Angeles, California	OLIN, Landscape Architect/Richard Meier & Partners Architects, LLP
242 T	Xochimilco Ecological Park	Xochimilco, Mexico City	Grupo de Diseño Urbano, S.C.
242 B	Boldwater Farm	Edgartown, Massachusetts	Stephen Stimson Associates, Landscape Architects, Inc./Mark Hutker & Associates, Architects
244 TL	Robert F. Wagner, Jr. Park	New York, New York	OLIN
244 TR	Blackcomb	Whistler, British Columbia, Canada	Design Workshop
244 BM	Xochimilco Ecological Park	Xochimilco, Mexico City	Grupo de Diseño Urbano, S.C.
244 BR	The Woodlands	Athens, Georgia	Robinson Fisher Associates
246	Green Diamond Residence	Paradise Valley, Arizona	Kristina Floor, FASLA, JJR|Floor
253	Minneapolis Waterfront Design Concept	Minneapolis, Minnesota	Kongjian Yu/ Turenscape
254 T	Heritage View Condominium	Singapore	Belt Collins
255 T	Novartis Headquarters Campus	Basel, Switzerland	PWP Landscape Architecture
255 B	John E. Jaqua Academic Center	Eugene, Oregon	Charles Anderson, Atelier PS
258–259	Novartis Headquarters Campus	Basel, Switzerland	PWP Landscape Architecture
260	Arizona Center	Phoenix, Arizona	SWA Group
264 L	Dallas West End Historic District	Dallas, Texas	SWA Group
264 R	Rancho Dulce		Pamela Burton and Company
266	Rio Grande Botanic Gardens	Albuquerque, New Mexico	Design Workshop
268 TM	Bunker Hill Steps	Los Angeles, California	Lawrence Halprin, FASLA
268 TR	Central Park, New York City/The Gates	New York, New York	Frederick Law Olmsted and Calvert Vaux/Christo and Jeanne-Claude
268 BR	Bunker Hill Steps	Los Angeles, California	Lawrence Halprin, FASLA
270 R	Vietnam Veterans Memorial	Washington, DC	Maya Lin, Architect
275 TL	The Promenade at Marion Oliver McCaw Hall	Seattle, Washington	Gustafson Guthrie Nichol Ltd.
275 TR	Nova Southeastern University Family Center Village	Davie, Florida	EDSA
275 BL	Private Residence	Aspen, Colorado	Design Workshop
275 BR	Elsie McCarthy Sensory Garden	Glendale, Arizona	Kristina Floor, FASLA, JJR|Floor
276	Maymont Park	Richmond, Virginia	Earth Design Associates, Inc.
277	The Gateway to the McDowell Sonoran Preserve	Scottsdale, Arizona	Phil Weddle, AIA, Weddle Gilmore Architects and Christopher Brown, FASLA, JJR|Floor
278 L	Taiyuan Yingze Streetscape	Taiyuan, China	AECOM

Page and Position	Project	Location	Landscape Architect/Designer
278 R	The Brazilian Garden at Naples Botanical Garden	Naples, Florida	Raymond Jungles, FASLA
281 L	MacArthur Place	Orange County, California	Landscape Architect M. Paul Friedberg and Partners
281 R	Waterworks/Beatty Mews	Vancouver, British Columbia	Harold Neufeldt
282	Centennial Olympic Park	Atlanta, Georgia	AECOM
284	Folk Art Park	Atlanta, Georgia	Pat Connell, Robinson Fisher Associates
285	Yongning River Park	Taizhou, China	Kongjian Yu/Turenscape
286	Central Train Station Plaza	Muragame, Japan	PWP Landscape Architecture
288–289	Buffalo Bayou Promonade	Houston, Texas	SWA Group
290 T	Boldwater Farm	Edgartown, Massachusetts	Stephen Stimson Associates, Landscape Architects, Inc./Mark Hutker & Associates, Architects
290 B	Stone River	New York	Jon Piasecki
297 L	San Francisco Residence	San Francisco, California	Lutsko Associates
297 R	Walt Disney Concert Hall	Los Angeles, California	Melinda Taylor and Lawrence Reed Moline, Landscape Architecture/Frank Gehry, Architect
300 ALL	Franklin Delano Roosevelt Memorial	Washington, DC	Lawrence Halprin, FASLA
303	Arctic Ring of Life, Detroit Zoo	Detroit, Michigan	Jones & Jones Architects and Landscape Architects, Ltd.
306 TL	Yerba Buena Gardens	San Francisco, California	Landscape Architect M. Paul Friedberg and Partners
306 TM	Overtown Pedestrian Mall	Miama, Florida	Wallace Roberts Todd, LLC
306 BL	Maymont Park Japanese Garden	Richmond, Virginia	Earth Design Associates, Inc.
315	Los Angeles River Revitalization	Los Angeles, California	Mia Lehrer + Associates, Civitas Inc., Wenk Associates, Inc.
316	Evans Restorative Garden, Cleveland Botanical Garden	Cleveland, Ohio	David Kamp, FASLA
318 TR	The Commons	Denver, Colorado	Design Workshop
318 BL	Baltimore Inner Harbor	Baltimore, Maryland	Wallace Roberts Todd, LLC
320	Extending the Legacy: Planning America's Capital for the 21st Century	Washington, DC	National Capital Planning Commission, AECOM
322 L	J. Paul Getty Museum	Los Angeles, California	OLIN, Landscape Architect/Richard Meier & Partners Architects, LLP
322 R	Bunker Hill Steps	Los Angeles, California	Lawrence Halprin
323	Anaheim Redevelopment	Anaheim, California	SWA Group
324	Park Avenue Redevelopment	South Lake Tahoe, California	Design Workshop
326–327	Hallelujah Concert Hall	Zhangjiajie, Hunan province, China	Kongjian Yu/Turenscape
329	Fanueil Hall Marketplace	Boston, Massachusetts	John Smibert for Peter Faneuil, 1740–42/ Charles Bullfinch, 1806/William Pressley and Associates, Inc.
331	Walt Disney Concert Hall	Los Angeles, California	Melinda Taylor and Lawrence Reed Moline, Landscape Architecture/Frank Gehry, Architect
338	Soka University	Aliso Viejo, California	SWA Group
340 TL	Zhongshan Shipyard	Zhongshan City, Guangdong, China	Kongjian Yu/Turenscape
340 BL	Chani Village Hotel	Singapore	Belt Collins
340 R	Coal Harbour Waterfront Walkway	Vancouver, British Columbia	Urban Design/Civitas; Concept Plan/Phillips Wuori Long, Inc.; Detailed Design/Phillips Farevaag Smallenberg
345	Stone Villa	Aspen, Colorado	Design Workshop
348	Gardens at El Paseo	Palm Desert, California	Design Workshop
349 TL	The Wilshire	Los Angeles, California	SWA Group
349 BL	Toad Hall, Santa Barbara Botanic Garden	Santa Barbara, California	Patrick Dougherty
349 TR	The Patra Resort & Villas	Bali, Indonesia	Belt Collins
349 BR	Spring Hill Farm	Casanova, Virginia	Earth Design Associates, Inc.

Project Credits

Page and Position	Project	Location	Landscape Architect/Designer
350	Mountain Retreat	Aspen, Colorado	Design Workshop
351 L	Conrad Bali Resort & Spa	Bali, Indonesia	Belt Collins
351 R	Bedon's Alley	Charleston, South Carolina	Nelson Byrd Woltz Landscape Architects
352–353	Private Residence	Aspen, Colorado	Design Workshop
355	Phil Hardberger Park	San Antonio, Texas	Stephen Stimson Associates Landscape Architects
356 R	Maymont Park	Richmond, Virginia	Earth Design Associates, Inc.
358 TL	Apollo and Daphne, Little Sparta, Stonypath	Pentland Hills, Edinburgh, Scotland	Ian Hamilton Finlay
358 TR	Walt Disney Concert Hall	Los Angeles, California	Melinda Taylor and Lawrence Reed Moline, Landscape Architecture, Frank Gehry, Architect
358 BL	Walt Disney Concert Hall	Los Angeles, California	Melinda Taylor and Lawrence Reed Moline, Landscape Architecture, Frank Gehry, Architect
358 BR	Apollo, Little Sparta, Stonypath	Pentland Hills, Edinburgh, Scotland	Ian Hamilton Finlay
359 TL	Polmood Farm	Santa Fe, New Mexico	Design Workshop
359 BL	Exxon Corporate Headquarters	Irving, Texas	SWA Group
359 BR	Private Residence	Aspen, Colorado	Design Workshop
361 L	Private Residence	Aspen, Colorado	Design Workshop
361 R	Copia, The American Center for Wine, Food, and Arts	Napa, California	PWP Landscape Architecture
362 R	5800 Third Street	San Francisco, California	Miller Company
362 L	The Children's Garden at The Oregon Garden	Silverton, Oregon	Mayer/Reed
363 L	Clark County Government Center	Las Vegas, Nevada	Civitas, Inc.
363 R	Ensley Avenue	Los Angeles, California	Orange Street Studio
364	Mirabella	Portland, Oregon	Mayer/Reed
365	John E. Jaqua Academic Center	Eugene, Oregon	Charles Anderson, Atelier PS
366–367	The Gates, Central Park	New York, New York	The Gates—Christo and Jeanne-Claude/Central Park—Frederick Law Olmsted and Calvert Vaux
374 L	Court of the Toads, Dallas Arboretum	Dallas, Texas	SWA Group
374 R	Portland Parks and Jamison Square	Portland, Oregon	PWP Landscape Architecture
375	Creekfront	Denver, Colorado	Wenk Associates, Inc.

Quotation Sources (page)

Adams, Henry: *The Education of Henry Adams*, Houghton Mifflin, Boston, 1928 (198)

Ardrey, Robert: *African Genesis*, Dell, New York, 1961 (14)

Aristotle: *Rhetoric* (235)

Bacon, Edmund N.: *Planning*, The American Society of Planning Officials, Chicago, 1958 (181)

Beck, Walter: *Painting with Starch*, Van Nostrand, Princeton, N.J., 1956 (333)

Bel Geddes, Norman: *Magic Motorways*, Random House, New York, 1940 (307, 309)

Benét, Stephen Vincent: *Western Star*, Farrar & Rinehart, New York, 1943 (4)

Bergmann, Karen: *Landscape Architecture*, May 1990 (275)

Berry, Wendell: *Another Turn of the Crank*, Counterpoint, Washington, D.C., 1995 (180)

Borissaviévitch, Miloutine: *The Golden Number*, Alec Tiranti, London, 1958 (334)

Bowie, Henry P.: *On the Laws of Japanese Painting*, Dover, New York, 1952 (republication of 1911 edition) (228)

Braun, Ernest, and David E. Cavagnaro, *Living Water*, The American West Publishing Company, Palo Alto, Calif., 1971 (13)

Breuer, Marcel: In conversation (328)

Bronowski, Jacob: *Arts and Architecture*, February and December 1957 (108, 229)

Carson, Rachel: *The Sea around Us*, Oxford University Press, New York, 1951 (8)

Church, Thomas D.: *Gardens Are for People*, Reinhold, New York, 1955 (312, 346)

Churchill, Henry S.: *The City Is the People*, Harcourt, Brace, New York, 1945 (181, 198)

Clark, Kenneth: *Civilisation*, Harper & Row, New York, 1969 (3)

Clawson, Marion: *Man and Land in the United States*, University of Nebraska Press, Lincoln, 1964 (62)

Clay, Grady: *Water and the Landscape*, McGraw-Hill, New York, 1979 (115)

Crowe, Sylvia: *Tomorrow's Landscape*, Architectural Press, London, 1956 (181)

Cullen, Gordon: *Townscape*, Reinhold, New York, 1961 (275)

Danby, Hope: *The Garden of Perfect Brightness*, Henry Regnery Company, Chicago, 1950 (108)

Eckbo, Garrett: *Landscape Architecture*, May 1990 (215)

———: *Landscape for Living*, McGraw-Hill Information Systems Company, McGraw-Hill, Inc., New York, 1950 (180, 219, 260)

Eiseley, Loren: *The Immense Journey*, Random House, New York, 1957 (41)

Gallion, Arthur B.: *The Urban Pattern*, Van Nostrand, New York, 1949 (198)

Gardner, James, and Caroline Heller: *Exhibition and Display*, McGraw-Hill Information Systems Company, McGraw-Hill, Inc., New York, 1960 (304)

Giedion, Siegfried: *Space, Time and Architecture*, Harvard University Press, Cambridge, Mass., 1941 (121)

Goshorn, Warner S.: In correspondence with Harold S. Wagner (61)

Graham, Wade: "The Grassman," *The New Yorker*, August 19, 1996 (48)

Gutkind, E. A.: *Community and Environment*, C. A. Watts & Co., London, 1953 (17)

Hilberseimer, Ludwig K.: *The New Regional Pattern*, Paul Theobald, Chicago, 1949 (186, 307)

Hubbard, Henry V., and T. Kimball: *An Introduction to the Study of Landscape Design*, Macmillan, New York, 1917 (106)

Kepes, Gyorgy: *Language of Vision*, Paul Theobald, Chicago, 1944 (106)

Landscape Architecture, October 1994 (160)

Le Corbusier: *The Radiant City*, republication, Orion Press, New York, 1964 (123, 328)

Leopold, Aldo: *A Sand County Almanac*, reprint, Oxford University Press, Fair Lawn, N.J., 1969 (64, 311)

Li, H. H.: Translation of Chinese manuscript (6)

McHarg, Ian L.: *Landscape Architecture* (quarterly magazine of the American Society of Landscape Architects), January 1958 (186)

McPhee, John: *Annals of the Former World*, Farrar, Straus and Giroux, New York, 1998 (18)

McPhee, John: *Coming into the Country*, Bantam, New York, 1979 (60)

Mendelsohn, Eric: *Perspecta* (the Yale architectural journal), 1957 (109)

Millay, Edna St. Vincent: "The Goose-Girl," *Collected Lyrics of Edna St. Vincent Millay*, Harper and Brothers, New York, 1939 (345)

Moholy-Nagy, László: *The New Vision*, Wittenborn, Schultz, New York, 1928 (108, 263)

Mumford, Lewis: *The Culture of Cities*, Harcourt, Brace, New York, 1938 (158, 181, 185, 186, 198)

Murphy, W. Tayloe, "Address to ASLA Virginia Chapter" (44)

Neutra, Richard J.: *Survival through Design*, Oxford University Press, New York, 1954 (5, 266)

Newton, Norman T.: *An Approach to Design*, Addison-Wesley, Cambridge, Mass., 1941 (6, 107)

Ognibene, Peter J.: "Vanishing Farmlands," *Saturday Review*, May 1980 (58)

Okakura, Kakuzo: *The Book of Tea*, Charles E. Tuttle, Rutland, Vt., 1958 (247)

Phillips, Patricia C.: *Landscape Architecture*, December 1994 (196)

Rasmussen, Steen Eiler: *Towns and Buildings*, Harvard University Press, Cambridge, Mass., 1951 (195)

Read, Sir Herbert: *Arts and Architecture*, May 1954 (262)

Reed, Henry H., Jr.: *Perspecta* (the Yale architectural journal), 1952 (97)

Saarinen, Eliel: *Search for Form*, Reinhold, New York, 1948 (103, 191, 331, 374)

Santayana, George: *The Sense of Beauty*, Dover, New York, 1955 (105, 107)

Sert, José Luis, and C.I.A.M.: *Can Our Cities Survive?* Harvard University Press, Cambridge, Mass., 1942 (196, 331)

Severud, Fred M.: "Turtles and Walnuts, Morning Glories and Grass," *Architectural Forum*, September 1945 (9)

Shigemori, Kanto: In conversation (345)

Simonds, Dylan Todd: In correspondence (207)

Simonds, John Todd: In conversation (2)

Sitte, Camillo: *The Art of Building Cities*, Reinhold, New York, 1945 (103, 197, 329, 334)

Spengler, Oswald: *Decline of the West,* Alfred A. Knopf, New York, 1939 (267)

Sullivan, Louis H.: *Kindergarten Chats,* Wittenborn, Schultz, New York, 1947 (107, 375)

Sze, Mai-mai: *The Tao of Painting,* The Bollingen Foundation, New York, 1956 (9)

Tunnard, Christopher: *Gardens in the Modern Landscape,* Charles Scribner's, New York, 1948 (16, 122)

Van der Ryn, Sim, and Stuart Cowan: *Ecological Design,* Island Press, Washington, D.C., 1996 (4, 7, 11)

Van Loon, Hendrik: *The Story of Mankind,* Boni and Liveright, New York, 1921 (8)

Veri, Albert R., et al.: *Environmental Quality by Design: South Florida,* University of Miami Press, Coral Gables, Fla., 1975 (13, 51)

White, Stanley: *A Primer of Landscape Architecture,* University of Illinois, Urbana, 1956 (13, 15, 127)

Whyte, Lancelot Law: "Some Thoughts on the Design of Nature and Their Implications for Education," *Arts and Architecture,* January 1956 (2)

Whyte, William H., Jr.: *The Exploding Metropolis,* Doubleday, New York, 1958 (198)

Wikipedia: "Water Resources," last modified July 20, 2012, accessed September 10, 2012, http://en.wikipedia.org/wiki/Water_resources (43)

Wilson, E. O.: *The Diversity of Life,* W. W. Norton and Co., 1992 (21)

Wittkower, Rudolph: *Architectural Principles in the Age of Humanism,* University of London, Warburg Institute, 1949 (336)

Zevi, Bruno: *Architecture as Space,* Horizon Press, New York, 1957 (277)

Bibliography

The titles listed give no more than a glimpse of the broad range of writings on the shaping of our living environment. While some books may be out of print they are available in most university libraries.

1. History and Theory

These selected references provide an insight into landscape planning history and thought.

ASLA: *Landscape Architecture* magazine, *Profiles in Landscape Architecture,* American Society of Landscape Architects, Washington, D.C., 1995.

Brubaker, Sterling: *To Live on Earth,* Resources for the Future, Inc., Johns Hopkins University Press, Baltimore, 1972.

Carson, Rachel: *Silent Spring,* Buccaneer Books, New York, 1994.

Clark, Kenneth: *Civilisation,* Harper & Row, New York, 1969.

Commoner, Barry: *The Closing Circle,* Bantam, New York, 1971.

Diamond, Henry L., and Patrick F. Noonam: *Land Use in America,* Island Press, Washington, D.C., 1996.

Dubos, René: *So Human an Animal: How We Are Shaped by Surroundings and Events,* Charles Scribner's Sons, New York, 1969.

Fein, Albert: *Frederick Law Olmsted and the American Environmental Tradition,* George Braziller, New York, 1972.

Howard, Ebenezer: *Garden Cities of Tomorrow,* M.I.T. Press, Cambridge, Mass., 1965. (Originally published in 1898.)

Hubbard, Henry Vincent, and Theodora Kimball: *An Introduction to the Study of Landscape Design,* rev. ed., Hubbard Educational Trust, Boston, 1959.

Jackson, J. B.: *Discovering the Vernacular Landscape,* Yale University Press, New Haven, Conn., 1983.

Jellicoe, Geoffrey, and Susan Jellicoe: *The Landscape of Man; Shaping the Environment from Prehistory to the Present Day,* Viking Press, New York, 1975.

Leopold, Aldo: *A Sand County Almanac: With Essays on Conservation from Round River,* Ecological Main Event Series, Ballantine, New York, 1987.

Marsh, George Perkins: *Man and Nature,* Harvard University Press, Cambridge, Mass., 1965. (Originally published in 1864.)

Mumford, Lewis: *The Culture of Cities,* Greenwood Publishers, Westport, Conn., 1981.

Newton, Norman T.: *Design on the Land,* Belknap Press, Harvard University Press, Cambridge, Mass., 1971.

Reich, Charles: *The Greening of America,* Bantam, New York, 1970.

Smithsonian Annual Symposium: *The Fitness of Man's Environment,* Smithsonian Institution Press, Washington, D.C., 1968.

Tunnard, Christopher, and Boris Pushkarev: *Man-made America: Chaos or Control?,* Yale University Press, New Haven, Conn., 1963.

Wilkes, Joseph A., and Robert T. Packard (eds.): *Encyclopedia of Architecture: Design, Engineering and Construction,* John Wiley & Sons, New York, 1988.

2. Environment

The field of environmental protection and planning has recently assumed increased significance as world conditions become ever more critical. The following publications are among the more telling.

Anderson, J. M.: *Ecology for Environmental Sciences: Biosphere, Ecosystems and Man,* John Wiley & Sons (Halsted), New York, 1981.

Berry, Thomas: *The Dream of Earth,* Sierra Club Books, San Francisco, 1990.

Berry, Wendell: *Another Turn of the Crank,* Counterpoint, Washington, D.C., 1995.

Berry, Wendell: *The Gift of Good Land,* North Point Press, San Francisco, 1981.

Bradshaw, A. D., and M. J. Chadwick: *The Restoration of the Land: The Ecology and Reclamation of Derelict and Degraded Land,* University of California Press, Berkeley, Calif., 1981.

Chase, Alson: *In a Dark Wood,* Houghton Mifflin, New York, 1995.

Clawson, Marion: *Forests for Whom and for What?,* Johns Hopkins University Press, Baltimore, 1975.

Curry-Lindahl, Kai: *Conservation for Survival: An Ecological Strategy,* William Morrow & Company, New York, 1972.

Fiedler, Peggy, and Subodh K. Jain (eds.): *Conservation Biology: The Theory and Practice of Nature Conservation, Preservation and Management,* Chapman & Hall, New York, 1992.

Gore, Al: *Earth in the Balance: Ecology and the Human Spirit,* Houghton Mifflin, New York, 1993.

Hiss, Tony: *The Experience of Place,* Vintage, New York, 1990.

Lewis, Philip H., Jr.: *Tomorrow By Design: A Regional Design Process for Sustainability,* John Wiley & Sons, New York, 1996.

Lyle, John Tillman: *Regenerative Design for Sustainable Development,* John Wiley & Sons, New York, 1994.

McHarg, Ian L.: *Design with Nature,* John Wiley & Sons, New York, 1995. (First published by the Natural History Press, 1969.)

Simonds, John Ormsbee: *Earthscape: A Manual of Environmental Planning and Design,* 2d ed., Van Nostrand Reinhold, New York, 1996.

Thayer, Robert: *Gray World, Green Heart: Technology, Nature and the Sustainable Landscape,* John Wiley & Sons, New York, 1994.

Van der Ryn, Sim, and Stuart Cowan: *Ecological Design,* Island Press, Washington, D.C., 1995.

Ward, Barbara, and René Dubos: *Only One Earth: The Care and Maintenance of a Small Planet,* The United Nations Conference on the Human Environment, W.W. Norton, New York, 1972.

3. Community

The arrangement and design of more agreeable homesites, neighborhoods, and communities are treated in the following publications:

Arendt, Randall G.: *Conservation Design for Subdivisions: A Practical Guide to Creating Open Space Networks,* Island Press, Washington, D.C., 1996.

Dowden, C. James: *Community Associations: A Guide for Public Officials Published Jointly by the Urban Land Institute and the Community Associations Institute,* Washington, D.C., 1980.

Hall, Kenneth B.: *A Concise Guide to Community Planning,* McGraw-Hill, New York, 1994.

Harker, Donald, and Elizabeth Ungar Natter: *Where We Live: A Citizen's Guide to Conducting a Community Environmental Inventory,* Island Press, Washington, D.C., 1995.

Hester, Randolph T., Jr.: *Planning Neighborhood Space with People,* Van Nostrand Reinhold, New York, 1984.

Little, Charles E.: *Challenge of the Land: Open Space Preservation,* Pergamon Press, New York, 1969.

Moore, Colleen Grogan: *PUD's In Practice,* Urban Land Institute, Washington, D.C., 1985.

Smart, Eric: *Making Infill Projects Work,* Urban Land Institute and Lincoln Institute of Land Policy, Washington, D.C., 1985.

Terrene Institute (and U.S. EPA): *Local Ordinances: A User's Guide,* Terrene Institute, Washington, D.C., 1995.

Whyte, William H.: *Cluster Development,* American Conservation Association, New York, 1964.

4. Urban and Regional Form

Urban and regional patterns and form receive attention in these references on land use, transportation, recreation, and resource planning.

Arendt, Randall: *Rural By Design: Maintaining Small Town Character,* Planners' Press, Chicago, 1994.

Bacon, Edmund N.: *Design of Cities,* rev. ed., Viking Press, New York, 1974.

Breen, Ann, and Dick Rigby: *The New Waterfront: A Worldwide Urban Success Story,* McGraw-Hill, New York, 1996.

Calthorpe, Peter: *The Next American Metropolis: Ecology, Community, and the American Dream,* Princeton Architectural Press, New York, 1993.

Collins, Richard C., Elizabeth B. Waters, and A. Bruce Dotson: *America's Downtowns: Growth, Politics and Preservation,* Preservation Press, The National Trust for Historic Preservation, Washington, D.C., 1990.

Harr, Charles M.: *Land Use Planning: A Casebook on the Use, Misuse, and Reuse of Urban Land,* Little, Brown, Boston, 1976.

Jacobs, Jane: *The Death and Life of Great American Cities,* Modern Library, New York, 1993. (Originally published 1961.)

Katz, Peter: *The New Urbanism: Toward an Architecture of Community,* McGraw-Hill, New York, 1993.

Kunstler, James Howard: *The Geography of Nowhere: The Rise and Decline of America's Man-Made Landscape,* Simon & Schuster, New York, 1993.

Laurie, Ian C.: *Nature in Cities,* John Wiley & Sons, New York, 1979.

Little, Charles: *Greenways for America,* Johns Hopkins University Press, Baltimore, 1990.

MacKaye, Benton: *The New Exploration: A Philosophy of Regional Planning,* University of Illinois Press, Urbana, Ill., 1962.

Mertes, James D., and James R. Hall: *Park, Recreation Open Space, and Greenway Guidelines,* National Park and Recreation Association in cooperation with the American Academy for Park and Recreation Administration, Washington, D.C., 1996.

Simonds, John Ormsbee: *Garden Cities 21: Creating a Livable Urban Environment,* McGraw-Hill, New York, 1994.

Spirn, Anne Whiston: *The Granite Garden, Urban Nature and Human Design,* Basic Books, New York, 1984.

Spreiregen, Paul D.: *Urban Design: The Architecture of Town and Cities,* McGraw-Hill, New York, 1965.

Whittick, Arnold (ed.): *Encyclopedia of Urban Planning,* McGraw-Hill, New York, 1974.

Whyte, William H., Jr.: *Rediscovering the Center City,* Doubleday, New York, 1990.

5. Site Planning

Among the many excellent source books on site and landscape planning and design, the following provide a working introduction.

Brown, Karen M., and Curtis Charles: *Computers in the Professional Practice of Design,* McGraw-Hill, New York, 1995.

Church, Thomas D., et al.: *Gardens Are for People,* 3d ed., University of California Press, Berkeley, Calif., 1995.

Collins, Lester A.: *Innisfree, An American Garden,* Sagapress/Harry Abrams, New York, 1994.

Crowe, Sylvia: *Garden Design,* Antique Collectors Club, Wappingers Falls, N.Y., 1994.

Dattner, Richard: *Civil Architecture: The New Public Infrastructure,* McGraw-Hill, New York, 1994.

Eckbo, Garrett, *Philosophy of Landscape,* Process Architecture Co., Tokyo, 1995.

EDAW: *The Integrated World,* Process Architecture Co., Tokyo, 1994.

Harris, Charles W., and Nicholas T. Dines: *Time-Saver Standards for Landscape Architecture,* McGraw-Hill, New York, 1988.

Kiley, Dan: *In Step with Nature,* Process Architecture Co., Tokyo, 1993.

Lebovich, William L.: *Design for Dignity,* John Wiley & Sons, New York, 1993.

Oehme, Wolfgang, and James van Sweden: *Bold Romantic Gardens,* Acropolis Books, Reston, Va., 1990.

Robinette, Gary O.: *Water Conservation in Landscape Design and Management,* Van Nostrand Reinhold, New York, 1984.

Van Sweden, James: *Gardening With Water,* Random House, New York, 1995.

Walker, Peter, William Johnson, and Partners: *Art and Nature,* Process Architecture Co., Tokyo, 1994.

Zion, Robert: *Landscape Architecture,* Process Architecture Co., Tokyo, 1994.

Other Publications:

(Bookstore catalogs available)

American Institute of Architects
1735 New York Avenue, N.W.
Washington, DC 20006

American Planning Association
122 S. Michigan Ave.
Suite 1600
Chicago, IL 60603

American Society of Landscape Architects
4401 Connecticut Avenue, N.W.
Washington, DC 20008

Community Builders Handbook Series
Urban Land Institute
625 Indiana Avenue, N.W.
Washington, DC 20004-2930

Process Architecture Publications
Process Architecture Publishing Co., Ltd.
1-47-2-418 Sasazuka,
Shibuya-Ku
Tokyo, Japan

Sierra Club Books
2034 Fillmore St.
San Francisco, CA 94115

Sunset Magazine: Sunset Gardening and Outdoor Books publish an enduring series of excellent paperback publications relating particularly to residential landscape design.
Lane Publishing Company
Menlo Park, CA 94025

Index

Page numbers in italics refer to illustrations; page numbers in boldface refer to pull-quote authors.

Abbot's Garden of Nikko (Japan), 265
Acid rain, 138
Activity centers:
  at airports, 322
  entrance plantings for, 359
  in planned communities, 150, 176
  plans developed for, 174
  public transit for, *319,* 325
  in regional plans, 188
  in urban revitalization plans, 171–172, 206
Adams, Henry, **198**
Afforestation, 84
Agriculture. *See also* Farmland
  advent of, 20, 81
  expansion of, 47
  impact of, 81–82
  irrigation for, 11, 40, 43, 44–45
  land planning for, 61
  land restoration for, 45
  pollution from, 138
  rectilinear survey of fields in, 63
  urban, 84, *84*
Air pollution:
  control of, 169
  as global warming factor, 36, *36, 37*
  health effects of, 138
  urban forestry and, 85
Airplanes:
  freight versus passenger, 317, 321
  travel via, 321–322
Airports:
  amenities at, 322
  transport at, 323
Alaska Purchase, 62
Alaska Statehood Act of 1958, 62
Alberti, Leon Battista, **267**
Allegheny Conference of Western Pennsylvania, 135
Altitude, 33, *33*
American Conservation Foundation, 135
American Society of Landscape Architects (ASLA), 383
Americans with Disabilities Act (ADA), 208

Amusement park design, 269–270
Animals. *See also* Wildlife
  biosphere as home to, 13
  climate change impact on, 36, 37
  environment needed by, 3
  in food chain, 77
  human dominion over, 2
  invasive species of, 82–83
Anthropomorphic module, 336
Approaches:
  to airports, 321
  to buildings, 330
  design of, 302–303, 311–314, *312–314*
  landscape plantings at, 359, *359*
  parking and, 315, 316
  for planned communities, 159, *184*
  at Rockefeller Center, 261
Aquifer replenishment, 46, 76, 77
Arc de Triomphe (Paris, France), 96, *96*
Ardrey, Robert, **14**
Aristotle, 6, 196, **235**
Arlington National Cemetery, *270*
Asia. *See also* China; Japan
  approaches designed in, 302–303
  cities in, 196
  nature-based design in, 342, *344*
  spatial design in, 271, 332
Assessments (land), 138
Asymmetry, 104–110, 333–334, 369
Atlanta Station (Atlanta, GA), 66
Atmosphere (Earth), 37
Atomic power:
  civic action against, *134*
  control of, *3*
  waste from, 138
Attiret, Jean Denis, 108, 110
Automobiles:
  cultural focus on, 180, 314
  driveways/approaches for, 311–314
  as hazard, 344
  land planning impacted by, 207–208, 308–309
  parking for (*see* Parking)
  in planned communities, *146,* 149, *149*
  proliferation of, 148, 307

Automobiles (*Cont.*):
  in rural site design, 238
  traffic flow planning for, *307,* 309–311, *310, 311*
Axis:
  asymmetric, 108
  characteristics of, 95–98
  design function of, 94, *99,* 99–100, *100, 101,* 333, 368
  examples of, *95, 96, 98*

Back-to-the-city movement, 207
Bacon, Edmund N., **181**
Balance, as design principle, 104–106, 332
Balconies:
  for sloped sites, 240
  for urban residences, 199
Base map:
  for landscape planting, 354
  in site planning, 225
Base plane:
  articulated by vertical plane, 284, *285, 286*
  characteristics of, 272–275, *272–275*
  coloration of, 268
  of exterior volumes, 272
  functions of, *275*
  pedestrian traffic on, 305, *306*
  plantings to define, *355, 357, 361*
  in site space design, 259, 260, *260*
Bauer, Catherine, **214**
Bauhaus, 367, 372
Beauty:
  versus decoration, 344
  experience of, 376
  form/function in, 267, 268
  harmony and, 113, 114
  human need for, 5, 120
  mathematical basis of, 334
  of natural forms, 337
  symmetry and, 101, 103
  in urban design, 186
  wabi quality in, 236–237
Beaux Arts system, 367, 367n
Beck, Walter, 332, 333n

395

Bedroom communities, 161
Beijing (Peking), China, 99–100, 108, *109*, 371
Bel Geddes, Norman, **307, 309**
Belluschi, Pietro, **97**
Bench mark (topographic), 67, 68
Benét, Stephen Vincent, **4**
Bergmann, Karen, **275**
Berry, Wendell, **180**
Bigger, Frederick, **307**
Bikeways:
　in community planning, 151, 159, 161
　on complete streets, 315
　along greenways, 172
　in integrated design, 253
　location of, *313*
　in neighborhood plans, 182
　plantings along, *358,* 360
　as safety measure, 138, *139*
　on site analysis map, 224
　use of, 324
Bioengineering, 79
Biology, 12
Bioretention, 252, 365
Biosphere:
　components of, 13
　overconsumption and, 21
　plant function in, 80
Bioswales, 252, 365
Blue Ridge Parkway (VA), 267
Blueways, in regional plans, *190,* 190–191
Boat travel, 319–321
A Book of Tea (Okakura), 90
Borissavlievitch, Miloutine, 334, 334n, 335
Botanical gardens, 80, *80,* 117, 201, 381
Botany, 12–13, 78–79
Bowie, Henry P., 228
Braun, Ernest, 13n
Breuer, Marcel, **328,** 367
Bridge design, 51–52, 122–123, *123,* 311
British North Borneo (Sabah), 17
Bronowski, Jacob, **108, 229**
Brownfields, 66
Brundtland Commission (UN), 18
Buckshot plans, 250, *250*
Buffers:
　in community planning, 159
　vegetation as, 77
Building codes:
　in comprehensive plan, 221
　disabilities and, 208
　enforcement of, 176–177
　as site analysis data, 224
　urban, 185

Building materials:
　in Asian architecture, 342
　for highway structures, 311
　in integrated design, 256
　for pedestrian paths, 305
　in rural site design, 238
　in spatial design, 271–272
　technology in, 329
　in urban site design, 236
　for vertical enclosures, 279
Building orientation:
　landscape character and, 117
　microclimate and, 31–32, 33, *33,* 35
　street frontage and, 145, 148, 159, 174, 176
Building site. *See* Site
Buildings. *See also* Structures
　as sculptural elements, 281
　solitary versus grouped, 339
Built environment:
　design elements for, 120–129
　suitability of site/surroundings, 120–121, 180
Burbank, Luther, 79
Burchard, John Ely, **96**
Bus trains, 323
Buses, 323–324

Cable cars, 324, *324*
Campuses, walkways on, 303
Canals:
　cities along, 321
　repurposing of, 50
　traffic in, 303
　in transportation network, 58
Canopy trees, *356,* 357, *358*
Carbohydrate production, 77
Carbon dioxide, atmospheric, 36, 77, 138, 363
Carnegie Mellon University, 383
Carrying capacity:
　of land, 64, 132, 191, 192
　of roadways, 310
Cars. *See* Automobiles
Carson, Rachel, **8**
Cascades:
　foliage, 357
　water, 53, *53,* 55, 241
Casey Trees, 85
Cavagnaro, David E., 13n
Cemetery design, *270,* 270–271
Central business district (CBD), 185, 198–201, *201,* 208, 210
Central Park (New York City), *199,* 281

Champs-Élysée (Paris, France), *96,* 96–97
Checkerboard plans, 250, *250*
Chicago Botanic Garden, 117, 381
Ch'ien-lung (emperor of China), 108
China, 6, 9, 99–100, 108, *109,* 116, 371. *See also specific locations and sites*
Church, Thomas D., **312, 346**
Churchill, Henry S., **181, 198**
Circulation patterns. *See also* Roadways; Traffic; Transportation
　for air travel, 321–322
　for automobiles, 307–317
　for bicycles (*see* Bikeways)
　to connect structures, *338,* 339
　design importance of, 289–290
　impelled motion in, 290–295
　landscape planting and, *355, 355,* 357, *358, 358,* 359, 360
　multimodal transport and, 323–325
　for pedestrians, 303–306 (*see also* Walkways)
　for railways, 317–319
　route design in, 296
　sequence in, 299–303
　space modulation in, 296–299
　for water travel, 319–321
Cities:
　asymmetric plans in, 108–109
　axial plans in, 96–98
　components of, 198–207
　contemporary planning for, 196–198
　defined, 184
　design of, 208–210
　experience of, 375
　forestry in, 85
　gardening in, 84, *236,* 237
　land use issues and, 170
　microclimate in, 85, *234,* 235
　open space in, 172
　placement of, 117
　population density of, 143–144
　regional planning for, 184–186, 188
　relationship with surroundings, 179–180
　revitalization of, 139, 171, *171*
　site development for, 234–237
　spatial design of, 260
　traffic in, *187,* 207–208
　vitality of, 195–196, 211
　along waterfronts, 321
Civic action:
　antinuclear demonstration as, *134*
　city beautification as, 209
　in environmental planning, 192
　function of, 135

Civic action (*Cont.*):
    proposed antiwar, 140–141
    in urban planning, 184
Civilian Conservation Corps (CCC), 139, 380, 382
Civilization, dawn of, 19–20, 81, 133
Clark, Kenneth, **3**
Clawson, Marion, **62**
Clay, Grady, **115**
Climate:
    defined, 23
    as design factor, 139, 238, 342–343
    elements of, 23–24
    human responses to, 24, 25
    microclimate, 34
    social imprint of, 26
    vegetation effect on, 77, 360
Climate change, 36–37, 138, 167, 363
Climatic regions, 25–29
Cluster housing, 180–181
Cold climatic region, 25, 26, 33
Collins, Lester A., 369n, 380
Color:
    contrasts in, 123
    of roadways, 310
    in spatial design, 268–269, 271
Colorado River, 45
Community. *See also* Planned communities
    culture of, 328
    evolving forms of, 144
    as human necessity, 143
    social activities in, 161
    urban spaces for, 186, 236
Community gardens, 84, *84*
Commuting:
    electric cart for, 324
    via rapid transit, 317
    suburban development and, 207
Compass and chain survey, 70
Complete streets, *315,* 314–315
Composition:
    buildings/spaces in, 329–330
    for groups of structures, 330–334
    rules for, 334–337
Comprehensive land planning:
    approach to, 228–229
    conceptual plan in, 226–227
    example, *220*
    function of, 220–222
    impact assessment in, 229–231
    site analysis in, 222–225, 226
Computer:
    for plan documentation, 225
    as planning tool, 231–233

Computer (*Cont.*):
    in structural design, 329
    visualization produced by, *232*
Computer-Aided Design (CAD), 233, 331
Conceptual plan:
    as collaborative, 226, *226*
    example, *228*
    function of, 233
    for landscape planting, 356
    process for, 227
    site-structure diagram in, 226–227, *227*
    three-dimensional translation of, 259
Conference facilities, 161
Conservancies, 167. *See also* Preserves
Conservation:
    credo for, 132
    defined, 61
    as environmental issue, 141
    green roofs in, 363
    jurisdictions for, 60
    in PCD community planning, 152, 153
    regional planning for, 188
    of water, 48, 190
Conservation easements, *135,* 135–136
Consumption, excessive, 21. *See also* Sustainability
Container gardening, 362, *362*
Contours:
    mapping of, *67,* 67–68, *68,* 70, *70*
    roadways following, 273, 313
    site design based on, 238–241, 342
Cool-temperate climatic region, 25, 27
Cooling:
    controlling, 33–35
    evaporative, 32, *32,* 35, 77, 137, 235
    natural versus mechanical, 33
    plantings used in, 357, 363
Corbusier, Le, **123, 328,** 371, 372
Corridor spaces, 195–196, *197,* 268
Counties, in regional planning, 189
Court of the Concubine (Beijing, China), 297–299
Court of the Lions, the Alhambra (Spain), 101, *101*
Courtyards:
    privacy afforded by, *236, 237,* 243, 278
    in site plan integration, 250
    space allowed for, 330
    as street frontage alternative, 144, 145, 180
    structurally defined, 341
    in urban design plans, 260
Cowan, Stuart, **4, 7, 11**
Croplands, irrigation of, 11, 40. *See also* Agriculture

Crosby Arboretum (Picayune, MS), *121*
Cross-pollination, 79
Crowe, Sylvia, **181**
Crystalline form, 103
Cul-de-sacs, *146, 182, 313,* 358
Cullen, Gordon, **275**
Culverts, 311
Cyclones, 139

Dams, 51
Dawson, Stuart, 380
Decks:
    residential, *348–350*
    for sloped sites, 240
Decomposition process, 11
Deduction, defined, 2
Deer, as invasive species, 83
Deforestation, 136, 137, 144
Deserts, 137
Design. *See also* Planning
    asymmetry in, 104–110, 333–334
    axis in, 94–100, 108
    climate change as factor in, 36–37
    for climatic region, 25–29
    conditioned perception in, 299–300
    cyclical nature of, 373, *373*
    defined, 214
    for disadvantaged, 139
    dynamic tension in, 332
    end result of, 376
    form and function in, 267, 328, 337, 344, 367, 373
    microclimatic factors in, 30–35
    in nature, 9
    objectives of, 6
    symmetry in, 100–104
    as three-dimensional, 259, 333
Design review board, 162
Developers, in planning, 174–175
Development. *See also* Planned unit development (PUD)
    in community planning, 152–153
    ecological balance and, 15
    growth management and, 164–169, 172
    of hill form, *116*
    lawn irrigation and, 45
    overall impact of, 80–81
    planning for, 59, 133
    pollution from, 138
    of reclaimed sites, 66, 202
    in regional planning, 188–189
    along rivers, 320–321
    suburban, 144
    transfer of rights to, 158

Development (*Cont.*):
   unrestrained, 5, *5*, 8, 58, 166, 170, 175
   water management and, 46, *46,* 47, 49
Development guideline manual, 163
Disabilities, accommodating, 208, *296,* 315
Disease, climate effects on, 24
Disneyland, 318
Disney World, 318
Distance, as design factor, 296, 305–306
DNA:
   bioengineering of, 79
   human programming by, 20
Documents:
   for community development plans, 163
   for comprehensive site plans, 225
Drainage:
   as design consideration, 252, *274*
   natural, preserving, 342
   along roadways, 310
   as site selection factor, 40
Driveway:
   as accessway, 308
   for city site, 235
   entrance to (*see* Approaches)
   opening on trafficway, 145, 174
Drought, 44, 48
Dubos, René, **5**
Dudok, Willem, **263**
Dwellings. *See also* Residences
   cultural design changes in, 180
   functions of, 341, 347
   ideal features of, 343–346, *344*
   locations of, 143
   nature integrated with, 342–343
   in reclaimed developments, 202
   water resources as consideration for, 45
Dynamic repose, 332

Earth:
   atmospheric composition of, 37
   biomass of, 61, 77
   carbon dioxide enveloping, 138
   climatic regions of, 25–29
   ecology of, 13–15
   habitations on, 342
   human relationship to, 2, 132, 168, 377
   oxygen production on, 12, 77, 85
   place in the universe, 15
   relationship with sun, 24
   surface variations on, 67
   vegetative covering on, 75
Earth plane. *See* Base plane

Earthquakes, 139–140
Easements:
   conservation, *135,* 135–136, 152
   for landscape plantings, *359, 360*
   in survey specification, 71
   for utility line placement, 146
Eastern versus Western philosophies:
   on approach to planning, 376
   on beauty, 17
   on composition, 333
   on nature, 17
Eckbo, Garrett, **180, 215, 260,** 380, 382
Ecology:
   as basis of life, 13–15
   damage to, 82, 83
   in landscape architecture practice, 13
   landscape plantings in, 354
   principles of, 61
   around water bodies, 50
   water resource management in, 45
Economy:
   climate effects on, 24
   as planning factor, 220
   unity of rural and urban, 180
   urban revitalization and, 172
Egypt, 278
Eiseley, Loren, **41**
Elder, Henry, 373
Electric carts, 324
Elevations:
   in design for level sites, 242
   in surveying, 67, 68, 70, 71
Emergency vehicle access, 317
Eminent domain, 202
Employment:
   in inner cities, 202, 203
   location of, 161, 200, 206
   sedentary nature of, 147
Energy:
   in community planning, 145, 146, 166
   consumption of, 33, 35, 364
   hydroelectric, 51
   from sun (radiant), 24
Enframement:
   clarity of form and, *283*
   of highway views, 310
   via landscape plantings, *354,* 357, 359
   as outward-directed, 280
   privacy and, *278*
   from structures, 341
   in unified landscape view, *89,* 89–90, 92, *92,* 286, 330
Entrances. *See* Approaches
Environment. *See also* Built environment
   aquatic, *42,* 78

Environment (*Cont.*):
   care for, 353
   dynamic nature of, 6
   ecology as study of, 13
   human relationship to, 376
   interdependence of life forms in, *14*
   organic growth in, 107
Environmental impact assessment:
   checklist for, 230
   in comprehensive plan, 229–231
   in regional plan, 191
Environmental Impact Statement (EIS), 229, 231
Environmental issues, 132. *See also* Pollution
   civic action to confront, 135
   climate as, 139
   in community planning, 162, 163, 166
   conservation as, 141
   conservation easements as, 135–136
   freshwater depletion as, 136–137
   growth management in, 133, 167, 168–169
   natural disasters as, 139–140, *140*
   regional planning and, 133–134, 186, 188
   safety as, 138–139
   in site analysis, 224
   soil loss as, 137–138
   in structural design, 329
   transfer of development rights in, 158
   war as, 140–141
Environmental Planning and Design Partnership, 381
Environmentalists, 153
Erosion:
   as growth management issue, 167
   rectilinear land survey and, 64
   as regional planning issue, 190
   as spatial design consideration, 272
   topsoil loss from, *60,* 60–61, *137,* 137–138
   vegetative protection against, 45, 75–76, 77, *77,* 311, 357
Escalators, *322,* 323
Europe:
   cities in, 196, 246
   climate change addressed by, 37
   Renaissance landscape design in, 109–110
Evaporative cooling (evapotranspiration), 32, *32,* 35, 77, 137, 235
Evolution:
   of plant life, 80
   timeline for (earth and human), 19–20

Excavation:
 geology and, 10, 342
 ill effects of, 176
 in landscape design, 65, *243*
 reclaiming land from, 151
 regulation of, 138
 for suburban sewer lines, 146
 for water bodies, 54
 waterscaping after, 49–50, *50*
Exotic plants, 358, 363
Experiences, planned, 371–372, 373–377, *374, 375*
Exploded plans, 250, *250*
Exterior space design, 271–272

Fairchild, David, 79
Fallingwater (Bear Run, PA), *124,* 125
Family, as social unit, 180
Farmland:
 in growth management plan, 165, 166, 169
 loss of, 82, *82,* 138
 preservation of, 207
 regional planning for, 188
 taxation of, 170
 transfer of development rights to, 158
Fault lines, 11
Fibonacci, Leonardo, 335–336
Field observation (site analysis), 221, 224
Finger plans, 250, *250*
Fish:
 contamination of, 138
 in food chain, 77
 habitat for, 40–41, 78
Fitch, James, **277**
Flattid bug, 14
Flexibility zoning, 158, 183
Flooding:
 as design consideration, 33, 53, 139–140, *140,* 343
 as hazard, 11, 44
 increased incidence of, 37
 management of, 46, 159, 169, 190
 as site analysis data, 11, 44
Florida wetlands, 40
Folger, Timothy, 8
Food chain, 77, *77*
Forestry, urban, 85, 173
Forests:
 depletion of, 136
 development potential of, 170
 establishment of, 84
 in growth management plan, 165, 167, 169

Forests (*Cont.*):
 national, 110
 preserves for, 117, 191, 207
 in regional plans, 188
 restoration of, 137
 site design in, *244*
Forms:
 design innovations and, 368
 function and, 267, 328, 337, 344, 367, 373
 motion impelled by, *290–294,* 290–295
 natural, 115–116, 337–338, 342, *342*
 spatial, 267–268
Fountains, 53, *54,* 55
France, Raoul, **15**
Franklin, Benjamin, 8
Freshwater:
 availability of, 342
 depletion of, 42, 43, 44, 48, 136–137, 362, 363
 global portion of, 39, 40, *40*
 replenishing, 159
Friends of Urban Forests, 85

Gallion, Arthur B., **198**
Gardens. *See also specific gardens*
 botanical, 80, *80,* 117, 201, 381
 community, 84, *84*
 container, 362, *362*
 experience of, 374
 Japanese, 265, **341**
 for privacy, 278
 rain, 252, 365, *365*
 residential, 348
 rooftop, 199, 347
 space allowed for, 330
 in United States, 362
 for urban sites, *236,* 237
 water features in, 350, *351*
Gardner, James, **304**
Gas Works Park (Seattle, WA), 66
Genetic code, 20
Geographic Information Systems (GIS), 64, 73
Geologic time:
 climate change throughout, 36
 eras in, 18–19
Geology:
 as climate element, 23–24
 in habitation design, 342
 in landscape architecture practice, 10–11
Geomancy, 9
Geometric design:
 in contemporary urban plans, 196–197

Geometric design (*Cont.*):
 versus experienced design, 374
 for level sites, 241
 purposeful application of, 249, 338
 revolt against, 368, 372
 in symmetrical plans, 103–104
 three-dimensional consideration of, 333
 for tree planting, 357, 358, *359*
Georgetown (Washington, DC), 203
Giedion, Siegfried, **121**
Global warming:
 factors in, 21
 implications of, 36–37
Globalization:
 consequences of, 82
 cultural evolution in, 168
Goethe, Johann Wolfgang von, **105**
Golden Gate National Recreation Area, *167*
Golden rectangle, 334
Golden Triangle (Pittsburgh, PA), 304
The Golden Number (Borissavlievitch), 334
Goshorn, Warner S., **61**
Government agencies/bodies:
 in community planning, 152, 153, 163
 complete streets promoted by, 315
 developers working with, 174
 eminent domain exercised by, 202
 land use planning by, 132, 133–136, 167
 map/survey information from, 73
 preserves established by, 83–84
 in regional planning, 186, 189, 191–193
 urban forestry under, 85
 visual resource management by, 110
Grade:
 of building site, 238–244
 design solutions to, 305, *305*
 at intersections, 149, 208, 311
 along rivers, 321
Grading:
 geological factors in, 342
 regulation of, 138
 for roadway construction, 310
Graham, Robert, 382
Graham, Wade, **48**
Grand Canyon (AZ), 267
Gravity:
 design base plane and, 273
 as water flow design factor, 40
Great Lakes, 138
Greece:
 ancient, architecture in, 336, *344*
 desertification of, 137
Green infrastructure, 85

Index 399

Green roofs, 252, 363–365, *364*
Greenhouse gases, 36
Greenways:
   in neighborhood plans, 182
   in planned communities, 145
   in regional plans, *190,* 190–191
   in urban areas, 172
Gropius, Walter, 367, 372
Ground covers, 357, *357*
Ground plane. *See* Base plane
Groundwater:
   bioretention and, 365
   determining presence of, 342
   recharging, 252
Growth management:
   defined, 165, 170
   guideline plan for, 164–165
   problems in, 164, *164*
   project review in, 165
   public services in, 165–169, 174
Gulf Stream, 8, 23
Gutkind, E. A., **17**

Habitations. *See* Dwellings; Residences; Structures
Habitats:
   in biosphere, 13
   for fish/wildlife, 1, 40–41, 78, 190, 337, 342, 365
   human, 2–6, 36
   land as, 61–62
   suburban development and, 144
   vegetation and, 76
Harbors, 170, 319–320
Harmony:
   in aesthetics, 267
   architectural, 335
   in built environment, *121,* 121–122, 351
   in Chinese philosophy, 6, 9
   as human pursuit, 5
   between humans and nature, 4, 16, 60
   in landscape character, 112–114
   of site and design, 233, 245–246
   symmetry and, 102
   violation of, 125
Harris, Walter D., **144**
Harvard Graduate School of Design, 367–368, 380, 382
Hatshepsut (Queen of Egypt), 369
Hazardous materials, 224
Heating, natural versus mechanical, 33
Heller, Caroline, **304**

Herbicides, 138
Hilberseimer, Ludwig K., **186, 307**
Hills, modification of, *116,* 117, 188
Historic landmarks, 162, *162,* 167, 189
Homeowners' associations, 163
Homestead Act of 1862, 62
Homo erectus, 19, 20
Homo sapiens, 1, 19, 20. *See also* Humankind
Horticulture, 80. *See also* Landscape planting; Plants
Hot-dry climatic region, 25, 29, 30–31, 33
Hotels, 161, 199
Housing. *See also* Dwellings; Residences; Structures
   in central business districts, 201
   in inner-city areas, 201, 202, *203*
   types of, 203–204
Howard, Ebenezer, **193**
Hubbard, Henry V., **106**
Hudnut, Joseph, 367, 368, 381
Human physiology:
   climate effects on, 24
   symmetry in, 101
Humankind:
   affinity for water, 39, 41–42, 51
   on American continents, 75
   animal nature of, 1, 3, 20
   cities designed for, 210–211
   effect on climate, 36
   evolution of, 19–20, 78
   intelligence of, 2, 6
   land ownership by, 61–62
   life span of, 20, 21
   privacy needs of, 279, 345
   relationship with nature, 3–9, 15–17, 20, 60, 346, 374, 376
   responses to climate, 24, 25
Humidity:
   as design factor, 139
   reducing, 33
Humus, 77
Hunter-gatherers, 20, 78
Hurricanes, 37, 139
Huxley, Julian, **133**
Hybridization of plants, 79
Hydrologic cycle, 11
Hydrology, 11

Ice:
   as global portion of water, 39, *40*
   polar, 24, 44
Impoundments (water), 51

Indoor-outdoor living, 346, *346–351,* 347–351
Industrial Revolution:
   land planning and, 207
   sustainability and, 21, 36
   timeframe for, 19, 20
Industrial sites, 66
Inner city, 201–202, 203, *244*
Innisfree Garden (Millbrook, NY), 332–333
Insulation:
   earth as, 33
   from green roofs, 364
Integrated plan, 246, *246,* 343
Intersections (traffic):
   design of, 304, *304, 308*
   landscaping at, 358–359
   on-grade, 138, 149, 208, 311
   three-way, 159
   turbulence of, 303–304, 307
Invasive species, 82–83
Irrigation:
   agricultural, 11, 40
   as design consideration, 55
   minimizing, 48, 362
   water depletion and, 43, 44–45, 136, 363
Israel, 137

Jacobs, Jane, **199**
Japan. *See also specific locations and sites*
   aesthetic sensibility in, 228–229, 236
   enclosed spaces in, 278
   form order in, 336–337
   housing design in, 204
   land preservation in, 117
   landscape planning in, 218–219
   moon viewing in, 346
   nature-design integration in, 250–251
   spatial design in, 265
   tokonoma in homes of, 344–345
Johnson, Lyndon, 382
Johnson, William J., **232**
Johnston, Paul, 381
Johnstone, B. Kenneth, **225**

Karnak Temple (Egypt), 331
Katsura Palace (Kyoto, Japan), 331, 371
Kepes, Gyorgy, **106**
Kiley, Dan, 380, 382
Kipling, Rudyard, **4,** 371
Kublai Khan, 99, 210n, 369

Kudzu, as invasive species, 83, *83*
Kyoto, Japan, 9, 331, *341,* 371, *371*

Lake George (Michigan), 115
Lakes:
    cities adjacent to, 321
    as landscape features, 51
    as water table recharge, 252
Land. *See also* Topography
    "banking" of, 188, 190
    carrying capacity of, 64, 132, 191, 192
    human impact on, 57–60, 81–82
    minimizing impact on, 252
    preserves for, 83–84, 117
    as resource, 60–62, 66, 141
    rights to, 62–63, 64, 131, 158
Land grants, 62
Land management, 64–65, 132–136
Land ownership:
    establishing, 61–63
    responsibilities of, 65
    in scatteration problem, 175
    transferring, 64, 138
Land surveys:
    computer access to, 231
    methods for, 70
    original U.S., *63,* 63–64
    in site analysis, 217, 223
    specification for, 70–71
Land use:
    in community planning, 163, 166
    evolving pattern of, 170
    planning for, 133–136, 138, 171, 179, 207
    in regional planning, 188
Land-use codes, 252
Land value:
    appreciation of, 174–175
    versus open space preservation, 210
    taxation and, 138, 170, 172
    zoning and, 176
Landscape:
    aerial view of, 321
    control of, 250
    in harmony with nature, 9, 15, *345*
    modification of, 114–119, 128–129 (*see also* Built environment)
    natural forms in, 115–116, 273, *311*
    preserving integrity of, 135–136, 328
    spatial design within, 286
    structures in, 330, 331, 337–339, 351
    symmetry in, 101, 102
    U.S. management of, 83
    visual (*see* Visual landscape)

Landscape architects:
    aesthetics of, 372
    in collaborative planning, 226, *226*
    goal of, 377
    knowledge needed by, 10–13
    site familiarity of, 223
Landscape architecture:
    American approach to, 220, 246
    defined, 372
    evolution of, 368–373
    function of, 252
    Japanese approach to, 218–219
    sustainability in, 18
Landscape Architecture book (Simonds), 382
Landscape Architecture magazine, 160, 382
Landscape art, 372
Landscape character:
    of building complexes, 339
    controlling changes in, *246*
    defined, 112
    geometric design imposed on, 104, 249
    land use and, 120
    of level sites, 243
    preservation of, *127,* 189, 343
    qualities in, 112–114
    in rural site design, 238
    scenic value in, 110
    trees and, 357, 358
Landscape planting:
    cultural influences on, 361–363
    guidelines for, 355–361
    installation of, 355
    in low-impact design, 363–365
    process of, 354–355
    purpose of, 353–354, *354–355*
Landscape type, 114
Landslides, 224
Lao-tzu, **263,** 369
Laser transit (surveying), 64, 70
Latin America:
    cities in, 196
    land ownership in, 63
Law of fitness, 337
Law of the same, 335
Law of the similar, 335
Lawns:
    edging for, *256*
    function of, 346–347
    irrigation of, 11, 45, 48, 136
    size of, 362, 363
Leakey, L. S. B., 14
Learning Through Landscapes Trust, 160
Léger, Fernand, **107**
Lenôtre, André, 369
Leopold, Aldo, 46, **64, 311,** 372

Level sites, design for, 241–244, *242–244*
Li, H. H., 6n
Light exposure:
    as design consideration, 32, *32,* 139
    in overhead plane, 276–277
Lighting:
    design for, 253–254, *254*
    in planned communities, 160
    residential exterior, 350
Line of approach, 312
Line of sight:
    at traffic intersections, 359, *359*
    visual balance and, 105, 106, *106*
Linear plans, 250
Linnaeus, 79, 79n
Living Water (Braun and Cavagnaro), 13n
London, England, 205
Long-range planning, 133–134
Los Angeles, CA, 140
Louis XIV (king of France), 94
Louisiana Purchase, 62
Louvre (Paris, France), 97
Low-impact design (LID):
    application of, 252, *253*
    landscape planting in, 363–365

Maillart, Robert, 122, 123, *123,* 125
Maintenance:
    of base plane materials, 273
    as design consideration, 256–257
    for planned communities, 162
Maps:
    axial plan for Washington, DC, 98, *98*
    base, for planning, 225
    contour, 69
    satellite, 73
    for site research/analysis, 215, *223,* 224–225
    Strata of England & Wales, 10
    topographic, 72
    from USGS, 72, 215
Mathematics, design role of, 334–336
Mayan culture, 44
McHarg, Ian L., **186**
McPhee, John, **18, 60**
Mendelsohn, Eric, **109**
Metes and bounds, 70
Metro government, 133, 134, 192–193
Michigan State Department of Parks, 118
Microclimatology:
    defined, 30
    as design factor, 30–35, *30–35,* 343
    plantings and, 360

Microclimatology (*Cont.*):
   in site analysis, 224
   urban, 85, *234,* 235
   water as factor in, 40
Military installations, 250
Millay, Edna St. Vincent, **345**
Mineral reserves:
   conservation of, 167
   as site analysis data, 225
Ming dynasty (China), 116
Minibuses, 323
Mixed-use communities, 150
Mobile home parks, 176
Models (topographic), 70, *70*
Modular systems, 336–337
Moholy-Nagy, László, **108, 263**
Monorails, 323, *323*
Mont-Saint-Michel (France), *120*
Montreal, Quebec, 318
Motels, 161
Motion:
   impelled by form, *290–294,* 290–295
   perception and, 289–290
Muir, John, 46
Mulch, 363
Mumford, Lewis, **158, 181, 185, 186, 198**
Murphy, W. Tayloe, **44**
Museum of Modern Art (New York City), 261

National Gallery (Washington, DC), 290
National parks:
   bridges in, 123
   landscape design in, 250
   in regional plans, 191
Native plants:
   defined, 363
   preserving, *355,* 355–356
   along roadways, 311
   in site landscape, 256, *354*
Natural resources:
   in community planning, 158, 166
   exploitation of, 131
   in growth management, 167
   land as, 60–62
   management of, 83, 110–111, 132
   in regional planning, 189
   renewable, 20, 21
   water as, 39–43, 60, 159
Natural Resources Conservation Service, 73
Natural sciences, 10–13
Natural systems, defined, 61
Naturalized plants, 363

Nature:
   in aesthetics, 372
   coloration in, 268–269
   efficiency of processes in, 15
   habitation integrated with, 342–343
   human relationship with, 3–9, 15–17, 20, 60, 346, 374, 376
   in Japanese design, 250–251
   preservation efforts for, 83–84
   in rural design, 237
   symmetry/asymmetry in, 101, *103,* 104, 106, 108
   in urban design, 211, *235,* 236
Nature preserves. *See* Preserves
Nautilus, 368, 376, *377*
Neighborhoods:
   character of, 204–205, 236, 357
   entrance plantings for, 359, *359*
   mixed-use, 203, *205*
   planning for, 181–182, *183, 184,* 188
Neutra, Richard J., **5, 266**
New Orleans, LA, *140*
New Urbanism, 315
New York City, 37, 195, *197, 199, 202*
Newton, Norman T., **6, 107**
Noise abatement:
   at airports, 321
   for city sites, 235
   along trafficways, *358*
North American climatic regions, 25
Nuclear power. *See* Atomic power
Nutrient yield, 61

Occult balance, 106
Ocean currents, 24
Ognibene, Peter J., **58**
Okakura, Kakuzo, 90, **247**
Olmsted, Frederick Law, *199,* 372, 380
On the Laws of Japanese Painting (Bowie), 228
Open space:
   in cities, 209–210
   components of, 172–174, *173*
   in growth management plan, 165, 168
   in landscape planting, 359
   negative, in structural design, 331, 340
   in New York City, *199*
   in planned communities, 150–152, *151, 153,* 159
   in regional plans, 189, 190
   structurally defined, 339–341, *340*
Order:
   as aesthetic quality, 334–335
   in Chinese philosophy, 9
   experience of, 376

Order (*Cont.*):
   human need for, 5
   mathematical, 334
   as spatial quality, 270
   symmetry and, 103
   in urban design, 186, 210–211
Organic growth, 107
Organic planning, 107–108, *108*
Ornamental planting, *355,* 357
Outer city, 206
Overhead plane:
   characteristics of, 275–277, *276–277*
   coloration of, 268–269
   of exterior volumes, 272
   implications of, 266
   planting to define, *354*
   in site space design, 260, *260*
Overlooks, 51
Overpasses, 311
Oxygen production:
   on Earth, 12, 77
   in urban areas, 85

Parking. *See also* Driveway
   at activity centers, 325
   in central business districts, 199, 200, 201
   for disabled persons, 208, 316, *317*
   off-street, 315–317, *315–317*
   on-street, 312
   in planned communities, 149
   plantings to shield, 360
   residential, 348
   space allowed for, 330
Parks:
   in growth management plan, 169
   land acquired for, 151
   national, 123, 191, 250
   in neighborhood plans, 182
   in regional plans, 189
   schools adjacent to, 150, 160
   structure design for, 311
   in urban areas, 172, 209–210
Patios, 53, 180, 199, 330, 347–348
Pavement:
   and harsh urban microclimate, 85, *234,* 235
   versus lawn, 363
   modular systems, *349*
   water runoff and, 49, 252
PCD (preserve, conserve, develop) planning, *152,* 152–157, 224
Pedestrian traffic. *See also* Walkways
   automobile impact on, 309
   in cities, 198, *201*

Pedestrian traffic (*Cont.*):
   planning for, 145, *146,* 149, *149,* 253, *303–306, 303–306,* 314
Peking. *See* Beijing, China
Pelican Bay, FL, *152*
People. *See* Humankind
Perception:
   conditioned, 299–300
   defined, 2
   design control of, 289
   experience and, 375–376
Pericles, 369
Permeable paving, 252
Pesticides, 138
Phillips, Patricia C., **196**
Photogrammetry, 64, *64,* 70
Photography, site information via, 215
Photosynthesis, 61, 77, *77*
Piazza San Marco (Venice, Italy), 246
Pittsburgh Point (PA), *170*
Pittsburgh Technology Center (Pittsburgh, PA), 66
Pix, 283, *284, 293*
Place de la Concorde (Paris, France), 96–97
Plane table survey, 70
Planes, in site space design, 260, *260,* 272–287
Planned communities:
   activity centers in, 150, 176
   criteria for, 148, 158–165
   efficiency in, 145–147
   examples of, *146, 152, 153*
   experience of, 374
   health benefits of, 147
   in inner cities, 202
   open space in, 150–152, *151, 153,* 159
   PCD approach to, 152–157
   recreation in, 151, 161
   regional approach to, *182,* 182–184, 188
   traffic management in, 148–149, *149*
   utility lines in, 146
Planned unit development (PUD), 148–149, 150, 151, 158, 176, 182
Planning. *See also* Comprehensive land planning; Planned communities
   aesthetic considerations in, 110, 111
   for agricultural production, 84
   for built environment, 120–129
   climate as factor in, 23
   climate change as factor in, 36–37
   developers' role in, 174–175
   empathetic understanding required for, 229
   essential components of, 2
   fully informed, 213–214

Planning (*Cont.*):
   growth management in, 164–169
   highways as factor in, 308
   integrated, 246, *246,* 343
   landscape character in, 114–119
   long-range, 152, 166, 189
   nature as element in, 4–5, 8, 9
   objective of, 6
   organic, 107–108, *108*
   phased, 161, 174
   philosophical approach to, 376
   for productivity, 61, 138
   property boundaries and, 179
   regional (*see* Regional planning)
   for site development, 59
   ten-step process for, 220
   as two-dimensional, 259, 333
   U.S. philosophy for, 131–132, 368
   water proximity as factor in, 46–47
   for waterscaping, 49–55
   zoning as component in, 175–177
Planning attitude, 228–229
Plants. *See also* Landscape planting; Vegetation
   beneficial effects of, 77–78
   container-grown, *362, 362*
   cultivation of, 79–81
   identification of, *78,* 78–79, 80
   in integrated design, *255,* 255–256
   invasive species of, 82–83, *83*
   native, 256, 311, 354–356, 363
   nonnative, in suburban developments, 144
   photosynthesis by, 61, 77, *77*
   rooftop (*see* Green roofs)
   selecting for landscape plan, 354–355, 356, 361
   in urban site design, 236
   in vertical plane, 277, 286
Plato, **267**, 273
Point of view:
   aerial, 321
   fixed versus moving, 289–290
Polar ice, 24, 39, *40,* 44
Political institutions:
   climate effects on, 24
   in regional planning, 191
Political jurisdictions:
   conservation by, 60
   land ownership and, 62
Pollination, *14*
Pollution. *See also* Air pollution; Noise abatement; Water pollution
   abatement of, 138, 343
   of cities, 170
   from development, 82

Pollution (*Cont.*):
   effects on ecologic balance, 14
   as global warming factor, 36, *36, 37*
   of land, 66
   laws governing, 65
   from light, 254
   population density and, 144
   water management and, 46, 365
Pompeii, Italy, 278
Pools, as landscape features, 53, 55
Population growth:
   community planning and, 166
   impact on land, 58
   regional, 133
   through time, 20–21, 133
   urban, 85, 143–144, 365
   water management and, 11
Postmodernism, 371, 372
Precipitation:
   as climate element, 23
   as design consideration, 343
   management of, 146
   retention of, 48, 76, 77, 137, 190, 252
Preserves:
   forest, 117, 191
   land, 83–84, 117
   nature, 162
   regional planning for, 188
   for wildlife, 190
President's Task Force on Resources and the Environment, 382
Privacy considerations:
   in dwellings, 345
   enclosure and, 278–279, *280*
   on level sites, 243
   in urban site design, 237
Program development, 213–214
Progressions:
   mathematical, 336
   in nature, 300–301, *301*
   of vistas, 93–94
Property boundaries:
   on base map, 225
   in design expression, *234*
   establishing, 63
   land use planning and, 179
   on site analysis map, 224
   survey of, *64,* 70
   in survey specification, *71*
Property titles, 63, 71
Property values:
   along complete streets, 315
   overdevelopment and, 144
   regional planning and, 191
   urban, 211

Proportion, in composition, 335–336
Public domain:
    greenways in, 172
    water bodies in, 41, 49
Public services:
    as growth management component, 165–169, 174
    in regional plan, 189, 190, 191
    urban sprawl and, 172, *187*
Public spaces:
    form suiting function of, 261, 333–334
    structurally defined, 341
    vertical reference points in, 283

Quality of life, 144, 147–148

Radburn, NJ, *146*
Rai, Sanyō, **9**
Railways:
    in developing landscape, 170
    freight versus passenger, 317, 319
    impact of, 82
    as people movers, 323
    rapid-transit (*see* Rapid transit)
    right-of-way for, 62
    stations, 319, *319*
    in transportation network, 58
Rain gardens, 252, 365, *365*
Rapid transit:
    in community planning, 159, 160
    function of, 317–319, *319*
    in regional planning, 185, 189
    in urban revitalization plans, 172, 206
Rasmussen, Steen, 333
Read, Herbert, **262**
Recreation:
    as growth management issue, 167
    in planned communities, 151, 161
    regional planning for, 188, 189, 191
    water as resource for, 41, *41, 46*, 51
Recycling, 166
Red Rocks Amphitheatre (Denver, CO), *116*
Redevelopment, 202, 203, 210
Reed, Henry H., Jr., **97**
Reference files. *See* Documents
Reforestation, 137
Region, plantings by (chart), 360
Regional planning:
    acceptance of, 207
    approaches to, 191–192
    for cities, 184–186, *187*

Regional planning (*Cont.*):
    commercial centers in, 161
    for communities, 182–184
    criteria for, 191
    environmental, *133*
    farmland preservation and, 138
    function of, 133–134, 186, 188
    governance in, 192–193
    growth management in, 167
    multimodal transportation in, 325
    for neighborhoods, 181–182
    PCD approach in, 152–157
    rapid transit in, 319
    rationale for, 179–180
    urban revitalization and, 172
Regional planning commission, 192
Renaissance:
    formalism of, 372
    geometric design in, 333, 336–337
    integrated planning in, 246
    major/minor axis used in, 368
    structure design in, 344
    symmetrical design in, 109–110
Renewable resources, 20, 21
Repton, Humphry, 369
Reservoirs, 51, 136
Residences. *See also* Dwellings
    in central business districts, 201
    exterior furnishings for, *350,* 350–351, *351*
    functions of, 347
    for indoor-outdoor living, 347–349, *347–350*
    inward/outward progression of, 245
    lawns with, 346–347
    in planned communities, 145, 150, 160, *160*
    in self-sufficient neighborhoods, 180–181
    street-facing, 144, 148, 159
    supplementary structures for, *349,* 349–350
    survey specification for, 70–71
Retaining walls, 311
Rhetoric (Aristotle), 196
Ribbon plans, 250, *250*
Right-of-way:
    landscape plantings and, 359, *360*
    for railways, 62
    residences facing, 148
    for roadways, 307, 310, *310,* 314
    in survey specification, 71
    for urban ring roads, 201
    utility lines in, 146
Ritual, function of, 9

Rivers:
    bank erosion on, 50
    depletion of, 136
    development along, 320–321
    for drainage, 252
    restoration of, 136–137
Roadways. *See also* Approaches; Circulation patterns; Intersections; Streets
    controlled-access, 138, 159, 174, 183, *189,* 325
    as design axes, 94
    on design base plane, 273
    development around, 5, *5,* 81–82, 144
    flow of, 307–308
    in growth management plan, 165
    landscape character and, 117, 253
    linear path of, 63, 250, 307
    in neighborhood plans, 182
    as planned experiences, 373–374
    plantings along, 358, *358,* 359
    in regional plans, 189
    on site analysis map, 224
    spatial design of, 259–260, 308–311
    in survey specification, 71
    in transportation network, 58, 159
    unrestrained development and, *133,* 170, *188*
    in urban plans, 172, 173, 185, 186, *188,* 195–196, 201, 206
    in visual resource management, 110
    water proximity of, *46,* 47
Rockefeller Center (New York City), 261
Rome, Italy, 195, *197*
Rooftops:
    gardens on, 199, 347
    green, 252, 363–365, *364*
    restaurants on, 199
    utilizing, *200*
Rose, James, 380, 382
Rudolph, Paul, **330**
Runoff:
    in blueways, 190
    as design consideration, 252
    erosion from, 77
    managing, 40, 45, 46, 53, 363, 365
    pollution from, 138
    on sloped sites, 241
    urban mitigation of, 85
Rural areas:
    landscape design in, *128*
    natural settings preserved in, 363
    site design for, *237,* 237–238, *238*
    versus urban areas, 180

Rural areas (*Cont.*):
   U.S. preference for, 196
Ryōanji garden (Kyoto, Japan), *341,* 371, *371*

Saarinen, Eliel, **103, 191, 331, 374**
Sabah (British North Borneo), 17
Safety issues:
   in bioengineering, 79
   on building site, 224
   for disabled people, 208, *296*
   for dwellings, 344
   environmental, 138, 147, 231
   in existing communities, 147
   lighting and, 253–254
   natural disasters and, 140
   in planned communities, 145, 147–148
   public services and, 165, 191
   in transportation, 138–139, 149, 159, 184, 296, 302, 307–308, 314–315
   in urban areas, 170, 171, 199, 201, 235
Saltwater:
   global portion of, 40, *40*
   intrusion into freshwater bodies, 44, 136
San Andreas fault, 140
San Francisco, CA, 140, 318
Santa Barbara Botanic Garden (CA), *80*
Santa Monica Mountains Conservancy (CA), *189*
Santayana, George, **105, 107**
Saprophytes, 11
Sasaki, Hideo, **248**
Satellite communities:
   public services for, 190, 202
   roadways interconnecting, 183, 189, 206, 308
Satellite maps, 73
Satellite plans, 245–246, 250, *250*
Scale:
   for base maps, 354
   for contour maps, 67–68
   on level sites, *243,* 244
   planting to define, *355*
   as project design factor, 234, *234*
   of public spaces, 281
   vertical plane and, 283, *284*
Scatteration:
   in conservation plan, 132
   defined, 172
   development of, 169–170
   drawbacks of, 161
   lack of planning and, 191
   reversal of, 166, 175, 189, 207

Scatteration (*Cont.*):
   tax yield and, 133
   zoning and, 176
Scenic value:
   accentuating, 343
   in conservation plan, 132
   as growth management issue, 167
   in regional plan, 188, 189
   resource management and, 110–111
   in roadway design, 310, *310*
   as site analysis data, 224
   of water bodies, *41,* 41–42
Schools:
   adjacent to parks, 150, 160
   in community plans, 184
   exploded site plans for, 250
   in neighborhood plans, 182
Screens:
   shrubbery as, 357, *357, 358*
   in spatial design, 279, *279*
Sea level rise, 36, 37
Sea Palace gardens (Beijing), 333, *333*
Seasons, as design consideration, 32, *32,* 35, 139
Sections (contour maps), 69, *69*
Seneca, **3**
Sequence:
   climax in, 301
   perception of, 299–300
   planning of, 300–303, *300–303*
Sert, José Luis, **196, 331**
Service courts, 330, 348–349
Setbacks:
   as site analysis data, 224
   in survey specification, 71
   for urban residences, 199
Severud, Fred M., **9**
Sewers:
   in property specification, 71
   for storm runoff, 146, 252
   suburban development and, 144
Shade:
   as design element, 33, *34*
   in landscape planting, *355,* 357, 358
Shelter, as basic concept, 343, *344*
Shigemori, Kanto, **345**
Shinjuku Gardens (Japan), 265
Ships:
   freight versus passenger, 317
   travel via, 319–321
Shopping:
   in downtowns, 199, 200
   in planned communities, *160,* 161, 184
   satellite malls for, 190

Shorelines:
   design treatments for, 52–53
   migration of, 51
   protection of, 50
Shrubbery:
   in landscape plan, 357, *357*
   line of sight and, 359, *359*
Sierra Club, 135
Signage:
   design of, 255, *255*
   at driveways, 312
   in planned communities, 160
   for roadways, 311
   standardized, 208
Siltation, 46, 77, 190
Silver Pavilion (Kyoto, Japan), 371
Simon, Guy Wallace, 379
Simon, Marguerite Ormsbee, 379
Simonds, Dylan Todd, **207**
Simonds, John Ormsbee, *379,* 379–383
Simonds, John Todd, **2**
Simonds, Marjorie Todd, *379,* 381, 382
Simonds, Philip, 381
Site:
   analysis of, 216–220, 222–225, 342
   character of, 354
   in comprehensive plan, 220–225
   conceptual plan for, 226–231, 233
   design development for, 233–244
   extensional aspects of, 217, *217,* 245
   multiple viewing points for, 289–290
   program development for, 213–214
   protecting quality of, 272
   reclaimed, 66, 202
   residential, 346–351
   selection of (*see* Site selection)
   ten-step planning process for, 220
   trees as framework for, 357
Site analysis:
   approach to, 217–220
   function of, 216–217, 226
   guidelines for, 222–225
Site analysis map, *223,* 224–225
Site design. *See also* Site-structure plan
   expression of, 233–234
   water as consideration in, 50–55
Site selection:
   climatic factors in, 25–29
   for dams/impoundments, 51
   environmental factors in, 141
   microclimatic factors in, 30, 31
   in planning process, 23, 214–216
   water proximity in, 40–43, 45–47
Site spaces, as volumes, 259–260

Site-structure plan:
  composition of, 330, *339*
  development of, 245–246
  evaluation of, 247
  unity of, 247–251, *248*
Site systems:
  building materials, 256
  defined, 251
  drainage, 252
  lighting, 253–254
  movement, 253
  operations/maintenance, 256–257
  plantings, 255–256
  signage, 255
Sitte, Camillo, **197, 329**, 333–334, **334**
Sky:
  defined space open to, 340–341
  as overhead plane, 275–276, *277*
Slopes:
  in building site development, 238–241, *238–241*
  protecting with vegetation, *354*
  along roadways, 310, *311*
Smart Growth, 315
Soil:
  as climate element, 24
  as design base plane, 272
  erosion of (*see* Erosion)
  for green roofs, 364
  pollution of, 138
  protecting with vegetation, 32
  stabilizing, 45, 146
  study of, 10, *11*
  in urban areas, 85
Soil Survey Reports, 73
Spaces:
  containment of, *271*
  enframement of (*see* Enframement)
  function of, 373
  occupants of, 265, *266*, 267
  organization of, 329–330
  qualities of, *263*, 263–265
  as related to structures, 330, 339–341
Spaciousness, as need, 345–346
Spain, 137, 278
Spatial design. *See also* Spaces; Structures, composition of
  abstractions expressed in, 269–271, *269–271*
  color in, 268–269, 271
  enclosure in, *271*, 271–272, *278*, 278–280, 286, 287, 297, 357
  form in, 267–268
  planes in, 260, *260*, 272–287
  plantings in, 360–361, *360–361*

Spatial design (*Cont.*):
  responses to, *261*, 261–263, *262*, 264, 267, 297, 301–302, 371–372
  sequences in, 299–303, *300–303*
  size in, *265*, 265–267
  transitions in, 296–299, *297*
  volumes in, 259–260
Spengler, Oswald, 13, **267**
Stabilization:
  of roadways, 310
  of sloped sites, 239, *239–241*, 357
  of soil, 45, 146
Stadia survey, 70
Stairway design, *274, 304*
Stein, Clarence, *146*
Stewardship:
  importance of, 132
  past record of, 2
Stinkbugs, as invasive species, 83
Stonehenge (England), 267
Storm sewers, 146, 252
Storms:
  as climate element, 23, 140
  as design consideration, 33, 37
Stormwater management (SWM). *See also* Runoff; Storm sewers
  as design consideration, 252
  landscape planning and, 365
  laws governing, 65
  natural versus man-made systems for, 40, 49
Strata of England & Wales (map), *10*
Streams:
  bank erosion on, 50
  for drainage, 252
  restoration of, *136*, 136–137
  in survey specification, 71
Street crossing design, 138, 208
Street life:
  in central business districts, 199–201
  planning for, 208
Streets. *See also* Intersections; Roadways
  in central business districts, 199
  complete, 314–315, *315*
  cul-de-sacs, *146, 182*, 313, 358
  lights/signs for, 255
  one-way versus two-way, 314
  in planned communities, 145–146, *146*, *149*, *149*, 159
  residential, 144, 148, 159, 235, *313, 314*
  tree plantings along, 358, *358*, 362
  as urban design focus, 260
  width of, 312

Streetscape:
  Japanese-style, 236
  utility lines and, 146
Structures:
  composition of, *329–333*, 329–337, *335–337*
  groups of, 330–333, 338
  in landscape, 337–339, *339*, 342, 351, 356
  open space defined by, 339–341
  postmodern, 372
  qualities of, 327–329
Subdivisions, 145
Subsidence, 224
Suburbs:
  development of, *59*, 144–145
  evolution of, 207
  inefficiency of, 161
  natural settings preserved in, 363
  rapid transit in, 318
  sprawl in, *206*
  U.S. preference for, 196
Sullivan, Louis H., **107,** 367, 375
Summer Palace (Beijing, China), 297–298
Sun:
  climate affected by, 23, 24
  as design element, *31–35*, 33, 242, 343
  in photosynthesis, 61, 77, *77*
Surveys. *See* Land surveys
Sustainability. *See also* Green roofs; Low-impact design
  defined, 18
  development and, 166
  global warming and, 36
  population growth and, 18, 20–21
  of regional plan, 191
Suzhou (Soochow) gardens (China), 331
Swales. *See also* Bioswales
  to manage runoff, 46, 49, 53, 252
  along roadways, 310
  in survey specification, 71
Symmetry, 94, 100–104, *102, 103, 106, 107*, 337
Syria, 137
Sze, Mai-mai, **9**

Tao (The Way), 9, 376
Tatami (Japanese mat), 336
Taxation:
  in cities, 207
  community governance and, 163
  land use and, 170, 172
  land value and, 138

Taxation (*Cont.*):
    regional zoning and, 189
    scatteration and, 133, 175
Technology, in structural design, 328–329. *See also* Computer
Tectonic plates, 11
Temperature:
    as climate element, 23, 24, 31, *31, 33*
    global increase in, 36
    in urban areas, 85
Temperature control, 32, *32*
Terraces:
    in site plan integration, 250
    for sloped sites, 239, 240
    space for, 330
    for urban residences, 199
Thermodynamics, 35. *See also* Cooling; Heating
Thoreau, Henry David, 46, 372
Tidal estuaries, 78
Time:
    geologic, 18–19, 36
    human comprehension of, 18–21
    perception of objects in, 289, 300
Tokonoma, 344
Topographic survey, 70–71, 223, 224
Topography. *See also* Land
    airports and, 322
    community planning and, 151, 166
    contours in, 67–68
    defined, 67
    development impact on, 81–82
    information gleaned from, 57
    land ownership and, 61
    land survey and, 63–64
    in landscape architecture practice, 10, 65
    light exposure and, *32*
    microclimate and, *31*
    minimizing disruption to, 342
    models used in, 70
    natural forms in, 115–116
    regional planning and, *187*, 188, *188*
    roadway design and, 310
    in rural site design, 238, *238*
    sections in, 69
    in site selection/analysis, 216, 217, 222
    storm sewers and, 146
    USGS maps of, 72, *72*
Topsoil. *See also* Erosion
    accumulation of, 77
    biomass in, 62
    geology and, 342
    removal of, 65
    replenishment of, 176
    vegetative protection of, 75

Tornadoes, 11, 37
Toronto, Ontario, 318
Town houses, 203
Towns and Buildings (Rasmussen), 333
Traditional Neighborhood Development (TND), 315
Traffic. *See also* Automobiles; Circulation patterns; Roadways
    in community planning, 148–149, *149*, 159
    as design consideration, 253
    efficient routing of, 208
    flow of, *307*, 309–311, *310, 311*
    in neighborhood plans, 182
    pedestrian (*see* Pedestrian traffic)
    reduction of, 172
    in regional plans, 188
    route design for, 296
    as site analysis data, 224
    in urban plans, 186, 199, 200, 207–208
Transfer of development rights (TDR), 158
Transitions:
    for driveways, 312
    indoor-outdoor, 346
    integrated design of, 251, 296–299, *297*
    in water travel, 320
Transportation. *See also* Automobiles; Railways
    multimodal, *318, 322–324, 323–325*
    by plane, 321–322
    rapid transit, 159, 160, 172, 185, 189, 206, 317–319
    route design, 126
    safety issues in, 138–139
    trucking, 159, 189, 317
    U.S. land allotments for, 62
    via water, 40, 319–321, *320*
Travel accommodations, 161
Trees. *See also* Forestry
    on complete streets, 315, *315*
    in landscape plan, *356, 357, 358, 358, 359, 359*
    on site analysis map, 224
    on suburban streets, 146
    on urban streets, 173, 234, 236
    in vertical plane, 285–286
Truck routes:
    dedicated, 189
    for delivery/parking, 317
    through-community, 159
Truth:
    mathematical basis of, 334
    in plan design, 103
Tunnard, Christopher, **16, 122**

Ugliness, source of, 114
Underpasses, 311
United States:
    Beaux Arts system in, 367, 367n
    contemporary dwellings in, *346*
    gardening initiatives in, 84
    land development in, 58, *59*, 170
    land grants in, 62
    land preserves in, 117
    landscape planning approach in, 220, 246, 368
    lawns in, 45, 48, 346–347
    lifestyle changes in, 361–362
    national parks in, 123
    pioneering stage in, 131–132
    residential patterns in, *59*, 144
    settlement of, 143
    suburban living in, 207
    topsoil loss in, 137, *137*
    urban design in, 260
    vitality of cities in, 195–198
    water resource management in, 47, 48
University of California, Berkeley, *104–105*
Urban agriculture, 84
Urban forestry, 85, 173
Urban planning. *See also* Cities
    asymmetry in, 108–109
    for city segments, 198–207
    contemporary approach to, 196–200
    human element in, 375
    inspiration from older cities, 196
    regional approach to, 184–186
Urban revitalization, *171*, 171–174, 202, 203, 204, 210
Urban sprawl. *See also* Scatteration
    alternatives to, 172, 190
    consequences of, 175
    history of, 169–170
    lack of regulation and, 177
    reasons for, 166, 170
    stopping, 132, 174, 199, 206
Urbanization. *See also* Cities
    rate of, 85
    water table level and, 136
U.S. Department of Transportation, 315
U.S. Forest Service, 110
U.S. Geological Survey (USGS) maps, 72, *72, 72*n, 215, 222, *222*
U.S. Soil Conservation Service. *See* Natural Resources Conservation Service
Utilities:
    in planned communities, 146, 169
    in site analysis, 224

Index 407

Utilities (*Cont.*):
  in survey specification, 71
  unrestrained development and, 133

Van der Ryn, Sim, **4, 7, 11**
Van Loon, Hendrik, **8**
Vaux, Calvert, *199*
Vegetation. *See also* Landscape planting; Plants
  biosphere as home to, 13
  climate problems and, 32–33, 37
  destruction of, 78
  erosion and, 50, 75–76, 77, *77*, 137, 252
  oxygen produced by, 12
  preserving, 40–41, 342, *355*, 355–356
  reestablishment of, 83–84
  along rivers, 321
  along roadways, 311
  as site analysis data, 224, 353
  variety of, 76, *76*
  water depletion and, 42, 49, *49*
Veri, Albert R., **13, 51**
Versailles Palace (France), 94, *333*, *333*
Vertical plane:
  to articulate base plane, 284, *285, 286*
  coloration of, 268
  to control environmental elements, 284–285
  as dominant spatial feature, 280–281
  for enclosure, *278*, 278–280, *280*
  of exterior volumes, 272, 281
  eye level and, 283–284, *284*
  function of, 277–278
  implications of, 266
  as reference point, *282*, 282–283
  in site space design, 260, *260*
  structures as, 281–282
  visual control from, 279–280, *280, 281*
Vetter, Hans, **6**
Victory Gardens, 84
Vietnam Veterans Memorial, *270*
View:
  in asymmetrical design, 106
  defined space open to, 341, 345
  as design element, 88–91, *88–91*, 250
  from drive approach, 313
  in landscape planting, 359
  nature of, 87
  along roadways, 310
  from sloped sites, 240
  suitability of, 88
Viewshed, 110

Villa D'Este (Tivoli, Italy), 249, *249*
Vinci, Leonardo da, 336, *336*
Vines, plantings of, 357, *357*
Virginia's Common Wealth, 381
Vista:
  defined, 91
  as design element, *92*, 92–94, *93, 101*, 250
Visual landscape design, 87–110
Visual resource management, *110*, 110–111
Vitruvian man, 336, *336*
Vitruvius, Marcus, 336
Volcanoes, *10*, 11, 140
Volumes. *See also* Spaces
  as enclosed, *271*, 271–272
  functions of, 266, 297
  objects placed in, 280–281, *281*
  in site design, 259–260
  structure groupings and, 330, 339–341

Wabi design quality, 236–237, 251
Wagner, Martin, 367
Waikiki, HI, *185*
Walker, Ralph, **184**
Walkways. *See also* Pedestrian traffic
  automobile isolation from, 309, *313*
  in central business districts, 200
  on complete streets, 315, *315*
  along greenways, 172
  in planned communities, 149, *149*, 160
  plantings along, *358*, 360
  as safety measure, 138
  on site analysis map, 224
War:
  as environmental disaster, 140
  preventing, 141
Warm-humid climatic region, 25, 28
Washington, DC:
  axial plan for, 98, *98*
  Georgetown homes in, 203
  rapid transit in, 318
Waste management technology, 176
Wastewater:
  in community planning, 159
  for irrigation, 11, 136, 363
  recycling of, 48
Water. *See also* Freshwater; Saltwater
  conservation of, 48, 190, 363
  cycle of, 11
  as design element, 53–55, *53–55*, 241, *249*
  as garden feature, 350, *351*

Water (*Cont.*):
  human affinity for, 39, 41–42, 51
  interrelated systems of, 43–46
  qualities of, 53
  as resource, 39–43, 60, 136–137, 159, 189
  as symbol, 55
  travel via, 40, 319–321, *320*
  vegetation and, 12, 77
Water, potable:
  availability of, 23
  distribution of, 45, 136
  as site analysis data, 225
Water bodies:
  carrying capacity of, 64
  as design consideration, 32, 50–53
  protecting/restoring, 47–48, 342
  in public domain, 41, 49
  recreational/scenic value of, *41*, 41–42, 45–46, *46*
  in regional plans, 188
  on site analysis map, 224
  in survey specification, 71
  in urban areas, 172
Water-edge paths, 51, *51, 52*
Water pollution:
  control of, 45, 138
  impact of, 44
  preventing, 46, 53
  wetland remediation of, 47
Water rights, 43
Water table:
  level of, 45, 49, 136
  management of, 167
  replenishment of, 46, 76, 137
Waterfalls, *55*, 241
Waterfronts:
  development on, *200*, 210, *320*, 320–321
  urban design for, *244*
Watershed management:
  blueways in, 190–191
  components in, 46–50
  importance of, 11, 44
  landscape planting in, *354*
  planning as component in, 167
  protection in, 84
  ten axioms for, 45
Weather:
  design influenced by, 25, 238, 343
  entrance court design for, 314
  increasing severity of, 36, 37
West Palm Beach, FL, 154–157
Western philosophies. *See* Eastern versus Western philosophies

Wetlands:
   constructed, *48*
   in Florida, 40
   loss of, 43
   protection of, 45, *45,* 137, 153, 169
   reestablishment of, *83,* 83–84
   for runoff retention, 46
   tidal, *43*
   in wastewater treatment, 46, 47
White, Stanley, **13, 15, 127**
Whyte, Lancelot Law, **2**
Whyte, William H., Jr., **198**
Wilderness:
   preservation of, 45, 82, 84, 207
   profusion of plant life in, 80
   remaining, 58
Wildlife:
   in food chain, 77
   habitats for, 40–41, 78, 190, 342, 365
   invasive species of, 82–83

Wildlife (*Cont.*):
   protection of, 84, 167
   in regional plans, 188
Wilson, E. H., 79
Wilson, Edward O., **21**
Wind:
   as climate element, 23, *34*
   as design element, 32, 33, 34, *34,* 343
   protection from, *354,* 357, 360, 363
   as site analysis data, 224
Wittkower, Rudolph, **336**
World Trade Center Memorial (New York City), *202*
Wright, Frank Lloyd, 125, **218**
Wright, Henry, *146*

Xeriscaping, 48, 363, *363*

York River Preserve (New Kent County, VA), *183*

Yosemite Falls, *111*
Yuan Ming Yuan (Garden of Perfect Brightness; Beijing), 108, *109*

Zen Buddhism:
   concept of beauty in, 90
   concept of perfection in, 476
Zero lotline homes, 203
Zevi, Bruno, **277**
Zoning:
   in comprehensive plan, 221
   flexibility, 158, 183
   in growth management, 167, 172, 175–177
   land value and, 138
   landscape character in, 117
   in regional plan, 189
   as site analysis data, 224
   traditional, 191
   uniformity in, 205–206

Printed in the USA
CPSIA information can be obtained
at www.ICGtesting.com
JSHW061147140823
46476JS00004B/25